CITY LIFE IN JAPAN

A Study of a Tokyo Ward

BY R. P. DORE

UNIVERSITY OF CALIFORNIA PRESS

Berkeley, Los Angeles, London

UNIVERSITY OF CALIFORNIA PRESS
BERKELEY AND LOS ANGELES, CALIFORNIA
UNIVERSITY OF CALIFORNIA PRESS, LTD.
LONDON, ENGLAND
© R. P. DORE 1958
THIRD CALIFORNIA PAPERBACK PRINTING, 1971
PRINTED IN THE UNITED STATES OF AMERICA
ISBN: 0-520-00341-1 CLOTH
0-520-00344-6 PAPER

Acknowledgements

THIS book was made possible by the generosity of the Treasury Committee for Studentships in Oriental Languages and Cultures, which supported the author during an eighteen months' stay in Japan, and also of the Central Research Committee of the University of London which provided a grant for the machine-sorting of some of the material obtained. The author is also greatly indebted to many friends without whose help this book could not have been written; to Professors K. Aoi, K. Iwai and T. Tsukamoto for their invaluable advice concerning the preparation of questionnaires; to the interviewers for their long and conscientious labours; to Mrs. R. Enoki, Mrs. K. Omori and Mr. H. Takagi for help in copying and tabulation; to Mr. Y. Kawashima and Professor Y. Yamada for many useful discussions and suggestions concerning additional material; and to Professor W. G. Beasley, Miss Carmen Blacker, Mr. Anthony Christie, Mr. F. J. Daniels, Miss Machiko Kubo, Mr. W. R. MacAlpine, Professor M. Maruyama, Professor W. J. H. Sprott, and Mrs. Sybil van der Sprenkel for reading the whole or parts of the manuscript and making many valuable suggestions. Finally, grateful thanks are due to the people of Shitayama-cho, whose kindness and friendly co-operation made the work of collecting the material here presented a personal as well as an academic pleasure, and in particular to Mrs. Kiyoko Nishitani who not only provided her lodger with a strict, if hilarious, training in the niceties of Japanese etiquette, but also suffered her house to be turned into an interviewers' centre and bore all the attendant inconveniences with something more than the usual human allowance of patience and good humour.

Contents

SECTION V RELIGION AND MORALITY

APPENDICES

Illustrations

Diagrams

Tables

Section I

INTRODUCTORY

1

Aims and Limitations

THE chief aim of this book is to give an idea of what it is like to be a Japanese living in Shitayama-cho, a neighbourhood of some three hundred households not far from the centre of Tokyo. It is concerned with what people do—how they earn a living and run a home, how they marry, how they amuse themselves, how they treat their relatives, their neighbours, and their gods—and with what people think and feel, in so far as this can be inferred from what they do and say. The account is based in part on direct observation of life as it is lived, in part on the information gained in the more artificial situation of the formal interview.

A neighbourhood study, such as this, has certain inevitable limitations as a means of approach to the study of 'city life in Japan'. Chiefly, there is the danger that the neighbourhood selected may be unrepresentative, and where the individual or the family is the unit of study a broader approach based on systematic sampling of, say, the inhabitants of Tokyo or of the urban Japanese population as a whole might be of greater value. On the other hand the neighbourhood study has certain advantages. In the first place it enables the results of formal interviews to be supplemented by personal acquaintance with the people concerned and a knowledge of the general background of their lives. In the second place it offers a means of studying a range of topics beyond the reach of a broader sample survey— patterns of community organization, for instance, friendships and neighbour relations, the functions of shrines and temples. There is a third general justification for the community study as a descriptive device; namely that the more the people studied are similar in background and outlook the more meaningful do generalizations about them become and the less is the 'average man' a mere statistical abstraction. This latter advantage, however, can hardly be claimed here, for, as Chapter 2 shows, the population of Shitayama-cho was, in origin, education, occupation and economic well-being not very much less heterogeneous than the population of Tokyo as a whole.

This heterogeneity of Shitayama-cho, although it destroys some of the advantage of the neighbourhood study approach, has its

3

compensations. Granted that no application of statistical techniques could give the results of a single neighbourhood study any precise validity as a description of 'the Japanese' or 'the inhabitants of Tokyo', still, since studies of urban Japan are rare it would seem preferable that the neighbourhood selected should not be too obviously exceptional. Shitayama-cho filled the bill in this sense. It was typical in the sense that many other wards like it could be found in Tokyo, and its population was representative in the sense that its class and occupational character was none too clearly defined. 'It's a nondescript sort of place,' said one of the ward leaders when I was discussing plans for the survey with them. 'It isn't a shopkeeper's ward like (the ward next door). It's not really a "salary-man's ward" either. Or a working-class ward. It's residential, but we have our workshops too. I suppose if you had to call the ward something or other you wouldn't go wrong if you said it was "towards the bottom end of the middle class".'

The result, then, is a compromise; a compromise between the contradictory aims on the one hand of deriving the maximum advantages of all-embracingness and personal familiarity which attach to the narrow neighbourhood study, and on the other of producing something which, even if it is taken as in some respects typical of a wider universe, will not seriously mislead.

It is to further the latter aim, and so to justify the title of this book, that Chapter 2 is concerned primarily with 'placing' Shitayama-cho in the context of Tokyo and of urban Japan as a whole by means of a few easily quantified characteristics. Throughout the book, moreover, where national or regional statistics or general institutional studies by other writers are relevant to the wider perspective of topics studied in Shitayama-cho—as in the discussion of income levels, housing, education and so on—such material has been quoted for purposes of comparison.

The inclusion of this more general material has another purpose in addition to the 'correction for sample bias'. A report of investigations into the church-going or courting habits of an English community could safely assume the reader's familiarity with the main outlines of the religious and family institutions of our society. It would be rash to assume the same familiarity with the major institutions of Japanese society and the information is not easily come by. Much of the more general material culled from secondary sources is included, therefore, for the purpose of providing such background information as is necessary to make the description of Shitayama-cho intelligible. The reader might wonder, for instance, why he is told so much about the almost non-existent conflict between mothers and daughters-in-law in Shitayama-cho if he were not told something about the traditional Japanese family. Such background information has a special importance in those parts of the book concerned with social change.

It is in its concern with social change that this book does attempt to go beyond simple ethnographic description. It does not try to confirm or to falsify any general theory of social change. It was, however, written, and the data were collected, within the framework of a loose theoretical picture of the sort of development which Japanese society has been undergoing over the last three-quarters of a century. At one end of this 'ideal' scale of development was a society based on peasant agriculture and domestic craft production, rigidly stratified and with only rudimentary means of central political control, a society in which traditional values and views of the world were rarely questioned, in which hereditary status was overwhelmingly important in defining the limits of a man's permitted behaviour and in which a man's relations with his kin and with his immediate neighbours made up almost the whole range of his life. At the other end of this scale of development lies an open competitive society in which the family plays no part in the economic productive activities of large sections of the population, in which codified law is a major element in social control and educational institutions outside the family play a major part in the training of new members of the society, in which a wide range of a man's daily contacts are of an impersonal kind, and in which a rising standard of material well-being produces a constantly changing set of material values and has created an expectation of continuing change and continuing progress.

From community to association, from status to contract, mechanical to organic solidarity; the basic notions are familiar. In filling out the concrete detail of these schematized types of society the 'traditional' end offers no difficulty. The comparatively good documentation of the society of the Tokugawa period, supplemented by observation of contemporary rural areas, provides an adequate picture of the base-line from which Japan's recent development began. My own picture of the other end of the scale—the goal in the direction of which Japanese society might be thought to be moving—was more vague and amorphous. It may be characterized as 'a society which differs from none of the Western industrial societies more than they differ from each other'. Inevitably, since England is the one of these societies which I know best, my picture of this end of the scale tended to be an abstraction of English social structure as I know it.

This assumption that the course of development was to make Japanese society in more and more respects like English society did not spring from a belief that the latter embodied the highest ideals of human progress. It rested, rather, on assumptions concerning the motive forces of changes in Japan in recent decades. These can be broadly classified under three heads.

(*a*) The chains of cause and effect set up by changes in economic organization.

(*b*) Changes in formal institutions (of law, government, education, etc.) only in part the result of economic changes and to a large extent accomplished by borrowing social techniques from abroad.

(*c*) Changes in attitudes which, though in part the direct consequence of the other two, are in part the result of contact with the ideas of foreign countries, percolated through an intellectual elite to increasingly wide strata of the population.

Each of these could be expected to have the effect of making Japan more and more like Western societies; the last two obviously since the West was the origin of the techniques and ideas, the first if one accepts as true the general notion that many of the common features of Western societies—contract relations, bourgeois democracy, the conjugal multilineal family and so on—are the inevitable concomitants of industrialization, 'functional prerequisites' for an industrial society in the East as much as in the West.

According to this picture, then, Japan started moving from the 'traditional' towards the 'modern' pole some three-quarters of a century ago, propelled by these three basic factors. Japanese urban society, it might be thought, had already moved a considerable way towards the 'modern' end.

Such a model has a limited use in this sort of study. It was not possible to observe social change as such during the six months of the study. All that could be hoped for was to document Shitayama-cho within the context of this model, to try to show, by explicit comparisons with traditional Japanese society and with other industrial societies (almost exclusively England) whereabouts on this hypothetical scale it stood, and to attempt, where possible, to test the validity of the model itself and the assumptions on which it rested; to answer, that is, such questions as: Is it impossible for traditional family patterns to survive in an industrial society? (i.e. Are there signs of strain where they do?) or: Is urban life in an industrial society inimical to the tightly knit form of local community life which existed in Japanese rural areas and to a lesser extent in urban areas of the Tokugawa period?

Another related problem within this general framework concerned the inter-relations, at the level of attitudes and ideas, between changes in different spheres of life: a question posed in the form: Are the observable differences in outlook between individuals in Shitayama-cho capable of being characterized as 'generally traditional' and 'generally modern' or 'progressive'? Are the individuals who manifest attitudes towards their employer which conform to what one would expect at the 'modern' end of the scale likely also to manifest 'modern' attitudes to their wives?

Certain sections of the book (in particular those on old age and the relations between parents and children) are also concerned with the 'problems' of change as they are experienced by the Japanese themselves: overt problems, that is to say, of conflict and adjustment which are recognized as demanding solution.

The topics selected for discussion have, then, been chosen primarily in the light of their relevance to these various aspects of social change. But this was not the sole criterion used. An exclusive preoccupation with applying to Shitayama-cho the yardstick of 'A society which differs from none of the Western industrial societies more than they differ from each other' would run the danger of ignoring the particular differentia of Japanese society, in particular those characteristics of outlook and way of life, more amenable to a 'cultural' than to a 'structural' approach and as easily portrayed in a novel as in the form of a scientific treatise, which make a Frenchman different from an Englishman and a Japanese different from both.

This book does attempt, then, if not to give an analysis of Japanese 'national character', at least to convey something of the flavour, the 'essential Japaneseness' of life in Tokyo. As a guide to observation and enquiry a list was first drawn up of 'What . . .?' and 'How . . .?' questions which the data collected should try to answer. These questions were of diverse origin. Apart from those which arose from the problems of change discussed above, some took the form 'Is it true that . . .?' followed by an assertion about the Japanese made by such writers as Ruth Benedict, some were the result of reading similar studies of other societies and attempting to formulate explicitly the questions about the community studied which their works were intended to answer (in particular, the Lynds' *Middletown* was a fruitful source, many echoes of which will be found in this book). Others concerned features of Japanese life which had struck me as 'significant' or 'interesting'.

The question of what is likely to strike a foreign observer as 'significant' or 'interesting' is worth pursuing since it points up the inherent relativity of all ethnographic description. If a well-trained anthropologist says 'the Japanese are indulgent to their children', this statement may be interpreted: 'if all studied peoples are ranged on a continuum with respect to the degree of indulgence they show their children the Japanese will be found at the indulgent end'. A good anthropologist, of course, would rarely make such unqualified general statements without concrete examples of the behaviour of Japanese parents to their children. But, nevertheless, if parental indulgence is selected for comment and illustration the reason is likely to be that it is felt in some way to differentiate Japanese from other cultures.

In this case, having only a limited knowledge of other societies, the yardstick by which I selected topics as 'characteristic' or 'interesting' was chiefly difference from what I knew of my own. When I say 'the Japanese are indulgent to their children', it means 'more indulgent than English parents'. Such general statements will, of course, as far as possible be avoided in favour of concrete illustrations, but it will be as well to remember that it is this criterion of difference from my own society which makes me choose to comment on the Japanese parent's indulgence to his children and not on the fact that Japanese mothers are proud of their babies, to say something about the social status of the priest and omit to mention that the doctor is accorded greater social prestige than a road-sweeper, to discuss the disposition of sleeping quarters within the family but not to point out that the Japanese sleep in a horizontal position. As a reminder of this relativity and the limitations it involves, it was thought best to make such lurking comparisons explicit. This runs the risk of arousing what the author of a book with intentions similar to this calls, in explaining his reason for avoiding the odium of comparisons, 'feelings of unfriendly criticism and Pharasaical self-satisfaction'.[1] But in the nature of the case this would seem unavoidable.

A warning should be entered concerning Section II which describes the contemporary material setting for the attitudes and behaviour discussed in the rest of the book. Since 1951, when this study was made, the increased tempo of industrial expansion has brought Japan well beyond the phase of post-war reconstruction. According to the Government's Economic Survey, the consumption level of the average urban family for the period October 1956–April 1957 stood at 156% of the 1951 figure. Section II should not, therefore, be read as an up-to-date account of present-day levels of living, though there has probably been less change in the attitudes and standards of consumption which are there discussed. In the field of social security, considered in Chapter 6, there has been some increase in assistance grants and an expansion of war pension schemes, but no major change in other areas of the state security system.

Finally, a word about the interpretation of the results of formal interviews. (Details concerning the schedules used, sampling and analysis, etc., are to be found in Appendix I.) Japan at the time of the survey was occupied by a reforming, 'democratizing', army. The reader may well be led to wonder how far replies to interview questions, in particular those touching on political matters, were distorted by the fact that those interviewed had a shrewd understanding of the prejudices of foreigners and simulated opinions which they did not hold in order to give the answer which they thought 'correct' from the foreigner's standpoint.

Subjective impressions that this was not often the case are, perhaps, of little value, but certain objective facts are relevant. In the first place the interviews were mostly carried out by Japanese students, and any distortion there was is as likely to have been in deference to their opinions as to mine. This may still give the results a somewhat false 'progressive' bias. Secondly, in so far as the respondents were, during the interviews, aware of myself as the prime mover, the prejudices imputed to me would not necessarily have been linked with the post-war reforms and the propaganda of democracy. America loomed so large in the closing stages of the war and in the occupation that Britain was largely forgotten. Moreover, in the minds of many people, particularly the older ones, Britain is still pictured in colours which belong to the days of the Anglo-Japanese alliance—the other island Empire, the friendly power of the West which shares with Japan many noble features such as respect for tradition and monarchy, and a code of restrained etiquette which has something in common with the 'way of the warrior'. It should not necessarily be supposed, therefore, that everyone would assume that the 'correct' line with me would be to show enthusiasm for all that had been done by the Occupation. Thirdly, some of the topics selected for investigation in Shitayama-cho have also been investigated by Japanese research institutes and sociologists. Their results (which are sometimes quoted in the text) do not show any great difference in the balance of opinions from those obtained in Shitayama-cho.

It should be emphasized, however, that these arguments are intended to suggest only that a special element of deliberate distortion of opinion due to the political situation at the time is not very probable. This is not to claim that the opinions elicited in interviews represent deep and unshakeable convictions. All the drawbacks inherent in opinion surveys anywhere were present in this case, the more so since little use was made in these interviews of devices for measuring the intensity or the consistency of opinions. It will be apparent, however, that in this book my concern has been less with the measurement of opinion as an end in itself, as with enumerating the differences of opinion which exist, with showing the attitudinal and structural backgrounds of different opinions, and, where possible, with speculating on the directions of change.

NOTE: Where statistical tests of association are used, the value of p (the probability that the association is due entirely to chance) is indicated in a footnote. Chi square was generally used, but in some cases the more approximate method of the standard deviation of the difference. Where the latter method was used, this has been indicated in brackets—as (s.d. of d.).

In the text, the following conventional phrases have been adopted:

A 'noticeable' difference or association: when $\cdot05 < p < \cdot2$, i.e. the chances of the result being due to sampling error lie between one in five and one in twenty. This is used when it is thought likely that a real difference is obscured by the small size of the sample.

A 'significant' difference or association: when $\cdot 01 < p < \cdot 05$, i.e. the the result could occur by chance more frequently than once in a hundred, but less frequently than once in twenty times.

A 'very (or highly) significant' difference or association: when $p < \cdot 01$, i.e. the result would occur by chance less than once in a hundred times.

The reference numbers for notes which contain only source citations or figures for independence values are italicized in the text.

2

Shitayama-cho

THE popular names for the major districts of large cities—East End, West End, South-side, the Left Bank—are not always capable of precise territorial definition. This is understandable since these names stand, more than anything, as symbols of different ways of life. Modern Tokyo, for the urban ecologist, divides satisfactorily into the concentric zones he seeks to find,[2] but as far as the ordinary inhabitant of Tokyo is concerned his city is divisible into two parts—*Shitamachi*, the 'down-town' districts, and *Yamanote*, the 'hill-side'. Of the various characteristics by which they are supposed to be distinguished from each other, we may briefly list a few.

1. First, the Shitamachi districts were, in origin, the districts inhabited by the non-samurai merchant and artisan families during the Tokugawa period. Yamanote districts were those in which were to be found the town mansions of the feudal nobility and the houses and barracks of the lesser ranks of the samurai class.

2. Geographically, the samurai districts were found in the rather more airy and salubrious higher ground which begins some way inland from the coast of Tokyo bay. The merchants and artisans were concentrated on the alluvial plain between this higher ground and the sea, a strip of land beginning as a narrow beach at Shinagawa in the south of the city, and widening out into a coastal plain three or four miles wide to the north-east. There were some commoners' districts, however, scattered among the samurai areas.

3. As a direct consequence of their origins, the typical Shitamachi man is still thought of as a merchant or an independent craftsman, perhaps a tailor or a restaurant-owner, a carpenter or the owner of a small workshop employing one or two workers. The typical Yamanote man, on the other hand, gets his living from the modern tertiary industries; he is the professional man, the official, the business executive, the sales assistant in a departmental store, the clerical worker in one of Tokyo's large offices.

4. There are differences in language too. The language of the old Yamanote districts has received the official cachet as standard Japanese. The Shitamachi districts preserve elements of the old Edo

11

dialect, and even when a Shitamachi man speaks standard Japanese, slight deviations from the received pronunciation are supposed to be noticeable—*hi* becomes *shi* and there is a tendency to double consonants.

5. Then there are traditional differences in temperament between the Shitamachi man and the Yamanote man. The first is hot-tempered, but warm-hearted, uninhibited in his enjoyment of sensual pleasures, extravagant and with no thought for the morrow. The Yamanote man is more prudent, more rational, inhibited in his enjoyments and in his friendships by the demands of a bourgeois respectability.

6. There are numerous other associated cultural differences. The wide-open, no-secrets, communal life of the Shitamachi family contrasts with the greater individualism and privacy of the Yamanote family. The close relations between neighbours and tremendous enthusiasm in the local celebration of festivities in Shitamachi districts contrasts with neighbourly diffidence and half-hearted participation in shrine festivals in Yamanote. Indeed, whereas the Shitamachi family typically lives in a crowded street in a densely populated area, the Yamanote family divides itself from its neighbours with a garden and a hedge. The Shitamachi taste is largely for traditional Japanese entertainments, the *kabuki* theatre, the *sumoo* wrestling, traditional sentimental music, the *geisha* houses; whereas the Yamanote man is more attracted by things Western, orchestral music, 'modern' dramas, foreign films, 'social' (i.e. ball-room) dancing, together with, in the more traditional Yamanote families, a taste for the more 'refined' elements of the indigenous culture—the *Noo* mime-drama, the tea ceremony, the music of the *koto* lute rather than the popular *shamisen* banjo. Shitamachi women are more likely to wear Japanese dress, and when they do they have a distinctive way of wearing it—the *kimono* is cut lower to disclose more of the nape of the neck (traditionally an erotic zone) and the *obi* waist-band is worn lower down on the hips.

It is tempting to sum all this up as lower middle class and below, versus lower middle class and above. But such categorizations can be very misleading. At least one needs the qualifications which distinguish not only the old from the new upper middle class as in England, but also the old from the new working class, the old from the new lower middle class. For here one is dealing with a society which, until three-quarters of a century ago, had an estate system whose main lines of cleavage did not entirely correspond with gradations in economic status (many of the 'inferior' townsmen were far richer than many of the 'superior' samurai), where modern industry has only partly displaced more traditional forms of production, and where 'Japaneseness', as opposed to 'Western-ness', is still a criterion of some importance for dividing men from their fellows and one which does not necessarily follow economic status lines.

At any rate, the above list indicates some of the general characteristics which the names Shitamachi and Yamanote suggest to Tokyo Japanese. The geographical areas with which they associate them are still respectively the low-lying and the higher areas within the boundaries of the old city of Edo (as Tokyo was called in Tokugawa times). Whether the new post-Meiji[3] industrial and working-class areas to the north-east and south of Tokyo would be called Shitamachi is doubtful. It is more common, however, to include in Yamanote the newer residential areas, both the predominantly white-collar suburbs lying on either side of the central railway line running approximately due west out of Tokyo, and the newer professional and business class areas in the south-west.

Many changes taking place within the old city boundaries have also had the effect of blurring these distinctions. The centre of the old Shitamachi has now become the governmental and financial centre; an area filled with office blocks, banks and ministry buildings, spreading over into three boroughs[4] which have a day population between two and three times their night population (for the centre alone the ratio is, of course, much higher). Then there has been a tendency for the more successful of Shitamachi merchants and craftsmen, whose business has expanded to the point where the separation of home from workshop becomes possible, to move out to the Yamanote districts and commute daily; for, although the 'real Edokko' like the 'real Cockney' is intensely proud of his own culture, his defiant rejection of the Yamanote belief in Yamanote cultural superiority does not always carry absolute conviction. This migration was considerably accelerated by the great earthquake and fire of 1923 and again by the bombing of 1945, both of which destroyed large sections of Shitamachi Tokyo.[5]

Thus there are many districts within the old city boundaries, even, which cannot be readily assigned to the Shitamachi or to the Yamanote category. Both these concepts are a composite of a number of variables, not all of them interdependent and each of them representing a continuum, so that although one can find districts which fairly fit the stereotypes, there are many others which may be more like Shitamachi in one respect, more like Yamanote in another, and halfway in between in yet another respect.

The borough to which Shitayama-cho belonged was clearly Shitamachi; to give one numerical indication of its general character, in 1940 it had the highest proportion of manufacturing enterprises employing fewer than five workers' (three-quarters of them without any electric power) of any borough in Tokyo—one for every 33 of the population.[6] Shitayama-cho, however, which lies on the edge of the borough, is one of the betwixt and between wards; it could hardly be called Yamanote, but it is not quite Shitamachi. Houses are close-packed around narrow streets, there is less privacy in family life and more solidarity in communal ward activities than one could expect in Yamanote districts; on the other hand, most of the inhabitants are wage and salary earners rather than independent shopkeepers and craftsmen, and the majority do not come from old Edo families. The composite name Shitayama-cho, which is not the ward's real name, will stand as a reminder that it represents, in many ways, a mingling of the two strains in Tokyo culture.

Geographically, Shitayama-cho stands on the dividing line between the old Shitamachi and the old Yamanote. It is in the valley of a small river, now piped underground, which makes a narrow indentation into the line of the higher ground. Old maps of the Tokugawa period show it as divided into four or five plots, the largest of which contained the town residence of a minor feudal baron, the others the houses of lesser Tokugawa vassals. A few hundred yards away from these samurai mansions were wards inhabited by commoners some of whose descendants still live there today.

At the Meiji restoration, the original residents were confirmed in their ownership of the land, but, with the commutation of feudal dues and the frequent failures of ex-samurai in their attempts to find some commercial solution to the problem of achieving a *modus vivendi* with a bewildering new world, the land changed hands rapidly. By the end of the century a large proportion of it had become the property of another ex-feudal-baron family which rented it out in—at first fairly large-unit—building lots. The population grew steadily.[7]

In the nineteenth century the residents seem to have been mostly well-to-do; the houses large enough to have been called 'mansions' (*yashiki*). The greengrocer remembers among the neighbours of his childhood about 1900, a Count, the president of a small bank, a retired army surgeon, the head of a private suburban railway and a large-scale labour contractor who built the longest tunnel in Japan. At that time the neighbouring hill-side was still dotted with fields of cultivated land—the district had its own 'famous local product', a special sort of ginger which was reputed to grow here better than anywhere else. There was a thatcher living in the ward; the river still ran beside the streets and was trapped off into fish-ponds which supported a flourishing gold-fish breeding industry. The main road from the centre of the city to some of the famous beauty spots towards the north then ran along one side of the ward and this road was lined with tea-houses and restaurants which aimed to catch such moon-viewing, plum-blossom viewing and cherry-blossom viewing traffic. 'The day we sold ten barrels of tangerines to people going up to the

Chrysanthemum Festival' is still a living legend in the greengrocer's family.

At about the time of the first world war the trams came past the ward and took the main road elsewhere—along the line of the former river, now piped underground. Then with the big expansion of industry and the growth in the population and size of Tokyo which came with the wartime boom, Shitayama-cho began somewhat to change its residential character. The first batch of Meiji houses had reached the end of their normal life-span. They were replaced by smaller ones. The land was parcelled into smaller lots and gradually sold off as the aristocratic landlord's fortunes declined. Some speculative builders came in and built rows of two-storey houses, others built *apaato*—apartment blocks containing twenty to thirty one-room units. Hotels were built, a bath-house, two small factories. Only two of the old 'mansions' remain and one has been turned into a hotel. The residents, as they became more numerous, tended to come from lower down the social scale.

Not unimpeachable, but probably not very inaccurate, figures for the population of the ward are shown in Table 1.

Table 1: Population of Shitayama-cho

Year	Number of households	Number of persons
1872	21	72
1875	91	348
1920	—	794
1930	—	862
1950 (Oct.)	344	1,302
1951 (Mar.)	310 (approx.)	1,225 (approx.)[8]

Shitayama-cho escaped both the earthquake fire of 1923 and the fire raids of 1945, but bombing and the housing shortage has brought over-crowding here as it has to every other part of Tokyo. Housing will be considered separately later on; here it will suffice to note that there would appear to have been little increase in the number of dwellings since 1930, only in the number of people inhabiting them. Apart from those families—nearly a quarter of the total—who live in one-room *apaato*, many other families share houses, there are (still excluding the *apaato*-dwellers) five households for every four dwellings, and the narrowness of the streets, together with the lack of gardens adds to the general sense of congestion.[9]

Some houses are well-proportioned, neat and trim. The tiled roof with its ornamental edge-tiles; the lower-floor eaves; the porch with its wooden gable and sliding doors of opaque glass and criss-cross wooden frame; the wide windows with at night their wooden-board shutters and by day their sliding panels of glass or white paper—all these can make an attractive composition, especially when they are set off by the shrubbery of a small garden spilling over the top of a six-foot wooden fence with a simple but interesting panel design and, as its central feature, an ornamental arched gateway made of the finest timber. But such 'gated' houses are rare (indeed, only 10 houses in Shitayama-cho have gardens bigger than 40 square yards, and 65% of the houses have no gardens at all). Most houses abut directly on to the narrow lanes. Nor are all made of wood of the quality which (always unpainted) mellows to a ripe brown without cracking or splitting; some are obviously patched, a few with corrugated iron; and some, with rotting boards hanging loose, are in obvious need of patching. A few tiles askew on the roof, the paper of the windows or internal partitions browned by the sun and jaggedly holed by children's fingers, show that keeping a Japanese house neat and attractive in appearance is something which requires a continuous expenditure of time and money.

But dilapidation as such is only a minor contributory factor to the general immediate impression of untidiness and disorder which a street in Shitayama-cho presents. Except for a few solid rows of terrace houses, building has been unplanned, and houses which have been fitted like jigsaw pieces into every viable space present themselves to the lanes at odd angles and in higgledy-piggledy order. There is a mass of overhead wiring for telephones and electricity; in the absence of gardens, washing is hung on rows of bamboo poles on special platforms which jut out at first floor level indiscriminately at the front or the back of the house. On fine days the bedding—thick eiderdowns, quilts and nightshirts—is hung from upper windows to air; cooking pots and pieces of furniture are pushed out on to the narrow upper floor verandahs from rooms where living space is insufficient. One house may have a low miniature chicken-run built in front of it in the three-foot width between the outer wall and the concrete paving slabs down the centre of the lane, while on the other side a grocer, strategically placed on a corner, further encroaches on the right-of-way with a wall of stacked crates and barrels along the whole side of his shop. Two of the roads were wide enough for motor-cars, but they were unmetalled, a source of choking dust in the dry and windy spring and a hazard of puddles in the wet early summer. The narrow lanes had a row of paving stones down the centre for rainy weather, and gutter ditches on either side, theoretically covered with boarding which in many places was rotting away or completely missing. One of these lanes was just wide enough for a car, but rarely used, except for an occasional midnight taxi fetching clients from the restaurant in the middle of the ward who were too drunk, or too important, to walk to the main road.

Shitayama-cho may not present a very attractive exterior, and the sense of style and colour harmony for which the Japanese are justly famed may not be immediately visible, but Shitayama-cho was made to be lived in and not to be looked at. Its streets are lively and friendly places. In sunny weather they become playgrounds for groups of young children—boys with shaved or close-cropped heads, girls with doll-like fringes who sit outside their homes on rush mats (wooden clogs, as tabooed on outdoor mats as on the indoor ones, neatly lined up at the edge) banging merrily with a hammer at pieces of wood, making mud pies, entertaining with broken pieces of china on soap boxes, blowing bubbles, queueing for their turn on a lucky child's tricycle. After school hours they are joined by groups of older children. Girls skipping or playing hop-scotch, ball-bouncing to interminable songs with a younger brother or sister nodding drowsily on their backs. Boys wrestling, poring over comics, huddled into con-spiratorial groups, playing games of snap with tremendous gusto and noise. There is generally, too, a group of their mothers passing the time of the day as they look benevolently on and prepare to mediate in quarrels. With their hair permanently waved or drawn into a bun at the back and clogs on their feet (nothing else could be slipped on and off so easily every time they enter and leave the house), a white long-sleeved apron obscures the difference between those (younger ones) who wear skirt and blouse, and those (older ones) who wear *kimono*. One of them, perhaps, standing as she talks slightly bent forward to balance the weight of a three-year-old tied astraddle her back, is on her way to the bath-house, a fact proclaimed by the metal bowl she carries in hands clasped under the baby's buttocks and by the washable rubber elephant with which he hammers abstractedly at the nape of her neck.

Sometimes there is a clatter of drums and the sound of a flute and the crowds in the lane are suddenly augmented by more white-aproned women and excited children flocking to see the 'tinkle-bang merchant'—the advertising man, dressed up as a samurai of the Tokugawa period with his son as flautist-cum-clown. Heavily made up, his hair tied in a well-greased top-knot, a swaggering scabbard at his side (and police permit in pocket with map showing proposed itinerary duly appended), he stops every fifty yards to address his hearers on the merits of the fishmonger's fish, or perhaps, if he is commissioned by the Anti-crime Association that day, on the dangers of leaving one's house unattended; speaking all the time in the old literary style which nowadays is heard elsewhere only on the stage of the *kabuki* theatre. Almost every day after school-time another drum announces the arrival of the 'paper-theatre man'. Children gather around his bicycle. A brisk trade in boiled sweets and lollipops ensues. Then he unfolds a wooden frame-work attached to the carrier and recounts to a breathless audience that day's instalment of his interminable serial story, illustrated with pictures which he shows them one by one. Umbrella-menders and shoe-menders come calling their business round the ward, spread a mat on the ground in a shady spot in one of the lanes and sit with their tools awaiting customers. Early in the morning, at any time after half-past six, one can hear the plaintive horn of the bean-curd seller, or the cry of the *nattoo* man selling a sticky substance made from fermented beans, favourite breakfast delicacies which, especially in the hot summer, are best eaten fresh. The fishmonger's barrow, the flower-seller's cart, sellers of children's toys and doll-shaped sweets, knife-sharpeners, junk men come along these narrow streets one after the other in a profusion symptomatic of post-war unemployment. Each one provides an excuse for some gregariously inclined housewife to join a gossiping group in the lane.

But despite the general appearance of neighbourly friendliness, and despite the general sameness of everyday dress and of the houses they inhabited (except for a few secluded ones), Shitayama-cho contained a fairly heterogeneous population; heterogeneous in origin, in occupation, in educational background and in way of life. Before going on, in later chapters, to consider differences between individuals and families, it may be useful to give some general idea of the composition of Shitayama-cho's population and to 'place' it by some comparative figures in the urban Japanese population and in the population of Tokyo as a whole.

Table 2: Birthplace* by Sex, Shitayama-cho (1951) and Tokyo Borough Areas (1950)

Population of: / Birthplace	Shitayama-cho		Tokyo, all borough areas†	
	M(%)	F(%)	M(%)	F(%)
Shitayama-cho	11·3	7·2		
Other parts of Tokyo prefecture	48·5	41·6	}57·3	58·2
Elsewhere	40·2	51·2	42·7	41·8
Total	100·0	100·0	100·0	100·0

* Birthplace—Mother's usual place of residence at time of birth.
† Bureau of Statistics, Office of the Prime Minister, *Population Census of 1950*, vol. VII, pt. 13, p. 141.

Table 3: Years of Schooling completed by Persons 25 years old and over, by Sex. Shitayama-cho (1951), Tokyo Borough Areas and All Japan (1950)

Years of schooling	Shitayama-cho M(%) (N = 297)	Shitayama-cho F(%) (N = 332)	Tokyo, all borough areas † M(%)	Tokyo, all borough areas † F(%)	All Japan* M(%)	All Japan* F(%)
0–6	17·6	21·1	22·4	35·8	33·1	51·5
7–12	54·9	71·7	56·3	59·1	56·7	46·6
13+	24·1	3·6	21·1	4·9	10·0	1·8
Not repted.	3·4	3·6	0·2	0·2	0·1	0·1
Total	100·0	100·0	100·0	100·0	100·0	100·0

* Bureau of Statistics, Office of the Prime Minister, *Population Census of 1950*, vol. III, pt. 1 (10% sample), p. 109.
† *Ibid.*, vol. VII, pt. 13, p. 154.

Table 4: Percentage of Population aged 16–24 attending School, by Sex, Shitayama-cho (1951), Tokyo Urban Areas, All Urban Areas, and All Japan (1950)

	Aged 16–18 M(%)	Aged 16–18 F(%)	Aged 19–24 M(%)	Aged 19–24 F(%)
Shitayama-cho	66·6 (N = 30)	41·2 (N = 34)	35·1 (N = 77)	3·6 (N = 55)
Tokyo urban areas*	45·8	38·0	26·6	6·8
All urban areas†	42·9	33·8	14·7	4·1
All Japan	34·4	28·2	8·5	3·4

* This includes, as well as the Tokyo borough areas, the three cities of Tokyo Prefecture, Tachikawa, Musashino and Hachiooji (Bureau of Statistics, Office of the Prime Minister, *Population Census of 1950*, vol. VII, pt. 13, p. 21).
† Bureau of Statistics, *op. cit.*, vol. III, pt. 1 (10% sample), p. 105. Urban areas are those under a city or metropolitan administration. City administrations were in principle established where (a) there is a population concentration of more than 30,000 inhabitants, (b) of which 60% or more are concentrated in a central nucleus, and (c) of which 60% or more get their living from commerce and industry (Isomura Eiichi, *Toshi Shakaigaku*, 1953, p. 7).

Table 5: Population by Age and Sex, Shitayama-cho; 1951, Tokyo, All Boroughs; Japan All Urban and All Rural Areas (1950)

Age	Shitayama-cho (N = 1,181)		Tokyo all boroughs*		Japan, all urban areas†		Japan, all rural areas†	
	M(%)	F(%)	M(%)	F(%)	M(%)	F(%)	M(%)	F(%)
0–4	5·42	5·84	6·26	5·99	6·69	6·41	6·98	6·71
5–9	5·00	5·42	5·33	5·18	5·57	5·43	5·95	5·80
10–14	3·89	3·13	4·22	4·14	4·68	4·55	5·66	5·55
15–19	4·40	4·31	5·53	4·93	5·21	5·18	5·15	5·05
20–24	5·50	3·81	6·00	5·21	5·05	5·07	4·31	4·46
25–29	3·81	5·25	4·35	4·81	3·80	4·49	3·13	3·76
30–34	4·23	5·42	3·49	3·96	3·17	3·77	2·62	3·20
35–39	3·47	4·06	3·43	3·49	3·20	3·45	2·65	3·08
40–44	3·13	3·30	2·99	2·90	2·87	2·88	2·52	2·65
45–49	2·88	3·05	2·70	2·50	2·55	2·47	2·35	2·33
50–54	2·88	1·95	2·20	1·95	2·09	2·00	2·05	2·02
55–59	1·27	2·29	1·63	1·48	1·57	1·54	1·70	1·70
60–64	1·35	1·27	1·16	1·16	1·19	1·27	1·42	1·54
65–69	1·10	0·59	0·67	0·82	0·78	0·98	1·07	1·28
70–79	0·85	0·85	0·50	0·82	0·68	1·08	1·14	1·58
80+	0·17	0·08	0·05	0·13	0·09	0·20	0·19	0·35
Not reptd.	—	—	0·01	0·00	0·02	0·02	0·02	0·02
Total	49·35	50·62	50·52	49·48	49·21	50·79	48·91	51·08

* Bureau of Statistics, Office of the Prime Minister, *Population Census of 1950*, vol. VII, pt. 13, p. 46.

† *Ibid.*, vol. III, pt. 1, pp. 30–1.

It will be seen from Table 2 that migrants from areas outside Tokyo are as common in the Shitayama-cho population as in the population of Tokyo as a whole, and significantly more common in the case of women, a feature which may be due to a higher proportion of domestic and hotel servants (mostly country-born) among the younger age-groups in Shitayama-cho than in the Tokyo population as a whole. The proportion born in Shitayama-cho itself is small, it consists mostly of children.

Average household size in Shitayama-cho (3·8) is smaller than in Tokyo borough areas as a whole (4·2), which is in turn smaller than in all urban areas of Japan (4·5; for rural areas the corresponding figure is 5·3).[10] Table 6 shows what this means in terms of household composition. The slightly smaller proportion of female 'spouse of children and grandchildren', if not due to sampling error, would indicate that the urban trend away from the three-generation family

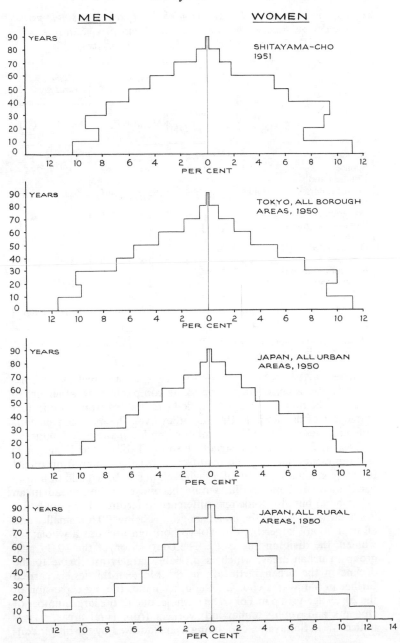

DIAGRAM 1—Population by age and sex (10 year age-groups)

Table 6: Population in Private Households (excluding single-person households) by Relationship to Househead and Sex, Shitayama-cho (1951), Japan, All Urban and All Rural Areas (1950)

Relationship to househead	Shitayama-cho		Japan, all urban areas*		Japan, all rural areas*	
	M(%) (N = 567)	F(%) (N = 576)	M(%)	F(%)	M(%)	F(%)
Household	46·0	6·4	38·2	5·1	33·2	3·7
Spouse	1·1	35·1	0·1	33·3	0·1	29·2
Children and grandchildren	40·6	39·9	53·0	46·1	58·0	48·2
Spouse of children or grandchildren	0·7	1·9	0·6	2·5	0·8	6·3
Parents and grandparents	1·1	5·9	1·6	6·5	2·9	8·4
Other related persons	2·8	4·2	3·8	3·8	3·8	3·9
Not reptd. and non-related persons	7·8	6·6	2·7	2·6	1·2	1·2
Total	100·0	100·0	100·0	100·0	100·0	100·0

* Bureau of Statistics, Office of the Prime Minister, *Population Census of 1950*, vol. III, pt. 1, p. 125.

is carried further in Shitayama-cho than in urban areas as a whole. There is also a considerable excess (as compared with other urban areas) in the number of unrelated lodgers, half of whom are in fact employees of the family with which they live. The most conspicuous difference lies in the smaller number of 'children and grandchildren', and as the figures for age structure show (Table 5 and Diagram 1) this represents not only the result of increasing atomization of the family (e.g. a married man of 30 who might still be a 'child of house-head' in a rural household, would be himself a househead in an urban area) but also some real difference in fertility. The population is somewhat older; all the male age-groups below 30 are smaller and all over 30 are larger than in Tokyo borough areas as a whole; for women, the dividing line is 25. The contraction of the 10–19 age-group in urban areas, which is probably largely ascribable to the decline in the urban birth-rate in the nineteen-thirties, is carried further in Shitayama-cho. On the other hand, the big expansion of the 20–29 age-group in Tokyo as a whole, due to the large number of students and young unmarried workers from rural areas, is less noticeable in Shitayama-cho, being overshadowed by the bigger concentrations in the 30–49 age-groups. Some of the peculiarities in Shitayama-cho age structure can be explained by the relatively high proportion of households living in one-room apartment houses, a type of housing which tends to attract younger couples at the beginning of their married career.

The figures for occupational distribution (Table 7) and for education (Tables 3–4) illustrate the point made earlier concerning the relative heterogeneity of the Shitayama-cho population. The reasons for this and its significance as a social phenomenon will be considered in later chapters dealing with neighbour relations; here we are concerned only with the extent to which it affects the representativeness of Shitayama-cho as a segment of the Tokyo population. The differences between Shitayama-cho on the one hand, and Tokyo borough areas and other urban areas on the other, are all in the same direction; Shitayama-cho contains a bigger proportion in the higher-prestige-carrying occupations, and its population is better educated. There is a smaller proportion of industrial workers and a correspondingly higher proportion of managerial, clerical, and sales, service and transport workers (though not of professional workers). The proportion of self-employed particularly among sales and service workers is considerably greater than for all urban areas, and, although the corresponding detailed figures are not available, considerably greater also than for Tokyo borough areas where the total proportion of self-employed workers is smaller than for urban areas as a whole.[11]

An interesting feature of the figures for years of schooling and for the proportions attending high school and university, is that, whereas Shitayama-cho men are only slightly better educated than the Tokyo average, their wives have a somewhat greater educational superiority, and the proportion sending their children to high school and university is noticeably higher. This suggests that Shitayama-cho contains a higher than average proportion of the upwardly mobile, men who have 'got on' via other routes than the educational ladder, have married 'above' them and are now able to give their children a better education than they had themselves.

To sum up this brief survey of the demographic characteristics of Shitayama-cho, it may give a better perspective to the contents of later chapters to remember that the 'average' citizen lives in a slightly more 'urban' type of household than the 'average' Tokyo citizen, is slightly better educated and in a slightly more prestige-carrying occupation. In what follows, however, statements about the 'average' Shitayama-cho inhabitant will as far as possible give place to more concrete descriptions of individual cases and the range of variability.

Table 7: Occupation of Employed Men, Shitayama-cho (1951) Tokyo Borough Areas and Japan, All Urban Areas (1950)*

Occupation	Shitayama-cho			Tokyo all borough areas† (%)	Japan all urban areas‡ (%)
	Not now work-ing§	Gainfully employed			
		(No.)	(%)		
Professional and technical workers	—	19	6·0	7·7	6·9
Salaried workers		*13*	*4·1*		*5·6*
Self-employed‖		*6*	*1·9*		*1·3*
Managers and officials	4	31	9·7	6·9	5·2
Salaried workers	*3*	*15*	*4·7*		*4·2*
Self-employed	*1*	*16*	*5·0*		*1·0*
Clerical and related workers	2	80	25·1	17·8	15·2
Sales, service and transport workers	5	97	30·5	23·9	21·1
Wage and salaried workers	—	*48*	*15·1*		*14·7*
Unpaid family workers	—	*6*	*1·9*		*1·1*
Self-employed‖	*5*	*43*	*13·5*		*5·3*
Farmers, fishermen, lumbermen, miners	1	—	—	2·3	11·7
Craftsmen and production process workers	7	78	24·5	35·0	32·2
Wage and salaried workers	*4*	*54*	*16·9*		*22·4*
Unpaid family workers	—	*3*	*0·9*		*1·7*
Self-employed‖	*3*	*21*	*6·6*		*8·1*
Unskilled labourers	—	6	1·9	6·2	7·4
Not reported	30	3	0·9	0·2	0·2
Total	49	314	100·0	100·0	100·0

* The classification used is that of the Bureau of Statistics as contained in the report of the 1950 Census (major occupational groups, with some categories combined). See Bureau of Statistics, Office of the Prime Minister, *Population Census of 1950*, vol. iii, pt. 2.

† Bureau of Statistics, *op. cit.*, vol. vii, pt. 13, p. 94.

‡ Bureau of Statistics, *op. cit.*, vol. iii, pt. 2, pp. 80–90 and 139.

§ Owing to retirement, illness or unemployment. Figures in this column refer, therefore, to former or usual employment.

‖ For Shitayama-cho, all self-employed workers with five or more employees were included among the self-employed workers in the Managers and Officials category. All self-employed workers with fewer than five employees were included among the self-employed workers of the Professional and Technical, Sales Service and Transport, or Craftsmen and Production Process Workers categories. The exact criterion used by the Census authorities to discriminate Managers and Officials from (say) Craftsmen and Production Process Workers who are also employers of labour is not clear, particularly since a small number of Managers and Officials are classified as 'Self-employed workers without paid employees' (vol. iii, pt. 2, p. 139). It is possible that the difference in the size of the self-employed managerial group, as between Shitayama-cho and all Japanese urban Areas (5·0% as opposed to 1·0%) in part depends on difference in the criteria used.

Section II

LEVELS AND STANDARDS OF LIVING

3

Some Sketches

BEFORE coming to averages and percentages, it may be useful to give first a number of individual portraits of the material lives of some Shitayama-cho families.

O is a policeman, 39 years old, the son of a carpenter. He went to a secondary technical school, but for reasons of family poverty had to leave before completing the course. He has spent a large part of his adult life in the army, and married during the war. His first son was born in 1944. Soon afterwards his wife was bombed out of their house in Tokyo and returned to her home in the country. When he was demobilized and rejoined the police he brought his wife and child to live in their present one-room apartment. Since then two more children have been born.

The five of them have one 'four-and-a-half-mat' room, that is, a room about nine feet square with one large recessed cupboard to contain the bedding, which is rolled up and stored away in the daytime. The *tatami* mats which cover the floor of the room—made of an inch and a half's thickness of rice straw, covered with a woven rush of superior quality and hemmed with cloth—are yellowed and frayed and bear the distinctive musty odour of mats which should long ago have been renewed. Apart from a table, the only other furniture consists of two large chests-of-drawers and cupboards. These contain all the family possessions except the cooking pots and utensils which stand outside the sliding door, making narrower the already narrow corridor from which half a dozen other similar one-roomed flats open off. On the top of one of these chests is a wireless. There is one gas ring on which Mrs. O cooks for the whole family.

Cooking means primarily preparing the rice. The O family can rarely afford meat, but they have fish four or five times a week, though generally the least expensive salted salmon. The rest of the time their 'secondary food'—as everything except the rice, the 'primary food', is called—consists of vegetables, fresh or pickled. Every day Mr. O takes some of this 'secondary food' in a tin for his lunch. His 'primary food' comes from a special ration cooked at the police station, rice for half the month and a type of vermicelli made from buckwheat for the other·half.

One sink with a single cold water tap, and one lavatory are shared with three other families. The latter is connected with the sewer and, although without a flushing mechanism, is so arranged that the waste from the sink regularly flushes it out. There are no baths, but Mrs. O takes the children to the bath-house every other day and Mr. O goes regularly once a week. Laundry is difficult, and the tiny drying platform at the end of the corridor where the washing has to be strung on rows of bamboo poles, is quite inadequate. Nevertheless, the eldest boy is always sent to school in clean, though unironed clothes. Mrs. O would like to be able to afford an electric iron, but she is even more envious of those of her neighbours who own a sewing machine. One widow next door makes her living as a dress-maker and will make things cheaply for close neighbours.

It is in winter that the discomforts and inadequacies of a one-roomed apartment are most deeply felt. A brazier burning charcoal or anthracite briquettes produces fumes but probably less heat than five human bodies. In the dark and cold evenings the children have to be indoors long before their energies are exhausted. At seven, four and three, respectively, they do not remain still and silent for long together, and with three children on nine square yards one is bound to develop a certain insensitivity to their noise. Constant nagging and interference in their tempestuous games would be emotionally wearing as well as ineffective. An embarrassing effect of this habitual tolerance, however, is that when a visitor comes it is very difficult to prevent the children from climbing all over him. But, eventually, one after another the children will curl up on the floor asleep. Mrs. O will pull out an under-mattress from the cupboard, lift them bodily on to it, then, pulling the top clothes from their inert bodies, cover them with a thick coverlet.

Meanwhile, Mr. O has been entertaining his visitor by showing his small collection of maps of the old Edo, as Tokyo used to be called, and of books containing the short satirical poems of the late eighteenth and early nineteenth century, the collection of which is his hobby and he hopes may one day be his profession, for it is his chief ambition in life to own a bookshop. His wife, who does not consider herself as included in the conversation except when specifically addressed has, in the intervals of tea-making and putting the children to bed, been sitting under the forty-watt bulb embroidering red flower patterns on bright blue socks which an enterprising Tokyo manufacturer exports to America. She has, in fact, been doing this for most of the day. By this means she is able to earn the few shillings a week which bring up their family income to about £11 a month.[12]

Ten shillings of this goes on rent, and another 15s. or so on water, gas, electricity and charcoal. Eight or nine shillings are given to the children for sweets, and apart from about 15s. for newspapers, cigarettes, and a monthly visit to the cinema, most of the rest goes on food, with what can be spared left over for clothes. This leaves no margin for saving, but twice a year, at New Year and Midsummer, there are regular bonuses of £10 to £15, a half of which they spend immediately on necessities such as clothes. The other half they save in the hope of one day having a house of their own.

A house of their own is the one dominant and recurrent ambition of their lives. They have some hopes of a police house, and they apply for a Tokyo municipality flat every time the lottery is reopened. So far they have failed in five draws. After the sixth failure they will be entitled to a special ticket and their chances will be increased in the next draw from something like a hundred to one to something nearer forty to one. They think they have a good chance of getting one of these flats within three years.

Mrs. A is a widow of 62. She was born of a farming family on the outskirts of Tokyo, married at the age of 22 and widowed some fifteen years later. Her husband had owned a small retail business not far from Shitayama-cho, but when he became ill they were forced to sell it and move into their present house, then newly built, thirty-five years ago. Her husband left her with three children. The eldest died, but by dint of economy, her own exertions and family help she has managed to send both her son and her remaining daughter to the secondary school. They are now 31 and 27 respectively, both still unmarried and both working as clerks in the borough office.

Thirty-five years is not much less than the average life of a Japanese town house, and theirs shows some signs of age in uneven floors and darkened woodwork which adds to the dimness of rooms, the small opaque glass windows of which look immediately on to the side of another house.

It is a small single-storey house. Apart from a tiny kitchen with a sink and two gas rings, and a sink-flush lavatory, there are two rooms, one 'four-and-a-half mat' about nine feet square, and one 'eight-mat' about twelve feet square. The furniture—a low polished table, tall chests of drawers and a wardrobe—is old, but solid and of good workmanship. The 'eight-mat' room has an alcove in one corner in which Mrs. A always keeps a scroll painting, changed regularly according to the season of the year. In winter it may be a snow scene, in spring a still-life of a fish, in autumn a single persimmon or a raging torrent pouring through a mountain ravine whose flanks are ablaze with the red of maple leaves. Below the scroll is a simple tea-bowl, or some other ornament of pottery or bronze sometimes replaced by a bowl of flowers. Flowers are also kept on top of one of the chests-of-drawers in front of the small altar-shrine which contains the tablets of her husband and her eldest daughter. In the lavatory, too, there are always one or two flowers stuck in a small holder attached to the wall.

There is a wireless and a sewing machine, but no ice-box, or electric iron or electric fan, which are the hoped-for and possibly attainable luxuries of many Shitayama-cho householders. There is no bath, so they go to the Shitayama-cho bath-house, but even Mrs. A does not go more than once a week for, not being fond of gossip, sociability does not add an extra motive to cleanliness and twopence-halfpenny is not lightly to be thrown away.

Like most white-collar workers since the war, her children do not earn a great deal. 'However, we manage to get along—just, with nothing much to spare. My son is very good. He doesn't smoke or drink and we live very economically.' Between them they give her £12 or so a month. Mrs. A knows very well how she spends this for she keeps a careful household account. Most of it goes on food, apart from 12s. for rent, 16s. for gas, water and electricity and about 8s. for newspapers and cinemas. Small items of clothing are bought by Mrs. A out of her housekeeping money, but larger items are bought by her son who, as 'head of the family' disposes of the funds for this sort of thing. They manage to save a little, but only by denying themselves such luxuries as repairs to the roof and new clothes. Saving is necessary, however. First of all, it is hoped that the children will soon marry, and that is expensive, particularly for girls. It is already a cause of some worry that her daughter is 27 and still unmarried. Secondly, there must be something to fall back on in case of illness, for neither of them are insured. Their savings are in the form of small blocks of shares. So great has been the shortage of capital since the war, that facilities for the small investor are well developed and share holdings are spread over a wide sector of the urban population.

T is far and away the wealthiest man in the ward. His life is lived on a plane so removed from that of most of the residents of Shitayama-cho that, although in the ward, he is hardly of it, is widely disliked and, apart from delayed and grudging contributions to various subscription funds, he has no part in ward activities. His geographical position in one corner of the ward helps to make this isolation possible.

T is the son of a provincial architect and engineer. His wife is the daughter of a small-town hemp merchant. Neither had more than an elementary school education, both have more than average intelligence, brashness, drive and, it was widely held, unscrupulousness. They were typical examples of the rewards of entrepreneurial virtue in a period of rapid industrialization, but untypical in the prominent role played in their activities by Mrs. T who is commonly thought to

Street in Shitayama-cho

Street in Shitayama-cho

be the driving spirit of the partnership. 'Mme Chiang Kai-Shek', as she is known to the ward, is a woman of forbidding appearance and dominant personality, director of several companies, including one which publishes a woman's magazine. Inclined to snap at servants and to lecture visiting Englishmen on the monumental iniquities of socialism, she divides her time between her various offices, the hair-dressers and dress-makers who come to wait on her at her home, the entertainment of business contacts, a Woman's Economic Union of which she is vice-president, and, once every month, an old woman with shamanistic powers who is brought down from the country to afford her spiritual comfort and to advise her on current business. The day of the first post-war election when 'Mme Chiang Kai-Shek' marched through the ward at the head of a small army of servants to record her first vote and to supervise the recording of theirs, has become a part of Shitayama-cho legend.

From small beginnings, manufacturing a powder shampoo in a back room, the T's ended the war in control of several companies, most of them the product of the war situation and good contacts, sedulously maintained, with the army commissariat. These contacts served them well at the end of the war when stocks of industrial materials controlled by the Services dissolved at the threatened appearance of Occupation troops. As soon as the Occupation was established, their well-appointed house, which had escaped damage when nearly all Tokyo restaurants had been burnt down in the fire raids, was frequently borrowed by government officials for the enter-tainment of Occupation officials. In 1951 a contract for the supply of dried blood plasma for the American forces in Korea (4s. and a good meal per contribution offered to any healthy vagrant) was their main, and a very lucrative, source of income.

Their household consisted of themselves, a son who studied music, switched to medicine to avoid the call-up, and is now learning theatre production, two daughters who are attended daily by teachers of one or other of the polite and maidenly arts, a young university student (son of a poor farmer and recipient of a prefectural scholar-ship from T's native prefecture, given lodgings in T's house at the request of prefectural officials), three male and six female servants, two secretaries, a carpenter and three chauffeurs. The secretaries, carpenter and chauffeurs are for taxation purposes employees of the company, but live in to be the more readily available at any time of the day or night. In addition a half-dozen other homeless employees of the company are quartered in various parts of the building.

The T's are well-off by any standards. The house, rebuilt to Mrs. T's designs after a fire two years before, contains twenty-nine rooms of which ten are let off to servants and employees. The largest, about twenty feet by thirty, has a grand piano and a dance floor. It was installed for the entertainment of members of the Occupation. All except the guest-rooms are in Western style; the sitting-rooms stuffed with bronze urns, skin rugs, leather armchairs and cut-glass candelabras, are dominated by enormous marble mantelpieces. The doors are heavily and ornately carved. The bedrooms (air-conditioned) have Western beds, the family eats Western food from Western tables and chairs in a Western dining-room.

A recital of their material possessions becomes tedious: three radios, eighteen electric fans, two telephones, two cars (American post-war models), three electric refrigerators (one, in fact, a refrigerated cellar immediately stocked with quantities of tinned foods on the day the Korean war broke out), a tiled bath that is almost a swimming pool, a private line to the fire station, a room equipped with a special stage for the daughters' dancing lessons and so on. Household expenses are estimated by Mrs. T at £300 a month, but there are other claims on their income to be met. For instance, art dealers, under commission from depressed members of the old aristocracy, are constantly bringing things to them in the hope of a sale. It is difficult to refuse. *Richesse oblige*, and the present checking off of the inflation may not be permanent.

A, by contrast, is one of the poorest men in the ward. His father, a merchant, went bankrupt just as he was leaving the elementary school. He was sent to become a tailor's apprentice, and after many years of strictly disciplined service eventually set up with a business of his own. It gradually expanded, but towards the end of the war bombing destroyed both home and workshop. With the insurance money he entered the field of general brokerage, like a high proportion of the rest of the Tokyo population immediately after the war. He, however, lost his money; tried to start up his business again before all his money had gone; failed, and, two years before the survey, was reduced to daily attendance at the Labour Exchange for public unemployment relief work, which, when he was lucky enough to get work, brought him 4s. 10d. a day. Earlier on he would vary this with an odd day at the docks where one could earn twice that amount. But poverty has its own vicious spiral. The work at the docks is too hard for him unless he is well fed, and he cannot begin to be well fed until he has worked a month at the rates they pay at the docks. In any case, some of his income has to go on drink, a taste which he acquired when it was, with an occasional visit to the cheaper brothels, the only relief from the rigours of a strict apprenticeship.

Seven months ago he stuck a nail into his foot, the wound festered and he could not work. Eventually he was forced to swallow his pride and apply for public assistance. The doctor designated by the assistance authorities had a clientèle almost entirely derived from this source; he had, said A, no great reputation for skill and his surgery was poorly equipped. At any rate his leg did not heal and he got permission to change his doctor. He had, admittedly, aggravated matters by tramping the streets as a scrap-metal collector.

When he was better he hoped to develop this business in which he was engaged with a number of friends. He thought his leadership powers would be a great asset; he had, for instance, been leader of the local union among the relief workers. At any rate, he wanted no more of the drabness of life as an artisan. He was going to branch out in something more speculative, where talent would command quicker and more ample reward. His apprenticeship background has given him something of the old Edo 'Shitamachi spirit', with its pride in impetuosity and its scorn of prudent accumulation.

His wife, whom he had married when his fortunes were fair and his prospects favourable, was well-born and well-educated, the daughter of a provincial bank-manager. Her only fault, said her husband, was that she was an imbecile. However, she was the wife his old employer had found for him; he had accepted her and that was that. This remark, although it embarrassed the interviewer, appeared to have no effect on his wife. Her expression remained as impassive as ever, in so far as it could be seen in the candle-light, for the electricity had been cut off.

In theory they occupied three rooms above the greengrocer's shop, but it is some time since they last paid any rent and they remain only on sufferance, for a landlord does not like to turn the hopelessly poor on to the streets. They are now confined to one 'eight-mat' room (twelve feet by twelve). Water has to be fetched from downstairs, and the only cooking facilities consist of one small charcoal brazier. The *tatami* mats have almost entirely lost their surface in the centre of the room and are a mass of frayed yellow ends. The two chests-of-drawers are of good solid workmanship with wrought iron decorative bindings, the only relics of former prosperity and probably part of the wife's dowry. The only other furniture is a table and a crucifix, for Mr. A has been a Christian for many years and was once, he says, pressed to enter the priesthood.

The youngest child, thin, listless, with a bald patch on the back of his head showing the open sores of a skin disease, lay back in his mother's arms. He is three, the youngest of three children. The girl aged eight and the boy aged four lay in their clothes among the tattered and dirty bedding.

With loans from his friends, occasional help from his wife's home in the country, the public assistance grant and the proceeds of his scrap collecting, they manage to survive. His wife, he claims, for she is not allowed to give an opinion on this matter, disposes of £9–£12 a month. Apart from food, the only other expenditure is on cheap

potato wine, and occasionally pocket money for the children.
Everything else goes by the board.

K works in a bank. He is 54, the second son of a farmer from a
village some forty miles from Tokyo. Since he left the elementary
school he has always been in some office job or other. He came to
the ward when he first married twenty-four years ago. His first wife
bore him five children, but died soon after the birth of the fifth. The
child also died soon after. Of his four remaining sons the eldest has
gone back to K's father's home in his native village. K's elder brother
having died, there is no one else to succeed to the headship of the
farm family. The second works with the next-door neighbour who
makes xylophones in a small workshop at the back of his house. The
third suffers from a wasting disease, is partially paralysed and sits all
day carving toys from blocks of wood. The youngest is still at the
primary school.

Mr. K has married again, a cheerful, placid and competent woman
of the same age as himself. It is her second marriage also. They live
in a two-storey, three-roomed house, downstairs a 'three-mat' (six
feet by nine), divided by a sliding partition from a 'six-mat' (nine feet
by twelve) and upstairs another 'six-mat'. During the daytime the
upstairs room is used as an extra workroom by the neighbouring
xylophone-maker, and Mrs. K also earns a little extra by helping in
the work in her spare time.

Mrs. K is fairly satisfied with her standard of living. She has two
gas rings, a wireless, a firewood-heated bath, an electric iron, an ice-
box daily refilled with blocks of ice in the summer months. She has
never been used to luxuries such as electric fans, and, although a
sewing machine would be a nice thing to have, she rarely has the time
to use it. Only a year or two before, the house was thoroughly
repaired; the leaking roof mended and the warped door-frames replaced. (The house had been built by a speculative builder in the late
twenties and much of the wood had been of poor quality.) They are
not over-crowded; the children can sleep in a separate room from
her and her husband. If they were to receive a sudden windfall the
first thing they would think of would be to build another house in a
quieter district. Here they have no garden, but they nevertheless
manage to keep half a dozen chickens by making a run the length of
the house-front, taking up a strip about a yard wide of the earth
path and reaching up to the level of the bottoms of the windows.

With her husband's, her son's and her own earnings, the rent for
the daytime use of the upper room and the interest on a small holding of industrial shares, Mrs. K disposes of about £16 a month. Her
husband probably spends an extra £3 or so as pocket money; she
does not know the exact amount. Of the £16, about £10 goes on food;
rent comes to 13s., gas, water, electricity and firewood to 26s., in-

surance 10s., pocket money for the children 10s. The cost of various school activities (Mrs. K is class representative on the P.T.A. committee), newspapers, cigarettes (her own), cinemas and entertaining her husband's friends takes the rest. Their needs are fairly modest and they are content to eat the ration rice, even though it does contain some Siamese rice and even barley mixed into it, rather than pay more for pure white Japanese rice on the black market as some of her more wealthy neighbours do. Mrs. K is proud of the fact that none of the people who call for rent, insurance, gas or water money has ever been asked to come back again the following week.

Mrs. A is a widow. Her husband died of tuberculosis while the survey was in progress. He was 43. For a year she had been nursing him in the one six-mat room (nine feet by twelve) in a large apartment block which constituted all the living space they had for themselves and four children. They were married not long before the war when they were both working in Tokyo. He was the son of a non-commissioned officer in the army; her father was a clerk in a small country town. During the war he was in the army. His wife stayed in Tokyo until their house was destroyed in a fire-bomb raid. She and her children then went back to her parents' home in the country, where they stayed, in full and uncomfortable knowledge that they were a burden on their parents' resources, until 1948 when her husband, who had been leading a precarious odd-job existence in Tokyo since demobilization, succeeded in finding a permanent job.

Soon he fell ill, however, and it became apparent that he was going to die. As he had been working in a small engineering workshop which was not covered by the government's sickness and unemployment benefit scheme, apart from a few small gifts from his previous employer, they had no income. Mrs. A went to the Tokyo municipal work centre, where she managed to get some 'home work' which brought in between £2 and £3 a month. Neighbours helped with gifts of food and clothing for the children; she was able to borrow a little from relatives, but not much. Very rapidly she was forced to apply for public assistance, and after being assured that she was absolutely destitute the public authorities gave her some £6 a month. With gifts and her own earnings, she had about £10 a month to spend on herself, four growing children and a husband who required special foods. The public-assistance doctor came to see him once or twice, but not very often; his time was limited and it was better to devote it to people whom he could cure. Basic costs amounted to 27s. for rent, gas, water and electricity. For this they have a room and the use of a lavatory, five taps and four gas rings shared in common with ten other households. Most of the rest went on food.

Now that she is a widow, Mrs. A is economically somewhat better off than she has been for the past year. She has not got to feed her husband and she has more time to earn money. Neighbours will look after the children while she goes out to do a full-time job. Even so, there is little chance for a woman with no special skills to earn enough to keep herself and four children without the help of public assistance. Remarriage is not easy at 35. If she had lost her husband in the war she would be eligible for a pension, but since he only ruined his health in the war and postponed his death until peacetime she is excluded from that prospect. Pensions in Japan are not primarily means of redistributing income with grants paid in respect of needs, and only a small beginning has been made with contributory insurance schemes. Pensions are rewards paid by 'the State' to those who have faithfully served 'the State'.

Life is reduced to the barest essentials. When asked if there is anything she badly needs for the home, Mrs. A does not, like many of her neighbours, talk of electric irons or ice-boxes, or even radios. She mentions a chest-of-drawers and a dresser. Their few possessions now have to be piled in wicker baskets and apple boxes in the corner of the room.

Mr. T is 54, a quiet, gentle university graduate with an equable temperament and unhurried ease which suggests that his life has been free from the pressures of poverty and overwork. His father was a lawyer and gave him a good start in life but, after he left the university, little financial support. For a time he made his living by writing —life and letters in eighteenth-century England are his main interest —but with marriage and the need to settle down he got a job in the national broadcasting corporation. He has been there ever since, although he still supplements his income by his odd literary activities; not that articles on eighteenth-century England are in very great demand.

His home has a warm untidy atmosphere of steady, but controlled, decay. The wood is darkened and the mats are yellowed with age, but the walls are lined with low tables piled with books and papers; there are two cats, photographs on the wall, one or two examples of old Japanese clocks and an alcove in the main living-room which, although encroached on for book-piling purposes, still fulfills its primary decorative function with a piece of pottery centrally displayed on a small wooden stand.

His wife is devoted and house-proud, well satisfied with her husband's provision for her housekeeping money—although they never discuss what proportion of his income that actually represents—and proud of her ability to keep the home running smoothly in a way which ensures the least possible intrusion of sordid domestic matters on her husband's exalted intellectual and professional life. They have three children. The eldest girl is doing hospital training in order to becoming a doctor; one son is at the university, and another at high school.

Their standard of living is modest. In Japan as elsewhere it is the professional classes who suffer most during and after periods of inflation. Their house has four rooms besides the tiny kitchen with its single gas ring, and there is a small garden about six yards square. But there is no bath, and the lavatory is one of the few in Shitayama-cho which is not connected to the sewer. They have a wireless and a sufficiency of essential furniture. Mrs. T wants an ice-box, but is not confident of being able to save up for one and does not wish to bother her husband. They feed fairly well. Mrs. T generally spends about £12 a month on food out of a total of about £18. They have fish every day and meat three or four times a week. 'It is better to spend a bit extra on food than to have to spend more later on medicines.' Things were tighter soon after the war. Then, she said, she had to plan carefully, 'getting protein from bean-curd, for instance, and giving up eggs'. Now she has a little more leeway and she occasionally tries out new recipes which she has heard on the wireless.

Mr. T is insured against sickness and unemployment; he will eventually get a small pension; their children are able and attached to their parents and can be relied on as a support for their old age. Mrs. T has reason to feel fairly secure and fairly contented. She is proud of the fact that she never has cause to borrow money; at the worst she is forced to go round the house collecting a few things for the rag-and-bone man to tide her over the end of the month.

4

Houses and Apartment Blocks

THE housing needs of the Japanese urban population during the period of industrialization and urban growth have never been adequately met. Nor, on the other hand, have they been so completely disregarded by State authority as was the case during the growth of the industrial towns of the north of England in the early nineteenth century. Mid-Meiji descriptions of the slum quarters of the growing industrial cities can be found to parallel anything in the Western literature,[13] but even from early times there was a certain amount of municipal control in the interests of public health, and although it was not until the nineteen-twenties that the government began tentatively to take positive measures to improve housing, negative controls had for some time been universal, if enforced with by no means uniform thoroughness. It seems that the squalor, disease, feckless irresponsibility and human degradation generally associated with slums remained a feature of relatively limited areas of Japanese industrial cities and never came to characterize the working classes as a whole.

Several reasons for this suggest themselves. In the first place, in the early period of industrialization, with the exception of mining and heavy industry, the typical form of factory labour was the temporary employment of single men or girls recruited from country districts and accommodated in dormitories by their employer. Many of these employees returned later to their rural homes to be replaced by others. Thus the development of a permanent urban working class was much slower than the development of industry, though it was much accelerated after the first world war and particularly in the thirties when, in fact, housing problems began to become acute.

Secondly, during her period of industrialization, Japan had the advantage of Western experience and techniques in the field of public health. Moreover, the gradual abandonment of *laissez-faire* in the West, and the acceptance of the desirability of governmental interference in welfare matters fitted readily into the Tokugawa tradition of interventionist paternalism and into the Meiji political leaders' wide interpretation of their responsibility for the development of industry and, to a certain extent, the welfare of the people. The manufacturing middle class never effectively captured control of the government in Japan as it did in England in the mid-nineteenth century. The development of industry owed much to government sponsorship, and the influence of the leaders of banking and industry and the political parties allied to them was always balanced by that of the army and the bureaucracy, two groups largely recruited from the samurai class.[14]

To the latter, industrialization was primarily a means of strengthening the nation *vis-à-vis* foreign powers, and to many of them the necessity was a disagreeable one, for they recoiled from a way of life the avowed end of which was not the fulfilment of status-defined duty or the performance of honourable deeds, but the accumulation of material wealth. Although these groups produced no Lord Shaftesburies, they did to some extent fulfil the role of the conservative landed gentry in England in exerting pressure for social legislation.[15] In the thirties, the army considerably increased its popular support by appearing as the champion of the masses against the corrupt and luxurious bourgeoisie. It had, moreover, a specific interest in promoting such social legislation, for it was concerned with the physical quality of the human material conscription brought into its ranks.[16]

A third relevant factor is the relative simplicity of traditional Japanese housing requirements compared with those of Western peoples, both as regards space and furniture. Moreover, the high value placed on personal cleanliness, the almost universal habit of bathing and the widespread provision from early times of cheap commercially-operated bathing facilities in the industrial towns, combined with the fact that a compulsory education system (in which instruction in elementary hygiene was always stressed) was already widely enforced before industrialization began to get under way, tended to make filth and squalor the exception rather than the rule except among the utterly destitute.

Some idea of the extent of slum conditions in 1925 can be gained from a Home Office survey of that date. In the twenty-four cities of more than half a million inhabitants surveyed, 217 slum areas were designated, containing 300,000 inhabitants, representing some 2·5% of the total population of those towns at that time.[17] Slum areas, or rather 'areas containing a congregation of unsuitable houses', were rather loosely defined in terms of 'overcrowded conditions detrimental to public health and morals', and since local authorities were used for the survey it is reasonable to expect that these figures to some extent underestimate the amount of bad housing. Nevertheless, simply in terms of the proportion living in houses considered grossly inadequate according to the standards of the society, Japanese urban housing at this time probably compared favourably with that of contemporary European cities.

This hard core of depressed areas remained despite legislation following this survey which enabled local authorities to receive loans for slum clearance. No more than one-tenth of the dwellings in the designated areas were rebuilt or replaced. Controls on new building designed to prevent the development of new slum areas were embodied in the City Planning Act, the Town Buildings Act and the Prevention of Tuberculosis Act, all of 1919, but though these had some effect enforcement measures were far from rigorous.[18]

The provision of houses for the urban population was almost exclusively in the hands of speculative builders and of paternalistic employers, but the government began in the twenties to do something to increase the quantity as well as regulate the quality of housing. Local authorities were offered grants to build houses to let and, for the middle classes, government protection and assistance was given to building societies. The total effect of these schemes was small, however. During the period 1920–30 when they were in force they effected the building of a total of only 100,000 houses, about a fifth of the number destroyed in the earthquake and fire of 1923.[19]

It was during the thirties, however, with the increased tempo of industrial expansion and the rapid growth of the urban population that the shortage of houses and the inadequacy of accommodation for industrial workers became acute. Governmental action chiefly took the form of loans to employers to enable them to build 'tied' housing for their employees, particularly in the case of armaments factories built in inaccessible suburbs; but neither this, nor the activities of speculative builders of houses to rent, adequately met essential needs. 'In the districts where the armaments factories were located there were many examples of seven or more living in a six-mat room, of families which had converted chicken-huts into "houses", of groups of men on shift work who paired off and took turns to sleep in beds which were never taken up off the floor, of men who found the overcrowding so intolerable that they slept twenty days of the month in a brothel.' [20]

The progress of the war meant the virtual cessation of new building, and finally, in 1944–5 there came the destruction of more than two million houses by bombing, and of another half-million by the authorities to make fire-breaks in densely populated areas. This meant a total loss of more than a sixth of the nation's houses.

Post-war chaos, the necessity of supplying the needs of the occupation army and the looseness and ineffectiveness of licensing and building-material controls did not provide the best background for attempts to repair these losses. Bank loans were available for the building of restaurants and 'salons'—a safe investment given the universal importance of entertainments in oiling the wheels of Japanese commerce and administration—but not for private housing. The wide gap between the cost of housing and the level of (government-controlled) rents caused the virtual disappearance of the speculative builder of houses to rent—the chief source of housing for urban workers before the war. Soon after the war some armaments factories were turned over to the production of simple prefabricated houses under government subsidy, but the scope of such government or local authority-sponsored schemes was limited. Of the million and a half houses—many of very inferior quality—built in the first three years after the war three-quarters were built by the prospective occupier.[21] Somehow or other houses got built; by May 1952 more than half the houses in Tokyo were post-war, but even then the number of houses in Tokyo was only 76% of estimated minimum requirements.[22]

HOUSING IN SHITAYAMA-CHO

The housing shortage was reflected in Shitayama-cho in 1951 in the large number of families 'doubling up'. Excluding apartment-dwellers, 186 households[23] were living in 147 houses. If one-person households are included the figures are 207 households in 155 houses, which is to say that only 53% of the total number of households and single-person households had exclusive possession of a house.

The disadvantages of sharing a house in Japan are legion. According to the most usual pattern, the owner or tenant occupies the ground-floor and the sub-tenant the upper floor of a two-storey house. A typical case is shown in Diagram 2. It is fairly typical in size as well as in layout, for the average number of rooms in shared houses is approximately 4·5.

As in this case, stairs are rarely situated near the entrance, so that access to the upper floor entails passing through that part of the house occupied by the other family. In the summer months the sliding doors between the matted rooms and the wooden corridor are generally removed to allow freer movement of air and even in winter they are often kept open for ease of access to the kitchen and the other rooms. Lack of privacy is, however, for many house-sharers, the least of the disadvantages. Individual privacy tends to be less highly valued than in England. Interviewers sometimes commented on the family-like relationships existing between unrelated house-sharers ('Mrs. T calls Mrs. S "auntie" and they seem more like mother and daughter than anything else'). Often more disagreeable than lack of privacy is the lack of adequate cooking and washing facilities. Most houses have only one or two gas rings in their tiny kitchens, the sharing of which is not easy. In some cases families living in one or two upstairs rooms do not share the kitchen at all, but cook on a charcoal brazier in their own room.

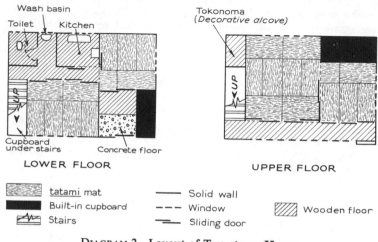

DIAGRAM 2—Layout of Two-storey House

All house-sharing in Shitayama-cho is voluntary, none the result of the small amount of compulsory requisitioning which took place after the war. In many cases the families living together are related, and in one or two cases the husbands are work-mates. Without this willingness to share—a reflection of Japanese family solidarity and the strength of 'personal' relationships in the non-kinship groupings of Japanese society—the post-war housing problems of Japan would have been greatly magnified. Apart from such sharing for non-profit-making motives, however, there are some families who put up with the inconveniences of having another family in the house for the sake of the income so to be derived. Such extra income is not very large (the average monthly rent paid by families sharing a house was 640 *yen*, about 13s.) but for some families it may mean the difference between just tolerable austerity and absolute privation.

Of the 147 houses in Shitayama-cho 57 were owned by their occupier, 12 were company houses tied to particular jobs, and the rest were rented at an average monthly rent of 880 *yen* (17s.). Rents were kept down by government rent-control legislation. In 1951 their permitted level was thirty times that of November 1940 when rents were first frozen, compared with a general price rise of more than two hundred times the pre-war level. Rents in Shitayama-cho were frequently greater than the controlled rent, but rarely twice as much and certainly not as high as one would imagine to be their 'economic' level. The sharp conflict of interest between tenants protected by the law and landlords who were its victims seems to have dealt the final blow to the traditional landlord-tenant relationship which in Edo times was more than a simple contractual economic relationship, involving as it did regular gift-giving on both sides and the assumption on the part of the landlord of some general responsibility for the tenant's welfare.

Apartment-dwellers have, as compared with those sharing houses, the advantage that the apartments were built for communal living, but the disadvantage that space is often even more restricted. There are four apartment blocks in Shitayama-cho. Of these, one is small, well-appointed, clean and select. There are only three children between the five households and the head of all except one of these households has a good white-collar job. Although each household has only one six-mat room, there is also a separate kitchenette attached to each, containing a sink with cold-water tap and a gas ring. The rent is 1,000 *yen* per month, well above the average house rent. The other blocks are three-storey buildings containing about twenty households in each. These are inferior in facilities, in state of repair and in 'tone'. The rooms vary from four-and-a-half to six mats (nine feet by nine and twelve feet by nine) with a very small number of eight-mat rooms. In these blocks the average number of persons per room is 2·9. Some families occupy two adjacent rooms, but the biggest family in these blocks—three adults and six children—is not one of these. Amenities vary, but washing and cooking facilities are in every case both communal and inadequate. In addition to the rent, which averages 500 *yen*, a gas and water levy is charged in proportion to the size of the family. Toilets, the nature of which is important in such crowded conditions, are in three of the blocks equipped with flushing apparatus, but in one of these it does not work and buckets of water have to be used. The fourth simply has a cess-pool which is emptied once a week. Toilets are shared, in the best block by two, in the worst instance by nineteen families. Corridors, which are always dark, cannot be kept clean because of the need of cramped families to store some of their kitchen utensils or household possessions outside their rooms. In addition, privacy is hardly guaranteed by the wooden partition walls, even though there is a cupboard between each room which provides some insulation.

OVERCROWDING

Overcrowding is a relative concept and before attempting to define it in Japanese terms something more should be said concerning Japanese living habits.

It will be clear from the sketches of the preceding chapter that the amount of furniture required is small. The *tatami* mats, with their smooth and hard-wearing rush covering are not unpleasant to sit on, particularly in hot weather. They have a certain springiness, but thin cushions are generally offered to guests to mitigate the hardness of which the sitter gradually becomes aware. Meals are taken at a table raised about eighteen inches from the floor. On the ground-floor, the table in the main living-room is generally placed over a boarded pit, about thirty inches deep. This provides (*a*) greater comfort by making possible an alternative sitting posture—legs dangling instead of squatting, and (*b*) a method of heating. The centre of the pit is made even deeper than the surrounding boards and in the winter a charcoal burner is placed in this central hole. The table top is then removed and over the frame on which it rests is placed a thin quilt which spreads out on all sides. The table top is then replaced. Enclosed by the quilt there is thus created a heat chamber which warms the lower half of the body (and the hands when unoccupied). In many households this is the only form of heating employed.

Other means of heating are, first, a variant of the brazier-and-quilt method which does not require a hole in the floor—the charcoal burner is placed in a wooden frame above floor level, and secondly, an open charcoal brazier; generally a china bowl about eighteen inches in diameter (though it may be as much as three feet) filled with ash, in a hollow in the centre of which charcoal is burnt. Charcoal, however, which is expensive, is in constant use only in middle-class homes and sometimes reserved for guests in poorer homes. The more common fuel is briquettes made from a mixture of anthracite and low-grade charcoal which are burnt in earthenware braziers. In theory, if these briquettes are 'started off' out of doors for half an hour, they can be brought inside and will give off heat without fumes for two or three hours. That heat is produced is undeniable, but the absence of fumes is illusory and many Japanese spend the winter with perpetual briquette headaches. In Shitayama-cho only the wealthy entrepreneur had central heating, and electric and gas fires were owned only by a very few families.

The heat which any of the traditional methods produces is limited and localized. In any case the opportunities given to draughts by Japanese domestic architecture make attempts to heat a whole room unrealistic as well as extravagant. The individual must apply himself to the source of heat rather than expect the heat to come to him. In the cold Tokyo winter this greatly restricts freedom of movement, though the opportunities for intimate family conversation when snugly gathered around and half inside the quilted heat chamber are considered some compensation. Sitting in the *kotatsu*, as this device is called, occupies much the same place in Japanese culture as 'gathering round the fireside' in England.

Cupboards and chests-of-drawers, sometimes Western-style wardrobes, are the most important articles of furniture. Built-in cupboards are always provided and are necessary for the daytime storage of the bedding which consists of stuffed quilts of which one is placed under, and one to four over, the sleeper. Ideally there should be one set of bedding per person, though two or three children may sometimes share one large set of bed-clothes. The youngest child generally sleeps with its mother, often, if not superseded by a younger child, until the age of five or six, though it is becoming increasingly common in middle-class families to give even young children a separate set of bed-clothes.

Although, generally speaking, one room is very much like another and can be used equally for day living and for sleeping, there is some differentiation of function. The living-room (*ima*) is generally small and near the kitchen; the cupboards in it contain most of the household goods other than clothes, and the table at which meals are taken. It is not generally used for sleeping. Pre-war surveys showed that the use of the living-room for sleeping was generally avoided even at the cost of over-crowding in the sleeping rooms.[24]

Where possible one room would be reserved as a guest-room (*oosetsuma, zashiki*). Preferably this would be of eight or ten mats. Furniture would be excluded as far as possible except for a polished low table of good-quality wood. The room would have as its central decorative feature an alcove, framed in pillars of fine polished wood, in which a scroll or a single bowl of flowers is placed as the sole ornament. Such a room would be used as a 'front parlour', for entertaining visitors, or the family might have its meals here on special occasions. It might also be used regularly for sleeping and in the summer as a general sitting-room for the family. Urban middle-class families often have as an alternative to such a 'front parlour', or in addition to it, a 'Western room' (*Yooma*) for receiving visitors. Such rooms, with their grey and brown wallpapers, plush, horse-hair, tiger-skin rugs, marble mantelpieces, gilt baroque clocks and anti-macassars, generally manage to combine all the ugliness of Victorian domestic furnishing with none of its comforts. If there are enough rooms for further specialization, the most usual form is the reservation of one room as the children's room where they can keep their toys, have a desk and a chair at which to do their homework and in which they may also sleep at night. A very few families have rooms reserved exclusively for sleeping which are fitted with beds.

It was on the basis of these fairly simple and elastic physical requirements that a 'People's House' Committee of the Architects' Association attempted in 1941 to define minimum housing requirements.[25] According to the standards it set up any household with more than two persons per room or less than three mats per person would be considered overcrowded (two children counting as one adult). If these standards are applied to Shitayama-cho 50% of households and single-person households were overcrowded on the person-per-room calculation (12% have four or more persons per room) and 45% according to the mats-per-person calculation. 42% are overcrowded on both counts and 53% on one or the other. Apartment-dwellers and room-sharers make up the majority of the over-crowded households, but nearly half the families who were sub-letting rooms do so at the cost of overcrowding themselves.

What comforts and advantages are first sacrificed in these over-crowded households? The 'People's House' Committee in 1941 arrived at its conclusions on the basis of the following list of desirable conditions:

1. That married couples be given a separate bedroom.
2. That a separate living-room be reserved and not used for sleeping.
3. That in order to prevent an excessive concentration of carbon dioxide each person should have at least 4·5 square yards of sleeping space.
4. That adolescent children of opposite sexes should not sleep together.

It would appear that the order in which these conditions are listed fairly represents the order of their importance to the Japanese. The last is the least important. It was doubtless incorporated in these housing standards because it was found in similar European lists of housing requirements and it was thought that Japan should not be slow in adopting standards which elsewhere were considered essential to civilized living. It would be very rare, for example, to find a family which used the living-room for sleeping in order to avoid having adult brothers and sisters sleep together in the same room, even in upper-class families. Modesty does not forbid uncovering the body in the presence of members of the opposite sex within the family, and, in any case, when the partitions between rooms are no more than sliding wood-and-paper doors, the difference between sleeping in the same room (in a separate set of bed-clothes) and sleep-ing in adjoining rooms is not very great. Incest is not unknown and it does appear occasionally as a subsidiary theme in novels, but it is far from being a general preoccupation.[26] Generally speaking, sleeping in the same room with a member of the opposite sex is not defined as a sexually significant situation to anything like the same extent in Japan as in the West. It is common after late-night parties, either family parties or *geisha* parties, for all the assembled company, men and women, to sleep in the same room. The valued feature of this 'mixed sleeping' (*zakone*) is the sociability it affords; the opportunity for conversation in fuddled comfort for as long as one feels like

Craftsmen re-covering *tatami* mats

A sunny morning in Shitayama-cho

He leaves for work

Living-room in a middle-class home. The 'salary-man' relaxes in
Japanese dress

staying awake. There is no assumption that anything improper will take place, though it sometimes does.

The first condition is considered more important, though perhaps less so than in European countries since it is common practice, even though not made necessary by lack of space, for children to sleep with their parents until they are five or six or are superseded by a more recent child. This is thought desirable in order that mothers can attend to the child's needs, and at that age children are not considered to impose restraint on their parents.[27] If the children have passed that age, however, the living-room would probably be used to avoid sleeping together. But such privacy is beyond the means of those couples, of which there are fifty-nine in Shitayama-cho, who live with children in one room.

As for the precedence of conditions two and three, there is the authority of the pre-war survey quoted on page 47. What is generally considered to constitute overcrowded sleeping quarters is, however, probably very different from a definition based on calculations of air-changes and carbonic-acid gas content. Although the Japanese are, generally, highly conscious of matters of elementary hygiene, the ill-effects of overcrowded sleeping quarters is not one of the things which has figured in school hygiene lessons (it would have been unrealistic to have stressed it, in any case) and for most people the only limitations considered are those imposed by the amount of available floor-space. Fresh air is not considered a positive good. At night the outer 'rain-doors' of solid wood which slide outside the windows of paper or glass are pulled along and fixed tight in order to prevent burglary as well as, in winter, the loss of heat. Beyond the limits of actual cramped discomfort, crowded sleeping seems to be considered to be more pleasant than isolation in separate rooms. The individual gains a comforting security and it is a sign that a spirit of happy intimacy pervades the family. A widow living with a 30-year-old son and a 27-year-old daughter in a two-roomed house, said, when asked whether they made any division of rooms, 'No, we all sleep together, we are a happy family all together, sharing everything and keeping nothing from each other. It's happier that way.' There is much to be said for the theory that this low evaluation of individual privacy is linked with the general preference for group, over individual, action and responsibility which characterizes Japanese society if compared with the 'individualistic' West. A Japanese newspaper writer once remarked that Japan will never be democratized or the principle of individual responsibility established until Japanese are brought up in separate bedrooms with solid sound-proof walls and locks on the doors.

At the other end of the scale, there were twenty households in Shitayama-cho which had at least one spare guest-room not normally used by the family. The allocation of rooms to individual members of the family was not common. Twenty-three households had what they called a 'children's room' (11) or a 'study room' (12). (The second word is as common as the first, an incidental indication of the importance placed on education in Shitayama-cho.) A separate room for the husband was found in seven professional workers' homes. Only three housewives said that they had anything which they regarded as their own room.

It is not surprising that housing figures prominently in the scale of felt wants in Shitayamo-cho. When housewives were asked the question: 'What do you find the biggest worry in life at the moment?' at the end of an interview on living standards and household management, accommodation easily headed the list, being mentioned by 32% of those interviewed. Of those who made specific complaints the majority referred to the inconveniences of sharing houses or of living in communal apartments: 'Having to go downstairs to fetch water', 'Not having any privacy', 'Having the people upstairs pass through the room whenever they go to the toilet', 'No gas', 'Being so cramped'. Some reflect standards just above the bare minimum: 'Nowhere for the children to play', 'Not enough sunlight', 'The rooms are awkwardly arranged', 'We have nowhere to entertain guests'.

Another question was: 'Supposing you won 300,000 *yen* (£300) in the government lottery, what would you do with it?' Of 219 housewives who gave concrete answers 61% said that they would either start buying or building a new house, or rebuild their existing house. Apartment-dwellers with children were almost unanimous in giving such a reply.

For most people, indeed, a win in the lottery represents almost the only chance of being able to fulfil these wishes. Almost none of those in housing difficulties have the capital to buy a house or to build one for themselves. It is not easy to find better rentable accommodation in Tokyo where the supply of houses is increasing less rapidly than the demand, and a move would mean a premium to pay and probably a higher rent. Two possibilities are provided by the government. In the first place, the Government's Housing Credit Bank is authorized to provide prospective builders of houses for personal occupation with loans of up to 85% of the cost of houses conforming to certain standard requirements. Applications have always far exceeded the available funds, but in practice the cost of land and other expenses limits this opportunity to the middle classes. A second possibility is provided by the government-subsidized municipal housing schemes. These are increasingly taking the form of concrete blocks divided into two- to four-roomed flats. The rent is not high, though more than that paid by the majority of the households in greatest need in

Shitayama-cho. These are allocated by lottery, and despite the requirement of a 10,000 *yen* deposit (£10), the number of applicants always vastly outruns the number of houses available. Moreover this scheme, too, has a middle-class bias. The Tokyo Government, to guard against rent-defaulting, stipulates a *minimum*, not a maximum, income-level for applicants.

The people of Shitayama-cho could, however, be worse off. The 1948 Housing Census showed that 2·6% of all households in Tokyo, containing 2·4% of the population, were living in 'non-dwelling-houses', that is, according to the definition of the census authorities, 'temporary housing, generally built by the resident himself', with a durability of less than three years, 'for example, sheds constructed with metal sheets, scrap lumber, etc., temporary shelters made in burnt buildings and those covered with tent or marshreed screens'.[28] Resettlement schemes in cheap low-rent houses were in progress during 1951, but the size of this submerged fortieth was probably not much diminished. The picture of misery presented by such a settlement of shack dwellers in the wet season, the mud and filth and the smell of the piles of rubbish by scavenging which many of them eked out a living, was one of the most depressing sights Tokyo had to offer in 1951.

HOUSEHOLD GOODS

To conclude this section on the more permanent aspects of living levels in Shitayama-cho, Table 8 gives a brief indication of the ownership of some of the household goods which are now part of most families' expected or ideal standard of living, but which are by no means universally to be found.

Table 8: Ownership of Household Goods by Type of Occupancy

Article	Percentage of households possessing it			
	Exclusive occupiers (%) (N = 108)	Subleasors (%) (N = 39)	Subtenants and flat-dwellers (%) (N = 123)	All households (%) (N = 270)
Wireless	94·4	89·7	66·6	80·8
Ice-box	25·0	10·3	2·4	12·6
Electric fan	23·1	12·8	2·4	12·2
Telephone	16·7	10·3	0·8	8·4
Sewing machine	44·4	33·3	24·8	32·8
Electric iron	89·8	82·1	62·3	75·2

Electricity is widely diffused in Japan, thanks to an abundance of hydroelectric power. There is therefore a ready market for electric appliances, which are produced cheaply and in large quantities. Quality is not, however, very high, and a large number of these radios were not in fact working. Many more, of low selective power, were due to be swamped when the number of broadcasting stations increased with the beginning of commercial broadcasting at the end of 1951. Ice-boxes are supplied with ice daily or every other day by the ice merchant from June until September. Although butter and milk do not hold an important place in the Japanese diet, so that cooling is not of such great importance as it otherwise might be in the hot summer months, an ice-box is useful for keeping meat and fish. Generally speaking, however, housewives tend to buy food for one meal at a time and cook it immediately. Ovens are a rarity, so that the roasting of large joints to provide food for several days is unknown. With Japanese urban-population densities, moreover, the butcher and fishmonger is rarely more than five minutes' walk away and the saving of time and labour does not yet occupy a very high place in most housewives' scale of values. An ice-box, then, is a luxury. The sewing machine is primarily a means of economizing on clothing expenditure rather than a means of enjoyably occupying leisure. Some wives use it to supplement their income and for two or three widows in the ward it is their sole income source. An electric fan is another luxury, though one which is widely appreciated as a more effective substitute for the paper fans which are universally carried in the hot weather. The electric fan is the article most highly charged with prestige value, and the pride with which some housewives claimed to possess it was unmistakable. Telephones are mostly installed for business rather than for social reasons, but are widely used for both purposes both by their owners and a wide range of their owners' neighbours.

5

Family Income and Expenditure

A LARGE number of families in Shitayama-cho (23% of the total) are supported by self-employed workers or by joint family enterprise. This proportion is by no means above the general average for Japan. Even if the agricultural population is excluded, self-employed workers and unpaid family workers make up almost a third of the total labour force.

In part this is a pre-industrial legacy, a sign of what is, by European standards, the underdeveloped state of the Japanese economy, or, as some would prefer, the one-sided development of the Japanese economy due to State-directed concentration of capital resources in heavy industry. At any rate, many of the old crafts remain unaltered: carpenters, plasterers, tub-makers, leather-workers, and umbrella-makers, work in much the same way as their grandfathers worked. Many of the goods which in more fully industrialized societies are mass-produced in factories are made in home workshops by family labour, aided by the minimum of machinery, and that often hand-powered. Writing-brushes, envelopes, wooden clogs, xylophones and children's toys were all being made in this way in Shitayama-cho. The production and marketing economies of large-scale manufacture of this type of goods still does not necessarily enable factory producers to undersell the products of this domestic industry, since the domestic workers are prepared to work longer hours and to take fewer holidays. They do not count their labour in the costs of production and consider only the relation between their trading profit and their needs, not the relation between their profit and the hours of work required to produce it. The same applies to the vast number of retail shops which are almost exclusively family affairs (the chain store is practically unknown), hire labour on a family-servant rather than on an hourly wage-rate basis, and are generally open from seven in the morning until nine or ten at night.

In part the high proportion of self-employed workers is a result of the war. The breakdown in the manufacturing industries and the disorganization of the supply routes of raw materials at the end of the war forced many—including large numbers of repatriated soldiers

—into precarious self-employment: small retail business, black-market trading, craft enterprises, the service trades, everything from boot-blacking to hairdressing, from scavenging to guiding American troops over beauty-spots. Side by side with this unnatural inflation of the service trades—the means whereby incomes were to some extent levelled down by a process of taking in each other's washing—there was a return to more primitive industrial forms in the manufacturing industries. Small family enterprises rapidly increased in number. In 1948, for instance, unincorporated manufacturing businesses accounted for 10·1% of the national income, compared with 3·8% for 1934–6.[29] It was largely these characteristics of the Japanese family enterprise—the ability for improvisation and the willingness to work long hours—which were responsible for Japan's relatively rapid recovery after the war. By 1951, the Japanese economy was getting back to something much more like its pre-war form, but still self-employed workers formed a larger proportion of the total labour force than before the war, and excluding farmers were taking 24% of the national income as opposed to 18% in 1934–6.[30]

As a group, self-employed workers are only slightly better off than wage and salary earners. (In contrast to, say, Britain, where the 'mixed income' groups, containing a much smaller proportion of independent artisans and retailers, are considerably the more wealthy.) Income per head for self-employed workers (still excluding peasants) was only about 9% higher than that of wage and salary earners in 1951,[31] though this comparison conceals a wide range of income levels within each group and is thus not very meaningful. The self-employed have, however, one definite advantage over wage earners—their ability to avoid taxation. The number and variety of taxes to be avoided is great, and despite the universal lament of the Japanese business man against the harshness of the tax officials, who are said to make arbitrary assessments based on the scandalous evidence of neighbours and outward appearances of prosperity, it is not difficult to show from published figures that the self-employed worker, on the average, pays proportionately less tax than the wage or salary earner whose income is fixed, easily discovered, and generally taxed at source.[32] Occupation costs, reconstruction costs and the general expansion of government have greatly increased the burden of taxation on the wage and salary earner. The families covered in the Government's Family Income Survey paid 10·7% of their income in taxation in 1951, compared with 0·7% in 1934–6.[33]

In Shitayama-cho the majority of households (71%) were supported by such wage and salary earners. Most employees of all kinds are paid by the month (though since the war fortnightly or tri-monthly payments have become more common) which both puts a premium on careful planning of expenditure in all types of households and makes impossible any useful distinction between wage earner and salary earner.

The distinction usually made in official statistics is between manual workers and white-collar workers, the latter including professional workers (provided they are employees) as well as office clerks. This is the distinction employed in the comparison of income sources in Table 9. As this table shows, the differential between these two broad groups is not very great; considerably less, probably, than before the war, for Japan has been no exception to the rule that the middle-class, in particular the professional employee, suffers more than the industrial worker in time of inflation. The change in their relative positions is shown in the difference in their savings habits. According to the Government's Family Income Surveys, savings from Nov. 1950 to March 1951 amounted to 72% of withdrawals of savings for office workers, and 112% of withdrawals for manual workers.[34]

This change in relative prosperity has taken place within the context of a general depression of urban living levels since the war. The real income of Tokyo employees in 1951 has been estimated as 76% of the pre-war (1934-6) level.[35] For the majority of workers income was insufficient to maintain pre-war standards.

The difficulty of maintaining a family on the earnings of its household is somewhat mitigated by the practice of most private employers of paying family allowances. This has become almost universal since the war for both white-collar and manual workers. The general level of wages was so far depressed that the arguments for sharing the total wages bill as far as possible according to needs seemed overwhelming. The practice also fitted neatly into the paternalistic pattern of employment relations, and in the early days after the war the unions, with no firmly established traditional adherence to rate-for-the-job principles, were in this case, as in many others, less concerned to destroy existing paternalistic relationships than to exact full performance of paternalistic duty from the employer. The wages-pool system of operating family allowance schemes is practically unknown, so that the married and philoprogenitive have only the union, if there is one, and the employer's *ninjoo*—his sense of 'human feeling'—to prevent them from being the first victims in times of retrenchment.

But despite family allowances some supplementary source of income besides the husband's earnings is essential for most families. Office workers are still, as the table shows, to a certain extent drawing on savings, but the biggest extra item of income—and one which has acquired much greater importance than before the war if pre-war budget studies are to be believed[36]—is the earnings of other members of the family. Children are a less important source of income than they used to be since there has been a big increase in school attendance

Table 9: *Expended Income of Workers' Families by source,*
March 1951*

		JAPAN, ALL CITIES	
		Office workers (N = 1,307)	Other workers (N = 825)
Persons per household		4·70	4·56
Earning persons per household		1·29	1·40
ACTUAL INCOME	Earnings of househead (yen)	13,739 (82·7%)	10,656 (80·8%)
	Earnings of other household members	1,301 (7·8)	1,954 (14·8)
	Home work (factory outwork, etc.)	271 (1·6)	180 (1·4)
	Rent, interest, etc.	154 (0·9)	42 (0·3)
	Social security benefits	64 (0·4)	79 (0·6)
	Money gifts	144 (0·8)	134 (1·0)
	Other income	530 (3·2)	254 (1·9)
BALANCE OF OTHER RECEIPTS	Withdrawal of savings and sale of assets less savings	529 (3·2)	− 50 (− 0·3)
	Borrowing less repayment	63 (0·4)	121 (0·9)
	Receipts from loan repayments less loans	65 (0·4)	53 (0·4)
	Other receipts + (balance at 1st March less balance at 31st March)	− 245 (− 1·5)	− 235 (− 1·8)
Total		16,615 (100%)	13,188 (100%)

* Source: Statistics Bureau, Prime Minister's Office, *Consumer Price Survey*, March 1951, pp. 17 and 23. This table combines Family Receipts with Family Disbursements to arrive at 'Expended Income', i.e. total outgoings during the month for all purposes except the increase of (monetary) assets or the decrease of (monetary) liabilities.

at the 15–18 level as well as an additional year of compulsory education. Wives, however, go out to work more than before the war. Even so, only about 6% of Shitayama-cho wives were in regular paid employment, compared with nearly a half of the widows. Many more, however, supplemented the family income by various forms of factory outwork at wages which, in 1950, averaged 10–13 *yen* per hour, or 10s. to 12s. 3d. for a 48-hour week.[37]

There are many other ways of supplementing the family income. Manual workers do odd-jobs in their spare time for more wealthy neighbours. Office workers seize every opportunity afforded by their

position to engage in profitable minor transactions on their own
account—something which is in part a legacy of the days immediately
after the war when black-market brokerage was almost the sole means
of livelihood for a considerable portion of the town population.
Public servants—even school-teachers—are sorely tempted to accept
gifts, and there is no lack of offers. Expense accounts, both in government service and in private companies, are generally considered a
legitimate means of adjusting income. In addition, since so much of
Japanese business is performed in restaurants, geisha houses and at
hot springs resorts, receipts in kind are by no means negligible for
administrative workers in business firms. Even clerical workers of
humble rank may share in these benefits, being taken along to such
functions less because the negotiations require their presence than as
a gesture of appreciation for their loyal service. For these workers,
several days' deficiency in their normal diet may be made good by the
protein and vitamin content of the meals provided on such occasions.
They are able to eat meat and fish and vegetable delicacies in quantities beyond their normal means—and beyond, also, the normal intake capacity of anyone without a stomach distended by long years
of bulk rice-eating. Such income in kind, the more accessible to office
than to manual workers, escapes the Family Budget Survey, so that
the difference in consumption levels for the two classes of worker may,
for that reason, be somewhat underestimated by Table 9.

Two other items in Table 9 require some comment. The need for
a separate category of 'money gifts' chiefly reflects the economic
importance of kinship ties. The normal and approved way for
children to take care of aged parents is by maintaining a common
household, but where this is impossible a regular monthly allowance
may be the means of performing their filial duty. It may be, however,
that in urban worker families the reverse process—gifts from a rural
parent to struggling children in the towns—is a more important
factor. At least three families in Shitayama-cho were receiving such
help regularly, and several more referred to it in an interview as their
immediate resort if they lost their present source of income.

These 'money gifts', as well as gifts in kind which (doubtless
underestimated) probably make up the bulk of 'other income', are
also a reflection of the prevalence of gift-giving between neighbours,
friends, or business contacts, between employers and employees and
in patron-client relations in all spheres of society. Such gift-giving is
primarily of importance for its symbolic function, which will be considered in a later chapter, but it is not entirely without economic
significance as well. Reciprocity in gift-giving is modified by differences in means and status; the wealthy man gives better than he
gets from his poorer neighbour. This custom, therefore, has a constant redistributive effect. This is in addition to the special function

of such gift-giving in times of crisis: in illness, unemployment, after fires, the gifts will be entirely one-sided, the givers receiving only the 'insurance' of similar help when they are similarly situated.

EXPENDITURE ON FOOD

Japan is no exception to Engel's 'law' that the smaller the total family income the higher is the proportion of it spent on food. The Japanese Statistics Bureau's tables of family expenditure by income group show that food expenditure ranges from 59% of the total budget in the lowest income group to 29% of the total for the highest.[38] There is, however, a very wide range of difference between income groups in the actual *amount* spent on food, a range which will be apparent from a glance at the family budgets given in Appendix II. Such differences in many cases represent real differences in standards of nutrition, but to a certain extent they represent differences according to some other criteria—of taste or of social prestige attaching to some foods rather than others. The chief such difference between families with a high and families with a low food expenditure is that whereas the latter accept the government ration of staple foods (partly in half-milled Japanese rice, partly in foreign rice, partly in barley, and partly in flour, bread or forms of macaroni) the former reject it in favour of the more expensive, but less nutritious, fully-milled 'white' rice available on the black market.

To the Japanese, 'food' and 'rice' are practically synonymous. The same word—*gohan*—can mean both. The Japanese meal consists of two elements; the 'main' or 'staple' food (*shushoku*) and the 'subsidiary' food (*fukushoku, o-kazu*). The staple food, traditionally plain boiled rice, is consumed in large quantities. (According to the Government's nutrition survey for 1951, grains provided in the towns 75% and in rural areas 78% of the total calorie intake.[39]) The subsidiary foods are looked on somewhat as extras, desirable, but at a pinch dispensable. Most important among them is a soup, the basis of which is *miso*, a bean-paste of high-quality protein content. To the soup can be added vegetables, edible fungi, or fresh or dried fish. Second in importance are vegetables pickled in salt and rice bran, chief among them the giant white radish (*daikon*). Other types of side dishes vary with the locality, but are mostly varieties of fresh vegetables, fish—fresh or dried according to proximity to the sea—algae, pulses and sometimes meat.

In the Tokugawa period it was a sign of superior status to consume 'white' rice (i.e. polished rice, milling ratio approximately 92%) as the staple food. The rice-producing peasants were expected to deliver their rice crop to their overlord's granaries as feudal dues and content themselves with inferior grains. By the thirties, however, white rice had come to be considered a part of the birth-right of every Japanese. Most of Japanese fastidiousness about food is centred on rice, the degree to which it is polished, washed and boiled, the size of grain, glutinosity and so on. A proper appreciation of rice (involving necessarily a horror for foreign rice) is valued as highly in a Japanese as a discriminating palate for wines in an upper-class Englishman. Of recent years 'white' rice has again become available only to those who can afford to pay black-market prices. As a result, its social-prestige value has been restored without, however, the belief that it is an essential part of Japanese 'normalcy' being in any way impaired. In 1951, a Cabinet Minister was almost forced to resign for saying that controls could be taken off before rice supplies were fully adequate, and 'people who couldn't afford rice would have to make do with barley'.

The full milling process which produces 'white' rice removes three-quarters of its vitamin B_1 content, the lack of which causes the beri-beri and the digestive complaints which are widespread in Japan. From long before the war, through the schools, through women's organizations and through the informal local government network, the Government had devoted much energy to pointing out the nutritional deficiences of fully-milled, and urging the use of partially-milled rice.

Eventually, what this propaganda failed to do by persuasion was achieved by compulsion. Since the beginning of rationing Japanese rice has been supplied half-milled. The victory has, however, been only temporary. The reluctance of the Japanese to accept 'black rice' as a permanent feature of the diet has been far greater than the British public's addiction to white bread. A recent report by a government committee admits defeat. 'The strength of the nation's attachment to white rice has proved irreducible', it says, and goes on to recommend that the Government abandons its propaganda campaign, provides white rice on the ration, and fortifies it with artificially manufactured vitamin B_1 by a process developed by Americans in the Philippines since the war.[40]

The increasing inadequacy of domestic rice production to meet the total needs of the Japanese population has also meant that the 'main food' ration has had to be supplied in part in foreign rice (long-grained and despised rice from South-East Asia, not the Korean and Formosan rice barely tolerated before the war), in part in bread, in part in barley and naked barley (to be mixed with rice) and in types of spaghetti, one (*udon*) made from wheat, the other (*soba*) from buckwheat.

Of these 'substitute foods', as they are called, the chief variation is found in attitudes to bread. Some families refuse it altogether and buy black-market rice; some families eat it with distaste, looking forward to a hypothetical future when they can enjoy cheap white rice again; some eat it because they believe the statements of government officials that it is good for them; some, particularly those who can afford the most expensive varieties, eat it occasionally because they like it. But in many households it is the daily breakfast food because the housewife values the extra half-hour in bed which she would otherwise have to spend preparing rice. Three housewives in Shitayama-cho mentioned bread along with gas and water as one of the things which have made the lot of the housewife easier over the past generation, and the importance of these positive factors is shown by the gradual increase in bread production in the thirties although there was then no question of compulsion.[41] Of the seventeen Shitayama-cho families from whom budgets were collected, one has no bread at all, five have it less than once a week, four have it slightly more often, and seven have it as often as once a day.

The seventeen budgets of Appendix II show other instances of variation in expenditure which are primarily due to variation in culturally determined food-habits, the reflection of different degrees of resistance to the changes of the last half-century. Chief among these differences are those in the consumption of meat, and of milk and milk products. There have been strong resistances to both these foods, particularly in rural districts. The objection to meat has largely rested on Buddhist prohibitions of slaughter. Fish has always been part of the diet of the laity, but there is perhaps a distinction between the nearly natural death which fishes die and the more blatant slaughter which meat production necessitates. Even now slaughtering, like the leather trade, is largely in the hands of a special caste-like group, the *eta*, which during the Tokugawa period was legally, and even today is socially, discriminated against.

In modern Tokyo prejudice against meat, either in the form of a diffuse antipathy or of explicit religious scruples, has practically disappeared. It will be seen that all of the seventeen households bought some meat, and when all Shitayama-cho housewives were asked what was the family's favourite food nearly a half mentioned some form of meat. Even in rural areas meat is now an accepted luxury. This change owes little to government nutritional propaganda (the high cost made it unrealistic to urge widespread consumption); it has been largely unengineered and may be explained by the intrinsic attractiveness of the food itself or by the fact that it formed a part of a 'Western' style of living which was a generally admired and prestige-carrying form of consumption in urban areas. The shortage of suitable pasture-land and the prevalence of coarse grasses keep the price of meat high, however—weight for weight it generally costs about half as much again as the most expensive fish—and it is now cost rather than prejudice which severely limits the ordinary family's consumption.

High cost is also partly responsible for the still low consumption of milk, butter and cheese, but here prejudice remains a stronger barrier than in the case of meat. The notion that humans being provided with human milk, cow's milk is intended for calves, has perhaps a certain prima-facie reasonableness. Butter and cheese were, in addition, deplored on account of their repulsive smell, considered to be the source of the peculiar body odours of foreigners themselves (hence the epithet for foreigners—*bata-kusai*—smelling of butter). Prejudice against milk has, however, been undermined by the same forces as have spread a taste for meat. Since the war it has been further attacked by the regular distribution of milk to school children as part of the school-meals scheme. But the still wide variation in consumption of these foods can be seen in the seventeen budgets of Appendix II. The amount spent bears very little relation to the general level of consumption and some families, such as 1 and 14, with a reasonably high expenditure on food have no milk, butter or cheese at all. No. 1 was also the household which took no bread; it was, too, very 'traditional' in general atmosphere, a three-generation household in which the relations between parents and children seemed very exactly to conform to the patterns of the old 'Japanese family system'.

Despite the failure of the 'black rice' campaign, it would perhaps be wrong to discount entirely the possibility that not simply imitative conformity to the tide of change, but also more positive beliefs concerning the nutritive value of new foods have been responsible for change in diets. Among Shitayama-cho housewives, at least, instruction in the rudiments of nutrition in schools and in women's magazines (40% of Shitayama-cho housewives were regular readers of some magazine or other) seemed to have produced a widespread awareness of the basic idea that diets may be judged in terms of nutritive value as well as in terms of taste and simple adequacy in allaying hunger. Words like 'protein', 'calorie' and 'mineral' appeared frequently, unsolicited and unprovoked, in housewives' replies to interview questions concerning the family diet. How far this general awareness is accompanied by concrete dietetical knowledge is, of course, a different question and one which has an important bearing on the problem of how far such diet deficiencies as do exist are 'primary'—due to an absolute inability to afford an adequate diet— or 'secondary'—due to a failure to secure the maximum food value for a given expenditure.

Some of the other items of expenditure detailed in the budgets shown in the Appendix will be dealt with in other contexts. Two may be singled out for mention here. The item 'education, stationery, newspapers' is in no case insignificant, and as such is a measure of the high prevailing degree of literacy. Expenditure on education ranges from contributions to the Parent–Teacher Association, and fees for children's calligraphy or abacus lessons to fees for the wife's lessons in flower arrangement. Another large item is 'entertainments, hobbies, pleasure travel and children's pocket-money' within which children's pocket-money generally predominates. This item accounts, for instance, for 10% of the expenditure of one family (Budget No. 2) with a very low standard of nutrition—a high proportion for expenditure which moralistic analysts of the budgets of the poor would regard as dispensable, if not reprehensible, luxuries. This does not mean that this family is satisfied with its poor diet. It is rather a reflection of the indulgence which parents commonly display toward their children, an indulgence which acquires greater significance in that it is the sphere of life which is most pervaded by the competitive desire to 'keep up with the Jones's'. The wish to make sure that one's own child does not lack what the neighbour's child has is one which weighs heavily on many family budgets in Shitayama-cho. Expenditure on children is perhaps one of the more attractive as well as functionally commendable forms of competitive expenditure, but the actual content of the indulgences often leaves much to be desired The most frequent destination of children's pocket-money is the purse of the street story-teller who regularly preludes his performances with a brisk sale of sweets and lollipops, as meretricious in colour as in content, and, manufactured as they are in dirty back-rooms, a frequent source of infection, With the sweets, however, the child purchases the right to hear with a good conscience that day's instalment of two or three interminable serial stories, and these, with the picture tableaux which accompany them, are value for money.

This brief survey of family budget expenditure has attempted to do no more than describe the level of consumption in a few random families and to indicate some aspects of the material scale of values which determines the choice between alternative expenditures. Evaluation of a different order—the degree of satisfaction with present consumption levels, the focus of aspirations or dissatisfactions, and the assessments of future prospects, will be dealt with in a later chapter. First it is necessary to give some attention to health and security, elements of the plane of living which in Japan, as in other industrial societies, it is increasingly considered the duty of the State rather than the individual family to provide.

6

Health and Security

O F the sounds which formed a constant daytime background to life in Shitayama-cho one was more strident and insistent than any other. This was the handbell of the borough refuse collector and, unlike the flute of the bean-curd seller or the kettle-drum of the sugar-doll man, it was more a command than an offer of service. Three times a week he moved round the ward, stationing himself for a few minutes at each corner and waiting until the house-wives from the neighbourhood had come from their houses to empty their buckets of refuse in his handcart.

One summer morning all Shitayama-cho was informed by mega-phone that the borough health department would make a free distribution of disinfectant that afternoon. Each household was to send one person with a bucket to the collection point and the disin-fectant was to be liberally used on refuse heaps and in lavatories. At the appointed time a queue of housewives and children were waiting with their buckets.

As these two illustrations show, a great deal in the operation of Tokyo health services is left to the initiative of the individual house-holder. This is partly because inadequate financial resources make it impossible to provide complete spoon-feeding services. It is partly due to the pre-war tradition of civic discipline and the ease with which voluntary co-operation can, in fact, be secured. The pre-war system of local government by descending chain of command—from Home Ministry to Metropolitan Office, to Borough Office, to the Ward officials, to each Neighbourhood Group leader, to each household— made possible, by means of a continuous face-to-face transmission of instructions reaching down to every individual householder, a form of 'voluntary' co-operation far more effective than the enacting and impersonal publicizing of by-laws and regulations.

The inverted comas round the word 'voluntary' in the last sentence should not be given too much weight. Although the element of coercion involved in the immediacy of the individual to whom each

63

person owed a duty of obedience was an important factor, the system would not have worked so efficiently had the mass of the populace not been fully identified with the aims of its leaders. The wartime use of the system to secure trench-digging squads and flag-waving parties and to organize civil defence obviously tapped a strong and universal will to victory. So, too, the orders to present babies for inoculation, to spread disinfectants on rubbish heaps, to perform the general spring-clean on the appointed day in time for the following day's police inspection, secured the more ready a response in that they appealed to an already existent desire for self-betterment (for want of a better phrase) and to a belief in the value of science, new techniques and the united co-ordination of effort as a means of attaining it. We shall be more concerned with this desire for self-betterment in the next chapter and in a discussion of education, but we may note in passing that the whole direction of internal government policy since the Meiji period—almost consistently modernizing and reformist in its emphasis—has played a big part in the development of such attitudes.

In 1951 the local government chain of command had in part broken down, but the desire for self-betterment and the sense of a duty to co-operate with one's immediate neighbours remained and was still largely relied on by the authorities to the exclusion of compulsory legislation. Even in the matter of sewage the metropolitan authorities contented themselves with laying the main sewer and leaving it to individual householders to provide their own connecting links, although they did add encouragement in the way of numerous posters proclaiming in every part of the city that 'A flush toilet is the first condition of Civilized Living' and offered short-term loans covering up to half the cost of installation provided that the cheaper sink-waste flushing system was employed. In 1951 some 90% of Shitayama-cho houses were connected to the sewer; the others still had to get their cess-pits emptied by private arrangement.

Public hygiene standards in Tokyo were sufficient to keep epidemic diseases within manageable, though still by no means negligible proportions. The summer peak of dysentery cases in August 1950 reached 2,500 a month in Tokyo. The origin of the infection was in most cases traced to foods and ice-creams manufactured in small and unhygienic establishments. Inadequate inspection and enforcement of existing legislation lies at the root of the trouble, combined, perhaps, with an undeveloped sense of any generalized civic responsibility. It is one of the things Japanese critics say of themselves that while the public is co-operative in health measures which can be seen directly to protect themselves or their immediate local community, they tend to be careless and resentful of restrictions when it is solely the safety of 'other people' in general that is at stake.[42] At the small-community level consideration for others is not difficult to mobilize; the good 'of the ward' as a whole is an easily acceptable goal. 'Other people' in general, however,—the people one meets in buses and trains, the members of other picnic parties in the park, the person one sells one's sweets to—these are in a different category. In that sphere it is every man for himself.

The relatively large amounts shown in the family budgets for expenditures on medicines and doctors' fees are an indication both of a quite high degree of health-consciousness and of generally low standards of health. Outwardly ill-health manifests itself less in a prevalence of sores and skin diseases as in a frequent air of lassitude and debility caused sometimes by malnutrition and sometimes by intestinal parasites, which are responsible for a considerable loss of human efficiency. A survey of Tokyo school-children in mid-1951 showed that 51% were suffering from such parasites and in one district the proportion was as high as 72%.[43] The use of human fertilizer is largely responsible, but the increased use of preventive and curative medicines is producing a gradual improvement with each yearly test. Vermifuges are the most widely advertised form of patent medicine and some Japanese take them regularly 'just in case' despite their very unpleasant incidental effects.

If the most common complaint is intestinal parasites, the most feared is tuberculosis. And this not without reason, since from the beginning of the century, when mortality statistics began first to be collected, until 1951 tuberculosis was the greatest single cause of death, with a death rate (all forms) hovering around 2 per thousand and reaching a peak of 282 per hundred thousand in 1945. In 1951 this rate was 111 per hundred thousand and for the first time was exceeded by one of the other groups in the intermediate classification, the degenerative diseases grouped under 'vascular lesions of the central nervous system'. Though this rate is still high by European standards (England, 32 per hundred thousand in 1951, Italy 71 per hundred thousand in 1950) it represents a considerable advance and the decline in the age-specific death rates for tuberculosis has been greatest in the critical 15–25 age-groups. In part this is due to the more energetic measures of the State, though facilities are still far from adequate despite the Tuberculosis Prevention Law of 1950 which voted funds (considerably less than the Welfare Ministry or the Opposition wanted) for mass radiography, BCG inoculation and expansion of hospital facilities.

The prominence given by the newspapers to all matters concerning tuberculosis (at the end of 1952 a fierce controversy over the merits of BCG vaccine between the Ministry of Welfare, the Ministry of Education's Joint Tuberculosis Research Committee, the Medical Section of the Japan Science Council, the Japan BCG Research

Association and the Welfare Committee of the Upper House made headline news for some weeks) is an indication of the fear which the disease provokes. In addition to the very real cause for fear—at best the loss of earning capacity for a long period and the bleak prospect of public assistance—there is also, though less in urban than in country districts, a considerable social stigma attached to the disease, inferior only to that attached to leprosy or insanity. This derives in part from a belief that tuberculosis is inherited and that a reputation for 'weakness of the lung' might seriously damage the family's chances on the marriage market. The attempt at concealment which this sense of shame induces is still somewhat of an obstacle to proper treatment and prevention of the disease.

The greater sense of shame attaching to certain illnesses[44] may be related to the generally higher degree of health-consciousness among the Japanese (as compared with, say, the English) which to some Western writers has seemed so marked as to deserve the term hypochondria.[45] The citizens of Shitayama-cho were certainly much given to self-medication, but it is disputable whether such difference as exists in this regard as between the Japanese and the English is due to a higher incidence of pathological hypochondriac tendencies or to the higher incidence of illness in Japan and the higher cost of medical advice. The latter factors are too easily forgotten by enthusiasts for explanation in terms of national character. At any rate, advertisments for patent medicines—advertisments much less legally restricted in the nature of their claims than in England—abound in the newspapers and magazines.

The majority claim their scientific character and the recency of the medical discoveries on which they are based as their chief recommendation, and many have foreign names. But still, even in medicine, where the pragmatic success of the new is perhaps most obvious, the forces of tradition are by no means routed and the old remedies deriving from Chinese medical lore still have their adherents. The ward next to Shitayama-cho contained a specialist in 'acupuncture, the moxa (pain is relieved by burning a small pyramid of powder on the affected spot), and breast massage' (presumably to aid the flow of milk). Even the peddling sales organization of the medicine manufacturers of Toyama prefecture, an organization which dates from the Tokugawa period, has remained intact despite the competition of modern chemist shops. Many Shitayama-cho households contained a 'home medicine bag' provided by one of these old patent-medicine firms. The peddler leaves it free of charge on his first visit and takes payment on his second and subsequent visits only for those medicines which have been used and require replacement.

The list of contents which the bag bears under the legend 'Health, the First Requirement for Building a New Peaceful Japan' shows the extent of the penetration of modern science and modern quackery even in this preserve of traditional lore. The 'Six Gods Pill' for 'heart diseases, stomach diseases and all fevers' jostles with what claims to be a santonin preparation for intestinal parasites and with the 'Universal Panacea' which 'lowers temperatures and has a good effect on all illnesses'. The 'Maternal Powder' is good for women in childbirth, the 'Life-Saver' deals with tantrums as well as fevers in children, and 'Whoosh' (*kerorin*) has a lightning effect on headaches and toothaches. Not forgetting the preventive as well as the curative aspects of medicine, the back of the bag is devoted to tips in *Old Moore's Almanack* style. One is warned, for instance, against combinations of foods which can prove dangerous; water-melon should never be eaten with fish or vegetable fritters, sparrows with peaches, herring with the fruit of the gingko tree, or eels with pickled plums.

More sophisticated middle-class households scorn anything which does not at least have the appearance of originating in the most modern of scientific laboratories. Most have their hypodermic syringe and ampoules of injections, for Japanese medicine follows German in its preference for the needle to the pill. Vitamin injections are also taken in large self-administered doses. The old Japanese belief that *seishin*—spirit, will-power—could conquer matter, that the human body could endure loss of sleep, starvation and physical pain to an almost unlimited degree provided the will was strong enough, has demanded some modification ever since the central wartime inference from this premiss—that Japanese spirit would be superior to American guns and bombs—has been falsified. The modern version is that spirit plus vitamin injections can conquer matter. 'Work hard, play hard, drink hard, and make up for loss of sleep with benzedrine and vitamin injections' seems to be the admired regimen of many middle-class Tokyo Japanese men, particularly those who would count themselves intellectuals. Ruth Benedict remarks on the Japanese belief in the superiority of spirit over matter and notes that they lack the American's tendency to consider the body as a machine from which one can only get out the equivalent of the energy one puts in.[46] But the Japanese are not lacking in this notion; rather the difference lies in their attitudes to machines. If the American treats them with respect and considers their requirements absolute, the Japanese treats them with familiar contempt, expects them to run with the minimum of maintenance in crises, and places great reliance on emergency patching up. This is true of attitudes to motor-cars as it is of attitudes to the human body. One may see as a reflection of such attitudes the easy acceptance of surgery in Japan; health-advice columns in the newspapers casually recommend the painful operation of skin removal and regrafting as a cure for axillary odours, and the increase in the number of abortions reported yearly since the operation became legal in 1948 has been of astonishing proportions.

The gradual improvement in Japanese health standards is undeniable. The crude death-rate is now of European proportions and expectation of life at birth according to the 1951 Abridged Life Table was 60·8 years for men and 64·8 for women. (Compared with 42·1 and 43·2 respectively for 1921–5.) Morbidity has correspondingly decreased. Illness remains a hazard, however; so does unemployment and old age, and the extent to which the individual can and does expect help from the State is still limited.

Some social security schemes for urban industrial workers existed before the war—the first Health Insurance Act was passed in 1922, and the Welfare Pensions Insurance Scheme (primarily a form of enforced saving to help finance the war effort) was started during the war—but their scope has been somewhat enlarged since. Details of the main social insurance schemes, for health, unemployment and retirement pensions in force in 1951, are given in Appendix 111.

These schemes are widely recognized to be deficient both in coverage and in scales of benefits and services provided. The lowest strata of urban workers, the day labourers and those employed in small family enterprises, are entirely excluded from their operations. Many more who should legally be included undoubtedly are not, owing to the employer's evasion. Treatment provided by overworked Health Service doctors is often inferior; in a national public-opinion survey three-quarters of those interviewed said that they 'had heard' that panel patients were discriminated against.[47] All monetary benefits are proportionate to contributions; that is, the schemes are consistently conceived as insurance schemes from which the individual draws benefits by a right established solely by virtue of his contributions. The principles of payment according to need or of guaranteeing a subsistence minimum are entirely absent. Equally, with Exchequer contributions kept to a minimum, there is little evidence of conscious intention to achieve some measure of income redistribution by means of these social services. Redistribution takes place only as between the sick and the healthy within the same income level rather than between income levels.

How much these schemes have done to bring about freedom from fear may be judged from the report of a Government public-opinion survey concerning these services. Actual knowledge of the schemes was found to be extremely limited; the Health Scheme was better known than the newer Pensions and Unemployment schemes, but, the report concludes, 'there is little evidence that they have been very effective in actually reducing the fear of illness'.

Table 10: Reactions to loss of Present Income-Source

Reply	Number
Wife or other member of family would go out to work, or do factory out-work	55
Fall back on savings	44
Seek help of relatives	43
Seek help from employer (in the case of two domestic craft workers; the wholesaler)	11
Wages would continue	8
Would get employees' insurance benefits	10
Other private insurance	5
Borrow money	7
Seek help from friends	6
Other replies	11
Never thought about it	29
Don't know	9
Total Replies	238
Total Respondents	218

The same conclusion emerges from the replies, tabulated in Table 10 of housewives in Shitayama-cho to a question asking them what they would do if 'your husband became ill or something (your shop was burnt out or something) and you lost your present source of income?' Although at least sixty-five of these housewives had husbands who were insured and would have been entitled to sickness benefits, only ten mentioned this in their replies, a reflection not only of the inadequacy of the benefits, but also of the limited extent to which these insurance schemes have been accepted as something to be relied on in emergencies, and, as the public-opinion survey noted, the small extent to which they have succeeded in reducing the haunting fear of mishaps. Several interviewers commented that the answer 'never thought about it' was given not with the gay abandon which it suggests on paper but with a look which suggested on the contrary that the question cut too near the quick to be easily discussed.

The general lack of concern with the State insurance services cannot, at any rate, be interpreted as a sign of lackadaisical improvidence or of a complacent failure of imagination. The large amounts devoted to savings and insurance in some of the family budgets are evidence of a more calculating foresight. So also is the fact that 75% of male householders in Shitayama-cho had taken out life insurance, and 55% of households held a fire insurance policy.

PUBLIC ASSISTANCE

Not one of the replies analysed in Table 10 made any mention of public assistance, the last resort of those who have no family, no paternalistic employer, no savings, and no insurance. A somewhat similar question in the government survey produced only 3% who said that they would turn to the State or to public assistance. This is not surprising, since public assistance is, for almost any Japanese, only a last resort in the extreme of distress. Grants are made only subject to a rigorous means test, and the essentials of life which the individual is not expected to sell in order to support himself before applying for a grant, are limited. The grants when given are insufficient for adequate nutrition; in one of the poorest boroughs of Tokyo in July 1951 the average per family was only 2,660 per month.

In addition, given the structure of Japanese local administration and politics, the system lends itself to various abuses. The granting of relief depends, effectively, on the arbitrary decision of a small number of people; the voluntary Welfare Commissioner (*Minseiiin*) and the local government official who is Welfare Secretary of the local authority. These are the all-powerful. One receives relief not by stating one's case objectively, submitting to an impersonal examination and obtaining a decision reached by the application of objective criteria to the facts (though that is the pattern legally prescribed) but by 'asking' these powerful individuals. The word *tanomu* is somewhere between the English word to 'ask' and to 'rely on'.[48] It means that you put yourself in the hands of the other person, that you will consider his decision not as the operation of legally prescribed machinery, but as the personal giving or withholding of a favour, that a favourable decision will necessarily entail a personal sense of gratitude and consequently the acknowledgement of a certain indebtedness. One small way in which this debt can be repaid is in accepting your benefactor's suggestions as to who to vote for at elections. The post of Welfare Commissioner is therefore a coveted one for budding local politicians, and he and the Welfare Secretary is generally 'worth' a fair number of votes at election time. The pattern is American, even the modern word for such men—'bossu'—is American, but this is not a part of the American way of life imported during the last few years. It has quite genuine indigenous roots. The etymology of the older Japanese word for such a person—a word which lacks the pejorative implications of the modern loan-word *bossu*—shows what these roots are. *Oyabun* is related to *oya* meaning parents, an indication of the pseudo-familial patron-client relations which ramified throughout every part of Japanese traditional social organization.

By traditional Japanese moral standards the submissive client's role is neither humiliating nor irksome. An old proverb—'wrap yourself up in something long'—gives it explicit sanction. But a growing individualism in urban areas is making it appear so to an increasing number of people. The *oyabun* becomes a *bossu*. There is nothing in the present Japanese public relief system comparable to the deliberate deterrent harshness, exerted with high moral purpose, which characterized the old British Poor Law, and the principle of granting out-relief for the maintenance of a subsistence minimum without removing any rights of citizenship in consequence[49] seems to be accepted. Nevertheless, a stigma attaches to the receipt of public relief and it remains a last resort.

STATE SOCIAL SECURITY; PLANS, DEMANDS AND ATTITUDES

In 1948, at the instigation of the Occupation authorities, the Japanese Government established a committee to study Japan's social security system and to make recommendations. Its report, published in October 1950, has become the Beveridge Report of Japanese reformers. It was, however, branded as too socialistic by the Occupation (since 1948 there had not only been personnel changes within Headquarters which had given it a somewhat different ideological colour, fiscal policy had also taken a turn towards stern retrenchment). The Japanese Government shelved the Report with no apparent sign of reluctance.

By any absolute standards, the Report was modest enough in the level of benefits it proposed, but in the general context of the Japanese economy it may be considered bold. It recommended the extension of unemployment, health and pensions schemes to all employees, not simply those in establishments employing five or more workers as at present. The national Health service was to be extended; there was to be some increase in the level of monetary benefits (though to some extent retaining the principle of differential contribution levels carrying differential benefits) and a limited beginning was to be made with widows', old age (over 70) and disablement pensions for the nation at large. The extra cost was to be largely met by the State. Whereas the existing social services (1950) absorbed 5% of the National Income and 5% of the Budget, the proposed schemes would have absorbed 8% of the National Income and 13% of the National Budget.[50] (This compares with approximately 9% of the National Income and over 13% of the Budget for Great Britain at that time.)

Even if the Government had had any enthusiasm for the extension of the social services, it might well have been cooled by the prospect of an 8% increase in Budgetary expenditure, but there is little solid ideological opposition to the creation and development of social services in Japan. Japanese capitalism has developed at a time when the optimistic individualism of *laissez-faire* liberalism was already on the decline as a political philosophy. In England, between the State interventionism of the Elizabethan period and the collectivism of the twentieth century there intervened a period when the principles of *laissez-faire* were accepted as axiomatic by the governing class. But in Japan the 'Elizabethan' policies of the Tokugawa period passed, by a smooth transition, into State Sponsorship of capitalism, and it has never been held as the central dogma of any party or class that it is only by giving free rein to the acquisitive instinct of each that one can best ensure the economic betterment of all, and that, consequently, poverty must always be given its full deterrent force as the penalty for non-acquisition; a necessary stimulus of thrift and industry.

On the other hand, just as Japan has never experienced the domination of the philosophy of economic liberalism, so the philosophical bases of the European collectivism which developed as a reaction against it in the social field have never been really potent factors in shaping either social policy or the course of political discussion in Japan; neither the argument from Christian charity (Confucian emphasis on family duty left little room for duty to one's neighbour) nor the secular arguments extending the doctrine of the 'rights of man' to the belief in economic rights inherent in the very nature of citizenship. The new American-written constitution proclaims that 'all people shall have the right to maintain the minimum standards of wholesome and cultured living. In all spheres of life, the State shall use its endeavours for the promotion and extension of social welfare and security, and of public health.' Ever since, these words have provided the starting point of every discussion of social security, but somehow they have a strangely alien ring which does not derive entirely from the 'translation Japanese' in which they are written. The idea of 'natural rights' and approval for the outspoken assertion of one's own rights does not come easily to a Japanese, for Japanese ethics and political thought has always been concerned to stress the importance of duties rather than to define explicitly the reciprocal rights. Translators of Western legal writings in the mid-nineteenth century were faced with an *embarras de richesse* when they came to choose a word for 'duty'. They had to coin an entirely new one for 'right'.

These arguments concerning natural rights—to minimum standards of living or to freedom from fear—the appeal to social justice, or the responsibility of the strong to care for the weak, have not been the main basis for proposals for social security measures in Japan. The moral arguments most easily invoked in Japan belong to a general context of benevolent despotism, or more properly, perhaps, State paternalism, since even in the hey-day of Emperor-worship the symbol *kokka*—the State—seems to have been charged with transcendental implications almost equal to those surrounding the word 'Emperor'. 'The old people have served the State well, so I suppose it is only right that the State should give them a reward in their old age' was, for one traditionally-minded Professor of Education, the natural justification for an old age pension system. It is significant, too, that the anti-tuberculosis campaign was launched in 1939 with a gracious letter from the Empress instructing the Government to try to alleviate the miseries of her people. And in 1951 it was the twelfth anniversary of the receipt of this letter which was chosen by the Government to launch a new campaign.

Modern Welfare-State philosophy in Japan, being thus the product of political battles fought not in Japan but elsewhere, is not surrounded by the same complex of moral conviction and political partisanship as in the West. It is accepted as something, like democracy, to the development of which Japan is committed by her general commitment to 'progress'. It is not recorded in the report of the discussion of the Social Security Advisory Committee that any of the ten politicians from all parties who were among its members issued any warning against undermining the family system or destroying the will to work.

But neither is there any really widespread popular political demand for social security measures. It is difficult for many older Japanese to conceive of the receipt of benefits from State schemes in any terms but those of *'o-kami no go-yakkai ni naru'*—to become a nuisance to *o-kami*, a word which until 1868 meant local feudal authorities and now means all officials in general, an amorphous respected 'they' whom it is every 'subject's' duty to honour and obey with a loyal self-effacement which puts 'making a nuisance' of oneself out of the question.

There are also other specific factors involved in the attitude of the public to social-security measures; factors which depend on the nature of Japanese employment relations, small community structure, and above all family structure.

The first two are important because they provide alternative mechanisms for dealing with the hazards of life. (They will be considered more fully in other chapters.) It is common for employers to take a paternalistic view of their duty to their employees, which involves the provision of some help in times of trouble. The close-knit community structure with carefully fostered relations of mutual obligation between families, ensures some help for those who have to meet sudden crises. Both these factors make State-run schemes of social security less essential. Gradually the 'depersonalization' of employment relations in large enterprises and the loosening of small-community structure are making these mechanisms less and less effective in the towns, but they are still not without importance.

The family not only provides a third and most important mechanism for dealing with the hazards of life and thus makes State-sponsored schemes less essential; in addition the morality of family relations in Japan also imposes certain positive hindrances on the acceptance of State aid. A small sample (102) in Shitayama-cho were asked the following questions;

1. I suppose you know the sort of pensions scheme civil servants have and the Welfare Pensions Scheme for workers in private firms; systems by which when people get old and can't work they still have some money coming in. But apart from the *Kan-i Hoken* (Post Office contributory insurance scheme) there is no pension scheme for the people of this country in general. Do you think some system like this is necessary so that everybody gets a certain allowance from the State as soon as he reaches a certain age? Or do you think such a system is unnecessary?
2. This ties up with the last question to a certain extent. Leaving aside for the moment people who don't have children, supposing an old person has a son who is well and working. From the point of view of such an old person do you think he would feel happier to be looked after by his son, or to live on the sort of old age pension I mentioned just now?

To the first question only seventeen people out of the hundred and two gave answers positively opposed to the establishment of such an old-age pensions scheme, and sixty-five said that they considered it necessary. In reply to the second question, however, seventy-eight thought that—'of course' as many of them said—a man would feel much happier to be looked after by his children. Only twenty thought that 'It's much better to have something like an old-age pension which you know there's no doubt you've got a right to draw,' or that 'It's less of a burden on the children and I should think the parent would feel more independent, too.'

It was in the replies of some of the seventy-eight that one found some evidence of the positive barriers of the family system to State-sponsored security schemes. Such, for instance, as 'If you take money from the State, people around start talking and look on you with contempt, and that's not a very nice feeling.' Public assistance given out of benevolence to 'failures' is still the only familiar form of State aid, and, indeed, by Japanese standards it is a sign of failure not to have a child which fulfils its filial obligations; either a failure in moral education of one's children, or a failure to give them the start in life which would make them able and—from spontaneous gratitude—willing to support one's old age. Nor is childlessness an excuse; one has the moral duty to ensure the succession by adopting an heir. It is significant that several of the twenty who preferred the impersonal dependance on a State pension added the qualification 'provided it really becomes general' if, that is, the existing social disapprobation is removed.

Other replies showed the scruples deriving primarily from political attitudes which were mentioned above. The word *o-kami* was not in fact used by anyone—one has to go to rural areas to find that level of unsophistication today—but the sentiment was there; 'One mustn't be a burden on the country,' 'It would make me feel *sumanai* to take money from the State.' *Sumanai* expresses overwhelmed gratitude, tinged with guilt at the thought of one's own unworthiness to receive the favour.

These questions referred specifically to old-age pensions. Filial piety forms the central core of Japanese family morality, and caring for parents in their old age is the typical concrete form of its expression. One must beware, therefore, of assuming that attitudes to old-age pensions typify attitudes towards all social services. During the same interview, a question immediately preceding the two quoted above asked who should bear the chief responsibility for looking after those who, through sickness or unemployment, were unable to look after themselves. The alternatives offered were; family and relations, the State, private charity organizations, or the employer.

Table 11: Who bears Responsibility for the Sick and Unemployed?

First choice	Men	Women
Family	14	23
State	27	11
Private charity	3	6
Employer	0	7
Don't know, or qualified replies	6	5
Total	50	52

Those who gave the State and those who gave the family as having the primary responsibility were approximately equal in number, but there is a significantly greater preference for the family over the State among women than among men. One 45 year-old woman expressed very well the theoretical basis for objecting to the State's interference in these matters. Having said that it was the responsibility of the family to look after its unfortunates, she answered the interviewer's next question: 'But supposing the person has no family or relatives?' as follows: 'Well, he should have some friend or acquaintance. He should go to them for help. If he hasn't, then I suppose there's nothing but the State. But if there's nobody to look after him, then it's the person's own fault. People aren't born out of the crotch of a tree. Nobody can go through life entirely on his own. If you are always kind to other people, then you will never want help yourself.'

The general preference for personal contacts over impersonalized procedures—the much-discussed 'particularism' of Japanese society—is, as this reply shows, at the basis of these hesitancies and objections to such essentially 'universalistic' institutions as State social services.[51] The inevitable widening of the sphere of impersonal contacts which results from urban life, the size of the city, the specialization of function, migration and the isolation of the individual, is undoubtedly bringing a change. The Government's Public Opinion Survey summarized the conclusions of a study of attitudes to the social services as follows:[52]

1. Generally speaking there seems to be no positive opposition to existing schemes.
2. Most families are worse off now (April 1950) than a year ago (the 'Dodge Line' deflation was getting under way) and are finding it difficult to make ends meet. Many look to the State to do something to secure their means of livelihood. Most people are well-disposed towards social insurance schemes and consider them necessary.
3. However, it cannot be said that any great interest is shown in this question. Most people are more concerned with stabilizing, and if possible raising, their present standards of consumption.

7

Progress and Planning

How far, and in what way, are the people of Shitayama-cho concerned with 'raising their present standards of consumption'? In traditionally oriented, technologically stationary societies, the standards of living (using 'standard' in its normative sense of 'level of living considered appropriate') of its members tend to be fixed. No overall improvement for the whole of society is expected or considered possible, and the relative wealth of its members is thought to be, and accepted as being, ineluctably determined by status, which is generally inherited and only exceptionally acquired.

Japanese society is obviously not technologically stationary, and few Japanese are entirely 'traditionally-oriented' any longer; wealth is increasingly looked on as the cause and not the expression of status, competition for wealth and status is increasingly thought to be normal and, indeed, laudable, and a general and continuing improvement in the levels of living of society as a whole is increasingly looked on as not only desirable but inevitable. This chapter will attempt to elaborate these generalizations by means of the answers of housewives in interviews in Shitayama-cho.

Theoretically, for a materially progressive society such as England at the present time, one might distinguish three 'standards' of living, three levels of aspiration. At the lowest level is what might be called the 'normative standard of living' which one may see expressed in such phrases as 'We have always been used to an X', 'Everybody has an X these days', or 'People in our position invariably have an X'. A lack of X is felt as a positive deprivation to be remedied at the earliest opportunity. Secondly, there is what might be called the 'aimed-at standard of living'—'Lots of people have X nowadays and they seem to be very useful (nice things to have, attractive, comfortable, etc.). We must get one as soon as we can afford it.' Thirdly the 'ideal standard of living' belongs to the dream world of vicarious living in the pages of illustrated magazines. 'Wouldn't it be wonderful to have an ... If ever I win a football pool. ...'

These three levels are, of course, only points on a continuum rather than levels proper, but they will provide a useful framework within which to discuss the reactions of housewives to a question asking them; 'Is there any article for use in the home which you often think to yourself you would like to have if only you could afford it?' Although the 'for use in the home' was interpreted liberally and some mentioned such things as organs and children's bicycles, not many answers could be interpreted as belonging to the 'ideal' plane. No-one wanted Cadillacs or diamond tiaras. For many, indeed, particularly those sharing rooms or living in apartment blocks—a good number of them victims of wartime bombing—the attainment of a normative standard represented the limits of their ambitions. They wanted furniture and clothing and radios and irons which for them have long been a part of the daily necessities of life. The most interesting replies are those of housewives of above average economic status who might be expected, if they took their normative standard from the general level of their neighbours, to have attained it. Their replies may be considered to indicate their aimed-at standard. There were some who mentioned electric refrigerators, washing machines, vacuum cleaners, an electric record-player, a piano, electric toaster, a telephone. But there were almost as many who wanted more or better clothing or furniture, not, that is to say, new gadgets, recent inventions or labour-saving devices, but greater fulfilment within the framework of a traditional pattern of living.

A rough classification of the possible motives for desiring new possessions might run as follows:

1. To secure an increase of physical, aesthetic, intellectual, etc., satisfactions of a familiar type (e.g. softer arm-chairs, new clothes—to those already used to wearing clothes, more books, etc.).
2. To secure physical, aesthetic, intellectual, etc. satisfactions of a new type (e.g. arm-chairs to habitual floor-sitters, gramophones for those who have never owned one, etc.).
3. To save time or physical effort in the performance of familiar tasks (e.g. vacuum cleaners, washing machines).
4. To acquire the prestige which goes with the possession of the article in question.
5. As a form of investment.

During the Tokugawa period, only motives (1), (4), and (5) were of any importance and of these (4) was often the dominant one. For those who had attained the maximum level of nutrition and physical comfort which contemporary knowledge and resources permitted, the only channel for further ambition was conspicuous consumption in the strictest sense—more and better clothes, rooms, furniture, ceremonial implements for weddings and funerals, paintings, tea-bowls and gardens. These things were a source of aesthetic satisfaction in themselves as well as being an important form of investment in a society in which banking facilities were rudimentary, but it was of their essence that they should be conspicuous, particularly in the lower reaches of the status hierarchy. In Tokugawa society, a society in which status was overwhelmingly important, it was also to a large degree hereditarily ascribed, but in the peasant and merchant communities (to a greater degree than among the samurai) there was considerable latitude for a man's status to rise or fall. Though the frontiers between the main estates—the samurai, the peasants and the rest—were fairly rigid, within the frontiers status could be acquired and lost. In any case it had to be affirmed by a suitable level of consumption in the things which 'show', in particular the clothes, the implements, the furniture and the physical setting provided when the family invites its neighbours to wedding feasts or funerals.

It is the legacy of these attitudes—excessive attachment to motive (4) to the exclusion of all others—which is being fought in rural areas by the Government-sponsored Reformed Living Campaign (*Seikatsu Kaizen Undoo*). Its reports often dwell on the extent to which concentration on this 'status-preserving' consumption prevents expenditure necessary for health or more directly related to physical comfort. They find farm households with carefully preserved sets of best china kept for entertaining, while the family makes do with an insufficient number of chipped and cracked pieces; bright sunny reception rooms which are never used, while the family confines itself to dark dingy rooms at the back of the house; enormous expenditures on wedding receptions by families which are normally half-starved. Whereas in England, at least as far as public housing policy is concerned, the battle against the Victorian front parlour seems to have been finally won, this is far from being the case in rural Japan.

In urban areas, however, two main changes in these attitudes take place: (*a*) The looser structure of the local community makes status, and hence the prestige attaching to material possessions, of lesser importance, and the other motives, (1)–(3), are given fuller play. Moreover, the particular form of 'rationality' exemplified in the Reformed Living Movement, which emphasizes material satisfactions to the exclusion of prestige considerations, tends to be fostered by the whole tenor of modern urban life.

(*b*) Secondly, a more important change is that the greater prestige begins to be attached not to the possession of articles which also satisfy motive (1), but rather to the possession of articles which also satisfy motives (2)–(3). The process of technical development and the impact of a Western scale of values in which the mere quality of novelty in itself has a high place, provide new objects of ambition; electric fans, refrigerators and washing machines, vacuum cleaners and gramophones. The new gadgets may be highly valued in themselves for the increased comfort or convenience which they bring, or for their effect in reducing household drudgery and saving time. But it is also important that prestige attached to them too. The pride with which some owners of electric fans in Shitayama-cho brought them out for visitors was unmistakeable. Conspicuous consumption can now take the form of possessing the latest invention which other people do not have, rather than more or better goods of traditional types. The time-saving motive, is still, probably, of the least importance, for Shitayama-cho housewives, generally speaking, have only limited opportunities for social or professional activities which compete with housework.

But the change is still in progress. There are housewives in Shitayama-cho who have their eye on a vacuum cleaner or a refrigerator. But for many household drudgery is an inevitable part of the woman's lot and their ambitions are not directed primarily towards relieving it. Their aim, rather, is to keep their home as attractive as possible by stocking it not so much with the latest gadget as with the traditional goods, the clothes and furniture which one could be proud to show to one's neighbours.

This does not imply any positive resistance to innovations. Certain innovations of the past few decades—electric light, gas, mains water, the radio—now form part of the normative standard of living for every Tokyo family. It implies only a negative attitude. The prospects of such innovations do not arouse their enthusiasms or direct their ambitions. It probably also implies that these housewives do not share the assumption, common in England and held with even more assurance in America, that society is gradually moving along an inclined plane of continuous progress towards greater and greater material prosperity achieved by advancing scientific knowledge. They are more prone to take the Tokugawa view by which society is seen as in a state of stable equilibrium likely to continue indefinitely unchanged, modified only by the short-run cycle of disaster (from famine, fire, war or earthquake) and recovery; a view which, indeed, the experiences of the last two decades have done something to justify.

Some more direct evidence on this score can be found in the answers to another set of questions which came later in the same interview.

1. Compared with your mother's day would you say that the housewife's job—cooking, cleaning and so on—had got easier, or that it had got more difficult, or that it hadn't changed very much?
2. In what way, exactly?
3. By the time your daughter is your age do you think the housewife's work will have got easier, or do you think it will get more difficult or do you think it won't change very much?
4. Why do you think so?

The generalized form of these questions proved difficult for the housewives interviewed. Almost every one in replying to the first two questions made some specific comparison between herself and her own mother, and replies like 'I don't know because my mother died when I was young' were not uncommon. This in itself is evidence that there is no strong stereotyped belief in 'tremendous material progress over the past few decades' to be immediately touched off by a question of this sort. Nevertheless, as Table 12 shows, a large minority of the total sample believe themselves to be better off than their mothers.

Table 12: Have things got Better?

	Type of Reply		Number	
Things have got better	1. Refers to general amenities such as gas, water, shops, etc.		44	
	2. Ditto, but specifically pointing a contrast between town and country		31	
	3. Refers to fortuitous personal circumstances, e.g. 'Mother was widowed when I was young so I am much better off.'		19	
	4. Refers to social changes		12	
	5. Non-explanatory explanations, e.g. 'I am not so busy', 'Economically better off', etc.		6	112
No change			19	
Things have got worse	1. General post-war economic decline		15	
	2. Other reasons, 'I am busier than mother was', 'Mother had servants and I haven't', Inconveniences of apartment life, etc.		42	57
Don't know, not reported			50	
Total			238	

Of those who do not, many are wives of middle-class families whose standard of living is generally depressed compared with pre-war days. Thirteen complained, for instance, that their mothers had domestic servants which they themselves could not afford. Others blamed the increased cost of living and their relatively lower post-war incomes, the difficulties of rationing or of room-sharing.

In the replies of those who saw themselves as better off, there were frequent references to the gas and water mains, as a great improvement on the well their mothers drew from and the firewood their mothers had to chop, or to the electricity which abolished the necessity of daily polishing a sooty oil lamp. Even a large number of apartment-dwellers thought themselves better off on this score, although they shared a gas tap and a water tap between anything from two to six families.

Some of the housewives who mentioned gas and water and electricity were brought up in Tokyo—for even in Tokyo gas and water mains were none too common in the early nineteen-twenties—but the majority were country-born and it was often explicitly in terms of a difference between country-life and town-life, rather than between Japan a generation ago and Japan today, that housewives compared their lot with their mothers'. For these people shopping was easier, pickles which used to be made at home could now be bought round the corner, and a dozen women mentioned that they had only a small compact town house or a single apartment room to keep clean, not an aged rambling farm-house. A further and cardinal point of difference was that their mothers not only had to do the housework (until a daughter was old enough to take over) but also had to work most of the day with the men in the fields. (On the other hand, one woman born in Tokyo saw things differently. 'Women go out to work these days, but they still have to do the housework just the same.') The positive replies of these women do not necessarily mean that they see any general material improvement. As they see it, they have simply bettered themselves by moving from the countryside to the towns.

An interesting group of replies are those which referred to social rather than economic changes as the cause of their betterment. 'We have fewer children nowadays' said one. Husbands are more co-operative; 'It's much easier being a woman these days. Men have come to have more respect for us. In the old days you could work yourself to the bone and all you would get would be a scolding for not working hard enough.' 'Men are much more understanding and help about the house and with the children and things.' 'My mother had to worry about everything herself. Now husbands and wives do the worrying together. To that extent the burden is lighter.' Again, there was no mother-in-law; 'nobody to complain of everything you do'. The etiquette of social relations was much simplified; 'In my mother's day all the details of etiquette were so precisely regulated. It was a great strain. Now housewives don't care, almost.' Even changes in women's clothing had helped; 'With Western-style skirts one can get around the house so much more easily,' and changes in diet: 'We eat bread instead of rice for one meal and that saves that much cooking.'

The variety of these answers is the best indication that an axiomatic acceptance of the reality of recent progress does not play a central part in the folk-lore or ideology of Shitayama-cho housewives. There were no ready-made answers to the question. On the other hand, there were signs of a general awareness that perhaps to agree that there had been an improvement was the right and expected answer. At any rate, of those who said that there had been no change, seven made elucidatory comments which gave particular reasons why they thought they were *worse* off.

Perhaps a better test of general notions of progress in the abstract is contained in the answers to the second pair of questions about the future.

Table 13: Will Things get Better in the Future?

Type of Reply		Number
Things will get better	1. Uses words like, 'advance of civilization', 'American civilization', 'convenience', 'scientific progress', 'machinery'	61
	2. Economic improvements in existing framework, e.g. cheaper goods, better wages, end of food rationing, stability, etc.	15
	3. Social changes (as in Table 12)	15
	4. Non-explanatory explanations—mere paraphrases of the original answer that things will get better	24
	5. Personal fortuitous circumstances—e.g. 'my daughter will be a doctor so she will have servants'.	8
		123
No change		41
Things will get worse	1. Due to economic deterioration; higher prices, political instability, etc.	6
	2. Others	7
		13
Don't know, not reported		61
Total		238

This time there is a bare majority committed to optimism and the positive pessimists are in a much smaller minority. Not surprisingly, many of the optimistic replies mentioned America as the country which has reached the apogee of material progress and offers an example of what Japan, too, might achieve. 'We shall be leading an Americanized life by then,' was a typical reply.

The impact of America on the people of Tokyo since the war has, of course, been enormous. The defeat itself is normally interpreted as the logical outcome of American technical superiority, and the wholesale transportation of the American way of life into Tokyo has enabled vast numbers to see directly what that technical superiority means in domestic terms. There are probably few members of the working classes and lower middle classes who have never met someone, a plumber, a telephone mechanic, a maid, a gardener, who has been inside an American house on one of the Occupation's housing estates.

Until the end of the war the organs of public opinion and popular education were scornful of the gross materialism of American culture in contrast to the fine spirituality of the Japanese way of life. Since, they have tended to be more admiring than critical. The magazines carried articles on home life in America by Occupation wives and by Japanese who had visited the United States under the Tours for National Leaders programme which gave the general impression that if the millennium had not already arrived on the other side of the Pacific, at least it was not very far off. *Reader's Digest* appeared in a Japanese edition from early on in the Occupation and achieved a high circulation; one of the largest Tokyo daily papers chose, as its one and only daily cartoon feature, the popular American Blondie strip cartoon portraying the vicissitudes of white collar life in America. 'Every time I see Blondie it makes me think,' said one woman, 'Things have gradually tended to get easier in the past and I suppose they will do in the future. Ordinary cleaning, for instance. People will make houses with fewer places to be cleaned with wet cloths. If the woodwork is varnished you can make do with a flicker-duster, or just a vacuum cleaner like Blondie.' [53]

The pessimists most commonly pointed to the prospects of continuing national economic difficulty as the justification of their views. 'Things won't be much different from what they are now, I should imagine. Of course, there are washing machines and things, but when are we ever likely to be able to buy them?' Another was sceptical about improvement in the social position of women. 'Wages aren't likely to improve, nor is the idea that it's the woman who has to do all the work.'

Again, many of those who said that there would be no change mentioned factors *inhibiting* progress as their justification. To sum up these remarks, then, we may say that the notion of a gradually progressing society, though not a firm and unshakeable belief, is at least a familiar one even to those who are sceptical of its truth, and more people are prepared to entertain the idea as an abstract proposition concerning the future than as an accurate description of what has happened in the recent past.

RATIONALITY

One would expect a belief in the continuity of material progress to be found in conjunction with a desire to share in its fruits. That is to say one would expect it to be found in conjunction with attitudes to housework which are 'rational' in the sense of not being bound solely by tradition, of being prepared to reconsider accepted patterns of behaviour if new and more efficient means of achieving desired ends present themselves. This is a part of the sort of rationality with which Max Weber was concerned as an essential prerequisite for the successful development of a capitalist society; and the recent history of Japan shows how adequately that prerequisite has been met in the sphere of economic productive activity—even in that most traditional segment of the economy, agriculture, productivity doubled in half a century as a result of adopting new techniques. That these attitudes have penetrated also into the home will have been clear from all this talk about refrigerators and vacuum cleaners. The 'desire for self-betterment' which the public health authorities were able to rely on to secure co-operation in public health schemes (see Chapter 6), the willingness to reconsider traditional food habits and to adopt new ways of evaluating foods, may all be considered to belong to the same family of attitudes.

As an attempt to measure the distribution of these attitudes, housewives were asked in an interview whether they read women's magazines, whether they listened to Woman's Hour on the wireless, and whether they had got any useful ideas, hints or recipes from either source which they had tried out in their home. 40% claimed to be regular readers of one of the monthly magazines, usually one of the more popular magazines, though with a sprinkling of the '*interi*-lady's' (*interi* is from 'intellectual') 'quality' magazines. Another 30% read magazines occasionally. (One or two of the negative replies were contemptuous, e.g. 'I never read anything but Goethe'.) 48% of the total sample gave examples of ideas which they had got either from these magazines or from the radio, and some were quite enthusiastic about the sweetness and light which these media had brought into their lives. (Others complained of the impracticality of the suggestions of middle-class experts; the mere fact that quantities were given in grams was enough to damn them as far as many housewives were concerned.) It is interesting to note that this figure of 48% is higher than the proportion who answered 'yes' to the next question asking whether they had ever got similar ideas from talking to neighbours. This was only 44%. Although there are also many other factors involved here (e.g. pride—'The average run of women round here are so common that I wouldn't be seen talking to them'), it is, perhaps, an indication of the extent to which personal have been replaced by impersonal channels of communication.

There are two other senses of rational management which one might expect to find related—the keeping of a regular account of household expenditure (50% of housewives said they kept such accounts) and the provision for future disasters in the form of fire-insurance (55% of households) and life insurance (75% of house-heads). But how related are they?

Some of these kinds of rationality are, indeed, very significantly related. The housewife who says that she keeps a budget is more likely to say that she has adopted suggestions from magazines and the radio.[54] And if she gives either of these replies she is likely to be younger and better educated than those who do not.[55]

Ideas about progress, however, seem to bear only a slight relationship to these other factors. The housewife who keeps a budget is more likely to discern progress in the recent past than those who do not,[56] and the housewife who expects progress in the future is more likely to be receptive to the suggestions of magazine and radio.[57] But the answers to neither of these questions about progress seem to be in any way related to age or education, and, indeed, the relation between optimism about the future and belief in progress in the recent past, though significant, is not in itself by any means a strong one.[58]

Private insurance, again, shows little relationship to any of these other factors. This one can understand. The kind of foresight which makes general preparation for possible disasters is not new in Japanese society. The Japanese of the infinitely more hazardous Tokugawa period were not lacking in such prudence. True—for a world of frequent famine, typhoon, earthquake, pestilence and fire may conduce to 'what's-the-use' give-up-the-ghost-ism or to devil-may-care live-for-the-moment-ism just as much as to prudence—the Edokko (the Tokyo cockney) made a cult of his scorn for financial security, and it was his proudest boast that he 'never carried money over from one day to the next', a phrase which has passed into the language as typifying the gay braggadocio of the young artisan. But this attitude never characterized Edo society as a whole—the house-wives pictured in Shikitei Samba's Sketches of the Bath-House were longsighted enough—and in any case, even in the towns where the money economy was fully established, the real source of security lay not in financial savings, but in the maintenance of correct personal relationships. 'If you are kind to other people, other people will always be kind to you.' If you carry out all your obligations of regular gift-giving and visiting, are kind to your kin, loyal to your patrons and neighbourly to your neighbours, then in emergencies you will always be able to count on their help. The growth of commercial fire insurance has, then, been not so much the result of the development of new attitudes of rational foresight, as of a change from personal, particularistic to impersonal, universalistic means of attaining traditional ends.

Finally, a further word about the relation of these rational characteristics to some of the more obvious manifestations of tradition in Shitayama-cho life. One might expect that, in so far as not having household gods within the home is a sign of scepticism, it would be linked with the presence or absence of the rational behaviour we have been considering. The only noticeable relation which emerges, however, is with the keeping of budgets,[59] and it is in the direction one would expect, that is, the housewives who keep budgets are less likely to rely on the protective power of household gods. The lowness of the association is due in part to the fact that scepticism is not the only cause for the absence of household gods; it is as often as not a sign that the family has not got a house which it is satisfied with and feels to be a proper home.

These latter considerations are doubtless relevant to an interpretation of the fact that there is a very significant[60] relation between having household gods and having the house insured against fire (that is to say, the more a family has what it feels to be a proper home, the more likely it is to insure it and the more likely it is to have household gods). Though here there may also be a common factor of prudence; the division being between those who take precautions against future calamities by all means possible, including guardian deities and fire insurance, and those who let the future take care of itself. At any rate, the dichotomy is not between the old and the new.

And this brings us to the moral of the story. The foregoing analysis of interrelations has been undertaken primarily with the intention of correcting the bias which a constant preoccupation with social change may have given to the preceding pages. While there is little doubt that changes in attitudes and in ways of life such as have been described are in progress, it would be wrong to give the impression that there is a fundamental cleavage in Shitayama-cho society between those who are consciously 'modernists' and those who are consciously 'traditionalists'. These changes in attitudes and behaviour are not as logically interrelated as the sociologist would like them to be; the most avidly bread-eating, blouse-and-skirted housewife may fill every nook and cranny of her house with fire-preventing deities and guardian Buddhas, while the conscious agnostics remain unmoved in their attachment to boiled rice and flowing *kimono*. It is true that a sort of modern-traditional dichotomy is recognized by the Japanese themselves. 'That is a very old-fashioned household." or 'They are very traditional, very (and this in spoken inverted commas) "Japanese" ' are common phrases, as also, are 'That is a very *modan* family' or 'She is a very emancipated (*kaihooteki*) house-wife' (a frequent interviewer's comment). But it is not a fundamental division, with frontiers clearly drawn and a foot in both camps impossible. The changes in attitudes and behaviour which are taking place are often discrete and unrelated to each other—unrelated both in the sense that they have different immediate causes, and in the sense that they are not related in the minds of the people who experience them. They are, moreover, taking place gradually; some are already thoroughly assimilated (like fire insurance), others (like scepticism concerning protective Buddhas and the lust for washing machines) have only just begun. Variations in attitudes and behaviour among housewives in Shitayama-cho are largely determined on each separate issue by differences in individual personality and background, differences in economic status and in means of livelihood, not by ideological commitment to one side or the other in a struggle between the forces of modernism and the forces of tradition. For, indeed, ever since the Meiji restoration, although interpretations of the word have varied, 'modernization' has been the accepted goal of the whole of Japanese society.

Section III

THE FAMILY

8

The Japanese Family System

ALL societies have a family system, but few are as consciously aware of their family system as the Japanese. The average Englishman would appreciate that the ways his fellow-countrymen get married, live together and have children follow certain fairly consistent patterns, but he would be likely to consider these simply as patterns of natural, normal behaviour. He would think it odd to hear this called the 'English family system' with all the suggestion of arbitrariness and uniqueness which such words imply. In Japan, however, the 'Japanese family system' is a widely used term. Those Japanese who were at school before 1945 have read about 'the family system of our country' in their school text-books; they have learned to recite the Imperial Rescript on Education which enumerates the values and obligations of that family system as virtues peculiar to Japan. Before 1945 they heard politicians, school-masters, the local mayor, the local battalion commander and countless publicists of press and radio stress the importance of 'the family system of our country' as the embodiment of all that was fine and noble in the national tradition, the only suitable training ground for patriotic and loyal citizens, the secret of the moral fibre of the Japanese people the core (foundation, pillar, bulwark) of the national polity. Since the war they have heard somewhat less assured voices (sometimes from the same politicians and the same publicists) denounce 'the Japanese family system' (it is in approving contexts that 'the family system of our country' predominates) as a hindrance to democracy, the last and strongest rampart of feudalism, symbol of a morality which ignores human rights, inhibits individual enterprise and responsibility, enforces the eternal subjection of women, and fosters the attitudes which facilitate the organization of a totalitarian state.

The historical reasons for this self-awareness are not difficult to find. The most obvious is the impact of Western culture. This has been of such a strength and extent that few individuals can have escaped the knowledge that foreigners behave in ways radically different from the Japanese. Moreover, it was natural that Japanese popular observation of differences between Japan and Western

91

societies should take especial notice of differences in family structure, since the family, of all forms of social organization, is the one in which every individual of a society must be to some degree involved and the one which tends to arouse the most intensely emotionally-toned attitudes. Differences, for instance, in the respect shown to women—immediately obvious to any Tokyo Japanese who had ever seen a foreigner hand his wife out of a carriage—stood out to the Japanese, and their awareness of these differences was heighted by the activities of a group of publicists—large in number at some times, smaller when the mood of the time swung back to reaction—who urged, at a time when Western techniques were being hastily and deliberately adopted in many other spheres, that Western family patterns, too, were superior to those of Japan.

Public discussion of the family system—what it was and what it should be—was further stimulated by the necessity which arose in the Meiji period of replacing the existing regionally-varying customary law governing the family with central state legislation. In 1890, after twenty years of 'Westernization', at the time when a traditionalist reaction was beginning to set in, preparations were completed for the enactment of Japan's first coherent civil code. The provisions concerning the family, however, provoked so much controversy that the code was withdrawn. Two opposed groups of lawyers, those who defended the original code and those who wished to alter it, struggled for six years in committee before a compromise code was enacted. This battle of the jurists has been represented as primarily a struggle between French jurisprudence and German jurisprudence,[61] between the historical school and naturalistic legal theories,[62] or simply as a clash of temperaments and ambitions rationalized into differences of principle.[63] It may have been all of these things, but it was certainly also, as far as the differences on many of the points at issue were concerned, a clash between those who wished to preserve and legitimize the traditional family structure and attacked the original draft of 1890 as being too much influenced by foreign ideas, and those who defended the original code as making the miniumum adjustments necessary to meet the requirements of a modern industrial state.

The code which originally came into force in 1898 was a compromize which satisfied neither side. The debate between the traditionalists and the reformists continued, until, when the nationalist reaction reached its peak in the early forties, the reformists were practically silenced. Then, finally, in 1948, the complete rewriting of the Civil Code brought victory to the reformists in a form more complete than they could ever have hoped for.

Throughout the years 1898 to 1948, the controversy was stimulated by the increasing discrepancy between the ideals of family organization upheld by the traditionalists and in part embodied in the 1898 Code, and the reality of family relations in Japanese society. Industrialization and urbanization were changing the economic basis of the traditional family and the economic sanctions of traditional authority patterns were weakened or destroyed. Widespread migration and female employment, no less than the growing influence of individualistic thought, popular education and the encouragement of individual enterprise helped to change the norms of behaviour, slowly but none the less surely. These seeds of change inevitably produced their crop of social problems—delinquency, disobedience of parental authority, problems of neglect and individual security. And all the time a running battle was fought against all such change by the conservative political leaders, and in particular by educationalists, who placed a high value on the maintenance of traditional patterns, and whose one answer to all social problems was to advocate the strengthening of the family in its indigeneous mould.

The reason why such a great emphasis was placed on the maintenance of traditional family patterns was not only that 'the family system of our country' stood, like calligraphy, *bushidoo* (the way of the warrior), Shintoo and the tea ceremony, as a symbol embodying the traditional Japanese virtues as opposed to corrupting Occidental influences, nor simply that strengthening the family offered an acceptable retort to the demands for social reform which developed under the influence of corrupting Occidental ideologies. Nor was it due only to the same clustering of attitudes as makes opinion pollsters in this country link opposition to easier divorce and belief in the virtues of parental flogging with Empire-firstism as criteria of a conservative orientation. There were other specific factors involved which can only be understood in the context of the history of Japanese thought, and in particular of the tradition of Japanese Confucianism.

It was one of the basic assumptions of Chinese political theory that the good State would automatically result if each individual punctiliously cultivated the garden of his own family duties. The Confucian text often quoted in illustration of this ('Their persons being cultivated, their families were regulated. Their families being regulated, their states were rightly governed. Their states being rightly governed, the whole kingdom was made tranquil and happy',[64] refers primarily to the rulers of principalities under Chou feudalism, but it was an axiom of Chinese political thought that stable families meant a stable society and that filial piety was a civic and not merely a private duty.[65] One of the senses in which the word *kazoku-seido* (family system) is used in Japan—and that given by most Japanese dictionaries to the exclusion of all others—clearly presupposes these political principles. The word is used to talk of '*the* family system' (as

one talks of *the* feudal system) meaning a system of legal and political
organization whereby the family is the major unit of social organization, is a legal personality in which property rights and duties are
vested, and is represented externally by a family head who exercises
wide powers of control over family members.[66]

The second factor is more specifically Japanese. In Japan the habit
of modelling the structure of social groups outside the family—
occupational, educational, recreational, political, artistic, criminal—
on the pattern of the family, has been developed with a consistency
rare in other societies. The terms for positions in such groups are
formed by analogy with terms for positions in the family (e.g.
oyabun and *anikibun*—'father-part' and 'elder-brother part', *iemoto*—
'family chief', etc.), the duty of obedience in these non-kinship
structures (*chuu*—loyalty) is equated with filial piety; and the love,
the favours, shown by the superior to the inferior are designed by the
same term—*on*—whether it is parent, teacher, master or feudal lord
who confers them.[67]

Even today, despite the development of more impersonal forms of
association, such explicitly family-patterned groups exist, among
dock-labourers, among the teachers of all the traditional Japanese
aesthetic pursuits and in trade union branches and universities. The
apotheosis of this tendency to 'familize' was reached in the family-
state symbolism surrounding the Emperor, deliberately fostered, at
first to create a sense of national unity in a society which had hitherto
consisted of a large number of semi-autonomous fiefs, and later to
maintain that sense of unity and prepare the nation for war and
sacrifice.[68] The legitimation of state authority in family terms was
thus an important tool of government. Explicit statements of the
argument abound in the works of pre-war writers. One meets constantly such phrases as 'the unity of loyalty and filial piety exem-
plifies the basis of our national polity' or ' "familism" centring
round the Imperial family is at the foundation of the Japanese
state'.[69]

The relationship between the family and the state was, moreover,
not solely one of analogy. In the extreme nationalist formulations
of history, the Japanese people are all descended from a common
ancestor. The Imperial Family represents the line of direct descent;
all other families in Japan are collateral branches founded by younger
sons of earlier generations. The whole nation, therefore, is one vast
lineage group. 'The Emperor embodies the Spirit of the Original
Ancestor of our race. . . . In submitting to the Emperor of a line
which has persisted through the ages, we subjects are submitting to
the Spirit of the Joint Parent of our Race, the Ancestor of our
ancestors.'[70]

'The Japanese family system', then, are not unfamiliar words to the Japanese. Their connection with the reality of daily behaviour is not, however, a direct one. They stand for an ideal pattern of family structure to which the actual patterns which exist and have existed in various groups of Japanese society approximate in varying degrees. The closest approximation can, perhaps, be found in the family of the samurai during the Tokugawa period, not unnaturally since it was in this class and at this time that the ideal took shape, and the work which more than any other embodies the norms and values of the Japanese family system—Kaibara Ekken's *Onna Daigaku*, 'The Greater Learning for Women',[71] was a book of moral instruction for samurai women. At the present day, the peasant family approximates more closely to the ideal concept than does the urban family.

When a Japanese talks about 'the Japanese family system', then, he is not necessarily describing what the Japanese do. When he tells a foreigner that 'in Japan marriages are arranged by parents', he might mean 'In Japan all marriages are so arranged' (which is false) or 'In Japan more marriages are arranged by parents than not' (which is dubious as far as Tokyo at the present day is concerned) or 'In Japan such a preponderant majority of marriages are arranged that those which are not are universally considered to be exceptional and generally disapproved of.' (This is probably true for certain segments of Japanese society, but not for Tokyo.)

If he means the last then one can say that the 'family system' which the Japanese is describing when he says that 'marriages are arranged' is a conceptualized set of behaviour patterns which have normative implications; they are standards by which actual conduct is measured and social disapproval is the likely result of deviation from these standards. But such social disapproval can vary in degree. The ways in which it varies are worth considering in more detail, for the Japanese family system is a somewhat odd phenomenon.

The distinction is frequently made between 'real' norms, the breach of which does entail disapproval, and 'ideal' norms conformity to which is highly admired but not really expected from everybody (extreme bravery and complete disregard for personal safety in the face of the enemy, for instance)[72] This one might call the real-ideal dimension of the normative strength attaching to any particular conceptualized set of behaviour patterns; the poles of the continuum (for it is a continuum and not a sharp dichotomy) being characterized by strong disapproval for deviations from the pattern at the 'real' end, and strong admiration for conformity to the patterns of the 'ideal' end.

But this is not the only dimension of normative strength. The behaviour patterns embodied in the concept 'the Japanese family system' are not remote from reality in this sense. They are not patterns of behaviour to which everyone's spirit would willingly conform were the flesh not so weak. There is another dimension of normative strength which one might, to distinguish it from the other, call the 'actual-indifferent' scale. In changing societies what is at one stage unusual and strongly disapproved behaviour often becomes gradually more common, and *pari passu* gradually ceases to arouse disapproval; it becomes a matter of indifference. (Women smoking in England, for instance.) This is what has happened to many of the behaviour patterns included in the 'Japanese family system'; non-conformity, in becoming more common, has gradually begun to excite less and less social disapproval. Nevertheless, it can happen that, particularly when the set of behaviour patterns forms an inte-grated and coherent system (as is the case with the 'Japanese family system') they can remain unchanged as purely cognitive concepts even though their evaluative accretions change and they move gradually along this latter scale of normative strength from actuality to indifference. Thus, for example, one might well hear Japanese say today without any I-don't-know-what-this-younger-generation-is-coming-to shaking of the head 'According to the Japanese family system marriages should be arranged, but of course in many cases nowadays they are not.' Arranged marriages are still a part of 'the Japanese family system' although few people nowadays have any strong moral feelings about their necessity.

The description of the 'Japanese family system' which follows in the next few pages, then, is not a description of how most people be-have today, nor even of how most (only some) people think people *ought* to behave today. It is rather a description of how most people think most people *used to* behave and everyone used to expect people to behave.[73]

The Japanese family (quotations marks will be dropped henceforth) is what Le Play called the *famille souche*, the stem family. That is to say, the domiciliary unit consists of a man, his wife, his unmarried brothers and sisters, his eldest son, his eldest son's wife, his eldest son's children and his unmarried sons and daughters. Sometimes it may also include the wife and children of one or more of his younger sons or younger brothers, but this is regarded as a temporary arrange-ment. As soon as possible, the younger son will have a separate home and establish a 'branch family' which for the first generation will be a single-nuclear conjugal family, but which thereafter will continue as a normal stem family.

Daughters leave the family and are taken into another already existing family as the bride of one of its sons. For a Japanese woman, marriage is conceived of less as an entry into conjugal relations with a particular man than as entry into another family group. Thus, she may be called the 'wife' (*tsuma, kanai, okusan*) of an individual man, but (as long as her mother-in-law is still alive) she is more likely to be referred to as *yome*, a term which defines her position in her husband's family group as a whole, and is best translated 'married woman of the youngest generation'. Thus a man might say 'if the harvest is good this year "we" must get a *yome* for Taroo' and he would be less likely when she has arrived to talk of her as 'my son Taroo's wife' as 'our *yome*' (*uchi no yome*).

Marriage is arranged by the parents, or, to give the proper perspective, by the heads of the two families who are exchanging a member. The financial arrangements, the size of the gift from the groom's family to the bride, the size of the return gift, the contents of the daughter's trousseau, the nature of the feast to be given at the groom's house, are decided through a go-between or go-betweens. The important elements of the ceremony centre around the journey of the bride from her parental to her new home, the ritual exchange of wine-cups between the married pair, their parents and the go-betweens, the feasting of relatives and neighbours, and the display to them of the gifts and the trousseau of the daughter. Marriage gives the husband exclusive sexual rights in his wife, but not *vice versa*. His children by women other than his wife could be adopted into his family.[74]

When she enters her new family, the bride goes through a period of explicit training by her mother-in-law in the 'ways of the family' (*kafuu*). (In substance there may be nothing to distinguish one family from its neighbour; nevertheless, the family tradition, the 'ways of the family', is a word of symbolic significance functionally important in maintaining the solidarity and emphasizing the continuity of the family group.) It is as well that a girl should marry young so that she may the more easily adjust to the ways of her new home and be more susceptible to the instructions of her mother-in-law. Submission to the mother-in-law's commands and obedient absorption of her instructions were the essential duties of the young bride. As in China the situation is such that conflict and ill-feeling between mother and daughter-in-law is considered almost normal. The mother's dominant position and her role as instructor *vis-à-vis* her daughter-in-law (combined with her own subordinate position *vis-à-vis* the males of the family) might be expected in any case to give rise to the sort of attitudes which in the army and in university fraternities are given institutional expression in the 'hazing' of new recruits. Add to this that the bride is a younger woman who appears as a competitor for her son's affection, and the possibilities of conflict may be readily seen. To a lesser extent the same applies also to the relations between the young wife and her husband's sisters, particularly if they are suffering the frustration of a delayed marriage. It is not for nothing that the husband's sister is referred to as the *kojuuto*—'little mother-in-law'. Adjustment may come eventually; if only in the form of an

uneasy truce liable to sporadic outbreaks of hostility until the day
when the headship passes into the son's hands and the management
of the household to his wife, who by then probably has her own
daughter-in-law to train up in the 'ways of the family'. Sometimes,
however, the outcome is divorce. The traditional formula for stating
the reasons for such divorce, and the reason sometimes explicitly
stated in the divorce bills of the Tokugawa period was 'she did not
fit into the "ways of the family" (*kafuu ni awanai*)'. Divorce, like
marriage, was a matter for the family, not just the husband; the
divorce bills of the Tokugawa period were issued by the head of the
family and began 'It is our pleasure to divorce . . .' [75]

Within the family much greater emphasis is placed on the parent-
child relationship than on the husband-wife relationship which is of
central importance to the Western family. This relative evaluation
finds symbolic expression in many forms—in proverbs such as 'the
womb is only borrowed' (*hara wa karimono*) contrasting with
'nothing can break the bond between parent and child' (*oyako no en
wa kitte mo kirarenu*), or in the code of mourning obligations, first
borrowed from China and made the prescribed etiquette of the Court
aristocracy in the seventh century, repromulgated in a modified form
in 1684 for the samurai of the Tokugawa period and finally reaffirmed
by the Meiji government in 1882 as the required practice of all
government servants. According to this a man mourned thirteen
months for his parents, but for only three months for his wife.[76] In
the Civil Code of 1898, the wife's right to maintenance from her
husband takes third place in the order of priorities, after his parents
and his children.[77] The relative importance of the two relationships
was, perhaps, never more unambiguously stated than by the Confucian Nakae Tooju in a seventeenth-century moral treatise for
girls; 'The fundamental reason for a man to take a wife is that she may
serve his parents and bear heirs to continue the succession.' [78]

In terms of required behaviour, this means that in disputes between
his wife—who for a long time remains something of an outsider to the
family group—and other members of his family, the husband should
range himself on the side of the family. This is not simply a moral
'should'; there is a reasonable expectation that his sympathies will
naturally incline that way, since ties of blood, of common ancestry
and shared childhood experience are thought to have stronger
emotional force than those generated by sexual relations. It is not
denied that sexual relations can generate strong emotional ties, but
such ties are not highly valued. The typical 'idyllic' picture of the
marital relationship, as exemplified in the old man and old woman
of Takasago, ritual symbols of the marriage ceremony, and in such
sentimental Kabuki plays as Bon-odori, is a desexualized Darby-and-
Joan one; only when all passion is spent and replaced by an affection

grown from the accumulation of shared experience is the marital relationship a respected and honoured one.[79]

Nevertheless, the development of emotional ties between young husband and wife is allowed to be so far within the bounds of possibility that tension between the mother-in-law (or sister-in-law) and daughter-in-law is also expected to entail some conflict of loyalties on the part of the son-husband, and if, in the last resort, the parents require the divorce of the daughter-in-law, this may well be a considerable sacrifice for the son, though well within the limits of what filial piety may legitimately demand.

Emphasis on the parent-child relationship is one aspect of the importance attached to the continuation of the family. The close connection between the two is apparent in the sentence from Nakae Tooju quoted above; the provision of heirs is as much an element of filial piety, as defined in Confucian writings, as actual service to one's parents. Important symbols serve to strengthen consciousness of this continuity, both as a duty for the future and as a fact of the past. The 'ways of the family' has already been mentioned. There are several others; the physical house itself, inhabited by the ancestors and to be inhabited by descendants (*ie* like the English 'house', means both family and dwelling), the 'family occupation' (*kagyoo*) (the 'Japanese family system' belongs to a state of society in which the family is the unit of production and occupations—agriculture, domestic crafts, commerce or samurai-hood—are handed on from father to son), the 'family property' (*kasan*), and in upper-class families a family constitution' (*kaken*), a written document in which some former outstanding member of the family has, often in the form of a letter to his son, left explicit instructions for posterity—mixtures of moral maxims, detailed rules of conduct, inheritance regulations and so on.[80] The 'family'—the *ka* of all these words—is not simply the actual living members of the family, but an entity which continues through time just as these things continue through time, with changing personnel but an unchanging identity. The 'family' includes the past and the future as well as the present generation.

The most important symbol of this sort, however, is the ancestors (*senzo*). They are commemorated by wooden tablets in the family altar and are the object of the family's ritual activities. Rites are carried out daily at this shrine by individual members of the family, and collectively at special seasonal festivals and on the anniversaries of ancestors' deaths.

The frequent use of words like *kagyoo*, *kasan*, *kafuu* and so on, and the importance attached to the ancestors, not only serves to strengthen a sense of the continuity of the family group. It also serves to emphasize the importance of the group over against that of the individual. Neither occupation, property, house tradition nor ancestors belong to the individual, but to the family as a whole. Another important word in this connection is *kamei* which means 'family name' both in the literal sense—the surname—and also in the sense of the family honour (in merchant families, for the latter sense an alternative word is *kamban*, literally 'shop-sign'). Honour, too, pertains not simply to the individual, but to the family. A man's acts bring praise and blame not only on himself but on his family, his parents and brothers, his ancestors and descendants. In Japan, where the local community has always been characterized by great solidarity and the existence of careful mechanisms for the smooth preservation of law and order, the fulfilment of one's duties to the wider community has always been considered an essential condition for the maintenance of honour. Concern for the family honour, therefore, becomes an important moral force operating on the individual in all his dealings with the outside world. He is always a representative of his family.

Given the emphasis placed on the family as a continuing entity, it is not surprising that continuation of the family becomes a moral duty. It was also a legal duty under the old Civil Code, which forbade any presumptive heir to the headship of a family to leave the family and enter another for purposes of marriage or adoption, a provision which had the incidental effect of making it impossible for two only children to marry.[81]

Other special mechanisms have been developed to ensure the continuity of already established families. A man who lacks heirs may adopt one. If he has a daughter but no sons, he will adopt a husband for his daughter. This is not considered a desirable fate for a young man—it is he, not the bride, who is then put into the invidious position of having to adapt to new 'family ways'—but younger sons could do worse, and their families are relieved of the burden of setting up a branch family. Strict patterning on the model of biological parenthood is not necessary. A man's adopted son may be only a few years younger than himself (it may be his younger brother—the practice of *jun-yooshi*), and should he be so imprudent as to die without providing a successor, his widow may still adopt one; so may a surviving daughter even if she fails to get a husband. If the family should die out completely it may still be revived at a later date. A friend of the family who has a younger son might make him take over the family name and the ancestral tablets of the extinct family. In a society where there is a fairly even balance of births and deaths and the rate of natural increase is at a minimum, these mechanisms absorb most of the younger sons, and the number of branch families which have to be created is relatively small.

Succession falls to the eldest male direct descendant, but widows may become househeads during the minority of their children, and daughters may also inherit the headship of the household; though, if they subsequently marry their husbands would normally replace them as head. As the phrasing of the last sentence indicates, 'succession' is considered less a matter of succession to property as of succession to the family headship. Property is thought of as belonging to the family. In so far as there is any division of property, this is not occasioned by the death of the household. When a daughter marries, she is given a trousseau sometimes of dowry proportions, or when a younger son is established in a branch family he may be given land or a start in business or a house. This may happen either before their father's death or after it, when their eldest brother has become the new head of the family. (Under the 1898 Civil Code, however, as a concession to the exigencies of capitalism, property was vested in the household as an individual, and he was able to dispose of half of it by testament, but rarely did. The right of other family members to hold property was also recognized, but exercised only in the upper classes.[82])

Succession to the headship of a family does not occur only on the death of a former head. A man in late middle or old age, whose son is sufficiently mature to handle adequately all the affairs of the family, may retire and hand on the headship to his son. At the same time his wife 'hands over the spoon' (*shakushi-watashi*) to her daughter-in-law. The old couple may move out to a separate neighbouring house to end their days. They will still continue to give their advice to the new household, but it is the son not the father, who will represent the family in local affairs and whose name (under the pre-1948 registration system) appears as household on the family register at the local government office.

The power of the household over other members of the family is great. His decisions are final in such matters as marriage and the choice of occupation. Under the 1898 Civil Code he was explicitly given the power to determine the place of residence of members of his family.[83] His authority is backed by the old samurai institution of *kandoo* or expulsion from the family, which also finds its place in the 1898 Civil Code. Expulsion is a formal act which, in modern times, took the form of the removal of the offender's name from the family register. One specified cause for such disciplinary action in the old Code is marriage without the household's approval[84] (if the household was also a parent he could force the dissolution of the marriage until a son was 30 or a daughter 25)[85] but it could be a device resorted to in all cases of defiance of the household's authority and more especially when the action of any member of the family threatened the family's good name. The family preserved its honour by cutting off the offending member.

The authority of the household over members of the family derives not from the biological relationship between them, but simply from their respective positions within the family. Thus the househead's authority over the children of subordinate members of the family to some extent circumscribes the authority of parents over their own children. The 1898 Civil Code drew a distinction between the parental authority and the househead's authority and it was the reformist groups' attempts to expand the former and contract the latter, and the traditionalists' attempts to reverse the process which provided a consistent theme in all the years of controversy.

In most cases, the househead's authority and the parent's authority coincide in the same individual, but this is not always so. A father who dies fairly young would leave a young eldest son as househead, having the power of direction over his younger brothers and sisters formerly exercised by his father. It is significant, for instance, that the word for 'parents', as in Parent-Teachers' Association, is *fukei*, literally 'father and/or elder brother', rather than 'father and mother'. It is perhaps a necessary corollary of the fact that eldest sons may have to assume formal authority over younger brothers and sisters that considerable stress is laid on relative age and sex distinctions within the family. Respectful behaviour is expected from younger towards elder brothers and from sisters to brothers. Older siblings are addressed as Elder Brother or Elder Sister, younger ones by their given names, generally without any polite suffix in the case of elder brother to younger sister, with polite suffix in the case of elder sister to younger brother. At meals and at the bath, men take precedence over women and elder over younger. Without this stress on relative age and on male superiority (which also prepares the girl for her position of subordination to her husband) the assumption of the headship by an elder brother could hardly be expected to proceed smoothly, given the powers which are vested in that position.

The other side of the medal of the househead's authority, however, is his duty to look after those under his jurisdiction. Widowed sisters, unemployed younger brothers would always have the right to fall back on his help in time of need. The property he inherits carries responsibilities with it.

The powers of the househead are to a certain extent circumscribed, moreover, by his awareness that he is only a trustee of the family affairs, responsible to the ancestors or to the family continuing through time, the fortunes of which are only temporarily entrusted to his care. In certain matters, and especially in richer families, there are institutionalized methods of limiting the personal responsibility of the househead; important decisions are taken by a family council formed *ad hoc* by elder members of blood-related and to a lesser extent of marriage-related families.[86] In any case, the moral restraint is there, and on his observance of that moral restraint depends the consent of the governed. The pressure of relatives can force the retirement of an unsuitable family head.[87] Given the basic assumption discussed above—that the family is an entity of greater importance than the individuals who temporarily compose it—the assurance that the object of the househead's decisions is to promote the good of the family and that they are not the result of private personal whims is a necessary, and usually a sufficient, condition for ensuring the compliance of the other members of the family.

The 'family' in the sense we have been considering—as a continuing entity like a church or a school—is called the *ie*. 'House' would perhaps be a better translation. *Ie* was also, from the early Meiji period until 1947, a legally recognized unit of living individuals quite simply defined in law in terms of the family registers kept at the local government office. All children born to members of the *ie* automatically entered it. Others could enter by marriage or adoption. Family members left the *ie* by expulsion, by marriage, by adoption or by establishing a branch family. The *ie* as thus defined, however, bore no relation to the domiciliary unit. Sons and daughters working away in the towns would remain on the register of their parental families. Even after younger sons have been socially recognized as the heads of new branch families, their actual removal from the register may not take place for some years, or even for two or three generations.

The *ie* as revealed in the local government registers, then—often a large joint family of considerable proportions—was little more than a legal fiction. Such kinship groups may, however, have a certain cohesion. The head of a branch family may still consult with the head of the main family in whose *ie* he legally remains whenever some member of his family is about to choose a marriage partner or a career, or before engaging in any transaction which might materially alter the fortunes of the family. There are ritual links too—although after the first generation each branch house has its own ancestors, the main family has ancestors which are common to all the branch families as well. Other bonds are provided by mutual obligations to give help in emergencies, and by continuing relations of economic interdependence.

These relations of economic interdependence are the result of inheritance of occupation and of the way in which branch families are created. Occupations, as we have seen, attach not to individuals but to families, for the 'family system' belongs to a period when wage labour is at a minimum and the typical occupations are farming, commerce, and domestic craft production. Even in the samurai class in the Tokugawa period, the income from the feudal lord's granaries (the *roku*) was an endowment of the family rather than of individuals and it did not necessarily vary in amount whether, at any particular time, there was one male from' the family in the lord's service or three. Likewise, the Japanese family system belongs to a time when the economy, if expanding at all, was expanding laterally; that is to say, any growth there was in the population took the form of an approximately proportionate increase in the numbers in the existing occupational groups, not in the creation of new occupational groups or the disproportionate expansion of some accompanied by the contraction of others. Thus, a branch family typically followed the occupation of the main family. A farming family gave the branch family

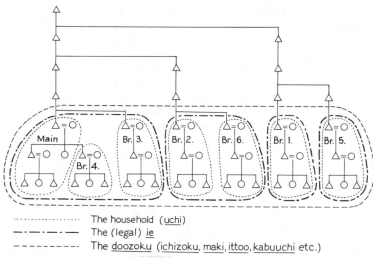

.... The household (<u>uchi</u>)
— · — · — · — The (legal) <u>ie</u>
— — — — — — — The <u>doozoku</u> (<u>ichizoku</u>, <u>maki</u>, <u>ittoo</u>, <u>kabuuchi</u> etc.)

DIAGRAM 3—Kinship Groupings

a portion of the family land, a merchant family gave the branch family a section of the main family's trade or at least offered all its wholesale buying facilities to help the branch family establish itself in a new area. Similarly, artisan families taught the craft, secured entrance for its branch family into the guild and helped in marketing its products.

Sometimes the establishment of branch families was a matter not of necessity—a means of disposing of younger sons—but of choice. A thriving family which had no younger sons expanded its business not by establishing branches on a purely commercial basis and hiring more wage employees, but by 'adopting' a promising employee and establishing him as a branch family.[88] (This did not, in fact, constitute a very big change in status, for employees in such families—

generally taken as apprentices at an early age—were always treated as members, though of inferior rank, of the family. When established in branch families, however, they would normally take over the surname of the main family.)

It was, however, an underlying principle of all this division that the main family should not be weakened and so, being always in a thriving condition, should have the resources to meet emergencies befalling any family in the group. Thus grants of land to farming branch families were often inadequate for subsistence; they were forced to work the main family's land to supplement their income, and to rely on the main family's granary in times of bad harvests. Branch families of merchant and artisan families likewise often remained dependent on the marketing or raw-material purchasing facilities of the main family. In certain crafts the main family developed the functions of putting-out capitalists, with the branch families as their dependent domestic workers.

These relations of economic dependence are backed by an explicit ideology of the superiority of the main family and the duty of the branch family to respond to the main family's leadership. They tend to be self-perpetuating and while they continue they help to maintain the cohesion of these groups of main and branch families through many generations, long after the relations between the individuals of the branch and the main families have become remote cousinships which cease to be taken account of. It is not the kinship relations between individuals which are important, but the main-branch relation between families.[89]

Large lineages of this sort, consisting of one main and a cluster of branch families (see example in Diagram 3— the *doozoku*) are common in Japanese villages, and, particularly in northern Japan, this form of grouping has great importance in the social structure of the village as a whole. Over the course of the generations they may grow to a considerable size, though powerful branch families with their own sub-branch families may break away when they cease to be economically dependent on the main family, and there seems to be a maximum limit to the size to which they can grow; beyond twenty-five or thirty there is a tendency to fission.[90] The groups are hierarchical in structure, the hierarchy being rooted in the main family's economic superiority, expressed in formal deferential behaviour required from members of branch to members of main families, and legitimized by the kinship relations existing (or thought to exist—genealogical traditions can change to suit changing economic realities) between the families. The numbering of the branch families in Diagram 3 indicates a possible ordering of the status hierarchy (as observed in the seating order at family gatherings) based on the twin criteria of antiquity of foundation and closeness to the main family—an order of precedence which can, however, on occasion be over-ridden by differences of wealth, age, education, or personality. (Generation differences are not taken into account, in contrast with the clans of southern China where they are all-important. In China the ceremonial head of the clan is the eldest male of the eldest generation, so that the headship does not necessarily rest permanently in the same constituent family. In consequence there is not the same permanent hierarchical ordering of families within these Chinese *fang* as there is in the Japanese *doozoku*.)

The apotheosis of this type of extended kinship group is to be found in the famous *zaibatsu* families, Mitsui, Mitsubishi, etc. In these, however, the solidarity of the lineage group as a whole has developed to such a degree, and central control of the group's interests, not by the head of the main family, but by a family council in which the main family's head may only nominally be given precedence is so strong, that disintegration by the breaking off of segments of branch and sub-branch families becomes unlikely.

CLASS DIFFERENCES

The inclusion of concrete descriptive material in the above account of the 'Japanese family system' should not be allowed to obscure the fact that it is only an attempt to present the ideal picture which most Japanese have of how the traditional Japanese family was organized.

How far does this ideal picture conform to the past reality? In the case of China, it now seems to be generally recognized that the so-called 'Chinese family' with its indefinitely expanding joint household was never the prevalent pattern. Only the gentry families had the economic resources to conform, but for the peasants it remained an 'ideal'—ways of behaviour which were valued because of their association with the prestige-carrying gentry class and which remained for the peasants an ideal in a normative, or at least in an aspirational sense, since there was always the theoretical possibility that they could rise into the gentry class.

The main institutions of the Japanese family system, as it has been outlined above, did not, however, require specially large economic resources. The forms of property-holding and property-division, the arrangements for succession and marriage and the formation of branch families, could be and in fact were, followed by all classes of Tokugawa society except the rootless indigent fringe.[91]

There were considerable differences in family structure between the various classes of Tokugawa society, but most of the basic elements described above were shared in common. The differences were in matters of lesser detail and some of them are listed below.[92]

The terms which will be used—the samurai family, the merchant family and the peasant family—are again generalizations of a fairly high degree of abstraction; there was, for instance, considerable class differentiation within each group, and even greater regional variation which often cut across class lines.[93]

1. *Expressive Behaviour*

Relations between family members were more formalized in the samurai than in the peasant or merchant family. In language, posture and gesture more deference was shown by children to parents, by wives to husbands and by younger to elder siblings. The expression of anger and the infliction of punishment by parents was more controlled and deliberate. The overt expression of affection between husband and wife was forbidden in all classes, but much more rigorously in the samurai family. Overt expression of affection for children was permitted, however, though again to a smaller extent among the samurai than among the peasants or merchants. The samurai father, who preserved his aloofness, thereby strengthened his authority. (And, of course, the more property a family has the greater is the occasion for the exercise of authority.)

2. *Pre-marital Relations between the Sexes*

Free unchaperoned relationships between unmarried men and women were not encouraged in any class and were particularly disapproved among the samurai, for whom the Confucian tag that 'from the age of seven boys and girls do not sit together' was at least accepted as an ideal. Secret love-affairs occurred, most typically, in the fiction of the Tokugawa period, between young apprentice, household retainer, living-in employee or student and the master's daughter. These were disapproved of as inconvenient complications of the difficult business of arranging marriages, and additionally in samurai families were considered a positive disgrace, particularly when—as was usual in the fiction at least—there was a wide discrepancy between the social status of the parties concerned. Virginity as such was not particularly highly regarded—there was no institutionalized demonstration of proofs of virginity on marriage, for instance—but unchastity showed a lack of discipline, an obedience to impulse rather than duty incompatible with the self-abnegating role imposed on women in samurai society. For males of the samurai class and also for the merchant and artisan classes, a system of open and regulated prostitution provided opportunities for sexual experience between puberty and marriage. Among the peasants, pre-marital sexual intercourse was permitted for both sexes—boys visited girls in their houses at night—but there were often institutionalized mechanisms to ensure a continuous circulation of partners and to prevent emotional attachments from developing between individuals.[94] The children of such unions were generally adopted into other families.

3. *Freedom of Choice of Marriage Partner*

That marriage was arranged by parents was true of all classes of society, but there were variations in the extent to which either the man or the woman concerned had the right to refuse an unattractive mate. Among the samurai, the wedding ceremony was often the occasion of the first meeting of the bride and groom, since the bride often came from a distant part of the country. Moreover, for the man, for whom attractive female company and permitted sexual experience was always available outside marriage, it was not unreasonable to accept without demur the marriage partner whom one's parents judged to have the right domestic and eugenic qualities and who came from a family of such a status that alliance with it was a 'good match'. As far as the girl was concerned, nothing in the whole of her upbringing had occurred to suggest that personal preferences had anything to do with matters of duty such as marriage. In the merchant classes of the towns, however, an opportunity for the prospective partners to survey each other and to express their personal wishes became an institutionalized part of the marriage process. The *miai*, as this was called, was a deliberately contrived, but by an agreed fiction accidental, meeting arranged by go-betweens for the prospective partners and their families. After the meeting either party could express displeasure with the prospective mate and the negotiations could then be dropped without either side necessarily feeling offended. Still, however, these meetings were as much opportunities for the parents to survey the suggested bride or groom as for these to survey each other. This system gradually became more general in urban areas, and the modern word for an arranged marriage is a *miai*-marriage (as opposed to a 'love-marriage'). Even in the Tokugawa period, however, among the poorer urban classes in which the family was already in a process of disintegration, marriage was often a tenuous and only half-formalized contract between individuals, concluded without benefit of go-between's negotiation, parental approval or even the wine-drinking ceremony in the presence of relatives which legitimized the match. 'Did you and your old woman get fixed up properly with a go-between, or did you just "get stuck" together'? is a not uncommon question in the humorous monologues of the old music halls which depict this sort of society.

4. *Concubinage*

For the upper-class male of the Tokugawa period the aridity of an arranged marriage might be compensated for in concubinage.

Although sometimes justified as a means of securing the succession,[95] concubines were a form of conspicuous consumption indulgence in which was expected to be consonant with social status, at least among the samurai. The so-called legacy of Ieyasu specifies the number of concubines appropriate to each rank.[96] Among the merchants, economic resources was the ruling factor. For the peasants (except a small number of richer village-headmen and landlords) and the poorer urban classes, monogamy was, perforce, the rule.

5. *Divorce*

Among the peasants, ease of divorce may also have provided some compensation for the rigors of arranged marriages, although against those cases where divorce resulted from a failure of relations between the married pair and was equally desired by both parties, must be set those in which divorce was a result of the parents' dissatisfaction with the son's wife and not necessarily desired by the son himself.[97] Divorce was, in any case, frequent among the peasants. It was an accepted part of the function of the marriage go-between to arrange a divorce if the marriage—his handiwork—came to grief. It is impossible to know how frequent divorce was among the samurai where the expression of personal choice in marriage was most completely restricted, but *a priori* one would expect it to be somewhat less frequent than in peasant communities. On the one hand there was a greater explicit stress in the samurai morality on the subordination of individual desires to the interests of the family; on the other, the greater formality in social relations between families in samurai society and the greater importance attached to family honour would have made the consequences of the slight implicit in 'sending back' a bride all the more serious.

6. *Power of Women in the Family*

The subordination of the young bride seems to have been common to all types of family structure. There were, however, considerable variations in the extent to which, having eventually had the 'spoon handed over' to her, on the death or retirement of her mother-in-law, she had direction of the economic affairs of the household and how far she shared control over the behaviour of other members of the family, in the first place with her husband while he was alive, and in the second place with her son when (as frequently happened, since a five to ten year age gap was common) her husband predeceased her and her eldest son became the new family head. The Confucian doctrine which summarizes the whole duty of woman in terms of the 'three obediences'—to her father when young, to her husband when married, and to her son when widowed—was still reiterated by the moralists of the Tokugawa period, but the reality was never so simple. Variation in this matter seems, however, to have been so wide and to such a great extent dependent on the unique combination of personalities involved, that the structural variations—variations in generally expected role behaviour—as between the various classes of Tokugawa society are difficult to epitomize. The following broad generalizations seem legitimate, however. In samurai families the househead's wife had fairly complete control over the consumption of the family, except that the demands of her husband would have an ineluctable priority. She would have control over the domestic servants and as soon as her eldest son married his wife would be under her direct command. In these matters her authority would not be challenged by her husband—they belonged to the woman's sphere in which his dignity would not permit him to involve himself. In other matters (such as questions of marriage, the disposal of capital, etc.) she would not express open disagreement with her husband, but might exert considerable influence on his decisions in private (women's wiles play their part in Japanese culture too). When she became a widow her authority was greatly enhanced, her son would be expected to consult her before taking any important family decisions, and not to go contrary to strongly expressed wishes. The history of the Tokugawa period contains some famous widowed mothers, notably that of the fifth Shogun, Tsunayoshi.

In those wealthier merchant families which consciously modelled themselves on the samurai class, a similar pattern prevailed. The original merchant family tradition, however, as it was still preserved in many quite wealthy families, allowed the wife much more say in the day-to-day running of the family business, and in particular allowed her to emerge as a widow with far greater power than in the samurai classes. Among the less wealthy urban classes, the small shopkeepers and the artisans, the general absence of formalized respect patterns as compared with the samurai class was accompanied by a much less severe subordination of women in general. If the humorous literature of the nineteenth century is to be believed, overt disagreement with one's husband, remonstrance and scolding, even husband-baiting, was by no means unexpected behaviour.

In peasant families, the wife probably had less freedom and less power than in any other class of society.

There were, however, great regional variations within each class. Gumma prefecture, for instance, is traditionally known as a place where the woman rules the roost (*kaka-denka*) in the peasant family. On the other hand, emphasis on sex distinctions and on female inferiority was carried so far among the samurai of the most martial province of Satsuma that in strict families it was forbidden to hang feminine washing on the same drying pole as men's.

INDUSTRIALIZATION

Adding together the generalized ideal principles of the 'Japanese family system' with which we started this chapter, and the more concrete generalizations concerning certain aspects of the actual structure of the family in various classes at the end of the Tokugawa period, we get an outline picture of the family in pre-industrial Japanese society. It will be immediately obvious that industrialization and urbanization, modernization and the impact of foreign ideas have altered family structure to a considerable degree. In the next chapter we shall, in considering the family in Shitayama-cho, illustrate the end-product of these changes in a concrete form. Before doing so, however, it may be useful first to list the ways in which, granted certain assumptions concerning the functional interplay of various features of the Japanese family, one would expect industrialization and the changes wrought by political action since the Meiji period to affect the structure of the family in urban areas.

1. *Demographic Changes and the Proportion of Branch Families*

When mortality is such that there is an approximate balance between births and deaths, given the possibility of adopting younger sons into other families, the proportion of new branch families in the population at any given time will be relatively small. When the demographic picture changes and falling mortality leads to a big increase in population, the proportion of new branch families in the population will inevitably increase. This means that there will be an increase in the proportion of the population which spends its life not entirely within the atmosphere of the three-generation stem family but—for twenty years of maturity—in a family of very different structure.

The new branch family has many points of difference from the three-generation stem family. It is smaller, the young household is not under the authority of an elder male, the wife is not trained in the ways of the family by a strict mother-in-law. The possibility of a division of loyalties on the part of the husband as between wife and mother is lessened. Children are not brought up in the same house with (often indulgent) grandparents. For the first generation there is no direct continuity and no established and directly inherited tradition. In such a family many of the symbols which uphold the traditional family morality and strengthen family solidarity—the ancestors, the family property, the physical house, etc.—lose their importance.

When branch families form only a very small minority of the total families, the deviant expectations of a small minority of individuals do not affect the common norms[98] of the society. Thus one would expect the relationship between husband and wife to be different in the single-nuclear family from what it is in the three-generation family. But when there are few branch families the common idea of how a wife should behave is likely to be wholly determined by the structure of the three-generation family.

The towns which have sprung up over the last two or three generations have been largely peopled by the younger sons of farmers.[99] Thus, not only has the proportion of branch families increased in the society at large; in the towns, in which these new branch families tend to be concentrated, they cease to be an insignificant minority and in periods of rapid urban growth perhaps form a majority of the total number of families. As a consequence, the common norms of family behaviour are likely to change in urban areas into something which conforms to the structure of the new branch family.

2. *Weakening of the Doozoku Group*

Traditionally, as we have seen, a certain element of continuity as between the branch family and its parent stem family is maintained within the framework of the extended *doozoku* group. An important element in maintaining these links is the economic dependence of the branch on the main family. Another is physical proximity. The branch family of a peasant main family traditionally builds its house in the same village and continues as a peasant family probably relying on the stem family for the loan of tools, for rented land, for grain storage and so on. During the process of industrialization, however, younger sons commonly move to the towns in order to establish branch families. They are geographically separated from the stem family, and since they follow different occupations are economically more independent. Only the affectual and ritual links remain to provide the solidarity of the wider *doozoku* group. These links may still be strong for the first generation when the head of the stem family is the father or elder brother of the head of the branch family, but are weaker in the next and tenuous in the extreme by the third generation. As a result the importance of these wider kinship groupings may be expected to disappear.

It should be noted, however, that this presupposes that the branch family established in the town is able to be self-sufficient in its new occupation. If the younger son becomes unemployed and cannot survive in the town, dependence on the stem family is his only resource in the absence of unemployment insurance. He returns with his wife and children to the countryside. He may not be welcomed, but at least the peasant family has some source of income and at the cost of a general lowering of living standards he can be accommodated. His right to call on the main family's help would not be in dispute. This is an important characteristic of the Japanese urban labour force and is partly responsible for the slow growth of working-class consciousness and militant trade-union organization.[100] Here again, by the second generation, the urban worker is less willing, and he has less claim, to call on the support of the main family, by then headed by his uncle or his cousin.

These considerations apply to the wider kinship grouping centring on a peasant stem family. The same applies, if with less force, to kinship groupings centred on urban stem families. With technological development, expansion of the economy ceases to take the form of a more or less proportionate expansion of each occupational group. New occupational groups are created, some groups expand rapidly, others decline. With the development of schools and universities, educational qualifications become the route of entry into certain occupations, not skills acquired in the family. Thus it ceases to be the normal and safest pattern for a younger son to follow the occupation of the stem family—with consequent weakening of the wider kinship group.

3. Inheritance of Occupation

The same changes in occupational structure affect the stem family itself as well as its relationship with its branch families. When the family was still the unit of production the 'family occupation' theoretically remained unchanged through the generations. This provided a strong bond between father and eldest son; it served as much as anything else to foster the sense of the *ie* as an entity continuing through the generations, and it provided a strong reason why the son should accept the authority of his father, since revolt left him little prospects of a livelihood outside the family occupation. In the families of wage and salary workers, however, occupation is divorced from the family; it becomes the occupation of an individual and 'preserving the business (land, craft) of the ancestors' ceases to be a reason why the eldest son should follow in his father's footsteps. Moreover, the number and variety of occupational groups increases; old concepts of fixed statuses and barriers between estates tend to be replaced by a picture of society as more open, composed of a large number of occupational groups lying somewhere on a continuous graded scale of monetary reward and social prestige; individuals succeed in moving up the scale by the exercise of skill or initiative or by good fortune, and the educational system operates to a certain extent to make it possible for children to enter the occupational hierarchy at a higher level than their parents. The ideal of following in father's footsteps is replaced by the ideal of doing better than father.

4. Changes in Source of Income

Another aspect of the change from family production to wage

employment is that the family income ceases to be the product of the co-operative effort of the family as a whole and derives from payments made to individual family members outside the family. This makes possible the growth of a sense of individual ownership as opposed to family ownership. The husband may reserve a portion of his wages for his own use; unmarried children may do likewise. The increased range of individual choice which this makes possible increases their sense of personal independence (quite apart from the effect of making it less disastrous in the extreme case to reject parental authority, as was noted in the last paragraph).

Moreover, the efficient operation of a capitalist economy requires the establishment of individual property rights. Family ownership becomes unwieldy and complicates the attribution of rights and liabilities in contractual relations. It has been mentioned that the Meiji Civil Code recognized individual property rights.

These are only some of the basic economic aspects of a general process of individuation which can be seen at work in other fields. It is the individual who receives education in State schools, the individual on whom lies the duty of military service (not the family as among the Tokugawa samurai), the individual who is responsible for his own crimes (not, as for certain purposes under the Tokugawa regime, his family) the individual who is elected to public office above the local level (though it is still, to some extent, *qua* representative of a family that a man is appointed to office at the informal village level), and the individual who is converted to Christianity (if it is still the family which performs the ancestor rites). All these implications of a modern industrial state tend to weaken the all-inclusiveness and the solidarity of the family.

5. *Increase in Time spent outside the Family*

There is a great increase in the participation of individuals in non-kinship groupings. Time spent in school, time spent in factories, time spent performing military service would all formerly have been spent within the family. In so far as continuity of personal interaction is an important element in maintaining the strength of affectual relationships between family members this would tend to have the effect of weakening family bonds.

Moreover, in these groups outside the family new patterns of relationship tend to prevail. Objective criteria of skill are likely to replace kinship criteria in determining the allocation of power and responsibility and reward. We have already noted that Japanese society has tended to a high degree to order the structure of non-kinship groupings on family lines, using pseudo-kinship terms for positions in the group and allocating power responsibility and reward on the basis of relative age and seniority. This is possible when such groups are of only minor economic importance and the pseudo-kinship structuring is not a barrier to the effective functioning of the association for the end for which it was created. These conditions do not hold, however, in a modern factory, bureaucracy, army or university. The efficient functioning of these organizations is of greater importance to the running of the society, and it becomes necessary to 'rationalize', to emphasize criteria of ability at the expense of criteria of age and seniority, and to allocate strictly defined authority to positions in a coherent chain of command, rather than to allow it to emerge from the personal semi-affectual relationships between specific individuals.

In other words, the effect of industrialization and accompanying changes in the political, legal, military and educational institutions is to make the non-kinship associations of the society less community-like and more association-like, less personal and more instrumental.

This can be expected to have its effects on the personality of the individual. He develops a capacity for engaging in impersonal relationships, for dealing with others solely by virtue of specific roles which they fulfill rather than as whole persons, a capacity which is not possible for an individual whose responses in inter-personal relations are developed within and maintained solely within the family.

The chief effects of this are likely to be found in the structure of intermediate associations, associations, that is, such as the local community or recreational groups, which are intermediate between the family on the one hand, and those which by their very nature need to be as impersonal and rationalized as possible.[101] But it is also likely that such a change in the modal personality will have repercussions on the structure of relations within the family. It may be that there will be an increasing tendency to view family relations from an instrumental point of view, to consider them as means to individual ends of economic security or sexual satisfaction. On a different theory of psychological need, it might be argued, on the contrary, that the increase in the portion of the individual's interpersonal relations which are depersonalized would cause him to emphasize the 'personalness', the degree of affectuality, in those personal relations which remain to him. The increasing emphasis on the value of romantic love between husband and wife in urban Japan might be ascribed in part to this cause.

6. *Women in Industry and in the Home*

The development of industry affects the position of women in the family in various ways. In the first place, the growth of the textile industries meant that many peasant girls, instead of moving, at an early age, directly from their parental family to the family of their husband, or at the most spending a few intermediate years in domestic service, married later, and entered marriage with four or five years' experience of factory dormitory life behind them. As industralization proceeds, the tertiary industries provide greater scope for female employment before marriage, especially in the towns. Office jobs requiring higher educational standards offer socially acceptable opportunities for middle-class girls. As the opportunities for employment grow and the expected standard of living rises, marriage is postponed as the length of the period of employment increases.

This opportunity for broader experience outside the family before marriage reduces the superiority of the husband's 'knowledge of the world' after marriage. The wife has more confidence in her ability to take decisions for herself. The more so if, as in some cases, she continues to work after marriage and so contributes *qua* individual and in her own right to the family income.

On the other hand, if wives do not take paid employment outside the home, the removal of productive activities from the family in the working classes tends to increase the emphasis on the differentiation of male and female roles. The wife's activities are confined to domestic matters. The education of children may become more exclusively her sphere—the father, being out of the home most of the time has little opportunity to exercise influence—but there may be a corresponding loss of authority in economic matters.

This process means, in fact, that an increasing number of women are placed in the same relation to the family's economic life as the wives of the samurai and some of the more wealthy merchants of the Tokugawa period. These were, quite naturally, the classes in which the 'essential femininity' of women was most emphasized and given expression not only in their exclusion from male activities, but more positively in the cultivation of such arts as flower arrangement, the playing of musical instruments, the performance of the tea ceremony. They became, in Veblen's terms, conspicuous performers of vicarious leisure for their husbands. With the increasing divorce of women from family production and the rising standard of living, the acquisition of these 'parts' becomes the object of ever-widening strata of society. The middle-class Girls' High School of pre-war days was almost exclusively devoted to such education.

Whereas, however, the same sort of economic changes and the same increasing emphasis on the different activities of men and women brought in the England of the seventeenth and eighteenth centuries a general depression in the position of women in the wider society (loss of legal rights, loss of monopoly of professions such as midwifery and so on), in Japan these economic changes coincided with the progress of female emancipation in the West. Japan could not remain uninfluenced by this. Indeed, equal compulsory education for both sexes was introduced in principle in 1872, at a time when there were as yet hardly a hundred factories in Japan. Although higher education for women tended to concentrate on the acquisition of polite accomplishments, still there was a constant pressure for the entry of women into the professions which had been opened to them in the West. It achieved some considerable successes; more intellectual and vocational higher educational institutions for women were founded, and medicine, school-teaching and nursing were fairly early opened to them.

The effects of industrialization on the status of women are thus extremely complicated. Different classes are affected differently, and for the middle classes employment before marriage and greater leisure afterwards may have effects which cancel each other out. Moreover, this is an instance where economic changes and foreign influences can be seen pulling in opposite directions with the weight of Japanese cultural traditions dragging in yet a third direction. None of these factors can be ignored in any discussion of the changing position of women in Japan.

LEGAL CHANGES

These, then, are some of the things one would expect industrialization to have done to the Japanese family. It must be remembered, however, that industrialization has not advanced so far in Japan as in most European countries. Quite apart from the fact that 45% of the population still maintain themselves primarily by agriculture, manufacturing is still carried on to a large (though decreasing) extent in small workshops which are little more than slight extensions (by the addition of apprentice-type living-in labour) of domestic production. In 1950 only 48% of male and 27% of female workers in Japan were in wage employment; the rest were either self-employed or unpaid family workers. Even in the manufacturing industries the proportions were only 79% and 76% respectively.[102]

The large urban centres such as Tokyo and Osaka, however, present a different picture. They are the children of industrialization. Wage-workers in Tokyo comprised 74% of all male and 66% of all female workers in 1950.[103] It is in the towns such as these that the factors enumerated above have been working with full effect to make the pattern of family relations something very different from that of the old type of peasant family from which the ancestors of most of these workers came, or even from that of the urban family of the Tokugawa period.

During the major part of this process of change, the legal institutions remained constant. The Civil Code of 1898 continued to embody many of the ideals of the old family system and in the limiting case to provide coercive sanctions for their maintenance. These ideals, however, did not go unassailed. Already at the time of the drafting of the Civil Code there was a considerable body of opinion to urge the liberalization of the family laws; to demand greater freedom of the individual from family control and an enhancement of the position of women *vis-à-vis* that of men. This body of opinion grew among lawyers and publicists, but it was, curiously enough, the reaction of the traditionalists who thought that the Civil Code of 1898 gave too much freedom to the individual and unduly weakened the bonds of the family which provided the impetus to reform.

In 1917, at a time when the industrial boom was leading to rapid urban growth and the attendant problems were exacerbated by the spread of socialist ideas and labour unrest, a Committee was established to 'enquire into educational matters'. Social unrest, according to the Committee, was due to the gradual abandonment of the 'noble moral customs (*jumpuu-bizoku*) traditional to our country'. These noble moral customs were enumerated as follows: 'to observe propriety and decorum and so maintan due order in the relation of superior and inferior; to value loyalty, filial piety and constancy; to be upright and frugal, forthright and fearless in personal conduct; in relations between rich and poor to use benevolence and mutual trust, mutual understanding and mutual concession'. These were the virtues embedded in and preserved by the family system, and the break-up of the family was the cause of their abandonment. In Japan of 1917, 'the ways of honesty and trust are losing ground, and vanity and luxury are taking their place. The rich fall into extravagance, the poor lack honesty, and the harmony of the classes of society is endangered.' This process of disintegration of the family was hastened by the Civil Code which should be revised to give more power of control to the househead over family members, and, possibly, by instituting a system of family ownership of property to enhance the functioning of the family as a provider of economic security for its members.[104]

After the Rice Riots had shown the extent to which the 'harmony of the classes of society' was endangered, an Emergency Legal Commission of Enquiry was established, in 1919, charged with recommending revisions of the Civil Code which would make it more in harmony with the 'noble moral customs traditional to our country'. Despite its terms of reference, however, the Commission's recommendations, published in 1925 and 1927, represented a victory for the 'modernizers'. The powers of the househead were to be restricted, the inequalities of property division were to be lessened, parental control over marriage reduced and the independence of women to be somewhat enhanced. Except in minor matters, however, these recommendations were never put into effect, and the likelihood of their implementation decreased as the army gradually gained power in the thirties. The voices of the reformers were silenced as the emphasis on the noble moral customs traditional to a martial Japan increased.[105]

This epoch came to an end in 1945, and the reformers emerged from retirement or a protective shell of conformity to find themselves supported, or rather pushed, by an Occupation bent on reforms far more sweeping than any they had themselves contemplated. The Constitution of 1947 contained as one of its clauses the promise that the parts of the Civil Code relating to marriage and the family would be drastically altered 'from the standpoint of individual dignity and the essential equality of the sexes' (Article 24).

The amendment of the Civil Code which followed was radical. Legal recognition of the 'house' ceased; so, automatically, did the position of househead and all the powers over family members which it entailed. Registration is still by household unit, but the family which is thus given legal recognition is the small nuclear family of man, wife and unmarried children. Each marriage now constitutes a new family, which has a new page in the local register. With the exception of a provision that the records, utensils and sacred objects connected with the worship of the ancestors shall pass intact to 'whoever shall perform the rites according to custom' and a provision allowing a husband to take his wife's surname on marriage (aimed not at establishing the 'essential equality of the sexes', but at permitting the ensuring of the succession by 'son-in-law adoption') all traces of the continuing family and primogeniture succession have disappeared. Property inheritance is now based on equal division between children of both sexes with a reserved portion for a surviving spouse. The 'essential equality of the sexes' is further established by the removal of the former powers of the husband to restrict his wife's exercise of property rights, by the provision that infidelity by the husband, not only by the wife, can be a ground for judicial divorce, and, as a necessary consequence, the abolition of the category of *shoshi*—illegitmate children of the husband which the old Code required the wife to recognize as her own. Husbands and wives now 'co-operate together' and determine their place of residence by mutual consent, and in their exercise of parental rights are on a footing of equality. Parental rights are much circumscribed in the interests of 'individual dignity'; parental consent is no longer required for marriage over the age of twenty, and below that age the consent of one parent will suffice.[106]

It is normal for changes in the law to lag behind changes in public opinion and to represent the moral standards of a former generation. In revolutionary situations, like post-war Japan, it sometimes leaps far ahead. The word 'ahead' implies the assumption that the new Civil Code represents a further stage along the road of development which Japanese family institutions were already travelling. Of that there can be little doubt; nor can it be doubted that the enactment of the new Code has had and will continue to have some effect in accelerating the rate of progress along that road. Western observers of General MacArthur's activities frequently tended to scorn the notion that fundamental changes in Japanese social institutions could be carried out by the decree of an occupying power. The somewhat over-sanguine tone of some official pronouncements on the achievements of the Occupation, and the impression often given by Occupation officials that they were engaged in some kind of competition to achieve the record for the number of villages democratized per week, were perhaps some justification for scepticism. But the new family laws had eager protagonists among Japanese lawyers and leaders of public opinion. The new laws represented what many had, in fact, been advocating for decades. Some were so enthusiastic as to object, during the Diet discussions, even to the vestigial traces of the old family system which still remain in the new Code. There seems, after a decade, little immediate likelihood that the laws will be substantially changed, and just as the old Code gave the full protective authority of the State to certain principles which were beginning to be challenged, so the new gives its authority to principles which were still emergent. It can be expected to assist their emergence in society and, in the limiting case, to uphold them by legal sanctions when they meet with the stubborn resistance of the old.

9

Household Composition in Shitayama-cho

How far does the family in Shitayama-cho, today conform to the ideal 'Japanese family system' we have been describing? The first and most easily measurable aspect is family size and composition. It will be remembered that Table 6 (p. 22) showed certain ways in which Shitayama-cho was more 'urban' than the urban areas of Japan as a whole, in that it carried even further the urban trends towards a smaller average household size, a smaller proportion of three-generation households, a smaller proportion of children, and a larger proportion of lodgers and employees unrelated to the families with which they were living.

The detailed analysis of household composition in Table 15 and the summary comparative figures of Table 14 modify and expand

Table 14: Composition of Households, Shitayama-cho (1951), Five Northern Prefectures and Six Large Cities (1920)

Composition of household	Shitayama-cho (1951) (%)	Five northern prefectures* (1920) (%)	Six large cities* (1920) (%)
1 generation household	26·2	8·1	27·4
2 generations and 1 (or no) married couples	60·0	40·0	58·7
2 gens. and 2 m.c.	0·3	4·7	0·7
3 (or more) gens., 1 m.c.	10·1	20·8	10·0
3 (or more) gens., 2 (or more) m.c.	3·3	26·4	3·2
Total	100·0	100·0	100·0

* These figures were calculated by Toda Teizoo from a ·1% sample of the 1920 Census data (*Kazoku Koosei*, 3rd ed. 1942, pp. 508 and 513). The Five northern prefectures are the rural prefectures of Aomori, Akita, Iwate, Miyagi and Yamagata. The cities are Tokyo, Yokohama, Nagoya, Kyooto, Koobe and Oosaka.

121

Table 15: Household Composition in Shitayama-cho

Type of household	Number of households					
	Alone	Collateral relatives	Lodgers	Domestic servants	Employees	Total
		Containing additionally				
Single generation households	69	4	0	2	3	78
Single person households	39					39
Bachelors	6					6
Widowers	6					6
Men temporarily separated from families	4					4
Spinsters	11					11
Widows	12					12
Married couples only	22	4		1	2	29
Brothers and sisters only	6					6
Others	2			1	1	4
Parents with non-married children*	136	17	10	5	8	176
Marr. couples & children	105	15	9	4	6	139
Widower with children	6					6
Widow with children†	25	2	1	1	2	31
Parents with married children	28	8	2	1	4	43
Marr. couple & one parent	2					2
Marr. child is (a) son	1					1
(b) non-inher. dtr.	1					1
Marr. Couple & marr. parents (of husband)	1					1
Marr. non-earning parents with child (child's spouse), and grandchildren	8					8
Marr. child is (a) son	5					5
(b) inheriting dtr.	1					1
(c) non-inheriting dtr.	2					2
Marr. earning parents with child (child's spouse) and grandchildren	3		1		1	5
Marr. child is (a) son	2					2
(b) inheriting dtr.	0		1		1	2
(c) non-inheriting dtr.	1					1
Single non-earning parent with child (child's spouse), and grandchildren	14	8	1	1	3	27
Marr. child is (a) son	8	6		1	3	18
(b) inheriting dtr.	2	1				3
(c) non-inheriting dtr.	4	1				6
Total	233	29	12	8	15	297

* I.e. unmarried or separated from spouse.

† Also including divorcees. Of these twenty-four widows and divorcees with children, eleven had more earning than non-earning children.

these generalizations. As the latter shows, the distribution of household types in Shitayama-cho is not very different from that yielded by the ·1% sample survey of the six big industrial towns in 1920, but very different from that of the five rural prefectures of northern Japan at that date.

The three-generation household 'typical' of the old family system would never, of course, be universal in any population however closely the prescriptions of the Japanese family system were observed —the wastage of normal mortality would see to that—but the figures for rural districts in 1920 (Table 14) give some idea of what the distribution of household types might be, allowing for a certain number of new branch families and for a certain number of normal stem families passing through a temporary two-generation phase.

Compared with these figures, the three-generation household in Shitayama-cho is very much under-represented. It constitutes less than 14% of the total number of households, and more than half of these are cases of a single surviving parent living with a married son or daughter.

In part this is to be accounted for, not in terms of a breakdown of the old family system, but as a result of the predominance of first-generation branch families. This does, in fact, immediately account for some 64% of the conjugal families, the husband of which is a younger son.

But it does not account for the other 36%, the sixty married eldest sons who have no parent living with them. In many cases, of course, their parents have already died. But there are other eldest sons who are living apart from still surviving parents. This departure from the prescriptions of the Japanese family system has two aspects, the first involving patterns of migration, the second new urban customs of neolocal marriage.

YOUNGER SON MIGRATION OR ELDEST SON MIGRATION?

It was said in the previous chapter that the urban labour force has been largely recruited from the *younger* sons of provincial, mainly peasant, families. This is easily substantiated in general terms by the fact that whereas of those men in Shitayama-cho who were born in Tokyo and Yokohama 45% are younger sons, of those born elsewhere 72% are younger sons; a very significant difference.[107] But there are still the other 28% to be accounted for; of the migrants to Tokyo, fifty-three are eldest sons, twenty-one of them the sons of farmers.

Their presence can be accounted for by two hypotheses; one concerning the poorer and the other the richer strata of peasants. The poorer peasant families have, probably, provided the bulk of the industrial labour force. Many families have no more land than can be

easily tilled by one man and his wife. The labour of the children is not
required on the holding. The eldest son matures first, and it is natural
that he should be the first to set off to seek his fortune. Later on, as
the family's economic position improves, a younger son may be kept
at home to help on the land and relieve the burden on his ageing
parents.

But the negative drive of poverty is not the only factor accounting
for migration. Education also plays its part, for migration from the
countryside takes the form not only of an influx of unskilled labour
from the poorest strata of peasant families, but also of students and
the educationally qualified from the middle and upper strata.

It is generally said that a peasant family which can afford to educate
some but not all of its sons concentrates on providing education for
its younger sons, in order to improve their chances in seeking some
other occupation in the towns. The eldest son does not need education
to the same extent, for he has the prospect of a secure future in
succeeding to the family's land holding. Moreover, payment for his
education is one way of giving the younger son his branch family's
share in the family property.

In many cases, indeed, this is what happens, but although this
arrangement best serves the ultimate purpose of securing smooth and
orderly succession to the headship of the family by the eldest son, it
conflicts with the general tendency to give precedence to the eldest
son in all matters of daily life. He is early given a sense of his own
importance as heir designate; he has the use of the family bath before
his brothers; he is given the most tasty part of the fish; he is generally
indulged more than his younger brothers who grow up expecting to
defer to his wishes; if money for education is scarce he would have a
superior claim. Moreover, in his ultimate position as head of the
family, his authority over his younger brothers would have somewhat
less weight if they were better educated than he.

Further, although money was of major importance for entry into
universities, at the secondary level, entry into the middle school depended not only on the parents having the economic resources to pay
fees and forgo earnings, but also on the child's success in a competitive entrance examination. Education is a generally valued good
in Japanese rural society, and the competitive element in entry to the
middle school made it more so. A farmer whose eldest son achieved
a place in the middle school would probably find it difficult to refuse
to send him there in favour of a younger son who might or might not
succeed in the examination when his turn came.

For these reasons then, one might expect that it was not always the
younger sons who were singled out to receive higher education. And
although among the small class of leisured landlords in Japanese
villages (before the Land Reform) there were many university-edu-

cated househeads, an eldest son from a moderately well-off farm family who had started on the educational ladder at his local middle school, gone on to university and there acquired qualifications which could only be used in the towns would be likely to stay there.

Some confirmation of these suggestions that 'migration by extreme poverty' and 'migration by education', working against the pressures of inheritance patterns, are largely responsible for bringing eldest sons to the towns may be seen in the educational backgrounds of migrants in Shitayama-cho. Provincial born eldest sons contain a higher proportion who received only an elementary education (52·8%) or who attended high schools, higher technical schools or universities (24·5%) than among the rest of the male population, (though the sample (53) is too small to draw any very precise conclusions).

Where an eldest son has migrated to the towns, ultimogeniture, rather than primogeniture, would provide the most convenient arrangement of inheritance. But primogeniture still being the socially sanctioned custom, the eldest son who has settled in the city is faced with a difficult choice on the death of his parents. Should he, in order to fulfil his obligations as eldest son, return to his home, to a job for which he is by now physically ill-trained and often to a lowered standard of living, in many cases knowing that he will thereby be displacing a younger brother who is in effective and efficient control of affairs? Or should he ignore his abstract obligations to continue the family line, confirm his younger brother in the headship of the main family, and relegate himself to the position of head of a subordinate branch family? Several eldest sons of provincial families living in Shitayama-cho had already had to face this choice and had decided to stay. Ten with parents still living were asked what they intended to do and only one proclaimed his intention of returning to his parental home—and in his case his home was just within commuting distance of Tokyo.

One reason, then, for the partial abandonment of the old family system can be clearly traced to the exigencies of the occupational changes and urban migration which industrialization has brought. But this is not the whole story.

NEOLOCAL MARRIAGE

There are other eldest sons in Shitayama-cho who were born in Tokyo and whose parents are still living elsewhere in the city. Likewise, one old couple in Shitayama-cho, now in their sixties, have four sons; the three eldest are married and living elsewhere in Tokyo; only the unmarried fourth son still lives at home.

This trend towards the conjugal family, quite divorced from the consequences of migration, can be fairly readily explained. The traditional family structure, as we have seen, contained one potential source of friction and conflict in the relation between mother-in-law and daughter-in-law, with lesser tensions between wife and husband's sisters. The early years of married life were not expected to be happy ones for the woman. Parents who were solicitous of their daughter's happiness tried to ensure that they married younger sons who would be free from the responsibility of living with parents. The 'mother-in-law-daughter-in-law problem' is a common phrase, although it was until recently simply considered a part of the natural order like earthquakes, not as a 'problem' in the sense of something to be dealt with and solved.[108]

Despite this internal source of strain the family held together, since, normally, the eldest son was economically dependent on his father, and the system of family production required that the family live together in order to be able to work together smoothly under the direction of the family head. When, with the substitution of wage-employment for family production, the one compelling *raison d'être* for the large family disappears, this centre of internal stress is likely to burst it asunder.

Some indication of the change in what is regarded as normal practice may be gained from the answers to certain interview questions in Shitayama-cho. One sample of a hundred were asked the following set of questions. The number giving the various replies is shown in brackets.

1. What do you think of this sort of situation? An eldest son is married and living with his parents. His wife and his mother don't get on together and his mother asks him to divorce his wife. But he is fond of his wife. What do you think the son should do? Do you think he should divorce his wife?

Yes (10)   Don't know (15)

|No (75)|

1a. But supposing that they were both strong personalities and neither of them would give an inch so that living together became impossible and the son was faced with the choice of either divorcing his wife or leaving home and breaking completely with his parents. What do you think he should do then?

Divorce her (15)
Leave home (60)

2. This is a similar sort of situation. Parents and a married eldest son are living together. The son's wife doesn't get on well with her mother-in-law and suggests to her husband that they should go and live somewhere else, even if it does mean living in rented rooms. But

his parents are against it because they don't like to be left by themselves. What should the son do?

Move out (52)   Don't Know (8)

Stay on (40)

2a.   But supposing his wife finds life so unbearable that she says that if he won't move out she will leave him. What do you think he should do then?

'Move out (18)   Don't Know (3)
Let her go (19)

The traditionalist views—those which in each case give absolute precedence to the parent-child bond over the husband-wife bond— are in the minority.[109] But they were often given with great confidence. 'The parents are the supreme consideration,' said one woman, 'and the daughter-in-law should do everything she can to co-operate with them. She should look after the parents with meticulous care. It's not a bad idea for the son to quarrel occasionally with his wife in front of his parents, either' (i.e. to pacify his parents by making a show of disciplining his wife). Another said, in answer to Question 2: 'The son should send her away. It's not as if she was the main support of the household or anything. The *yome* has no right to behave so selfishly.'

Emphasis on the selfishness of the young wife in demanding that her husband take her out of his parents' home was common in such replies. 'If she is so lacking in patient endurance, then she would be no good to him anyway.' Some saw it as a test of moral uprightness for the husband; 'A man should have the strength of mind not to give way to his wife's demands.' It is typical, too, of the background to such attitudes that some viewed the question not simply as a matter affecting the individual marriage partners, but as—primarily even— a matter between the two families concerned. The *yome's* parents should be called on to help discipline their recalcitrant daughter, said one man, and one woman in her thirties, who related her answer to her own situation, said, 'In my case, my own parents would not allow me to be divorced'; in the situation described in the first question because it would be an insult to her family if she were sent home as unworthy, and in the second because the daughter's irresponsibility in walking out instead of bearing her troubles with adequate meekness would redound to her own family's discredit.

Opposed to this there are three main views which make up the majority of the replies. In the first place there are those who consider that the happy large family is the ideal, but that if trouble arises to make this impossible, a man should stick to his wife. A modification of this view, and one which places even greater stress on the ideal of harmony in the joint household, is held by those (9%) who gave intermediate replies, that is, considered that a son should stick to his wife despite parental attempts to separate them, but, on the other hand, that a man should let his wife go rather than yield to her requests to him to leave his parents. Harmonious coexistence is the greatest good, and it should be the person who, for selfish and personal motives, destroys that harmony—in the first case the mother and in the second the wife—who should be made to suffer.

The third view, expressed in some replies, is that it is always better to live apart in the first place.

There is little doubt that the majority opinion is Shitayama-cho, as represented by the last three views detailed above which all have in common the belief that a man's relation with his wife is of more importance than his relation with his parents, is a view which, though contrary to the principles of the traditional family system, represents the majority opinion at least of Tokyo society.

These questions, however, represented situations of enforced choice, where the stresses of the traditional family structure have broken through to the surface. In the course of a different interview about children, seventy-seven parents of unmarried boys were asked, 'Do you hope that when your (eldest) son gets married he will live with you or live apart?' Only seventeen (22%) said that they hoped their son would live with them. A noticeably, but (with this small sample) not quite significantly,[110] high proportion of these were women. Some of them remarked that the bonds between parent and child would grow weaker if they lived apart, one that otherwise it would be impossible to train the young bride to be a good housewife, and one complained that 'you couldn't even get to know your own grandchildren properly' if your son lived elsewhere. The rest (apart from one 'don't know') said that it would be best, if economically possible, to have separate households. 'Newly-married youngsters don't want to have old people around—I know from experience.' 'It only leads to unpleasantness and quarrels.' A sixth of this group, however, added the qualification that they hoped to live together again when their son was less newly-married and they themselves were no longer able to work.

One might have expected that of all instances of change in the family this was one most likely to give rise to conflict. The older generation would not only have their stronger attachment to tradition, but also strong emotional and economic motives for resisting such a change. Yet we find a widespread acceptance of the new patterns among parents, at least as far as their replies to interview questions are concerned. One cannot too readily accept their replies as indications of probable behaviour, but they can be considered as representing the common norms of the society in the sense that they give the answer which they believe is expected in their society (rather than it is to be hoped, the reply which they believe is expected by the British organizer of the Inquiry). That is to say, if they do try to keep their sons at home after marriage, they will not do so in the full confidence of having the whole weight of prevailing social custom on their side.

Conflict does, of course, sometimes arise; one case was known in Shitayama-cho which ended in the divorce of the young couple, but general observation would seem to confirm that it is not at all widespread.

For this there are good reasons, for nowadays the mother-in-law too has grounds for wishing to live apart. The speed of modern changes has meant that her traditional supremacy *vis-à-vis* her daughter in-law has been considerably undermined. The young bride in the traditionally-oriented society of a hundred, or even fifty, years ago, accepted her mother-in-law's advice concerning the care and weaning of her children as the accumulated wisdom of the centuries, observed the superstitions she was taught and was generally prepared to grant that the mother-in-law always knew best. But in modern Japan new authorities have arisen to challenge tradition. The school and the woman's magazine teach new methods of hygiene, a new 'nutritional' way of looking at food, new theories about the appropriate time and ways of weaning children, new ideas about the arrangement of kitchens. These all have the backing of the authority of science, and in the acceptance of that authority is implied the assumption that the newer a theory is the more likely it is to be right, in contrast to the old view that tradition alone is an adequate guarantee of truth.

The young daughter-in-law, with her more recent schooling, is more up-to-date, more converted to the progressive attitude than her mother-in-law. The latter, in Tokyo commonly a country-born and country-educated woman who came to Tokyo soon after marriage, is often completely disorientated. The rapid changes in society in her lifetime, the backing given to the new ideas by the school which as an organ of 'the authorities' commands her respect; all these things have destroyed her confidence in traditional ways before she has acquired knowledge of the new. One mother-in-law, in answering the questions about progress mentioned earlier, said that she thought things had got gradually more difficult for the housewife since she 'no longer just has to go on doing the same cooking and cleaning; she has got to find out new things about clothes and about the new education. She's got to use her spare time to read the newspapers and magazines in order to keep up with the young ones.'

To a certain extent, then, the nature of the 'mother-in-law-daughter-in-law problem' has changed. It still does arise in its traditional form, and readers' advice columns in women's magazines are often devoted to it. But the reply by a member of the Tokyo Family Tribunal to the complaint of one woman about the unbearable tyranny of her mother-in-law is an interesting indication of the turning of the tables. 'Today when the power of the daughter-in-law has become so strong and there are many families where the poor mother-in-law can hardly hold up her head, houses like yours which still exhibit the old traditional pattern really present a problem.' [111] In July 1951, the Japanese Broadcasting Corporation devoted its 'What the man in the street thinks' programme to 'The Mother-in-law-daughter-in-law Problem'. A majority of the passers-by who were stopped and asked to give their opinion suggested that the daughter-in-law should be more tolerant and understanding, should realize her debt of gratitude to her mother-in-law and so on. The general assumption was that it was aggressiveness on the part of the daughter-in-law which was today at the root of the problem.

When this is the generally accepted appraisal of the situation, prospective mothers-in-law may well have second thoughts about the desirability of living with married children, and be only too willing to allow them to set up separate households.

A further relevant factor is the fact that the generation getting married in Tokyo today is composed largely of the sons and daughters of migrants from rural areas. More than three-quarters of women in Tokyo between the ages of 45 and 54 today are provincial born, and so are their husbands. Most of them migrated in their twenties and established a new branch family in Tokyo. They are not mothers, therefore, who are just emerging from the dominance of their own mother-in-law in a family with a long tradition which always has expected its brides to be brought into the family. Here is a typical case where the discontinuity inherent in the establishment of branch families can assist the transition from the old to the new.

CARE OF THE AGED

Living with one's married eldest son in the traditional family, (or rather, keeping one's son at home after marriage) was not simply a matter of emotional attachment, nor of convenience of domestic economic production. It was also the automatic means of providing for old age. The approach of old age meant simply that one ceased, perhaps gradually and imperceptibly, to be a producing member of the family group, but continued to have undiminished—and even enhanced—rights as a consuming member. This change might take place before actual physical incapacitation. If the family was prospering and the heir was mature and reliable, the parents would formally relinquish the headship of the family to the son and look forward to *raku-inkyo*—easy retirement—with diminished tasks and responsibility, but enhanced prestige in the local community and more leisure for amusement, for playing with grandchildren, and for social activity.

This automatic form of provision for the aged undergoes a considerable change as the new patterns of neolocal marriage develop. The desire for the security which it gives was doubtless prominent among the motives of those parents in Shitayama-cho who hoped that their eldest son would live with them after marriage, and it will be remembered that a fair proportion of those who hoped their son would be able to have a separate household 'at first', also added that they hoped to live with him again later on, when they were too old to work. This, indeed, is one form of adjustment within the traditional pattern. Another is to maintain separate households, but to depend on financial support from the eldest son.

A slightly more radical adjustment, and one which follows to its logical conclusion the equal inheritance provisions of the new Civil Code, is to depend not simply on the eldest son but on all children equally. The clearest rejection of tradition is made by those who look to their own efforts, or to the State, to provide for their old age.

Table 16 below, may give some impression of the relative attractive-

Table 16: Prospective Provision for Old Age by Parents in Shitayamacho

Reply	Number	(%)
Rely on eldest son	35	(50)
Intend to be as independent as possible, but if necessary will rely on eldest son	14	(20)
Rely on all the children collectively	2	(3)
Intend to be as independent as possible, but if necessary will rely on all children collectively	4	(6)
Rely on child other than eldest son	1	(1)
Intend to put some savings by for old age	1	(1)
No intention of ever being burden on children	7	(10)
Don't know, depends on circumstances, never think of it	6	(9)
Total	70	(100)

ness of these various prospects to parents in Shitayama-cho. Seventy parents of boys were asked 'Which of your children do you expect to depend on in your old age?' The form of the question itself gave the respondent a strong push towards the traditional pattern, and it is perhaps a further convincing proof of changing ideas that only a half simply answered 'eldest son'.

It is impossible to say whether the replies which spoke of depending on all children equally are the result of a gradual change in family institutions, or of the acceptance, and logical extension, of the new Civil Code's prescription of equal inheritance by all children irrespective of sex. It has, however, long been common for widows to tour the houses of their children, staying a month or two in each. One woman specified that this was her intention—'to stay with each of them in turn, taking a hand in looking after the grandchildren—if you settle with one child it leads to all sorts of complications'. Often married daughters are not only included in the tour but occupy the major place in it—for reasons which will be considered later.

It may be expected that this way of spending old age or widowhood will become even more prevalent as the provisions of the new Civil Code gradually assert their influence and equal inheritance, implying a right to call on all one's children for help in old age, replaces primogeniture with its reciprocal right to depend on the eldest son. There are strong obstacles to the adoption of equal inheritance in rural areas where the duty of maintaining holdings intact through the generations has strong traditional as well as economic supports and where strict enforcement of equal inheritance would in fact lead to all the difficulties which Le Play deplored in the working of the Napoleonic Code in nineteenth-century France—in a form much aggravated by the already tiny average size of holdings. But except in the case of owners of retail or craft businesses, in which there is an occupation, property and a family tradition to inherit, in the towns the obstacles to equal division of property are not very great. As compared with farm families, moreover, the Tokyo eldest son does not receive such consistently preferential treatment and he is not so consciously groomed for his future position as head of the family.

As we noted above, there are good reasons for thinking that daughters are in future likely to play a bigger part than sons in looking after parents. We have mentioned the woman in Shitayama-cho whose three eldest sons had all married and left her. She complained bitterly to the interviewer and remarked that her hopes now rested on her daughter who she thought would probably give her a home.

For her this was obviously a second-best, but it is, in fact, becoming a widespread custom. Of those forty-three families in Shitayama-cho in which parents are living with married children, thirty-four, as Table 15 shows, do conform to the patterns of the 'family system'. That is to say, the married child is either a son (in twenty-seven cases) or, in the other seven, an inheriting daughter who has taken an adopted husband—a husband who takes his wife's surname and succeeds his father-in-law (rather than his own father) as head of his wife's family. The remaining fifth of these families, however, do not conform to these patterns at all. Although in form the daughter has married out of her family into her husband's, the young couple live with her, and not with her husband's, parents.

There are several reasons for expecting this to become gradually more common nowadays when the chief reasons for parents to live with their married children is to solve the young couple's housing problem or to make some provision for the parents' old age, rather than simply because 'it is the proper thing to do'. Firstly, in joint households it is the women who are most in contact with each other and friction is much less likely if they are mother and daughter than if they are mother and daughter-in-law. Secondly, women generally lead more family-centred lives than men and their bonds of attachment to their parental family at the time of marriage tend to be stronger than in the case of men. Thirdly, the new-comer into the on-going family circle is the man, rather than the woman, and, particularly in Japan where the tradition of male dominance compensates for the subordinate status of the newcomer, he is better able than the woman to adapt to his new environment other than on a basis of complete but unwilling submission. The 'mother-in-law problem' in the English sense—as a problem for the husband—may eventually become a Japanese music-hall joke too, as matrilocal or neolocal patterns of marriage spread, but as long as the traditional dominance of the male is upheld, it is likely to be less serious.

However, to return to Table 16, there were a large number (37%) who (again, remember, despite the form of the question) would prefer not to be dependent on their children at all. Some of them expressed a strong determination always to provide for themselves, though the majority recognized that this might be impossible and saw reluctant dependence on their children as the inevitable result. Whence derives this reluctance? Why do some people no longer believe that they have a natural right to depend on their children?

One reason is undoubtedly the separation of households. There is no longer a gradual transformation of the aged into non-producing but still consuming members of the on-going family group. Instead, some overt action initiating a relation of dependence—going to live with a son or receiving money gifts—becomes necessary. Another is that the transmission to the son of a family craft, land or business was a simple justification of the parents' assertion of their right to support which no longer exists for most wage-earning urban families. Another that crowded living conditions in the towns often make impossible the allocation of separate and architecturally somewhat isolated rooms to the older married couple, as is a common rural custom, so that the actual extent to which joint families are liable to cause friction may be greater. The decline in the explicit teaching of the Confucian ideology which laid so much stress on filial piety and on caring for aged parents as its chief expression; the influence of Western individualism with its general emphasis on the individual pursuit of happiness rather than on the fulfilment of duty to the family; all of these factors may be expected to have played their part.

The logical consequences of a reluctance to depend on children and of the practical impossibility of continuous self-support, are the alternatives of private savings or State assistance, which, the table suggests, play only a very small part in the scheme of things for parents in Shitayama-cho. Only one man (a 35-year-old departmental chief in a factory) mentioned savings and none the prospects of pensions, insurance annuities or State aid. Individual savings, although far from negligible (see the family budgets of Appendix II), are intended to meet short-run emergencies; few Japanese, except possibly in the upper-middle classes, expect to save enough to secure them a comfortable retirement.

It is hardly surprising that State aid does not loom very large in the Shitayama-cho consciousness since existing provisions are hardly adequate. Apart from the schemes for outdoor relief which were mentioned in an earlier chapter, there were four municipally operated homes for the aged in Tokyo in 1951. Vastly overcrowded as they were, they still accommodated only one in every 350 of the Tokyo population aged over 60.

One may sum up these changes as follows. The traditional methods by which the family cares for the aged are being altered by new patterns of economic activity and inheritance and by new views of the relative importance of marital and parental relations. Other methods are developing by which the family fulfils the same function, but these, by their very nature, are bound to be less certain and less effective in their operation. The number who are forced to look outside the family for help is growing without, as yet, any adequate growth in public provision to meet their needs.

It is not surprising that this is one of the most discussed of contemporary family problems. The author of a recent collection of essays on various aspects of the family called her book, significantly enough, *'Children Who Do Not Look After Their Parents'.*[112] Newspaper articles frequently refer to the problem, usually attributing it either to 'democracy' or, more specifically, to 'the new Civil Code which prescribes equal inheritance so that the responsibility for looking after parents rests squarely on no-one in particular'.[113] The family Tribunals will hear appeals for maintenance by abandoned parents and can effect conciliation and order money payments (which cannot, however, be enforced unless the case is subsequently taken to the ordinary courts). But the number of such appeals is small.[114] The sense of a legal right to maintenance which it is not unnatural to insist on irrespective of the presence or absence of affection or gratitude on the part of the child, or at least the willingness to assert such a right would not seem to be widespread. Only the extremities of want are likely to drive parents to the courts and thus publicize to the world their failure to raise up truly filial children. The distress and insecurity of the aged and the ageing, though like all the unfortunate effects of 'democracy' somewhat exaggerated in the public mind, are more widespread than figures for appeals to the Family Tribunals would suggest.

COLLATERALS AND LODGERS

Before leaving consideration of Table 15, two more points may be briefly noted. Firstly, that collateral relatives outnumber lodgers. Table 7 shows that this is much more noticeably the case in Tokyo as a whole than in Shitayama-cho. One conclusion which can be drawn from this is that individuals coming from the provinces to Tokyo for work or study are more likely to seek lodgings with relatives, however distant, than with strangers on an impersonal contractual basis —a further aspect of the general tendency to confine social relations as far as possible to family or pseudo-family relations.

Secondly, there is a slight tendency (not significant with this sample size) for collateral relatives to be found more frequently in the three-generation families than in the small conjugal families.[115] This may have something to do with house size, but it may also be the outcome of differences in the structure of family relations.

One would expect the affectual bonds between members of the small conjugal family to be stronger than those between members of the three-generation families; both because it is smaller in size so that interaction is concentrated within a smaller number of people, and because within it the relations most prone to produce strong affectual links (husband-wife, parent-child) predominate. The child has only its own mother to look to for love and attention, not additional grandmothers and aunts; the wife is used to having only her husband to get along with, not his brothers and his father as well. In the three-generation family with its more varied relationships, one would expect a newcomer from outside to be more easily absorbed and to be less likely to be felt as an intruder than in the smaller, more tightly knit and more emotionally integrated conjugal family group.

10

The 'House'

I N the last chapter changes in family relationships were studied as they manifest themselves in household composition. This will be concerned with questions of authority within the family, with some of the ideological concomitants of the traditional family patterns—such as the symbols of family unity and continuity, and the merging of individual interests and responsibilities in group interests and responsibilities—and also with the related topic of relationships within the framework of the wider kin group, the *doozoku*.

AUTHORITY IN THE FAMILY

In the traditional family the househead[116] directed both the economic and social activities of all the family members, and also had ultimate control over the distribution of the family income in consumption as between family members. It was suggested earlier that the removal of the family's productive functions and the earning by subordinate family members of independent incomes might tend to diminish the authority of parents or househead and lead to an increased exercise of individual choice and individual responsibility. The relative fall in middle-class incomes since the war may be expected to have much accelerated this process in middle-class families. Daughters and even, sometimes, wives now go out to work whereas formerly they would have been wholly dependent on the househead's income. Sons who might formerly have been educated at their father's expense now work their way through college.[117] Moreover, in the particular case of daughters, not only economic pressures but also the sweeping changes of ideas since the war have had their effect. The principal of a former Girls' High School (now co-educational) in one of the best residential districts of Tokyo remarked that before the war any girl who worked after leaving school would have been practically ostracized at class reunions. Now, however rich the family, a girl who does not 'get out and see the world' feels very small among her more sophisticated ex-class-mates.

136

But does a certain amount of economic independence in fact increase the range of individual choice and weaken family control? Table 17 may give some answer. It shows what housewives in fifty-nine households said happened to the wages of working children.

Table 17: What happens to Your Children's Wages?

Reply	Number of households*	Child concerned is	
		Son	Daughter
Child gives mother whole wages and receives pocket money for specific purposes	13	10	5
Child gives mother whole wages and receives a lump sum as pocket money	11	9	2
Child gives mother a fixed sum for its keep and retains the rest	22	15	10
'It is entirely up to' the child	5	2	3
Money saved for child's future benefit	3	1	2
Not reported	5	3	2
Total	59	40	24

* Cross-totals do not add since some households contained both a working son and daughter.

Obviously the practice most in conformity with the traditional family structure is the first, wherein control over the child's activities is at a maximum. In total effect there is little difference between answers two and three, but still symbolically the parents' right to control the whole income of the child is recognized in the second but abandoned in the third. As will be seen there is no noticeable tendency for sons to have more freedom to dispose of their income than girls (a contrast, as we shall find, with the findings concerning choice of mate).

In the previous chapter doubts were implied whether the small number of three-generation households in Shitayama-cho could be considered as strongholds of the traditional family ideals, or whether they were merely the result of necessity, of the economic difficulty of maintaining separate households as the individuals concerned would have preferred. Some information gained concerning the control of expenditure in these families can help to throw light on this question. In those households where the parents are no longer working and have no independent income of their own, the son's wife often, though not invariably, keeps the purse and controls the family expenditure. In one case at least the son spoke of occasionally giving his parents 'pocket money'. In the other families, in which the older parents were still active and had no sense of dependence on their children, a variety of patterns was found. At one end of the scale were three families in which, though living together, the two nuclear families maintained separate households as far as money matters were concerned and even cooked separately. At the other end of the scale was one household in which the son gave the whole of his wages to his mother. Clothes for his children and for his wife, school expenses, sweets, cigarettes and cinemas were all paid for by the mother. Most of the fifteen families concerned were some way between these two extremes. In one the young married couple always kept 2,000 *yen* (about one seventh) of the husband's wages for their own 'pocket money', out of which the wife bought her own clothing, but in this household the mother-in-law paid for, and herself bought, the clothing for her grandchildren. It was indeed noticeable that the mother-in-law provided the money for clothing for the son's children (in five cases) more frequently than for the son's wife (in only two of these five cases), an indication, perhaps, of a feeling that the children born in the *ie* are more fully members of it than women brought in by marriage, or, alternatively, the relevant distinction may be that clothes for the children are a necessity and are therefore provided in the same way as other necessities—by the mother-in-law—whereas clothes for the wife are in the nature of indulgences which come best from her husband.

There is, then, no uniformity of behaviour in these respects, but even in those households which by virtue of their composition might be expected to conform to the traditional type, the traditional submission by the married son and his wife to the direction of the parents in matters of consumption is found in only a small number of cases.

One crucial area in which it is generally admitted that customs are changing is parental control over marriage. In one interview parents were asked what they intended to do about their own children's marriage, and their replies, roughly classified, are tabled below (Table 18). They suggest that family control over marriage is no longer considered desirable even by the majority of parents, or at least, if they do consider it desirable they hesitate to say so.

Traditionally, in the small closed local community, all marriages into and out of the family were important to the family as such and hence required the househead's control, for a number of reasons. The following are suggested by Dr. Kawashima:[118]

1. The need to affirm the family's position in the status hierarchy by an alliance with a family of appropriate status.
2. The affinal links formed between the two families were new channels for the manipulation of the family's social and political influence in

the community. (e.g. 'How many votes would the girl's family be good for if I stood for village headman?')

3. The affinal links formed between the two families can have economic importance—giving and receiving help in emergencies, and so on.

Table 18: When the Time comes for Your Son (Daughter) to get Married, who do You think should decide whom He (She) Marries? Yourselves? Or he Himself (she Herself)?*

Reply	Child concerned is	
	Son	Daughter
Parents should take the initiative and look for a marriage partner	8	32
The child should be left to find its own partner, but parents should exercise a power of veto	24	8
The child should be left to find its own partner and, though the parents may give strong advice, they should exercise no ultimate veto power	32	23
The initiative should be taken by either as opportunity occurs	3	4
Don't know	5	5
Totals	72	72

* This question was elaborated with the follow-up probes: 'But suppose he doesn't like the girl you choose?' or 'But suppose you don't like the girl he chooses?'

In addition, for the marriage of an eldest son family control was of particular importance in so far as the bride who was to be brought into the family was destined eventually to take control over its domestic affairs, and her quality might thus have a considerable effect on the family's fortunes. Moreover, when the parents eventually went into retirement and the headship of the household passed to the eldest son, they would, to a certain extent, be dependent on the goodwill of the daughter-in-law for a comfortable old age.

One or two parents who said that they expected to have a final say in their son's choice added as an explanatory reason 'he is, after all, the *atotori*, the "successor" ', and one woman, widowed owner of a retail shop, quite explicitly drew a distinction between her eldest son whose bride would be found by her, and her youngest who could marry whom he liked.

But in urban areas status considerations (of the traditional local-community type) are of diminished importance, and the growing acceptance of neolocal marriage reduces the insurance-for-old-age motive for controlling the eldest son's marriage. And as for the 'family' reasons, most families in Shitayama-cho have no extensive family property, no family occupation, no proud family tradition which might be jeopardized by the incompetence or misbehaviour of a son's bride. 'I don't think that just because he is the eldest son, his parents should compel him to do anything.' 'After all, it's his wife, not his family's wife.' There always was a tendency in the traditional family for the enforcement of family control to be somewhat weakened by a contrary tendency for the mother to indulge every wish of her sons—the mechanism whereby male dominance was perpetuated in Japanese society. A son's desire to marry a girl with whom he had fallen in love was sometimes given covert support by the mother against the father. This traditional indulgence, working from inside, as it were, combines with new individualistic ideas and new views of the nature of marriage to reduce family control. One woman in Shitayama-cho, the wife of a small home-manufacturer whose unmarried son is also in the business (one of those cases where one might have expected family control to be enforced) said that she would not interfere with her son's marriage—'I've always brought up my *boys* to have their own way.'

Not so her girls. Indulgence has never been a marked characteristic of the upbringing of daughters in the Japanese family. They have been trained to a subordinate and submissive role, and it has been part of their education not only not to express, but not even to become conscious of potentially disruptive personal desires. It is partly a reflection of this that parents of daughters tended to want to exercise control over their marriage more often than the parents of sons. The reasons given were often related to the stereotyped feminine personality of traditional Japanese culture; girls have no power of judgement, they are 'negative', shy, 'unlike men in that they are incapable of saying frankly what they think and doing what they want to do'. The follow-up question 'But suppose she didn't like the person you had chosen?' was greeted with derision by one mother—'What, our Suzuko!' Another recurring reason was that marriage is a far more serious matter for women than for men and should be for that reason even more carefully deliberated over by her parents, particularly since girls normally marry younger than boys. All these reasons implied that parental supervision was an expression of solicitude for the daughter's happiness. None suggested that it was necessary to prevent the daughter from making an unworthy match which might redound to the discredit of the family, or from choosing so badly as to bring on herself and her family the shame of being 'sent home'.

Throughout the struggles in the legal-reform committees of the last half century between the upholders of the traditional 'family system' and the reformers, one central point of conflict has been the relative weight to be given to the powers defined as 'househead's right' (*koshuken*) and 'parental right' (*shinken*). The reform proposals of 1925 recommended the expansion of the latter at the expense of the former in such matters as the power to determine the residence of children, to withhold permission to marry, and so on.[119] This was considered a victory for the reformers in their effort to extend the freedom of individual, for, underlying the debate was the assumption, made by both sides, that where there was in fact conflict between the parent and the househead (as could happen, say, concerning the grandchild of the househead) the househead would be more likely to exert his authority in the interests of 'the family' as a corporate continuing entity, whereas the parent would be more likely to consider the welfare of the individual child. The reformers thought the latter desirable; the traditionalists valued subordination of the individual to family ends as a positive good in itself. It is this dichotomy which is exemplified in the change from traditional types and motives of control over children's marriages to those of the present day. Many parents still wish to control the marriage of their children to some extent, but they think of this control as necessary for the child's own good, not for the good of 'the family'.

THE FAMILY IDEOLOGY: SYMBOLS OF CONTINUITY

A concern with the honour or the interests of 'the family'—not the immediate household group, but the transcending entity including ancestors and descendants as well—is most likely to be preserved when there is some continuity of occupation through the generations. Thus, when a widow who ran a *saké* shop in Shitayama-cho began having an illicit affair with a shop assistant her elder brother arrived from the main family shop in the country to sit in judgement on her conduct which was deplored as 'dirtying the shop-sign'. Simple continuity of residence may have the same effect. Thus, until some years ago one of the largest houses in the ward was occupied by a wealthy wholesaler who had always taken the prominent part appropriate to his relative wealth, in ward subscription lists. He had, however, gone to live in the country and his house was occupied by a nephew. The nephew was not particularly rich; nevertheless he considered it his duty to maintain the family's traditional place on the subscription lists. It was not *qua* individual that he was contributing, but *qua* representative of 'the K family'.

But where sons follow different occupations from their fathers and go to live elsewhere on marriage, such consciousness of family tends to be attenuated. This was clear in replies to questions relating to the *kafuu*—the ways of the family—which, traditionally handed on in the patrilineal line, is one of the symbols which help to keep alive a sense of family continuity. Properly, the young bride should adapt to the ways of her husband's family, but, since these matters belong primarily to the domestic sphere, there is every reason to expect this to cease to be so when the young couple live apart, from the husband's parents.

When housewives were asked whether, in preparing the foods and decorations for the annual festivals, they followed their husband's family's customs or their own, 45% (of a total number of 202) said that they followed their husband's family customs. In some cases, the traditional training of the bride by the mother-in-law was replaced by correspondence. One man in Shitayama-cho who had recently had his first child, was receiving frequent letters from his parents reminding him of the various rituals which should be gone through, the visits to the shrines, the special foods on the hundred-and-tenth day, how the baby should be dressed, who should be visited, and so on. It may be doubted very much whether all of these ninety-one housewives were really following their husband's family customs in such a conscientious way. But at least they showed an awareness of what was the proper answer in terms of traditional family institutions, and gave it. In this they were unlike the 26% (excluding the small number of wives with 'adopted husbands') who said that they followed their own family customs.

Others (19%) in their replies showed no notion that ties with the husband's family were, or should be, more important. Their family customs were neither one thing nor the other, or a mixture of both the husband's and the wife's family customs. One or two stressed not simply the equality of the patrilineal and matrilineal links, but also their unimportance. They and their husbands, they said, were making a new *kafuu* together. Some young housewives were faintly amused and scornful of the idea that they should have a *kafuu*, a reaction which may be interpreted as a conscious rejection of the whole complex of family institutions of which the *kafuu* is a symbol. It may, alternatively, be primarily self-deprecating; the *kafuu*, like, indeed, most manifestations of strict familism, being for these people associated with high social status which they were at pains to disclaim.

(The remaining 10% is made up of 5% who said that they learnt how to do things from neighbours and the rest not reported.)

Another important symbol of the continuity of the family is the ancestors. Ancestor worship in Shitayama-cho will be considered in more detail in a later chapter, but some general conclusions on its relation to family consciousness may be given here. In the first place, practically every family in Shitayama-cho which had an obligation according to the traditional family patterns to look after the ancestral tablets of direct ascendants (i.e. all families except younger-son branch families) were in fact doing so. This is not surprising. However attenuated consciousness of family tradition may be there is a difference between gradually ceasing to observe family customs and making an overt and unequivocal gesture of rejection by disposing of the ancestors' tablets. For some of them bombing in the war had made such a gesture unnecessary, but of these the greater number had since replaced the tablets and the Buddhist altar-shrine to house them. It would appear from questioning, however, that not all families observe the ancestral rites as punctiliously as tradition requires, and in the observance of the rites there are a great many elements involved besides the nurturing of consciousness of family tradition.

For instance, many either hold, or have only incompletely rejected, conscious or half-conscious beliefs about the magical productive or protective efficacy of ancestral rites. For many more, the cognitive accompaniments of the ritual acts are almost exclusively centred on memories of recently deceased close relatives—children, wives or brothers—as often as on direct ascendants, ancestors in the proper sense of the term.

Others, however, when asked the meaning of their acts of worship, will indeed talk of expressing gratitude to, or recalling their debt to, 'the ancestors' collectively; those who have laid the foundations of the family's present livelihood; who are responsible for the physical existence of the present members of the family, who have built up its traditions and established it in the status which it enjoys in the local community and the world at large. Others spoke of their acts of worship as in some sense acts of self-dedication. The awareness of a debt to the ancestors crystallizes into a sense of duty to preserve the family's honour, status and material wealth for the sake of the descendants in order 'not to let the ancestors down'. Some went on to tell the interviewers of the age of their family, of the fact that it had samurai status in the Tokugawa period, and of the stories they had been told in their childhood of the deeds of individual ancestors.

Generally speaking, however, it would seem that it is only families which have, in fact, a long, a romantic or an upper-class history, whose idea of the ancestors is given this degree of concrete embroidery. It would seem probable, although, without private access to the minds of others, such a statement is impossible to verify, that despite the replies given concerning the purpose and meaning of ancestor worship, for few was there any cognitive accompaniment to their daily ritual act which involved a notion of the ancestors; though it may be that in moments of stress, when they are required to make moral choices in which the interests or the honour of the family may be involved (and, indeed, all a man's acts can involve the honour of his family) the rites take on an added significance. In any case, a large number of individuals no longer perform these rites. One man who did not explained that he had been brought up to do so in his parental (peasant) home. Since he had come to Tokyo (into a new house, a new district, a new job, all breaking continuity with the old) he had gradually become less punctilious and eventually given up altogether. 'Life is too busy, nowadays, one can't spend all one's time running round with offerings of rice and water for the ancestors.'

Besides these individual acts, with their possible but by no means inevitable relation to family symbolism, there are also certain collective rites connected with the ancestors. These, which are held on the anniversaries of the ancestors' death-days do, by the mere fact of assembly, foster a consciousness of membership of the existing family group, while the nature and occasion of the assembly should foster a consciousness of membership of the family as a corporate entity which transcends its individual members both in life-span and in importance. But these collective rites are no longer observed as punctiliously as in former times. With the exception of the general summer feast for all the ancestors, they are held only for individuals whose memories remain alive among family members and not for 'the ancestors' in general. Celebrations extending up to the traditional limit of fifty years after death are rare. The individual ancestors so celebrated are, then, with their idiosyncratic and personal associations, less effective as pure symbols of 'the family'.

The decline in the observance of these rites, if it means nothing else, at least means a decrease in the number of occasions on which it is possible for the individual to be reminded of his duty towards the ancestors and to unborn generations, and to have his cognitive notion of the 'family' as an entity transcending the generations reinforced, as it is also a reflection of the decreasing importance attached to such ideas.

PERPETUATION

This decreasing importance of the 'transcendental' concept of the family means also that the duty of perpetuating the family becomes of lesser importance. It has already been mentioned that this obligation was formerly more than a moral one; by the Civil Code of 1898 it was reinforced by State legislation. As well as the permissive clauses making adoption and the 'revival' of an extinct house possible, the heir to an existing house was forbidden to leave it for marriage or adoption.

Traditionally, the stress placed on perpetuating the family was reflected in the fact that child-bearing was pre-eminently defined in terms of providing an heir to continue the line. It was surprising to find how little this figures in explicit statements about the importance of child-bearing in Shitayama-cho. When a hundred parents of both sexes were asked: 'Do you think childless couples are to be pitied?—Why?' the answers dwelt almost exclusively on the two factors of the value of children as supports in old age, and on the emotional satisfaction of bringing up children. Only one person said anything unprompted about continuing the family line.

Nevertheless, some provision for the continuation of the family is still generally made. A childless couple[120] will generally adopt an heir, and a couple with daughters but no sons will 'adopt' a husband for a daughter, i.e. the man will marry into the 'house' of, and take the surname of, the wife. The provision in the new Civil Code which permits a married couple to adopt the family surname of either party, though it might appear to carry equality of the sexes to doctrinaire limits unknown in the West, is, in fact, expressly designed to cover such cases.

In the traditional family the adopted child was not merely the perpetuator of the family line, he was also the provider of support and emotional comfort for the parents in their old age. It is in the latter capacity rather than the former that adopted children were notoriously a poor substitute for children of one's own. Despite lip-service to the Chinese notions of the importance of blood-relationships, and the consequent insistence that the adopted son should be a patrilineal kinsman, in actual fact blood ties have not been considered an essential for formal perpetuation of the family.[121] It is, however, a very different matter to be in one's old age dependent on someone who is fundamentally a stranger. A device frequently practised in childless families is first of all to adopt a daughter. If she proves uncongenial she can be married off, and another attempt made; if she proves congenial then a husband can be adopted for her. There is not only the possibility of a second chance; there is also the consideration that for parents who look forward to living in a common household with their adopted children in their old age, to have an affectionate relationship with the daughter is of even greater importance than an affectionate relationship with their son.

The complications of lineage and affinal relations which the practice of adoption involves could be illustrated by many examples from Shitayama-cho. One will here suffice. (See Diagram 4.)

C was the third son of the M family, peasants not far from Tokyo. He came to Tokyo, married D and his surname remained M. Later, however, E, heir to the K, family, died. CD thereupon changed their name to K, and C became the heir to the K family. He retained the name K although his first wife D died and he remarried with F. Later both of his elder brothers, A and B, died, leaving no-one to succeed to the headship of his parental family. His eldest son, G, then approximately 12 years old, was sent back to the farm,

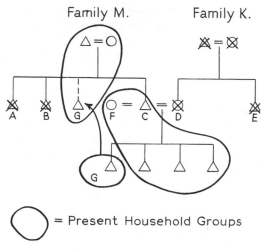

DIAGRAM 4.—Adoption

changed his name back to M, and will succeed to the headship of
the M family on the death of the parents.

As perpetuation of the family becomes a decreasingly important
value, however, the willingness to take the complicated steps of
adoption and name-change necessary to prevent families from dying
out will also decrease. There were two cases in Shitayama-cho of
families which were being allowed to die out. The first was that of
the wife of a couple who had been unable to marry under the old
Civil Code since both were only children and hence presumptive
heirs of their families. As soon as the law permitted, in 1948, she
took her husband's name. This left no present bearer of her family
name and she apparently had no plans for reviving the family in
future with one of her own children. In the other case, a couple had
been married eighteen years before on the understanding that the
husband (family name A) was to take the wife's name (B). For a
long time, however, the marriage was not legally registered. In the
interval the wife's parents suffered financial misfortunes and it
eventually appeared that the inheritance prospects were better for
the couple as a third son of A, than as sole heritor of B. The husband,
therefore, refused to take the wife's name and the B family became
extinct on the death of the wife's parents.

The former heads of these dead or dying families were respectively
a doctor and a schoolmaster. For these families, 'letting the family
die out' meant no more than that the family name was not handed
on and their ancestral tablets (if, as members of the more sceptical
middle classes, they cared about such things) would be looked after

by someone not bearing their name and not looking on them as direct ancestors. To a peasant, however, 'letting the family die out' means something more; it means also that the ancestral land passes into other hands, that the ancestral house is lived in by others and that the family not simply ceases to exist, but also loses the position in the local community which it has traditionally held.

In the old family system the practice of son-in-law adoption and matrilocal marriage always involved a certain conflict of structural principles; the principle of male dominance on the one hand, and on the other of the inferiority of the non-blood-related stranger-member recruited into the closed society of the family group. In the last resort the principle of male dominance generally proved the weaker and such households were proverbially expected to be those in which 'the wife was king' (*kaka-denka*).[122] In one prominent Shitayama-cho household in which the wife, as director of several companies, appeared to eclipse her husband in economic and social activity, gossip had it that the husband was an adopted son-in-law. This was not true, but their relationship obviously fitted the stereotype of the adopted son-in-law marriage. An old proverb says 'do not go to be an adopted son-in-law while you still have three *goo* of rice bran to your name'.[123]

The proportion of adopted son-in-law marriages was declining at least between 1920 and 1930.[124] Declining mortality, particularly infant and child mortality, was doubtless in part responsible in that it reduced the occasion for such adoptions. Increased opportunity for younger sons in industry may also have led to a reduction in the number of candidates for such marriages. The decline may also reflect a decreasing emphasis on the duty of perpetuation of the family, leading to a reduction in the number of offers of such marriages. Probably the dominant factor, however, is the growing divorce of the family from economic productive activity. Son-in-law adoption into a peasant family, or an urban craft or commercial family, meant that the adoptee was offered a secure future as prospective head of the family business in return for his potential loss of male prestige. Adoption into a wage or salary worker's family offers no such prospects, and while male dominance, however attenuated, continues to be a feature of Japanese society, we may expect the practice of son-in-law adoption to decline *pari passu* with the increase in wage employment. More and more families will be allowed to die out, and fewer people will be much perturbed by the fact.

THE WIDER KIN GROUP

In discussing the *kafuu*, the ancestors and perpetuation of the family we have been chiefly concerned with the importance attached to direct continuation of the main family line. Another important aspect of family continuity and inter-generation solidarity lies in the relationship between branch families and the main family. The typical form of such relationships in the village has already been discussed. The grant of land and of a house to a younger son was considered a 'favour' of the main family; it left the branch family in a position of economic dependence on the main family and as long as this economic dependence continued, even after the passage of many generations had made the actual lineage relations between the heads of the two branch families extremely remote, the relation of branch to main family continued to be explicitly recognized in deferential behaviour by members of branch to members of main family, by labour service and reliance on the one hand, and by the assumption of authority and the acceptance of the duty of protection on the other.

The form which these relations still take in old-established commercial families is well illustrated by the following account by a resident of Shitayama-cho of the minor Oosaka *zaibatsu* family to which she belongs.

There hasn't been much change in my family since the war. The power of the main family is still absolute as far as the branch families are concerned. It is still the old sort of master-servant relationship. For instance in the main family, as soon as their elder brother becomes head of the family he is no longer just 'elder brother' to his younger brothers and sisters, he becomes 'the master of the main family', or just 'the master' or 'the chief' and they no longer feel at ease with him. . . . The other day my nephew in the H family finished university. His (widowed) mother took him off to Oosaka to the main family to discuss his future. There all ten branch families were gathered in family council. They eventually decided that he should go into the technical branch of one of the main family's firms at Nagoya. None of the branch families can do a thing without the main family's permission. If a son is ready to enter the university, the main family has to be consulted about which university it should be. University fees are all paid for out of an education fund which all the branch families contribute to. Nowadays the children of the employees of the family's firms can also get money from the fund as well as children of the family. Of course, with marriage it is even stricter. When one family arranged marriage and then asked for the main family's approval *after* everything was fixed they didn't even get a greeting telegram. And at New Year everybody, not only the branch families but the managers in the Tokyo offices too, is expected to go up to Oosaka to pay his respects to the main family.

But families such as this in which the main family still retains its economic stranglehold are now a rarity. A study of the kinship ties of families in Shitayama-cho (ties being defined by virtue of the recognition of another family as the main or the branch family *vis-à-vis* one's own, by statements as to whether or not visiting took place between the two families and whether or not there had been economic assistance rendered or received) suggests, broadly, that as soon as the economic implications of the traditional main-branch family relations cease to hold good, main and branch status are mutually recognized and visiting is continued only so long as there are personal affective links between members of the two families, and the implications of super- and sub-ordination in the traditional main-branch family relationship tend from the very beginning to be very much modified. The stress is now on personal links whereas it was formerly essentially a question of relations between family units. (There is thus, perhaps, a significant relation between this tendency away from the conceptualization of relations as existing between family units to an exclusive emphasis on relations between individuals and the general tendency towards individualization apparent in all spheres of Japanese society.)

In the first generation, when the branch family in Tokyo typically has a main family in the country, the relationship is still a close one. Several young couples who had not long left their husband's parental family found it difficult to conceive of themselves as a separate household complete in itself rather than as a temporarily detached fragment of the parental household. They would say 'Yes' when asked 'Have you an Altar of the Buddhas in your house (*o-taku*)?' and it would appear only later that they were talking of the Altar of the Buddhas in the husband's home in the country. By the time that the branch family has grown children, however, its sense of independent existence is generally fully developed. Visiting may continue. After the death of the husband's parents, the anniversary services on their death-days provide occasions on which the head, and if possible other members of the branch family visit the main family.

But by the time of the second generation of househeads,—when the head of the main family and the head of the branch family are first cousins—relations are already somewhat attenuated. The branch-family head does not make a very special effort to attend the death-day anniversary of his grandfather. By the next generation these ritual links have almost completely disappeared. The individual death-day celebrations for the last common ancestor (the branch househead's great-grandfather) have probably ceased altogether (they are continued only for fifty years after death). The ceremonies for all the family ancestors of the main family are the only ones which have any relevance for the branch family and by this time it already has two generations of ancestors of its own to care for on these 'all souls' feasts.

It is not surprising, therefore, that of all the families in Shitayama-cho which had what they recognized as a main family, in only two cases was the branch family in its third generation; in twenty-nine it was founded by the father of the present househead; and in all the others (110), the branch family was founded in the present generation. There were other families which had not more than two generations of ancestors in the family altar and could not, therefore, be of any great antiquity, but which nevertheless recognized no main family. The rapid attenuation of main-branch family relations was even more marked in the case of branches of Shitayama-cho main families. This is not surprising since the town main family has even less to offer its subordinate branches than the rural main family which has, at least, a solid basic annual income from the land and can provide the basic means of existence and shelter in an emergency. When housewives were asked if they had branch families, the vast majority mentioned were families founded by the sons or the younger brothers of present househeads. In only four cases (out of twenty-five) were families recognized to be branch families which had been founded by an uncle (father's younger brother) of the househead, and in only one case was a branch family of two generations standing mentioned—'a grandfather's younger brother who used to be in Oosaka, though we haven't heard from him for years'.

What this means, in general terms, is that the range of kin recognized by urban Japanese today is now little, if at all, wider than in England. It still remains true, however, that the patrilineal relationships which are maintained tend, where appropriate, to be structured in traditional main-branch family patterns. This is generally true as far as the terminology used is concerned. A mother talking to her children would be likely to refer to the main family as 'the main family' (*honke*) rather than as 'uncle ——'s house' (. . . *oji-san no uchi*) which would be appropriate if she were referring to her own brothers, and she would refer to their paternal cousins as 'the eldest son (etc.) in the main family' (*honke no o-niisan*) rather than by their given names. The status superiority of the main family, which is an integral part of the traditional pattern of main-branch family relations, is not, however, universally accepted. Sometimes it is: 'for instance,' said one man, 'if I were at the main family and my elder brother was smoking Hikari cigarettes (at 40 *yen* for ten) I should have to switch to Shinsei (20 *yen* for ten). It would be presumptuous of me if I didn't.' On the other hand, very many members of new branch families denied, when asking a leading question, that there was any difference between their relations with the husband's eldest brother's family (i.e. the main family) and the families of his other brothers.

It is an obvious hypothesis, though one not clearly demonstrable from Shitayama-cho material, that this recognition of inferiority is related in part to the degree of security or insecurity of the branch family in the town, or the extent to which the branch family has received economic help from the main family when it was established or subsequently. Some examples tend to support this. One younger son of a farm family, when asked if he had a main family said that he had not. He had left home when he was young and had made his own way in the world; he was not indebted to his elder brother for anything and did not consider him as his main family; he had not been home for years and he expected nothing from him. But in an industrial society with only rudimentary social services, such defiant independence is not so easily maintained. In the depressions of the twenties and thirties many precariously established younger sons took their families back to their elder brother's home in the country and main families absorbed a large number of the four million people who flocked out of Tokyo as the air bombardments were intensified at the end of the war. For families for whom the possibility of unemployment or a disabling two years of tuberculosis for the main wage-earner is not a remote one, the main family as a possible source of help and in the last resort shelter, is an important source of psychological security. And this prospect of possible economic dependence can help to maintain the relationships between main and branch families on a traditional footing of subordination and super-ordination.

When the economic tables are turned difficulties may arise. One younger son in Shitayama-cho who had made good and was now the owner of two prosperous bath-houses, admitted that he had an elder brother in the country who could, he supposed, be called the main family. But in name only. 'He is very poor compared with us and it was we, not he, who paid for father's grave'. Moreover, the surviving mother lives in Shitayama-cho, not with the indigent elder brother, and it is to Shitayama-cho that the Altar of the Buddhas and the ancestral tablets have been brought.

Difficulty is caused by the time-lag between changes in economic conditions and changes in ideas. Implicit in the idea of a main family and a branch family in the model of such relations which the people carry in their heads, is the notion of hierarchical ranking. Also, where relations between families have been important elements in the social structure, they have been accompanied by economic relations of dependence. It would be wrong to expect that attentuation of the relations of economic dependence would lead *pari passu* to non-recognition of the hierarchical nature of the relationship. Models do not change so easily. Moreover, in the first generation, the branch family's deference to the main family is no more than a continuation of the attitudes towards father and elder brother which have been instilled since childhood.

There was obviously a functional interdependence between primogeniture inheritance, the nature of main-branch relations, and the birth-order distinctions insisted on in the traditional Japanese family. But the disappearance or weakening of the one does not of itself lead to the abandonment of the others. The traditional precedence given to the eldest son was not solely justified in terms of 'as he is the successor he is destined to be the head of the house'. There was also considered to be something intrinsic in the very nature of seniority which made the eldest son superior to his siblings. And this belief would not be automatically eradicated by the decline in the importance of primogeniture inheritance and economic dependence of younger-son branch families on their elder brothers. What has weakened the force of traditional birth-order distinctions would appear to be, more than anything else, Western egalitarian ideas. In the legal committees of the twenties Minobe Tatsukichi and others argued passionately for the abolition of primogeniture on purely ideological grounds,[125] and this was by no means an isolated phenomenon. One intellectual friend in Tokyo forbids his children to use the traditional honorific terms of address to their elder brothers and sisters and insists that they all address each other equally by their given names. Though egalitarian ideas are not often held so strongly or put so rigorously into practice, their permeation has been deep. Even most rural mothers will now deny to interviewers that they give any special attention to their eldest sons, and in rural areas the functional importance of the eldest son's pre-eminence is little changed. We can perhaps see here, at least, an instance where the influence of ideas in altering the pattern of social relations has been of greater importance than the influence of economic changes, though even here we cannot ignore the possible reinforcing effects of tendencies towards 'universalistic' and 'achievementistic' criteria in other spheres of society—birth-order has had little effect on the private's chance of becoming a corporal, the schoolboy's chance of getting through the middle-school entrance examination or the reporter's chance of becoming assistant editor.

To sum up, then, this discussion of patrilineal kin relationships; the range of kin recognized today is narrow and though the relationships still maintained are, where appropriate, still thought of in main-branch family terms and described in such language, the element of sub- and super-ordination implicit in the traditional relationship is now considerably weakened.

MATRILINEAL AND AFFINAL TIES

According to the old 'family system' a man's relationships of greatest solidarity were with his patrilineal kin. In actual fact, however, the emphasis on patrilineal ties, on the completeness of the transfer of a woman's allegiance by marriage and on the non-concern of the woman's lineage with her children, was never so complete in Japanese society as would seem to be indicated by the codified institutions deriving from China—the early laws defining degrees of relationship (paternal grandparents, second degree; maternal grandparents, fourth degree) and the mourning regulations still current in 1945 (five months for paternal and three for maternal grandparents). Toda, in his work on Japanese kinship terms, points out that although the Japanese have for a milennium used on paper the Chinese kinship terms differentiating maternal from paternal grandparents and uncles, no differentiating terms have ever developed in popular speech.[126] Father's elder brothers, father's younger brothers, mother's brothers, are all *oji* to a Japanese even though, if he were sufficiently learned in these matters, he would write *oji* with different characters according to the precise relation involved. Similarly maternal and paternal grandparents are equally referred to as *ojii-san* and *o-baa-san*. In rural areas, the wife makes regular visits to her parental home, often taking her children with her, and in the case of divorce her, or her lineage's rights, in her children were not entirely negligible, though she was generally permitted to take only the less desirable girl children.

The measurement of the relative strength of patrilineal and matrilineal ties is by no means easy. There are, however, two pieces of relevant information from Shitayamo-cho. First, in answer to a question to housewives: 'Would you say, on the whole, that you saw more of your husband's brothers and sisters or of your brothers and sisters?', of the 176 to whom the question was relevant, 137 said that there was no difference, twenty-four that they saw more of the wife's and fifteen more of the husband's brothers and sisters. Geographical distance and relative size of families are obviously important factors, but assuming that their effects were randomly and independently distributed, the conclusion would seem to be justified that (*a*) there is no special tendency for the visiting relations of a married couple to be exclusively directed towards the husband's family, and (*b*) there is no indication that there is any traditional, normative 'proper answer' to this question.

The second piece of evidence has more substance. It was suggested above that main families were chiefly responsible for absorbing the four million emigrants from Tokyo, and those from the other large cities at the end of the war. The efficiency of the Japanese family system was widely praised on these grounds, just as it was praised before the war for siphoning off the potentially dangerous unemployed and so preventing the development of a rootless and class-conscious proletariat. The elder brother who inherited the family property also inherited the responsibility of supporting his non-inheriting younger brothers in emergencies. And this is, indeed, what often happens.

One finds, however, that of the fifty-two families in Shitayama-cho who, during the war, were evacuated from Tokyo, sixteen went to the husband's main family, but twenty-eight went to the wife's home. There were here, certainly, special circumstances—often the husband was in the army and it was only the wife who went back to mother. But this does not explain the answers to another question in which housewives were asked what they thought they would do if their house was destroyed in a fire. Of 201 housewives who had husbands living with them, 26% said that they would probably go to the husband's main family, and 21% said they would probably go to the wife's home.

From these facts one may conclude, first (and this is a point of current political rather than sociological relevance),[127] that the Japanese family system with its primogeniture and its implicit emphasis on patrilineal ties, was by no means as effective a mechanism of social security as is often suggested. The ties of solidarity in fact brought into play in these crisis situations did not necessarily run along the channels defined by the Japanese family system, but as often as not cut across them. Secondly, that the bias towards patrilineal ties in the old family depended primarily on the practice of patrilocal marriage. The neolocal conjugal family tends automatically to be multilineal. If anything, there is, perhaps, a tendency for the new family to have relations of greatest solidarity with the wife's parental family and with her siblings; a tendency which can be in part ascribed to the nature of the division of labour in Japanese, as in Western, society, to the difference between the expected personalities of men and women in Japanese society and perhaps, to the fact that the girl's psychological development within the family does not require the same sudden wrench in her relation with her mother as does the boy's.[128]

FAMILY, HOUSEHOLD AND INDIVIDUAL

All the evidence presented above tends to the conclusion, which should occasion no surprise, that the notion of the 'transcendental' unity of the family group across the generations is already greatly weakened and that the honour and the interests of 'the family' in this sense has ceased for most people to be a value of any motivating importance. This, however, does not of itself necessarily imply anything which can be called a 'triumph of individualism'.

In a small country town the head of a climbing upper-middle family was entertained to lunch by a definitely upper-upper family. The next day, when his wife (who was not, of course, included in the invitation) met the 19-year-old youngest son of the upper-upper family (who had nothing whatever to do with the invitation), she bowed deeply and used the politest possible form to say 'many thanks for your very kind entertainment yesterday'.

A woman in Shitayama-cho was asked to join a new religious sect of doubtful character by a girl who lived in the ward. She had no interest in the sect and no wish to join, nevertheless she thought she ought to since she had an obligation towards the keepers of a spaghetti restaurant in the ward, particularly strengthened by certain wartime favours they had done her, and 'the spaghetti restaurant's wife's sister is the wife of this girl's brother'. Such a tenuous relationship would not normally have been taken into account had it not been that in this case the two families lived side by side and for obligation purposes could be treated as one unit.

An interviewer sent to interview Mrs. K calls at her house. 'Mrs. K?'—'That's right.' Half-way through the interview (on household management, children, etc.) the interviewer grows gradually aware that some of the answers are inconsistent with the personal data on the face sheet with which he has been supplied. He asks about this. 'Oh, yes. My name is S really; I live here; I'm Mrs. K's sister-in-law. She's had to go out. But it's all the same really you know. I'm sure she'd tell you the same as I, we think alike on everything.'

The point of these examples is to suggest that despite the diminished importance of the transcendental family the identity of the individual can still be deeply merged in the *household* to which he belongs. It is still possible for transactions between individuals to be viewed primarily as transactions between households and for obligations for favours, opinions, as well as status, religious affiliation and politics, to appertain not to the individual but to the family group. Attitudes of 'collectivity-orientation' can still survive in a new form.

A certain merging of the identity of the individual in that of the group is an essential prerequisite for the existence of the group. Group solidarity implies psychological identification on the part of its members. The common statement that in Japan the individual is subordinated to the group makes into a sharp dichotomy what is really a question of degree. When Mr. A in Surbiton buys a rattle for B's baby, it is towards B's household rather than the baby as an individual that the gesture is directed. But the principle would not normally in England be carried to the extent illustrated in the examples above.

Nevertheless, it is perhaps significant that in order to fill out a paucity of illustrative examples from Shitayama-cho I had to fall back on a small country town. The process of individuation is proceeding as the individual's education, employment, recreation and political activity become increasingly divorced from the household, and the number of overlapping groups in which he is involved, each claiming a separate allegiance, increases. The decline in parental authority, with the consideration of which we began this chapter, is only one aspect of this. Today the main stronghold of 'household-orientation' of behaviour is the sphere of neighbour relations within the local ward community, a topic which will merit a separate chapter later on.

11

Husbands and Wives

THE greatest single change in Japanese family institutions lies in the increased importance attached to the emotional relationship between husband and wife, at the expense of the relationship between parents and children which was of overwhelming importance to the traditional family. We have already discussed this in general terms and shown the relative balance of 'traditional' and 'modern' opinion in this matter (see p. 127). It remains to consider in more detail the changes in ideas which have taken place, and to examine some aspects of the footing on which marital relations were actually being maintained in Shitayama-cho.

It was no accident that the previous discussion of the change in the nature of the marital relationship arose from a discussion of household size and composition. For the change in household size and composition is undoubtedly one factor of great importance in bringing about change in the nature of the marriage relationship. In the large family the husband-wife relationship has to be fitted into a large number of other relationships of the same 'personal', face-to-face type. Any excessive intensity of this one relationship would upset the equilibrium of the whole.[129] This functional reason for not giving the husband-wife relation great institutionalized importance and for minimizing the overt display of affection between them disappears in the small conjugal family, and it is, as we saw before, the small conjugal family which is becoming the normal household type, at first by the mere mechanics of branch-family formation and later for various reasons including (circularly) changes in the ideal of the marriage relationship itself.

Not only is the need for restraint removed. In the traditional family there were many roles in which a bride could be successful. She could be a good daughter-in-law, a good sister-in-law, a good house-cleaner, a good rice-planter, a good link with another rich and influential family, an efficient performer of ceremonial duties *vis-à-vis* the ancestors or neighbours, as well as being successful as a source of emotional and sexual satisfaction for her husband—if, indeed, the latter counted for much at all. In the new conjugal family she can

157

still prove her worth as housekeeper, as mother and as maintainer of her husband's prestige, but the number of roles is whittled down. It is natural, then, that as the definition of wifehood becomes more circumscribed the function of providing emotional and sexual satisfaction for the husband should assume greater importance in it.[130]

Along with this we must put the influence of ideas. Here, perhaps, is good support for the theory that a culture always selects its borrowings in the light of its predispositions or its needs. The Western ideals of marriage as the culmination of romantic love, a relationship the *raison d'être* of which lies in the subjective feelings of two equal and independent individuals, might not so easily have found favour had their introduction not coincided with the structural changes outlined above and with the aspirations of a sex whose traditionally submissive role had in other respects undergone some change with universal education and the growth of industry.

There was, as we have seen, considerable class variation in traditional values. One basic assumption, however, was that women are biologically inferior. 'The five diseases of the female mind,' says the Greater Learning for Women, 'are disobedience, anger, slander-ousness, jealousy and lack of intelligence. Seven or eight out of every ten women suffer from these faults. That is why women are inferior to men. In particular lack of intelligence is at the root of these other faults.' Feminine inferiority was, of course, given more marked in-stitutional expression in the upper classes, as also was the strict differentiation of male and female spheres—in the upper samurai class extending to the rigid division of the house into the master's quarters and the women's quarters. Sex was by no means sinful; it was a natural and pleasurable function, in the enjoyment of which, however, women, as part of the self-abnegating role imposed on them by the culture, were necessarily restricted. Chastity was expected of them, but men were permitted great freedom before and outside of marriage. The only form of affection towards women which the re-spectable man would permit himself, however, was the affection of a master for a domestic pet. A 'love' which placed the woman on a footing of equality, much less on the pedestal of European romantic tradition, offended against the canons of masculine superiority. It was an effeminate emotion, for adoration of the superior being and the inability to control emotion were essentially feminine attributes. For the upper classes it was possible further to differentiate the functions of woman *qua* domestic manager and breeder of heirs, and of woman *qua* charming play-thing, in the separate personalities of wife and concubine.

For the peasants and the urban commoners this was impossible. Moreover, economic factors prevented the same rigid division of male and female spheres, and the same extreme emphasis on feminine inferiority. The villages were characterized by freedom of pre-marital sex relations for women as well as for men, and by widespread phallicism often involving institutionalized periodic promiscuity. The novels and the drama of the towns portrayed with sympathy the man in the grip of passion, and the object of his passion (generally, however, a geisha or at least a girl with whom marriage was impossible) was a personality in her own right and not merely a negative plaything.

From the Meiji period until 1945 four separate trends in ideas can be distinguished.

1. A diffusion by deliberate government policy and via the schools and the police, of certain aspects of the samurai code;—the insistence on the rigid division of male and female spheres, involving a taboo on social intercourse between the sexes, and an emphasis on the purity of womanhood, scorn of love as a detraction from masculine dignity, tacit approval of male sexual freedom, but a strict localization of the opportunities for sexual stimulation and enjoyment to brothel or semi-brothel districts whose existence was justified as an essential means of preserving the purity of the home. This entailed the cleaning-up of rural phallicism and ritual promiscuity, and the control of obscene publications.[131] Rigid educational segregation, separate youth clubs, even separate seats in cinemas, were part of the policy. Clandestine meeting with girls other than prostitutes was adequate reason for expulsion from high school; where factory organization made some contact between the sexes necessary, strict watch was enforced and (until the wartime pro-natalist policy brought a change) the man who fell in love with a fellow-employee and tried to marry her was liable to be dismissed. Husbands and wives lived separate social lives; it was a cause of shame to be seen walking together in the street. At one stage during the war police in some districts took it upon themselves to arrest '*abekku*' (from the French *avec*, i.e. couples travelling together) once, by mistake, arresting a professor of an Imperial university travelling with his wife for the impeccable Confucian purpose of visiting his father's grave.[132]

2. Coinciding to some extent with this in its effects, at least on rural customs, was the attempt, again by government policy, to enforce such modifications of traditional morality as were necessary to forestall the criticism and moral disapproval of foreigners, many of whom in the early days of Meiji had reported that Japan was a land of 'nudity, rudity and crudity'. This was of particular importance in the period when it was the over-riding aim of Government policy to secure for Japan the prestige in the West which would earn for her the renunciation of extra-territorial rights. Numerous edicts and city by-laws of the period, forbidding nakedness in the streets or mixed bathing in public bath-houses, specifically state that although 'this is the general

custom and is not so despised among ourselves, in foreign countries this is looked on with great contempt. You should therefore consider it a great shame.' Fukuzawa Yukichi, in an attack on the lewd behaviour of many of his contemporaries, reminds them that with the modern growth in communications, 'sooner or later such conditions in our country will come to the ears of foreigners, exposing us to who knows what attacks and reproaches'.[133] The same sentiment is far from dead. In 1951, when a Tokyo haberdasher filled his shop window with masculine models perpetually removing and replacing their trousers to display the merits of their underwear, the immediate newspaper comment was 'what will foreigners think of us?'

This tendency had its more positive side. In the 'Rokumeikan'—the 'ballroom'—period, when officials sought to impress the foreign diplomatic community by throwing lavish fancy-dress balls, wives came out of their seclusion to dress as Venetian noblewomen, to learn to waltz and to be bowed to by their husbands. Foreigners' parties were an exception to the rule of segregated entertainment which affected a fairly wide section of the middle class (most towns had their missionaries, every high school had its foreign teachers), though defensive tactics were soon developed;—women gathered at one end of the room and men at the other.

3. Deference to the values of foreigners inevitably ran the danger of admitting the intrinsic superiority of those foreign values, particularly at a time when Western industrial and social techniques were being deliberately adopted because no one doubted their superiority. Missionaries, too, had their sincere adherents.

Open concubinage was the first victim. Concubines, regarded as second degree relatives in the early Meiji period, disappeared from the Criminal Code in 1892 and from the Civil Code in 1898. The matter was finally clinched by a judgement of the Supreme Court in 1897. 'Concubinage is a private relation between a man and a woman, and one which offends against the excellent principle of monogamy. It is therefore a relation to which the law cannot lend its recognition, and the status of concubine is one which we cannot recognize as a legitimate status. Hence all contracts in relations involving the status of concubine are null and void and the Court may not countenance their enforcement.'[134]

Strict monogamy, involving a single standard of marital fidelity, became an increasingly accepted ideal, and criticism of licensed prostitution grew. In the Legal Reform Committee of the early twenties, after a fierce debate, in the course of which the sacred symbol of the Imperial House Laws had been invoked by the traditionalists, a draft clause was passed making the wife's permission necessary before a husband could 'recognize' a child by another woman and adopt it into his own family.[135] The attempt was also made to make adultery by the husband a grounds for divorce equally with adultery by the wife. Most of the lawyers agreed that this was desirable, and it was only with the solemn expression of deep crocodile regret that they threw the proposal out as impracticable given the prevailing state of society. The chief upholders of this new morality were middle-class women; a writer who has analysed the middle-class women's-magazine serial novels of the pre-war period notes how consistent they were on this point.[136] The growth of the ideal was largely a manifestation of feminist aspirations: unable to make the outrageous demand of equal freedom for themselves, women contented themselves with demanding equal restriction for men. The Christian terminology of 'purity' and 'soiling' which (male) educators of women had gratefully seized on in their inculcation of feminine chastity, recoiled on its users.

4. Allied with this was a change in attitudes to romantic love. La Rochefoucauld wondered 'combien d'hommes seraient amoureux, s'ils n'avaient jamais entendu parler d'amour'. In translations of Western literature men came increasingly to hear love talked of, and to hear it talked of not as an effeminate sign of weakness, or as an inconvenient complication of the difficult business of getting married, but as a noble emotion, a fulfilment, an enrichment of the personality. Such ideas were most widespread among students and intellectuals, particularly in such periods as the twenties when the tide of samurai traditionalism was beginning to ebb. The result was sometimes the advocacy and practice of a Bohemian free love, but more often these ideas struck deeper at the roots of prevailing morality by combining with the ideal of monogamous marriage, and seeing marriage as the culmination of love, and love as a condition of marriage. A typical expression of these ideas was the series of essays by the poet Kuriyagawa Hakuson which appeared in the Asahi daily paper in 1922 and were later issued as a separate work under the tittle *A Modern View of Love*.[137] The English title of his first essay (*Love is Best*), his references to Romeo and Juliet, Pelleas and Mélisande, and Dante's Beatrice, to Browning, Stendhal, and Schopenhauer, and also to Freud, Havelock Ellis and Marie Stopes, show clearly the source of his inspiration. Such ideas certainly never gained widespread acceptance—the moral fury with which men like Kuriyagawa were attacked showed all the violence and irrationality of the 'authoritarian personality' at its text-book best—but they achieved sufficient strength for it to be impossible for even the sort of guide to marriage which rated a preface from the President of the Patriotic Women's League to ignore them. 'Nowadays,' says one of these 'there are many people who say "Love is the basis of marriage; for a women to marry without love is to allow her purity to be soiled at the hand of a demon." But these are extremely dangerous words. . . . This is not to say that love

has never led to a good marriage. But to make this your object would be utterly reckless.' [138]

The prevailing morality was essentially an officially bolstered one. It is doubtful if there has ever been a totalitarian state with such a didactic flavour as that of pre-war Japan. Not even Victorian England produced such large numbers of moralizers, or gave them such complete control of the police forces, the means of education and the organs of public opinion. The paralysis of government which followed the defeat in 1945 removed the props of the old morality. It did more. The connection between the unique Japaneseness of Japanese family and sex morality, and the unique Japaneseness of Japan's military supremacy, her glorious traditions and her magnificent future destiny, had been too explicitly pointed out by the pre-war moralists for the discrediting of the latter not to have disastrous effects on the former.

The confusion which followed the defeat was catastrophic to the old morality. In some cases it was catastrophic to moral restraint of any kind. For many individuals, indeed, patriotism was so predominantly the centre of their moral emotions, that defeat left them entirely disorientated. Crime of all sorts, exacerbated by famine and shortage, rapidly increased. Prostitution, driven from the licensed quarters, became an expanding industry of the side-streets. The taboos which had maintained sexual segregation broke down, and promiscuity was a frequent result. A new school of literature arose called the 'Literature of the Flesh' (*Nikutai-Bungaku*). It was ordinary pornography with streaks of sadism, but it was an interesting sign of the moral confusion of the times that its exponents could pose as the heralds of a new philosophy which aimed at the liberation of the instinctual human being from the artificial restraint of a feudal morality. [139]

But the pattern of the future began to emerge. As local community pressures regained their strength and a more settled social order reduced the intensity of the immediate struggle for survival and began to hold some promise for the future, the more responsible of pre-war trends began to reassert themselves with a new force derived from the sweeping legal reforms of the Occupation. Co-education was established in schools at all levels. Feminine equality was embodied in election laws, in labour laws and in the Civil Code; while the latter abolished house and househeads, primogeniture and all the other legal supports of traditional 'familism'. Women became Diet members and civil servants. A new female-staffed branch of the Labour Ministry—the Women and Minors' Bureau—made it its business by research, by the organization of Women's Weeks and by public meetings to 'fight feudalism' in workshop and home and, after the Occupation had ended, successfully weathered a campaign to make it the first victim of administrative retrenchment. In 1953, a translation of Simone de Beauvoir's *Le Deuxieme Sexe* was top best-seller for some months in succession.

The swing in public opinion has been unmistakable. Ten years ago, the questions asked in Shitayama-cho concerning living with parents and the choice of a mate (pp. 126, 139) would have produced very different answers. A few quotations from various sources will help to illustrate the change in opinion on the point which chiefly interests us here, the proper nature of husband-wife relations.

In Tokyo, nowadays, (1954) it is an absolute commonplace for husband and wife to be seen out together, and no one would any longer look askance.[140]

In one of his newspaper essays, Takata Tamotsu tells the story of a diplomat who was found dead in mysterious circumstances in the late twenties. One of the reasons which finally persuaded the Court to give a suicide verdict was that a photograph of his dead wife was found in the man's pocket.

I don't suppose it would seem odd to anyone nowadays for a man to carry about with him a photograph of a dead wife whom he had loved. Today it is a commonplace and not in the least peculiar. But at the time this perfectly ordinary action was counted among the causes of the very extraordinary action of suicide. And this only twenty years ago. Was there ever a place where relations between husband and wife have changed as much as they have in Japan?[141]

In 1953, the Asahi carried the following report of the ceremony at which an Oosaka Professor of Psychology was presented with the Asahi prize for research.

'There is one more thing I must say,' the Professor said, and, after thanking the Asahi for the invitation to the ceremony addressed to Professor 'and Mrs.' Kurotsu, he went on, 'For twenty years I have lived a life of research. The laboratory has practically been my home. Until I saw this invitation card it had never occurred to me to question my way of life— that was how things were. But when I came to the words "and Mrs." Kurotsu, I was brought up with a jerk. Looking back over these twenty years—there have been the children, there was the war with all its troubles and all the difficulties of the post-war period. Everything I have left entirely to those around me. When I read those words "and Mrs." I was suddenly overcome. Ah! I do not know what to say. Yes, I . . . I . . .' Dr. Kurotsu suddenly gulped and dropped his eyes. Several times he tried to continue but the words would not come.

Below the platform, Fumiko, his wife (aged 46), who had at first been watching her husband with a very special sort of smile, looked down too. Then, as she raised her eyes filled with tears, her husband looked straight towards her.

The hall was filled with an immense silence. When the audience looked up again it was to see Mrs. Kurotsu, now all smiles again, make room for a weeping husband in the seat next to her—together on their first trip *a deux* in twenty years of married life.[142]

A government-approved text-book, published in 1952 for use in the Social Studies course in secondary schools (ages 12–15) deals with the family. In the author's evolutionary historical presentation monogamy is represented as the product of 'modern civilization' and as such is given all the authority of inevitability and all the associations surrounding the word 'progress'. The following extract will give an idea of the reformist tone of the book.

It cannot be said today that mistresses have entirely disappeared. Nor can it be honestly said that marriages no longer take place in which the wishes of the individuals concerned are ignored. . . . It is our task to build a real, and not simply a formal, system of monogamous marriage. . . . That men and women should be truly equal, that marriage should be guaranteed economic security, that marriage should be free—these are the foundations of a healthy and undistorted system of monogamous marriage. Only on such foundations can the union of two people who truly love one another be assured.[143]

The change in the values now upheld by the organs of mass opinion is obvious, so is the change in the general nature of normative judgements of behaviour among the town population at large. But practice does not change so rapidly. Established patterns of marital relationships are not easily modified. One of today's standing jokes is the liberal intellectual who shouts 'Oi!' to his wife. A newspaper leading article comments:

It is easy enough, today, to get up in meetings and in public places and expound the advantages of democracy. But how do the people who do this behave in matters which affect themselves? What sort of attitude do they take within the home towards their wives and children? Of course, there are exceptions, and particularly among the younger generations in the towns the changes have been immense, but in many cases the sad truth is that these 'democrats' of the market place are the absolute despotic rulers of the home.[144]

On the other hand, although the change in behaviour has not been so sudden as the change in opinion, it has been going on longer. Whereas it now lags somewhat behind opinion, formerly it was some way ahead. Table 19, although the sample is not very large, suggests that as far as concerns the way marriages are made, a change has been under way for a long time. Before going on further to discuss marital relations in Shitayama-cho, it may be useful, by way of elaboration of this table, to discuss the mechanics of getting married.

THE LOVE MARRIAGE AND THE ARRANGED MARRIAGE

The word 'love marriage' as it was used in the question to Shitayama-cho housewives, the results of which are tabulated below, implies that the initiative is taken by the couple themselves, and that their subjective feelings for each other are a prime condition of the match. In most cases in Shitayama-cho, as will be seen from the table, the parents' permission was obtained (a 'good' girl might never allow her parents to know that it was all a put-up job when the go-between appointed by the groom's family came to ask for her hand). In such cases a go-between would then be appointed by agreement between the families to settle the details of the bride's trousseau, the size of the *yuinoo* money gift from the groom's family to the bride's, and the division of the expenses of the wedding feast. Sometimes the same go-between, but often someone else—someone who could stand in a fatherly position to the married pair and perhaps help the husband in his future career (the groom's employer is a frequent and obvious choice)—presided over the wedding ceremony. The presence of such a go-between is an essential for the social recognition of the marriage. A university professor about to be married during the war applied to the local borough office for the special wedding rice-wine ration. In the space provided on the form for name and address of go-between he wrote 'none'. The borough office held that a wedding without a go-between was not a proper wedding and refused to give him his ration until he invented one.[145]

Several couples in Shitayama-cho had, as the table shows, dispensed with such social recognition. 'Individualism by default', to borrow Marion J. Levy's phrase, is often the cause of their unconventional marriages rather than the 'individualism by conviction' of the university professor.[146] Themselves the children of impoverished disintegrated urban families, or single individuals separated from a provincial home, constrained by no bonds of kinship or local community pressure, propertyless and practically rootless, they have no status to lose. The women are often waitresses or members of the 'water-trades', the entertainments industries which supply food, drink and sex in proportions varying with the type of establishment. Six of these marriages in Shitayama-cho started from acquaintances between waitress and customer in a 'Milk Hall', spaghetti restaurant, or 'social tea-house'. Most of these couples lived in the one-room apartment blocks. In many cases they have children, the marriage appears to be stable and is perfectly respectable by Shitayama-cho apartment-block standards. Although the formalities of go-betweens and so on are dispensed with, the marriage may not go entirely unmarked and uncelebrated, a few friends may be called in for a small informal party. Other unions are less stable, never formalized either socially or

Table 19: *Form of Marriage of couples in Shitayama-cho, by Year of Marriage**

Type of marriage		Date of marriage						Totals
		Before 1921	1921–30	1931–40	1941–5	1946–51	Not rptd.	
LOVE MARRIAGE	Not formalized by relatives or go-between	1 }11%	2 }23%	2 }28%	3 }33%	3 }46%	0	11
	Formalized by relatives or go-between	2	12	11	16	13	1	55
ARRANGED MARRIAGE	Preceded by some acquaintance	4 }86%	13 }72%	8 }70%	10 }64%	8 }46%	0	43
	Less than six meetings before marriage	20	31	25	27	8	1	112
Not reported		1	3	1	2	3	13	23
Totals		28 (100%)	61 (100%)	47 (100%)	58 (100%)	35 (100%)	15	244

* The form of the questions was as follows:

How long is it that you have been married?

I'm afraid it's a rather personal question, but was it a 'love marriage' or an 'arranged marriage'?

LOVE

When you had decided to get married did you both tell your parents and ask them to arrange it, or did only one of you tell his parents? Or did you marry without consulting anyone at all?

Who was it who actually arranged the details—your parents or a go-between?

ARRANGED

Was the 'mutual-viewing meeting' the first time you had met?

How long was it from the 'mutual-viewing meeting' to the wedding?

How often did you meet in that time?

legally,[147] and for the woman little more secure than the only likely alternative for someone of her social situation, the position of kept mistress of a married man.

Such a marginal class existed in the Edo of Tokugawa times, and, as was noted on p. 108, shifting, socially unsanctioned unions were common within it. The size of this class, or at least the degree of rootlessness of its members, is not, however, as great as the speed and conditions of industrialization and urban growth might lead one to expect. Unlike the French industrial towns of the nineteenth century where, according to Le Play's description of the 'anomic' state of their proletariat, it was 'patrons not clients who were wanting',[148] there has been no shortage of patrons in Japan. The employer's initiative lies at the origin of a number of arranged marriages in Shitayama-cho.

'Arranged marriage' (*miai-kekkon*) means that the parties were brought together expressly for the purpose of marriage on the initiative of parents, a friend of the family or a go-between. It means also that the initial criteria of selection were objective ones; not only the 'family' considerations which were discussed in previous chapters— questions of status and lineage, of the value to the family of the new connections to be forged, the suitability of the bride as a preserver of family tradition and as a breeder of heirs—but also, and increasingly as 'the family' declines in importance, the personal qualities of the individuals concerned—looks, health, intelligence, the bride's domestic abilities and her accomplishments (a girl's diplomas for the tea ceremony and flower arrangement would invariably be included in the go-between's recital of her virtues),[149] the absence of leprosy or madness in the family's history, the man's earning power and also the suitability of their respective temperaments. In addition there are numerous horoscopic and geomantic considerations which have an important function since they are sufficiently complicated to forbid any match if 'worked to rule' and therefore provided face-saving excuses for breaking off negotiations.[150]

The first suggestion of a match may come from a common friend of the two families or from a go-between whose good offices have been requested. This initial 'bridge-building' (*hashi-kake*) go-between performs essentially the functions of the English marriage bureau, though his services are requited not by a fixed fee but by a suitably large present of money on successful completion of the negotiations. Some people find in the work a rewarding, and even profitable, hobby. Many successful marriages were first conceived in Shitayama-cho by a widow who had a wide acquaintance among students to whom she often let rooms, and a friend who taught in a Girls' High School and visited her periodically with a sheaf of photographs and personal histories of her ex-pupils.

When a marriage is proposed, the first step is for both families to make discreet enquiries in order to substantiate the go-between's recital of the other party's virtues. Always maintain good relations with your neighbours, advises a pre-war guide to marriage, since it is always of your neighbours that the first enquiries will be made.[151] In the impersonalized world of the city special detective agencies (*kooshinjo*) now exist to make the business easier.

The next stage of the process has undergone a considerable change. Within the framework of an arranged marriage, having ascertained that the objective conditions of a good match are fulfilled, the opportunities for the prospective partners to accept or reject the proposed marriage have increased. The development of the custom of holding a *miai*—a 'mutual-viewing meeting'—among the merchants of the Tokugawa period was mentioned earlier. Photography later provided a chance for an initial eliminating process before the *miai* was arranged. Most of the couples in Shitayama-cho whose marriage was arranged were married on the strength of the *miai* without further meeting. Indeed, as some explained, to have met would have been bad manners towards the go-between in whose hands the whole conduct of the negotiations had been placed. Cousins who were known to each other before the marriage was proposed deliberately avoided meeting in order to prevent any embarrassment between the families. But nowadays it is not uncommon for the young couple to be packed off to the cinema together after the *miai*, or even for a period of some weeks or months of courtship to intervene before the intermediaries carry the final verdict. But withdrawal, once a *miai* has been held, requires some strength of mind to resist the pressure of parents and go-between who are convinced of the appropriateness of the match and would find extrication from the negotiations embarrassing—a strength of mind not often to be found in Japanese women. At that stage horoscopic excuses sound somewhat hollow, although no open unpleasantness will ensue provided that the fiction is politely maintained. Refusal after a *miai*, the more so after a *miai* followed by an unchaperoned cinema visit, can be a severe blow to self-esteem. One young man in Shitayama-cho was deeply hurt by such an experience, but blamed it all on his father's meanness in promising him as his *yuinoo* (money gift to the bride's family) a sum which he thought far smaller in proportion to his elder brother's than was justified by his position of second son.

The final decision having been taken, the subsequent steps of the process are identical with those for a 'love marriage'.

THE GO-BETWEEN

The injection into the business of marriage arrangement of the preferences of the individuals concerned—as a necessary and a sufficient condition of a 'love' marriage and increasingly as a necessary condition of an 'arranged' marriage—is having an effect on the functions of the go-between who is rapidly becoming as formal a part of the wedding ceremony as the striped trousers and frock coat which for every middle-school graduate bridegroom is *de rigueur*. Traditionally, the go-between (not the 'bridge-builder' but the one who had handled the delicate negotiations and presided at the wedding ceremony) took some responsibility for the marriage. It was, after all, his handiwork. The couple would continue to visit him at New Year and in the summer; he would make ceremonial god-father-like gifts to their children, and when any trouble arose in the marital relationship it was to him that either of the parties, or preferably their families, took their complaints and their request that he should make the other side see reason. As individual choice, implying individual responsibility, is given more weight, such appeals to the go-between begin to seem inappropriate. For perhaps the majority of couples in Shitayama-cho the go-between still had not lost these functions; most were still keeping in touch, often by regular correspondence, although not many housewives when asked whether they had in the past or would contemplate in the future calling on the go-between's help, gave replies like 'I went to him when I had trouble with my mother-in-law', or 'I would if there was any question of divorce'. There were only fifteen such replies (out of 200) which is not, however, a very reliable index since even in Japan many would hesitate to admit to such facts or possibilities to casual interviewers.

Three times as common, however, were references to economic help from the go-between—loans given, jobs found, business connections made, or worn clothes passed on—and it was clear that the help was reciprocated not only by traditional 'service'—'if there is a marriage or a funeral at his house we all go along to help'—but also by financial help to go-betweens who have fallen on hard times, or to the go-between's children. Indeed, although the go-between's functions as a mediator decline in importance, the patron-client aspect of the relationship loses its importance more gradually, with the only slowly declining strength of such relations in the business, professional, educational and political worlds. Even now, a research student is well advised to get his professor to perform the office, a docker his labour-contractor boss, a young diplomat an Ambassador, or better still a rising Minister or Counsellor whose beneficent influence will continue longer.

THE 'LOVE MARRIAGE' SINCE THE WAR

As emerged from the previous discussion of parents' views on their children's marriage, the 'love marriage' which maximizes the importance of spontaneous individual choice is now the majority ideal in Shitayama-cho. Among the youth of the towns it is an almost universal ideal. This does not mean, however, that the romanticization of marriage has been carried very far. As an analyst of Japanese popular songs notes, golden dreams, blue skies, honeymoons, moonlit kisses and sultry palm beaches are symbols as yet imperfectly assimilated despite some years of education in American musicals.[152] The institutionalized importance of the objective criteria of a good marriage in the old *miai* system has to some extent ensured that these factors are not ignored. Saikaku's seventeenth-century dictum that marriage is 'a commercial transaction that only comes once in a lifetime'[153] might still meet with agreement today. Women, in particular, are well aware that given the present constitution of society marriage is for them a means of livelihood. When asked to enumerate the desirable qualities in a husband 21% of factory girls and 27% of non-working girls mention 'earning capacity' first.[154]

There is another factor of importance. Despite the acceptance of the love-marriage ideal, there are no established patterns of courtship. Before the war opportunities for meeting members of the opposite sex were extremely limited. Of forty-one Shitayama-cho love marriages most developed from acquaintanceships struck up at work, between neighbours or with the relative of a friend of the same sex. The only exceptions were the six waitresses previously mentioned, one acquaintance which sprang from a 'comforts letter' to the troops during the war, one started in a railway train after many months of travelling the same line to work, and two which began at youth meetings. Since the war, institutionalized segregation of the sexes has perforce broken down under the pressure of co-education, and even in the villages joint youth clubs are now common. But although group mixing is now accepted, unchaperoned pairing off is still disapproved, particularly in middle-class society. A public-opinion-survey sample 85% of whom saw nothing wrong in husbands and wives going out together, contained only 16% who thought it was all right for a young man and a young woman to walk the streets arm in arm.[155] Moreover, there are no established patterns of behaviour in such relationships and embarrassment and frustration mixed with a sense of guilt is a frequent result. The new co-educated generation will doubtless find it much easier to manage its calf-loves and its flirtations but many now in their middle and late twenties are acutely conscious of, to use the terminology of Merton's definition of *anomie*, the absence of 'socially structured avenues . . . for realizing culturally pre-scribed aspirations'.[156] The solution of one university research assistant is interesting. He resigned himself to an arranged marriage, but went to his *miai* somewhat drunk on the grounds that it was giving the girl a fair chance by showing her the worst she could expect.

In accepting the old, he nevertheless made a gesture of his ideological solidarity with the new.

One may note, in passing, that in Shitayama-cho both for men and for women 'love' marriages are more common among the younger (as one would expect from Table 19) and among the better educated. For both men and women, however, the younger are also the better educated. Partial correlation does not yield significant results with this size of sample, but it would appear that educational level has little independent relation with the form of marriage; the only group within which there might be a tendency for those with high school education to contract 'love, marriages more frequently than those of the same age but of lower educational attainment is among men in their thirties.[157]

HUSBANDS AND WIVES IN SHITAYAMA-CHO

The increased importance attached to subjective sentiment as a condition for entering marriage is part and parcel of changes noted earlier in ideals of the marital relationship. It is now time to offer what evidence there is of the nature of husband–wife relations in Shitayama-cho. That there was great variety was obvious. The persistence of traditional attitudes was made clear at the start of the survey. In the first meeting with ward leaders at which plans for the survey were discussed I was warned by one of them that interviewers should take care to call only when the husband was at home. 'Otherwise you will never get the truth about Japan. Of course, nowadays we have feminine equality and I'm beginning by now to get used to the idea that my wife has the right to go out and vote. But the old ideas are still there and I should think a lot of women wouldn't have any opinions of their own and wouldn't know about the things you want to find out. Even if they did know, they wouldn't be sure if it was all right to tell you. . . .' (The advice was ignored, but the warning may be pertinent to the evaluation of interview replies.) That some men might have additional reasons for such a warning, other than a solicitous desire to ensure the accuracy of the survey, was apparent from some of the interviewers' experiences. There was, for instance, the woman who complained that 'Japanese men are tyrants. A wife isn't allowed to do anything or to have any interests without her husband's permission. I was fond of going to flower and tea classes, but one evening I got held up and it was ten o'clock before I got back. My husband was furious and for about six months he wouldn't let me go anywhere at all.' There was the mother who explained that she brought her girls up to understand that 'Men are beasts. If you grow up not to expect too much out of life you will be all right. Husbands are creatures who say that black is white, and all the wife has to do is listen in silence and say "Yes, I see." ' There was the wife asked whether birthdays were celebrated in her household who said that they were, but added as the most natural thing in the world 'but only my husband's of course'. There were others who told interviewers who went enquiring for their husbands that he had not come home the previous night and as they had no idea where he might be they could not say when he would be back.

Equally there was plenty of evidence on the other side. The women who saw as the greatest improvement in the housewife's lot over the past generation the fact that 'husbands are more co-operative' or 'husbands and wives now do the worrying together' have already been mentioned. (pp. 82–3). The gentle twigging by one young man of another on the grounds that he was an *aisaika*—in love with his wife—was certainly far from received as an insult or a reflection on a man's masculinity. There were husbands who did the washing-up and consented to be trailed on shopping expeditions, husbands who never went out to enjoy themselves without their wives; wives who expected to receive their husband's pay packet intact—and got it.

More systematically the attempt is made below to consider Shitayama-cho marriages, by means of necessarily somewhat superficial indices, in the light of three dimensions.
1. The extent of the wife's autonomous direction of domestic matters defined as a feminine preserve.
2. The extent to which the wife maintains her own personal social and economic relationships outside the home as an individual on an equal footing with her husband.
3. The extent to which there is a merging of personality and interests, a sharing of leisure activities and of domestic and social responsibilities.

1. *Domestic Autonomy*

The control by the wife of the domestic economy—at least the consumption side of it—varied greatly as between classes and districts, as was noted before. In samurai families it was considerable and in the new urban middle classes it, for obvious reasons (the separation of the husband's employment from the home), became more so. The security and the satisfaction from the exercise of power which this provided was for many women adequate compensation for the lack of any emotional satisfaction from their relationship with their husband. It often gave them a quiet dignity, a certain confident self-sufficiency and inner serenity. The professor's wife in the post-war novel *Jiyuu-gakkoo* is well observed. She is telling her niece about her own marriage. Her husband, having been made Faculty dean, had become insufferably pompous, both inside and outside the home. One morning she reaches the limits of tolerance and attempts to quarrel with him. But he ignores her and begins to shave. She goes on:

I used always to soap his face for him when he shaved, but that morning I just sat there fuming and watched him. He tried to look dignified and began scraping away. Stretching his neck, pinching his nose, pulling the skin, making pop-eyes, pouting . . . Have you ever watched a man shaving? It is fantastic the faces they pull. Suddenly as I sat there I burst out laughing. It wasn't so much the funny faces he was making; all of a sudden it occurred to me what comic creatures men are. Their silliness, their gullibility, their unreliability, their childish boasting, their vanity, and on top of that their stinginess and pettiness and their fondness for you know what . . . Ever since that day, whatever Haneda did it didn't seem to make me so angry. I even came to see a certain quaint charm in him.[158]

Most Shitayama-cho wives, too, had a secure basis for developing the same good-natured contempt for husbands who deserved it. In most cases their control over family expenditure was fairly complete. In no case, for instance, did any of the earning children in the ward hand over their wages to their father rather than to their mother. The replies to questions concerning what happened to the husband's wages were even more revealing. Seventy-eight wives (45% of all wage-earners' wives asked) said that they received the whole of their husband's wages and doled out their husband's pocket money. These results may represent some exaggeration of the truth—some housewives may have wanted to claim an authority which they did not in fact possess—but the frequent circumstantial details of how much the husband was given every morning as luncheon money or tobacco money were too convincing to leave any doubt that this is what often happens. In the other households the wife generally had a fixed housekeeping allowance either with or without the possibility of claiming more from her husband. In only seven (4%) households did the wife have to apply for money to her husband every time it was necessary. It was fairly common for wives to receive the whole of their husband's wages, but not his 'side-earnings' of various sorts which remained his own. Some wives had no idea of what their husband's total income might be, but gave no indication that they thought this anything other than a proper state of affairs. 'Of course, I've got a good idea how much he spends; I know the number of times a month he goes out to parties and I've a shrewd idea how much they cost, but I would never dream of asking him outright. He might start worrying about the housekeeping and he ought not to be worried.' The possession of private undeclared funds by the husband permits him the private pleasures of male drinking parties and the like. This is nowadays more predominantly a part of white-collar than manual-worker culture (though well within the traditions of the old working

class—the Edo artisan). It is not surprising, therefore, to find that
the wife receives the whole of her husband's wages significantly more
frequently in households of lower than in those of higher economic
status. Provincial-born husbands are also significantly more likely
to hand over their wages than those born in Tokyo or Yokohama.

2. *Relations Outside the Home*

Three indices bearing on the second dimension—the extent to
which the wife maintains economic and social relations outside the
home on a footing of equality with her husband—were; whether the
wife claimed any property of her own, whether the wife sent New
Year cards in her own name to her own friends, and whether the
wife had her own friends home to meals.

Only forty-six wives (23%) claimed to have any property, ten of
them house property, ten of them 'all that I brought with me when I
was married', and seventeen some form of savings. There are two
quite separate factors involved here, however. Modern notions of
feminine equality may be one. Another is the tradition of rural
society. Divorce (which was frequent) permitted the wife's family to
reclaim all the trousseau—the clothes, chest of drawers, cupboards,
etc.—which the bride had taken with her. That the latter factor may
be dominant here is suggested by the fact that there is a noticeable
tendency for provincial-born wives to claim to have property more
often than those born in Tokyo and Yokohama.[159]

New Year cards were sent in their own name to their own personal
friends by sixty-seven wives (34%). In 33% of households all were
sent in the husband's name. In 20% some were sent jointly in the
name of both husband and wife. Here the wife's educational level
has some importance. High-School graduates are very significantly
more likely to send New Year cards than graduates of lower schools.
A noticeably higher frequency of New Year card sending among the
higher economic groups also supports the assumption that this is a
predominantly middle-class characteristic. It is slightly more frequent
among younger wives.

The replies to the questions concerning visitors who were invited
to meals in the home are best dealt with by a table. It will be seen that
only about half as many wives had friends in to meals as husbands.
We shall return to the small number of 'equally friends of both of us'
replies in the next section.

As indices of the third dimension—the extent to which there is
a merging of personality and interests, and a sharing of leisure
activities and of domestic and social responsibilities—there is first
of all the answer 'both of us' to the question: 'Who decides on the
amount of the "condolence money" gift?' (The gift made to neighbours when a death occurs in their family, the appropriate amount

Table 20: Friends invited to Meals in the Home, Shitayama-cho

Reply	Number (%)
All visitors are equally friends of both husband and wife	6 (3)
Both husband and wife have friends to meals	52 (26)
Only the husband has friends to meals	59 (29)
Only the wife has friends to meals	8 (4)
The only visitors are relatives	22 (11)
No visitors ever come to meals	33 (17)
Not reported	20 (10)
Total	200 (100)

of which is a tricky thing to decide.) This answer (from 38% of housewives) comes significantly more frequently from the younger and not quite noticeably more frequently from the provincial born rather than from those born in Tokyo or Yokohama.

Secondly, questions were asked concerning the extent to which the husband helped with housework. Here is a case in which traditionally, in middle and upper class families at least, the differentiation of spheres was rigid, and for the husband to help in the home was as much a serious reflection on the wife's competence as it was on the husband's masculinity. One woman said that when she first came to live in their apartment block she had not fully recovered from an attack of pleurisy some two years before. Her husband used therefore to help her in the weekly communal cleaning. She discovered, however, that this was leading to a good deal of talk behind her back to the effect that she was lazy or that it was a household where 'the wife wore the trousers' (*kaka-denka*). This made her so unhappy that she had to ask her husband to stop helping her.

However, according to housewives' reports, in only 32% of Shitayama-cho households (including 1% with domestic servants) did the husband never help. In another 24% he was said to be capable of turning to in an emergency but normally left everything to his wife. Regular help by husbands was often confined to spreading and rolling up the bed mattresses, others helped in cleaning and cooking, but only 3% ever helped with washing clothes. ('Minding the children' —the most common of male domestic activities—was entirely excluded to improve comparability.) Younger husbands help more frequently (to a noticeable extent) than older husbands, and clerical and managerial workers more than manual workers.

The small number of 'equally friends of both of us' replies shown in Table 20 is another indication that in sociable and leisure activities husband and wife traditionally moved in different spheres. Ruth Benedict's thesis that for the male, life was divided into the mutually exclusive 'circles' of 'duty' and 'human feelings' is a good characterization of traditional attitudes. The family belonged to the former sphere; male friendships, usually involving alcoholic conviviality and hired feminine entertainment, belonged to the latter; and the two spheres were not allowed to overlap. The husband might do formal 'duty' entertaining at his home, in which case his wife played the self-effacing role of waiting on the men at table (herself getting the left-overs in the kitchen afterwards) and speaking when she was spoken to. But boon companions would be entertained not in the home, but in a geisha house, at the house of a mistress, in a restaurant, brothel or potato-wine bar according to economic resources. As, with changing views of marriage, the home tends increasingly to become a centre of the man's interests and emotional life as well as a means of performing his duty, it becomes more common for the husband to entertain his own friends at home.

THE EXPLANATION OF DIFFERENCES

Before going on to consider one or two other aspects of this third, or 'merging' dimension, it will be useful to summarize what has been said above concerning the relations between these various indices and other characteristics, such as age, education, birth-place and economic status of the husbands and wives concerned. Table 21 lists the independence values of the various associations discernible, in terms of the probability that the association could be due to chance. It will be seen that it is only deciding together about 'condolence money' which shows a significant correlation with age. This suggests, what one might indeed expect, that the long-term trend of change in marital relationships is a change in the third of these dimensions. This is the only case where differences between households in Shitayama-cho easily lend themselves to interpretations in terms of 'old' and 'new' (and even here the explanation could be not that the younger generation manifests new characteristics which it will carry with it, but that the differences are characteristic of different phases of the marital relationship). Many of these differences are likely to be due, not to changes in progress, but to personality differences, or to established and continuing class differences.

It has been suggested that change along the 'merging and sharing' dimension is related to the increasing importance attached to love as a condition of marriage, but it will be seen from Table 21 that although the relation between the form of marriage of Shitayama-cho couples and these indices shows the same consistent tendency (i.e. the wives of 'love' marriages are more likely to send their own New

Table 21: Factors Associated with Indices[160] of Marital Relations*

	Dimension 1		Dimension 2			Dimension 3		
	Husband hands over wages	Wife has own property	Wife sends own New Year cards	Wife has own visitors	Husband has own visitors	Husband helps with household chores	Condolence money jointly decided
Wife is younger rather than older	+·3<p<·5	+·3<p<·5	+·3<p<·5	+·2<p<·3	—	0	+·02<p<·05
Wife is better rather than less well educated	0	0	+·001<p<·01	0	—	0	0
Wife is born in Tokyo or Yokohama rather than provinces	0	−·1<p<·2	0	0	—	0	−·2<p<·3
Husband is younger rather than older	0	—	—	—	+·2<p<·3	+·1<p<·2	+·02<p<·05
Husband is better rather than less well educated	0	—	—	—	+·5<p<·7	+·5<p<·7	+·05<p<·1
Husband is born in Tokyo or Yokohama rather than provinces	−·02<p<·05	—	—	—	0	+·3<p<·5	0
Couple are recently—rather than long—married	+·3<p<·5	+·3<p<·5	+·3<p<·5	0	+·1<p<·2	0	+·05<p<·1
Household is of higher rather than lower economic status	+·02<p<·05	0	+·05<p<·1	−·3<p<·5	0	0	0
Couple were married 'for love' rather than by arrangement	+·1<p<·2	+·5<p<·7	+·05<p<·1	0	+·02<p<·05	+·1<p<·2	+·2<p<·3

* + indicates a positive, and − an inverse association. 0 indicates that no association is discernible. For p, see note on p. 9. For economic status index, see Appendix I.

Year cards, have their husband's visitors to the house, get help from their husbands in housework, have more complete control over the husband's wages and say that 'condolence money' amounts are decided jointly), the association is only a weak one. This suggests the qualification that the 'love' insisted on for the 'love' marriage is not necessarily a love between equals implying equal regard for the wishes of both partners and the sharing of responsibilities and interests which is the Western romantic ideal. It can be no more than an assertion by the man of the right of individual choice of the woman who shall be his bondmaid. A love marriage is not a precondition for greater sharing of interests and responsibilities; this trend affects the relations of couples married by arrangement too.

SEX AND MONOGAMY

It might be expected that the new role of love in marriage and the tendency towards greater sharing of responsibilities and pleasures between husband and wife would have an effect also on sexual relations in marriage. Something more nearly approaching the Marie Stopes ideal of 'married love' might be expected to replace the idea that sexual enjoyment is the husband's prerogative, to be indulged by the wife on the same level as her indulgence of his needs for food and warmth (as implied by the professor's wife in the novel quoted above), or alternatively the more specifically upper-class definition of marital sex relations primarily in terms of breeding heirs, with the concomitant expectation that the husband seeks emotional and physical satisfaction in relations outside marriage.[161]

Fuufu-seikatsu—the word translated 'married life'—is one commonly heard and has primarily sexual connotations. Taboos on the discussion of sex have always been much weaker in Japan than in Christian countries, and the removal since the war of police controls on the publication of works which discuss sex in the context of a romantic view of marriage has led to a great increase in their number. Stopes and van der Velde sell in large quantities, and they have many Japanese imitators. Such general notions as that the nature of a couple's sex relations have an important determining influence on their adjustment to one another in all other respects, seem to be widely diffused. Newspaper reporters interviewing famous divorcees regularly ask if they were dissatisfied with their sex life and, if they fail to get serious answers, invent them or substitute speculation, for the public expects such information. It seems also to be an accepted axiom that all marriages go through a 'fed-up period' (the *kentaiki*)—generally around the seventh year—and that this is something to be consciously anticipated and provided against. The Japan *Woman's News*, in inviting essays from its readers, suggested

as one of five topics 'How I prevented a crisis in marital relations in
"the fed-up period" '.[162]

There has also been a great increase since the war in the publication
of pornographic magazines and books, some of which deliberately
cash in on the boom in well-intentioned scientific works on sex in
marriage. One monthly magazine, for instance, is called *Fuufu-
seikatsu*, but its articles on Fifty Arts of the Bedchamber, and
Virginity Old and New, leave no doubt of their pornographic intention. Although this particular magazine was taken regularly by one
couple in Shitayama-cho, literature of this sort is produced primarily
for the male market. Long-distance trains generally arrive at their
destination littered with such *ero-zasshi* ('erotic' magazines) which
travelling business men buy to console the tedium of their journey
but hesitate to take to their homes. It is significant that one sociologist whose post-war activities have been dedicated to the extirpation
of feudalism and repression, particularly in the sphere of the family,
and who generally welcomes all weakening of traditional restraints,
concludes a recent book by expressing concern at the hedonistic
tendencies which provide such a ready market for such commercial
sexual stimulation. In what he calls the 'oversexualization' of contemporary Japanese culture he sees signs of a decadence which
prompts him to invoke the parallel of the declining Roman Empire.[163]

While it is true that this 'hedonistic' tendency is leading on the
one hand to a reduction of moral restraints on sex relations before
marriage, in particular among young isolated individuals of the
cities,[164] there is a solid countervailing tendency in 'respectable'
society towards a strengthening of the ideal of monogamous fidelity
within marriage. It may be worth considering in detail the replies
given by a sample of a hundred in Shitayama-cho to the following
questions:

Do you think it is all right for a married man to have a mistress?

No—74 Yes—20 Don't Know—6

But supposing the man looked after his wife properly and wasn't a
particularly bad husband to her, would you still object to it?

Still objectionable—60 Then permissible—14

Implicit in the reasons and qualifications offered from both points
of view in answer to this question is the assumption of three different
motives which might prompt a man to keep a mistress.

1. As a luxury indulgence.
2. As a means of seeking sexual or emotional satisfaction not fully
   obtainable in marriage.
3. As a means of begetting children.

The replies showed that it was the first type of situation which the
question immediately suggested to most people and it may be

assumed that it was this which was being accepted by the majority of the twenty immediate and the fourteen reluctant approvers. According to one woman, 'It's all right provided a man can afford it. I'm not one to worry much about these matters. It wouldn't matter to me in the least if my husband did it.' Other women, however, while not being aware of any moral objections, thought themselves entitled to have emotional ones. 'I don't see any objection to it, or at least, I don't mind saying so now when I know my husband couldn't afford it, but if it actually happened I'm sure I shouldn't feel so happy about it.' As several, on both sides of the fence, agreed, 'Women tend to be monopolistic about men.'

'Higamous Hogamous, Woman is monogamous, Hogamous Higamous, Man is polygamous', dreamt the philosopher, and he would hardly have been hailed for the originality of his perception in Japan. It is sometimes on the basis of such a view of the nature of the man that the question is approached. 'I suppose you have to overlook these things,' said one woman, 'provided a man doesn't ruin himself.' Though a sign of weakness, it is a venial sin and, as the frequent qualifications of the 'provided he can afford it' type indicate, much less reprehensible than failure to keep these indulgences within the limits appropriate to status and means.

By the same token, this form of indulgence can, in certain business circles, become almost an essential means of conspicuous consumption whereby a man demonstrates what his status and his means are. Business associates can be better entertained at the house of a mistress, particularly if, as is frequently the case, the mistress is a geisha or is set up with her own little restaurant or tea-house. There is, however, something which smacks of the sententious in this reply from a 33-year-old man: 'To a certain extent it is necessary for a man's work, but he should always remember that his life is based on his home and he should always get his wife's permission first.'

Others consider a mistress permissible only on one of the other two grounds listed above—when a man is unable to find adequate sexual or emotional gratification in marriage, or for the purpose of begetting children.

The latter receives only two mentions; one man considers it the sole justification, another is more doubtful, explicitly says 'monogamy is best', but thinks a mistress preferable to the alternative expedient of adoption. The other reason is mentioned with greater frequency—'It is wrong except where a husband does his best for his wife and she fails to satisfy him in return.' 'If a man cannot find satisfaction in the home, then I suppose it can't be helped.' 'It is wrong unless a man's wife is ill or something.' The assumption seems to be that no man can be expected to abstain from seeking other means of sexual gratification if he fails to find it in his home. This may apply equally when his failure to find adequate satisfaction can legitimately be blamed on the wife's remissness, or is simply due to the wife's illness. 'We aren't made of wood and stone' said a young printer whose wife had tuberculosis, talking in another context about his visits to brothels.

Several add, from this point of view, that it is up to the wife; it is a test of her powers to keep her man. As the conception of a mistress as a legitimate piece of extra self-indulgence is replaced by the conception of a mistress as a remedy for a dissatisfied home life, so it becomes harder for a wife to accept the situation with equanimity. One woman in Shitayama-cho whose husband kept a mistress was noticeably nervous in the company of other women, and it was remarked that this change dated from the time of her husband's defection and she was very much to be pitied.

The majority of those who condemn the keeping of a mistress made it clear that their objection was a moral one. One man disapproved on the grounds that it destroyed the 'fine virtues' of the 'Japanese family system', though, as we have seen, the moralists of the Japanese family system have been somewhat ambiguous on this issue. Most, however, base their condemnation on the newer ideals of monogamous marriage, implying exclusive sexual rights for both partners and trust and confidence between them. The dreaming philosopher is explicitly repudiated: 'It is impossible for a man to love two women at once.' From which one man drew the conclusion that if a man did love someone other than his wife 'he should do things properly and get a divorce'. Another clearly rejected the double standard with the words, 'If my wife had a lover, I know how I'd feel.'

The sample was too small for significant analysis, but as it stands the distribution of replies by both sex and age is fairly even.

Here again a caveat must be entered against assuming too readily that these replies can be interpreted in the context of a traditional-modern dichotomy. This sample was the same one as received the questions on p. 126 presenting a choice between maintaining good relations with the mother or good relations with the wife. The latter questions immediately preceded those on keeping a mistress. It was expected that those who took a 'traditional' view on the first question (i.e. evaluated the relation with the mother as the more important) would take a 'traditional' view on the second (i.e. show tolerance of keeping a mistress). In fact, however, the tendency of association (though a weak one—·2<p<·3) is in the opposite direction. If this association is not due to chance and would reach a higher level in a wider sample, the explanation might be that the relevant distinction is not between 'traditional' ideas which give little importance to love between husband and wife, and 'modern' ideas which give it great importance, but between what one might call a 'hedonistic' attitude and 'moral' attitude. That is, the hedonist might see the satisfactions of his relation with his wife as more important than fulfilling his duties to his parents, and the satisfactions of his relations with his mistress as not to be foregone in deference to his duties to his wife.

DIVORCE

The increasing importance placed on subjective factors in the definition of the husband–wife relation cannot fail to affect the nature and frequency of divorce. It is not only that the functions of the family are whittled down in reality, as was suggested at the beginning of this chapter. Of those which remain to it attention is increasingly directed to the emotional satisfactions of the marital relation itself, to the exclusion of the family's economic or child-rearing functions. As the whole *raison d'être* of marriage is increasingly seen as the fulfilment of love, so the absence of love becomes sufficient grounds for divorce. We have already quoted the opinion that a man who loves someone else more than his wife, should 'do things properly' and get a divorce. A newspaper writer commenting on the divorce of a member of the Japanese Royal Family reveals the same attitude when he remarks that Prince K in letting things slide and continuing the marriage after it became obvious that he and his wife were not suited to each other showed that he 'was lacking in a serious attitude towards his own and his wife's human nature'.[165]

This is familiar ground; familiar also is the increase in divorce rates which it implies. It is a process, however, which has only just begun in Japan. From the beginning of statistical records to 1945, Japan was the only country in the world in which the divorce rate showed a steady and continued decline—from 1·4 per thousand in 1901 to about ·6 per thousand at the beginning of the war.[166] (Compared with an American increase from ·7 in 1900 to 4·3 in 1946.) During all this period divorce was possible by the simple act of registering consent. To complete the reversal of the Western pattern, in 1930 the divorce rate was lower in towns with more than 50,000 population than in agricultural districts.[167]

The probable reasons for this decline lie in later marriage, a more 'responsible' attitude to marriage with the growth in education and the diffusion of new standards of respectability, and the effect of the whole complex of changes summed up in the words 'improved status of women' on the traditional form of divorce, which amounted in fact to dismissal by the groom's family of a bride whom they found unsatisfactory.

Since the war, which has brought no legal changes except in the grounds for judicial divorce—which in any case accounts for only a small fraction of the total number of divorces[168]—the divorce rate has risen from the pre-war ·6 per thousand to a figure very close to 1·0 per thousand for each of the five years 1947–51.[169] The new 'Western' trend towards increased divorce would seem to be beginning to assert itself—and for the same reasons as in the West.

Nevertheless, it is still only beginning. More 'realistic' conceptions of marriage still play a large part at least in feminine attitudes to marriage and divorce. We have already quoted the factory girl's concern to get a man 'with earning capacity' for a husband. For women marriage is still a means of livelihood. The writer of a personal advice column in the newspaper, for instance, answers a woman with children whose husband is persistently and flagrantly unfaithful with a sympathetic denunciation of faithless husbands who 'do not realize that equality of the sexes means equal recognition of the personality of each partner in marriage'. But she concludes by advising the woman that with three children divorce might be the greater evil and her best course is to try to win back her husband with extra attentions.[170]

Japanese feminists in their discussions of divorce are often concerned to point out that the equality which the law prescribes is a hollow mockery given the biological arrangement of reproduction and the existing economic and educational ordering of society which make it difficult for a woman to acquire a skill, or having acquired a skill to get a job, or having got a job to earn a living wage. Many divorces 'by consent' are no more than the discarding by a selfish husband of a defenceless and dependent wife who is as yet unused to the idea that women in Japanese society have any rights to assert.[171] Many feel that the remedy lies in making divorce by consent conditional on the approval of a Family Tribunal.

EXPECTED PERSONALITIES

The nature of the traditional expected personalities of men and women in Japanese society obviously bore an intimate relation to the expected relations of dominance and submission between husband and wife. With change in the latter one can expect change also in the former. Contrariwise, unless there is change in the former it is impossible for change in the latter to be complete. It may be worth considering here in some detail the answers from a sample of a hundred to the questions, 'What sort of man (woman) do you admire most?'

The great diversity of expressions used in describing the ideal man shows that there is no accepted stereotyped form of words which springs readily to the tongue. The replies are not, however, devoid of pattern. Although each mentions only one or two or at the most four traits of character which they most admire, it is possible, by relating these to the hero type of popular films and novels,[172] to the type of individual who acquires power and prestige in national and community life, and to the sort of evaluative judgements of character which are made in everyday life, to build up a composite picture of the admired type to which most of the answers may be deemed to be partial references.

Thus the ideal man is the leader type, the 'manly' man, one who has suffered, a man of courage and endurance, strong-willed, quick, decisive and forceful in situations where lesser men would hesitate out of scupulous regard for detail, frank in the expression of his opinion without excessive regard for etiquette or convention, disdainful of underhand scheming, direct in the expression of his emotions, a good loser, generously lacking in petty resentments, but ready to avenge insult whenever it is proffered, capable of deep passions but able to conquer them if necessary, a loyal friend, ready to act on the promptings of the heart, as a leader of men ready to give his life for his subordinates and chivalrous in his protection of the weak. In all, over half the respondents mention one or other of these traits and a just significantly greater number of such replies come from men than from women.

There is a tendency for women to favour what one might build up into a secondary pattern as the 'safe-and-sound' type—the man who is faithful, loyal and sincere (11 respondents), who is punctilious in his personal relations (6), a man of integrity (1), a man of just dealings (2), thoughtful (1), a hard worker (6), a steady reliable man (3), to which should perhaps be added the 'serious-minded man' mentioned by nine women and no men. This word (*majime na*) is the one recurring most frequently in these replies. It means specifically a man who does not spend his time and money on women and drink, particularly women—an eminently reasonable preference from the wife's point of view.

Two other groups of answers which do not fit into either of the above categories are gaiety and cheerfulness (7), and kindliness and consideration for others. It is noticeable that of the twelve people who mention this latter trait, ten are women.

The pattern of admired feminine types emerges more clearly than the masculine, which is perhaps an illustration of a general tendency for the lower statuses in any society to be more clearly defined than the higher. It is, for one thing, generally those who occupy the higher statuses who do the defining. Moreover, the greater the restriction of choice which any role entails, the easier becomes its concrete definition and, perhaps, the greater the need for defining and enforcing it. Thus, in the writings of the Tokugawa moralists—Kaibara

Ekken of the seventeenth century, for instance, or Nakamura Tekisai of the eighteenth—we get a very clear picture of what they expect of women, but a much vaguer picture of the ideal masculine character. The same is true of the ethics text-books on which the present generation was nurtured.

The essential qualities of womanhood stressed by Confucian moralists were especially those of loyal obedience and service, and it is these qualities which predominate in the replies. Twenty-six people out of a hundred used words such as 'quiet', 'reserved', 'obedient', 'submissive', 'loyal', 'modest', 'quiet-mannered', 'open and trusting' (*otonashii, juujun, ninjuu, chuujitsu, kenjo, odayaka, sunao*). Eight mentioned 'gracefulness' (*shitoyaka*). Ten stressed the qualities of the ideal servant—'noticing' things (anticipating the wants of others), consideration, a woman who can look after people, gives of her best for others, devotes herself to her home and her children. Eighteen used the word *yasashii* which has a wide range of meaning; graceful, gentle, tender, affectionate, qualities which hospitalized males in our society are expected to find epitomized in young nurses. Other traits mentioned which fit into this picture are lack of vanity, non-extravagance, lack of affectation, being a hard worker, not being 'brainy', gaining the trust of neighbours. Each received one mention.

This does not, however, entirely complete the picture. Just as the heroine of the *kabuki* plays, for all her grace and submissive loyalty, nevertheless carries a short dagger in her bosom and is prepared to use it with grim determination (though most probably on herself) whenever the honour of her family or the life of her lord is at stake, so we find that eleven of those who mention one or several of the above characteristics add, 'but on the other hand . . .' or 'but combined with this . . .' a certain strength, spirit, solid reliability, a hard core, something positive about her, no weakling. The 'but' is always there; the contrast is always pointed.

It is presumably this type of personality to which the six people who used the word 'womanly' were referring. These qualities are the specific differentiating characteristics of the female sex. (In fact, only eight people used entirely the same terms and only nine others partially the same terms in describing both their ideal woman and their ideal man, though it must be remembered that the nature of the questions perhaps suggested that a contrast was expected.) It is interesting to notice the suggestion here (as in the case of the 'Japanese family system') that such a pattern of feminine character is peculiar to Japan and (together, one suspects, with the *kimono*, the tea ceremony, the cherry trees and Mount Fuji) to be counted one of her chief glories. Five people, all men, in introducing one or other of the above traits said 'a really Japanese type of . . .' or 'a real

Japanese woman'. One even used the phrase *Yamato nadeshiko*
which has about the same ring and if used in earnest would arouse
about the same titter in sophisticated circles as 'a true English rose',
with the difference that the *nadeshiko* or fringed pink, is more slender,
more pale and more modestly retiring than most roses. The belief
that the Japanese woman was a unique and superior product was
put forward explicitly by one man who quoted as evidence his
experiences of the women of other parts of Asia during the war. There
is an aphorism which the Japanese man of the world can rarely resist
the temptation offered by the presence of a foreigner at a party to
quote; it is to the effect that a man's physical wants are most adequately catered for by living in a Western-style house with a Japanese
wife who can do Chinese cooking.

This ideal of what I shall call the Confucian pattern seems to be
shared equally by both men and women. The only significant difference concerns the use of the word *yasashii* which women use more
than men (fourteen to four). The reason may possibly be that the
term implies a certain protectiveness, a positive tenderness springing
from individual initiative, a role in which women like to picture
themselves but which is hardly consistent with the subordination and
the negative virtues of willing obedience which figure most prominently in the man's estimation of the ideal woman.

To that extent it might be doubted whether *yasashii* really belongs
to the Confucian pattern or whether it is really part of another quality
referred to by other respondents in such terms as 'a capacity for love',
'depth' or 'delicacy' of feeling. (*Aijoo-yutaka, joo-bukai, joo ga
komakai, ninjoo ga aru.*) One might point the distinction between the
Confucian pattern proper and this emphasis on a loving nature in
terms of Ruth Benedict's thesis that for the Japanese all social action
falls into one of two mutually exclusive spheres, that of duty and that
of 'human feeling'. ('Human feeling' is, indeed, a translation of one
of these words, *ninjoo.*) Alternatively, and less abstractly, the Confucian pattern might be considered to belong to the samurai sub-
culture and the warmly-feeling woman to the urban plebeian sub-
culture of the Tokugawa period. The difference in heroine types is
quite clear in the *kabuki* drama. The heroines of the *buke-mono*—
the dramas of intrigue and battle set mostly in the Kamakura and
Muromachi periods—belong to the Confucian pattern. Rarely do
they display emotional attachment towards a man. The 'human
feeling' which is allowed is almost entirely confined to their love for
their children which, however, often serves only as a counterpoint
to their duty of loyalty to lord or husband to which it often has to
be subordinated. (The nurse who delivers up her own child to assas-
sins who are searching for the heir of her master.) In the *choonin-
mono*, however,—dramas which reflect the culture of the town classes

of Edo and Oosaka during the Tokugawa period—the wife of the merchant or artisan typically shows much greater freedom and independence of action and is allowed to express feelings of love and jealousy vividly and forcefully.

But although the Confucian pattern predominates in these replies, there is, nevertheless, a feeling that it rather belongs to the past. Two people spoke of the 'old type' of Japanese woman. But though in decline the old norms are far from displaced, and those whose replies deviate from the above patterns frequently feel the need of explicitly pointing out, or even of justifying, their deviation. Thus one woman of 24 says 'I dislike the old "good-wife-and-wise-mother" type', and another, 'I like someone who is not dependent on a man.' 'I don't like *even* women to be indirect and roundabout in their speech,' said one man, and another, 'It used not to be the thing for women to work, but as soon as I married my wife I set her to work. I treat her as an equal.' (This particular man may be making the best of a bad job. He was the man previously mentioned who was so eclipsed by his wife in their business and social activities that he was falsely rumoured to be an adopted son-in-law.) There is too, a note of defiant overstatement in the replies of two young women who deviate from the traditional patterns. One used the word *jajauma* —'I like a woman to be a bit of a virago' and the other, 'a woman who speaks her mind, even to the point of being cheeky'.

The other character traits mentioned by the deviants are those which appeared as characteristics of the ideal man. *Sappari shita*— someone who is simple and direct, does not fuss or cry over spilt milk, *hakkiri shita*—someone who speaks her own mind, makes her intention clear and sticks to it, *hakihaki shita, tekipaki shita*—a sharp, bustling, managing type. Finally there are various odd remarks such as 'someone with enough manliness about her to stand up for herself', 'someone with as much ability as a man', a 'thoughtful person', a 'solidly reliable person'. Altogether there are nineteen such replies. All of the eleven women who give them are under 35 (highly significant difference) and of the eight men, five are under 25. For the rest, ten were unable or unwilling to give replies, and seventy-one gave answers falling within the traditional pattern.

CONCLUSION

If the picture given above is one of confusion, it has done no more than reflect the confusion in normative ideals which exist in Tokyo today. There is not only the fumbling, experimentation and uncertainty which inevitably characterizes human relations in growing cities, cities which lack the established patterns of response to stock situations of the small local community and lack also the group pressures which give training in these responses, secure their enforce-ment and afford the individual the security which comes from the expectation of his group's approval. To all this is added the sudden subversion of an official morality which was formerly inculcated at high pressure, the sudden release of tendencies which had been undermining the official morality for decades, and the sudden in-flux of Western ideas which in themselves present a confusion of ideals ranging from extreme individualistic hedonism at one end, to Catholic insistence on the indissolubility of the marriage sacrament and the predominantly procreative function of sex on the other. It is not surprising that the Don't Know group should be large for all questions in opinion-surveys about the family. Journalists, scholars and publicists of various sorts have exerted the whole weight of their influence to the destruction of 'feudalism' in the family, a preoccu-pation which has prevented very careful consideration of the prob-lems of the new non-feudal family which is emerging. The ideal of marriage as the fulfilment of the mutual love of two independent and equal personalities is generally accepted, but how this ideal is to be fitted into the structure of the new conjugal family with its existing economic and child-rearing functions, is a question which has received scant attention. It will probably continue to be largely disregarded as long as the battle against the 'remnants of feudalism' has still to be won, particularly in rural areas. But the rise in the divorce rate and the increase in juvenile delinquency suggests that the problems of the next stage are beginning to raise their head in the cities, and that the concern over family disintegration familiar to Western societies will increasingly occupy attention in the future.

Section IV

THE WIDER WORLD

12

Getting on

'JAPAN'S confidence in hierarchy', wrote Ruth Benedict in *The Chrysanthemum and the Sword*, 'is basic in her whole notion of man's relation to his fellow man and of man's relation to the State. . . . The hierarchical arrangements of Japanese life have been as drastic in relations between the classes as they have been in the family. In all her national history Japan has been a strong class and caste society.' Again, later, remarking that the Japanese scorn the *nouveau riche* who has no 'hierarchical right' to his wealth, she comments, 'Japan provided a place in her hierarchy for great wealth and kept an alliance with it; when wealth is achieved in the field outside, Japanese public opinion is bitter against it.' [173]

In a review of her book, one of Japan's foremost historians has this to say:

I was born in a little village in West Japan in the year of the promulgation of the Japanese Constitution (1889) and I spent my childhood there. To me then, not only the Tokugawa period, even the Meiji Restoration itself seemed to belong to the distant past. . . . From that time until my present sixtieth year I have rarely come across what the author calls 'Japan's confidence in hierarchy'. My grandfather, born in 1830, certainly had that confidence. But my father and the men of his generation were no longer men content to take their 'appropriate position in the hierarchy'. Although, by force of circumstances, my father did stay in his 'position', it was not for want of attempts to get out of it. And for the young men of my generation—and this in the village and in the small country town—it was taken for granted that all strove to get out of their 'position' and climb to the greatest heights. . . . A translation of Theodore Roosevelt's *The Strenuous Life* had a great vogue, and we middle-school students burnt the midnight oil with a book of extracts from the original English. There was a magazine called *Success* which sold a good many copies in the nearby country town. . . . [174]

The criticism is not necessarily damaging to Ruth Benedict's main thesis. The tendency to insist on rigid hierarchical distinctions of authority and prestige between the positions in any existing social organization, does not necessarily imply that these positions are filled by the criteria of birth and class affiliation and that the opportunities for reaching the higher positions are unequally distributed among the population at large. It is one thing to insist that sergeants should unfailingly obey captains; another to insist that only those born in upper-class families have the right to become captains. Ruth Benedict is most concerned to stress the former aspect, and although she does point out that in the Japanese army, for instance, strict criteria of ability rather than birth determined promotion, she remains ambiguous in her assessment of the extent to which opportunities for the individual to improve his class-position existed in pre-war Japan, and of the extent to which 'getting on in the world' was considered a legitimate aspiration, or when accomplished a laudable achievement. Tokugawa society, the society of Professor Watsuji's grandfather, certainly had confidence in hierarchy. It depended for its stability on the observance of birth-determined status distinctions and birth-determined relations of lord and vassal. The 'each-in-his-proper-station' ideal was explicit and practically unquestioned. But for all that, Tokugawa Japan had its mechanisms of upward social mobility. Even if they were limited forms of social capillary action rather than broad avenues of advancement, they nevertheless existed. One of these, the amassing of wealth in trade, has received considerable attention from historians. By the end of the Tokugawa period wealthy merchants were able, in increasing numbers, by adoption or by outright purchase of rank to infiltrate the samurai class. 'Getting on' was always an accepted part of the ethic of the merchants of the Tokugawa period. Saikaku's *Muna-zanyoo* and *Eitaigura* were written, at the end of the seventeenth century, to tell them how to do it. At that time the merchants' was a closed society with sufficient self-confidence to oppose its own values to those of the samurai. Saikaku's remark that 'the merchant who is content to live off the wealth inherited from his father (i.e. without increasing it) is *no better than* the samurai living on the rice stipend he gets with his ancestral tablets' [175] is a typical expression of that—perhaps compensatory— self-confidence. By the end of the period the richer merchants were able not merely to gain the satisfactions of power and prestige within their own world which enabled them to affect to despise the values of those beyond the frontiers, but also to go further, to sally beyond the frontiers and penetrate the world of the samurai itself.

The second means of rising in the world has received less attention but it was equally important in laying the foundation for later developments. Success was also possible through intellectual training. The priests and scholars of the Tokugawa period formed an intermediate class which did not fit into the theoretical division of society into samurai, peasants, artisans and merchants, or the main practical division into the samurai and the rest. The Buddhist Churches, like the Church of medieval England, provided opportunities for the poor scholar to achieve some eminence.[176] Fukuzawa Yukichi, one of the most influential intellectual leaders of the Meiji enlightenment, undoubtedly got some of his drive from his ambitious but impoverished and frustrated lower-samurai father. It was the latter's original intention to put Yukichi into the priesthood for he had heard of instances of even the sons of fishmongers becoming abbots.[177]

But the Buddhist Churches were of lesser importance in this respect than the secular Chinese, or later Dutch, learning. It was possible for lower samurai, and even for merchants and peasants of sufficiently outstanding ability, to become the favourite Confucian lecturer of a feudal lord with a taste for learning, and so gain an assured place with a stipend in the fief school. If such a man turned his intellectual ability and mastery of verbal symbols to practical rather than academic and philosophical ends, he might become the lord's commercial manager, his doctor, his adviser on agricultural technology, or gunnery, or mining, or simply political intrigue. In its upper reaches the hierarchical rigour of Tokugawa society was modified by an element of competition in the conspicuous display demanded by the social whirl of the feudal capital at Edo. This gave the feudal lord a strong incentive to exact the maximum material wealth from his fief, and as a consequence a high premium was placed on the ability of his fief administrators, even sometimes at the cost of setting aside traditional emphasis on birth-determined status. Opportunities for such advancement were, of course, greatest for the lower grades of the samurai class for whom the fief schools provided the necessary education and for whom the social barriers to be crossed were not so formidable. But such opportunities were not entirely absent for the commoners of the towns who had their own private schools, and in some go-ahead fiefs education was provided by the fief authorities to selected commoner children.[178] The moralists of the period did not approve of study for the purpose of personal advancement. For them moral perfection and the training necessary to fulfil the duties implied by one's inherited status were the only legitimate ends. But the fact that they were moved to inveigh against 'study for fame and profit' is proof that Tokugawa society afforded such possibilities and rewarded such efforts.[179]

These two channels of social mobility—the individualist's route via commercial or industrial skill and the dependent employee's route via advancement within a bureaucratic organization—were both greatly expanded in the Meiji era. And of the two it was the latter which received the sanction and even the encouragement of government authority.

The leaders of the Meiji Restoration were for the most part men who themselves had risen by sole virtue of their ability from the lower grades of the samurai class to positions of power within their own fiefs and eventually in the nation at large. They had no vested interest in the existence of the feudal hierachy as it stood; on the contrary their own power could only be assured by destroying a system which decentralized authority and allocated it on the basis of hereditary status, a criterion which could be used to deny their own legitimacy.

They were thus most immediately concerned to dismantle the class structure from the top. But they did not stop there. Their reforms showed what was, in the context of the times, a sweeping egalitarianism. For all their humble origin, they were nevertheless samurai and as such they might have been expected to show some desire to preserve some of the institutional supports of the traditional superiority of the samurai as a class. But such legal privileges as lingered through the first decade seem to have been reluctant concessions to conservative opinion among the rank-and-file samurai; the leaders themselves, and certainly the propagandists of the enlightenment who took it upon themselves to expound the new national policy to the people, seem to have believed that the basic aim of their policy—to strengthen the country by modernization—required that talent from every stratum of society be sought out and set to the task of absorbing the new learning and the new techniques. The first moves of the new Government in the field of education betrayed a traditional class bias—it was envisaged that the old distinction between the more academic fief schools for the samurai and the practical three-Rs schools for commoners would be perpetuated.[180] But the edict of 1872 outlining the school system of the future no longer contained any traces of this idea. A unified non-discriminatory school system was established and has persisted to the present day with, at the primary and secondary level, only a very limited development of private-school alternatives.

The new compulsory-education system which was thus launched in the seventies, and which by the end of the century was catering for some 95% of the children of the appropriate ages,[181] was not, then, like the contemporary English system, imbued with the atmosphere of 'charitable relief, disciplining of the poor, and education in elementary hygiene'.[182] It catered for the children of the samurai as well as for the lower orders. Its goals were positive and reformist. Belief in human perfectibility has never, perhaps, held such sway as in Japan in the early days of Meiji. The new education was the means by which everyone could theoretically gain the means of self-improvement, and by improving himself improve the nation. And, although status considerations in the early period and economic considerations throughout the whole period prevented the poorer peasants from taking advantage of the higher reaches of the educational system, as far as the overt intentions of the central Government were concerned, 'everyone' included commoners too. One of the propagandists of the enlightenment, in *A Country Dialogue on Civilization*, tells his sceptical peasant, 'In human society (*ningen nakama*) all men, from prince and minister at the top to peasant and merchant at the bottom, are human beings of equal worth. A prince, for all he is a prince, is not by virtue of his position born with three eyes; a commoner does not have one ear less than other people just because he is a commoner. Stripped to the skin, what is the difference between the feudal baron's daughter and the kitchen maid, except that one is white-skinned and the other tanned in the sun? The only distinction of worth among human beings is between those who, having learning and ability, are useful to society, and those who are not.' Everyone, he goes on, both men and women in all walks of life, need reading, writing and arithmetic. Everyone, therefore, should attend the elementary schools. 'Thereafter, everyone should study the speciality of his own choice in order to prepare himself for his livelihood'—politics, law, military affairs, etc.—'according to his aptitude and aspirations (*seishitsu nozomi*). . . . Those who do not enter schools for the study of such specialities continue the industry of their forefathers.' [183]

Risshin Shusse 'rising in the world', was a legitimate and even a laudable aspiration in the Meiji period. Smiles' *Self Help*, was one of the first books to be translated into Japanese, in 1871, three years after the Restoration and thirty years before Professor Watsuji and his school friends wrestled with Theodore Roosevelt in the original. Ambition found explicit sanction in the framework of traditional morality from two points of view. The first is apparent in the *Dialogue* quoted above—'getting on' was a matter of giving one's best to the State in the position in which one was best fitted to serve the State. The second, again legitimizing ambition in the framework of a 'collectivity-oriented' rather than a 'self-oriented' morality, was the justification in terms of bringing honour and wealth to the 'family of the ancestors'. Or more immediately of achieving the wealth which would make it possible to repay all the favours (the *on*) of one's parents by assuring them of comfortable old age. The strength of this drive as a real motivating force and not simply as a rationalization is apparent in some of the success stories. Boys sent to study in Tokyo on the meagre hard-earned surplus of a frugal peasant household economy never dare to tell their parents that they have 'let them down' by failures in examinations, and plod on year after year, working in their spare time, until they at last succeed.

But although the motive of personal ambition with the aim of personal enjoyment of prestige and wealth and power was not so often given explicit approval, it was given institutional support. In the Tokugawa period status and wealth appertained to the family not to the individual. When Ogyuu Sorai, who started life, so the legend goes, as an impoverished scholar, living on the scraps from his bean-curd-manufacturing landlord's tubs, rose to the position of adviser to the most powerful feudal lord in the land, it was a hereditary stipend and a hereditary seating position at the lord's levees which were granted him. But status in the Meiji bureaucracy or army, or even in the growing bureaucratic organizations of industrial firms belonged to the individual not to his family. And legal steps were early taken to permit the individual to enjoy personally not only the status, but also the wealth which his efforts achieved. By 1877 it was already legal for individuals other than househeads to become the titular holders of government bonds,[184] and the Civil Code of 1890 instituted a thorough-going system of individual property rights which remained intact in the later revised code. Critics of the law who attacked these provisions as a fatal blow to the sacred institution of the solidary family were met with the argument that individual property rights were necessary as an encouragement to individual enterprise, and the encouragement of individual enterprise was necessary to the State.[185]

That it was considered laudable during the Meiji period to strive to get on is unquestioned, that large numbers did so strive is equally unquestioned, nor do the biographies of the time leave any doubt that some succeeded, but just how many is a question which must await detailed studies of the social origins of the elites of the first decades of this century. There can be no doubt that, particularly at the beginning of the period, the prestige of samurai ancestry and the cultural traditions of the samurai family, as well as the access of capital when feudal stipends were commuted into government bonds, were all important factors favouring the chances of those of samurai stock.[186]

The prestige and cultural tradition factors were of special importance in the early period because of the particularistic nature of the avenues of advancement. Before the routes of entry into the bureaucracy and the armed services became fully formalized, the only sure route to success—granted the requisite ability—was by securing a powerful patron. The story of one poor boy's successful climb to fame was told by his surviving sister who lived near Shitayama-cho. He was the eldest son of a doctor, but defied his father's insistence that he should follow him in his practice, ran away to Tokyo and presented himself at the house of Itoo, the most powerful of the surviving Restoration leaders. His sole link was that they were born in the same fief, but in those days fief solidarity was a force of some importance. Itoo took the lad into his house as one of his many *shosei*—student secretaries, employed as copyists, for secretarial work and for errand-running of all sorts, in return for which they were bedded, boarded, given time to study and allowed to learn the practical conduct of affairs by hovering in the milieu of the great man. This particular boy had the talent to make the most of his opportunities and responded with unfailing loyalty to Itoo's patronage (*hikitate*, the word used, means etymologically 'pulling up on one's feet'). He eventually achieved a post in Itoo's last short-lived Cabinet. This *shosei* apprenticeship system was responsible for many successful careers in the bureaucratic, political, literary, academic and other professional worlds.[187] But it is doubtful if any but the sons of samurai, or at least the headman class of peasants, were able to form such essential links.

In addition to the expansion of this channel of upward mobility—the dependent employee's route—the Meiji period also offered greater opportunities for advancement by the other route of the Tokugawa period—via industrial or commercial entrepreneurship. Here again, with the Government controlling so much of the country's capital investment, and frequently taking the initiative in starting new industries which it afterwards sold out to private individuals, patronage was of the greatest importance, and although it was to some extent selective patronage in the sense that it operated in favour of those who had some ability, it was also selective in the sense that fellow samurai or already established wealthy merchants were the most likely to be favoured by Government officials. But outside of this sphere of government initiative and protection there was, particularly in the light industries, the whole shadow-world of small-time business enterprise where individual initiative counted. Shitayama-cho's second richest inhabitant, the owner of a glassworks employing some fifty workers, was very proud of his career. His father was one of those samurai who failed to adjust to the new Meiji world. He had eked out a precarious rentier's living from the Government bonds received in commutation of his feudal stipend and had no occupation. He considered himself a failure, but he was insistent that his sons at least should go out into the world, earn their own living and restore the family's fortunes. The eldest was sent to the Middle School, but the second, my informant, was sent to Tokyo at the age of 13 and through an uncle's good offices got a job with a glass manufacturer. Working hours were from 7 a.m to 9 p.m. His request for time off to attend night school was at first refused until the uncle again intervened. He was then freed from 5 to 9 p.m. every night, but on the understanding that he worked from 9 until midnight delivering glass whenever necessary. He lived in and received pocket-money wages at first of some 40 *sen* (contemporarily, *c.* 1912 = 9d.) on each of his two monthly holidays, the 1st and the 15th of every month. The first world war came and a great demand for clinical thermometers. Only three small firms in Tokyo had the secret of making the constriction at the base. His own firm's thermometers always broke off at this point. At night he secretly got out of bed and experimented with a gas burner behind a curtain. At last he succeeded, but instead of giving his secret to his employer he contacted a chemist who put up the capital and employed him as chief technician at a princely salary. Thereafter he never looked back. When permit and licensing regulations drove them out of the thermometer business he had enough savings to join his brother in starting a firm of their own. Thus, he said, he had 'restored the family's fortunes' (*uchi wo okoshita*).

Risshin-shusse, 'getting on in the world', like *Bummei-kaika*, 'Civilization and Enlightenment', was one of the catch-phrases of the Meiji period. Both slogans stood as symbols of a bold determination to reverse the traditional order of society in the interests of rational human improvement. But by the beginning of the twentieth century the climate of opinion had changed. Those who moulded the official morality began to place less importance on the encouragement of individual enterprise and ambition.

For this there was an obvious reason. After the great shake-up of the early days of Meiji a new settled class system had developed with new vested interests. The new officials, the new industrialists, established and sure of their own power, had no strong motive to insist that ability was the sole justification for the possession of wealth or power. Moreover, the drive to strengthen the nation by the mobilization of all talent began to have less urgency as Japan's international position became established. The ethics text-books of the schools began to lay greater stress on the duty of service to the Emperor and the State. It is interesting, for instance, to compare the 1918–30 edition of the Elementary School text-books with the 1905–6 edition for Upper Elementary Schools.[188] The story of Hideyoshi, the peasant's son who became the late sixteenth-century dictator appears in both, but in the later edition the title is changed from the earlier *Mi wo tateyo* ('Raise yourself'—the Japanese equivalent of the Chinese word *Risshin* as in *Risshin-shusse*) to *Kokorozashi wo tateyo* ('Make endeavours') with its lesser emphasis on personal success; the story is shortened and much greater emphasis is placed on Hideyoshi's devoted respect for the Emperor. The sections on Hard Work and Honesty (in the earlier volume the latter had the title *Honesty is the Key to Success*) in the later volume extol these virtues as ends in themselves without a final sentence pointing out that they are a prerequisite for *risshin* or for *shusse*. The problem of the early twentieth-century governments, faced with the first stirrings of class-consciousness among the industrial workers, was not to ensure adequate mobility between classes but to ensure the coexistent 'harmony of the classes'—a concern clearly apparent in the educationalists' memorandum quoted on p. 118.

The changing emphasis in the official morality was not immediately reflected in a change in the values of the population at large; the official morality did not, in any case, change so far as to condemn ambitious striving. In the early thirties, candidates for the High School entrance examination still invariably read Smiles' *Self Help* since it was well known as one of the examiner's favourite sources for unseen English translation pieces. But there had, by this time, been a change in the opportunities for 'getting on'. With the growth in educational institutions the routes of entry into the professions had become formalized. It was no longer enough for a bright boy to come to Tokyo from the provinces, attach himself, like the doctor's son, to a prominent politician or bureaucrat and work his way by loyal service and spare-time study into a place in the official class. It was no longer possible to become a doctor or a lawyer after a decade's apprenticeship with an established practitioner. It was now necessary to pass, through selective entrance examinations, into Middle School, High School and University and emerge at the age of twenty-four with a qualifying degree. Entry into the bureaucracy was almost the exclusive prerogative of graduates from the Law department of Tokyo Imperial University. Moreover, the big industrial corporations, the newspapers, insurance companies and department stores increasingly recruited their managerial staff direct from the universities and by the nineteen-twenties most big firms ran their own entrance examinations for new graduates. The chances of promotion to managerial rank within the firm were greatly decreased as a consequence. Educational qualification become all-important, and although the competitive examinations for entry into State schools were strictly fair, public maintenance grants for poor students were few in number and small in amount. Hence the opportunities for achieving these qualifications were limited to those whose parents could afford to support them, or at least—for many students worked their way through the university—to forego their potential earnings until they were 24.

The growing demand for education led to the foundation of large numbers of private universities which catered for middle-class children unable to pass the entrance examination to the Imperial Universities. Some of these were of very inferior quality,[189] but the great growth in their numbers led eventually to an over-production of work-seeking graduates. 'What chance is there today', writes the author of the *Story of the Salary-man* in 1928, 'of getting back all the capital poured into school and university fees? All these parents down in the country who expect their son to walk into a provincial governorship or a directorship with Mitsui as soon as he leaves the university are going to be somewhat surprised when they at last get the letter announcing that he has got a job as a tram-conductor or a policeman.'[190] With the expansion of the economy in the thirties, the situation was somewhat eased .(though, as we shall see, the same conditions are now being reproduced in the fifties).

Meanwhile the other route of upward mobility—via independent industrial or commercial enterprise—offered fluctuating opportunities; widening in times of economic prosperity, contracting in times of depression, but with an overall secular trend for such opportunities to diminish as the hold of the large corporations on the economy was strengthened. The typical small industrial entrepreneur was a maker of parts, dependent on one of the big combines. Fortunes were made, however, though Ruth Benedict is probably right in suggesting that the industrial *nouveau riche* was not as easily accorded social recognition as the man who won his position via educational qualifications and promotion within the ranks of a salaried bureaucratic organization.

These, then, are some of the factors which must be taken into account in considering the values and aspirations of the citizens of Shitayama-cho—a high official evaluation of ambitious striving in the Meiji period catalysing tendencies already present in the status society of Tokugawa times, a soft-pedalling of this motif in the twentieth century as a new capitalist class system solidified, as the routes of entry into the elite classes became formalized in a way which put a greater premium on parental wealth, and as the opportunities to make good in industry declined.

Two questions intended to test general attitudes to personal ambition were asked in the course of an interview on religious attitudes and general value outlook. They were as follows:

1. Some people say that for everybody there is a proper way of life, for the farmer there is the farmer's way of life, for the aristocrat the aristocrat's way of life; everyone ought to live the life appropriate to his position (*bun-soo-oo na seikatsu*) and not expect anything more. Other people say, on the other hand, that nobody is born with a 'position' ('status'—*mibun*) or with a proper way of life, and everyone, according to his ability, should put forward his best efforts to get on in the world (*shusse*). What do you think?

   Should be content with position—10   Don't Know—6
   Should strive to get on—83

The second question came some twenty minutes later in the same interview.

2. Which of these two do you think is the most to be admired. The son of a blacksmith who works steadily all his life at his smithy and dies a blacksmith, or the son of a blacksmith who gives up the family craft, starts a business and ends as the owner of a big company?

   The Blacksmith—12   Don't Know—17
   The Company Owner—70

Although there may be some doubts about the validity of these questions as a measure of the attitudes they were intended to test,[191] there seems little doubt where the general weight of opinion lies. It is interesting, however, to note the qualifications and justifications which were offered in response to the further questions 'Why do you think so?' which followed each of the above. Some clearly reflect the values of the *Country Dialogue on Civilization*, i.e. not personal ambition but service is the only legitimate motive. 'One should take the course which most benefits the national society (*kokka-shakai*). If a man's talents are such that he could best continue to be a farmer, then he should be a farmer. But if a higher position would give better scope to his abilities, then he should be in a higher position.' There is further the view that the truly worthy aim is personal development, realization of one's full potentialities: 'One should not strive simply to 'get on'—that is wrong—but it is the duty of modern man to develop his talents as fully and as freely as possible.' Thirdly there is the view that hard work is the greatest virtue, the loyal performance of duty in whatever station of life one finds one-self—'even a rickshaw-puller can become the finest rickshaw-puller in the world'.

Although such qualifications—clearly reflecting the teaching of Elementary School ethics courses—were not infrequent, straight-forward approbation of 'getting on' was more common, in one case justified in family terms—'Of course everyone should try to get on; it's not only he himself who benefits, but his family as well'. (The word used was *ikka* which can only mean the wider, and not the conjugal, family.) Only a very few gave the typical Tokugawa answer in terms of the *honshoku* (proper occupation) or *tenshoku* (Heaven-sent occupation).

Cynical disillusionment was expressed in these replies but rarely. Some may be considered to reflect the individual's own frustrated experience, but only one reply saw the source of frustrations in the present constitution of society. 'One should strive to get on, but in the world as it is you can't get far on effort alone, can you? You must have connections, too.'

Another question, asked of a different sample (of 103) during the political-attitudes questionnaire, is relevant here.

In the world today some people get on and make a name for them-selves, some people remain poor all their lives. What do you think is the biggest factor making for success? Is it ability? Or education? Or having wealthy parents? Or having good connections? Or being lucky? Or just cunning? Which of these do you think counts for most?

Again the number disposed to question the justice of society was not very large. Only twenty-one said that parental wealth, good con-nections or cunning were the most important, whereas fifty-one thought that ability counted for most. (Five education, fifteen luck, the remainder didn't know.) Emphasis on ability came as often from the declared supporters of the Socialist and Communist Parties as from supporters of one of the conservative parties (though a larger sample might have revealed some differences).

Is Japan, then, the land of business opportunity, in which ability and effort will inevitably find its reward? The disruption of the economy at the end of the war, and the real success of many of the 'new *Yen*' class who seized the opportunities open to those able to manipulate the black or the grey markets in raw materials and in finished goods, may well have been a recent stimulus to such a view. Certainly, whatever may be the truth about the hold of monopoly capitalism on the heavy industries, the proportion of small businesses in the light industries is still very high, and although the death rate of such small businesses is high too, fortunes are nonetheless made. In the retail trades the independent retailer is still the norm. Department stores take over an increasing amount of the trade in durable goods in the large cities, but the chain store is practically unknown.

In Tokyo (and perhaps even more in Osaka which is reported to have one company for every twenty inhabitants and where it is said that to enter a restaurant wearing a collar and tie is generally sufficient to get oneself addressed as *shachoo-san*—Mr. Director[192]) the self-employed worker forms a sufficiently high proportion of the population for it to be his, rather than the white-collar worker's preference for security in obscurity, which constitutes the dominant ideology. This at least would seem to be the case in Shitayama-cho. A haphazard collection of forty-two male employees below managerial rank were asked in an interview which they thought best; to be a wage or salary earner, to be an independent trader, or to be an independent craftsman or service worker. Only eleven (including one who confessed to a miserable failure as a rice merchant) were satisfied with the wage-earner's life. Of the eighteen who thought it better to be a trader and the twelve who preferred the independent craftsman's lot (one not reported), thirteen said in reply to a further question that they had concrete ambitions which they hoped one day to fulfil, the rest had only vague and uncertain hopes.

The way in which the 'entrepreneurial spirit' pervades the atmosphere of some homes is perhaps best illustrated by the following essay of an 11-year-old girl in the local Ikegami Primary School on the subject *My Hopes for the Future*.

When I have left the Primary School I shall study for another six years at Middle and High School. Then I shall start learning dress-making. I shall study it for all I am worth, thinking of nothing but dress-making. To be a proper dress-maker is really something. If possible I want to save up some money and buy a sewing-machine. Then I shall be able to make clothes for my younger brother. When I feel confident enough I shall do dress-making for the neighbours, and save the money until I have got a lot of money and can open a shop and set up on my own. If the business prospers I want to take a pupil-apprentice. Even with a pupil-apprentice it will be no easy life, but the two of us will work for all we are worth. But two people and one sewing-machine is unreasonable. So by cutting down and economizing I hope to get an extra machine. Then we shall make low charges and make the business prosper. My hope is that everyone will say 'That's a very skilful dress-maker, and cheap, too.' I want to learn knitting too at the same time as dress-making. My hope is to learn knitting and dress-making and be independent.

The attraction of working on one's own is strong. It depends less on the pleasures of independence, of not having to take orders from others (though complaints about the arrogance of superiors did come up once or twice in lists of dissatisfactions with present jobs) as on the prospect of an income the upper limit of which is determined not by the low post-war wage rates, but by the extent of the individual's efforts. The independent worker is not bound by Labour Standards Laws. The shopkeeper keeps his shop open for fifteen hours a day, all the year round except for a couple of days at New Year. But the reduction in leisure is for most men adequately compensated for by an increase in income. Wives, as we saw on p. 78, have a full list of unsatisfied wants, and some are articulate enough in giving them expression. (The marital quarrels of one of my neighbours which the inadequacies of Japanese domestic architecture permitted me to hear with considerable frequency, often centred on the weak-kneedness, the good-for-nothing lack of initiative and drive of the husband, a commission salesman for a firm of chemists.) Moreover, a slight increase in income might make all the difference to the children's educational chances.

EDUCATION

For many families, indeed, hopes are fixed less on the husband's bettering himself by business enterprise than on the children's taking advantage of the other route of upward mobility—getting educational qualifications and eventually a good salaried job in the professions or in business. Many frustrated parental ambitions are projected on to sons and daughters. One man in Shitayama-cho whose boyhood ambition to become a lawyer had been frustrated by poverty intended his son to study law.[193] The pride with which mothers spoke of children who had got on was unmistakable.

Moreover, apart from unadulterated concern for the child's future welfare, education also plays some part in the competitive indulgence of children mentioned in earlier chapters. Like chocolates and clothes, education is something which parents wish their children to have the best of. Occasionally, too, shrewd calculating investment may be a conscious motivating factor. A 49-year-old cook at an American officers' club, asked if he could make do on his present earnings said that he could not, but he had some savings to draw on and he could manage until his children finished the university (of three sons, the eldest had just graduated)—after that he would be all right; his children would do the rest.

The post-war university system, remodelled on American lines with earlier graduation at a lower academic level and specialized education in effect postponed to graduate departments, has made a university degree necessary for entry into an increasingly wide range of white-collar occupations. This, in turn, has brought a great expansion of private universities in addition to the new public prefectural universities. The very high percentage of the population receiving a university education (far greater than in England) is shown in Table 4 (p. 19). In 1950, over a third of the male population of Tokyo between the ages of 19 and 21 were at a university, and 17·8% of those aged 22 to 24.[194]

The enthusiasm of Shitayama-cho parents for their children's education was unmistakable. It will be remembered that a 'study room' for the children was one of the most frequently expressed housing wants. The wife who frequently scolded her husband for his lack of backbone was equally outraged by her nine-year-old son's lack of enthusiasm for his homework. Every morning throughout the summer holidays, she set him to do a daily stint of arithmetic, his weak subject, before he was allowed out to play. Public elementary schools in Japan have always given homework; parents insist on it.

Every time I meet one of my parents [complains an elementary-school teacher writing in the newspaper], I hear the same complaint—'Teacher, I wish you would pile on the homework a bit more. My boy simply won't sit down and study unless he's got to.' Of course one understands the sincerity of parents' desire to do the best they can for their child. But if the child, after giving all his brain-power to his school work, comes home only to have to start all over again, the result will be a deep dislike for study of any sort. As long as this continues, the familiar problem of the child who seriously damages his health over entrance examinations will always be with us.[195]

The attention given by the press to the education system and its problems is symptomatic of the parental eagerness for their children to get on. The index of the *Asahi*, a paper with a four million circulation, for the ten months Oct. 1950 to July 1951, gives 313 references to articles and reports on education (including, however, one large batch of 67 concerning student demonstrations which were of political rather than educational interest); this compares with 318 references to murders, 21 to aviation, 125 to Trade Unions (excluding a much greater number concerned with T.U. disputes), and 137 to the Imperial Family (including 63 on the death and funeral of a Dowager Empress).

This interest was reflected in the readiness and detail with which parents answered questions in interviews about the new educational system, and the knowledge which they displayed of the prospects of success in the higher reaches of the educational system. It was a revelation to hear three mothers of boys now at the Primary School, only one of whom had been to a Girls' High School herself, discuss the prospects for their children's secondary education. One said that the local High School was not at all bad; thirty-seven children from it got into Tokyo University the previous year. Another capped this with the story of another High School which secured 119 successes. The conversation ranged on to the quality of the local Middle School as reflected in its ability to get children into the best High Schools, the fees at some of the better private Middle Schools, the advantages of one of the 'Attached' Middle Schools belonging to a private university, entrance to which ensured a smooth passage right through to the degree stage, the ratio of applicants to available places at some of the more famous of these 'attached' schools, the amount of the contribution to the school's 'Memorial Fund' which secured certain success in the entrance test—and so on.

The rapid decline in fertility since birth-control propaganda was permitted after the war, and particularly since the Eugenics Protection Law of 1948 made legal abortion possible, undoubtedly owes much to parents' ambitions for their children and the high cost of education. (The crude birth rate has fallen from 34 per thousand in 1948 to 22 per thousand in 1954, figures for which a great increase in abortions is largely responsible, although annual surveys of a newspaper research institute show a steadily increasing proportion practising contraception.[196]) It is not without relevance, for instance, that there is a significant correlation between the number of legal abortions per head and the proportion of the children of the relevant ages attending High School for the 46 prefectures for 1950.[197]

The new educational system, established since the war, is strictly egalitarian up to the age of 15. For the compulsory six years of primary and three years of secondary education, all children receive the same tuition in large schools drawing their pupils from a fixed geographical area and in classes constituted on an alphabetical or random basis. Streaming according to ability is scrupulously avoided in all schools with the exception of a few experimental ones. Selection according to ability does, however operate to a certain extent in Tokyo and the larger cities at the High School entrance level. High Schools (age 15 to 18) are non-compulsory but State-maintained [198] and in theory open to all (but fee-taking and thus closed to the poor.[199]) In 1951, 40% of Tokyo Middle-School leavers went on to full-time and 10% to part-time High School.

The whole of Tokyo is divided into only three catchment areas for the purpose of High School entrance. Any child may apply for entry to any of a large number of schools in his area, but whether or not he gets to the school of his choice depends on teachers' reports and on his performance in the standard *achiibumento* (achievement test) taken on Middle School graduation (with the greater weight placed on the latter). In practice, applicants for entrance into the 'best' High Schools (those with a good record for getting their pupils into the 'best' university—(the ex-Imperial) Tokyo University— graduation from which is the means of entry into the 'best', i.e. the most highly paid and most prestige-carrying jobs) outnumber and excel in quality applicants for the inferior High Schools. As a consequence, a higher standard in the achievement test is required to get into the better High Schools and pupils are thus graded according to ability as between schools. The process is a circular one, since the differential quality of the student material increases the differential success rates of the different schools in the university-entrance examinations, thus increases the differential in their reputations and so exaggerates the tendency for the brighter to concentrate on getting to the best school regardless of geographical location. There has, too, since the war, been a considerable growth in private schools at the secondary level and above. Parents who can afford it send their children to a private Middle School to increase their chances in High School entrance, to a private High School to increase their chances in University entrance, or, if they have little hope of gaining a place in the ex-Imperial Universities with their greater prestige, to private universities.

This form of grading of pupils according to ability at the High School level, has the obvious social advantage of speeding the advance of the bright pupil; but the introduction of a competitive element at this stage, in a school career in which hitherto competition had been generally avoided and in an atmosphere over-loaded with parental ambition, lays a severe strain on the child and breakdowns are not infrequent (as Ruth Benedict noted of the Middle School entrance examination in pre-war days). The form of the examination, moreover, puts a premium on cramming and so operates to the advantage of the child from the better-off home.[200] (Though this has an incidental advantage in that private tuition of secondary and High School children provides the easiest form of part-time *arubaito* (ar- beit) for impoverished university students.) Of seventy parents of boys in Shitayama-cho, thirty said that they had given, were giving, or intended to give their children extra tuition outside the school.

Many more said that they would very much like to, but could not afford it.

Not all of this out-of-school education was of the cramming kind. Some parents were sending their children to learn to use the abacus, others to teachers of brush calligraphy. These are subjects no longer taught in schools, though both have a vocational value for the humbler commercial and white-collar jobs, while the latter has purely aesthetic values too. Indeed, the view of educational interests and aspirations given here in the context of this chapter is necessarily a one-sided one. Education is certainly important to parents in Shitayama-cho as means of gaining the qualifications necessary for getting on in the world. But it is also greatly valued as an end in itself. The scholar has great prestige, and conscious philistinism, scorn for 'la-di-dah nonsense', is an attitude rarely met with. But these broader perspectives of education will be dealt with in a later chapter.

PERSONAL CONNECTIONS

A good university degree and the ability to do well in the entrance examinations for the civil service or a private company offer a fairly sure means of entry into a good job. These plus the right personal connections offer an absolutely certain one. The *shosei* system of Meiji times—a means of 'getting on' entirely by dependence on patronage—was mentioned earlier. So, in another chapter, was the importance of the marriage go-between in this respect. One indication of the importance of personal connections in determining an individual's life-chances may be seen in the fact that of forty-two employees interviewed in Shitayama-cho, four got their present job by replying to an advertisement, two through a Labour Exchange, two through an entrance test, and thirty-three by personal introduction. (One not reported.) Another survey (scope not stated) showed that only 13% of new jobs were found through a Labour Exchange.[201]

The importance of personal relations does not cease with getting a job. A, who gets his job in the United Glass and Steel Corporation through the influence of B who was, perhaps, at the same High School with A's uncle, is thereafter marked as B's man. This not only means that B is the obvious man to ask to be his marriage go-between, the obvious man to go to for advice when he is in trouble over a girl, or the obvious man to ask for a loan, nor only that he takes it as a matter of course that he is expected to run personal errands for B, or even for B's wife. It means also that he will join the rank and file of the B group in its cold war against the X group and the Y group within the firm, and that his own chances of success will depend on the B group's maintaining its power, in particular on B maintaining his influence in the highest councils. Such *habatsu*, as these groups are called, are a frequent topic of discussion; their existence in private firms and political parties is taken more or less for granted, their existence in the civil service and universities is more actively deplored. This is a phenomenon to be found in a greater or less degree in organizations of the bureaucratic type almost anywhere. The only difference between Japan and England is that in Japan, where such relations hold it is almost impossible to exist in the organization without being clearly identified with such a group and accepting the identification explicitly, and that loyalty to such a group is often explicitly counted a higher value than the honest expression of personal opinion.

Professor Takeyoshi Kawashima, a sociologist and a professed admirer of the work of Ruth Benedict, has, in one of his more scathingly anti-Japanese moods, written an illuminating article on this topic.[202] One could not do better than summarize his enumeration of the essential elements for the maintenance of these patron-client relations.

1. A high degree of affectivity. In a *gemeinschaftlich* society such as Japan, the solidarity of the family implies social distance from, if not active hostility towards, other families. Relations outside the family can only be entered into by making them as much like family relationships as possible. The means of achieving this are (*a*) the granting of special favours (*on*), to one's subordinates (*b*) eating and drinking together, especially drinking which removes inhibitions to the display of affectivity. The etiquette of male drinking parties requires drunkenness, and even, if the rice wine is not strong enough, a simulated display of drunkenness. Games such as mah-jong, Japanese chess or cards also help. So do lewd jokes. At contemporary business parties, he notes, it is not uncommon for guests to be given pornographic books as a parting gift.

2. Strict hierarchical order. The subordinate bolsters the superior's authority by the use of respect language,[203] by periodical visits, by seasonal gifts and by accepting the superior's orders and his favours (for example by not attempting to repay hospitality as one would to an equal). This implies also an attitude of circumspection towards a stranger until one has established his age, date of graduation or date of entry into the firm. Once this is established the niceties of the etiquette required are fairly closely determined. Kawashima also notes that the essential role of ritual gift-giving in these relations gives the problem of official bribery in Japan a very special character.

3. The avoidance of conflict. The subordinate should always give way to the superior when there is objectively a potential conflict of interest. When there is a conflict of opinion within a group where such relations prevail, the subordinate should never be seen to win an

argument. Skill lies in giving the superior an escape route, and allowing it to appear that the final solution was what the superior first proposed. This is the sort of skill on which success depends in Japanese society.

CONCLUSIONS

It will be apparent from the foregoing discussion that any attempt to characterize Japanese society as being more, or less, a 'status society' or a 'competitive society' is in danger of obscuring important distinctions. Few people in Shitayama-cho are influenced by, or seek verbal rationalizations in, ideas of a 'proper station' determined by birth. Nor do many people take the view that there are enforced 'stations'—whether proper or not—imposed by an economic system which guarantees that the poor shall remain poor and the rich remain rich. Most people have a strong desire—either for themselves or for their children—to get on, and a majority believe that society makes it possible for the man of ability to rise to the top, at least if he gets his foot on the right educational ladder early enough in life. But the emphasis on status traditional to Japanese society still remains as an essential ingredient of the patron-client relationships which provide the ambitious individual with a—no longer essential but still useful—additional lever to success. Thus are both Ruth Benedict and Professor Watsuji in a sense vindicated.

All this has important consequences for political attitudes, which will be the topic of the next chapter. Meanwhile it might be as well to add here the reminder that the population of Shitayamo-cho, the subject of the foregoing generalizations, contains somewhat more of the upwardly mobile (see p. 23) and somewhat fewer of those who cannot afford to give their children High-School education (see Table 4) than the population of Tokyo as a whole.

13

Political Attitudes

THE explicit acceptance of status inequalities, the receipt of favours acknowledged to create an obligation of indebtedness but in no way detracting from the individual's sense of self-respect, and the granting of favours in conscious expectation of a return in loyal service, the genuine and positive approval of the sentiments of personal loyalty to superiors and protective solicitude for inferiors, combined with clear 'sociological' insight into the material implications of such relationships—all these features of the patron-client relationship just described as a useful tool for 'getting on' in Japanese society are equally characteristic of employment relations over a large sphere of Japanese industry.

The traditional relation between the employer and the employee is a personal one more closely corresponding to the ideas suggested by the English words 'master' and 'servant'. It is an 'affective' and a 'diffuse' relation, a relation of the whole man which requires the employer to take a personal interest in the employee's family affairs, giving him financial help when he becomes ill or on retirement, perhaps keeping him on the books when a strict concern for profit would prompt his dismissal. It requires the employee also not to begrudge a little unpaid overtime work when the firm is busy, and not to complain if the payment of wages is delayed for a few weeks when times are bad. The atmosphere is one wholly inimical to hard economic bargaining for the sale and the purchase of the employee's labour on the assumption that each party pursues his own interest and his interest only to the point of compromise determined by market conditions.

Several scraps of evidence illustrating the existence of such relationships can be quoted from Shitayama-cho. There was the man whose family photograph album gave pride of place to a birthday picture of his employer's daughter. There were the eleven housewives (out of 200) who said that if by an unlucky chance their house burnt down in a fire it would be their husband's employer rather than relatives to whom they would turn. There were several cases of employees living with their employers, in one or two instances married employees with their families shared a part of their employer's house (and at the same time were on call for odd jobs at all hours). One employee, living near his employer, was regularly allowed the use of his employer's bath.

The following note, written after an interview with a section chief in a cosmetics firm (covering the two schedules on religious attitudes and on employment) perhaps gives an idea of the personality type of the perfect Japanese employee.

If B, is a typical Japanese worker, one can understand why S, the glass-works owner, should have remarked the other day as the fruit of thirty years' experience as an employer of labour, 'Japanese have a certain simplicity about them, don't you think—obedient, easy to employ.'

At any rate, B appears to have dedicated his life to his work. Until recently he would, he says, stay at the office doing 'left-overs' until ten o'clock or so on most nights of the week, and although he has recently become section chief he frequently does so still. (At his request the interview began at a quarter to midnight since he had no certain prospect of being free at any other time in the near future.) He considers the chief duty of man to be to 'work conscientiously' (*majime ni*); by doing so he repays his *on* to his parents and to the Emperor as well as to his schoolteacher. His morning prayers at the Shinto god-shelf are for 'Safety in the Home' and for the protection which will see him through the day in safety. The chief prerequisite for happiness is health, and health means for him not the avoidance of pain and suffering, but the ability to continue his work and maintain the *status quo*. He is extremely careful of his health. His rest days he considers chiefly as a means of recuperating himself physically for the labour of the next week, and it is only when he feels well and is sure that there is no need for such recuperation that he would take it into his head to go off to enjoy himself, or even to pay a visit to his parents' graves. He is sure that the Buddhas will understand that it is not idleness but industry which keeps him from frequently visiting their graves and temples.

He is proud of the trust which his superiors have in him. Trouble-makers are often sent to him from other departments because he is known to have a way of dealing with them. He was to have been appointed section chief three years ago, but the union's insistence on seniority prevented it. This is only one of the unfortunate consequences of introducing unions into what was formerly a perfectly harmonious atmosphere.

With his twenty-one years' service he is entitled to twenty days paid holiday per year (exclusive of national holidays). Previously to 'hand back' this would mean extra pay, but the Labour Standards Regulations now forbid this. Nevertheless he last year 'handed back' eighteen of his twenty days and intended to sacrifice all twenty this year. He cannot feel happy about leaving his job to other people. The suspicion that the company has probably found some way of circumventing the Labour Standards Law in this respect is, in B's case, not even a necessary hypothesis.

Of forty-two employees below managerial rank, sixteen said in an interview that there was no union at their office or factory and that they thought, moreover, that a union was unnecessary; everything was fine without one; 'our firm has a really family atmosphere', said one or two. On the other hand there were seventeen working in firms where a union was organized and of these ten expressed themselves as well satisfied with the union's activity and instanced concrete benefits which they owed to it. Another eight were working in firms without a union and had strong dissatisfactions which they thought a union might do something to cure. 'But what a hope!' said one, 'there were the beginnings of a union once, but thirty sudden dismissals the next day and that was the end of that.'

The successful maintenance of the paternalistic system requires that the employer be paternal. There was something quite genuine in the gratitude with which some of these employees spoke of the family atmosphere of their firm. But the man who forestalled the organization of a Trade Union by dismissing thirty employees is no longer a paternalistic employer. His employees no longer identify themselves with his fortunes, the conflict of interest is consciously appreciated by both sides, but, in an economy with a large under-employed labour reserve, he has the bargaining strength *vis-à-vis* an unorganized mass of employees to prevent them from becoming organized. He can also count on the existence of a large number of individuals who, given the training in the acceptance of status distinctions provided by pre-war Japanese society, think it wiser to maintain an attitude of subservient compliance towards tyranny, and even to act as the tyrant's informer, rather than to risk the emotional as well as the material insecurity which overt opposition to the tyrannous authority would entail.

Some obvious factors make for this transition from more or less stable paternalism to naked and less stable authoritarianism. The increasing size of the firm makes personal relations between the employer and his employees difficult to maintain. The necessity for rationalized principles of management which competitive production for the market demands strengthens the tendency to treat labour as a commodity to be bought for a fixed price without regard for the individual selling it. The profit-seeking drive of the up-and-coming competitive entrepreneur induces a certain ruthlessness which prompts him to minimize the financial burden of his paternalistic obligations in a way which would be unthinkable to the employer in a fully status society, unthinkable for, say, the merchant or the master-craftsman of the Tokugawa period, operating for a guaranteed market under guild-regulated prices and accepting his duties towards his employees as for him as essential a part of his inherited status as his wealth.

The man who dismissed the thirty men attempting to organize a union (T, of pp. 32–4) employs a total of 500 workers, and the ruthlessness of his business methods is a byword among those who know him. His is no longer a paternalistic firm. The rot has set in even within his own personal entourage. The following is an interviewer's report of a conversation with his chauffeur.

I have to be on call all the time. I never get to bed before twelve and I am supposed to start at eight in the morning which means starting to get the car ready at half past seven. This includes Sundays, too; altogether I get about one day off a month. The wages are low—even though I get my food here, how could I keep a wife and family on 7,000 *yen* a month? And what food! A chunk of bread and a tasteless *miso* soup for breakfast. Foreign rice for lunch and for supper one bowl of *soba* spaghetti just cooked in salt and soy sauce with no extras. If I come in late I just have to have it cold and then it's practically uneatable. It's not enough to keep a man alive—I have to buy extra food for myself. This is the same all the year round. Not even at New Year do we get anything like a special treat. With them it's like that every night (he pointed to the dining-room through the window of which the employer and his wife and guests could be seen sitting under an enormous chandelier, around a white linen-covered table studded with beer bottles and large plates of food). And we get food fit for pigs.

One of the office people went to hospital the other day with cancer of the stomach. The boss doesn't give him a penny to make up his insurance benefits, and he made him pay for medicines that the firm makes.

The firm is a joint-stock company, but he and his wife own all the shares and it's as pretty a fiddle as you could imagine. Practically all their household expenses go on the firm's account—gas and water, fur coats for his wife, furniture and all the rest. That's why the firm itself is always in the red and often behindhand in paying wages. A year or two ago people came from the Tax Office without warning and seized the books. We were delighted. We thought they'd got him this time. But within three days he'd bribed the lot of them and the books were back in the office. I know because I drove him round.

The other day we were caught speeding after he'd told me to step on it. The fine was stopped out of my wages.

'What a hope!' was this man's opinion of the prospects of forming a union. His own solution was a personal rather than a collective one. He hoped somehow to be able to get hold of a car and set himself up as an independent taxi-driver. In his case there was no question of the permanent acceptance of ineluctable status relations, nor of moving to seek an employer who would take his paternalistic duties seriously, nor did his hopes rest on the organization of a power which could counter the employer's power, make overt the conflict of interest and institutionalize the means of improving the employee's lot by bargaining on a more equal footing. His solution was to escape from the employment relation altogether. His employer himself had started from nothing. One day the position might be reversed.

The variety of employment relations in modern Tokyo is great. At one end of the scale are the workers in large unionized firms who have little or no sense of personal loyalty towards, or dependence on, an individual employer and who are identified with the union's aims of protecting the workers' interests. In Shitayama-cho the men who belonged to a union and were appreciative of its activities were workers on the Tokyo municipality trams, workers in government offices, the employee of a large firm of fruit wholesalers, of a firm of road hauliers, an electricity company, the broadcasting corporation. They may within these organizations have something like a patron-client relationship with an immediate superior, indeed the union organizations themselves are riddled with such relationships.[204] but their employer is an impersonal corporation with which such a relation is impossible. At the other end of the scale are the employees in the small firms untouched by union organization, who live by the light of the proverbial injunction; 'wrap yourself up in something long'. They may receive smaller wages,[205] but they are secure in the 'family atmosphere' of the paternalistic firm. Nearly all those in Shitayama-cho who said that they belonged to no union and thought a union unnecessary were workers in firms employing less than forty workers. In between these two extremes there are others like the chauffeur who lack the security of the paternalistic relation and certainly lack all sense of personal loyalty to their employer, but lack also the security of union support and protection. Some may look to union organization for the solution, though the prospects are not good in a country in which the craft and the general union have made only small beginnings (most of the post-war unions are on the basis of the individual firm and the large national federations often have only loose control of constituent unions) and in which employers are actively hostile, have official support in their hostility, and enjoy the advantages of a good reservoir of unemployed. Most, like the chauffeur, look for a personal solution and believe that their society—in which, indeed, nearly a third of the non-agricultural labour force is still self-employed—offers opportunities for individual enterprise.

CLASS AND CLASS-CONSCIOUSNESS

The relevance of these considerations to political attitudes and the development of class consciousness is obvious. The consciousness of a community of interest among fellow employees, at variance with the interests of a common employer, and the attempt to create a union organization which will actively further those common interests can be considered a necessary first step towards a consciousness of a community of interest between all workers at variance with the interests of all employers, and the attempt to create a political organization which can further the interests of 'the workers' at the level of central government politics. In the worker who fully accepts the paternalistic values of loyal dependence and protective leadership one can find, certainly, a consciousness of status, a consciousness, if one likes, of class position; but it is one which implies an acceptance of inferiority and an identification with the protecting leader, rather than with others of one's own status against a common enemy. On the other hand, in the individual who has the ambition, and believe he has the opportunity, to rise out of it, consciousness of his status position, and an awareness that his own interests are similar to those of others of like position, can exist without producing a class-consciousness in the accepted sense—personal identification with the interests of the class to which one belongs.

It is in this context that it is interesting to consider the replies of a sample of 102 men and women to the following questions.

1. One often hears the words 'something-or-other class'. If you were asked what class you belong to could you give an immediate answer?
2. If you *had* to say what class you belonged to what would you say?
3. If you had to choose between upper, middle and lower, which would you choose?

Only 21 people out of 102 gave what could be called an immediate answer to the first question, 36 gave a more grudging 'Well I suppose . . .' type of answer and 14 did not name their class until prodded by question 2. Six, although they gave replies at some stage, were marked by the interviewer as taking the questions as a joke, while 25 either persisted in saying that they didn't know or said that they did not believe in classes. 'There is no such thing as classes *any longer*. I'm just a good citizen.' 'I think it's silly to talk about classes. "Model your aims on those above, but model your life (habits of expenditure) on those below" is my motto for life.' The latter 25 included, also, one highly sophisticated reply to the effect that 'economically I'm at the bottom, but as far as ideas go, I'm *puchi-buru* (petit-bourgeoise)'.

The small number of immediate replies to the first question is in itself, perhaps, evidence of the rarity of positive class identification. The great variety of words used as names of classes may be considered further evidence. They are listed in Table 22 overleaf.

'Middle class' is the most common answer, and, indeed, this is where a large number of the inhabitants of Shitayama-cho would belong by Marxist criteria of their relation to the means of production. Others, humbler white-collar workers, are doubtless prompted to such a reply by a desire to dissociate themselves from the manual workers. That 'proletarian' should be the next most common word, just outnumbering 'working class', is an indication of the dominance

Table 22: Class Identification

Reply to Questions 1 and 2	Reply to Question 3			
	Upper	Middle	Lower	Don't know
Middle class (*chuuryuu, chuusan*)	—	30	—	—
Proletariat (*puro, puroretaria*)	—	5	6	—
Working (*kinroo, roodoo*)	—	7	3	—
Common people (*shomin, heimin*)	—	3	5	—
Lower (*kasoo*)	—	—	5	—
Merchant (*shoonin*)	—	2	—	—
Others (leader, intellectual, citizen, salaried, ordinary, propertyless)	1	4	1	—
Joking reply	—	3	3	—
Don't know, other replies	—	13	8	4
Total	1	67	31	4

of Marxism in Japanese left-wing thought and the extent to which its terminology has gained general currency. It should not, however, be taken too seriously since, it will be seen, half of these proletarians count themselves middle class.

The terms *shomin* (7) and *heimin* (1) are relics of Tokugawa feudalism—they were used to describe the 'common people' as opposed to the samurai, and, indeed, until quite recently the municipal office registers recorded for each family whether it was of *heimin*, of samurai, or of aristocratic stock.[206] (It was to the formal abolition of these distinctions that the woman referred who said that classes do not exist 'any longer'.) People who seriously identify themselves as members of the 'common people class' must do so with a clear sense of society as divided into the rulers and the ruled. They, the *shomin*, are content to be ruled.

The impression gained from the answers to these questions is that the language of class has few evocative implications and the tendency to view political questions in class terms is little developed. The impression might be somewhat different if the same questions were asked in a mining town or in one of the factory workers' suburbs of a heavy-industrial district, but there are good historical reasons why class distinctions should be more blurred and consciousness of class membership less distinct in Japan than in, say, England. It may be of interest to enumerate some of them here.

1. The first is that the Japanese upper class has been less culturally homogeneous, and the cultural gulf between it and the middle and lower classes has not been as great as in England. There are, that is to

say, fewer of those distinguishing criteria of U and non-U which prompted the recent English discovery of class differences. For this the discontinuity in the development of the Japanese class system due to the Meiji upheaval is chiefly responsible. During the Tokugawa period there had been clearly identifiable differences of outlook and way of life between the samurai, the merchants and the peasants (though even then there were considerable cultural differences between the upper and the lower samurai, and the class differences were to some extent cut across by regional differences). But the class system of the twentieth century (the 'objective' class system defined in terms of the relation to the means of production and the sources of political power) was not a gradual outgrowth of the class system of the Tokugawa period. The abolition of legally sanctioned estate distinctions found many of the formerly 'inferior' merchants in possession of greater economic power than the majority of the samurai. A small aristocratic rentier class—made up of the old Court nobility and the upper crust of the Tokugawa feudal nobility—persisted until the 1946–8 inflation served it a mortal blow, but its function was largely honorific and it was not in its hands that the sources of political and economic power lay. The bureaucrats of the twentieth century, the new leaders of business and industry, the new staffs of the army and navy, even if of predominantly samurai origin, were from all grades of the samurai hierarchy and contained a fair admixture of men from merchant or rich peasant stock. Thus there has not been in Japan as there was in England, a landed aristocracy with political and economic power, to act as a solid continuing core of the upper class, setting the cultural standards to which parvenus learn to conform.

A second important factor which has contributed to the lack of upper-class cultural homogeneity is the influence of the West. Frock coats for ceremonial occasions, Western table manners, Western education, wall-papered and sofa'ed 'Western rooms' in private houses, Western ideas of family and sexual morality have had their chief impact on the upper classes. Such Western cultural influence tended to undermine the confidence in traditional Japanese culture on the basis of which the upper class might have become culturally unified. Moreover, this penetration of Western culture has in itself had a divisive effect. Although all sections of the upper class were to a certain degree affected by it, some have been more eagerly cosmopolitan than others. At times of international tension between Japan and the West differing degrees of Western influence has been a cause of hostility and suspicion between the ruling groups. The ideological rift between the army and the leaders of finance and industry in the twenties and thirties, at basis a struggle for political power, was exacerbated by the fact that the militarists made themselves the champions of tradition, the defenders of the faith in the 'Japanese spirit' against the insidious luxury and decadence of the cosmopolitan business class. Within the bureaucracy the Foreign Office, with its polished Western manners and its foreign tastes in wines and music and literature, was constantly on the defensive against the suspicion of disloyalty.

A third factor, affecting both the homogeneity of the upper class and its differentiation from other classes, has been the nature of the educational system. There has been no system of independent education exclusively *serving the upper classes as there has been in England. With the exception of one aristocratic school (the Gaku-shuuin) to which a small number of children of officials and industrialists were admitted, the institutions of higher education which carried the greatest prestige—the State High Schools and the Imperial Universities, have stood at the apex of a system of universal public education which catered for all classes. It was not until the twenties and thirties that private middle-class primary and secondary schools began to be developed in the large cities (and even then they lacked the prestige and traditions of the best State schools). Most of the present élite groups went to the same primary schools, followed the same standardized curriculum, read in their ethics text-books the same stories of former Emperors, of Jenner, Benjamin Franklin and Florence Nightingale, as their peasant and industrial worker contemporaries. One effect of this has been to minimize language differences. There is no gulf such as separates English Received Pronunciation from the language of Aldgate or Tooting Bec. Apart from the elimination of one or two minor consonant differences, the Tokyo lower-class child in order to be 'received' has only to learn proficiency in the use of respect language, which is not difficult. Business men and bureaucrats at all-male drinking parties lapse into the same slangy vowel distortions as the grocer and the fishmonger. Regional dialect differences still remain strong, but these have less relevance to class distinctions.

What educational differentiation has existed has been largely at the higher level and has been such as to contribute to the differences within the upper class. The army and the navy had their own academies, the bureaucrats were drawn almost exclusively from the Imperial Universities and, although perhaps the top managerial stratum of the large banks and corporations were also drawn predominantly from the Imperial Universities, a large part of the business class was trained by the (State) University of Commerce and the private universities.

2. A second factor which, given the diversity of the elements of which the upper class was composed, has tended to hinder the development of an upper-class solidarity is the strength of kinship ties. It is obvious that, in the limiting case, in a society so organized as to

ensure 'perfect mobility'—the allocation of the members of each generation to the class position for which they are best fitted by ability, irrespective of parental situation—class cultural differences and strong class solidarity could only be maintained on the basis of a great attenuation of family bonds, at least as soon as adulthood is attained. The two features of sharp class differences and strong family bonds are incompatible where there is a great deal of mobility. In the Japan of the last century, in which the maintenance of family ties been given high moral priority, it is the rigidity of class distinctions and the strength of class solidarity which have suffered. The peasant's son who becomes a civil servant still has strong emotional and ritual ties to his peasant family; ties which may continue after the death of his parents. So has the son of a small-town merchant or of a samurai turned policeman. To that extent their ability to acquire new cultural patterns is reduced, their need for psychological identification with their occupational equals is weakened, and the emergence of common upper-class values and symbols and ways of life overriding diversities in the origins of its members is consequently hindered.

The same considerations apply to the continued strength of local community ties. This was a phenomenon of considerable prominence, particularly in the early period; witness the constant attacks continuing into the nineteen-twenties, on cliquish sectionalism (the *hambatsu*) in the bureaucracy and the armed forces. The basis of the solidarity of these cliques lay in regional cultural peculiarities and the remnants of fief loyalty. Although it has somewhat given place in importance to a more 'functional' solidarity based on common High School or University membership, this is still a by no means negligible factor. For practically every district in Japan there is in Tokyo a Society of Men of . . . Prefecture (. . . *kenjinkai*) and still an almost inevitable question in the first few minutes of a new acquaintanceship in Tokyo is 'Which is your province?' If the individual himself happens to be born in Tokyo he is as likely as not to answer by naming the district in which his father or even his grandfather, was born.

We may summarize the argument of this section in terms of the predominance of 'particularistic' relations in Japanese society. With the exception of such solidary relations as have their basis in common High School or University membership, these have been such as to cut across the occupational divisions of society and hinder the development of a sense of solidarity based on more 'universalistic' criteria of occupational similarity or identity of economic interest.

3. A third factor which has already been sufficiently hinted at in this and the previous chapter is that the opportunities for upward mobility either through the educational ladder or via industry and commerce, whether or not they were great in reality, have been

sufficient to prevent the class divisions from seeming rigid predetermined barriers which the individual can never hope to cross, and this has weakened any sense of the injustice of the social system, which is an essential precondition of militant working-class consciousness. Moreover, it may well be that the 'familism' of Japanese society, by giving an explicit moral sanction and strong group support to individual ambition to 'get on' has made this a more common way of resolving dissatisfaction than the sentiment of solidarity with non-kin-related fellows.

4. On the other hand, the changes of the last three-quarters of the century have not entirely removed the 'each in his proper station' attitudes among those who failed to get on and had little real prospect of doing so. The status consciousness of the *shomin* who accept the system as a just, or at least an ineluctable one, and identify with their superiors on whose benevolence they rely—a status consciousness which accepts and is strengthened by paternalism in industry and authoritarianism in politics—is very different from class consciousness in the accepted sense of the term.

5. A further obvious source of difference between Japan and England lies in the different structures of the economies. Firstly, 'the masses' to whom the left-wing propagandists appeal are divided into a conservative small-land-holding or land-renting peasantry, and a smaller number of urban industrial workers, a large proportion of whom are only one generation away from a rural background, look to a parent peasant family as a source of security, and may even have hopes and prospects of returning eventually to the land. Moreover, secondly, the urban population itself contains a high proportion of self-employed workers. Small shopkeepers, service workers, and domestic craft workers, they form an intermediate class between the employers and the employed, sufficiently large in number for theirs to be the dominant ideology of mixed communities such as Shitayama-cho, affecting the outlook of, and providing a model for the aspirations of, the industrial worker. Add to this, thirdly, the predominance in Japanese industry of small enterprises,[207] strongholds of the paternalistic relations which serve more to foster the feudal attitudes of status acceptance than class consciousness in the usual sense.

6. A sixth factor of importance has been the direction of internal government policy, central government propaganda and the exigencies of Japan's international position. Before the war left-wing activity was severely controlled, strikes were broken up by the police, and trade unions either destroyed or reduced to subservient furthering of the government's interests. At the same time Government propaganda stressed the need for unity, spread a belief in the superiority of the Japanese people as a whole, fostered conceptions of the Family State in which the Emperor had supreme symbolic significance, directed

resentments outwards against Japan's enemies abroad, and offered as
a cure for present frustrations not a reordering of the internal structure of the country but expansion abroad. The policy worked; a strong
sense of national unity developed, the industrial worker was a Japanese
first and a member of the proletariat second; Japan's wars were his
wars, her victories his victories. Just as in the wartime English village
the lady of the manor will entertain the grocer's wife at W.V.S. tea-
parties, so in Japan, something of the same sort of atmosphere of
local community and national solidarity cutting across class lines was
maintained for decades during which Japan, a solitary Asiatic power,
was struggling to find her place in the sun in a hostile world organized
on a basis of white supremacy.

POLITICAL ATTITUDES

Given the conditions outlined above, one would not expect to find
it common to view political parties as legitimately organs for the
representation of class interests, and the process of central government politics as a means of adjusting the conflicting interests of
different classes. Although, after seven years of political freedom, the
left-wing parties gained more than a quarter of the votes in the 1952
elections, they are parties with a very small membership and they gain
a large proportion of their votes not on the basis of political principles
or an objective appeal to reason and self-interest, but in the same
way as the traditional conservative parties—by the candidate's
personal base (*jiban*), his network of personal connections with local
'powerful men' or 'bosses' (*yuuryokusha, bossu*) who can be relied on
to use their own personal connections to rally voters to his cause.
Within the parties themselves, personal loyalties seem to count for
more than differences of principle in determining the composition of,
and the shifting alliances between, cliques.

This is not to say that nothing has changed since before the war.
This is not the place, and a few conversations and a hundred interviews in Shitayama-cho do not provide the basis, for an exhaustive
discussion of political tendencies in contemporary Japan, but some
limited generalizations may be attempted.

First of all, people in Shitayama-cho are not uninterested in or
uninformed about politics. The mass-circulation newspapers which
most of them read give greater prominence to political news and are
generally more 'serious-minded' in tone than their English equivalents.
In answer to the simple question 'Are you interested in politics?' only
42 (out of 102) said that they were not. Only 20 (13 of them women)
did not know the name of the successful candidate in the Tokyo
Municipal Governorship election, an election fought on party
political lines some three months before the interview. Only 16 (12 of

them women) would not name a party which they generally supported. (Of the others, 17 supported the Socialist, two the Communist and the rest one of the conservative parties.) On the other hand, only three men have ever been members of any political party and only seven men and three women have ever taken part in electioneering. As far as voting behaviour goes, more people vote in local than in national elections (in the former the network of face-to-face connections which the candidate can mobilize has fewer loopholes than in the latter). In questions of national politics, interest centres on international more than on internal politics. Of a total of 140 references by the same sample to the current political questions they were most interested in only 32 concerned internal politics, about a half of them relating to personalities or internal party issues, the other half to political and economic questions proper. This was perhaps inevitable at a time when the Japanese Peace Treaty was being negotiated and a war was raging just across the Japan Sea in Korea. It is also a natural consequence of Japan's economic dependence on foreign trade. But it is also, perhaps, a legacy of pre-war days when the—in part deliberately calculated—focusing of public attention on foreign affairs (in which it is *Japan* which acts as a unit and the honour and interests of *Japan* which are involved) helped to paper over internal divisions and strengthen the solidarity of the nation.

Indeed, there is evidence from interview answers that some of the basic political attitudes which were fostered by, and at the same time made possible, the pre-war regime have not greatly changed. One question asked of the sample of 102 ran as follows.

I'm afraid this is a bit vague, but of the four things written on this card, which two do you think are the most important for Japan at the present time?
(Interviewer reads aloud the following:)

	Men	Women
1. The spiritual unity of the people	39	45
2. The firm establishment of individual freedoms	23	14
3. Strong leaders	24	32
4. Destruction of the power of the bosses	14	11

The figures to the right indicate the number of times each slogan was chosen. Spiritual unity, the most popular, was the watchword of the pre-war military leaders, but it was sufficiently vague for it to have escaped explicit denunciation by the post-war propagandists of democracy. It will be seen that not many people react sceptically towards it. Altogether nearly half the sample (45) chose the combination of 1 and 3, the answer which would have been unquestionably the proper one in pre-war days. 2 and 4 were post-war slogans and those who approved them must consciously have been expressing approval of the post-war reforms of which 2 in particular stood as an obvious symbol. Only six, however, chose a combination of 2 and 4. It will be noticed that women tend to be more unregenerate than men.[208]

Answers to other questions, however, suggest that some of the symbols which have been subject to explicit attack since the war have lost their magic. One of these is the Emperor. The defeat, the Emperor's visits to General MacArthur, the radio speech in which he renounced his divinity, his embarrassed essays in the hand-shaking, appreciative-word-for-everyone style of European mon-archs, the impunity of the Communists who have reviled him; all these things could not have failed to have some effect on popular attitudes. In a series of questions concerning *on* (the 'favours' which, according to the teachings of the primary-school ethics course, everyone received from the Emperor, from parents and from school-teachers—favours which put the individual under an everlasting debt of obligation) not many people spontaneously recognized that they had any such debt towards the Emperor and only one offered a concrete instance of such indebtedness—the fact that it was the Emperor's decision which ended the war and saved his people from utter destruction.[209] Of those who did, when prompted, acknowledge such indebtedness, a few had no hesitation, in reply to a further ques-tion, in explaining how the debt should be repaid by loyal subjects—by preserving the honour of the country ('behaving in such a way that foreigners will not say, "Huh, these Japanese!" '), by preventing the country from falling a prey to false ideologies (*hen na shisoo*, i.e. Communism), by working hard and living justly, by being a useful member of society. These were the pre-war text-book answers. Some, however, were vague and admittedly bewildered. 'Now that we are supposed to treat him as a man', 'now that there is no conscription', it is difficult to know how the debt should be repaid. More than half the sample, however, refused to admit that an *on*-incurred debt to the Emperor had any meaning for them, and some were vehement in their rejection.

Another set of questions was intended to elicit the associations surrounding another favourite pre-war political symbol, the word *kokka*. The word corresponds to 'State', but its overtones are some-what removed from the Orwellian implications which that word has in Britain. The characters with which it is written show clearly its etymology, literally 'nation-family'. Before the war it was unmis-takably a 'hurrah-word' and 'to serve the State' (*kokka ni tsukusu*) was practically equivalent to 'serve the Emperor', as expressing the supreme duty of the citizen. The questions were as follows

1. What do you think should be the politician's chief concern
   (*a*) to further his own interests,
   (*b*) to further the interests of his party,

(c) to further the interests of the people, (*kokumin*) [210]
(d) to serve the *kokka*.
2. Do you think there's ever any difference between doing things for the *kokka* and doing things for the *kokumin*? When, for instance?
3. The next is about the duty of the people, I suppose you would call it. It's really a question of words; which do you think is the best way of putting it 'to do one's best for society (*shakai*)' or 'to do one's best for the *kokka*'?

Numerical analysis of the first two questions is not very meaningful since some answers could be ambiguous, but it is perhaps a rough measure of the extent to which the word *kokka* has lost its magic and even acquired bad odour that 65 people answered 'Society' to the last question and only 18 '*kokka*'. (Twelve said they were the same; seven didn't know.) The rejection of the *kokka* and all it stood for was explicit and even vehement in some cases; some said that it sounded 'militaristic' or 'nationalistic' (*kokka-shugiteki*, a word almost only used in disapproving contexts). 'The Tojo government was out to serve the *kokka*, but look what it did for the people.' 'We always used to be told that to do things for the *kokka* was to do things for the people,' said one woman who had lost a son in the war, 'but I wonder. I must say I've no intention of serving the *kokka* any more. I would say no thank you. Look what's happened to me. I even bear a grudge against the Emperor over my boy.' Some simply said that 'society' sounded more 'familiar' (*mijika*, i.e. presumably, not surrounded with an aura of military band music, flags, solemn hush and ceremonial bows). A few were either cynical or bewildered. 'Society seems to be the fashionable word nowadays'; 'These things change. Nowadays it's best to say "society", but it may be that one day it will be best to say *kokka* again, mayn't it?'

A small number of those for whom *kokka* was still a positive symbol made comments which would not have been out of place in pre-war speeches. 'The State comes first' or 'Without the State there wouldn't be a people'. Of more significance was the fact that many more people who revealed no positive attraction to the *kokka* symbol nevertheless showed in their replies to the second question that the cognitive connotation of the word was for them much the same as it had been in pre-war Japan; the *kokka* was a transcendental entity with an identity, interests and even a volition of its own. Thus, it was for the sake of the *kokka* that the Government was concluding a Peace Treaty without Russia although this was far from being in the interests of those of the people who had relatives still held prisoner in Siberia. It was not in the interests of the people to pay taxes, but it was necessary for the *kokka*. The same applied to the recent raising of electricity rates. Secret diplomacy was another necessity for the *kokka*. Austerity programmes could hurt the people, though the interests of the State demanded it. One or two who made such remarks added as an afterthought, 'though I suppose it's ultimately for the benefit of the people', but it was left to the editor of a small left-wing paper to give the reply: 'The *kokka* is only an association for furthering the welfare of the people.'

The rulers and the ruled; the leaders and the led; *o-kami* and the *shomin*. Traditional status concepts are still not extinct, and ten men and fifteen women agreed with the sentiment of a question put in the following terms; 'Some people hold the view that politics are a difficult business which ordinary people cannot expect to understand, and it's best to leave these things to politicians. What do you think?'

On the other hand, as was made clear in an earlier chapter concerning the Social Services (Chapter 6) there is, if not a strong vocal demand, at least a latent desire for improved State welfare services. To the evidence there given may be added the fact that only three people (of the same 102) said that they thought the State should not interfere with the employment situation. But welfare services can be fitted into the old authoritarian patterns—with, for instance, gracious letters from the Empress instructing her servants the Government to take measures to mitigate the ravages of tuberculosis among her people—as well as into the new democratic ones.

The suspicion held by many European observers that post-war Japanese democracy was a vast conspiratorial façade designed to secure the rapid ending of the Occupation and to lull the rest of the world into a false sense of security, was certainly a mistaken one. The symbols of the old regime, the *kokka*, the Emperor, have lost their rallying power, and the propaganda activity of people with some positive conceptions of what should replace them, propaganda which still, in 1954, has the general support of the Press, is making its mark on public opinion despite the failure of the present political leadership to do more than display their bewilderment in and their unfitness for democratic political institutions. But are the authoritarian attitudes so deeply ingrained that, given new opportunities— new national ambitions which can catch the imagination of the people and offer a new illusion of glory—the old symbols could be resuscitated, or the new ones—'society', 'welfare', 'democracy' and the rest—mobilized to produce the same political system as before the war? Is it only, as one pessimistic Japanese social scientist observed in 1949,[211] the 'talismanic' symbols which have been changed while the users of those symbols, their basic outlook and their intentions remain unaltered? At present the national ambition, and the only feasible one, is to gain the friendship and the trust of the outside (Western) world which will give Japan the place of honour among the nations promised by General MacArthur, and ensure her a reasonable standard of living. It will be a long time, if ever, before those ambitions can take a 'glorious', a military expansionist, turn. What will happen if such a time comes will depend in part on the quality of the political leadership which develops in the meanwhile. It will also be affected by the fact that by that time the new post-war-educated generation will form a larger proportion of the population. And, as we shall see in the next chapter, there is reason to believe that they will grow up with somewhat different attitudes towards authority from those of their elders.

14

Education

THE educational system was singled out for special attention by the reformers in Occupation Headquarters. It was believed that those features of the Japanese state—authoritarianism and militaristic nationalism—which were considered morally the most objectionable, and expediently the most dangerous in a Pacific neighbour, had their roots in the training given, and in the values and beliefs implanted by, the pre-war schools. In 1946 a large committee of American educators was invited to make a lightning tour and report on the modifications necessary to turn the educational system into one more befitting a democratic state. It was largely on the basis of its recommendations that the Fundamental Education Law of 1947 (a statement of general principles) and the School Education Law of 1948 were enacted. Meanwhile, by administrative regulations, thorough-going changes had been made in school organization and curriculum, the most noteworthy being the replacement of the former ethics, history and geography courses by a combined 'Social Studies' course.

The changes enforced in the system of higher education were generally deplored by the Japanese, but the new primary and secondary system less so. They set about making the new system work with perhaps more enthusiasm than was shown for any other of the post-war changes. Large numbers of new secondary schools were built, in villages often at the cost of a direct levy on the villagers and sometimes with the help of voluntary labour. There was a great vogue in American educational theory; Dewey became almost a best-seller and words like 'home-room', 'recreation', and 'core curriculum' were used with great fluency and determination, if not always with full comprehension, by teachers in the far corners of the land.[212] Possibly the bewilderment of the ordinary primary schoolmaster, but certainly his anxious desire for enlightenment, are reflected in the vast number of books on educational practice and theory, averaging thirteen a week in 1950, or 5% of the total number of titles produced in that year.[213]

A few visits to schools near Shitayama-cho and some conversations with teachers and parents hardly provide sufficient material on which to base a detailed and systematic analysis of the education Shitayama-cho children were receiving. They were, however, enough to gain some impression of the problems, the bewilderment, the enthusiasms and hesitations which go to make up the atmosphere of the modern Tokyo school.

The Ikegami primary school (catering for Shitayama-cho and four other wards) has just short of a thousand children (aged 6–11) divided into twenty classes (three or four for each age group). The average size of class (forty-nine) is about the average for the borough, though some schools have classes of seventy. Of the twenty-seven teachers (sixteen men, eleven women), three have largely administrative and secretarial duties—the headmaster, the senior master and one other teacher. There are three specialists, an art teacher, a music teacher, and a 'nurse teacher' who is chiefly concerned with the pupils' health.

Before the war it was one of the model schools for showing to foreign visitors, and as such was well provided with equipment, but it was burnt out in the bombing. With gradual rebuilding it progressed from three-shift to two-shift, and now finally to one-shift working. It is still bedraggled in appearance, and one wing remains a mass of scarred walls and twisted window-frames, but the drab classrooms with their resounding wooden boarding, are made gay with maps and drawings, flowers, models and insect cages. There is the inevitable loud-speaker system [214] (provided by the Parent-Teacher Association) and the school still has a good reputation, which prompts some parents from neighbouring districts to send their children here by getting them officially registered as 'lodgers' with relatives or friends within the Ikegami school district. The source of the school's comparative superiority, says the headmaster modestly, lies in the type of homes the children come from. The parents are all more or less of the same lower-middle-class level and they are all keen supporters of school activities.

Discussions of education in Shitayama-cho nearly always led round to a comparison of the present with the pre-war state of affairs. In our first conversation the headmaster, a very forceful and articulate man in his fifties, seemed very anxious to stress how far the spirit of the modern education was removed from the old inculcation of formal knowledge and abstract principles of loyalty and filial piety. Nowadays, he said, he is concerned to impress on the children their rights as citizens—the parks they go to on school outings belong to them, not to the Government—he believes not in rigid authoritarian discipline nor in the encouragement of moralistic precocity, but in awaiting the natural burgeoning of the child's moral sense. There are stages of development, . . . tender plants . . . fertilization . . . hot-house blossoms . . .

Certainly there was nothing rigidly disciplinarian about the assembly with which each day began. The pupils lined up in class formation and raggedly and haphazardly measured distance from the front on the orders of the senior master. As the headmaster came on to the platform, the head boy (President of the Pupils' Self-Governing Council) stepped forward to say 'Good morning, Headmaster' and all the pupils bowed. After the headmaster's few remarks on the fact that it was the day the Japanese plenipotentiaries were due back from the San Fransisco Peace Conference, that the next day was old people's day, and that parents had complimented him on the efficiency of the Traffic Section of the School's Self Government Association, they filled off in ragged line talking and laughing the while.

Until the end of the war strict military discipline prevailed on these occasions. After the war they stopped lining up altogether and just gathered in higgledy-piggledy groups. Then someone discovered that the children were lined up at one of the American schools in the Occupation housing estates. So they started lining up again, but they keep such discipline to the 'minimum necessary to maintain group life'. The headmaster, having elicited from me the information that children did not bow to the head teacher in English schools supposed that 'there is still a lot of unnecessary formalism we could do away with'.

Nor was formal discipline very marked in the class teaching. One class of fifty seven-year-olds presented a scene of good-natured chaos as the teacher attempts to tell a story about a sparrow, but eventually gave way to the persistent interruptions of one boy who had a story of his own that he wanted to tell. In the art room 10-year-olds were making a sort of propeller toy which rises up into the air as it is twisted. They were scraping away absorbedly at pieces of bamboo with penknives, kitchen knives, table knives, anything they had been able to persuade their mothers to let them have. Their 23-year-old teacher was wandering round the room giving advice, and occasionally shooting his own propeller into the air with boyish whoops of delight.

Another class, of 10-year-olds, was doing arithmetic. Problems were written on the board. When they had done them or wanted advice the pupils came individually to the teacher. But there was no question of working in silence; the problems were obviously being worked on, but to the accompaniment of conversation, consultation, shouts across the room and tussles over rubbers. There seemed to be a good many children walking about the room, not all in the direction of the teacher. One boy, convinced that he had been misinformed protested 'Teacher, that's wrong!' The teacher ignored him, having turned by that time to one of the other pupils crowding round him and shouting 'Teacher! Teacher!' like a press of autograph-hunters. One certainly did not get the impression that these children were being brought up in the fear of authority.

The quietest room in the school, in fact, contained the boys of a class of 11-year-olds left alone to work out some arithmetic problems while the girls were away for a domestic class. (Boys and girls take domestic classes together until the age of 10. The fact that boys are now taught to sew was often commented on by male parents as one of the least comprehensible whimsies of the new education. It is generally justified, and approved by many mothers, on the grounds that it should help to induce in men an understanding of the woman's lot.) These were working with quiet concentration which my entry and interrogation of one of them did little to interrupt. One boy, obviously recognized as an authority, would occasionally be asked if such and such was the right answer for number so-and-so. Once he adopted a very elder-brother tone, did not give the answer, but said instead, 'Look, you see that . . . Well, multiply that number by that number . . . See?'.

This much would seem to provide some confirmation of Ruth Benedict's theories concerning the discontinuity of child training in Japan—the undisciplined freedom of early childhood suddenly replaced at about the age of ten by rigid repression which breaks the spirit and prepares for the strict formalism and obedience to convention of adult Japanese life. The period may mark a change, but it is doubtful, however, if sudden repression plays much part. If this were the case, then this could not be other than conscious parental and pedagogic policy, based on commonly held views concerning the nature and responsibilities of the child. But there was little trace of this in parents' answers to interview questions, questions concerning the teaching of respect language, bowing to guests, silence at meals or the age at which they thought the child's *monogokoro ga tsuku* (not quite the same as 'develop a sense of right and wrong'; it means something more like 'develop the ability to behave with discretion and responsibility'). The answers (from 100 parents) show a great variety in which it would defy any statistician's ingenuity to discern a predominant pattern. Girls certainly seem to be taught manners more strictly than boys and from an earlier age, but there was no suggestion that the age of 10 or 11 had any particular significance in parents' eyes. Nor, one gathers from teachers, in their eyes either.

It seems though, that boys at least develop a certain sense of responsibility and self-importance at about this age—perhaps the Pupils' Self-Government Association helps in this. They also develop a sense of sex-separateness. An 11-year-old-boy once answered my question asking when they stopped playing with girls in unhesitatingly precise terms—in the third term of the third year (i.e. at about the age of nine), and he affirmed that this was 'fixed', a convention of the School Teachers also remarked that by the fourth year girls almost without exception used more respectful women's language, not the rougher language of boys.

Corporal punishment is not used in the school, the only punishments being scolding or making children stand in a corner or outside the room. They are invoked, said a group of teachers, chiefly as a means of dealing with quarrels or unco-operative behaviour in group activities—when children 'make a nuisance of themselves to others'. It is, indeed, surprising how often, in modern Japan, one hears *hito ni meiwaku wo kakete wa ikenai*—'one must not make a nuisance of oneself to other people' quoted as the cardinal principle of morality. Of all the traditional moral precepts, this, in itself somewhat negative and unsatisfying, seems to be the only one which has come unscathed through the fire of 'democracy'.

Each class has a Self-Government Association. (*Jichikai* sounds somewhat less pompous in Japanese.) A president and three vice-presidents are elected every term, the elections being preceded by speeches by each of the candidates declaring his policy and what he will do if elected. These act as monitors when the teacher is absent, and (except for the two lowest years) sit on the School Self-Government Council. Teachers are careful to confine the Self-Government Council to the making of the rules—no running in corridors, no leaving of litter, etc.—and to organize the performance of duties such as school cleaning or traffic control. (Every morning in the main road outside the school a 10- or 11-year-old boy or girl would appear with a large red flag inscribed *Ikegami Primary School, Pupils' Self-Government Association, Traffic Section* to hold up the traffic while the children crossed.) They do not give these councils any judiciary powers. In some schools after the war there were class courts in which children judged rule-breaking fellows. They were far too reminiscent of Communist self-criticism meetings—the 'stringing-up' of unpopular children against whom the whole weight of out-raged group sentiment was brought to bear, an experience of trau-matic proportions for the emotionally insecure child. They also have to be on their guard against the class president developing too great a sense of his own importance and becoming a gang-leader of the worst sort.

The children are not allowed, moreover, to write penal provisions into the rules, though they have often asked to be allowed to do so. One teacher said that if he asks the class 'What shall we do with him?' of some offender, they are usually in favour of punishment. There is very little sense of pupil solidarity *vis-à-vis* the teacher, except among girls in the top classes.

This, teachers insisted, used not to be so. The elder-brother attitude was not considered consonant with the teacher's dignity. There was a smouldering state of war between pupils and teachers. Children used to hate having to go to the staff-room. Now they thought nothing of it. Parents have remarked how impressed they were at seeing the headmaster walking away from the school hand in hand with one of his charges.

In the School Self-Government Council, the 10- and 11-year-olds obviously take the lead, but teachers do their best to correct for their predominance and bring the younger ones forward. No powers over lower forms are given to upper forms:—so much for the 'traditional emphasis on seniority' of Japanese society.

No teacher bothered very much about respect language. It used to be part of the ethics course to teach it and they used to insist on it in the class-room. Now there is a certain amount of teaching of respect language in the Japanese language periods, but they do not go out of their way to insist on it in the class-room. Children learn it at home, and there is a considerable difference in this respect between the 'well-spoken' boy from the professional class home and the children from, say, the Public Assistance Hostel.

There is no streaming by ability. It is, said teachers, a bad system. Effective from the intellectual point of view, but man does not live by intellect alone. Feelings have also to be considered. The sense of inferiority of the down-graded and the arrogance of the élite are to be avoided at all costs. Marks are not given in positional order. In reports a child's performance is compared not with that of other children but with his previous term's record. (Teachers fill in the most ludicrously complicated reports sheets for parents, each child being assessed in each subject on three or four criteria, e.g. for the Japanese language, on 'Ability for verbal expression', 'Ability for written expression', 'Ability for comprehension', 'Attitude to study' etc.) The head stressed as a cardinal principle the importance of not letting any child feel inferior or unappreciated. Even if a child was good at nothing but sweeping floors, he would be praised for that. (The really sub-normal are supposed to go to a special school, but the number of places at such schools is insufficient.) At a recent summer Handicrafts Exhibition about a third of the children got prizes—awarded more for effort than for skill.

The complaints of parents suggest that the teachers are not exaggerating in saying that there has been a big change in the disciplinary atmosphere of the schools. The majority of parents are, on the whole, favourable to the new education. The innovations are generally summed up in the phrase that whereas education used to be guided on 'packing-in' principles—the mere cramming of a lot of information down children's throats—now teachers made children study by themselves and gave them guidance. One mother described with unmistakable delight how her 10-year-old son had set off alone to interview the stationmaster at Tokyo station to get material for a social studies period. Another group of mothers agreed that intellectual training probably suffered—whereas the old was narrow and thorough the new education is broad and shallow—but they marvelled at their children's sense of independence and were pleased to see them enjoying their schooling far more than they themselves did in their youth. On the other hand, when asked whether the pre-war ethics course should be reinstated in the curriculum, more than eighty parents out of a hundred said that it should, and the most frequently expressed reason was that the children are 'badly behaved', 'don't know how to be polite' and 'have no respect for their elders'.[215] The other most common theme in justifying the need for an ethics course was that the children are no longer told the stories of famous men to inspire them—the old stories of Ninomiya Sontoku, Benjamin Franklin, Jenner or Noguchi. (Of these the most frequently mentioned was the first, the 'peasant sage of Japan', an agricultural productivity expert and moralist of the early nineteenth century, himself a shining example of upward mobility overleaping all the feudal barriers of estate distinctions, whose statue—always showing him reading a Confucian classic as he walks down from the mountains, back bent under a load of firewood—stood before the war outside nearly every primary school. At Ikegami it was destroyed in the bombing and has not been replaced.) The necessity of teaching children to be filial to their parents is the next most common theme. Two people thought that children ought to be taught to respect the Emperor and another thought it shameful that children nowadays did not even know the national anthem.

The post-war Parent-Teacher Associations have, at least, brought parents into frequent direct contact with the schools. At the Ikegami school the most common form of meeting was by class, the 'home room' teacher meeting the parents (almost exclusively mothers) of his pupils at regular intervals. There were also three parent representatives for each class who, in addition to arranging outings and social activities of their particular class, also sit on one of eight committees concerned with 'general affairs', 'education', 'culture', 'welfare', 'equipment', 'school meals', 'out-of-school activities' and 'finance'. It was apparent from the remarks of some mothers that they derived a good deal of both pleasure and information from these class meetings, but answers to a few interview questions about the P.T.A. suggested that the organization as a whole was not altogether popular.

Very few parents have nothing to do with it at all. On the other hand most go out of a sense of duty, i.e. it is on the same level as the Ward Association—a meeting at which it is necessary that *one* representative from each household should 'show his face' as a matter of obligation to the local community. Thus, of fifty-five parents with children at school, only six said that nobody from their house ever went to the P.T.A. meetings. In thirty-six houses only the wife went, in seven only the husband, and in five either the husband or the wife according to circumstances. But in only one case did husband and wife go together. (This may also to some extent be due to lingering ideas of the impropriety of married couples being seen out together, and to the necessity for someone to stay home to look after the children.) One woman said at the interview that 'everybody grumbles about *having* to go to the P.T.A. Nobody likes going.'

There were, too, a fair number of specific criticisms of the running of the P.T.A. Only about a dozen of the fifty-five proclaimed themselves fully or even mildly satisfied with the way the Association was being run. The criticisms were very much on the lines familiar from newspaper comment. Chiefly, first of all, that it was primarily a means for wringing money out of parents. This had been especially the case at the Ikegami school where parents bore a large share of the cost of the first stage of rebuilding. With the gradual rehabilitation of its finances, the borough had taken over the whole burden of the later stages of rebuilding, as, of course, it was its responsibility to do from the beginning. (A Ministry of Education survey of educational expenditure for 1949 showed that the money derived from P.T.A. and other contributions amounted to 72% of the amount provided from public funds for primary schools, 66% for secondary schools, and even 15% for high schools.)[216] The contributions were more or less proportionate to means, but since this involved a public self-evaluation of one's standing in the community, it was naturally unpopular. There were complaints that the rebuilding fund targets and the general level of contributions had been decided by the small clique of relatively wealthy members who run the affair and on whom the eventual publication of the subscription list would be most likely to reflect honour and prestige. Such criticisms applied especially to the *per capita* contributions for class activities the collection of which was the class representatives' chief function. Each parent of 11-year-olds, for instance, was asked to contribute 500 *yen* (About 10*s.*) towards the cost of a graduation photograph album, a graduation outing and a memorial present which each class of school-leavers presented to the school.

The very widespread complaint, which recurs in newspaper comment, that the P.T.A. is 'boss-ridden' and run for individual ends, also came up in these interview replies. One or two said that the accounting was distinctly loose and the annual statement left scope for quite sizable speculation. How justified such suspicions were it was impossible to tell, but it would seem more likely that the leaders of the P.T.A. (the President was also President of the Shitayama Ward Association) were attracted more by the opportunities for the minor exercise of power and for 'improving their connections' than by possibilities of financial profit. The former P.T.A. President had already reaped the fruits of his presidency in election to the borough council. There were possibly other advantages, too. The headmaster's room at the school was liberally provided with ashtrays, each of which bore an advertisement for the former President's glassware and kitchen equipment.

Another criticism of the leadership was that too much was spent on unnecessary and expensive conviviality for the exclusive enjoyment of the officials. That 'the women seem to have very little say in what goes on' was the complaint of another man whose wife always represented his household at the meetings. And, indeed, there did seem to be a strong tendency for the meetings to be composed of a small oligarchy of managing men, and a large number of docile women. This is, perhaps, one reason why women rather than men go. It would be somewhat humiliating for the man to have to join the docile herd of those not in the inner circle and it is not easy to lead an opposition in local community organizations of this sort in Japan.

Nevertheless, in spite of these criticisms—most of them justified—the P.T.A. does succeed in bringing parents and teachers together. Of forty-eight parents of primary school children, only ten (eight of them men) had never talked to their children's teacher in the past year.

Co-education, one of the chief post-war innovations, seems to be generally accepted and approved by parents, to judge from replies to interview questions. Women, in particular, approve on the grounds that their daughters are now able to enjoy an education equal in quality to that given to boys. It is most anxiously watched at the high school level, where, if anywhere, the new conventions governing adolescent friendships appropriate to a society which marries 'for love' rather than 'by arrangement' will have to be created. Some local authorities went over to co-education with a single thorough-going reorganization. In Osaka half the pupils and staff were transferred all at once from one school to another. Tokyo, however, believes in gradualism, with the result that a former boys' school (referred to hereafter as the Ueno School) takes two-thirds boys and one-third girls, and a former girls' school (the Mita School) takes two-thirds girls and one-third boys. Moreover, since the former boys' schools still have the reputation of being the best for boys, and the former girls' schools the best for girls, owing to the nature of the entrance examination (see p. 206), the Ueno school tends to consist of two-thirds bright boys and one-third dull girls, and the Mita school of two-thirds fairly bright girls and one-third boys who could not make the grade for one of the better former boys schools. Although this was denied by teachers, there seem some grounds for suspicion that the Municipal authorities were not keen to have the system work successfully. There are, at least, some headmasters who are strongly opposed to the change. At Hibiya, for instance, which formerly had the reputation of being the best boys' middle school— the sure route for entry into the First High School and thence into Tokyo Imperial University—the headmaster has publicly said that he has no intention of starting domestic studies or providing other special facilities for girls. Only one woman teacher has been appointed and a firm line is taken with girls who do not reach the standards required, fifteen of whom were expelled in 1950.

The boys at the Mita school were a very depressed group. The girls despised them, which suited the teachers since there was little probability of 'problems' arising. In the early days there were rumours that a third-year girl had written love-letters to a first-year boy, but since then there had been no difficulties. All classes except those in physical education and domestic studies were taken together and seating was determined by height with the sexes mixed. There were also joint class excursions, but the school definitely frowned on 'pairing off'. The school rules had the following section on 'friendship'.

1. With respect to friendships, always consult with your parents or your class teacher and respect their advice.
2. If you have specially intimate friends, always introduce them to your family.
3. In relations with members of the opposite sex, always observe proper decorum.
4. Relations with members of the opposite sex should be open and healthy. Always observe strict decorum and etiquette.
5. Strive to build a happy school atmosphere, each helping the other and supplementing the other's short-comings.
6. It is not proper etiquette to be alone in a room with a member of the opposite sex. If it is unavoidable, see that the door is left open.

Girls did have boy friends outside the school—mostly boys older than themselves and most frequently students of nearby Keioo University. It was considered bad form to have a boy friend who is working. Prohibition of make-up and permanent waves was written into the school rules, but was not very effective. Girls could be observed tying up their hair at the school gates and letting it down as they leave.

The *essu* ('s') or *shisutaa* ('sister')—the 'very special' adolescent girl friendship which were so much a part of the pre-war Girls' High School culture, seemed to have disappeared. The all-female Takarazuka troupe still performed its insipid musicals, but it no longer aroused the passionate interest of the High School girls, and 'pin-ups' of its leading stars—always Eton-cropped and dressed in dinner jacket and black tie—were no longer in favour. 'Crushes' can now, presumably, take a more adult heterosexual course without too great an accompanying sense of sin.

At the former boys' school at Ueno (where the intellectual inferiority of the girls fits more neatly into established cultural patterns) the atmosphere was somewhat different. In the second year of co-education there were the beginnings of particular friendships between boys and girls. Sometimes they would go to the cinema together, but more commonly (for economic reasons) call at a tea-shop for a cup of tea and a cake on the way home from school. Often it was the girls who paid and frequently the dominant feature of the relationship was a protective solicitude of the girl for the boy. The girl would often bring cakes for two to eat together during the break. (Perhaps freedom of adolescent courting in a society where male superiority is well established necessarily tends to make the girl the 'admirer'.) The attitudes taken by teachers vary; some made clear their disapproval of paired visits to cinemas. But the general policy of the school was tolerance provided there was no attempt at secrecy and the parents approved. On one occasion, when the relations between one third-year boy and a first-year girl appeared to be developing excessive intensity, they were both given a talking-to, but there was no question of repressive measures.

Club activities and class outings were all mixed. One teacher who had recently taken a class on a trip to the mountains said that there was no tendency to split up into separate sex groups; boys and girls came down the mountain hand in hand. On the other hand mixed groups for school group study was not a success, the girls were boycotted by the boys, who refused to take them seriously or allow them to do anything. Class seating was segregated. The four double rows or desks were alternately boy rows and girl rows, and during a break of five minutes in one class when there was much talking and joking going on, no boy appeared to speak to any girl.

At both schools, particularly the Ueno one, the children are very much examination-oppressed. At Mita before the war, according to the headmaster's estimate, about 10% of the girls went on to a women's university, 3–4% took jobs, about 15% stayed on for the Supplementary Course—in which they learnt flower arrangement and the tea ceremony and other polite accomplishments—the rest stayed at home to be trained for an early marriage by their mothers. In 1951 about a third went on to university and a third took jobs—not for family economic reasons so much as to 'see the world'. Every afternoon from 3 to 4.30 there were special examination classes for those who want to take university entrance examinations. There was still a supplementary 'bride's school' course, but the girls showed little eagerness to enter it.

At Ueno 95% of the boys aimed to get to a university. Many had private teachers and there were again special examination classes every afternoon. The whole school curriculum tends to be organized around the needs of the university entrance examinations. The teachers deplored this, but saw no way out. The parents want it, the children want it and the school, to maintain its reputation, must keep up a good record for getting its pupils into Tokyo University. It was even difficult to get boys to take on the jobs of officials in the Self-Government Association so reluctant were they to spare time from their studies.

Competitive personal rivalry becomes keener with the approach of the highly competitive university entrance examinations. There was a curious system of allocating positions only to the upper strata in examination results. In the trial run for the university entrance, held in the third year, the first fifty were numbered, the also-rans were simply classified as 'upper', 'middle' and 'lower'.

The most worried men in these schools were the teachers of social studies. It is not an easy subject at this level, where they can no longer stick to the safe primary school topics of the transport system and the fire brigade. 'What is the ultimate object? That's what bothers us,' said one. 'What is the "good citizen" we are supposed to produce? The person who is obedient to his leaders? Someone who has enough powers of independent criticism not to be fooled by his leaders? Or someone who is capable of rubbing along with his fellows and merging co-operatively in his group?' The Ministry of Education produces its Outline Course of Study (see Appendix IV). but it only lists the scope to be covered with little guidance as to the object in view. As one of them said, 'It used to be easy enough in the old days when everything centred on inculcating "loyalty" (he used the English word—the same psychological mechanism as produces a new polite word for "lavatory" every generation), but now it's impossible to bring everything coherently together.' Another showed the circumspection of a Vicar of Bray. 'Who knows how Japan is going to change in the future? [This was in the last year of the Occupation.] It is impossible to visualize what sort of society it will be like, or what will be the type of good citizen which that society will demand.' Too much is left to the teacher, and at the same time prudence demands care in the expression of his political opinions. (Most schools are still fairly liberal, but in others left-wing opinions have been the end of a promising career.) But the real trouble is that most of them have not got any firm opinions. As one of them said, their *nayami*—their worried confusion—transmits itself to their pupils.

Sometimes, indeed, it seemed in 1951 that only the Communists and the American-worshippers had succeeded in really finding something to believe *in* since the defeat. For them it was easier since it was not so much abstract principles or values as a source of authority to which they were required to pin their faith. But those who tried to get some clear idea of the moral implications for the individual and the political implications for contemporary Japanese society of the 'democratic' outlook were often as much at sea, and as insecure, as the conscious trimmers—than whom, was one's impression, they were rather more numerous.

The result, at any rate, was that the Social Studies periods tended to concentrate on the retailing of nearly packaged factual detail. The mere description of the established order was thought to be 'safe' and 'non-political'. It may be safe, but it is certainly not non-political. A general conservative bias is inevitable, which, however, the *nayami*, the worried confusion of the teacher may do something to subvert.

One first-year class, for instance, was being taken through the taxation system. (General Social Studies continue through the Secondary School to the first year of High School. For the last two years of High School it is split into Japanese History, World History, and Human Geography.) The explanation was based on pamphlets provided by the Tokyo Municipality and the Ministry of Finance, copies of which every child had. They explain the mechanisms of taxation. The teacher did promise to touch on the 'social policy aspects' in a later lesson, but today there was no approach to normative questions except in discussion of the system of graduated income tax, when the teacher said that the alternative system of equal *per capita* taxation might cut some people's income below the minimum, and so the progressive system was designed to meet this objection. His only comment on indirect taxation was that it was originally the most common form and was easier to apply since people were taxed without noticing it.

There was no mistaking the feelings, in any of these schools, that things had changed. Nor did one feel prompted to doubt the genuineness of frequent statements that the change was for the better. Many really felt that a dead weight of oppressive formalism had been lifted. In the former Japan the sacred had expanded its sphere of competence too far at the expense of the profane. The most frequent adjective used to describe the old days was *kyuukutsu*—'stiff', 'crampingly formal'. So much of life was sacrosanct;—the transcendental supremacy of the Emperor and his scriptural utterances, the glory of the army and the nobility of Japan's destiny, the principles of the established order and the ideals of the educational system, even the authority of the teacher. To treat these sacred symbols lightly and objectively, verbally to criticize or in behaviour to fail to conform, was unthinkable outside a small stratum of intellectuals. To do so was not only prudentially dangerous in a local community in which sententious solemnity held absolute sway and reacted with hostility against non-conformity, it was also to cut oneself off from the emotional security of identification with the aims and values of a thoroughly integrated society carving its way to success against a hostile world. The teacher, on whom devolved a special responsibility for upholding the values of the society, was more especially circumscribed by the solemn formality which the sacred elements of life demanded.

Now the frontiers of the sacred have been rolled back; the dreadful consequences of sacrilege no longer follow a joke about authority or a confession of honest fumbling doubt. A lapse from dignity is no longer a betrayal of the ideal role of the teacher which society formerly imposed. Many undoubtedly feel freer and happier. But there must also be some, both among the conscious trimmers and among those who honestly confess themselves uncertain in their basic value beliefs, who find this new freedom painful and distressing. Implicit acceptance of the sacred symbols undoubtedly gave many an assurance and a security for which the new age provides no substitute. How many are now in the grip of Erich Fromm's 'fear of freedom'?

And how many such individuals will the new generation now being educated contain? What was to be seen in these schools certainly did not suggest the educational system which one associates with an authoritarian society. The freedom and the gaiety of the primary school child does not foreshadow the adult personality which fears authority but stills its fears by appeasement, by subservience to and identification with authority, directing the hate which accompanies its fear towards external objects. But perhaps this is not the whole story. It may be that the new methods were the more easily assimilated in the primary school in that they fitted into already established patterns of tender indulgence for the young child. But there was something a little ominous in the deadly earnestness of the High-School boy whose life, with the whole weight of parental ambition behind him, centres on approaching competitive examinations. It was an earnestness which left little time for questioning, little time for anything but the amassing of knowledge primarily related to its instrumental value for 'getting on'. It was necessary for them to prepare themselves to answer the question: 'The present system of income tax is a (regressive, progressive, indirect) system of taxation. (Put a ring round the most suitable)' rather than to concern themselves with the question whether the present system of taxation was just or unjust. And what if the society whose workings are thus being

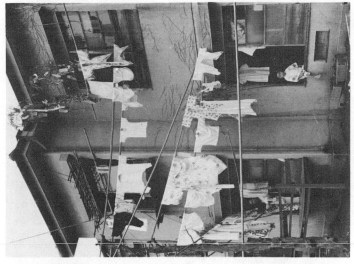

An apartment block

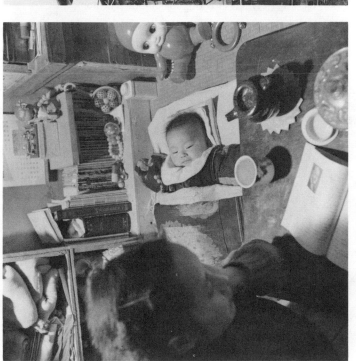

Living in one room

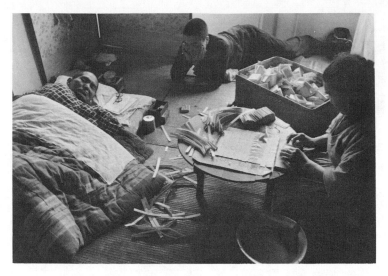

A poor family. The husband is sick and the family is largely supported by the wife's earnings making match-boxes at home

The street story-teller shows his pictures

taught in much the same way as the laws of physics are taught—a society whose prospects of economic expansion are rigorously limited by poverty of natural resources and by defeat—fails to offer some satisfactory fulfilment of their strivings to a large number of those now caught up in the greatly expanded higher-education system? Will there be sufficient fluidity in the economic system to enable such individuals to go on hoping for something to turn up, or at least to secure a working-out of their own thwarted ambitions by projecting them onto their children? Will the training in school self-government associations be sufficient to enable the frustrated to express themselves in the organization of democratic political parties and economic pressure groups? Or will their understanding of the forces which control society be so imperfect, will they feel so strongly the need for an immediate inspiring hope, the need, as the traditional proverb has it, 'to wrap up in something long'—to find some reassuring symbol of inviolate authority as an escape from the powerless isolation of the individual—that a new regime of authority and conformity develops? It need not necessarily be on the pre-war Japanese pattern —for the resuscitation of the old symbols would require an act of salesmanship of which the present political leaders are probably incapable—but the recent history of Europe and of Russia provides no lack of suitable alternative models.

15

Leisure

THE growth of commercial forms of passive mass entertainment is as much a feature of Tokyo as of any other modern city. And the development is not new. The old Edo of Tokugawa times compared well with any of the contemporary capitals of Europe in the number and variety of its forms of popular commercial entertainment. There were the restaurants, brothels and geisha-houses which provided private entertainment in the form of food and drink, music and dancing, juggling and jesting, and feminine company trained to be amusing and skilled in the literary arts as well as sexually attractive. There was a considerable production of wood-block-printed fiction, and commercial lending-libraries for those who could afford to borrow but not to buy. There were also well-developed forms of impersonalized mass entertainment. There were the popular theatres with their constant new productions and their repertoire of well-known classics—colourful dramas of samurai chivalry or merchant passion, played with rhetorical declamation and vociferous stylized dance by star actors whose block-printed portraits sold briskly on the streets. There were street booths with their freaks of nature, and music halls featuring jugglers and acrobats, story-tellers with their epic tales of battle and intrigue among the feudal lords, and humourists with their mimed anecdotes full of the broad Chaucerian humour of fleas and farts and unplanned pregnancies. There were wrestling matches between professional wrestlers whose short sharp bouts were preceded by ritual muscle-flexing dances and courteous civilities.

All these persist today. The *kabuki* drama shows no sign of declining popularity and is easily the most patronized of all the forms of live entertainment. The 'music halls' now sometimes have rows of seats in sloped auditoriums instead of the old *tatami-matted* hall and the bill includes cross-talk acts in the Western music-hall style, but still the core of the programme is provided by the old reciters and humourists telling stories their great-grandfathers told (often literally so, since the professions are hereditary) and in the language in which their great-grandfathers told them. The same wrestling matches take place but now in big covered stadiums, and the fortunes of the champions are followed not only by the thousands who pack the benches or squat on the *tatami* of the boxes, but by millions who listen to radio commentaries and read the sporting editions of the papers. The brothels and the geisha houses are now supplemented by large numbers of taxi-dance halls, 'salons', 'cabarets' and 'social tea-houses' which still provide hired feminine entertainment to an almost exclusively male clientele, but in a modernized, more garish, if cheaper form. The taste for fiction is now served, not only by the productions of the 'literary' novelists whose work appears in long instalments in the monthly magazines, nor only by the works of the 'semi-literary' and 'intermediate' novelists serialized in the daily newspapers, but also by a vast industry of 'popular' paper-backed fiction which, despite its adoption of Western 'true-confession' and thriller techniques, still finds an ever-popular source of material in the settings and legends of Tokugawa Japan.

To these have been added many new forms of entertainment. Cinemas are plentiful and are supplied not only by Hollywood and Europe but also by a home industry which, in 1950, produced as many films as Britain and France put together. The 'New Theatre' produces modern naturalistic and poetic drama by Japanese writers along with translations of Chekhov and Ibsen, Shaw, Priestley and Sartre. There is a new, slightly jazzed-up, more violent and exciting, form of the old *kabuki* drama. The Noo plays, the sedate mimed lyrical dramas which in Tokugawa times were almost the exclusive private entertainment of the samurai, are now performed by semi-professional companies and can be seen by all at commercial theatres. Most houses have a radio, for which an official Broadcasting Corporation and a large number of commercial stations provide news and political debates, classical and modern drama, parlour games and quizzes, sports commentaries and family serials, Chopin recitals and traditional ballads intoned to the accompaniment of the Japanese *shamisen*-banjo. Three television companies cater for a small minority with private sets and for the habitues of cafés drinking coffee at a shilling a cup. There are revue shows with hit songs and precision-drilled choruses, strip-tease shows, art exhibitions, zoos, opera, ballet and orchestral concerts. There are baseball matches between professional teams and university rugby and athletics meets. Gamblers are catered for by professional bicycle races, by a state lottery and by vast numbers of pin-table saloons and housey-housey halls.

A cheap railway service provides a widely popular form of entertainment. A day at one of the beaches within twenty or thirty miles of Tokyo is a favourite outing for Shitayama-cho children, and most large Tokyo firms have a 'House by the Sea' for their employees.

There are numerous hot-spring resorts and beauty-spots well provided with hotels, some cheap and of the cook-your-own-food hostel type for hikers, others of the more expensive kind, providing all the pleasures of the 'water-trades', including some whose advertisements claim a 'thousand-person bath' as among their chief attractions. (Mixed bathing, which was a normal and accepted feature of Japanese life eighty years ago, has now, under the influence of more sophisticated notions of sexual modesty, acquired an aspect of adventurous depravity.) Visitors to such resorts range from parties of school-children on the school's annual two-day outing, and groups of male friends or business associates (such resorts are a favourite place for business entertainments) to young couples and occasionally family groups.[217] Most trips are for two or three days only. Despite paid holidays for employees covered by Labour Standards Laws, the week or the fortnight's family holiday away from home is practically unknown except for visits to relatives, which are, in fact, generally made *en famille* and belong to a different category from visits to hot springs.

There are certain obvious divisions into which all these various forms of entertainment fall. In the first place there is a class, or at least an educational-level, dividing line. Opera, ballet, 'modern theatre', orchestral concerts, and the Noo theatre are generally patronized only by the middle-class high-school and university-educated groups. And for the first three, at least, audiences are predominantly youthful, with a preponderance of students.[218] Then there is an equally obvious sex division. Many traditional forms of entertainment—in particular the 'water-trades', the brothels, geisha houses, salons, cabarets and road-side potato-spirit bars—cater almost exclusively for men. So do most sports, though young women are to be seen at baseball and rugby matches, particularly at university matches, and the old *sumoo* wrestling matches have always been a favourite entertainment of the women of the 'water-trades' who are taken along by their patrons. There is, however, an increasing tendency for visits to cinemas, theatres, zoos and the seaside to be made *en famille* or by husbands and wives together.

Throughout the whole range of those forms of entertainment which provide fictional experience in vicarious living—the theatre, the cinema and printed fiction—run parallel lines of division between what are, in the case of films, generally labelled as the three categories 'foreign', 'period' and 'modern'. Foreign films have a ready market in Japan, not only the American productions which predominate, but also European films, though the audience for the latter is largely confined to the big cities. In 1950 the total number of foreign films shown equalled the total number produced in Japan, and they would appear to be popular. When a Shitayama-cho sample (of 104) were asked to name their favourite film actor, if any, forty-three mentioned foreign stars, compared with twenty-one who named a Japanese star. The foreign category of printed fiction—the large number of translations of European and American novels of which the nineteenth-century Russians and the modern French seem to be the most widely read—has not the same broad appeal. Its readers approximately coincide with the high-school and university-educated groups who patronize the opera and the 'modern theatre'.

But the 'modern' and the 'period' categories more or less equally divide between them both the output of the Japanese film industry and of the popular magazine and paper-backed fiction industry. 'Modern' fiction has its setting in present-day Japan and appeals to much the same basic emotions, and compensates for much the same frustrations as popular fiction in the West, though with significantly different centres of interest deriving from the special nature of Japanese family relations. The 'period' films and novels, and, of course, the *kabuki* theatre, though not basically different in their appeal from the 'modern' ones, have a special element of romanticism which derives from their setting in the feudal—usually the Tokugawa —period. Their heroes are men of action, courageous upholders of the right, resourceful swordsmen, protectors of the weak, and flawless examplars of the virtue of absolute loyalty.[219] The popularity of this type of fiction is one example, as it is also, perhaps, one cause, of the awareness which the ordinary Japanese has of the customs and the values of the feudal past (even the local street advertising man generally appeared in *samurai* costume and used Tokugawa language to extol the fishmonger's wares). Such an awareness is not, perhaps, surprising in view of the recency of the feudal past contrasting so clearly with the whole tenor of modern urban life.

Some of these forms of entertainment enter into the lives of every Shitayama-cho citizen. Nearly everyone has a radio and reads a daily newspaper and one of the monthly magazines. In an interview only six people out of 104 were not able to name any place of commercial entertainment which they had visited in the previous six months. All but twenty had been at least once to the cinema during that period. Nevertheless, with the possible exception of magazine and fiction reading, commercial forms of entertainment still play a smaller part in the lives of the citizens of Tokyo than in the lives of Londoners—primarily, doubtless, a reflection of the general difference in levels of living. To give some rough quantitative comparisons, whereas one Londoner in forty attends one of the League football matches on an average winter Saturday, all of Tokyo's baseball stadiums, if packed to capacity, would not accommodate more than one in fifty of the population. Whereas England as a whole has one cinema for every 11,000 of the population (1953), even Tokyo in 1951 had only one for every 31,000 inhabitants.

Much the same may be said of non-commercial organizations which provide opportunities for leisure activity; it is again a difference chiefly in the number of such organizations and the degree of participation which separates urban Japan from urban England. Clubs and societies exist—from an Eating With the Wife Luncheon club of business men and officials pioneering a new route to marital felicity to a Friends of the Postal Services Society of stamp collectors, from Family Planning Associations to fishing Clubs—but their number is relatively small. Generally speaking, the organization of recreational clubs and societies is common within limited communities whose members are already brought together for purposes other than recreation, but the number of associations for specific recreational social or political purposes which exist to bring together strangers of like interests for the sole or primary purpose of indulging or promoting those interests is small. Thus youth clubs are generally the youth clubs of a particular ward or neighbourhood. There are also associations participation in which is conceived more as a matter of civic duty than as ways of using leisure time—associations such as the Parent-Teacher Association, the Ward Association, Mothers' Meetings and so on—all organized on a narrow neighbourhood basis. Other more or less formal associations such as social savings societies and outings societies are organized among groups of neighbours. Within large firms there are often active sports clubs, film clubs, choirs and hiking clubs.

But of a sample of 104 adults in Shitayama-cho, only seven mentioned a club or society to which they belonged, membership in which was not confined to a closed territorial or occupational circle. These were a fishing club, a cookery-study club, a *kabuki* appreciation club, a music society, a Bible-study group, a Buddhist moral culture group, and a dancing club.[220] Political societies are rare; party branches have few members and organize almost no social activities. Temple membership, as will appear in later chapters, is hardly association membership in any sense of the term. A small number of religious societies exist, some of the traditional type which are concerned primarily with the organization of shrine pilgrimages, and some of a more modern doctrinal complexion, but there are almost no social clubs centring on temples. Charitable societies, and organizations to promote particular ideas and good causes, are confined to a small number of upper middle-class women. To sum up, then, the Japanese are not great 'joiners', though they do show considerable skill in the formal organization of associations within existing limited face-to-face groups—even the small social savings societies of fifteen to twenty neighbours have carefully formalized rules and keep meticulous records.

Another form of leisure activity, intermediate between the commercial and the voluntary organization and chiefly important for middle-class women, is the taking of lessons—in the tea ceremony, flower arrangement, music, dancing or calligraphy. Above a certain social level the acquisition of such 'parts' is an essential prerequisite for marriage, but some women develop an intrinsic interest in these pursuits and have the resources and the leisure to continue them after marriage. The sole form of recreation for many such housewives is a weekly or fortnighly gathering at the house of a teacher of the tea ceremony—not really for new instruction, but simply to spend a pleasant afternoon drinking tea and gossiping with the teacher and fellow-pupils. Such groups are not formal associations; they are held together by the bond of common (fee-paying) discipleship of a particular teacher. Membership is not entirely confined to women; men also learn the tea ceremony, and some of the traditional arts, such as Noo chanting or calligraphy, are more commonly practised by men than by women. Casual observation would suggest that the proportion of the population who cultivate arts and accomplishments such as these and derive from them all the satisfactions of positive creative activity is much higher than in a comparable English population. Sometimes the intrinsic satisfactions may be subordinated to the prestige value of these accomplishments or even to ambition— the latter particularly, apparently, in West Japan, where having the same interests and going to the same teacher as a superior may be as important a means of advancement within the firm as belonging to the right golf club.

But even if these forms of leisure activity are included, the Japanese are not enthusiastic joiners of formal leisure-time associations, a fact which may be partly explained in terms of the general characteristics of social relations in Japanese society. The solidarity of primary groups implies feelings of separateness from people who do not belong to the group and a certain wary circumspection in one's dealings with them. A Japanese, who tends to make all his social relations as 'personal' as possible, and hence also to confine his social relations to those which can be 'personal', hesitates to enter into relations with strangers for specific recreational purposes. Moreover, if he is able to find warm personal contacts at work and in his neighbourhood, he has less need to do so. Another factor involved in this difference between Japan and, say, England, is the difference in levels of living. Membership of such associations as exists costs money, particularly since the core of their members consists of the wealthier middle-class men and women who have received the necessary training in such association activity in high schools and universities.

Some importance may also be attributed to a difference in conceptions of the nature of leisure. Many Japanese do not see their lives as divided into two mutually exclusive parts, work and leisure, the former detestable and the latter desirable and to be used in as enjoyable and entertaining a way as possible. For those who are employed for fixed hours in routine jobs in offices and factories, such may indeed be the case. But for housewives and for the by no means negligible proportion of shopkeepers and domestic craft workers there is no such clear dividing line. The working day lasts from early in the morning until late at night, but the monotony is broken by chats with neighbours or customers, odd quarters of an hour spent trying to amuse a crying baby, pauses to watch the advertising man come down the road in his extravagant period costume, to prepare and eat meals or listen to something of special interest on the wireless.

Personal intercourse is still perhaps the staple source of leisure-time enjoyment of the people of Shitayama-cho. Not only odd chats in the course of the day's work (the willingness of officials and business men to interrupt their work for a sociable cup of tea with visitors appeared shocking to American Occupation officials and all of a piece with other evidence of unrationalized inefficiency such as bad time-keeping), but also evening visits to friends and neighbours, sometimes for a game of Japanese chess or cards or *mah jong*, but often simply to pass the time in pleasant gossip. It is gregariousness as well as cleanliness which induces many people to make prolonged daily visits to the ward bath-house. Although there is little deliberate cultivation of conversational techniques such as the conscious collection and polishing of anecdotes, the general level of verbal fluency is high and it would be rare to find a group of three or four neighbours or relatives who could not entertain each other with talk for hours at a time.

In traditional Japanese society, leisure which is consciously conceived as such is seasonal rather than daily, weekly or monthly. The farmers explicitly divide the year into 'busy seasons' and 'slack seasons' and it is in the slack season that come the occasions specially set aside for enjoyment—the festivals of the family and the local community. The change to daily leisure or weekly leisure and the opportunities for a vast range of leisure activities besides the traditional feasting, talking, singing, dancing and love-making, does make these annual festivals of lesser importance in places like Shitayama-cho. But it does not by any means cause them completely to disappear. The family groups which come together on these occasions are still large enough and generally contain a high enough proportion of young children for them to be gay and lively affairs. And there is still enough sense of community in the ward for the festival of the local shrine to be the occasion for carefully prepared ward festivities widely participated in.

Children are usually the centre of the small-family celebrations, not only those such as the Boys Festival and the Girls Festival which are held especially for their benefit, but also of the New Year's Festival, the most important in the calender. Then they are given presents of kites and battledore sets, and amused with a variety of games, from an ancient kind of snap based on the matching of cards inscribed with the separate halves of famous short poems, to snakes-and-ladders and rummy played with Western playing cards. The first few days of New Year is also a time for visiting of various degrees of formality, and a large part of the time is spent in talk while eating and drinking at one house after another the special foods and wine which each household prepares for the occasion.

In many ways the Japanese have the best of both worlds. Not only do they have a wealth of indoor games, with all those of the West to supplement traditional pastimes; the festival calendar itself has been augmented by borrowings from the West. Many households now celebrate Christmas as well as New Year, giving presents to the children and preparing special food and perhaps a Christmas tree. This is largely a result of the salesmanship of the departmental stores (one in 1950 had a stupendous Christmas display of pápier mâché angels spiralling up to the heavens with a juke box playing heavenly choir hymns below), and the celebration has, of course, in most households little connection with organized Christianity, though most of those who celebrate Christmas are aware of it as the festival of the birth of a very great man in the West. Individual birthdays, too (which were formerly not of much importance, since ages were counted from the first of January of the year of birth) are now often marked by a special family celebration.

It is a frequent and not unnatural assumption that Western culture and Japanese culture present themselves to the Japanese as somewhat inimical alternatives. It is an assumption which would seem to be confirmed by the pendulum swings of Westernizing fervour and nationalist reaction which have characterized Japanese history in the last eight decades, and by the fact that in popular speech 'traditional' (*dentooteki*) and 'Japanese' (*Nipponteki*) are often used as synonyms (though 'modern' (*modan, kindaiteki*) and 'Western' (*seiyooteki*) somewhat less so). It is generally assumed that those who read translated Western novels tend not to appreciate Japanese 'period' fiction, that the patrons of the 'modern theatre' are not often also the patrons of the old Japanese *kabuki* theatre. In the case of family celebrations, however, in Shitayamo-cho, at least, it seems that the more punctiliously a household celebrates traditional festivals (of a selected ten about which questions were asked) the more likely it is to celebrate Christmas and birthdays also.[221] There *is* a certain element of 'traditionality' involved in the celebration of traditional festivals, as is shown by the fact that celebrating such festivals correlates very highly with having household gods in the home,[222] whereas the celebration of Christmas and birthdays shows no relation to having household gods. But there is no contradiction between the old and the new festivals, and the more important dividing line would appear to be not between the 'traditionally-minded' and the 'modern-minded', or between the 'pure Japanese' and the 'Westernized', but between the more 'celebratious' households who are more likely to celebrate both the old and the new festivals, and those who are less punctilious about either. It would seem that whether or not there are children in the family has a lot to do with determining the 'celebratiousness' or otherwise of the household, but the level of living as shown in the economic status scale used in Shitayama-cho shows no consistent relation at all.

Apart from the fixed festivals of the calendar there are also such seasonal events as the viewing of the cherry blossoms in the spring. Tokyo's tiny parks on a fine Sunday in April become packed with people of whom perhaps 5% are sufficiently extraverted to perform the expedition in the traditional manner, and thus provide for the more inhibited 95% an additional spectacle besides the blossom and the booths and sideshows. The traditional manner requires large quantities of food and wine and a *shamisen*-banjo or an accordion to accompany the songs and dances which begin when everyone is happily tipsy. A variety of such parties was to be seen in Ueno Park on one cherry-viewing Sunday in 1951—large family groups containing all generations, neighbour groups of middle-aged men and women, and groups of young working men. The members of these parties were of the 'real Shitamachi' type—tattooed young men making a show of gay and raucous bravado, blowsy women of the 'water trades', uninhibited old grandmothers clowning suggestive dances—types now becoming sufficiently rare for their lively parties to attract crowds of spectators and for the dancers and singers to become aware of themselves as performers, at least to the extent of making a mock passing round of the hat.

The same contrast between abandoned jollity and more respectable restraint characterizes the differences in the way shrine festivals are celebrated in different parts of Tokyo. It was mentioned in the introduction that a difference in the scale and nature of the shrine festival celebrations is one of the features which distinguishes typical Shitamachi from the typical Yamanote ward. One of the phrases used to characterize the typical Edokko—the 'real Shitamachi' type —is that (as well as 'never carrying money over from one day to the next' and taking pride in 'fires and fights') he would 'even sell a daughter' to find the money to do himself proud at festival time. In wards not far from Shitayama-cho, near to the heart of the Shitamachi district and containing a high proportion of shopkeepers and domestic craftsmen, something of this spirit still prevailed. All through the day relays of young men, well primed with rice wine and all wearing a cotton *yukata* of uniform pattern, their faces made up and a towel tied tightly round their foreheads, carried the heavy gilt god-cart on their shoulders, displaying their strength and virtuosity as they careered in a heaving rhythmically shouting mass from one side of the road to the other, narrowly missing trams and fences and deriving from their vociferous team action the exhilaration of a rugby scrum or of a bayonet charge. The main procession touring all the wards of the shrine parish is a splendid affair with choruses of firemen, priests on white horses, small orchestras on decorated floats, and traditional costumes of all sorts. The children of each ward have their own wheeled god-cart to pull round in procession, well provided with big drums which they take turns to bang with great gusto, when they are not stuffing themselves with an endless supply of cakes and sweets. In the evenings, family and neighbour parties turn out to watch the hired performers on the open-air stage built for the occasion, and to join the press of dancers swaying and revolving round the central band tower to the accompaniment of the dull mesmerizing rhythm of the drums and the plaintive appeals of the flute and the ballad singer.

The two-day Shitayama-cho celebrations were tame and sedate by comparison, and the total expenditure of some £35 was less than a fifth of the expenditure of a ward of similar size in the heart of the Shitamachi district. Nearly every house, it is true put out its festival paper lantern for the occasion, and most gave their contribution to the expenses. But only one or two of the organizers took time off from work; there was no god-cart for the young men to heave round the ward on their shoulders—it had been burnt in a fire some years before and everyone agreed that it was too expensive to replace. The last occasion on which the ward had bought a uniform cotton *yukata* for the young men was in 1935.

As the President of the Ward Association said at a meeting called to make preparations for the celebrations, 'the main thing is that the children should come first', and someone else added as a commentary for my benefit that the festival used to be an occasion for adult merry-making, but this was less so everywhere now, and especially here, where 'salary men' predominated and shopkeepers were a small minority—'salary men' don't care much for 'making a splash'. The children were provided with cheap 'beer-barrel and crêpe paper' god-carts to shoulder and pull, with plenty of drums to bang and with liberal supplies of cakes and lemonade. In the evening many families invited friends and relatives to a festival supper with rice-wine and beer and special red rice cooked with sweet beans. And later on there was dancing. But the band tower around which the dancers circulated contained only a solitary drummer beating time to recorded music relayed through amplifiers, and the old country dances were varied with square dancing led by high-school students, and with fancy-dress competitions. A good time was had by all, the atmosphere was gay and cheerful, but it was restrained and proper compared with the rumbustious and somewhat orgiastic hilarity of a festival in a 'real Shitamachi' ward.

The higher proportion of 'salary men' is, as the people in the ward themselves suggested, undoubtedly in part responsible for this. The 'salary man' tends to be a more transient resident, and it is among his fellow-employees or perhaps among friends dating from his schooldays, rather than among his neighbours, that he has the more intimate contacts and is more likely to 'let himself go'. But there may be more to it than this. The better-educated 'salary man' is less likely to let himself go under any circumstances. He is a psychologically more complex character than the average Shitamachi inhabitant; more complex in that he is more completely an individual, his sources of restraint are more completely internal and he does not so easily drop the barriers of privacy which surround his inner self and merge himself in the identity of a wider group. This is a topic which will be touched on again in the final chapter. Meanwhile, in the next, some further consideration will be given to the nature of relations between neighbours in Shitayama-cho.

16

Neighbours and Friends

THE Japanese word *giri* has become known to sociologists and anthropologists as a result of the prominence it received in Ruth Benedict's brave and percipient attempt to describe Japanese notions of moral obligations by means of an analysis of some of the key words used in talking about them. Her researches led her to the conclusion that *giri* is 'one of the most curious ... of all the strange categories of moral obligations which anthropologists find in the cultures of the world' and that 'it is specifically Japanese'.[223] The methods of verbal analysis which she employs have, however, serious limitations. To take an English example, it would be difficult to draw any confident conclusions concerning English ideas of moral obligation from the fact that the Englishman (unlike the Japanese) uses the same word—'ought'—both in sentences of the type 'If he left on the 2.30 he ought to be here by 4', and in sentences of the type 'If he married her he ought to support her'. The word *giri* has had many uses at different historical periods and in different sub-cultures in Japan. In Ruth Benedict's account, these various uses, embodied in phrases to be found in dictionaries, were all given equal weight as 'common sayings' and, these, together with the explanations of them by her Japanese informants, provided the raw material out of which she sought to create a unified 'category' of moral obligation. The method is a logical extension of her basic assumption—surely a mistaken one —that there is such an entity as a homogeneous 'Japanese culture' or 'Japanese culture pattern' which persists through time and pervades all regions and all social classes; as such, the result could not be other than 'curious'. But *giri* loses most of its curiousness if one does not expect it to represent a moral category in the sense that it is used of, and used only of, a set of obligations which are conceived by the Japanese as all having the same compulsive nature and as all being enforced by the same sanctions.

There is, however, one type of situation in which the word *giri* is often, though by no means always and certainly not exclusively used, which can be treated as a unified category since it is possible to enumerate certain constant defining characteristics. Acts are often said to be done 'from *giri*' when they have the following characteristics:

1. They spring from a sense of obligation rather than from spontaneous inclination.
2. The obligation is spoken of as an obligation *towards* a specific person or group of persons.
3. The immediate sanction which would attend non-fulfilment of the obligation is the displeasure or the distress of this specific person or group of persons.

It will be convenient to talk of *giri*-acts for acts which spring from a sense of obligation of this type, and of a *giri*-relation of A to B to describe a relation such that A is likely to have feelings of this sort about acts which affect his relation to B. So far there is nothing very curious in this type of obligation. 'We really ought to go and see Auntie Mabel when we are in London. She's a bit of a bore, but she will be upset if we don't' is a perfect example of a *giri*-act and a *giri*-relation. The difference between Japan and England is that the structure of Japanese society is such that *giri*-relations arise with greater frequency and have greater importance for the individual's material well-being in Japan than in England, that the acts required in such relationships are more clearly formalized, and that the obligations to perform such actions are often given a higher place in the scale of values of a Japanese compared with such 'universalistic' obligations as 'loving one's neighbour', 'speaking one's mind', or 'pursuing truth' or 'justice', than in an Englishman's scale of values.

Giri-relationships may be 'ascribed' in the sense that they are implied in the very nature of the positions occupied by two parties in any kinship, community or economic organization. Such are relations between relatives not of the same household group, relations beween employer and employee, between landlord and tenant, between neighbours or between fellow-employees. They may also arise as the result of a particular favour conferred, for example, relations beween marriage go-between and married pair, or between an employee and the man who found him his job. Some of these relationships have already been discussed in other chapters, in particular those patron-client relationships—as between employer and employee or marriage go-between and married pair—in which the character of the *giri*-relationship is determined by the status inequalities of the individuals concerned. In this chapter we shall be chiefly concerned with relations between neighbours, relations within which *giri*-acts may be required but which are based on approximate equality of status.

FORMAL RELATIONS BETWEEN NEIGHBOURS

'The neighbours around here are terribly kind,' said a young machinist who had come with his wife to Tokyo some two years before, 'they soon taught us all the customs of the neighbourhood and made us feel at home.' *Kinjo no tsukiai*, the words used, would be more accurately translated as 'the social-intercourse customs of the neighbourhood'. *Tsukiai* is a word used much more frequently than *giri* of neighbour relations and acquaintanceships; to have *tsukiai* with someone is to be in a *giri*-relationship with him, and the noun can be used, as here, to describe the etiquette of such relations, and also, sometimes, the material gifts the exchange of which play an important part in that etiquette. The machinist's remark illustrates the point made above that the acts required in *giri*-relationships are in Japan formalized to a high degree. The etiquette of neighbour relations is a 'social fact' in Durkheim's sense in a way in which it rarely is in any but the politest of English society. It is something which is conceived as an objectively established body of rules, subject to local variation and capable of being learnt and taught, not simply as 'natural' ways of behaving which can safely be left to the spontaneous promptings of the individual heart to take care of.

The highest degree of formalization of neighbour relations is, of course, to be found in settled village communities. There the prescribed social intercourse has the function of 'keeping sweet' relations which have great importance in the context of the manifold forms of economic co-operation which are to be found in Japanese villages.[224] In the Tokugawa period, the towns had something of the same system of formal neighbour relations as the country. The small wards into which Tokyo is still divided had their origin in the Edo of Tokugawa times. They exercised a certain measure of self-government albeit under the distant supervision of samurai magistrates, and as such their organization resembled that of the villages. In both village and town the solidarity of neighbour relations was further strengthened by the 'five-man group' system—or better 'five-household group' system—of collective responsibility. This technique (familiar also to European feudalism) was first borrowed from China in the seventh century and reimposed by the Tokugawa rulers as a means of enforcing obedience to regulations and the paying of taxes.

The same ward unit of relatively small size remains today. (In 1935, of the nearly 3,000 Tokyo wards, 60% contained less than 300 households and only 20% more than 500).[225] In the nineteen-thirties, as the nation became organized for war, ward associations were given legal recognition and entrusted with the functions of organizing civil defence and rationing and in other ways ensuring the co-operation of the citizenry in the war effort. Within the ward associations

tonari-gumi—neighbour groups of from ten to twenty households—
were formed as subsidiary organs of the ward association.

The working of the ward association will be the subject of the
next chapter. Here we shall be concerned with the way in which the
smaller *tonari-gumi* has become the framework of formal neighbour
relations, the forms of which are much older than the official organization of these groups in the last two decades. These forms may be
briefly outlined.

First of all there is a prescribed form for becoming a member of
the group very similar to the leaving of cards by new residents in
English polite society. When a family moves into a new neighbourhood the househead or his wife will make a round of the other houses
in the *tonari-gumi* leaving his name-card and a small present—a cheap
towel, a few boxes of matches, a bar of soap or a fan. (In Japan the
use of the name-card is so widespread that the absence of one might
almost serve as the criterion of the rootless 'lumpen-proletariat'.) At
each house he would introduce himself, 'My name is . . . We have just
come to live at the house on the corner. Henceforth I expect we shall
have occasion to call on your assistance in various ways. I beg your
kind indulgence.' After this *o-hirome*—'advertisement'— he is a member of the group. (At a Ward Association meeting when a list was
being made of the houses in each *tonari-gumi*, the question arose
whether a certain new-comer should be included. The *tonari-gumi*
chief said that the individual concerned had made his rounds of the
neighbours, so he undoubtedly 'should be recognized'.)

At New Year the same formal visits to convey greetings are expected. 'Congratulations on the New Year. During the last year we
have had occasion to call on your assistance in various ways. Henceforth, too, I beg your kind indulgence.' On the birth of a child, or at
a wedding, neighbours make congratulatory visits taking a small
money gift with them. Generally, in the case of congratulatory gifts
and funeral condolence gifts a lump sum is given by the *tonari-gumi*
chief to which everyone in the group contributes, but this does not
preclude individual gifts as well, between particularly intimate households. When there is an illness in one of the households, someone
from each of the others (preferably the wife if it is the wife or a child
who is ill, the husband if it is a man) would pay a visit and take an egg
or some fruit as a present.

At funerals the *tonari-gumi* comes into its own. As soon as someone dies the housewives of the group gather at the group-chief's
house or at the house of the most intimate neighbour of the deceased
and apportion the jobs to be done—who is to help lay out the corpse,
who is to arrange for the undertaker's men to come, who is to send
the telegrams informing relatives, who is to lend what dishes and prepare what foods for the funeral feast and what would be the appropri-

The Shitayama-cho festival. Children
pull the 'god-cart' round the ward

Meeting of a Primary School Pupils' Self-governing Committee

A middle-class family at supper

ate sum for each member, or the group as a whole, to give as an 'incense-money' condolence gift. Then, after the coffin and the temporary altar have been set up, each member will go formally to burn a stick of incense and to offer condolences which generally follow a uniform formula. 'This is really a terrible thing. Despite all your efforts, finally it has come to this. It must be a great blow to you. I feel deeply sorry.' To be answered: 'Thank you very much. We are sorry to have caused everybody so much anxiety, but finally it has come to this. It is very good of you when you are so busy to call to burn incense.'

All of these gifts and visits require some formal acknowledgement. My own gift of a towel to all the households being interviewed was explicitly acknowledged when next I visited with the words 'The other day you were very polite to us.' As I discovered, it requires some months of training before, on meeting an acquaintance, one automatically thinks back to the previous meeting and has ready either the phrase, 'Thank you for your kind entertainment the other day', or, if one happens to have been the entertainer rather than the entertained, 'I was rude to you the other day.' In the case of wedding or funeral gifts, a return gift of approximately equal value is expected.

This etiquette is not, of course, confined to relations within the *tonari-gumi* group. With the exception of funeral help, the same rules of seasonal visiting and gift-giving apply to acquaintanceships with neighbours, friends and business acquaintances outside the immediate neighbour group. Indeed, answers to interview questions about New Year visits suggest that people in Shitayama-cho are more likely to be remiss about relations with neighbours than about relations with fellow-employees or business acquaintances. For this there is an obvious reason. In the foregoing definition of a *giri*-relation it was said that the *immediate* sanction for the performance of a *giri*-act is the displeasure or distress of the person towards whom the obligation is felt. It is generally also the case that there is additionally the *ultimate* sanction of possible material disadvantage. To revert to the English example given above, Aunt Mabel may be 75 and tolerably well off. An awareness of the possible ultimate sanction may or may not consciously affect motivation, but at any rate a clear appreciation of the economic implications of *giri*-relations was apparent in some of the replies to interview questions about *giri*-relations—'support and be supported', 'live together, prosper together' were traditional phrases quoted as justifications for maintaining such relationships.

In districts like Shitayama-cho the formal maintenance of neighbour relations still serves some important economic ends such as dealing with emergencies like death and illness, as well as being a means to the less calculable satisfactions of meeting smiling faces instead of blank stares as soon as one steps outside one's back door.

But these economic considerations are far less important than they are for the farmer whose livelihood depends on various forms of co-operation with his neighbours. Fire insurance, life insurance and post-office savings schemes are widely employed; in the last resort there is always public assistance. The *giri*-relations of greatest economic importance are now those with one's employer or fellow-employees, with the wholesaler or with the bank manager. The weakening of the material sanctions certainly does mean an attenuation of neighbour relations (an attenuation which is, of course, greatly speeded up by the transience of residence of a large part of the urban population). But it does not cause the old patterns to disappear entirely. An awareness of the material sanction backing a *giri*-obligation is not an essential for experiencing a sense of obligation, and the high degree of formalization of the etiquette of neighbour inter-course acts as a brake on the attenuation of such relations. Since everyone knows exactly what should be done, failure to follow the rules amounts to an overt act of rejection.

The existence of established patterns of neighbour relations as a 'social fact' also makes it easier for newcomers to initiate formal re-lations within the framework of which informal relations of in-timacy may grow. Like the machinist from the country, it is not difficult to attain in the new urban environment some substitute for the security and sense of belonging which a rural community pro-vides. Herein can be seen one reason why Japanese industrial towns, largely populated by rural migrants, have not shown the same ex-tremes of social disintegration as characterized the early industrial-ization of Western Europe or recently of Africa.

FORMAL *GIRI*-RELATIONS ELABORATED

Before pursuing the subject of neighbour relations from the formal to the informal level, it may be permissible to digress slightly to con-sider in more detail the three differences between Japan and England which were suggested as a substitute for the idea that *giri* is a 'curious category' of moral obligation. They were:

1. That *giri*-relations arise with greater frequency and have a greater importance for the individual's material well-being in Japan.
2. That the acts required in such relationships are more clearly formalized.
3. That the obligations to perform such actions are often given a higher place relative to other more universalistic obligations.

1. The first point has already been sufficiently illustrated. The greater economic importance of *giri*-relations is clearly connected with the undeveloped state of the social services and the small margins

with which most household budgets operate. And, as we saw, the importance of *giri*-relations goes beyond mere security; they are also important for 'getting on'. The greater a man's *tsukiai*—the wider his network of *giri*-relations or, as the Japanese say, the 'broader his face'—the greater is his power and influence and the greater the prestige accorded him. The breadth of one's *tsukiai* is important in determining status, and important also for political and business success. Only if one's *tsukiai* is broad enough and contains enough key individuals with large subsidiary *tsukiai* networks of their own, can one hope to have a sufficient 'base' (*jiban*) to gain election to public office. The right sort of *tsukiai* helps to get a bank loan, a telephone or an export licence. The extent to which social action in Japan naturally gravitates towards particularistic rather than impersonal procedures was made clear in a conversation with some Shitayamacho friends. An expedition to the *kabuki* theatre was proposed. Tickets are, of course, on sale at the box office and in ticket agencies in the department stores, but my friend's immediate reaction to the proposal was, 'I know someone who's got some shares in the *kabuki* theatre, I'll ring him up.' Even if the acquaintance had provided free seats the return gift would have had to be more than equivalent to the price, so that there was no question of economy involved.

Expansion of social services and of private saving will certainly have the effect of further reducing the importance of *tsukiai* as a means to security. It might be thought, too, on *a priori* grounds, that as the drive for profits enforces greater 'rationality' on industrial activity, as the ideals of efficiency and justice are increasingly imposed on a civil service brought under watchful Parliamentary control, and as the expansion of educational facilities increases political consciousness and the tendency for voting behaviour to be determined, at least overtly, by political beliefs or an appreciation of interest, so also the importance of nepotism and jobbery, of the 'right' connections and personal loyalties—in a word the importance of *tsukiai* as a means of 'getting on'—may be expected to recede still further. On the other hand it is a familiar fact that in Britain and America, with the growing expansion of government in the economic and social field and the consequent increase in the application of controls; with the growing tendency for the 'managerial demiurge' to replace the 'entrepreneurial spirit' in industry and business, the 'contact man', the 'fixer', the 'inside-dopester', whose stock-in-trade is a 'broad face', a wide *tsukiai*, becomes a figure of growing importance.

Here again, if one may for the moment be forgiven the logical fallacy of assuming that the history of Western Europe represents a 'natural' form of social development, the greatly accelerated timing of Japanese industrialization has consequences similar to those noted in connection with ideas of social welfare. Before the traditional village ethic of 'support and be supported' could be replaced by the liberal *laissez-faire* ethic of 'every man for himself and let right and justice prevail', already the age of the 'contact man' has arrived; the system of political and economic organization in which he can flourish has been established. But there is a difference. For the contact man of today, *tsukiai* have been entirely instrumentalized; they have become the means to the end of material advantage. His techniques of visiting and gift-exchange are the traditional currency of *giri*-relations but the moral element is removed. The modern 'fixer' does not take a return gift for a friendly favour received 'out of *giri*'—from a sense that it is the right thing to do and because he is *katai* (or *giri-gatai*), literally a staff man, a man of strict principles who finds it irksome to be under a debt of obligation to any man. He takes a return gift as the price for an advantage obtained and to strengthen a connection which he may need to manipulate again in the future. In the aetiology of the rash of official corruption which so frequently occupies the attention of today's newspapers, the traditional patterns of *giri* acts play an important part. We shall return to this at the end of this section.

2. The high degree of formalization of *giri* acts will have been clear from the description of proper neighbourly behaviour given above. One more example might be given which illustrates the extent to which formal procedures exists to cover not only seasonal occasions and *rites de passage*, but also emergencies of a less common kind. One night in 1951 there was a fire in a shopping centre not far from Shitayama-cho. The next morning, there was great activity, not only of salvage and reconstruction, but also of condolence visits. Outside the ruins of the shop at which the fire had started all that was to be seen was a notice proclaiming: 'Owing to our negligence a fire started which spread to our neighbours. We do not know how to apologize for the trouble we have caused.' Outside the ruins of the nearby shops stood other notices saying, 'Grateful thanks for condolence visits on the occasion of a "spread fire".' (*Ruishoo* is a clear repudiation of the responsibility of having started the fire.) The disconsolate shop-owners sat at tables under the notices with a charcoal brazier and tea-making implements, receiving all the friends and acquaintances who came to offer their condolences and recording their names in a register so that a postcard acknowledging the visit could later be sent. Even the shops on the edge of the burnt-out area had notices outside saying, 'Grateful thanks for condolence visits on the occasion of a near-by fire,' and were similarly engaged in entertaining those who came to enquire after their safety. Gifts are not taken on such condolence visits, though money or household goods may afterwards be sent to enable the victims to get on their feet again.

Another aspect of the high degree of formalization of *giri*-behaviour is the great elaboration of conditions governing the reciprocity of gift-exchanges, and the explicitness with which the duty of such reciprocity is acknowledged, a feature which was pointed out by Ruth Benedict. Some examples of gift-exchanges may be given.

Mr. A called at the B's household for a friendly chat and brought a gift of a very special sort of water-melon. He said that he just happened to be passing the fruiterers and thought they would like it. The next day Mrs. B went to the fruiterers to enquire how much such a melon would cost. She was told between 300 and 350 *yen*. She thereupon took to the A's a return gift of two bottles of beer, costing approximately 250 *yen*. She explained that as A had brought the gift of his own accord the return gift should be of slightly less value than the original gift, but if she had asked A to get the melon for her it would have had to be considerably more expensive. She added that one had to be extremely careful where Mrs. A was concerned, for she had the reputation of being very 'close'. She would, for instance, frequently bring food for the C's chickens, but although the amount she brought was small and often so rotten as to be unusable, she nevertheless showed considerable displeasure if she did not get the two or three eggs which she considered her due. 'But still, with four children, all sent to good schools, and on A's salary, I suppose it's understandable.'

Mrs. C was ill. Her daughter came to Mrs. B to ask if she would get an acquaintance of hers, an assistant professor at the Tokyo University Medical School, to call. He did so, and gave his advice and a prescription *gratis*. Mr. C then brought a 1,000-*yen* gift token from a department store, asking Mrs. B to pass it on to her friend the doctor. After he had gone Mrs. B inspected the gift token and decided that the amount was too much. She explained that the C's had given this out of *giri* to her, i.e. so that her 'face would stand up' *vis-à-vis* the doctor by giving him the generous thank-you present. On the other hand, since the gift was in fact over-generous for the nature of the service, it would be 'bad *giri*' on her part towards the C's if she accepted it. She therefore took it back and explained that 'I know it was very rude of me to open it but . . .'

Mrs. B wanted to have a new gas point installed. The gas company said that it would take three or four months. She then asked Mr. D, the factory owner, who is a good customer of the gas company, if he could do anything. Within two days the gas point was installed. Mrs. B took to the D's an expensive fish as a thank-you present. Some time later Mrs. B, Mrs. D and Mrs. E were talking at a funeral party.

Mrs. B to Mrs. E: Did you know we had a gas point put in the other day—thanks to D-san's kindness. (D-san could mean Mr. D, Mrs. D, or 'the D household'.)

Mrs. E to Mrs. D: Really? That was good of you Mrs. D.

Mrs. D to Mrs. E: Oh, but no. Mrs. B gave us a present and everything.

A lady called to see an old professor in his study, a gentleman who was known to have a great deal of influence. She was accompanied by her 18-year old son and carried a box of cakes with appropriate ceremonial gift wrappings. It appeared that the professor had already been warned of her approaching visit by a mutual acquaintance. Her son was anxious to enter the philosophy department of another university, but it was said to

be very difficult to get in and if the professor could possibly do anything
. . . He accepted the present with a formal nod and promised to see what
he could do. 'But I am an old man now and I tend to forget things. Don't
think to yourself, "I've 'asked' [for the word *tanomu* see p. 70] Tsurukawa
so it's bound to be all right." You must send me a postcard occasionally
to remind me.'

The theory of gift-exchanges and favour-gift exchanges requires
that they should be expressions of good-feeling towards people with
whom one is on a basis of *tsukiai* interaction. The favour done is in
the real sense of the term a favour, the return gift is a 'mere token'
(*shirushi dake*) of gratitude. Spontaneity of feeling is not inimical to
the relation, but it is not required. It is enough to realize that such
behaviour is enjoined by the interdependence—the 'indebtedness' in
Ruth Benedict's terms—of each to all which is entailed by living in
society. No-one, as an official of the ward association said to a young
man who objected to making gifts to the police and the fire brigade,[226]
is living in this world all by himself. To acknowledge this fact explicitly by a constant readiness to perform favours for others and
punctiliously to requite favours received with material gifts is proper,
and morally right, behaviour.

3. Conflict naturally arises when the favours which are given and
expected—the granting of public assistance, the installation of a gas
point, entrance to a university—are such as, according to the overt
and publicly upheld norms of the society, should be allocated on the
basis of universalistic criteria—the fulfilment of certain objective
qualifications; fair shares; first come, first served. Only a hair-line
separates the 'mere token' of gratitude from the bribe, and that hair-
line disappears as soon as the 'mere token' precedes the granting of
the favour. In the political-attitudes questionnaire a hundred people
were asked what they thought was the best way of dealing with the
corruption scandals which were being frequently reported in the press.
Then followed the question: 'Apart from big frauds of that sort, what
do you think of the sort of practice of, say, when making an application for a licence from a government office sending along a bottle
of whisky with the application form, or inviting the official to a party
and so on. What do you think of that sort of *tsukiai*?' Seventy out of
a hundred condemned the practice; six said that regrettable as it was,
that was the way of the world. Ten could not answer. Fourteen saw
nothing wrong in the practice. Of these a few added the qualification,
'but only if it is an expression of gratitude'.

INFORMAL NEIGHBOUR RELATIONS

One factor of great importance in determining the nature of relations between neighbours is sheer physical proximity. Few houses

have gardens; the disposal of rubbish, hanging out the washing, sitting out in the sun, is as likely as not to bring one into immediate contact with neighbours. The closeness of the houses and the acoustic properties of their wooden walls make it impossible to keep one's prayers or one's parties, one's sorrows or one's quarrels a secret from neighbours. My neighbour Mr. O, the commission salesman, and his wife could not pretend that they did not quarrel; they had to face it out. 'Who was it that had the "histeri" last night?', one woman asked slyly at the meeting to elect a new *tonari-gumi* chief. 'Me, of course,' said a glum Mrs. O, 'I'm the histeri-merchant around here.' [227] Mr. O referred to his wife when talking to neighbours as 'our thunder-rumble', and when they brought a puppy, another neighbour congratulated him. 'Lucky for you, Daddy. Half the thunderbolts will fall on the dog now.'

Privacy becomes impossible, intimacy inevitable, and no holds are barred. The machinist who went on to expatiate on the good nature of his neighbours remarked that there was no sort of trouble you couldn't discuss with them. 'But sometimes they say things that cut pretty near the quick, and then it hurts. But you know that there's no real malice behind it and you get over it.' A snatch of overheard conversation illustrates the sort of thing that can hurt: 'Did you know Mrs. T is going to have her seventh? I told her, "You're a fine one," I said, "What are you going to do with it? Haven't you heard there's medicines and things? You don't have to go on having them." Was she angry! "What comes, comes," she said, "and none of your business." She wouldn't speak to me for a couple of days.'

Close intimacy of this sort has little or nothing to do with the formal organization of the *tonari-gumi*. It is generally only with three or four close neighbours that one is on such close terms. 'The three houses opposite and the one on either side' is the traditional definition of the people one expects to be one's best friends (and the title of a popular radio programme in 1951). In answer to interview questions some housewives said that their near neighbours were 'much closer than relatives' and some interviewers commented on the evidence that this was so—sometimes neighbours came into the house and sat themselves down during the interview without a knock or an 'Am I disturbing you?'

Neighbours on such terms help each other in various ways. They act as guardians when someone has to leave the house; for people in Shitayama-cho, though they have an implicit trust in their neighbours, harbour a great distrust of the world outside, and, inspired too by a great deal of police propaganda against giving opportunities to thieves they will never entrust the safety of their homes to the feeble locking devices on their doors. They borrow and lend freely. When an unexpected visitor comes and you happen not to have a kettle boiling, it is always worth looking in next-door to see if they have one on the hob. When the gas-man comes too near the end of the month, someone else whose payday was more recent will probably be able to stand in. A household which installs a telephone cannot expect to have exclusive use of it. For every man in Tokyo who has his own telephone number written in the bottom left-hand corner of his name-card, there are three or four who have a neighbour's number with the bracketed qualification 'call-out'. In serious illness help is generous and unstinted. 'People will worry on your behalf as if it was they themselves in trouble,' said the machinist. One woman recommending her neighbour, a hard-up widow, as a domestic help, detailed her good qualities, 'and she's absolutely reliable; all the neighbours say they will take responsibility for her.' Perhaps this (which was meant literally) is a relic of the old days of five-men groups responsible for each other's good conduct; it is certainly (like the pre-war marriage guide's advice to keep on good terms with your neighbours because they are bound to be asked to give you a 'character' when there is any question of marriage) an indication that close neighbours are likely to know one's most intimate affairs, and support one up to the hilt if one is deemed worth supporting.

Such intimate relations prevail in general only among housewives, or shopkeepers and domestic craftsmen who are at home all day. Men who work outside the ward seek their friendships with fellow-employees. But it would be wrong to give the impression that all housewives, even, were on such terms with their neighbours. For one thing, it takes some time before such relations develop, and though the formal *tonari-gumi* system provides an immediate means of initial acceptance into the neighbourhood, and the framework within which informal relations can grow, some of the shifting population of Shitayama-cho do not stay long enough to cultivate such relations or do not have a sufficient sense of settled residence to wish to do so.

But there are others who find such intimacies irksome. One woman said that she rarely went to the bath-house because she did not like meeting neighbours. Another, not long married and living in one of the apartment blocks, went to a dress-making school in the daytime solely to avoid having to attend the so-called 'well-side gatherings' of the housewives on her floor—the 'gossip-meetings' which it was impossible not to join if you were at home, and at which she, the youngest, felt constantly bullied by her elders. Some housewives were extremely anxious in interviews to ensure that the information about domestic affairs would be confidential, and at the same time often showed great anxiety to know what answers had been given by their neighbours. Lack of privacy featured not infrequently in the complaints of apartment dwellers. With communal cooking facilities, 'even what you have for lunch becomes common knowledge'.

Altogether thirty-two housewives (out of 238) said in answer to a question asking if they ever got any useful household hints from neighbours that they 'never talked to neighbours', and another eighty-six said in answer to other questions that they were not more especially intimate with immediate neighbours than they were with anybody else in the ward. Length of residence, at least if measured in five-year periods, seems to have little to do with this. The difference between the housewife who has no secrets from her neighbours and the housewife who desires to 'keep herself to herself' is probably due primarily to differences in individual personality.

Japanese psychologists construct introversion-extraversion tests which show much the same distributions as in other societies. Sociometric studies of small groups, in Japan as elsewhere, show some individuals who never become 'popular choices' or participants in a 'mutual choice'. For such individuals withdrawal may seem a preferable alternative to involvement in personal relationships which bring only frustration and the jealous suspicion that one's confidence in Mrs. B are being retailed with gusto and enjoyment to her more intimate neighbour Mrs. C. It is, however, a truism that both the development of the personality and its expression in concrete situations is socially as well as genetically determined, and it is possible to discern some structural features which may be expected to exacerbate or modify personality differences in this respect.

1. Differences in background may differently predispose the individual towards involvement in personal relations with neighbours. The present inhabitants of Shitayama-cho did not grow up together in homogeneous surroundings. Some were brought up in villages or Shitamachi wards where something like an open communal life prevails and no great store is set by family secrets which are not, in any case, easy to preserve. Others were born in middle-class Yamanote wards where each house shuts itself off with a garden and a fence from the neighbours and keeps itself very much to itself. Even as between villages in different parts of Japan, there are considerable differences in the closeness of personal relationships between families and the extent to which kinship ties take precedence over neighbourhood ties in determining the individual's or the individual family's relations of greatest solidarity.

2. Differences in background may in themselves be an obstacle to the development of close neighbour relations, and regional differences can be as important in this respect as class differences. Cultural variations are still considerable, and the farmer's daughter from the country may well feel somewhat afraid of her more sophisticated town-born neighbours. The importance of such differences is, however, greatly minimized by the fact that all have received essentially

the same primary school education from identical text-books, and by the recent spread of the radio and the newspapers.

3. Current differences in economic level or educational background may operate as a barrier to the development of informal relations of intimacy. It was significant, for instance, that some housewives answering the question about household hints said that they never gossiped with neighbours, because 'the women round here are of a very low level'. This may be a rationalization of withdrawal into one's shell, but, although the pre-war Girl's High School education, which some Shitayama-cho women had and others had not, did not have sufficient intellectual content to make much difference in the interests and range of discourse of its products, it did impart airs and graces, cultural symbols the possession of which may be a ground for snobbery and the absence of which may be a ground for jealousy.

The relative weakness of class differences in outlook and way of life (as compared with England) was commented on in a previous chapter (see p.216). The effect of the *tonari-gumi* organization in bringing neighbours together on a footing of equality irrespective of wealth, education and occupation, is further to minimize the importance of such distinctions as between neighbours. That is not to say that economic and educational differences have *no* importance. To take one obvious implication of income differences, the few more wealthy families in Shitayama-cho who live in houses with gardens, surrounding fences and outer gates, tend automatically to be precluded from the intimacy of their neighbours who live the open life of the small terrace houses, gardenless and giving straight on to the street.

It would seem, indeed, that the importance of economic and educational differences as an obstacle to close relations between neighbours has gradually increased. The greengrocer was certainly of that opinion. In his youth in Shitayama-cho, thirty or forty years ago, he was, he said, on very friendly terms with some of his rich neighbours and customers. There was the bank president, for instance, who lived in the next ward in the big house with a stone wall, now a railway workers' hostel. Often on his way home from parties in the evening he would shout out as he went past in his rickshaw, 'Come round and have a drink!' 'Our *reberu* [levels] were as different as this [he raised one hand above his head and stretched the other towards the ground] and yet we were as close as if we had been brothers.' But nowadays people of that sort don't consort with their greengrocers. The only people he sees at the big houses in the next ward are the maids or sometimes the mistress of the house. To anticipate the conclusion of a fuller discussion of status in the next chapter, the change may be summarized thus. Formerly, as between the greengrocer and the rich business man, warm relations were possible because both sides had a clear, and an identical, definition of the status differences between them, and accepted such differences as part of the natural order. Now, although there is probably no lessening of economic differences, their significance has changed. What is felt as the proper pattern of relations between neighbours in the city are relations between equals. Where this equality of economic status is manifestly absent, the act of a person of a higher level in associating with a person of a lower level comes to seem like 'demeaning himself' for the one party and a possibly offensive act of condescension from the point of view of the other. (A similar change in English society would seem to be reflected in the history of the English word 'condescend' which, according to the examples given in the O.E.D., would seem to have acquired its present pejorative implications only during the seventeenth century.)

4. Changes in the relations between husbands and wives may be expected to have an effect on the nature of relations between neighbouring housewives. In households where the traditional patterns of marital relations prevailed, the wife who lacked any warm personal relationships with her husband might seek compensation in intimacy with her female neighbours. Just as the domestic servants of neighbouring households may become close friends on the basis of a fellow-feeling and a common interest in discussing the faults of their masters, so wives who are treated as a superior sort of domestic servant might seek solace in comparing notes on the tyranny of their husbands. Now in so far as, in the words of one woman quoted earlier on, 'husbands and wives do their worrying together', there is less need to seek someone to worry with among the neighbours. Wives have not only *themselves* to keep to themselves, but also a cosy and satisfactory home life which satisfies their emotional needs and of which privacy is an essential ingredient.

We may sum up the general burden of this discussion of relations between neighbours as follows. Despite the working of all those forces which tend to make city life anonymous and atomic—the rapidity of residential changes, the increase in secondary contacts, the tendency for the man's primary contacts to develop on occupational lines and to be independent of territorial propinquity—nevertheless, housewives, at least in Shitayama-cho, do frequently develop with their neighbours relations of a degree of intimacy which is usually associated with village rather than with city life. The fact that many of them were brought up in small settled communities in which close relations between neighbours prevail is one obvious reason for this. Equally relevant is the fact that the settled towns of the Edo period developed a formal etiquette of neighbour relations resembling that of the village and thus provided a model for urban living, a basis on which new immigrants could be absorbed, and a framework in which informal neighbour relations could grow. Increasing occupational differentiation and the removal of male productive activities from the family has meant, however, that men play an increasingly small part in the life of the neighbourhood, a tendency which is reflected in the relative tameness of Shitayama-cho festivals, in the large numbers who go individually to the bath-house and sit silent in the bath, and in the general indifference to the ward association, which will be the subject of the next chapter.

17

The Ward

SHITAYAMA-CHO was, of course, in no full sense of the word a community. On the other hand, it was something more than a postal district. Although the majority of the inhabitants satisfied most of their economic needs and many of their recreative needs quite outside the ward and in contact with persons other than their ward neighbours, most of the more settled residents had a sense of belonging to the ward in a way in which the Londoner only rarely in wartime has a sense of belonging to his streets or his buildings. In Shitayama-cho young men who are keen on group activities think automatically in terms of 'getting the youth of the ward together'; it is often as 'Shitayama-cho-ites' that children engage in gang fights and insult-exchanges with the children of other wards; at the time of the borough council elections the question is discussed which of the hundred-odd candidates can be most relied on to do his best for 'the ward' and deserves to have the backing of 'the ward'; it is for 'the children of the ward' that outings and film-strip shows are arranged (and voices are raised in protest when children of other wards gate-crash); it is because 'she was an old resident of the ward' that people regret an old lady's having to sell her house to settle a mortgage, and wish that they had known earlier so that they could have arranged to lend her the money; it is from the hereditary 'chief' of the ward that people buy their New Year's decorations, and it is in 'the ward's' celebrations of the festival of the local shrine that they participate. There is, moreover, a formal association which performs for the ward inhabitants such services as street lighting not provided by the borough, arranges that 'the ward' shall not be neglected by the police, the fire brigade or the borough office, and ensures that 'the ward' does its bit when contributions are being collected for the Red Cross or the Community Chest.

The origin of the wards as the semi-self-governing units of the capital in Tokugawa times was touched on in the previous chapter. These old Edo wards were, of course, socially as well as politically, much more self-contained communities than those of the present day. Most of their residents worked as shopkeepers or domestic craftsmen within the ward, and the organization of communal life was of an advanced level. Each ward (or sometimes each group of two or three wards) had its guardian gate-keepers who closed the ward to strangers at night and let out residents who had legitimate business with a clatter of sounding boards which assured the neighbouring gatekeepers of the authenticity of the approaching visitor. The ward had its fire-chief, who also had the monopoly of the right to provide labour for all house-building in the ward—a right enforceable, if necessary, by the fists and daggers of his labourers—his sworn 'children'—who also made up his fire-fighting team. There was a ward secretary in his office, which also served as a ward meeting place and the repository of all the registers—those showing the composition of every household and the birthplace, age and religion of each individual, those showing the apportionment of the ward's tax assessment among the households in the ward, the account books for the water-supply, for the repair of fire-fighting equipment, refuse disposal or expenditure on shrine festivals. It even had its ward barber who, in the odd way that barbers have of combining other incongruous employments with their main occupation, had the traditional duty of ensuring the safety of all official documents in case of fire, a responsibility which, in some places, was requited by a traditional right to receive his cut when any property transactions took place in the ward.[228]

Self-government was not absolute; the householders who took it in turn to supervise ward affairs as the 'month's functionary' were responsible to one of about 250 hereditary 'headmen' who controlled an average of five or six wards each and were in turn responsible for some purposes to the three hereditary non-samurai 'town-elders', who in turn were ultimately responsible to the two samurai 'magistrates'.[229] Down this hierarchical channel came a stream of edicts—warning against luxury and licence, forbidding abuse of monopoly rights, commending certain districts for reductions in their crime rates, attempting to fix rents, or explaining the correct procedure for dealing with abandoned babies or incapacitated vagrants. Within its sphere of competence, moreover, ward self-government tended to be oligarchic. Only a limited number of citizens had the right to participate in ward affairs as members of the ward-governing association,[230] or to become the 'month's functionary'. These were firstly the land-owners, and secondly the agents of house-owners—who had always to be employed to manage property owned in wards other than that in which the landlord was living. Tenants (either of land or of dwellings) who made up more than 80% of the population,[231] paid feudal taxes and ward rates only via their rents and had no part in running ward affairs. The division between the governors and the governed was thus a clear one. (In one of their many edicts, the samurai magistrates directed landlords, as part of their paternalistic duties towards their tenants, to call them together periodically and lecture them on the evils of gambling.)[232] In practice, power was often wielded by one or two wealthy landlords who had the fire chief, the ward secretary, and even the local 'headman' in their pockets.

Vestiges of the system remain today. Although Shitayama-cho is a post-Meiji ward, the former 'fire-chief' (*kashira*) of a neighbouring ward extended his 'rope-stretch' to cover it, and his present-day successor, though a man of no great prestige or authority, is still customarily held to have the monopoly right of providing the pine-trees which adorn Shitayama-cho houses at New Year, the decorations for the Shitayama-cho festival, and the banners and streamers which are a *sine qua non* when a new shop is opened in the district. He belongs to the Firemen's Union, a nostalgia group whose fire-fighting activities are now confined to leading shrine festival processions and to a ceremonial parade with ladder acrobatics before the Imperial Palace each New Year's morning. He still acts as works foreman for building operations in the district, and although his local monopoly can no longer be enforced, since the police forbid the traditional coercive means of enforcement, a neighbouring 'chief' who is hired for a job within his 'rope-stretch' will always come to seek his agreement and bring a suitable pacifying present.

The ward associations, too, although few now extant can claim direct ancestry stretching back to one of the *gonin-gumi* or *kumiai* of the Tokugawa period, owe their existence to the Edo tradition of ward self-government. The Meiji period, of course, saw great changes in the organization of the city. As a modern municipal administration was developed, many of the activities which had formerly been managed within the small face-to-face ward community were taken over and organized on a large-scale impersonal level by the police, the new professional fire-brigades, the utility undertakings, and the roads, sanitation and welfare departments of the borough and city governments. But there were still—as there are today—gaps in the city and borough administration which left ward associations useful services to perform, while the organization of shrine festivities remained a continuing centre of their activities. The new wards which were created as the city expanded generally formed such associations: Shitayama-cho started with a Hygiene Association in the late nineteenth century. The earthquake of 1923, when the existing associations showed their value in organizing help for the police and for rescue work, provided a big impetus to the growth of such associations.[233] At the beginning of the thirties such associations existed in nearly every ward. They had no legal status, but unofficially were widely used by the borough administrations as a channel for the transmission of information and for securing public co-operation in health and other matters. As the nation became mobilized for war they were increasingly so used, and in 1938 city by-laws gave them official status and laid down regulations for their management which provided also for the formation of the smaller *tonari-gumi* as subsidiary units.[234] Finally, in 1940, Home Office regulations made such associations compulsory for the whole country and defined their functions in the local administrative system.[235]

These ward associations played an important part in the war effort. When air raid shelters were to be dug the ward association divided its assessed cubic footage among each of the *tonari-gumi* which then set to work with teams made up of one representative from each household. (As in all Japanese community organizations, the household is the unit.) When someone in the ward was called up for military service, ward officials and representatives of the *tonari-gumi* were there to see him off; if he came back from the front as a handful of ashes in a little white box, there would be a ward deputation to welcome him again. (The wartime ward President, a gentle and likeable man who became President because the two real 'bosses' of the ward could neither of them agree to let the other take power, said that it was his intense antipathy to the task of performing these funerary celebrations which prompted him to retire before the war's end on grounds of ill-health.) For the distribution of rations of household goods, for the organization of pump-and-bucket fire-fighting teams, for getting the citizenry to the shrines (again one per household) to hear the Imperial Rescript read on the anniversary of the declaration of war, for the collection of comforts for the troops, saucepans for aeroplanes, and voluntary contributions for this, that and the other, the ward association and the *tonari-gumi* were used. Information of all kinds, about rationing, call-up, or civil defence, was rapidly disseminated from Home Ministry to Local Authority, from Local Authority to Ward Association; and from the Ward Association there went out one copy to each *tonari-gumi* chief who attached it to a wooden 'circulating notice-board' and sent it on its way from house to house within the group. If the matter was of some importance each householder would be expected to append his seal as a receipt for the information or order.

The possibilities which the system afforded of exerting pressure on the individual were exploited to the full. Failure to comply with a directive could not be excused on grounds of ignorance, for ignorance was impossible. Deliberate refusal to comply would have been 'to let down' one's immediate neighbours of the group, not simply a vague, impersonal and distant 'they'. And the people were so solidly behind their leaders, so fully identified with the aims of 'Japan', that it was unthinkable that groups of neighbours could become unitedly unco-operative or look with equanimity on an individual's traitorous defection. In the same way, when a drab khaki 'national dress' was suggested and officially encouraged as proper dress for the 'home-front' citizen in wartime, it needed only that official encouragement for it to become practically obligatory. No-one could afford to let it appear to his neighbours that he was lacking in a proper sense of patriotism. The Japanese word for 'national dress' 'ought', says a foreign observer of the Tokyo Japanese during the war, 'to be trans-lated "suit of patriotism" to indicate the spirit in which civilians thus voluntarily put themselves into uniform. Their unanimity came less from a reasoned sense of discipline than from an instinct of gregariousness. With frightening ease they adopted the ways of the ant-hill.' [236]

The ways of the ant-hill are not the ways of democracy. The Occupation ordered the disbanding of the ward associations and the *tonari-gumi* as integral elements of the totalitarian administrative structure which it was bent on reforming.[237] But there were still many of the functions of the former ward associations which had somehow to be provided for. There were festivals to be arranged; with the partial breakdown in borough finances during the inflation, refuse collection became inefficient; and in the unsettled post-war period with its rocketing crime figures, a ward night-watchmen became an even greater necessity. In Shitayama-cho, two or three energetic young men in their thirties took the lead in organizing a Youth Culture Society for the young men and young women of the ward. As well as forming English-language-study groups, poetry meetings, baseball teams, film-study groups and handicraft groups, the Youth Culture Society also ran the festival and made up work teams for rubbish disposal and the like. It had the blessing of the older leaders of the former ward association who, however, kept circumspectly in the background and were not, in fact, much consulted by the leaders of the youth group, who enjoyed their new-found sense of power.

The borough and metropolitan administrations adjusted them-selves to the new situation. Essential information concerning health matters and elections was posted on notice-boards, broadcast through megaphones throughout the street, or, later, included in the *Tokyo Metropolitan News* delivered free with the newspapers to each home every month. But gradually the old patterns began to assert them-selves. Not all the details of the following account could be checked, but there is no reason to doubt its general accuracy.

The police and the fire brigade which had formerly received good-will contributions from the ward association were only too delighted when prominent citizens in the district proposed to form a Crime Prevention and Fire Prevention Co-operation Society for the purpose of collecting such contributions. The wealthy manufacturer T (see

p. 32), who otherwise took little or no part in local activities, had by this time completed a prison sentence for wartime peculation, and was foremost in the foundation of this society. Most of the other officials were men who had formerly been active in the ward associations. The individual collection of contributions from each household, was, however, a laborious proceeding, and the main burden fell on a small number of the more wealthy. Then, in 1948, officials of the borough welfare department are said to have approached the ward leaders and explained that the Occupation was very keen on charities. The Red Cross Service Committee of the borough (ostensibly a voluntary body; in fact run by the welfare officials) wanted to make a good show that year, and it would be helpful if Shitayama-cho could form a Red Cross Service Sub-committee. The sub-committee was established with a chairman, two vice-chairmen (one of whom, in deference to the spirit of the age, was to be a woman) and 'section heads', one man and one woman, in each of the former *tonari-gumi*. Contributions were collected with great speed and efficiency. Shitayama-cho fulfilled its target.

Thus resuscitated in form, it was not long before the ward association was resuscitated in name. Informed opinion in the borough office held that voluntary associations of householders were by no means undemocratic. It was only compulsory membership and the use of the associations as an instrument of authoritarian government which were objected to by the Occupation. And in any case, American counter-intelligence was too busy hunting Communists to bother itself with ward associations. The advantages in saving time and labour by collecting all these various contributions in one consolidated monthly ward subscription naturally appealed to the ward leaders who, in the absence of complete collection, had often felt obliged to contribute more than they felt to be their fair share. The Youth Culture Society, too, with its membership confined, as a result of self-imposed notions of its function to foster ward solidarity, to the young men of Shitayama-cho—many of whom had more congenial opportunities for leisure activities in their university or office— was much too narrowly based for its many paper plans to flourish. It was in need of funds and welcomed the prospect of a block grant from a ward association. The old-guard leaders were glad of the opportunity to bring the upstart young leaders into a position of dependence on them.

So the Shitayama-cho Association came into being again, though care was taken to call it the Shitayama Association (*Shitayama-kai*) rather than Shitayama *Ward* Association (*Shitayama-cho-kai*) for the word *chokai* was too immediately reminiscent of the wartime pattern. In 1951 the 'circulating notice-boards' were out again, though far less frequently than in former times and, except for the occasions of the Red Cross and Community Chest weeks, exclusively for matters connected with the Association and not for borough affairs. These boards still bore, pasted on the back, the wartime exhortatory definition of the aims and purposes of the *tonari-gumi*.

A. The *Tongari-gumi* is a friendship group for neighbourhood *tsukiai* [for *tsukiai*, see p. 255].

Let us make sure that all members attend the general meetings, get to know each other well and maintain intimate relations.

The occasions for sadness and rejoicing (i.e. funerals and weddings or births) of any member of the group are occasions for sadness and rejoicing for the whole group. Let us show a warm generosity in helping one another.

B. The *Tonari-gumi* is an executive organ of the Ward Association.

Let us make sure that information and instructions are circulated speedily and to everyone, and let us carry them out promptly and efficiently.

For all the various consultations and activities which are necessary let us arrange duty rosters in order to carry out the work with the minimum delay.

C. The *Tonari-gumi* is a front-line home defence group.

Let all members be ever watchful for themselves and for others to prevent fire and burglary and epidemics.

Let us be in a constant state of preparedness and let each household appoint a person responsible in order to go into action immediately to deal with all emergencies.

The *tonari-gumi* chief was formally elected annually, but what could be distressing competition was eliminated by tacit agreement that the office should circulate on an annual roster. Nevertheless each *tonari-gumi* held a formal election meeting every year and solemnly held a paper ballot to confirm the foregone conclusion. The main task of the *tonari-gumi* chief was the monthly collection of contributions. These averaged 30 *yen* per household and the total ward budget amounted to some 140,000 *yen* (£140) annually.

This money was used for a variety of purposes. Some of it went in condolence money, or 'incense offerings'; gifts made by the Ward Association to households in which a death occurred. Some was spent on maintaining street lighting and on the hire of night-watch-men—members of the Youth Culture Society who took it in turns to patrol the ward on winter evenings carrying a metal staff with jangling rings and calling 'Take care of fire!' [238] Some was spent on the ward festival and on such items as tea and cakes for the temporary centre at which Shitayama-cho children were vaccinated.

But something like a half was paid out in donations to such bodies as the Crime Prevention and Traffic Co-operation Association (hereinafter the C.P.T.C.A.), the Fire Prevention Association, the Mothers' Society, the Borough District Office and the Borough

Refuse Department. These were essentially organizations for giving tips to the police, the fire brigade, rationing officials, dustmen, etc. (The Mothers' Society was no exception being organized at the instigation of the Juvenile Guidance Department of the Police.) They had other ostensible purposes, too; the C.P.T.C.A., for example, organized anti-crime propaganda weeks, hiring sandwich men to tour the streets with posters advising householders not to leave their homes unlocked. But these activities absorbed only about one-tenth of the £380 which the Association collected annually from Shitayama-cho and the fourteen other wards in its district. The rest was spent on various forms of police welfare—a fund to provide policemen on night beats with pocket money to buy themselves the odd dish of spaghetti, gifts to retiring members, a subsidy towards the purchase of land for a police hostel, and so on. The statement of accounts published by the leaders of the C.P.T.C.A. was, however, extremely vague, and one policeman employed at the district H.Q., though grateful for the occasional dish of spaghetti, had the impression that a disproportionate amount of money found its way directly into the pockets of his superior officials or was spent on parties for police officials and officials of the C.P.T.C.A.[239]

There was a certain amount of resentment against these gifts in the ward, largely based on the suspicion that the benefits of such *tsukiai* which the Ward Association maintained on behalf of the ward accrued disproportionately to the ward leaders. It was their 'face' which 'stood up' *vis-à-vis* the police when they took along a good contribution to the C.P.T.C.A. It was they who enjoyed the food and entertainment on which part of this money was thought to be spent, and it was they who improved their connections—'broadened their face'—on these occasions. In particular, in the case of the C.P.T.C.A., it was they who could expect (as a policeman in Shitayama-cho expressed it) 'not to feel the draught' (*kazeatari*) so much as a result of their connections. (In much the same way local factory owners might have hoped not to feel the draught so much from the local office of the Labour Standards Inspectorate after the Factory Owners' Association had sportingly offered to provide furnishings when the office was newly built.)

This did not, of course, mean *carte blanche* to commit arson and mayhem with impunity. This *tsukiai* with the police was chiefly important at election time. The gap between the very rigid prescriptions of the Election Laws and the traditional mode of electioneering was so great that the large number of prosecutions for election offences was commonly believed to represent only the protruding part of the iceberg. Good *tsukiai* enabled one to remain submerged. It was thought in Shitayama-cho that there might be other advantages too. The Ward President owned a factory the chimney of which had to be cleaned every three days. For this it was necessary to get the wind in such a direction that it was not blowing over the ward. If the wind remained in the same quarter for a long period and the cleaning was delayed or had to take place with the wind blowing over the ward, sparks sometimes flew out which had on occasions started small fires. Complaints had been lodged with the police, but no action had ever been taken.

This resentment smouldered into open hostility towards the Ward leaders at the annual meeting to consider the 1950 accounts. (The discussion is recorded in Appendix V.) The attack avoided in any way impugning the motives of the Association's leaders, and concentrated on the arguments that, first, the police, the dustmen and the firemen and so on were only doing their jobs and if they were remiss then it was the duty of the Ward Association leaders to make representations through the proper channels, not to make presents of money. Secondly, as a diversionary tactic it was urged that all the money which the Association could collect could be usefully employed in a campaign to rid the ward of flies and mosquitoes, and could ill be spared for gifts to the police.

The president's answer in respect of the dustmen was that 'theoretically' and 'logically' (*riron ya rikutsu kara ieba*) the objector was probably right. But you had to consider 'the times' (*jisei* is sometimes best translated 'the way of the world'). If you wanted to get things done you had to go the right way about it. Another voice from the floor agreed. 'Everything, like a sheet of paper, has its front and its back. Even the Borough Office has its "back". You have to recognize this. Even the Borough Office has its shady (*kitanai*) side.'

Later there came a more positive argument in support of these contributions from another member of the leadership circle, this time an argument which appealed on moral grounds to a sense of *giri*-responsibility. Since everybody was in a state of dependence on everybody else, and in particular since all would receive the benefit if some made these contributions, then it was only just for everyone to show a proper willingness to contribute. Thus accused of lacking a proper sense of responsibility to his neighbours, the objecter hastened to explain that he had been misunderstood and he was not opposed to the whole principle of making these contributions— which, according to his private conversation, was exactly what he was opposed to.

Overtly the question at issue was a conflict between the ideal of an impersonally organized society in which each individual performs fixed services for fixed fees, and the ideal of society as a harmonious web of personal relations sedulously maintained by mutual conciliation and the direct exchange of 'favours' and gifts. We have already discussed in the last chapter the confusion of moral ideas which results as the newer universalistic norms invade the province of the particularistic. The difference between the token of gratitude and the bribe is one of evaluation and not of substance. The confusion was clear in these discussions. Both the pragmatic argument that the 'shady side' had, unfortunately, to be recognized, and the moral argument that one should take proper cognizance of one's indebtedness to others received their nods of assent, and the discussion as it is recorded in the appendix shows that the ward leaders were uneasy and uncertain how their departure from the universalistic norms institutionally incorporated in the city administration—norms which 'theoretically' and 'logically' they could not but accept—should be justified.

But only two of the two hundred and fifty householders in Shitayama-cho appeared at the General Meeting to challenge the leaders' administration of the Association. The attitude of the vast majority was one of apathy. Only two households refused utterly to have dealings with the Association or to pay any contributions. They were considered somewhat peculiar and their householdheads had no dealings at all with neighbours. One had only recently come into the ward, the other was a resident of long standing who had, moreover, maintained his isolationism throughout the war years when the pressure to conformity was at its peak. On one occasion during the war, it was said, the Ward Association had sent a 'comforts parcel' to the house for their son at the front. The wife received the parcel with polite expressions of gratitude, but when the husband returned he ordered her to take the gift back immediately.

There were others in the ward who were entirely hostile to the Ward Association, but did not dare to court the unpopularity and isolation which a refusal to join would bring. One woman said, for instance, when asked what her household did at the time of the ward festival, that the Ward Association 'made you' put out lanterns, but otherwise her household took no notice of what was going on.

But the attitude of the majority was one of negative acceptance. They were glad to have their streets lit at night and most of them enjoyed the annual ward festivities. Some resented the pressure which the organization was able to use to exact contributions, but this was no new thing in their lives, and few had any firm individualist convictions on the basis of which to make reasoned objections. Some were resentful not so much because of the pressure brought to bear, but because the contributions were a strain on an over-extended household economy and they felt that the burden ought to be more equitably distributed according to means. Most considered those aspects of the Association's activities described above as something of a racket, but the usual reaction was to shrug the matter off as a necessary concession to the 'shady' side of life. Themselves involved at the personal level in a network of *tsukiai* relations the ethical status of which was analogous to those objected to, they had no clear basis for confident moral indignation. So they paid their subscriptions, took their turn as *tonari-gumi* chief and pasted on their doorposts, along with the metal discs showing that they had paid their wireless licences and their water-rates, the subscription receipts for the C.P.T.C.A., the F.P.C.A., the Red Cross and the Community Chest, and thus demonstrated for all the world to see that they had done their duty by their neighbours.

The exceptions to this generalization were a group of fourteen men who showed interest in and participated in the activities of the Ward Association. Of these twelve were 'in'—members of the controlling clique commonly referred to (though sometimes half-jokingly, since, to the sophisticated inhabitants of Tokyo, ward politics were on a somewhat petty scale) as *yuuryokusha*—'powerful men'. Two were 'out'—the two vocal critics of the leaders at the General Meeting who had formerly been leaders of the Youth Culture Society and rather resented their eclipse by the old-guard leaders when the Ward Association was reformed.

These fourteen were all men who had, over a period of settled residence—all had been in the ward for more than ten years—developed a sense of 'belonging' to the ward. Words such as 'for the good of the ward' sprang easily and naturally to their lips. Unlike the wealthy manufacturer (of p. 32) who had bigger fish to fry, or the few professional men or active trade unionists whose sources of desired power and prestige lay in spheres outside the ward, they valued the rewards which membership of the controlling circle could give. Most of them were of middle-to-upper economic status (only the President was in the upper tenth, but nine of the others were in the upper quarter according to the economic status scale) and most of them were self-employed and so lived their working as well as their leisure lives in and around the ward.

For the ambitious, membership of the inner circle with its opportunities to represent the ward externally at meetings of the C.P.T.C.A. or of the shrine Worshippers' Association provided a means of building up useful connections. It could be a first step towards a seat on the borough council; a step which Sakura, the Ward President, just failed to mount in 1951.[240]

The status of leader also carries in itself a certain amount of prestige within the ward. There is the satisfaction of being 'in the know', of being one of the chosen few entitled to go to the little room behind the 'branch altar' at ward festival time and there, sipping the *saké* which had been offered up to the gods, look benevolently on while the inhabitants of the ward enjoy themselves. One is referred to as a *yuuryokusha*—'a powerful man'—or a *kaoyaku*—'a man with a face' in the ward. Some of them obviously derived great pleasure from manipulating meetings. And it was with unmistakable pride that one once described to me the virtue of the Ward Association as a technique of social organization: a decision was made by the *yuuryokusha*, they communicated it to each *tonari-gumi* chief and the latter informed each householder; in no time, said he, the whole ward was brought into line. (Proof of this, for which I had every reason to be grateful, came in the very small number of refusals experienced by interviewers once I had got the approval of the *yuuryokusha*.) The Americans, he added, had been very shortsighted. If only they had used the ward associations instead of abolishing them, democracy would have been diffused in no time.

Membership of the circle of *yuuryokusha* also provided the satisfaction of sociable gossip at its meetings. One or two of the circle also obviously derived genuine satisfaction from making themselves useful to other people. The Vice-President once remarked when I took him a thank-you present for his help in arranging the interviews, 'Oh, but you shouldn't have done that. I enjoy doing all this sort of thing.' (This not being at all the usual formula of polite acceptance.)

Financial reward was not directly involved. Dishonesty in the accounting appeared to be always for other ends than the personal profit of the *yuuryokusha*, who were not, in any case, a sufficiently cohesive body for there to be concerted peculation. On the contrary, the position of *yuuryokusha* involved a certain financial burden; in order to set a good example, slightly larger-than-average contributions were required at festival time and for the Red Cross and Community Chest collections; and on the President, at least, devolved the cost of entertainment—tea and cakes and sometimes rice-wine and savouries—when the *yuuryokusha* gathered at his house.

For all practical purposes the *yuuryokusha* were the association, and the association were the *yuuryokusha*. It was they who effectively took all important decisions, decisions arrived at not by any formal procedures—even membership of the group was very hazily defined, and at none of the five meetings of the group which I attended was there ever any question of a vote being taken or even of a difference of opinion sufficiently overt for a vote to be possible—but by the chairman getting the 'feel' of the opinions of the others, or rather of the most important of the others, and everyone agreeing when he expressed what he believed to be the general sentiment.

It was typical of the type of leadership they exercised that when they met to draw up the accounts and discovered that they had a large surplus, it was suggested, and immediately agreed, that the figures should be juggled to scale down the amount since there might be a demand at the general meeting for a reduction in membership fees if such a surplus was admitted to. It was typical, too, that the general meeting was not called to consider the budget until three months after the financial year had begun. The system for electing officers was foolproof; the President and Vice-President were elected by the unanimous decision of an Election Committee appointed by the Chairman—always one of the *yuuryokusha*. The Treasurer, Assistant Treasurer and a discretionary number of 'auditors' and 'managers' were then nominated by the President. This system is akin to that of the P.T.A. and more or less that prescribed by the pre-war government model rules for ward associations. Secret or impersonal methods of election were avoided and the crucial decisions confined to an easily controlled face-to-face group. The *yuuryokusha* not only made policy; they made their own rules as well, though when they were challenged on this score at the General Meeting it was explained that the absence of a formal constitution was temporary and due to the unsettled political situation. In 1951 it was not clear, it was explained, how the situation would change when the Occupation came to an end and Japan was fully democratized. It was possible that there might be legislation affecting the position of ward associations and until the situation became clarified it was thought better not to commit any definite principles to paper, but to leave everything to the decision of the general meeting. The extent to which ordinary members were expected to participate in the general meeting was indicated by the President at the beginning of the second meeting after the first had been adjourned. Announcing that the meeting was to be tape-recorded and that the recording was going overseas, he asked that the meeting should be as lively as possible—'please let us have plenty of clapping'.

Such leadership is typical of small community organizations throughout Japan; and in villages, where the *yuuryokusha* generally hold economic power *vis-à-vis* their fellow-villagers, it is accepted and co-operated with, that is to say obeyed. In Shitayama-cho, however, although few attempt to rebel against such leadership, not many can be found willingly to accept the position of the led. Men who are not invited into the charmed circle of the *yuuryokusha* generally avoid contact with the Association altogether. If their position as *tonari-gumi* chief imposes on their household a duty of attendance at the general meeting, they send their wives, in whom docility will be proper and becoming. Thus, despite the fact that a notice was circulated to every household showing the budget accounts and announcing the general meeting which it was hoped all would attend, when the meeting began an hour late (one of the 'out' group was, characteristically, the only person there at the time announced) only twenty-nine people were present. These incluudeed nine of the *yuuryokusha* who sat at the front, fourteen of the nineteen *tonari-gumi* chiefs (or rather in most cases their wives), who came from a sense of duty, the nigger-in-the-wood-pile who came to object, a young man and his wife who were newcomers to the ward, and three others. Even when the adjourned meeting was resumed the following week, despite the promise of some fireworks, the number present was only thirty-six, of whom only twenty-six voted on the one occasion on which a vote was taken.

Nevertheless, it will have been clear from what was said about the criticisms directed at the Fire Brigade and Police gifts, that the leaders could no longer count on a mixture of apathy and docility. And the report of the meeting (in Appendix V) shows that, although the two critics were known not to be in any real sense spokesmen of an organized opposition, the President, at least, was not sufficiently confident of his own position (or not sufficiently anxious to hold on to it) to attempt to ride roughshod over their complaints, partly because he was aware that (as one of these critics himself claimed during the first meeting) they were voicing resentments against the leadership which were shared by many other people in the ward, and partly because the critics appealed to principles such as popular election of officers and open-and-above-board dealings with the police, which, in a Japan committed to 'democratization', could not be directly challenged.[241] It was significant that the adjective 'democratic' occurred several times in the suggestions of the opposition leader at the first meeting. The President conceded the justice of his claim that the election of officers should be held before consideration of the next year's budget and the implication it carried that the leaders' assumption of automatic re-election was unjustifiable; he himself made the proposal at the second meeting that the election committee should be bigger and chosen by objective random methods; at one point he offered to cut out all the 'goodwill' contributions from the budget 'if that were the general feeling', and he made a determined attempt to resign the Presidency when he was re-elected.

These observations may be summed up by saying that the *yuuryokusha* of Shitayama-cho were by no means the accepted and deferred-to leaders of recognized superior status that the *yuuryokusha* of an Edo ward were, or the *yuuryokusha* of many villages are today. They would no longer, for instance, presume, or be allowed, like their Edo counterparts, to lecture fellow-residents on the evils of gambling. And whereas in the Japanese village it is often only necessary for a Parliamentary candidate to win over the *yuuryokusha* whose influence can be counted on to bring all the other voters to heel,[242] in Shitayama-cho, although the *yuuryokusha's* sponsoring of the local candidate in the Borough Council elections certainly influenced the votes of many in the ward, this was because they could plausibly argue that the local candidate was the best man to get something done about the appalling ward roads, and there is no evidence that the *yuuryokusha* influenced anyone's vote in the Metropolitan Governorship elections fought on party lines at about the same time.

Although, as was mentioned in an earlier chapter, hierarchical rigidity remains a feature of most secondary groups in Japanese society, status differences are not easily accepted in relations between neighbours in a segment of a large city. It is now necessary that an overall fiction of equality should be maintained. Every man must be allowed to be as good as his neighbour. The reasons for this are clear enough; other chapters have already considered changes in the social structure and in officially encouraged ideologies which have contributed to the general development of egalitarian ideas. In the specific sphere of relations within a territorially defined group of neighbours there is one particularly relevant change. In the village community and in the old Edo wards differences of wealth were directly related to differences of power. Decisions of the wealthy could directly affect the material well-being of the less wealthy. In the city, as between neighbours, there are normally only differences of wealth, divorced from relations of economic interdependence.

We have already had occasion to note, in considering the green-grocers relations with his wealthy neighbours in the last chapter, this development of the idea that the only proper relations between neighbours are relations between equals. The principle of equality was implicit in the strict reciprocity of obligations within the *tonari-gumi*. But the principle was one which it was difficult to incorporate in the framework of the Ward Association in one particular respect. The old recognition of status differences had implied differential financial burdens. The traditional method of collecting money for, say, the rebuilding of a shrine, was to go first to the person of highest status in the community. The size of his contribution heading the list provided a yardstick by which others visited in order of their status could assess the proper amount of their own contribution. The amounts on the contribution list (which was always prominently displayed on the walls of the rebuilt shrine) represented a self-assessment of status influenced by the collector's assessment of status implicit in the order in which he brought the collecting register round.

A similar procedure was used in Shitayama-cho for collecting donations for the rebuilding of the parish shrine, for the rebuilding of the local primary school, and for the annual festival celebrations. The subscription list was always prominently displayed, and in the case of the festival the Ward Association prepared a special festival-budget account recording each individual subscription and sent this round the ward by circulating notice board. But in these cases, although the order of collecting the first two or three subscriptions would be decided by the collector's assessment of status ranking (see, for instance, the discussion reported on p. 298), thereafter there was no fixed order, and although there were individual problems—the insecure were never sure whether they were not the target of their neighbours' gossip because they had failed in their duty by giving too little or 'got a bit above themselves' by giving too much—these were individual decisions, and individuals' assessments of their own status. It would have been a different matter formally to recognize differences in status by levying differential membership dues for the Association in which, theoretically, all members were on a level of equality. And yet the tradition persisted in some degree that those who were of higher status (and greater wealth) should contribute more.

In practice the amount of the membership fee was left somewhat indefinite, 30 *yen* per household a month was the generally stated amount, but *tonari-gumi* chiefs were allowed to use their own discretion in taking less from poorer households, and the general level for one whole apartment block was 20 *yen* per household. Thus, those willing to accept the status of second-class citizen were permitted to do so. Such people did not, however, attend the Ward Association's general meeting and they often showed strong private resentment against the leadership.

The difficulty caused by the conflict between the old principle of acceptance of status differences and the new principle of equality was clear in a discussion which took place when the *tonari-gumi* chiefs met to receive instructions for the Red Cross collecting campaign. It was agreed that the contribution should be 20 *yen* per household. 'But,' said the Vice-President, 'there are some houses where even 10 *yen* is more than can be easily managed. We leave that to the *tonari-gumi* chief's discretion.'—'Best to avoid houses like that altogether,' said someone. 'No, on the contrary,' said another, 'that would only give them a feeling of inferiority. They would say you were slighting them. It's best to go to everyone.'

On the other hand, a common complaint, expressed in the ward against the Ward Association was that it was a means whereby the more wealthy residents, through the consolidated ward contributions, shifted on to others the burden of making gifts to the police or to the fire brigade, a burden which, if contributions were collected individually, would tend to fall disproportionately on their own shoulders. And this, it was argued, would be only right and proper; the more wealthy should be expected to pay more.

Formerly, it was possible for individuals of disparate economic levels to co-exist and maintain personal relations within an integrated small face-to-face community because differences of status were acquiesced in and explicitly recognized (in, for example, respect language and gesture.) It is the persistence *in a certain measure* of these status-accepting attitudes, together with the fact that there existed in the institutions of the Ward Association and the *tonari-gumi* convenient conceptual models for the formal organization of relations within small territorial groups, which explain why neighbourhoods such as Shitayama-cho, containing a population widely heterogeneous in occupation and economic level, manage to maintain something of a community sentiment. Nevertheless, the attenuation of status-accepting attitudes causes strain. The 'feelings of inferiority' of the second-class citizens in the apartment blocks are something different from the traditional acquiescence in lower status. They imply resentment rather than humility.

Strain also results in the management of the Ward Association from the clash between, on the one hand, the traditionally authoritarian patterns of the community-association model—the pre-war ward associations were expressly formed to secure efficiency in the *downward* transmission of instructions and information—and, on the other, the principle of equality of status of all members in an organization which exists to serve certain needs shared equally in common. It was the latter conception which was appealed to by the critics at the General Meeting and their criticism carried the more weight and extorted greater concessions in that democracy was in the air. The ward leaders had recovered from the first shock of the new age which induced them to go to the length of appointing a female vice-president in their first moves to resuscitate the ward association, but it was apparent that things were unlikely ever to be the same again. The official-sounding and authoritative high literary style of the wartime circulated notices had (like that of official documents proper in post-war Japan) given place to a simpler, more colloquial, style; and neither the demand for wider participation in decision-making and elections, nor the notion that 'speaking one's mind frankly' was more important than preserving a happy unanimity, could any longer be rejected out of hand. Even if there is a further change in the political atmosphere, and 'democracy' again becomes a 'boo-word' rather than the 'hurrah-word' which it was in 1951 and still apparently is at present (1954) an attempt to strengthen authoritarian leadership in city ward associations is not likely to be easy, for the opposition has deeper causes than the mere ideological influence or top-level institutional changes of the Occupation years. It is the product of a complex of changes—the increasing division of labour, the attenuation of economic links between city neighbours, the tendency for stratification to follow occupational lines as part of a nation-wide and not purely a local system, and the institutionalization of equality of opportunity in the educational system—changes which cannot be easily reversed.

It is arguable that the whole institution of the ward associations is already anachronistic—an attempt to apply to a group of heterogeneous individuals, whose principal contacts ramify widely over the whole city, institutions which properly belong to the self-contained village. There was already, on these grounds, opposition to the official recognition of ward associations before the war, and it was suggested that official purposes would be better served by the strengthening of more association-like associations for specific groups and purposes—reservists' associations, youth groups, women's groups, civil defence corps and the like—on a wider district basis.[243]

Nevertheless, there is still enough community sentiment in many wards like Shitayama-cho for associations to have been revived spontaneously since the war. One obvious condition for their revival was the existence of a traditional model for their organization. Another was the inadequacy of the borough and metropolitan services in the matter of street-lighting and so on. And a third was the existence of a not insignificant proportion of self-employed workers who spent their working life within the ward. In the more exclusively *sarari-man* wards of the Yamanote districts the revival of ward associations seems to be much slower, and already in large parts of Tokyo there appears to be little likelihood of their being re-formed unless there is positive official encouragement again.[244] It seems probable that as city administration becomes more complete in its coverage, and as industrial development reduces the number of self-employed workers, the mere momentum of established institutions will not be enough to prevent the ward associations from dying a natural death.

The revival of *tonari-gumi* and ward associations has received occasional attention in the press. The general tendency of newspaper comment has been to deplore the revival of such associations as a throw-back to the former totalitarian regime; an unwelcome means of exerting social pressure on the individual [245] (an interesting contrast with the trend of discussion of neighbourhood organization in this country which is generally concerned with how to develop *greater* integration and *foster* the growth of community sentiment). It is certain that many people are adequately satisfied with their primary contacts within the family or with their work-fellows and resent being forced into formal relations with their neighbours.[246] It is certain, too, that the notion of the ward as being properly a community and the natural unit for all social activities acts as an obstacle to the development of leisure-time associations which could more effectively be organized on a wider basis. Something, for instance, is clearly needed for the young men and women who have no opportunities for organized leisure activity in a university or large firm; but there are simply not enough such people in Shitayama-cho for a *ward* Youth Culture Society to be a workable proposition.

On the other hand, many people develop informal ties with their neighbours which are of emotional and material value to them, only because the formal institutions of the ward association and the *tonari-gumi* give them a means of breaking the ice. The insecure new immigrant from the country, faced with the emotional shock of the death of a child or a husband, may find great comfort in the assurance of help from neighbours and even from the formal gesture of a ward official's visit with a condolence gift from the ward. Though attenuated, some sense of 'belonging' to the ward, annually stimulated by the gaiety of the two-day festival celebrations, may well enrich the lives of some people and help to counteract the generally deplored psychological effects of the increasing atomization and depersonalization of city life.

RELIGION AND MORALITY

18

Main Trends of Religious Development

THE long and complex history of Japanese religious institutions can be only briefly considered here, but some general outline of the main trends of their development is perhaps necessary for an understanding of the religious practices and attitudes of people in Shitayama-cho.

The earliest religious practices of which there is evidence were those of the so-called Shinto tradition. In the society existing before the development of close cultural links with Korea and China, the clan was the ritual, as it was the political unit. Apart from lesser shrines dedicated to nature gods—animals, the spirits of rivers and trees, of mountains and the growing rice—the main shrines were clan shrines, and their objects of worship were clan ancestors. The rites, closely linked to the agricultural cycle, were characterized by a great emphasis on ritual purity. With the emergence to supremacy of the clan which became the Imperial Family, the *kami* (as the objects of worship were called) of the various clan shrines became amalgamated into a cohesive pantheon which functioned to legitimize the existing political structure. Later, as the clan organization gave way, in the seventh century, to a more centralized system of administration and still later, in the eleventh and twelfth, to a feudal system, shrines became increasingly linked to a territorially defined community rather than to a possibly-scattered clan.

In the fifth, sixth and seventh centuries, Chinese and Korean priests and returning Japanese travellers brought from the Continent the literature, the sacred objects and the ritual practices of Buddhism. Its well-developed metaphysic and ethic—both elements lacking in the indigenous religion—together with its association with the admired Continental culture, rapidly gained for it the patronage of the leading clans. Several sects were established, and as their influence grew, Buddhist priests came more and more to take over control of the shrines of the indigenous cults; many Shinto *kami* were found room in the Buddhist pantheon, and there was much intermingling of rituals and objects of worship, though at no time did what claimed to be a pure Shinto tradition entirely disappear from the Imperial

Court. As the clan organization crumbled and the patrilineal stem-family group became important, Buddhism secured its hold on the masses of the people by associating itself with the family rites for the dead.

The Buddhist sects were never united into a sufficiently cohesive organization to exert an influence on the political structure comparable to that exercised by the medieval Christian Church. The peak of Buddhist development may be said to have come in the thirteenth to fifteenth centuries. At that period the Zen sect exerted a powerful influence in moulding the outlook of the military class, evangelical reformist movements such as the Shin and Nichiren sects gained wide support among the agricultural masses, and the Buddhist monasteries alone kept alive the legal, ethical and literary traditions of earlier times.

In an increasingly military world these monasteries themselves became increasingly militarized, and it was the final defeat of the monkish armies by Nobunaga and Hideyoshi in the second half of the sixteenth century which presaged the decline both in the secular power of the Buddist sects and also in their hold on the spiritual allegiance of the people. Their resistance to the growth during this period of an active proselytizing Christianity was slight and unorganized, and the later suppression of Christianity was dictated more by political than by religious motives. In the seventeenth century, when the Tokugawas were establishing their new, more centralized feudal regime, problems of law and administration and ceremonial were frequently referred to Buddhist priests, who alone were competent to give opinions based on the precedents of Chinese and Japanese history. With remarkable speed, however, there developed outside the framework of the Buddhist sects an entirely new class of professional advisers, literati and preachers, who, drawing their inspiration from the Chinese Confucian tradition, rapidly acquired a mystique, a scholarly tradition and a professional consciousness of their own. As a result the Buddhist priesthood gradually lost social prestige, though Buddhism retained its connection with family rites, and this connection was in fact strengthened by the authorities, who required as part of the measures against Christianity and for general administrative and census purposes, that all commoners should be registered as the parishioners of a Buddhist temple.

In the eighteenth century, when Confucianism was firmly established as the official ideology, there came into being a group of scholars who, in a nationalist revulsion against the prevalent atmosphere of universal respect for Chinese traditions, began to study and to claim importance for the early Japanese records, particularly those collections of legends centring around the *kami* of the Shinto shrines. They tried to develop a Shinto philosophy and a Shinto ethnic which they claimed to be implicit in the early legends, and they advocated the freeing of Shinto shrines and their associated rites from their Buddhist accretions. On the political level they gave their support to the movement to restore power to the Emperor, the lineal descendant of some of the Shinto *kami*.

When this political movement reached a successful outcome in the Meiji Restoration, it carried into positions of influence these advocates of a revived Shinto. Their initial attempts to eradicate Buddhism and fill the gap with Shinto were a failure. Nevertheless Shinto shrines were removed from the control of Buddhist priests and endowed with public funds, and the religious enthusiasts' policy of building up Shinto as a national religion was ultimately much more successfully and subtly continued by the political leaders in the later years of the century. They clearly recognized the political advantages to be derived from a national and nationalistic religion which could be exploited to help concentrate loyalties in a single national state; no mean problem to the Meiji leaders who took over a segmentalized feudal society. Those shrines which had always been closely associated with the Imperial Family became national symbols, and in addition new national shrines were created, such as the Yasukuni consecrated to those who died in battle. At the same time, the local community shrines, purged of what could be easily recognized as Buddhist elements, were organized in a hierarchical pattern corresponding to the administrative system of the country and—while still continuing to be the centre for the rites of the local community, traditionally performed in connection with the agricultural cycle— they were entrusted with the performance of *national* rituals on *national* festival days, ceremonies which were attended by local government officials or their proxies.

The essentially political nature of these later developments of Shinto (as distinct from the abortive attempts of the Shinto advocates in the first few years after the Restoration) meant that it was not in direct competition with Buddhism. The latter, despite some attempts at revival which have in part borrowed Christian techniques and organization, has gradually declined in influence as a personal faith, though its association with family rites remains intimate.

At the same time, Christianity, which does compete with Buddhism, has gradually extended its influence; so also have a number of other sects which derive their inspiration from Shinto, Buddhist, and Western sources, and which, having distinct theological doctrines, may be properly called religions and their followers properly called 'believers'.

Since the war there has been some further growth in these latter sects. The other big change in religious institutions has been the disestablishment of Shinto. The description in the following chapters of the religious life of the inhabitants of Shitayama-cho will attempt in part to show the nature and direction of these recent changes. The attempt will be made to treat separately:

1. Those religious rites, and their accompanying beliefs, in which an individual partakes *qua* member of a social group; his family, his local community, or the nation.

2. Those rites in which an individual partakes and those beliefs which he holds *qua* individual; an individual who has to resolve individual moral conflicts, has individual sorrows and is destined to die an individual death.

The same shrines and temples, even the same rites, may sometimes appear to be important at several levels and it is not always easy to allocate particular pieces of religious behaviour to the appropriate level. Nevertheless, the effort is worth making in order to bring out the differential prevalence of religious behaviour at different levels, and to obtain some idea of its wider social implications in Japan.

19

The Local and the National Community

ATTEMPTS have been made, notably by Durkheim and some of his functionalist followers, to explain the emergence, or at least the survival, of religions in human societies by reference solely to their function in maintaining solidarity within the group, and in creating symbols—collective representations of the group itself—which have constraining effects on the group's members and thus provide an essential means of social control. Few, perhaps, would hold that this is the only function which religion has in society and later chapters will be devoted to the examination of Japanese religious behaviour which can hardly be fitted into the framework of such an 'explanation'. Nevertheless, it would not be denied that this is one most important aspect of religion, and Shinto, indeed, has become known to the West as almost a type case of a religion which has performed this function with the greatest efficiency at the level of a modern national community.

Originally, however, the Shinto rites were of far greater importance for the small local community, and even today, despite the declining importance of many of the old rites (insecticides and weather-forecasts have taken the urgency out of insect-repelling and rain-invoking ceremonies), the festivals of the village shrine have considerable importance in maintaining community sentiment within the village. The shrine is, or contains, or is dedicated to—there is some confusion on this point—the *kami*-protector of the village (*uji-gami* literally, 'clan-*kami*', reflecting the fact that the ritual community was earlier defined by lineage rather than by residence) and all the villagers are 'children of the god-family' (*ujiko*, literally, 'clan-children'.)

In the towns, too, something like the village system was created in the Meiji period. In the old Edo, before the institution of the State Shinto system and the grading of shrines, there were a large number of shrines of varying size and fame—the latter depending on their reputed magical efficacy and the magnificence of their annual festivals—each with a following which could not be territorially defined. The larger shrines had devotees all over Tokyo and thousands flocked to their festivals. In the early years of the Meiji period a territorial definition of their parishes was required, initially for the purpose of a new civil registration system which was to replace the Tokugawa system of registration at Buddhist temples.[247] Shrines were graded, the larger ones becoming Metropolitan Shrines and the lesser ones District Shrines, while a few became National Shrines. Only the larger shrines (roughly, those having a permanent priest) were allowed to have a parish (*ujiko-kuiki*) and the parish boundaries were drawn by mutual agreement between the priests of neighbouring shrines, in accordance with the general loyalties of the inhabitants of the neighbourhood. Parishes were for the most part quite large, often containing twenty or thirty of the wards like Shitayama-cho which were the real face-to-face community groups.

Lesser shrines which had no priest attached to them either fell into disuse or were kept up by interested residents in the immediate vicinity. There was one such in Shitayama-cho, tucked away at the end of a passage in one corner of the ward. It was looked after by four hereditary 'managers' who collected subscriptions from wealthy residents whenever rebuilding was necessary. One of these attributed to the virtue of this shrine the fact that Shitayama-cho had escaped destruction both in the earthquake of 1923 and in the fire-bomb raids of 1945 (adding, defensively, 'You might say it's superstition, but, anyway, I believe it'), but the shrine was rarely visited except by the pious few who call in passing from a feeling that all the *kami* of the neighbourhood, however humble, should be shown respect, and the few who make it the centre of a private productive cult. It was in no sense a ward shrine and the ward association had no part in its upkeep.

The ward as such was, however, officially concerned with the *uji-gami*, the Soga shrine to whose parish it belonged. Shitayama-cho had been included in its parish because it formed part of an estate stretching towards the shrine. The latter was twenty minutes' walk away, and unlike three closer shrines did not lie on the natural lines of communication out of the ward. For this reason relations between the shrine and the ward have always been somewhat less intimate than is usual for the district. Nevertheless, like the other twenty-two wards which made up the parish of the Soga shrine, Shitayama-cho contributed to the shrine's upkeep; its residents, by virtue of their residence, were all 'children of the god-family' of the shrine; and the ward as a whole participated in the shrine's annual festival.

THE UPKEEP OF THE SHRINE

Before the war the shrine was managed by a council consisting of representatives (*ujiko-soodai*) appointed by the ward association of each of the twenty-three wards in the parish. Contributions for the shrine were collected and the shrine's *fuda* (amuletic paper or wooden tablets bearing the name of the *kami* of the shrine) were distributed through these representatives, the ward association, and the neighbour groups, all the subtle pressures which the use of these channels offered being utilized to secure a full collection of contributions. Information concerning the activities of the shrine was conveyed through these representatives to the ward association, from the ward association to each neighbourhood unit, and thence, by circulating notice-board to each household.

In obedience to S.C.A.P. directive, this system of shrine administration and upkeep was abolished. In its place, a new body was formed called the 'Worshippers' Association' (*Suukeikai*). It is a small body of prominent men in each of the twenty-three wards who are, as the priest of the local shrine put it, 'sort of' representatives of the wards. Not all the twenty-three wards had revived their ward association since the war, but where such an association existed, the priest had approached its leaders and asked them to appoint a member of the Worshipper's Association. Where there was no ward association the priest had directly contacted prominent men (*yuuryokusha*) and asked them to join. There was now no longer a fixed number of these 'unofficial' representatives per ward. Advantage had been taken of the flexibility of the new organization to recruit as many wealthy men as possible. Thus, as well as preserving the substance of the old, some advantage was derived from the form of the new.

Some idea of the way in which this informal organization operates may be given by describing how contributions were collected for the rebuilding of the Soga shrine. The shrine was burned down during the war, and in 1951 the broad steps, flanked by an imposing concrete balustrade and the guardian 'Chinese lions'. led only to a small wooden temporary altar which stood forlornly in the middle of a broad concrete base. Plans to rebuild the shrine had long been complete, but with rising costs the original estimate of 2 million *yen* (£2,000) had increased to 3 million *yen* and in mid-1951 only one million had been subscribed. For fifty yards along either side of the approach to the shrine a slatted wooden framework about ten feet high had been erected. It was divided into twenty-three sections and over each section was written the name of one of the wards which were part of the parish of the shrine under the old dispensation. For every contribution received a wooden board was hung in the appropriate section and on it written the name of the donor and the amount.

In mid-1951 some sections were well-filled—mostly those devoted to wards very close to the shrine. The Shitayama-cho section bore only one board recording a donation of 30,000 *yen* (£30) by Sakura, the President of the Ward Association who was also a Vice-president of the Worshippers' Association. (He himself said he had given 20,000 *yen*. Whether this was a lapse of memory, or whether judicious inflation of the amounts of contributions was a common method of stimulating the generosity of others, I could not discover.) It was apparent, however, that Sakura had little interest in the shrine itself and never visited it. His support of the Worshippers' Association and of the rebuilding fund appeared to be more an expression of his sense of public duty as a prominent citizen, as it was also a means whereby his prominence as a citizen could be affirmed and enhanced.

Another official of the Ward Association, Kataoka, was also a member of the Worshippers' Association and by contrast conscientious, if not enthusiastic. Kataoka, with his obvious delight in occupying positions of authority and his committee-man skill, was nevertheless barred from higher positions of authority by his limited means combined with a tendency to arouse resentment by a slightly overbearing and pompous manner. Nevertheless he was doing his best, by taking an active part in the Worshippers' Association, the P.T.A., the C.P.T.C.A., and the Ward Association, to develop his connections against the day when his means should make a wider scale of activities possible.

At a meeting of the officials of the ward association, Kataoka reported the decisions of a recent meeting of the Worshippers' Association. So far only a third of the money had been collected, and there was a noticeable absence of contributions from Shitayama-cho. Each ward had been allocated a target on the basis of the number of households contained in it. Shitayama-cho's target was 90,000 *yen* or 300 *yen* (6s.) per household. The discussion ran somewhat as follows (for the people concerned, see Appendix V):

Okazaki: 'Have we really got to pay up?'

Kataoka: 'Well, I don't know. That's our apportionment, and when so many of the other wards have contributed we can hardly hold our heads up if we don't (*katami ga semai*).'

Nakazawa: 'Sakura [the ward president] has given us a good start anyway. [Hear, Hear!'s.] But it's no good going round asking other people to contribute until T is settled. [The T of p. 32; the richest man in the ward.] Once we get him to pay out we can go to S [a hotelier] and K [a fairly affluent wholesaler]. Then we can start generally.'

Okazaki: 'How is it best to collect the money, though?'

Izumi: 'I don't see what's wrong with K going round and collecting it as *ujiko-soodai*.' [Representative of the children of the god-family, i.e. the title of the ward association representative under the old system.]

Kataoka (apparently embarrassed, perhaps by the writer's presence): 'Well, there aren't any *ujiko-soodai* any longer. There's only a Worshippers'

Association. Of course there's talk that there will soon be a new law to make it possible again, but I don't know.'

Sakura: 'Yes, I think it's best to keep the ward association out of it for the time being at any rate. It would be best for someone from the shrine to come down collecting. One of us officials could go round introducing him, of course. I shouldn't think anyone would grumble about that. If the worst comes to the worst and the money doesn't come in, I suppose we shall have to take it out of ward funds a bit at a time, so much a month.'

The general feeling of the meeting seemed to be unanimous. No one felt any enthusiasm for the rebuilding of the shrine, and there was no suggestion that it was a worthy object. In most cases this was the result of a general lack of interest in any matters connected with shrines and the *kami*. In one or two cases it was the result, not of a lack of interest in all shrines but of the lack of any interest in this particular Soga shrine. One of those present, Izumi, was a member of the council of one of the shrines nearer to Shitayama-cho and a conscientious visitor for what appeared to be genuinely religious reasons.

But, though lacking in enthusiasm, all appeared to accept the duty of making contributions to the shrine. 'Have we really got to pay up?' was the nearest approach to a note of protest. No one suggested that religious faith was a private matter and should be left to individuals. It is doubtful if 'religious faith' entered anyone's head as a relevant factor in the situation; contributing to the upkeep of the local shrine has long been accepted as part of the duty of a good citizen on much the same level as paying taxes. Nor did anyone suggest that the ward as a whole should transfer its allegiance to a more convenient shrine and one to which more residents would be likely to pay spontaneous visits; only an emergency would ever justify such an unfriendly act towards the Soga shrine. In other words, long years of association had created what was called earlier a *giri*-relation between the ward on the one hand and the priest and the *kami* of the local shrine on the other. To break off that relation or neglect the duties which that relation involved would be to lay the ward open to the charge of 'not knowing *giri*'.

The reluctance to use the ward organization should be noted, however. This was not simply a question of temporary obedience of the statutes of the Occupation. It was equally forbidden to collect money through the ward organization to be used as gifts to the police, the fire-brigade and the food-office. Yet this was done. The reasons are not difficult to guess. In the first place, from the personal point of view of the ward leaders there was very little to be gained by sedulously maintaining good relations with the Shinto priest, though much to be gained from being 'well in with' the police, the fire-brigade and the borough office. In the second place, at Ward

Association meetings criticism of the gifts from ward funds to the police, etc., was answered by pointing out the concrete benefits which supposedly did accrue to the residents as a result of these contributions. The ward leaders presumably judged, and doubtless rightly, that if they made contributions to the shrine, firstly there would be an even greater amount of criticism, and secondly, not one of them would be prepared to maintain seriously that the residents of the ward were getting their money's worth in the *kami's* protection.

THE INDIVIDUAL RESIDENT AND THE SHRINE

There was, indeed, little evidence of any belief in a special relationship between the people of Shitayama-cho and the *ujigami* of the Soga shrine. Fifty-three per cent of households in Shitayama-cho had *kamidana*—the 'god-shelves', plain wooden boxes with ritual decorations which contain the *fuda* of the shrines for which they act as substitutes—and eighty per cent of these *kamidana* did contain the *fuda* of the Soga shrine. But explanations by seventy-five people of the purposes of worship at the *kamidana* contained no reference at all to the Soga shrine. Most parents took newly-born children for a *miya-mairi* ceremony, a registration rite at which the *ujigami* is asked to take note of the baby's arrival and extend it his future protection,[248] but most went to one of the nearer shrines rather than the Soga shrine. One woman explained that it was too hot a day to go so far, and added that she intended to make up for it by going to the Soga shrine for the child's next ceremony at the age of three. But here, again, 'local patriotism' was the operative notion; there was no suggestion that anything was actually lost by not going to the *ujigami* supposed to be responsible for protecting her particular district.

What such protection used to mean is well described by the ethnographer Yanagita Kunio in his description of the village in which he grew up.

It would sometimes happen in the summer evenings that children would go out to play and get lost and fail to come home. Then there would be great consternation, but generally the child would come back. The first thing the people of the village would think of then was the '*ujigami-sama*'. People would say that it was the *ujigami-sama* who saw that he came back; there would even be plausible-sounding stories going round that the child had met an old man with white hair who had told him that everybody at home was anxious and that he ought to go back. There was this idea that the *ujigama-sama* was the ruler of the village, a sort of hidden protector of the villagers . . .

It would be difficult for people living in Tokyo today to imagine the importance the *ujigami-sama* had for the people of my native village.[249]

This idea is not entirely dead in Tokyo. One woman who said that she had made one visit to the Soga shrine in the past year added as an explanation: 'After all, it is thanks to the *ujigami-sama* that we are able thus to live peacefully in this district.' But this was a rare instance; the only other piece of evidence of any such belief concerning the relation between the *ujigami-sama* and the community came, not from Shitayama-cho but from a neighbouring ward. The shrine of this parish had been destroyed during a fire raid while surrounding streets had been left untouched. It was considered that the *kami* had taken all the fire bombs on to itself in order to spare the local inhabitants, its children, and it was said to be for that reason that the general level of contributions to the rebuilding fund was so high; the shrine building had been almost completed by the summer of 1951. Perhaps the Soga shrine was too far away for it to be thought to have performed the same function for Shitayama-cho.

The *ujigami*, in theory, not only provides general protection for its *ujiko*, but may also be the object of personal prayers by any one of them. However, as far as individual visits to the shrine were concerned, the Soga priest knew of only one resident of Shitayama-cho, a middle-aged widow, who came regularly to pray at the shrine on the traditional shrine-visiting days, the 1st, 15th, and 28th of each month. And of all the shrine visits which a hundred respondents said they remembered having made in the past year (averaging less than ten per person even including the 365 visits of one individual) only 11% were to the Soga shrine.

THE ANNUAL SHRINE FESTIVAL

The Shitayama-cho celebrations of the festival of the Soga shrine—with dancing and fancy-dress competitions and children's parties—were briefly described in a previous chapter. Probably because of the predominantly recreational rather than religious character of the festival celebrations they have undergone little change in the postwar years, and the specifically religious elements of the celebrations are in large part preserved as traditional ritual trappings without which the occasion would be felt to be incomplete. Moreover, being, before the war, outside the sphere of State Shinto, the festivals received no artificial support for political purposes; rather the central government frowned on them and sought to prune them of their more extravagant features which tended to detract from the atmosphere of solemnity with which it wished the shrines of the State Shinto system to be invested. The collapse of State Shinto since the war has, therefore, had little effect on them.

The link between the ward and the Soga shrine at the time of the festival is provided by a 'branch shrine' (*o-miki-sho*) set up temporarily in the ward in a shop given over for the occasion. The job of establishing the shrine belongs to a few older inhabitants, one of whom looks after the ritual objects during the year, while the provision of certain decorations is the monopoly of the old fire-fighting 'chief' of the district (see p. 271). A *fuda* of the local shrine is placed in this branch shrine and blessed by the local priest (or rather 'purified'). Below it are ranged tiers of shelves on which are placed gifts of fruit, cakes or wine bearing a piece of paper marked 'Before the Holy Presence', followed by the name of the giver. In front is a tray for money contributions which are wrapped in an envelope also marked 'Before the Holy Presence' and bearing the name of the donor on the back.

In theory, the *o-miki-sho* exists for members of the ward to come to pay their respects to the Soga *kami* as an alternative to going to the shrine. They certainly come, but the object is rather to make their contribution which will later be published in the Ward Association's report of the festival budget. The *o-miki-sho* also acts as an office where the officials of the ward can sit and confer on the progress of the celebrations and the state of the universe—with the effect of gradual diminution of the bottles of wine which had been placed 'Before the Holy Presence'. Apart from the original purification ceremony which is formal and perfunctory and attended only by one or two officials (the priest has to visit twenty-three such shrines in one day) there are no communal religious celebrations at the *o-miki-sho*.

The large gilt, highly ornamented *mikoshi* of the Soga shrine, weighing about three-quarters of a ton and containing the ritual symbols which are spoken of as the 'body of the *kami*' (*go-shintai*), used to be carried round the parish on the shoulders of thirty or forty strong men hired for the occasion. The last occasion on which this happened was in 1935. After that date a more prosaic bullock-cart was resorted to. Labour costs became too high, said one theory; men aren't as tough now as they used to be, said another. Since the war, however, the *mikoshi* has toured the parish only every other year and then in a much reduced state. It is expensive; the procession of horses, masked dancers, and groups of members of the old fire-fighters' association singing their mournful dirge, all have to be paid and entertained. The Worshippers' Association is less efficient than the old *ujiko-soodai* system as a means of collecting donations, and the maximum is needed for the rebuilding of the shrine, so that even when the procession does tour the parish it is in an abbreviated form. This procession in theory strengthens the relations between the *kami* and its 'children'; popularly it is supposed that good fortune comes during the following year to those outside whose house the *mikoshi* halts. Such halts are arranged outside the houses of the most generous contributors.

At the main Soga shrine rites are held on the day of the festival. Formerly these were attended by the *ujiko-soodai* who each represented their own ward and presented their ward's joint offering at the ceremony. Since the *ujiko-soodai* system was abolished by Occupation ordinance, this festival rite is now attended by members of the Worshippers' Association. It was quite obvious, however, that the assembled worshippers were there not as individuals but as representatives of their ward. In the enclosure to which the worshippers were ushered to drink tea before the ceremony, the President of the Worshippers' Association, a wealthy antique dealer, immaculate in a white linen suit, strolled among the delegates enquiring with an air of authority, 'You are the —— delegates are you? Have you got ——'s contribution for the Building Fund yet?'

Shitayama-cho sent three 'representatives' to the rite; Kataoka, who has been mentioned before as acting as liaison between the Worshippers' Association and the Ward Association, and two older men, who appeared to have appointed themselves and to be motivated by a genuine interest in ritual and religious affairs. (It was significant for instance, that they, unlike Kataoka, knew the names of the instruments which were played during the ceremony.) The ward's offering which they bore, was not however, a large one. Of all the money which had been placed 'Before the Holy Presence' at the Shitayama-cho *o-miki-sho*, some 95% was spent within the ward on food and drink and entertainers' fees.

The ceremony at the Soga shrine was a simple one. Half an hour after the appointed time the worshippers (some in linen suits, some in cotton *yukata* and one only in the traditional formal dress of hempen *kimono* and *hakama*) filed out of the enclosure, rinsing their hands as they left under a tap installed for the purpose. They then lined up under an awning erected beside the temporary shrine which was decorated with a small amount of the usual offerings of fruit, rice-cakes, and vegetables. The priest, becomingly dressed in old Court robes, accompanied by two assistants and three musicians with *hichiriki* (a primitive oboe) soon appeared and began the ceremony. It lasted about ten minutes and consisted of the utterance of a number of prayers, much changing of position between priest and assistants and much waving of the branches of the sacred *sakaki* in the direction of the representatives' awning and of the small crowd of bystanders.

Even allowing for the great handicap of the dilapidated, bomb-damaged surroundings and the shack-like nature of the temporary shrine structure, the ceremony was brief, graceless and lacking in dignity. It evoked little interest among the general populace who thronged the stalls and peepshows in the forecourt of the shrine.

These stalls and peepshows are a regular feature of shrine festivals in every part of Japan. They are the nearest approach to the European fair. The large courtyard of the shrine and both sides of the approaching roads are filled with stalls and booths, whose goods are primarily for children. It is the fond parent who is aimed at with pink celluloid dolls, pink celluloid doll's furniture, pink balloons, windmills, toy soldiers, wooden tanks, goldfish, paper flowers that expand in water, kaleidoscopes, printators and sweets and cakes of all sizes and types. There are also peepshow booths and competition booths—snake-charming women, formalin-bottled foetuses, five-legged sheep, gold-fish catching games and ring-throwing games and on this occasion a 'People's Scientific Laboratory' which demonstrated how, by means of mirrors a girl's head could be made to appear to be stuck on a wooden pole ('Roll up everybody. Many Americans have seen this interesting exhibit and been impressed'). Each of these booths was equipped with loudspeaker apparatus which made up in volume for what it lacked in fidelity of reproduction. Simultaneously, on a stage in one corner of the forecourt a performance was in progress of one of the traditional *kagura* dances, mimed legends of great antiquity and, with their lions and foxes and long-nosed devils, full of the atmosphere of the Shinto mythology. In some country districts these are still the staple recreation at the local shrine festival, and the youths of the village will spend many months practising for these performances. Even in Tokyo they are still sufficiently felt to be an integral part of the festival for the shrine authorities to provide for their performance, though on the afternoon of the ceremony they were obviously in no position to vie for popularity with the 'People's Scientific Laboratory'. Questioning of five of the small number of onlookers failed to elicit any notion of the name or portent of the drama being performed at that moment. One expressed his complete lack of sympathy with what he called the 'fool's dance' (*baka-odori*) and added that it would be better in the evening when the stage was given over to a concert party who strummed mandolins and did quarrelling husband-and-wife acts.

In so far as a legitimate distinction can be drawn between the sacred and the profane in what went on at and around the shrine on festival day, the sacred, as represented by the shrine ceremony, seemed to have little of the atmosphere of solemnity and dignity or of awesome mystery with which it is invested in many societies, and seemed not to be given any transcendental importance as against the profane. While the ceremony was going on no attempt was made to silence either the loud-speakers or the *kagura* dancers. The noise was such that the sound of the *hichiriki* was drowned at a distance of four yards. Nor was any interest in the ceremony displayed by the public at large, nor, indeed, was anything done to inform the public at large that such a ceremony was to take place; it was performed exclusively for those assembled under the awning by invitation. The shifting crowd of onlookers in the immediate apron of the shrine was never more than fifteen in number, in contrast to the crowd of hundreds which moved among the showmen and salesmen in the forecourt.

But participating in, or showing interest in, religious rites is one thing, and paying one's respects to the *kami* is another. Many, perhaps the great majority, of the holiday-makers in the forecourt went, on their arrival at the shrine, to pay their respects to the *kami*. (Though not all; one man, asked if he had 'paid a worshipping visit' (*o-mairi*) to the Soga shrine in the past year, said that he had been there to the festival, but that 'worship' had nothing to do with it.) Even during, and quite independently of, the ceremony, there was a trickle of people who came to clap hands and bow and throw their mite (literally a mite; the usual offering is one *yen*—a farthing) into the large coffer-like offertory box. On this occasion, especially for the festival, there stood just in front of the shrine, a little table at which one of the priest's assistants, also dressed in the old court robes, sat with a register, recording the names and contributions of those who considered their offerings large enough to be recorded, and dispensing *fuda* of the shrine in return. This type of register-keeping is, as it were, a substitute for the issue of receipts, a formal acknowledgement that a social obligation has been performed. In a similar way, after a fire or a funeral, a member of the family will sit at the entrance to record the names and gifts of all those who come to offer condolences.

However, whether in this way respect is paid to the *kami* or not, the fact remains that for those who do go to the shrine at festival time (sixteen out of a hundred Shitayama-cho residents said that they went the previous year) the rites that take place there do not interest them and have no particular meaning for them.

Enough has been said to make it clear that in the towns Shinto rites have little to do with the maintenance of community sentiment. Unlike the villages, where the *ujiko* of the small natural-village *ujigami* do form what are, at certain levels, effective communities,[250] the same formal system has practically no meaning in the towns where the twenty-odd wards which make up a parish are far from forming a community and do not even correspond with a local government unit.

The situation might have been different if, at the reorganization of the Shinto shrine system in the early years of Meiji, small shrines with single-ward parishes had been established instead. Had it been the primary object of policy of the early Meiji government to maintain the tight integration of the small community such a scheme of organization might have been adopted; but in fact it had other objects in view. The loyalty which it was most concerned to foster was a national loyalty overriding the more limited loyalties to the local community. Such loyalties were, in fact, a threat to national integration. Thus, in rural areas, the shrines of the small *buraku* were 'ungraded' and only one shrine per local government unit was endowed with public funds as the village shrine. And in Tokyo, although the *ujigami-ujiko* system was formally institutionalized, official shrines with their large parishes were not intended to foster local loyalties which might compete with a higher loyalty to the nation.

THE NATIONAL COMMUNITY

Shinto rites no longer have any meaning at all for many people in Shitayama-cho. Before the war everyone had to have a *kamidana* in his house—the police, although they had no statutory authority to do so, often made a point, in their routine checks of household composition, of ascertaining whether there was one, and of reprimanding delinquents. But today 47% of households in Shitayama-cho have no *kamidana*. (59% of households who have moved into the ward since the end of the war.) And of fifty-five people in a sample of one hundred who said that they had *kamidana* in their houses, less than a half said that they bowed to it every day. Still, however, seventy-five out of the hundred said that they 'sometimes' worshipped at the *kamidana* or at Shinto shrines, and their explanations of their motives (given in response to the question: 'How would you describe your "feeling", would one say, or "intention", perhaps, when you bow before the *kamidana* or at a shrine?') will provide the best introduction to a discussion of the national aspects of Shinto worship. To put this aspect in its proper perspective, however, first of all a brief mention of other elements of *kamidana* worship which were revealed in these replies:

(a) Habit

Nineteen out of the seventy-five replies amounted to saying that it was merely a question of habit. Some such replies showed a certain introspective objectivity. Having been trained to bow at shrines since childhood, 'I automatically feel on my best behaviour when I approach one', said one man; and a woman said that she 'would feel uncomfortable' or would feel that 'something unfortunate was going to happen' if she failed to perform the appropriate worshipping act at the *kamidana* every morning. Most of these replies carried the suggestion that the habit was an eminently proper one which did not require any justification or explanation, but a few showed signs of a nascent, but suppressed, rejection of such behaviour in saying that it was 'only a question of form' or that they only worshipped because everyone else did so and 'you feel awkward if you don't.'

(b) Respect

A somewhat smaller number of replies, while still implying the basic idea that worship at the *kamidana* and at shrines was a matter of custom, specified the attitudes which such worship was intended to symbolize as 'showing respect'. Respect is, indeed, the keynote to a great deal of Japanese religious behaviour. Children are taught to bow to the *kami-sama* as they are taught to bow to visitors, and they grow up with an idea of the *kami-sama* as important beings to whom deference must be shown without necessarily ever receiving explicit instruction concerning the nature, abode or function of the *kami*.

This insistence on respect as the key to the appropriate attitude towards supernatural beings has a long tradition going back to Confucius at least. ('While respecting spiritual beings, to keep aloof from them may be called wisdom.')[251] During the Tokugawa period, the appropriate attitude which should be displayed towards Shinto and Buddhist shrines was a topic of discussion among the sceptical Confucian scholars. Their general attitude is perhaps best revealed in the story told of Itoo Jinsai who one day made a sight-seeing trip to a Buddhist temple accompanied by several disciples. Jinsai bowed towards the Buddha, at which his disciples asked how he could do such a thing in view of all his attacks on Buddhism. He is supposed to have replied, 'Certainly Buddhism and Confucianism are incompatible. But it would not be right to pay a visit to a place and not pay the proper respect to the master thereof.'[252]

It is not difficult to see why these thinkers who laid the foundation for modern Japanese ethics should have taken such a view. Insistence on respect for the *kami* was part of a general requirement of submissive respect towards all socially accepted authority. Just as it was held that 'A filial son makes a loyal retainer',[253] so the same transference of attitudes could be reasonably expected in this case—'a man who respects the *kami* will respect his father and his lord'.

There is some evidence for the truth of such a hypothesis in the results of these interviews. The people who say that they bow daily at the *kamidana* are significantly more likely to give answers to questions about marriage which show a traditional acceptance of parental authority.[254]

(c) Prayer

Another common group of replies were those which spoke of worship at the *kamidana* and at shrines as occasions for personal productive or protective prayer—prayers for sick relatives, for general protection from harm or for success in examinations. The reply of one man, who had never, presumably, read Malinowski, illustrates with text-book precision the latter's interpretation of the psychological functions of magic. He said that he prayed every morning that he might be able to live out the day in peace and safety, and that having done so he 'felt fortified at heart' (*kokorozuyoi*). More will be said of productive and protective prayer in a later chapter.

(*d*) *The Kami and the Nation*

Four replies in the fourth and last category are the relevant ones for a discussion of the relation between *kami*-worship and membership of the national community. They may be quoted in full.

I worship out of a feeling of respect for the famous men in Japan's history.
It is a case of giving thanks to our great forerunners to whom we are so much indebted. It's not a request for protection or anything like that.
I used to pay my respects because they used to say that Japan was the land of the *kami* and they ought to be worshipped.
I pray for the safety of the nation and my family.

These replies may be considered as some small evidence of the success of the policy of the political and military leaders since the Meiji period deliberately to cultivate the Shinto religion as a means of fostering a sense of national unity. Shinto obviously played a minor part in the whole process of welding a number of diverse fiefs into a national whole; the mere appearance of foreigners in Japan and the threat which expanding Occidental nations represented in the middle of the nineteenth century, the development of a national conscript army and of a national education system with standard text-books, in particular the opportunities of fostering patriotic sentiments afforded by the Sino-Japanese and the Russo-Japanese wars, were probably more weighty factors. The build-up of the position of the Emperor, another important device, was accomplished in part by means of Shinto ritual and teaching (for the important Shinto *kami* were, after all, the Emperor's ancestors) but in part directly through the schools and the army, by such devices as the ritual reading of Imperial rescripts.

The mechanism by which the Shinto ritual was mobilized for national purposes was simple. The peasant at the beginning of the Meiji period, whose life was circumscribed by his local community, was aware of his local *ujigami* as the guardian deity of himself and his fellows, knew of but was not much concerned with, the *ujigami* of neighbouring communities and may even have heard of an exalted Emperor whose ancestors were worshipped in great shrines in central Japan, but he was not greatly interested in them. The Japanese citizen of 1940, however, had developed a new concept of a large number of *kami*, of varying rank and importance, but all the protectors of the Japanese people and guardians of their fortunes.[255] He was made aware, by schooling, press and radio, of the existence and importance of the national shrines, especially the Ise shrine to the Imperial ancestress, Amaterasu, to which the Emperor regularly reported affairs of State (in 1951, half of the *kamidana* in Shitayama-cho still contained *fuda* of the Ise shrine), and the new shrines in the capital;—the Yasukuni-jinja enshrining all those who had died in battle for the Emperor, and the Meiji-jinguu enshrining the Emperor during whose reign Japan had fought the two wars which had brought her into the ranks of the great Powers. Schools, women's organizations, youth groups and factories organized outings to these shrines and their festivals were attended by vast crowds drawn from all over the country. At the local shrines which had been integrated into the national system ceremonies were regularly held on national occasions, the Spring and Autumn festivals of the Imperial Ancestors, the birthday of the Emperor Meiji, the Anniversary of the foundation of the Japanese Empire, and the birthday of the ruling Emperor.

These ceremonies were attended by officials of the local ward associations and other prominent citizens. After 1941, on each anniversary of the declaration of war, each house in Shitayama-cho had to send one member in procession behind the President of the Ward Association for an hour's ceremony at a nearby shrine. A new recruit to the army would be accompanied to a local shrine before his departure by a group of neighbours, generally including officials of the Ward Association. There a short ceremony would be held with prayers which were elaborations of the phrase *Bu-un Chookyuu*—'May military success be continuous and lasting'. In the minds of relatives, however, prayer for the recruit's return was the more dominant thought, as is evidenced by the popularity for such ceremonies of certain shrines whose amuletic *fuda* (afterwards given to the prospective soldier by the priest) were famed for a special protective power. Nevertheless, this rite, like all the others, helped to foster the concept of the *kami* as national symbols rather than as the symbols of a local community or as the objects of private personal cults.

Given this concept of the *kami*, it is easy to understand the reaction of one man who, at the end of the war, tore his *kamidana* from the wall and stamped on it. Less dramatically, the defeat has led to a decrease in visits to shrines, and—as already mentioned—in the number of *kamidana* in private homes and the amount of worship at the *kamidana*. As far as shrine-visits are concerned, fifty-five people out of a hundred said that they went less frequently now than during the war. Of these fifty-five, thirty-two said that the greater frequency of their war-time visits was due to compulsion—for to refuse to partake in an organized visit was to lay oneself open to being branded a *hikokumin*—un-Japanese—as did anyone who failed to show enthusiasm for air-raid precautions or refused to adopt the drab civilian uniform which became *de rigueur* in the later stages of the war. The other twenty-three said that their war-time visits were spontaneous. A significantly high proportion of these were women; not unnaturally, since women had the specific motive of praying, not simply for the welfare of the nation, but for the safety of sons and husbands at the front.

Not only have the gods failed, the new Constitution forbids State support of Shinto shrines and State compulsion of participation in any Shinto ritual. *Kamidana* have been removed from schools and offices and all shrines are now reduced to the same level and are not used for the celebration of occasions of national importance. The Spring and Autumn festivals of the Imperial Ancestors, though still national holidays, are called simply the Spring and Autumn Equinoctial Holidays (and the Emperor worships his ancestors as a private individual), Meiji-setsu, the birthday of the Emperor Meiji, is now Culture Day (though still the occasion of the Festival of the Meiji shrine).

But attitudes of long standing are not destroyed in a day, and, as the replies quoted above indicate, it is still consciously as citizens of the Japanese nation that some people pray to the *kami*. The great national shrines, symbols of Japan's former successes, still remain.

These national shrines are now financed by 'Worshippers' Associations' (*Suukeikai, Hoosankai*, etc.) with nation-wide organizations running parallel to the administrative system and largely officered by men prominent in local government. The aim of these associations is primarily the collection of contributions which are requited by a *fuda* from the shrine. In 1951, however, considerable difficulty was being found in collecting adequate funds. It was reported that the fund which was being built up for the ritual rebuilding of the Ise shrine was unlikely to reach its target, and it was hoped to raise a third of the £600,000 required from Japanese emigrants in Brazil.[256]

The defeat, the collapse of national ideals and the removal of compulsion have then, weakened, though without entirely destroying, what may be called nation-centred ritual attitudes. Shrine visits and *kamidana* worship in 1951 have to be understood primarily in terms of the attitudes outlined earlier. Under the Occupation there was no Resistance, and whereas the association between Shinto worship and military prowess has always been close, it would have been difficult to take over the Shinto symbols and mobilize them for the new national endeavour to win the respect and confidence of Japan's conquerors by proving how democratic the nation could become. Recent reports suggest, however, that since the end of the

Occupation, now that Japan is again in direct competition with the other nations of the world, there has been a big increase in the numbers attending the festivals of the national shrines, though whether this is, indeed, a manifestation of a rising tide of national consciousness or rather of a rising standard of living which enables more people to afford the fares and pocket-money to enjoy the booths and sideshows must remain open to doubt.

20

Family Rites

THE wife of the priest of the Soga shrine was apt to complain of the financial embarrassment which the apathy of post-war parishioners brought to her family. On one occasion she re-marked wryly, that the Buddhist temples had less to complain about; 'They look after the *hotoke-sama*.' The implication that it is their stake in the *hotoke-sama* (the spirits of the dead) which keeps the temples on their feet is probably a just one. The religious rites and beliefs with which the Buddhist temples are chiefly concerned are those which centre around the worship of the spirits of the dead. They are, that is, rites in which either the family is the worshipping unit, or, at least, consciousness of membership of the family is an important constituent of the worshippers' attitudes.

THE BUTSUDAN

The Buddhist rites in the home centre around the *butsudan*, the 'Altar of the Buddhas', which may be a simple wooden box or an elaborate lacquer-and-gilt altar, six feet high and of careful and ex-pensive workmanship. This contains the *ihai*, tablets bearing the posthumous names of former members of the family. Sometimes there are their photographs as well, and occasionally family heir-looms. One man in Shitayama-cho kept in the *butsudan* the swords which were the symbols of his family's former samurai status: another had a history of his native district. There were also genealogical scrolls, and 'registers of the past' (*kakochoo*) recording the death-days of former members of the family. (One family also kept its money in the *butsudan* under the ancestors' care.)

In addition to all these *family* symbols, some *butsudan* contain the symbols of the Buddhist faith, scroll paintings or brass images of Kannon, Amida and other Buddhas and Boddhisattvas; photographs, often of a very high quality, of famous Buddha statues in Nara or Kyooto, brought back from a sight-seeing tour; sometimes the amuletic *fuda* of some famous temple. (And, in one case, the similar *fuda* of a Shinto shrine. Another woman had a photograph of Christ

312

—'The priest knows about it and he says it's all right.') Whereas every butsudan had *ihai* of the family dead, however, only a very little over a half had any of these symbols of the Buddhist faith proper.

In ordinary speech no distinction is made between the spirits of the dead and the Buddhas and Boddhisattvas of the Buddhist faith. They are both called *hotoke* (—*sama*). There is evidence, though, that the two are differently conceptualized,[257] and it will be convenient to distinguish the two as *hotoke* and *Hotoke* respectively. A further distinction can be made among the *hotoke*, between Grandpa, Father, or brother Jiroo on the one hand, and 'the ancestors' (*senzo*)—all the *hotoke* who have been dead for so long that no surviving member of the family has personal memories of them—on the other. These will be distinguished as 'close-relative *hotoke*' and 'ancestor *hotoke*'. The distinction is reflected in the *ihai* kept in the Altar of the Buddhas. After a certain length of time (in theory, after the fiftieth year, though there is great variation in this respect) the *hooji* rites on the anniversaries of the death-days of particular ancestors cease to be held. Thereafter the individual *ihai* is removed and the ancestor is subsumed under the one general *ihai* bearing the legend, 'Ancestors of the various generations of the —— family' and thus become the object only of the general rites for the ancestors at the equinoxes and at the summer Bon festival.

Not every household necessarily has a *butsudan*. The governing principle is that all dead spirits must have their *ihai* kept in some *butsudan*, preferably that of their most direct descendants, rather than that all households must have a *butsudan* at which they can worship their forebears. Where family consciousness is strong, however, younger sons who set up house away from the main family, may take duplicates of the *ihai* (generally those of parents or equally close relatives) in the main family altar. But of the 45% of younger sons in Shitayama-cho who did have altars, only a few had them for this reason. Most of them installed altars on the death of a child or a wife.

Of those families in Shitayama-cho which have been established for more than one generation (and must, therefore, have at least one direct ancestor) 80% had a *butsudan*. The remaining 20% (twenty-four families) did not have one for a variety of reasons. A few were Christians. There were also a small number of families who were 'out-and-out' Shintoists, who that is to say, follow Shinto, rather than Buddhist, funeral and ancestor rites. Shinto rites are essentially similar in nature to Buddhist rites and clearly modelled on them,[258] but the memorial tablets are kept in an elaborated *kamidana* (a *soreisha*) instead of in a *butsudan*.

Sometimes, again, an eldest son who has left his rural home and allowed a younger brother to succeed to the *de facto* headship of his parental family has left the ancestral tablets to be cared for by him, too. But there were other families which had no such 'excuse'. Families which were bombed out during the war and lost their *butsudan* as a consequence, have not always replaced them in their new homes. Some had simply had new *ihai* made and kept them on a temporary wooden shelf. One man gave as his reason the fact that there was a 'superstition' (his word) that if a *butsudan* was bought on any other occasion than on that of a death in the family it would be likely itself to cause someone to die. Others had no explanation to offer. 'Since we've moved here we haven't bothered to get a new *butsudan* or new *ihai* or anything,' said the owner of a small cosmetics factory, adding, 'I'm ashamed to say.'

As this implies, a certain amount of apathy there may be, but positive rejection of the duty to look after and pay respect to the ancestors' *ihai* is rarely met with. The only expression of such an attitude in over two hundred households, was the remark of one woman that her husband 'has strong objections to people worshipping before *butsudan* and *kamidana*', and that for that reason the family's *butsudan* was being looked after by his sister in the country. This man, interestingly enough, a lawyer and one of the few professional men in the ward, was also marked out from his neighbours by the strong antipathy which he displayed towards all forms of ward community activities.

There were, however, few such instances. It is a fairly safe generalization that conformity to traditional religious practices centring round the *butsudan* and the *ihai* is much greater than conformity to those centring round Shinto shrines and the *kamidana*.

THE FAMILY TEMPLE

The worship of the spirits of ancestors, though in all its forms much influenced by the Buddhist religion and by Confucian ideas partly absorbed via that religion, can exist independently of Buddhist institutions. The Emperor's ancestors, to whom essentially similar rites are addressed by the Imperial family, are not *hotoke* but *kami* and they are enshrined in Shinto shrines. Ieyasu, the founder of the last house of Shogun, was also a *kami* to whom several shrines were devoted, so was an even more recent national hero, General Nogi, and, indeed, all those who died in battle are enshrined as *kami* in the Yasukuni shrine. Apart from these national associations some ordinary families, for a variety of reasons (see note 258), follow Shinto burial and ancestor-worshipping practices. Nevertheless, in the vast majority of families, these rites are associated with the Buddhist religion, and it is necessary for their full performance to have some connection with a Buddhist temple.

From this family temple the priest comes to perform funeral ceremonies and the rites held in front of the family *butsudan* on the anniversaries of ancestors' death-days. Alternatively, these latter ceremonies are held actually at the family temple. In some sects a part of the ashes are deposited at the family temple. In others an *ihai*, a duplicate of that in the family *butsudan* is also left at the family temple. It is from the fees for such services that the priest derives his income. It is one of Japan's perennial jokes that a priest is a man who does business in funerals. In a somewhat merciless humorous monologue, a favourite of Tokyo music-hall audiences, one priest says to another, 'If this goes on much longer I shall have forgotten the taste of decent wine. I haven't had a funeral for weeks. I must say, though, that I admire your enterprise, going round and finding out where people are ill. Here, what about a quick one, just a sort of advance celebration like?' [259]

The business, if not highly paid, at least guarantees a living. At some of the Tokyo temples with a large number of parishioners it is quite efficiently organized with an advance booking system and waiting rooms in which the latest magazines are provided for families waiting their turn for an anniversary ceremony.

Most Buddhist temples are almost exclusively concerned with death and the family cult, and few people in Shitayama-cho ever go to a temple for any other reason. Thus, when a family migrates from the country to Tokyo it normally only seeks a new family temple nearby when a death in the family makes it necessary. Many families in Shitayama-cho gave as their 'family temple' that of their parents in a distant part of the country. Ninety-four people out of a hundred acknowledged that they had such a family temple. (Of the others, two were Christians, two Shinto, and two just said they had nothing to do with that sort of thing.) Of these, however, sixteen did not know the name of their temple and seven did not know which of the many Buddhist sects it belonged to. In theory, loyalty to a sect persists through the generations, so that a migrating branch family will pick a family temple of the same sect as that of the main family, but so blurred are sectarian distinctions and so irrelevant are they to the actual purpose of family temples as a part of the family cult, that several cases were found in Shitayama-cho where the sect had been changed for reasons of convenience.

Of these ninety-four people, fifty-three said that they had visited their family temple in the previous year. They estimated that they had made 241 visits between them. Of these 206 were in connection with anniversary ceremonies. The other thirty-five visits, shared by nine people, were on the occasions of temple services (four people), casual visits 'when I happened to be passing' (four people) and 'a sight-seeing visit as guide to some business acquaintances up from the provinces'. This last was the astute Mr. T (of pp. 32–4) who had realized the advantage of having a 'smart' family temple to impress provincial connections. His temple was famous for the fact that it contained the graves of the Forty-seven Ronin, the most famous of all samurai heroes in Japanese legend.

Some Buddhist temples do have functions other than those simply of 'family temples', but these are aspects of 'individual' religious belief and practice which will be considered in a later chapter.

WORSHIP AT THE BUTSUDAN AND AT GRAVES

Apart from the death-anniversary rites for particular ancestors, general festivals for the worship of all the family dead are held at the spring and autumn equinoxes and at the Bon festival in mid-August. Graves are also visited on these occasions. In addition, in many families, incense is lit at the family *butsudan* every morning and offerings are made of rice and tea or water. Sometimes, apart from these offertory rites which are generally performed by the househead or his wife, all members of the family may make a brief formal bow to the *butsudan* every morning. (A fuller account of these rites is given in Appendix VI.)

People in Shitayama-cho are, it was said above, considerably more punctilious in performing the traditional ceremonies connected with the *butsudan* than they were about worship at the *kamidana*. Thus, of seventy-eight people who lived in houses which had a *butsudan*, only nine said that they never performed any individual worshipping act before it. Of these nine, eight were under 25 and only two were heads of households or the wives of heads of households. It is unlikely that this significant relation between youth and non-worship can be legitimately interpreted as an indication of a growing scepticism which the younger generation will carry with it. A more probable explanation is that although the daily bowing at the *butsudan* by all members of the family may be, and often is, omitted, the duty to perform the offertory rites, a duty which belongs to the house-head or his wife, remains as strong as ever. Many people do not begin to perform any acts of worship at the *butsudan* until they become heads of households and it becomes clearly their duty to do so. The remark of one man is significant. As a second son, he said, he 'didn't have much to do with that sort of thing'.

Worship at the *butsudan* is, that is to say, more a matter of family duty than one which concerns religious belief. This much was clear from people's own explanations of the significance which such acts of worship had for them, explanations given in the answers to the following questions which were asked of the sample of a hundred people.

Do you remember when you were a child being taught to worship at the *butsudan* by your parents? How did they explain the meaning of worship?
What do you (or would you) tell your children when you are teaching them?
How would you describe the 'meaning' should one say, or your 'intention', when you make a visit to a grave?
Have you ever made a grave-visit or worshipped at the *butsudan* for the purpose of making a report about family happenings—or do you think you are likely to? What sort of happenings?
Would you (or do you) hold *hooji* ceremonies (rites at which priests are hired to read sutras and prayers in the presence of the assembled family) on the anniversaries of your parents' deaths?

In answer to the learning and teaching questions, there were many who said that there was nothing to be specifically taught; children just learned naturally what they should do. Only thirteen of the hundred people showed a consistent attitude of hostility to any form of worship, insisting that they would teach their children nothing and that if they ever visited a grave it would be merely a matter of form; because it was a social custom or because relatives would expect some conformity to the usual proprieties. Only two of this thirteen were sufficiently rebellious to assert that they would not hold anniversary ceremonies for their parents if they died. These thirteen were significantly youthful, containing ten of the thirty-four under 25's, but the same reservations concerning the interpretation of this fact must be made here as above.

Underlying the replies of the other eighty-three (four only could give no reply) could be seen a variety of attitudes and assumptions which will, perhaps, repay detailed study.

1. Worship is an act primarily undertaken for the benefit of the spirits of the dead.

Some of the common phrases to describe such worship—'to give sustenance to the *hotoke*', 'to pray for the happiness of the *hotoke*'—imply such a belief. It is sometimes held that the 'spirits' (*reikon, tamashii*) of the dead do not immediately 'become *hotoke*'. This is sometimes thought not to happen until the forty-ninth day after death, and some families keep the ashes of a dead person in the house until that day. The ceremonies held on every seventh day until that time, as well as certain ritual abstinences on the part of members of the family, are sometimes explained as necessary to ensure the successful completion of the process of become a *hotoke*. (Under the pressure of modern life, this period is sometimes shortened to thirty-five days, and ritual abstinences are often entirely omitted.)

These beliefs are implicit in the form of death-anniversary and of funeral services. At an *o-tsuuya* feast after the death of a child in Shitayama-cho (held before the funeral, on the first night after the coffin and all the ceremonial offerings are prepared) one neighbour who had some facility in the recitation of sutras and prayers put on a priest's *o-kesa* sash and offered up a catholic selection of sutras. Then came a song in which the child was pictured crossing the seas to Paradise with various Buddhas and Boddhisattvas acting as its oars and sail and rudders,—and finally there were prayers some of which appeared to be addressed to the spirit of the dead child, wishing it god-speed to Paradise, some to the Buddhas asking their help for this child in its journey.

When a spirit successfully becomes a *hotoke*, it does not, however, cease to have wants; offerings (*kuyoo*) are made to them for their 'sustenance' and a special feast is prepared for them with a special display of offerings at the Bon season when the dead come to visit the family. Few people actually mentioned this offering element as of primary importance in *butsudan* worship, but somewhat more gave it as the chief purpose of visiting the graves.

Another need of the dead is companionship. One woman said that she was taught to pray at the *butsudan* 'to comfort the spirits of my brothers who had died when I was young'. 'I go to the graves,' said another, 'because I think that the *hotoke* will be pleased to be visited.'

2. There is a hint in one or two replies that such acts as those described above should be undertaken not only out of a spontaneous concern with the welfare of the dead, but also from enlightened self-interest since the dead, if not satisfied, can be malignant and vindictive.

It may be a corrollary of belief in the delayed attainment of *hotoke*-hood, that until the forty-ninth day the spirit remains as an uncomfortable and potentially dangerous presence in the house where it died. A breach of the ritual abstinences may have evil consequences. It is the trace of this belief, presumably, which underlies the reply of one woman to the effect that grave visits are undertaken to ensure that the dead 'become *hotoke* satisfactorily'. The words used could have the implication 'for our sakes' (*joobutsu shite kureru yoo ni*). One might render the sense 'to pray that they would be so good as to take themselves off into *hotoke*-hood'.

But, like the need for sustenance and attention, the potential dangerousness of the dead spirits does not necessarily cease with their attaining *hotoke*-hood. 'Some people say,' said one woman, thus giving a hint of her scepticism about this, her suggested reason for worshipping at the *butsudan*, 'that if anything happens in your house it is because you haven't taken enough care of, say, the second generation, or the third generation.' She was referring to pro-fessional diviners who sometimes make a speciality of exploiting the human need to see some sort of logic in suffering by giving explanations of misfortunes in such terms as these, lending verisimilitude to their findings by specifying the precise ancestor involved.

There is, even, a certain group of sects, chief among them the Reiyuukai, which have gained a large number of adherents chiefly by these means. The doctrines of the Reiyuukai are not exclusive; its members (it claimed 1,816,000 in 1949) may belong to any other sect as well. As an organization it is of minor proportions with only one church but sixty-eight priests or officials whose function is to distribute ritual paraphernalia and collect contributions[260] with, according to the sect's enemies, the emphasis on the latter.

Such sects, being aimed chiefly at women, also exploit the fact that the married woman, separated from her parental home, has no symbols to which she can address ritual acts on behalf of her own blood relatives.[261] The *butsudan* is supposed to contain only the *ihai* of the family she married into. The woman who mentioned the possible evil results of neglecting the second generation was a member of the Reiyuukai 'because they let you worship your own father and mother'. Another woman described her experience on entering a very similar but smaller sect as follows.

Most people seem to join it as a result of some misfortune, but in my case about eighteen years ago I began to have dreams of my father. In the dream he used to drag me by the hand and say, 'Come, come.' I couldn't sleep and gradually got into a nervous condition. Then I met someone who was a member and she told me that the reason why I had these dreams was because my father's spirit wanted to be worshipped. I joined and they gave us a 'register of the past' called a 'Mirror of the Spirits'. There they wrote down the posthumous names of all my relatives back at home and gave them new posthumous names. Every month I say prayers to the 'Mirror of the Spirits' and ever since I've never once had a dream of my father. Also, when there is something wrong with any of us I pray before it and the illness disappears. Not one of us has had anything to do with a doctor for twenty-five years. We cure ourselves by faith.

This very practical and superstitious concern with the welfare of the dead has ancient origins in the spiritualistic practices which survive despite police attempts at suppression before the war, and, possibly to a lesser extent, since. Spiritualism has long existed as a folk tradition particularly in the agricultural areas of the north, but, apart from the *miko* priestesses which were formerly to be found at some Shinto shrines, it seems not to have been given central importance—at least overtly—by any particular religious sect. The Reiyuukai, however, appears to make use of it. Another woman gave the following reasons for her own conversion:

My elder brother died after the war and exactly on the 'hundredth day' (after his death) a woman friend of his came to see us. She said she didn't know anything about his death but she'd seen him in a dream and she'd gathered something was wrong. She didn't know our address, either, she only knew the name of the borough and she said that it was her faith which brought her to the right house. She was a member of the Reiyuukai. Then there was a woman who lived opposite us, who was also a member of the Reiyuukai. She 'turned into' (*baketa*) my brother and started talking just as he did when he was alive, about what a bad time he had at the front, and he said that as he wasn't buried in the proper place his spirit was still wandering. It was through her that I joined.

Descriptions of the activities of medums in northern villages (*hotoke-oroshi* or 'bringing down the *hotoke*' as the process is called) suggest that the *hotoke* who are brought down also dwell on the difficulties they have of attaining *hotoke*-hood owing to ritual deficiencies in their survivors.

The extent and importance of these beliefs concerning the possible malignancy of the dead should not, however, be exaggerated. They seem to form merely an undercurrent activated only in the nervous and excitable.

3. The other side of the medal to the pacification of possibly malignant spirits, is prayer for their protection and guidance.

Such replies are slightly more frequent than the last type. Four people out of six specifically say that it is good health that they pray for; the others speak of general protection. Half spoke of the individual praying for his personal protection, half of praying for the health and happiness of the whole family. One 50-year-old woman who admitted to this intention showed that she did not take it very seriously, adding as an afterthought, 'It may be superstitious to think that the ancestors are "watching through the leaves". I don't know: if it isn't you would think we ought to be a bit better off than we are.'

4. Far more frequent than request for protection in prayers to the *butsudan* is the expression of gratitude for favours received from the ancestors. Some of these replies may be quoted verbatim:

It is thanks to the ancestors that we are what we are today. You must never forget your debt of gratitude to the ancestors, my parents used to say, and I was told all sorts of stories about what our ancestors had accomplished. I am the thirteenth of the F line.

The *hotoke* are the spirits of our ancestors and are continually protecting us, so you must show your gratitude to them and pay your respects.

As far as religion is concerned, I don't intend to teach my children anything or force anything on them; that wouldn't do any good anyway. As far as the *hotoke* of the ancestors are concerned, however, I shall teach them that they must be grateful to them, quite apart from any question of faith.

I teach them that they must be sure that bowing to the shrine never becomes a mere formality and that they never lose a sense of gratitude in their hearts. The *hotoke* are the spirits of the ancestors and it is one of the duties of man to express his thanks to them as a repayment for their kindness in making us what we are.

It is thanks to the ancestors that I am able to live in such a dirty little one-room flat as this and still be happy—and spiritually I really am happy.

In these replies the favours of the ancestors are sometimes interpreted as their past work in building up the property, the social position and the traditions of the family, sometimes as their continuing protection from beyond the grave.

This type of reply—the most frequent, given by twenty-two of the eighty-three—is a more sophisticated form of belief than those so far considered. The theme is a recurrent one in all spheres of Japanese religious behaviour; the word *arigatai* as an expression of awed gratitude is used equally of one's feeling towards the Emperor, towards the ancestors, or towards the *Hotoke*. Educated Buddhists will often try to explain to a foreigner that the worship of, say, Amida is not a magical productive rite, but simply the outward and manifest form of an inward and subjective gratitude. One might link this stress on humility, on thankfulness for those favours vouchsafed to the unworthy by the beneficient powerful, with the authoritarian structure and the emphasis on loyalty to superiors which was perhaps more explicit in Japan than in any other feudal society. This loyalty meant unquestioning and selfless service to the superior from whom one might occasionally receive grateful favours, but from whom rewards or *quid pro quo* could never be demanded as of right. Without trying to see one as the cause of the other we may find here an instance of a 'significant congruence' in institutions.

The functional relations of these attitudes to family structure will by now need little elaboration. The more firmly the consciousness of a debt of gratitude towards the ancestors is inculcated, and enforced by the solemnity of ritual acts, the stronger the individual's identification with his family and his sense of moral responsibility not to 'let the family (or the ancestors) down' can be expected to become. Such a sense of responsibility is of particular importance as a restraint on the authority of the househead.

For married women, who are not born into the family, but are recruited into it in adulthood, *butsudan* worship may have a special meaning. One woman said that she offered up tea and rice every morning, 'in gratitude for the fact that we live our lives in health, to requite the favours of the ancestors in protecting us. And I pledge as the bride of the house (*yome*) to preserve the family.' Thus unlike China where the married woman is only gradually allowed to participate in the ancestor rites, the Japanese bride is expected to perform them from the beginning as part of her training for the day when she will eventually become mistress of the household. In some parts of Japan, when there are two married sons living in the same household, the wife of the eldest is distinguished as the *hotoke-mori* or 'guardian of the *hotoke*'.

5. The last remark quoted belongs also to the next category, viz. worship is envisaged as a form of pledge to the ancestors to conform to certain moral standards. Thus, one man said that he was told in childhood to 'pledge before the *ihai* to become a splendid person the ancestors need never be ashamed of'.

The importance of the family in providing motivation for the individual to 'get on' in Japanese society receives some confirmation from one man's remark that he tells his children to 'go and pay your respects to the *hotoke* and promise them to study with all your might.' It is not just the immediate family, but also the ancestors who have a stake in the individual's success.

6. An extension of this idea is to regard the *hotoke* as external arbiters. 'The *hotoke* are always watching; if you do anything bad you will be scolded and if you do anything good you will have good done to you.'

7. There are some replies which bear a certain resemblance to these last, but refer not to moral benefit received from *butsudan* worship but to some sort of mystical experience which it brings. Thus one man said that he used to be taught in childhood simply to pay his respects to the ancestors, but now he does it to 'enter the realm of not-self'. Another said that it was a sort of 'spiritual training' which helps one to remain calm and quiet at moments of emotional stress.

The terms in which these replies are couched betray their ultimate origin in Buddhist contemplative thought. They are a measure of the extent to which some knowledge of the ideas and practices of such sects as the Zen have permeated all layers of Japanese society. The diffusion is not likely to be direct, thought it is still not uncommon for examination students to preface the final few weeks cramming with a period of meditation in a Zen temple 'to enter the realm of not-self'. The route of diffusion is most likely to be via the samurai code—*bushidoo* as it is called in modern times—which was subject to strong Zen influences. And also via the popular historical novels describing the deeds of famous swordsmen of the feudal period which are even today the most popular reading matter for the majority of novel-reading Japanese. Complete perfection in any art, particularly the military arts, only comes to one who is in the realm of 'not-self'. It is a popular tradition in Japan which has far outgrown the confines of institutionalized Buddhism that meditation can give great spiritual strength which can triumph over matter, the appetites, and especially the sufferings, of the flesh.

8. The keynote of some replies is again 'respect'. Worship is considered a matter of paying due respect to one's ancestors.

This theme has already been elaborated in the discussion of

kamidana worship. Except in the case of a small number of fervent Shinto nationalists, respect for the *kami* and respect for the *hotoke*, far from being mutually exclusive, generally go hand in hand. A phrase to describe a pious and upright man which has much the same connotations as the English 'honest, God-fearing' is *keishin-keibutsu no nen no aru hito*—'a man who respects the *kami* and respects the *hotoke*'. The relation of the inculcation of such respect attitudes to the moral importance of the family for the individual is as clear as in the case of the sentiments of gratitude which were considered above.

9. The last five categories of replies all presuppose that the object of worship at the *butsudan* is the 'ancestor *hotoke*'. Some people, however, made clear that their concern was primarily or exclusively with 'close-relative *hotoke*'. The normal English connotations of 'worship', indeed, hardly seem appropriate to the attitudes expressed in the reply of the man who said, in explanation of his own first childhood recollections of worshipping at the *butsudan*, that after the death of an elder sister of whom he was very fond, 'whenever I felt how much I missed her I would pay my respects to her *ihai* and her face would come floating to my mind,' or of the woman who said: 'For us old people, visiting the graves is like going to the pictures and so on for the youngsters. You go to meet your dead: you can see their faces in your mind's eye and you can talk to them—you don't get any reply, of course, but it feels good.'

The idea that the dead of whom one still has strong personal memories can and should be treated in very much the same way as when they were alive is often implanted in childhood, even before the child is taught the correct forms of ritual behaviour. In one house in Shitayama-cho a year-old child died. Its two-and-a-half-year-old cousin who lived next door frequently asked for the cakes which were ranged as offerings on the temporary altar for the child's ashes. He would say, 'Can I have *non-non*'s cakes?' (*Non-non* (—*chan*) is a baby word used by mothers for the *kami*, the *hotoke* and the moon, though not the sun. The popular theory of its etymology is that it means anything which is prayed to with a vague *non-non-non-non* sort of mumble.) Sometimes he would be allowed to take the food; sometimes he would be told, 'No, you mustn't, baby Mitomi will be cross if you take it!' Children are also taught to make offerings at the *butsudan* whenever they receive any special delicacy. Whenever the eight-year-old sister of the dead child was given sweets, she was told 'Go and offer some up to Mitomi (or sometimes "the *hotoke*") first.'

We have already considered the explanation of ritual offerings at the *butsudan* as a response to the *hotoke*'s need of 'sustenance'. A different explanation is that the *hotoke*, being still present among the family, should be treated as nearly as possible as they were when still alive. As respected members of the family, they should not be left out of anything—the doors of the *butsudan* are opened when, for instance, a marriage is celebrated in the house—and they have a right to the first share in all delicacies the family enjoys. In a recent novel a second wife who has trouble in disciplining her stepchildren lines them up in front of the *butsudan*, which contains a photograph of their mother, and begins to tell her of her children's naughtiness. It is easy to see how the photographs in the *butsudan* can help to foster this sense of personal communion.

The importance of these elements in *butsudan* worship has led some Japanese authorities, and Ruth Benedict, to suggest that 'ancestor worship' is a misnomer and that the correct term would be 'worship of close relatives'. It is probable, indeed, that the latter form has historical priority and that ancestor worship proper is a later Confucian-influenced development, but today the rites performed before the *butsudan* cannot be wholly considered as either the one or the other. Ritual, it is often said, is primary and belief secondary. Good evidence for one of the many senses which this ambiguous statement may have might be seen in the unity of ritual behaviour and the diversity of interpretations of its significance detailed in the foregoing pages. Some people who performed the rites, indeed, had no interpretation. Worship was 'just a question of habit', though fewer said this about worship at the *butsudan* than about *kami* worship. To the extent, however, that the ritual is not merely habitual and is accompanied by some conceptualization of the object of worship, when there has been a recent death in the family it is most likely to be the image of the known dead relative which springs to mind. But the same ritual forms continue as the memory of the living person begins to fade and he merges into the 'ancestors'.

'The ancestors' are not a meaningless symbol for everyone. In answer to the questions concerning *butsudan* worship, eleven people mentioned as the object of worship the undifferentiated *hotoke*, twelve specified particular dead individuals, and twenty-seven specified 'the ancestors'. Consciousness of, and gratitude for, the favours of 'the ancestors' is one of the essentials of the moral life according particularly to the old samurai codes, the diffusion of which has been aided by the deliberate ethics teaching of primary schools. Mothers do tell their children that they must be grateful for all the ancestors have done for them. The extent to which they do so and to which the ancestors become significant symbols probably depends on the antiquity of the family tradition, the degree of continuity in location and occupation of the family and the amount of property the family has. The man who knew himself to be of the thirteenth generation of a samurai family, or the carpenter whose forebears had been carpenters in the same house for several generations, would have a more lively awareness of the ancestors than the son of a younger son who had migrated from the country to become a factory worker.

10. Sometimes the purpose of worship at the *butsudan* or at the grave is said to be to report recent family events to the ancestors. One of the questions quoted above specifically asked about such practices. Thirty-two out of a hundred said that they had made such reports, a further nine said that they hadn't yet but probably would in the future. The sort of things they report are 'getting through the University entrance examination' (remember also the boy who pledged to the ancestors to study hard) 'how the family business is getting on', 'when anyone in the family is ill', 'when a baby is born or there is a marriage', or 'when we do any building work on the house'. (The actual fabric of the building in which the family lives—which in typical eldest-son families is the ancestral home—has a special symbolic significance for the family. The word *ie*, like 'house', can mean the actual physical house as well as the family.) The relation between these rituals and internalized moral sanctions are again very clearly shown in one reply, 'I go to apologize when anything has happened which I feel has let the ancestors down.'

Here, too, it is sometimes individual *hotoke* who are thought of as the recipients of the information, sometimes the ancestors collectively. This practice of reporting events is obviously not as widespread as ordinary worship at the *butsudan*. It is not one of those things which mark off a righteous man from an unrighteous man, though it seems to have been considered as such in certain pre-war government circles. Then, as long as it was an official government ritual for the Emperor to report affairs of state to his ancestors at the Ise shrine, the official mythology had to be supported by the conduct of government officials. Ambassadors, before they went abroad to take up a new appointment, were expected to take time off to visit the graves of their ancestors to inform them of their departure, and often travelled hundreds of miles in the midst of their preparations in order to do so.

CONSISTENCY OF BELIEFS

Many of these replies seem clearly to carry the assumption that some sort of spirit survives the body after death. Twenty questions later, about twenty minutes later in time, a further question was asked: 'When a man dies do you think that is the end, or do you think that in some form or other something like a spirit lives on?' The cross-classification of replies is interesting.

This table may be interpreted as showing simply the futility of this sort of questioning. It might be reasonably argued that the whole assumption that it is possible to discover people's 'beliefs' about subjects which do not normally occupy their thoughts is mistaken.

Table 23: Butsudan Worship and Survival after Death

Question 1 ＼ Question 2	Death the end	Don't know	Spirit lives on	Total
'*Butsudan* worship is meaningless, a mere custom'	9	3	1	13
'Worship is an expression of gratitude or respect'	9(31%)	3	17	29(100%)
Answers implying the existence of spirits who watch over the living, are prayed to for aid, are helped to become *hotoke*, are informed of family events, etc.	8(21%)	3	28	39(100%)
Answers implying the existence of spirits only in use of certain conventionalized phrases:, *kuyoo*, *meifuku*, etc.	7(47%)	1	7	15(100%)
Don't know		2	2	4
Total	33	12	55	100

But there are other explanations, and, in particular, some tentative conclusions might be drawn, concerning the differences between various groups of the above table. (Tentative because, with this small sample, the differences do not reach the level of statistical significance.) In the first place, the people who are most liable to logical inconsistency are those whose answers to the first group of questions were in terms of conventional phrases commonly used to describe the function of such worship in general terms, equivalent, perhaps, to such English phrases as 'to pray for the soul of . . .'. It may be assumed that these replies did not necessarily have for them any meaning as precise as their reply to the second question. And from this it follows that the explanation of ancestor worship in terms of giving sustenance to the spirits probably represents a real belief for only a very few people.

But still this leaves the eight people who are most explicit in their earlier replies assuming the existence of spirits and yet later on deny that such spirits exist. Is it, particularly in the case of 'personal communion' type of worship, that the important thing is the psychological need to express feelings in action—'it feels good', as the old lady said, to imagine that you are talking to the dead, irrespective of whether or not you believe in the real existence of some spiritual being taking cognizance of your acts? Or is it—and this particularly in the case of worship of ancestor-*hotoke*—that the rites derive their validity from the fact that they serve as the expression of sentiments —of gratitude and respect—which are morally approved, and the existence or non-existence of spirits is of minor importance? Or are the rites performed as customary and socially-enjoined acts which have no meaning for their agnostic performers but which will be explained to interviewers in terms which are thought generally acceptable? Or does the denial of the existence of spirits conceal a sceptical uncertainty which nevertheless permits productive prayer 'just in case'? Did the stimulus of the interview reveal the inconsistency for the first time? Or were the answers simply haphazard and dictated solely by a desire to get rid of the interviewer as quickly as possible? These questions must remain open to doubt (though one fact which may make the last solution unlikely is that these eight people who gave the most clearly inconsistent replies were all marked by the interviewers as 'extremely co-operative').

It is perhaps an argument in favour of the second explanation (that the validity of the rites derives from the moral values they serve to express and maintain) that scepticism concerning the existence of spirits is greater among those who interpret worship as the expression of gratitude than among those who speak of spirits giving protection, becoming *hotoke*, or being informed of family events. (Though the difference is not statistically significant; $\cdot 2 < p < \cdot 3$). It is easy to see that there is less strain involved in giving thanks to, than in asking for the help of, something in whose existence you do not fully believe. It is the inward and spiritual state of an awareness of one's indebtedness to all that has gone before which is important and which marks off, in his own eyes as well as in others', the morally upright man from the irresponsible. The demonstration and the strengthening of this state of mind is the purpose which the ritual serves; the actual existence or non-existence of spirits who accept the gratitude is largely irrelevant.

Something like this seems, indeed, to underlie the attitude of the sceptical Confucian scholars of China to ancestral and sacrificial rites.[262] In the Li Chi and in Hsün Tzu the idea is clearly expressed that the spirits 'have neither substance nor shadow', but that rites are performed '*as if* the deceased enjoyed the sacrifice' and '*as if* the deceased drank from his goblet'[263] because sacrificial rites represent 'a state of mind in which our thoughts turn with longing (towards Heaven, the Ancestors). It is the supreme expression of loyalty, love and respect. It is the climax of all those ritual prescriptions we embody in patterned behaviour.'[264] Such rites are necessary because they are the most important 'of all the ways of keeping men in good order'.[265]

This conscious 'sociological' awareness of the function of the rites for society was not expected to be widely diffused among the lower orders. 'The nobles know well enough that it (sacrifice) belongs to the way of man. Only the common people regard it as a service rendered to the spirits of the dead.' [266] The degree of double-think required is, indeed, a difficult one. For socially useful fictions to be maintained it is, perhaps, necessary that only a small minority should be aware that they are fictions and should keep the knowledge to themselves. It is difficult to imagine a society in which everyone performs rites towards supernatural beings which they believe not to exist *as if* they did exist, solely because they consider that the sentiments which they are thereby inducing *in themselves* are necessary to society. In ancient China Mo-tzu, whose rationalistic approach led him to assert that 'to hold that there are no spirits and learn sacrificial ceremonies is like learning the ceremonies of hospitality when there is no guest, or making fishnets when there are no fish', [267] explicity attacked the scepticism of the Confucians because, diffused among the common people, it led to an abandonment of moral standards and the disintegration of society in unfilial conduct, wickedness and rebellion.[268] For the common people to hold a sceptical Confucian outlook and yet train their moral responses by performance of the rites he clearly held to be impossible.

But are we to conclude from the evidence of the above table that among the more educated 'common people' of modern Shitayama-cho there are many for whom such a degree of sophistication is not impossible? The answer is already implicit in what was said three paragraphs back. The performance of ancestor rites serves not only to *strengthen* in the individual the attitudes of respect and gratitude (which, as the sociologist may discern, is important for the functioning of society), but also to *demonstate* such attitudes (which, in a society in which such attitudes are held to have intrinsic value, may have greater importance for a consideration of the motives of the worshipping individual).

And yet one is led to wonder whether this can continue for long. In a society in which 'rationality' is increasingly emphasized in all spheres, the view may be expected to spread that to worship non-existent beings—albeit as an expression and demonstration of socially-approved attitudes—is 'like making fishnets when there are no fish.' Moreover, since, ultimately, the social approval accorded to these attitudes—the belief in their absolute intrinsic value—is logically linked to a body of ideas which involve the existence of spirits, scepticism on the latter score cannot fail to affect the absoluteness of the value attached to the attitudes. This is a problem which confronts many societies other than Japan. Equal difficulty is found in the West in maintaining belief in the absolute validity of the Christian ethic while abandoning the revelationary basis which was its original claim to such absoluteness.

21

The Individual and the *Kami*

IT is a common characteristic of the rites which have been discussed up to this point that they are not only primarily social
in function, they are also generally considered by the people who
perform them to belong to the sphere of social obligation or hallowed
custom rather than to the sphere of religious faith. This is abundantly
clear from the following fact. The question: 'What religion are you
in your family?' produces in overwhelming proportions the reply
'Buddhism' which refers to the fact that the family has a family
temple on whose services it calls if need by. On the other hand, the
question: 'Do you personally have any religious belief?' [269] produces
eighty-eight noes out of a hundred.

The operative word here, . . . *wo shinjin suru*, means 'To believe in'
anything from the power of an Inari shrine to bring customers and
prosperity to a restaurant, to the power of an Amida or a Christ to
ensure salvation in an after-life. The next three chapters will describe,
first, some of the individual protective and productive cults, secondly,
some of the alternative explanations of the purpose of life and the
meaning of death which are presented to the citizens of Shitayama-
cho by the various religious sects, and thirdly, the beliefs which the
inhabitants of Shitayama-cho actually hold concerning some of the
problems with which religious faiths are generally concerned.

TYPES OF PROTECTIVE AND PRODUCTIVE CULTS

(a) Household Gods

Apart from the *kamidana* which was discussed in an earlier chapter
on community rituals, very old farmhouses are often full of household deities, the chief of which are the *kami* of the kitchen (Koojin-
sama), the *kami* of the well or the water-pipe, and the *kami* of the
lavatory. In form, simply small offertory shelves below a *fuda* bearing
the name of the *kami*, these shrines are supposed to ensure the purity
of the places they guard. Generally, they are refestooned with Shinto
ritual decorations at every New Year and offerings may be made
once or twice a month, or, in the case of the kitchen *kami*, more

frequently. In more strictly traditional families, someone would make it his duty to do the rounds every morning paying his respects to each *kami* in turn. (At the head-temple of the Hossoo sect of Buddhism in Nara, the priest's quarters contain a large number of *kami* of this type. One of the under-priests has the task of making a tour of these *kami* every morning making the correct hand-clap and bow—i.e. the Shinto, not the Buddhist ritual—to each.)

Of these *kami*, it is the kitchen-god, Koojin-sama which has shown the greatest survival power in an urban environment. Sixty-eight of 255 households in Shitayama-cho had one, and a further seventeen said that they used to but gave it up. Bombing and removal was the reason given by the majority of these; others said that they 'just could not be bothered these days' or had 'ceased to believe in it'. One woman explained her abandonment of the cult in these terms: 'Before I married I used to be a regular worshipper of Koojin-sama, but my Grandmother warned me. She said, "If you worship Koojin-sama you must continue it all your life. Now you're not very strong and I don't know that you will really be able to keep it up. Rather than be rudely neglectful (*burei ni naru*) of him it might be better for you to give it up with your marriage." So I took her advice.' Similar ideas were expressed in other contexts in relation to personal cults of particular *kami*. It has been argued in a previous chapter (see p. 64) that the Japanese tend to divide the outside world into people with whom they have '*giri*-relations' which involve certain obligations, not least the frequent acknowledgement and strengthening of the relationship by visits and gift-interchange, and those with whom they have no such relation. Ideally the distinction should be clear-cut, with no blurring of categories; a *giri*-relation that is left to fade into non-existence leaves a nagging sense of duty unfulfilled. The remark just quoted seems to show that the *kami* are treated in the same way. If you enter into a *giri*-relation with one of them, then you must be prepared to keep it up, if you are not, it is best not to enter into such a relation. There is no sense here, it will readily be seen, that the *kami* are in any way forces controlling our fate whether we like it or not. Grandmother's notion that marriage is in some sense a rebirth is also interesting.

The water *kami* and the lavatory *kami* have suffered rather more. Six households have and eleven used to have the former, ten have and eleven used to have the latter. Again, the reasons given for abandoning the *kami* are the same. One can easily appreciate that strongly over-chlorinated water issuing from a tap would seem less likely to require the attentions of a *kami* than spring-water trickling from a rotting bamboo-pipe, and the lavatory *kami*, too, may seem a little of an anachronism in an age when the Tokyo Municipal Authority fills the town with advertisements for its sewage installation grant-in-aid scheme reading, 'Install a flush toilet; the first condition of a civilized life.'

(b) Other Cults

In addition to these traditional household *kami*, some houses have other minor shrines or offertory-shelves in which are placed a *fuda* bearing the name of a *kami*. When such *fuda* are collected in casual visits to shrine festivals they are generally placed in the *kamidana*. If the *fuda* is given a special shelf to itself, it indicates that the family considers itself a regular devotee of the particular *kami*, makes special visits to that *kami*'s main shrine, and places special reliance on the *kami*'s protective agency. Some of these *fuda* are from shrines which are the centre of a flourishing annual festival. One common *fuda* in Shitayama-cho is that of *O-tori-sama*, a shrine near the old brothel quarters in Asakusa which attracts such vast crowds, particularly at the third of its three yearly festivals that regiments of police, equipped with loud-speaker cars are required to control the crowds and to keep them circulating in a fixed direction. At this festival, it is the custom to haggle with the priests who sit outside the shrine selling *fuda*. There is no attempt to maintain a pretence that amuletic protection is not a marketable commodity like any other.

It is often said that one worships the *kami* at Shinto shrines to get immediate this-worldly results; one prays to the *Hotoke* at Buddhist temples for long-term other-worldly results. The distinction holds generally good; nevertheless, some of the centres of the more flourishing of these essentially this-worldly productive cults are Buddhist in origin. One of the *fuda* most frequently found in Shitayama-cho (in forty-two of the 255 houses; in eight of these placed in a separate shrine or shelf, in the others merely placed in the *kamidana*) was that of the temple of Fudoo, on Mt. Narita in Chiba prefecture, some forty miles from Tokyo by electric train. At the time of the festival, excursion trains leave every few minutes, the crowds are enormous, and so, apparently, is their enthusiasm. A Japanese sociologist who recently made the pilgrimage has this to say:

I was astonished to see how earnest everyone was. The man in charge of the party said quite clearly, 'anyone without greed or desires might as well stay away. It is because we all have desires that we are here today, so wish away to your heart's content.' There were some people who when they got in front of the temple and put their hands together gradually started to tremble. They were all mumbling something unintelligible which I afterwards discovered to be repetitions of phrases like 'Safety in the Home', 'Prosperity in Business', and 'Excellence in the Arts' (dancers, singers, shamisen players, music-hall performers, etc., are generally devotees of Mt. Narita). They intone it in a sonorous voice and with a very clear rhythm. . . . In front of the temple one of the pilgrims was 'possessed by the *kami*' and started crying 'Japan has lost the war. Lost! The *kami* are mournful.' and then, 'The Japanese will rise again. The *kami* see through all', all the time waving a *gohei* (Shinto ritual wand). Others came crowding round this new *kami-sama* still intoning 'Prosperity in Business' and 'Safety in the Home' quite unconcernedly . . . I suppose when the chances of securing a happy daily life by one's own efforts are limited you have to ask the *kami* to secure it for you. The astonishing part of the experience for me was to see the way in which material interests and faith were so closely bound together, and they with the 'Japan, the land of the *kami*' type of ideology.[276]

There are many such cults involving pilgrimages to mountain-tops, On-take-san, Nantai-san, Minobu-san and several more. Frequently, as at Narita, the object of worship is a Buddhist deity in a Buddhist temple.

Not all the *fuda* found in Shitayama-cho homes are the products of such mass pilgrimages. Some people have their own favourite shrine or temple in Tokyo to which they make frequent visits alone or *en famille* for quiet personal prayer. One of the many temples and shrines in Asakusa, one of the oldest parts of Tokyo which has always been the centre of the entertainment industries of the city—among those engaged in which *kami*-worship is traditionally strong—is the Nichigen Soshidoo. In the grounds of this Buddhist temple there are:

1. A 'hundred-times stone', placed some distance from the steps leading to the main hall, opposite the main Buddhist image. Those who have some particular desire which they wish to have granted, take a bundle of a hundred pieces of string and, using this as a rosary, count off a hundred journeys from the stone to the foot of the steps where they each time bow to the Buddha and repeat a short prayer.

2. A Jizoo-bosatsu, one of the most popular of the Buddhist deities, common as a wayside god and a protector of children. This Jizoo can generally be seen receiving the attention of women, many with the Japanese-style hair-dressing worn now only by geisha. They pour water over him and rub some part of his body with one of the many scrubbing brushes provided. It is held that scrubbing his head cures a head-ache, scrubbing his mouth the toothache and so on.

3. An Inari shrine to the Shinto rice-god, covered, or rather, untidily littered, with offerings of fruit, and a sort of fritter (*abura-age*) and also with little white china foxes (foxes are traditionally associated with Inari) which were being sold nearby.

4. A smaller shrine, built into a large rock. Of obscure, but undoubtedly Shinto, origin, it was called Frog Mound (*kaeru-zuka*). Here there were fewer offerings of fruit and brown baked-clay frogs than at the Inari shrine. From the names on the list of donors to a recent repair fund, which stood beside the shrine, it appeared to be

largely supported by proprietors of establishments in the brothel quarters.

All of these shrines, of course, also have offertory boxes for the receipt of money offerings.

These are all the sort of *kami* with whom one might establish an obligation-bearing *giri*-relationship which would entail the reciprocal obligation on the *kami's* part to provide general protection. Some *kami* are specialized. There is, for instance, the Suitenguu shrine to which one goes to pray for easy child-birth, the Toge-nuki Jizoo who specializes—most improbably—in the removal of thorns stuck in fingers, or Kishimojin who is good for children's complaints. One woman in Shitayama-cho told how her son after being 'given up as hopeless by four or five doctors' was eventually cured by Kishimojin. Her story illustrates very clearly the element of formal entry into relations which is involved.

The way you do it is this. You go along to the temple and you say to the priest, can your child be his disciple [*deshi*—as contract-implying a terms as 'apprentice' in English]. Then he says, 'For seven years or ten years?' Then you say, 'Ten years', and that means the child is a disciple until he is ten years old. When you become a disciple you get a small pair of *zoori* sandals and a stick which you keep, and you must make a visit to the temple three times a month, on the eighth, eighteenth and twenty-eighth. It doesn't cost anything to become a disciple, but you make an offering every time you pay a visit. There is no abstention from any foods. I'm thankful to say my boy wasn't ill all these years, which has made us even stronger believers. Even after the ten years were over, we still call in whenever we happen to go in that direction and if anyone we know happens to be going over there we give them some money for an offering and ask them to bring us back a *fuda*.

Ritual abstinence, mentioned in this last description, is a feature of some cults. One woman who had put the fate of an ailing daughter into the hands of a *kami* had pledged to drink no tea until her daughter had successfully grown up, a pledge involving no mean hardship to the tea-drinking Japanese.

The *kami* are not solely concerned with sickness, however, more especially nowadays with modern improvements in medical science. Some shrines, particularly the Shinto Inari shrines, the most common of the small non-priest-attended shrines in Tokyo are visited not only when in trouble, but regularly in order to get the balances of fortune weighted in one's favour. It is part of the stereotype of all members of the 'Water-trades' (*mizu-shoobai*)—the food, wine and women side of the entertainment industry—and also of Kabuki actors, *sumoo* wrestlers and other exponents of indigenous arts with a long tradition, that they are regular in their devotion to Inari shrines. So also are the small business men, particularly the descendants of old Edo merchants. 'Ninety-nine per cent of the secret of success may be good business, but the other one per cent may be luck. You never know, you can't lose anything anyway' was the explanation of one devotee.[271]

The performance of protective or productive rites is not always the sole motive of shrine visits, particularly when they take the form of pilgrimages to distant provincial shrines. Then, piety and the enjoyment of travel and sociability are mixed in much the same proportions as for Chaucer's pilgrims to Canterbury. Small societies (*koo*, a word also used for savings societies) are often formed for the purpose of making annual trips to particular shrines, either by priests or by private individuals. As with all *koo*, even the more informal groups in villages, the rules are carefully drawn up and the registers are carefully kept. The rules of one Tokyo *koo* are translated below. It was organized by a professional pilgrimage-leader-cum-geomancer-cum-fortune-teller, and made a yearly pilgrimage to the Kasama shrine on the north Japanese coast.

1. The aim of the society is to secure the safety of members' families, the prosperity of their businesses, the expansion of their enterprises, and to promote friendly relations among them.
2. Members of the society make monthly payments towards the cost of a group pilgrimage to the Kasama shrine which is made every year in the middle of May.
3. The monthly contribution shall be 110 *yen* (2s. 2d.) of which 10 *yen* shall be used for the lighting of the meeting place and other *koo* expenses.
4. The yearly accumulation of 1,200 *yen* shall be used exclusively for the expenses of the pilgrimage.
5. Should any member of the *koo* be unable to make the pilgrimage, his money shall be returned to him with the exception of 100 *yen* 'sacred fire money' (*goma-ryoo*) which shall be used for an offering to be made on his behalf.
   N.B. It is possible that there may be some alterations in the above due to price fluctuations.

Other religious *koo* are simply organizations, involving no distant pilgrimage, by means of which the devotees of a particular shrine or temple are bound to it by formal ties. It is thus a spur to the regularity of their devotion and sometimes a means whereby a number of such worshippers are brought into social and sociable association to their general advantage. The members of one such *koo* gathered monthly at a temple near Shitayama-cho for the worship of Daikokuten whose laughing bronze image, with its mallet and its money-bags and bales of rice, appeared to receive more attention than the image of Shaka—Gautama, the original Buddha—to whom the temple was ostensibly dedicated. Part of the members' contributions is used to provide concert party entertainment on a stage in the temple's forecourt on summer evenings. An old prospectus of the *koo*, however, does not dwell on the recreational side of its activities. 'The wealth of this world is limited and has been likened to the insubstantial nature of the fleeting clouds. But the *fuku* (happiness, luck; it carries both connotations) of Heaven is without limits: it gives both spiritual wealth and material wealth, and can lead everyone to real and complete happiness.' The members of the *koo* also have *fuda* bearing the name of Daikokuten installed in a separate little shrine at home. One shopkeeper in Shitayama-cho kept his directly above his safe.

Installation in a household shrine is not the only use of such *fuda*. Some are purely amuletic in character. They may, in form, bear the name of a *kami* like other *fuda*—e.g. 'The *kami* (or "spirit"—*shinrei*) which prevents robbery'. Alternatively they may have simple formulas written on them such as ' Prevention of Robbery'. Two 'spirit which prevents robbery' *fuda* were prominently displayed over the clothes lockers in the men's changing room of the Shitayama-cho bathhouse. Other examples were a lightning-deflector *fuda* placed in the roof, a fire-preventor, and a general prevention-of-disaster *fuda* (*sainan-yoke*). These are simply pasted or nailed to the walls; a favourite place is above the main entrance to the house since it is from the entrance that many forms of disaster are likely to insinuate themselves. These *fuda* may also be carried as amulets on the body. The Narita *fuda* was supposed to have a special efficacy in preventing injury, and some mothers tie the *fuda* which they receive from the *uji-gami* shrine at *miya-mairi* registration ceremonies round the waist of their child.

SCEPTICISM AND BELIEF

Visits to temples and shrines is still one of the most common forms of Japanese outdoor expedition and one which does not necessarily imply a 'religious' motive. Similarly, the presence of a *fuda* in the *kamidana* does not necessarily imply that any great importance is attached to it by the household. A *fuda* brought back from an outing would be put in the *kamidana* as the proper place for it, just as wild flowers would be put in a vase in the *tokonoma*.

The fact that a *fuda* is placed not just in the *kamidana* but in a separate shrine, however, does indicate that someone in the family sets some store by it. Thirty-six houses in Shitayama-cho had such shrines. Of these, twenty-two were also possessors of one of the household *kami* (kitchen, lavatory, water) with the consideration of which we began this section. Thus all these additional shrines are concentrated in a relatively small number of households in the ward. Almost exactly two-thirds of the households had no such shrines and of the eighty-seven who did, a third had more than one type.

These are also the households which most conscientiously maintain traditional festival practices. There is a highly significant correlation between the possession of a shrine and keeping more than half of the festivals which were discussed in Chapter 15.[272] But mere traditionalism is not the sole factor involved. There is also a significant correlation between possessing an extra shrine and depending on income other than a fixed wage or salary.[273] One man revealed this connection quite explicitly. Asked if he had any *kami* in his house he replied that he had an Inari-sama, but as he had now given up his private business he intended to take it back to the Inari shrine.

Some indication of individual attitudes towards the *kami* and their *fuda* may be derived from the answers given to the following questions, by a hundred people.

1. Have you ever been to a shrine and been given some sort of protective *fuda* and brought it home? What sort of *fuda*? What have you done with it? Put it in the *kamidana*, or worn it as a charm, or what?
2. Do you think they have any effect?
3. [If 'yes' to (1) and 'no' to (2)] Then why do you get them? [274]

Only nineteen people said that they received such *fuda* and believed in their efficacy. Again there was no association with age, sex, or rural-urban origin, though a nearly significant association was found between lack of higher education and belief in *fuda*.[275]

Some were passionate defenders of their favourite shrine's *fuda* and ready to substantiate their claims for it by recounting personal experiences:

Yes, I am sure they have an effect. One day when I had the Narita *fuda* on me, I was at work and fell off a high shelf with a pile of things in my hands. Fortunately the things I was holding fell underneath me and I wasn't hurt. But the *fuda* was broken in two. I was overcome with awed gratitude (*mottainai to omotte*) and burnt the *fuda* and buried the ashes in the earth.

Three other people told similar stories of how the Narita *fuda* had saved their lives (though one introduced his story with the disclaimer, 'I expect it is just coincidence, but . . .') and two had similar stories about relatives. The power of the *fuda* depends on mere possession rather than on personal receipt of the *fuda* at a shrine. One woman described how she had once given a Taishaku *fuda* to a friend who, twenty years later, had come to thank her for his survival in a bad train accident, which he attributed entirely to the power of the *fuda*.

Other people are satisfied with more coincidental proof: 'They do have an effect. Once we had a burglar in, but we surprised him before he could take anything and he ran away.' 'My child wears a charm next to his skin and he is healthy.'

The completely amoral character of the *kami* and its power comes out clearly in one man's claim that the *fuda* must have some effect because he had not only survived the war, but had also 'done wrong without paying for it'. Perhaps it was this aspect of belief in *fuda* which prompted the following reply which had a moral tone absent in any of the others: 'I don't think they are entirely without effect, but I don't like such things; I believe that one should always go through life relying on one's own efforts.'

Twenty-five other people who said that they took *fuda* from shrines but had no belief in its efficacy, produced a variety of rationalizations of the function of *fuda* in answer to the second and third questions. Some, particularly women, said that they 'took them because they give them to you', and one spoke of being 'talked into buying' a *fuda*. Yet another brought them home to stick in an album as souvenirs.

There were others, however, who provided more subtle justifications for keeping a *fuda*. 'They have no effect, but they give you a sense of spiritual security.' 'There's no harm in it and it makes one feel settled in one's mind.'

The most developed type of rationalization was that which saw the *fuda* as a means of moral self-exhortation. Thus one man who had bought a *fuda* as a charm for his children, but believes that they have no effect, said he supposed it was 'just an expression of parental love, and also, I think, the psychological effect it has is not entirely meaningless, in that it makes one even more concerned for one's child's welfare and more careful in bringing it up.' And from another man, 'In themselves I don't think they have any effect, but they are a stimulus to take care of one's health. It is for that reason that I receive them; they have a bracing effect on one.'

Finally, a quite different argument was provided by one man for whom the *fuda* were obviously not simply charms but symbols of the *kami* of the shrine from which they were issued. His point was that in times of difficulty it is a beneficial thing to pray to the *kami* 'in order to purge oneself of all emotion'. But simply resorting to the *kami* in one's hour of need is unworthy. In between whiles one should, in recognition of one's possible need to pray to the *kami*, 'treat the *fuda* with respect'. That is to say, in maintaining a *giri*-relation with a *kami*, 'treating the *fuda* with respect' is a substitute for regular shrine-going, just as the sending of New Year and Midsummer cards is a substitute for visiting, in maintaining a *giri*-relation with men.

It appears, therefore, that it is possible for only a small number of people to believe in the immediate protective efficacy of such *fuda* and openly and naïvely to admit the fact. A somewhat larger number of people take these *fuda*, but scepticism concerning these matters is sufficiently widespread for many of these to feel the need to explain their action in a way which implies no assumption of the existence of supernatural forces.

'Rationalization' may not be the right word to use for the statements of those who see the effect of the *fuda* as purely subjective— as confidence-inspiring or self-exhortatory. For these people describe as their own experience what most anthropologists would agree is an important function of magic in many societies. Should one perhaps say that scepticism concerning the existence of supernatural forces has prompted an introspective enquiry which has arrived at the correct conclusions? But then these people implied that they would continue to use charms despite their unbelief in their direct efficacy. Again the same sort of questions arise as were noted on p. 327. Do such charms continue to have the desired psychological effect despite a thorough-going scepticism concerning their supernatural power? Are cognitive beliefs of little importance compared with the psychological need for reassurance and therefore easily shut out of consciousness in times of stress? Are these people practising conscious self-deception? Was their scepticism stimulated for the first time by the direct questioning of the interview, a situation which does not often occur in real life? Or are these cognitive beliefs which they express only half-beliefs, conflicting with other half-beliefs that 'there might be something in it', so that they receive these charms in order to be 'on the safe side'?

22

Present-day Religious Teachings

IN this chapter an attempt will be made to summarize the various types, the media and the varying 'volume of impact' of explicit religious teachings available to the residents of Shitayama-cho.

As will clearly emerge, the direct influence of religious organizations in moulding their religious beliefs is small. The family is obviously the most important milieu for the transmission of such ideas. Another factor which in Britain could not be ignored is the school, but in Japan the influence of the school in the formation of religious beliefs is small. Before the war, largely by means of ritual but also to a certain extent by explicit religious teaching, there was inculcated what might be called a religion of nationalism. But this teaching, as we shall see, did not constitute a coherent world-view; it could not become (and, indeed, the pre-war Ministry of Education was constantly declaring, in the face of Christian objections, that it was not intended to be) a satisfactory personal religion, capable of dealing with the problems of suffering and guilt and explaining the purpose of human life. Since the war, even this has disappeared and religious teaching of any sort is forbidden in schools provided by the public authority.

There must obviously be some transference of attitude as between teacher and pupil, but it is doubtful if the attitudes of teachers differ greatly from those of parents, except that they possibly lean a little more towards agnostic scepticism. It appeared from discussions with the teachers of the local elementary school that the problem of maintaining neutrality in religious matters was far from being in the forefront of their minds. They seemed quite genuinely unable to think of any occasion on which it had caused them embarrassment. When asked what they told the children about, for instance, the Spring Equinox Holiday—popularly known as the Buddhist *Higan* festival—they said that they simply talked about the sun and the length of night and day. Sometimes they discussed and compared the different sorts of celebrations in the children's various families— but quite objectively, with Christian children explaining what their families did too. Religious controversy and doctrinal differences have

339

so little power to arouse enthusiasm in Japan, that it is not difficult to accept the picture of children from Christian and Buddhist families being encouraged to describe to each other their families' different ritual activities with no more reserve or deep feeling than if they were describing the disposition of the furniture in their houses or what they have for breakfast.

BUDDHISM

It would be impertinent, if it were not impossible, to attempt to summarize here in a few pages the metaphysical and ethical developments of Buddhism in the course of its fourteen centuries of history in Japan. These doctrines are in any case fully described elsewhere.

It must be remembered, however, that the bulk of the doctrines which appear in histories of Japanese Buddhism were evolved by priests and monks, and recorded for the benefit of other priests and monks. It was only in a simplified form that they ever reached the mass of the people. This might be said of any mass religion, but it is more especially true of Japan, where preaching seems never to have played a very great part in the practice of the Buddhist sects.

Until the twelfth century, preaching was not part of the regular practice of any sect, although there were occasional revivalistic campaigners. There were also two families of specialist 'preachers', but these seem not to have been ordinary priests—for one thing they openly married—and they seem to have aimed more at oratorical brilliance than at successful doctrinal guidance. It was not until the twelfth century and the rise of the Joodo sect that preaching became at all important. The Joodo, Shin, Zen and Nichiren sects all owed their growth to the activities of proselytizing preachers. 'Preaching to the converted', however—sermons as a regular institution in established religious communities—persisted only in the Joodo and Shin sects and even in them declined in importance. The typical sermons of the Tokugawa period were not Buddhist. The *kooshaku*, which had a great vogue under Shogunal patronage at the end of the seventeenth century, were moralizing sermons on a Confucian text by Confucian scholars, and the *doowa*, which had a wide popular appeal in the next two centuries, were the sermons of the syncretist Shingakusha. It may be that the mystical nature of much of Buddhist doctrine militated against any attempt to explain it to the masses.

Since the beginning of the Meiji period, however, the competition of Christianity has had some effect. Buddhist Sunday schools have been started and new-style Buddhist hymns written. To a limited extent more importance has been placed also on sermons, at least in the Shin and Nichiren sects, the two which have attempted to put up some resistance and even make advances against the encrouching power of other religious, of scepticism and of apathy.

Generally these sermons are given at special festivals and anniversaries, rarely more than two or three times a year. In those villages with a Shin temple which really commands the loyalty of the villagers, the main festival of the sect, the two or three days of the *Hoo-on-koo*, is a village holiday, and the hour-and-a-half sermons are attended by practically the whole of the village. In Tokyo, audiences at such ceremonies are smaller and mostly composed of older people. A new type of doctrinal guidance which is probably more important than festival sermons in the towns is the 'lecture meeting' type of sermon. In the more active sects 'lecture courses' are held extending over two or three days, generally in the evenings. The speakers are often supplied by a centrally directed proselytizing organization of the sect, priests who may have no temple of their own but circulate among the temples of a given region organizing and lecturing at such courses.

One session of such a lecture course at a Nichiren temple not far from Shitayama-cho, was divided into two parts. The first was a scholarly disquisition, by a white-haired priest who breathed gentleness and gentility, on the distinctions between some of the terms used in Nichiren metaphysics. The blank expressions on the faces of his audience suggested that his sermon meant as little to them as it did to the writer, and unfortunately the soft gentleness of the priest's voice and his frequent turning to the blackboard to write difficult words defeated the tape recorder so that further analysis is impossible. The second priest had a wholly different style. There was something about his appearance—a slight shabbiness, two days' beard and a mixture of bad and gold teeth—which marked him as a man of the people. His method was essentially the same—the explanation of special Nichiren terms—but the terms he selected were ethical in character and he used the occasion for a series of little homilies delivered in a style which derives directly from that of the *koodanshi*— the reciters of dramatic monologues in the old Edo music-halls. Unfortunately it is impossible to reproduce in translation the sense of exaggerated dramatization and humourous old-worldly wisdom which this style of delivery automatically suggests, but one or two extracts may be worth while as an indication of the content. Unlike his predecessor he held the attention and frequently aroused the laughter of his audience.

The next word is *fuse-shoo*—to attract by charity. This character, *shoo*, as you may know, means to attract. Doubtless there are many of you here tonight who keep a business. Business! In order to do business it is first of all necessary to make your shop look nice; to have a pleasant manner and to sell cheap, so that even the man who stands outside to poke fun will be lured into making a purchase. I don't know if any of you see any of these books on the 'Retail Trade Today' or 'The Something-or-other of Business',—I see them occasionally—but you will find all this explained there. Most important, more important than the manager or the boss, the thing that makes the biggest impression is cheap service to the customer. For the merchant that is the most important thing of all. That is to say, charity, being kind; to give an example; here they are in the shop, busy with their work. Up you go to ask the way—at Bon I often have to ask the way and, you know, there are some people who are kind and there are some who aren't. They're busy in the shop, they're all rushed off their feet, 'What is it, priest? Can't you see we're busy? Move out of the way there.' —That's what you get. (Laughter) On the other hand there are some, busy as they are, who will say, 'Ah, yes, now you see the tobacconist's on that corner, well you turn right there and Minagawa's is the second house on the left.' Some will even call their errand boy. 'Hey, nipper, go and show the Father, here, where Minagawa's house is.' I often find this. And when you are treated as kindly as that you begin to want to buy something. This is a sort of *fuse-shoo*. When the customers come in front of your shop the 'the money's yours, the goods are mine' sort of attitude doesn't lead to prosperity in business, does it? There are a lot of headaches in business today. They come down on you for taxes, so that you sometimes wonder how anybody ever does any business. And competition is extremely keen. You can see that in the neon signs. 'If neon signs means prosperity in business, then the electrician will never know a slump'—Don't you think? (Laughter) It's one of the signs of an approaching slump to see so many neon signs about. It means that competition is getting fierce.

Fuse-shoo, then, the spirit of the merchant, kindness, a pleasant manner, by these means you attract. To make yours an attractive shop—this is by the way while we are on the subject of *fuse*—is the secret of 'prosperity in business'. However, I could go on talking about the secret of prosperity in business for another two hours. Arrangements could perhaps be made if there is a special demand. . . . (Laughter)

This concluded the discussion of *fuse-shoo*. He then went on to *shin-fuse*—charity by physical service.

Another example. There are people today who say all sorts of things about the Emperor system. Nevertheless, people from the countryside, simple honest people from the country, have vied with each other—I hear that the list is full for the rest of this year and up to next March—to do 'service'—cleaning up and weeding in front of the Imperial Palace. . . .

Then there is *zai-fuse* (charity by means of wealth). The Swedish scientist, who founded the Nobel prize and died at the age of 63 about fifty years ago—the 10th of December is his death-anniversary (*meinichi*)—this Mr. Nobel before his death at the age of 63, invented dynamite, built explosive factories in every country, and by making these products he amassed a, well, a *vast* fortune. This Mr. Nobel—the Nobel prize is a man's name, you see—this man Nobel invented dynamite in order to contribute to industry and mining. He wanted, for the sake of human happiness, as one might say, to build canals and to extract the hidden resources under the earth.

But before long it was used in weapons of war. Whereupon he was very distressed—if you look at this Mr. Nobel's biography you will see that he was a man full of compassion and kindness; he had a very beautiful side to his character as you will see from the fact that on his mother's death-anniversary he invariably did his filial duty by visiting her (grave). Since he was that sort of person he was upset by this. 'I invented dynamite for the happiness of man and society. Nevertheless, it is used in weapons of war to take the lives of many human beings. I cannot forgive myself.' That was the way he felt. And he gave his vast wealth, his house and property and everything, to found the fund for the Nobel prize. If you reckon in our money how much it all amounted to—this is as money was fifty years ago—171,360,000 *yen*. I don't know how much that would be today, but it is something enormous. This is divided into five equal parts; technology, culture, medicine and physics, and given as prizes to famous men throughout the world. Moreover, from our country, Japan, on the 10th of December the year before last, Mr. Yukawa received an award. And this 10th of December is the day Mr. Nobel died, his death anniversary; I want especially to draw your attention to that. This sort of thing, and, for example, Rockefeller in America, these are all included in *zai-fuse*.

There was much more in the same vein; stories of the great, anecdotes of famous merchants of the Tokugawa period, worldly advice on topics like 'prosperity in business' and 'harmony in the home', topical references to such things as the recent and widely deplored increase in the price of entry to public bath-houses, all mixed in with the occasional moral injunction, on humility towards instruction, on smoking in non-smoking compartments of trains, on being kind to others and on post-war moral irresponsibility. (Man is charged with murder of four women. Maintains 'right to keep silence' as prescribed in new criminal code through three days of police questioning. Exasperated policeman taps him on the chest. Criminal sues policeman for 'infringement of human rights'. 'Not only does the man kill four women, not only does he not have the decency to admit it, but when a justifiably exasperated policeman taps him on the chest he sues for the infringement of human rights! *His* human rights! What about the human rights of his victims? If this is democracy it is time it was altered.')

The values which are upheld are those of the patriotic, public-spirited old-school merchant. Worldly endeavour for worldly gain is approved of. Great success and enormous wealth, if only pipe dreams, are acceptable ideals. But such endeavour should be tempered by a sense of obligation to maintain close personal relations with all with whom one has personal dealings. At the same time one should show a proper respect for social conventions, for the convenience of *hitosama*—'other people', the people one meets in buses and trains. Charity is also desirable, though this is generally towards the people with whom you have close personal relations than towards *hitosama.* Loyalty to a superior, particularly the Emperor, and gratitude for favours received, are praiseworthy qualities. Humility towards the teachings of one's elders and superiors is equally desirable. Everyone should know his station and accept his duties, the kind of selfishness which breaks social conventions and which is particularly prevalent in the post-war world is deplorable.

To say that most sermons to be heard in Japanese temples today are like this would be for me to generalize from this and two other instances and ignore the quiet metaphysican who preceded this last preacher and a high dignitary of the Shin sect whose sermon in a small town in central Japan consisted mostly of stories of the life of Shinran, the sect's founder, somewhat less 'earthy' than the example quoted and containing some references to the Shin doctrine of salvation. One can say, however, that these quotations are at least not untypical.

It is both a cause and an effect of this that the social status of the Buddhist priest carries very little prestige in urban Japan.[276] This has indeed been the case since the Tokugawa period; the quotation made above from a music-hall monologue of the period (p. 315) gave some indication of the contemporary stereotype of the worldly priest. In some sects hereditary succession to temples has contributed to the decline in the quality of the priesthood, and despite the creation of Buddhist universities, many priests have little or no higher education. In some villages dominated by a Shin temple the priest may have considerable prestige, and in the traditional Buddhist centres, Kyooto, Nara, Kamakura, Kooya-san, and even in remote and unlikely village temples, one can sometimes meet priests who, if of no great intellectual qualities, nevertheless possess, in a dignified simplicity of living, a sensitive aesthetic refinement and a contemplative and gentle tolerance, qualities which earn them wide respect. But such men are rare in Tokyo temples. When a hundred parents in Shitayama-cho were asked what they wished their son to be when he grew up, not one suggested the priesthood. At a funeral service in Shitayama-cho the priest was treated with no more formality than the ragged toughs who came in as undertaker's men to remove the coffin. I can recall only one conversation in which a Buddhist priest was praised in Shitayama-cho—the greengrocer's story of a conscientious local priest who was deeply troubled when called up for the army, by the conflict between his patriotic duty and the Buddhist prohibition of slaughter. His resolution of the problem was to go into battle with an *o-kesa* praying robe over his uniform. Every time he fired his rifle at the enemy he threw a *fuda* in the direction of the enemy's lines saying a short prayer as he did so for the soul he hoped he had just despatched to eternity.

The typical priest is not the sort of man to whom people in trouble are likely to go for spiritual guidance. Nor are their sermons likely to attract many hearers or hold their attention. Of a hundred people in Shitayama-cho nearly a half said that they had never heard a sermon in their lives Apart from two Christians, only seven had heard one in the preceding year. It will be seen from this that doctrinal instruction plays only a very small part in present-day Buddhist practice. The Buddhist Sunday Schools do something on these lines, but they are rare and I heard of no Shitayama child going to a Sunday School.

This general lack of contact with Buddhist teachings among people who, it has been shown, are mostly regular participants in the family rites for the ancestors and also, to a somewhat lesser extent in various productive and protective cults centring on Buddhist temples, reinforces the argument that these rites have not very much to do with the Buddhist faith, with, that is to say, the body of doctrine which the Buddhist sects are ostensibly organized to promote.

Some temples also organize prayer meetings and memorial meetings unconnected with the family rites. At the Gokokuin, which was mentioned previously as the centre of a Daikokuten cult, the priest held a memorial meeting on the 15th of every month (the war ended on the 15th of August) for all those who died during the war (irrespective, he said, of race, creed or allegiance, friend and foe alike). In this he was consciously carrying on an earlier tradition, for it is recorded that in 1639 on the occasion of the twenty-fifth anniversary of the fall of Oosaka castle, the Shogun Iemitsu visited the temple for a memorial service held for the souls of all who had died in the battle. At these ceremonies the priest reads prayers and sutras, beating gongs and wooden blocks to punctuate his reading. If more than ten people comes he brings out a gigantic set of prayer-beads which all the participants tell together, sitting round in a circle. Rarely are there as many as ten present, however, and those who do come are mostly war widows. Another temple, the Nichigen Soshi-doo, the shrines in the forecourt of which were previously described, held regular 'Prayers for World Peace' and these were becoming popular in temples in 1951 when rearmament and the opposition to rearmament was a political issue.

Priest-led movements have, in fact, become active in the anti-rearmament campaign. There are several reasons for this; the traditional Buddhist prohibition of killing, the fact that the Buddhist priesthood, unlike its Christian counterpart in this country, has closer links with the mass of the people than with the 'ruling'—the upper and middle—classes, the fact perhaps, that the priests feel that they are losing their religious *raison d'être* and feel the need to assert themselves in another sphere, and also the fact that their most devout followers are women and among women those who have suffered most distress and anxiety as a result of the last war. The following quotation from the leading article of the *Yomiuri* (11 August 1951) a national daily newspaper, gives some indication of the trend. It also gives a further illustration of the social status of the priest and of the general disinclination to see any importance in institutionalized Buddhism in Japan today.

Noticeable lately have been 'peace speeches' by Buddhists of a distinctly political complexion. In post-war Japan, Japanese Buddhists (in particular professional priests) who formerly bore the heaviest responsibility in the religious sphere, have played almost no useful role, and nothing has emerged from the religious world of a socially practical nature. It is a fine thing for Buddhists to show enthusiasm for peace, but one would think there were other duties awaiting them than making swim-with-the-tide speeches. Should they not first concentrate on improving themselves and on carrying out practical social work, before they begin to stir up the masses. Peace cannot be saved by sentimental speeches.

This would appear to be not quite fair; some of the Buddhist sects, again perhaps from an awareness that their purely religious *raison d'être* is wearing rather thin, and certainly partly as a result of the example of the Christians, have undertaken a great deal of social work. In maintaining schools they lag well behind the Christian sects, despite the fact that the total declared membership of all the Buddhist sects is almost a hundred times that of all the Christian sects. In other activities which require goodwill rather than intellect or skill —crèches, hostels, orphanages, homes for unmarried mothers, convalescent homes and so on—they are well ahead of the Christian churches, at least in so far as the number of such institutions is concerned.

Another notable feature of post-war Japanese Buddhism and an indication of great organizational instability, is the growing frequency of sectarian divisions. In 1936, there were fifty-six separate registered sects. In 1939 these were more or less forcibly amalgamated by government directive into twenty-eight more easily controlled units. At the end of the war a change in the law made registration as a separate sect easy, provided certain simple conditions were fulfilled. As a result, by the end of 1949, there were 156 registered sects. Of these ninety-one were breakaway movements from existing sects, and thirteen entirely new sects which claimed to be generally Buddhist in doctrine. In addition there were about 200 temples which had broken away from their sect and established themselves as independent religious bodies.[277] Some of the reasons for this great increase in the number of sects are as follows:

1. Many of the divisions had in fact existed long beforehand. The amalgamations of 1939, for instance, immediately fell apart in 1945. Other new sects claim to have existed as separate entities within

the larger sects for many centuries. Typical of these is the Nyorai sect, a branch of Soodoo (Zen) Buddhism which now controls seventy-four temples. In its reply to a Ministry of Education questionnaire, it has this to say: 'The Nyorai sect is a branch of Buddhism which was founded in 1717 by Kino, the third daughter of a farmer Chooshiroo. The priests of the founding temple have continued her traditions to the present day and it is now a flourishing faith.' [278] This statement is typical of many of these questionnaire answers, in that it mentions the founder of the sect but gives no indication of the doctrinal differences which distinguish the sect from others. It might not be going too far to say that it is generally true of Japanese Buddhism that the general conception of the tie uniting the members of a given sect is less the fact that they share certain doctrinal views in common as that they share the characteristic of being all the followers of a certain sect founder. In the most flourishing of modern sects, the Joodo, Shin and Nichiren, the legends of the founders play an important symbolic role and are perhaps the most frequent topics of sermons. If one asked a Japanese the difference between the Shin and the Joodo sects, the most probable answer would be that the one was founded by Shinran and the other by Hoonen.

2. In an impoverished post-war world the prospect of freedom from the obligation to contribute to central sect funds has been a strong inducement to priests to seek independence. In addition to the large number of single-temple religious bodies, it is significant that fifty-five of the new full-scale sects boast less than five temples.

3. Some sects are of the magical/faith-healing/dancing variety which have flourished since the war. The financial advantages of being the head of such a sect are widely advertised; a possible incentive to the achievement of independence by any priest who is neither overscrupulous nor attached to his own particular sect.

SHINTO

We have hitherto considered the Shinto shrines as places associated with rites of symbolic significance for the local and national communities, and as the centres of protective and productive cults. We have made no mention hitherto of Shinto doctrine as it has been described in several European works.[279] This Shinto doctrine, first developed by scholars of the Tokugawa period, was later elaborated not only by their modern equivalents in universities, but also by generals and politicians and publicists of all sorts who had an interest in making it the metaphysical foundation of a Japanese state destined to conquer the world. In its final stage of development, by the political rather than by the academic writers, the emphasis was shifted from the teachings of 'sincerity' and 'purity' as the norms of personal relations to the political requirements of loyalty, patriotism, harmony and the martial spirit.

Perhaps the most comprehensive and most authoritative statement of the doctrine in this, its final form, is to be found in the *Kokutai no Hongi* (The Cardinal Principles of the National Entity)[280] a book which was widely distributed with government backing and was required reading in every teachers' training course in the late thirties. Like all forms of Shinto doctrine, it laid emphasis on the cosmological myths, the legends of the Imperial Ancestors and of the 'saints' of Shinto, the loyal servants of past Emperors. It laid great emphasis, too, on the sanctity of the national shrines, the importance of ritual as the foundation of the national morality and the definition of that morality in terms chiefly of the (Confucian-derived) virtues of loyalty and filial piety. It also attempted to give an interpretation of legal, economic, political and military institutions in Shinto terms.[281]

This was, however, essentially a political religion. It is an example of the type of symbolic belief which can prove an effective means of ideological integration, particularly in a period of war or approaching war when the external circumstances help to foster a sense of national solidarity. But as a personal religion it has obvious defects. It may provide sense and 'meaning' for death on the battlefield in the name of the Emperor, but it can give no 'meaning' to death under a tramcar and can provide no consolation for the bereaved. Its only way of dealing with the problems of suffering is to let in by the back door the beliefs in harmful and malignant spirits which the academic writers on Shinto had been trying to play down as superstitions.

Moreover, the diffusion of these doctrines was limited. Shinto priests were forbidden to teach or preach, at the same time as they were forbidden to perform funeral ceremonies, in 1882. In any case, there was no place in the traditional shrine ritual for sessions of public preaching. Apart from the armed forces, the chief medium for the diffusion of these ideas was the schools, and here it was taught only indirectly. Teachers who had read and understood the *Kokutai no Hongi* (the abundance of commentaries suggests that this was by no means easy) might well have implanted some of these ideas in the minds of their pupils. The occasions and excuses for so doing were not lacking; for example, the ethics course teachings concerning the Emperor, the ceremonial reading of Imperial Rescripts and bowing to the Imperial Portrait, school visits to shrines and so on. But the teaching of Shinto doctrine as an integrated whole played little part in the school ethics course readers, except possibly in the wartime *Shimmin no Michi* (The Way of the Subject). Even if most of these ideas were imparted in the course of school education it was not as an integrated body of belief, nor was it firmly attached to the rituals and symbols associated with the Shinto shrines.

The failure of the national aspirations which these doctrines had attempted to legitimize would probably have led to their discredit and disappearance even had there not been an Occupation to take positively prohibitive action. The shrines were disestablished, cut off from State aid and forbidden to utilize organs of local government for the collection of funds. The Emperor made a broadcast renouncing the divinity which had been imputed to him. To replace the Bureau of Shrines of the Home Ministry, a new, non-official, Central Bureau of Shrines (*Jinja Honchoo*) was established. By the end of 1949 86,000 shrines had accepted its jurisdiction,[282] 500 belonged to one of fourteen other large-scale organizations embracing more than one shrine, and about 1,200 had set themselves up as entirely independent bodies. It is estimated that about 20,000 shrines have simply fallen into disuse, at least no steps had then been taken to secure for them the financial advantages of incorporation as religious bodies. The reasons why independence is often preferred are, according to the Ministry of Education's report, similar to those of Buddhist breakaway movements; personal differences and avoidance of the obligation to contribute to central funds.[283]

The Central Bureau of Shrines has the allegiance of some of the main national shrines—though not the Yasukuni, which is independent—publishes a weekly newspaper (for priests), issues prayer books, sells ritual implements and makes detailed regulations concerning the conduct of shrines and the performance of rites in much the same manner as the old Home Ministry Bureau used to do. It also subsidizes the old Shinto university, the *Kokugakuin-Daigaku*, which has been and presumably continues to be the centre for the academic elaboration of Shinto doctrine and for the training of Shinto priests.

But the influence of these priests on the mass of the people is negligible; they are no higher in social prestige than the Buddhist priests and it has never been part of the role of the Shinto priest, except for a few years in the eighteen-seventies, to act as spiritual advisor or moral instructor. The enforcement of Shinto rituals and the teaching of so-called Shinto ethics in text-books has ceased to be a feature of the schools. Eight months after the end of the Occupation booksellers' lists continue to fill their philosophy sections with translations of Jaspers, Heidegger, Kierkegaard, Buber and other Western metaphysicians, but there is rarely a work on Shinto.[284]

The only opportunity which presented itself in a year's residence in Shitayama-cho to hear anything which could be called 'Shinto teaching' was at the festival of an Inari shrine close to Shitayama-cho. As part of the celebrations there was a lecture on 'The Inari Faith' by a professor from the Kokugakuin-Daigaku. The most striking feature of the talk was its apparently sceptical objectiveness. He gave an account of the origin of Inari worship which, however accurate it might have been, was certainly positivistic in attitude and impressive in its handling of etymological evidence and its application of the classical anthropological theory of cultural survivals. His talk was spattered with the words, 'People believed that . . .' 'It is said that . . .', or, 'The fox is supposed to be . . .' The impression of objectivity was reinforced by his reference to parallels in Ancient Egyptian and Hindu mythology, also, perhaps, by the fact that he rejected all the half-dozen or so Japanese equivalents in favour of the English word 'spirit' (*supiritto*), and by his little joke about the shrine in Asakusa which claimed superlative protective powers for its amulets, but had lost most of its devotees when battalions of local lads had been annihilated in the war.—'You have to be very chary how you go about these things, you know,' was his advice to the priest, given and received with uninhibited laughter.

On the other hand, there was a hint of real belief in his remark that the principle of the 'unification of government and ritual' was only practised in the Nara period, when Emperors did actually govern according to the dictates of the *kami* as relayed through priestesses, and the fact that this principle was perverted from its original purity in the Meiji period accounts, said he, for the defeat. However, this was only a remark dropped in passing which he hadn't 'time to go into here'. The only positive statement of any belief was contained in the last two sentences in which he said that the object of worshipping at an Inari shrine was to purify one's heart so that one could face the daily task in a true spirit of piety.

Even a lecture such as this is rare at shrine festivals. There were about twenty people present at this one, mostly old men and middle-aged or old women.

It will be seen that Shinto—what remains today of the old State Shinto—has practically nothing to offer to the average Japanese as an explanation of the meaning and purpose of human life, human suffering and human death.

SHINTO SECTS

In addition to State Shinto, the associated doctrines of which we have just been considering, there also existed before the war thirteen registered religious sects, each having shrines or churches of their own, a separate priesthood and distinctive ritual practices and doctrines. Since the essentials of their doctrines and practices were mostly derived from the Shinto tradition they are called 'Shinto sects' and sometimes the doctrine and practices of all the sects collectively are lumped together in the not very meaningful term 'Sect Shinto' (*kyooha-shintoo*).

Most of these sects were in origin rump movements of the nineteenth-century Shinto revival, founded by groups of people who were dissatisfied with the emasculated type of 'civic Shinto' which, rather than the comprehensive and exclusive Shinto religion which at first found official favour, it later became the Meiji Government's policy to promote.

Holtom, in his description of these sects, describes them under five headings each of which singles out one of their dominant characteristics.[285] These are 'Pure Shinto', three sects which claim to continue the ancient doctrines in their purest form, sects whose doctrines are similar to those of State Shinto and which have no personal founders; the 'Confucian Sects', two which not merely take most of their ethical doctrines from Confucianism but frankly acknowledge the fact; the 'Mountain Sects', two based on Mount Fuji and one on Mount On-take, elaborations of the type of mountain cult mentioned in the previous chapter; the 'Purification Sects', two sects which lay a great emphasis on rituals aimed to remove impurities which are considered to be the source both of sickness and moral evil; and, the most important perhaps, the 'Faith Healing Sects', the Kurozumi, Konkoo and Tenri sects which Holtom collectively designates as having 'a tendency towards extreme emotionalism, a basis in revelationalism, monotheistic and pantheistic trends in doctrine and a centre in faith-healing '.[286]

These labels refer, of course, only to the emphases in the doctrines of these sects. Perhaps the last group has moved further from the Shinto tradition than the others. In addition to the characteristics already mentioned, they share among other features the deification of the founder (who in every case lived in the first part of the nineteenth century), the importance given to legends of the founder's life and the scriptural sanctification of the founder's writings, the tendency away from an ethnocentric to a universalistic standpoint, and the doctrine of a unifying spirit in the universe of whom the various *kami* are manifestations. But in Japanese society, where '*kami*' normally carries the connotations which have been illustrated on previous pages, it would be difficult indeed for any sect to maintain in its original purity any doctrine as sophisticated as the last.[287] In fact, even these most developed sects share many of the common features of the others—the acceptance of the traditional Shinto pantheon (with each sect selecting a particular *kami* or group of *kami* as the focus of its attention), the emphasis on the correct performance of ritual as a means of purification, at once of bodily and spiritual ills, the repetition of magical formulæ, the high value placed on trance-like 'possession', their strong patriotism and the interpretation of the (pre-war) political system as decreed and sanctified by divine will, the importance placed on the Emperor (in some sects he is worshipped as a *kami*), the incorporation of Confucian moral principles and terms, the 'Shintoification' of ancestor rites, and generally, too, the cultivation of some of the traditional Japanese aesthetic pursuits such as the tea ceremony, the *noo* drama, flower arrangement and even *sumoo* wrestling.

These doctrines are 'taught'. The meeting places of these sects are called, not 'shrines', but *kyookai*, the word used also to translate 'church' and written with two characters which suggest the meaning 'teaching-meeting'. They also have large numbers of 'teachers'. According to the 1949 returns by the various sects, there is a ratio for the thirteen sects of 110 members per teacher.

Before the war these sects showed a gradual increase in membership. According to the official figures of the Ministry of Education, the sixteen and a quarter millions of 1933 had grown to seventeen and a quarter millions by 1937. In 1949 the total membership claims of these sects amounted to only nine and a half millions. One factor in this decline is the increase in sectarian schism. No less than 120 splinter sects were registered between 1946 and 1949, all acknowledged breakaway movements from one of these thirteen existing sects. The reasons for this proliferation of sects seem to be similar to those previously given concerning the new Buddhist splinter sects, but it is noticeable that two of the mountain sects, the Fusoo and the Mitake have been the most prone to division, producing an additional ninety-six splinter sects between them. These sects appear to have disintegrated into a number of pilgrimage-making *koo* each concentrated in one geographical area. More of these breakaway sects have been registered since, but at the end of 1952 the total claimed membership of the original thirteen and their splinter sects amounted to less than 15 million,[288] a 15% decline compared with 1937, since when there has been an increase in population of more than 20%.

OTHER NEW SECTS

In addition to the many sects which have been founded as breakaway movements from existing sects, there are a number of new sects, the parentage of which, according to the Ministry of Education's *Year Book of Religion*, cannot be assigned to any existing sect. Eighty-five such sects had been registered up to the end of 1949 with a total claimed membership of nearly three million.

Not all of these sects are entirely new post-war creations. At least a quarter of them claim to have been in existence as some form of association for some time previously. Six of these sects were first registered during the war, after a law of 1940 made this possible for sects which were close enough to Shinto in character and to the military faction in ideology.

But the licensing authorities, the Home Ministry and the Ministry of Education of that time, were careful to withhold registration from and even forcibly to suppress any new sect of a spiritualistic or orgiastic character, any sect which worshipped a deity not in the Shinto pantheon, or any sect which attempted in its doctrines to use the basic Shinto deities for purposes of which the militarists did not approve. It is precisely these which are among the common characteristics of the sects which have arisen since the war. Several, in fact, claim to be the direct descendants of sects which were actively suppressed by the police before the war, and some of their leaders have served prison sentences for their activities.

The following description of the general characteristics of these sects is based on their replies, of varying length and detail, to a questionnaire concerning the sect's origin and principles issued by the Ministry of Education. These replies are printed in the Ministry's *Year Book*. It should be remembered that these descriptions give only the declared aims, beliefs and practices of the sects; the reality may be otherwise. Nevertheless they do give some useful indications.

Some of the sects are little more than large-scale *koo*, of the type considered earlier, for the worship of, or pilgrimage to the shrine of, some particular already established deity. Such, for instance, is the *Kenkoo Senju Kannon-koo* (The *koo* for the Thousand-armed Kannon of Health) whose founder 'was born as a result of prayer by his parents to the Thousand-armed Kannon of Health and as a result has always been her ardent worshipper. Having now reached the age of 45, the average expectation of life for Japanese males, he considers this as entirely due to the favour of Kannon, and has established a separate sect' [289] for her worship.

Other sect founders claim to have arrived at their beliefs by the purely cognitive processes of theology and metaphysics. Japan's position as a melting-pot of ideologies is well brought out in the life histories of many of the founders. There is, for instance, the founder of the *On-naka-Kyoodan*, who

... graduated from the Law Faculty of Waseda University in 1928 and entered the office of the *Osaka Evening News*. During this period he was an untiring student of all religions, Shinto, Buddhism, Christianity and Mohammedism, but was most impressed by the Buddhist work the *Mujoo Muga Engi* (The Origin of Ephemerality and Self-Extinction) and became convinced that the true principles of economic guidance were to be found in Buddhism. It was then that he established the Buddhist Economics Study Group in Koobe. Later he had occasion to study Nestorian Christianity and was much struck by its doctrine of the Trinity. He then became convinced that religion is not a dualistic entity divorced from actual life, and that the only possible way of life lay in fusing oneself with the highest reality in the universe, God (Power). It is by making oneself one with infinite power that it is possible to live a complete, harmonious and happy life. Recently connections have been established with the 119th Pope in Chicago and the sect has become the founding branch of the Nestorian Church in Japan. It is hoped that by the spread of Nestorianism it will contribute to the fostering of American-Japanese relations.[290]

This type of sect rarely has a large number of adherents.

Some of these sects are earnest and respectable, with a slight mystical tinge of a type familiar in the West. Such, for instance, is the *Fukkoo Kyoodan* (The Light of Happiness) which holds to the principles:

1. To believe in a God, the creator of the universe and all living things, who is absolute and eternal and indestructible, and the guiding principle of the human spirit. To reject all false beliefs in superstition, spiritualism and prophecy.
2. To inflict no harm physical or spiritual, on oneself or on others; to reject revenge and to love one's neighbour.
3. Not to desire the possession of others.
4. To eschew lewdness.
5. To avoid falsehood.
6. To reflect constantly on thought, word and deed, that they may always accord with the dictates of conscience.

As methods of carrying out these principles,

A. To take deep breaths every morning, and thus compose the body and the spirit.
B. By contemplation to strive to realize the state of *sammai* (samadhi, trance), and to practise a transcendentally religious life.[291]

Yet others, mostly of Shinto tendencies, seem to be merely the prewar right-wing political secret societies forced with the collapse of their temporal ambitions, to seek fulfilment on a more spiritual plane. The present leader of a Shinto sect with sixty-three thousand adherents, the *Sumera-kyoo*, is the former would-be assassin of the politician Ookuma Shigenobu, a fact of which he boasts in his description of the sect's origins.[292] These sects frequently mention as a motive for their formation the degradation and collapse of morals in postwar Japan, but it is notable that none of them mentions by name the old virtues of loyalty and filial piety among those they are most anxious to inculcate.[293] Perhaps they feared Occupation displeasure; at any rate, when the Confucian virtues are mentioned it is generally the older and more comprehensive set of Benevolence, Righteousness, Propriety, Wisdom and Trust (*jin-gi-rei-chi-shin*) which are specified. There is a parallel between these sects and some of the earlier Shinto sects founded in the nineteenth century, again by men with an extreme nationalist tinge to Shinto belief. These earlier sect-founders were men who had been ardent workers for the Restoration but were dissatisfied with the way in which—in their case the success of the movement—had failed to lead to the theocratic state they desired.

The models for the majority of these post-war sects, however, are to be found not in these quasi-political groups but in those of the earlier sects such as Tenri and Konkoo which stemmed from the revelations of a divinely inspired founder. Some of these founders —most of them claim to have had their religious experiences long before the war—are 'possessed' and utter words in a trance. Others hear words spoken to them. The content of the message is most commonly simply the name of a *kami*—generally a newly-invented *kami* rather than an already established one—which is supposed to be the underlying principle of the universe. Sometimes these revelations come only after long years of study of such esoteric disciplines as Buddhist economics, sometimes only after ascetic pilgrimages to shrines throughout the length and breadth of the land, sometimes to uneducated peasants working in the fields. Whereas sects of other types are generally founded by men, these revelationist sects are often founded by a woman. These are the sects which generally practise faith-healing and fortune-telling. Twenty made specific claims concerning the former in their questionnaire answers and eleven concerning the latter. One imagines that many more have discreetly omitted such references. To this type belongs the more orgiastic sects which have attracted most popular attention in post-war Japan; sects at whose meetings audiences are whipped into a frenzy of emotion, not by doctrines of hell fire or eternal bliss, but by the use of stage effects and by the fanatical magnetism of their leaders, and in some cases by rhythmic and ultimately trance-inducing dancing. With this generally goes the practice of personal witness in the Buchmanite manner, with the emphasis less on consciousness of sin than on the attestation of miracles which demonstrate the goodness and power of the *kami*.

So regular appear to be these main characteristics that we may be justified in believing that the theological and ethical teachings of these sects are of only peripheral importance. At least twenty-three of them proclaim some sort of monotheistic doctrine. Sometimes it is a Bergsonian life force which is worshipped, sometimes a Creator God, sometimes a *kami* whose name, although it has the usual Shinto titular trappings, means something like Great Originator. In five cases this fundamental principle is supposed to be embodied in, or to reside in, the sun, in one case in the Pole Star. Sometimes the *kami* of Shinto, the Buddhas and Christ are all accepted as equal incarnations of this underlying principle. If one can accurately speak of syncretism in sects for which theological and ethical doctrine is not important but only the belief in their peculiar possession of the one cabalistic key to the ultimate, then they are syncretic. Many claim to have 'taken the best from' all the world religions. One sect has in its main hall images of Zoroaster, Confucius, Socrates, Christ, Mahomet, Gautama and (the Shinto) Ninigi-no-mikoto.[294] Of sects which maintain polytheistic traditions, perhaps the strangest is the 'Holy Garden of All Souls' (*Banrei Saien*) which numbers among its objects of worship, Rutherford Alcock, the first British ambassador to Japan, Townsend Harris, the first American ambassador, and Hendrik Heuskens, the latter's secretary.[295] Perhaps it was hoped that they, with their longer association with Japan, might intervene to mitigate the wrath of the occupying powers.

There is repeated emphasis on worship of ancestors and also on the dangers of impurity and the necessity of purification rites. These, as we have seen, are traditional elements of Japanese religious thought; and the way in which one of these sects, the Reiyuukai, is built entirely around ancestor worship was discussed on p. 319. Few sects mention a life after death, but far more promise happiness in this life, relief from illness and from suffering, both spiritual and physical. A recent Japanese writer on these sects considers this as the fundamental common characteristic of them all. He divides them into three types; those which are blatant and naïve about their promises of this-worldly gain and proclaim it as the object of religious 'faith' which is identified with the productive cult as such, those which proclaim these benefits to be not the object but the incidental results which the happiness of true faith brings, and those which teach that these worldly benefits are merely heuristic devices whereby the eyes of the believer are opened to the truth.[296]

More than half of these sects give no hint of any ethical teachings. Those which do are often traditionally Confucian in tendency, though, as was noted before, the formerly most emphasized and now discredited virtues of loyalty and filial piety are omitted. The most common ethical word is *hoo-on*—grateful awareness of favours received. 'Charity' occurs occasionally, so does 'universal love'. It is remarkable, too, that sixteen of these sects claim directly to 'promote world peace', a significant indication of the circumstances, the sufferings and the aspirations which surround their origins. With 'world peace' is often linked the phrase 'to contribute to the welfare of human society', a phrase which in post-war Japan generally carries the authentic hollow ring of hypocrisy.

Another characteristic which some of these sects share with such Western groups as the Buchmanites is an emphasis on a hearty jollity as the spiritual cure for all physical ills and the one cement which can bind humanity together in the bright and cheerful atmosphere of 'one big happy family'. With this bright jollity, in half a dozen cases, goes the claim to have incorporated the teachings of modern science.

One example of this type is the P.L. Sect (*P.L. Kyoodan*) with nearly a quarter of a million adherents. P.L. stands for 'Perfect Liberty' the name given to the sect by its leader after his release in 1945 from a jail sentence for his religious activities.[297] One issue of the sect's magazine, 'The Artistic Life', (*Geijutsu-seikatsu*), gives an outline of the sect's doctrines and activities.

It is one advantage of the Japanese language that it is easy to make up *ad hoc*, from two characters already known in other contexts, new and plausible-sounding words which, though they never convey a precise meaning, still have vaguely meaningful connotations and carry an aura of esoteric originality. The key-terms of P.L. theory are such creations. 'Self-phenomena' (*gashoo*—'self' having here all the Buddhist connotations as in such words as 'not-self') means nothing more nor less than suffering, illness, disasters and unhappiness. These 'self-phenomena' are all the results of 'self-attachments' (*gashuu*), subjective states which arise out of conflict between natural laws and laws imposed by men. The ill and suffering tell their troubles to the P.L. priest who, by a sort of short-cut psychoanalytic technique, points out the particular 'self-attachment' which is the underlying cause and gives specific instructions as to how to avoid it in the future. This removes the 'self-phenomena' symptoms. In the interval the symptoms may be slightly alleviated by prayer, and charms are also issued although their exact relation to the prevention of 'self-phenomena' is not explained. Another term explained in the magazine is the 'Treasure-Growing Pouch' in which members make their regular contributions, in return for which they are assured that the sect leader—the 'Teaching Father'—will intercede with the *kami* on their behalf and ensure that they shall receive the blessings of the *kami* 'on both the material and the spiritual plane'.

The testimony of science is invoked in the correspondence columns. An anonymous lecturer in medicine at an anonymous university describes how his general scepticism concerning religious movements has been overthrown by his recent persuasion of the truth of P.L. claims. He tells the story of Professor S of another anonymous university who has found in the P.L. theories of psychosomatic phenomena the explanation of the fact that *post mortem* dissections frequently do not correspond with the diagnosis of the final mortal illness. Now, after considerable study, Professor S is able by *post mortem* dissection to isolate the particular 'self-attachments' which led to the subject's death. He can say with precision, 'During his life this man did such and such, he was swayed by this or that emotion,' and enquiries into the man's life always prove him to have been right. The writer concludes that the laws governing these phenomena must be empirically ascertainable and he hopes that P.L. will devote some funds to research.

The magazine also shows traces of a bright modernism and sentimentality which suggests that the sect's leaders may well have learnt something from some of the Californian practitioners such as Amy Semple Macpherson. There is a graphic description of the celebration of the 'Teaching Father's' birthday (birthday celebrations themselves are a sign of modernity). The service of dedication was held in a theatre-like building and at the climax of the proceedings, as the band played the hymns of the sect, the curtain went up on the stage to disclose, picked out in silver letters, the words, 'Perfect Liberty' (in English, and therefore also up to date). This was followed by a fancy-dress ball at which each couple dressed to represent a nation. England was represented by a woman as Mr. Chamberlain and a man as Mrs. Simpson. The 'Teaching Father' appeared as Shirley Temple while his lady partner was dressed as Uncle Sam.

These new sects are regarded with considerable suspicion in Japan. Newspaper reports concerning their activities generally reveal the implicit assumption that they are organized by unscrupulous charlatans. According to the common stereotype the sect-leader is a man of magnetic personality who lives in a luxurious palace and is attended by large numbers of devoted female worshippers with whom his relations are, to say the least, ambiguous. And indeed the fact that several such sects have ended their career with the founder's imprisonment for crimes as diverse as fraud, tax evasion, obscenity, rape and contravention of the pharmaceutical regulations[298] provides some justification for these views. How far there is conscious exploitation of gullibility and how far these leaders are the victims of their own charisma it is impossible to say.

It can at least be said that these sects manage to generate in at least a hard core of their followers a degree of 'enthusiasm' which gives them a hold over these worshippers unlike that exercised by any other religious associations in Japan, even the Christian. This explains both their success in enriching their founders out of the contributions of believers and their rapid growth. In some sects it is a condition of 'grace' that the believer should prove his faith by 'works' and the proving 'works' generally consist in securing new members, many of whom are not 'converts' in any real sense, but what might be called '*giri*' members—people who join because they are asked to do so, as a personal favour, by people with whom they are in a *giri*-relation. As was noted earlier on, joining a religious group or a political party as a neighbourly favour, is something well within the scope of what a quite ordinary *giri*-relation may require. Members thus recruited may be induced to go to meetings and eventually brought into the core of enthusiasts.

CHRISTIANITY

The nature of Christian doctrines and beliefs needs no introduction here, although if more material were available an examination of the modifications which Japanese culture has imposed on Christian teachings would prove a fascinating study in itself. The need to find God on Japan's side in wartime has effected the same sort of modifications in Japan as in the case of other national Christian churches, though the transformation of the Trinity into a Quaternity by the inclusion of the Emperor—the solution of some theological extremists —would seem to be a rare type of radical adjustment.

At any rate, it can be said that the modifications of Christian doctrine in the process of transplanting in another culture are much less in the case of Japan than in that of pre-literate or barely literate societies. Proselytism in Japan is carried out on a higher intellectual level than in most parts of the world; converts have more often been educated townspeople who could and did read the translated Bible than peasants who could not.

It is partly for this reason that Christianity has had effects which are out of proportion to the actual numbers of its converts. Many more people than have been actually converted have been directly or indirectly influenced by Christian ideas, for, particularly at the end of the last century and the beginning of this, Christian teachings had a considerable prestige among the educated middle classes. The recognition of the West's technological superiority created the climate of opinion which enabled Japan's leaders implicitly to recognize the superiority of many of the West's legal, political and familial institutions by explicitly studying and copying them. This in its turn created a climate of opinion which predisposed those who were aware of the changes that were taking place, at least to consider with toleration claims for the superiority of the ethical and religious ideas which were generally considered to be the basis for the admired and imitated institutions.

Moreover, Christian missions were active in the development of educational institutions in Japan and it was they who founded some of the earliest private universities. Even today, approximately 9% of the universities, 7% of Specialized High Schools, nearly 4% of Senior High Schools and nearly 1% of Middle Schools are controlled by Christian bodies. One of the most fashionable girls 'finishing schools' for the daughters of the upper class in Tokyo, is run by Catholic nuns.

The indirect influence of Christianity may be sought everywhere. Even in the school ethics text-books from which children were supposedly taught traditional Japanese morality there was a section on 'universal love'. *Hakuai*, the term used, is found in Chinese writings, but it has never fitted into the basically particularistic system of Confucian ethics which has held sway in China and Japan and thus has never figured prominently in Confucian writings. It is unlikely that it would have had a section to itself, but for the influence of Christianity, and certain that it would not have been illustrated by the story of Florence Nightingale.

Christian ideals have seemed to have a greater attraction for women than for men, and here, perhaps, Florence Nightingale is of some importance. Although no distinction was made between the sexes in the public compulsory education system, there was sharp segregation at all levels of higher education. Men were given professional training; the education of women was aimed at the 'realization of the ideal of womanhood'.[299] The only professions open to women were medicine, nursing and school-teaching. It was into these ideals of public service that their aspirations had to be channelled, and for this purpose the best models and the best teachings were those of the Christian tradition. The code of the Confucian *retsujo*—the woman whose aspirations were limited to the fierce and unyielding defence of her husbands honour and interests—was too narrow in outlook.

The resultant 'interest in Christianity', never quite becoming Christian belief, which was common among women who had received higher education, is well caught in the following description of some of the female characters in pre-war novels (written mainly for female audiences) by Kikuchi Kan and Kume Masao:

> None of the characters in these works has any clear religion. But the women are all 'interested in' Christianity. Michiko in *Tsuki yori no Shisha* (Kume) becomes a nurse at the Fujimi Convalescent Home because, she says, 'it is only fitting that we should all bear the suffering of the cross'. Keiko in *San-Katei*, who can no longer bear to live with her unfaithful husband and goes home to her mother, tries to assuage her despair as she waits to bear that husband's child by reading the Bible. Emiko, whose mother is a Christian, sometimes reads the Bible, but in her case it is generally enforced reading as a punishment for coming home late. She reads the Old Testament stories—as literature. But interest in Christianity does not develop into Christian faith. The Christian Madame Isago is said to be 'pompous in everything, prejudiced, lacking in understanding and unable to make allowances; her judgment of sin is swift and cuttingly ruthless'. Christianity is even held to be narrow and oppressive.[300]

The number of Japanese, women or men, who have been attracted into Christian communities wherein such as Madame Isago are in fact only too often to be found, has never been large despite the much wider interest in Christianity as a body of ideas. Membership of Christian sects, has, however, increased somewhat since the war; in 1949 the claimed membership was 371,000, an increase of 17% over the 1935 figure. During the war the activities of Christians were somewhat circumscribed, and administratively, all sects were amalgamated into one. At the end of the war they reverted to denominational independence and again began to receive material help and new missionary personnel from foreign missions. In 1949 30% of Christian teachers and workers were of foreign origin.

It was perhaps natural that the number of Christians should rise at a time when the prestige of things foreign was raised by the defeat and the nation was committed to the duty of internal reform along lines prescribed by foreigners. Even General MacArthur's sonorous pronouncements which spoke of democratization (already accomplished) as but the first stage in the eventual Christianization of Japan may have had an influence on some people. More particularly, missions often disposed of relief goods which were important in the days of semi-starvation immediately after the war. Also, in a society in which a knowledge of English has become increasingly a marketable asset, missions have provided unique opportunities for the aspirant to English conversational practice.

There was only one Christian family in Shitayama-cho, whose househead had been converted when quite young. One other family used to be Christian but, they said, 'changed to Shinto' during the war. The daughter is still a regular churchgoer, but she nevertheless bows to the *kamidana* at home. Membership of a Christian sect should properly preclude this. Another woman who had been to a Catholic Mission School, told how she had been on the verge of conversion at the persuasion of one of the nuns. But the Catholic faith forbids the offering of incense to the dead, and prayer is expected at various awkward times during the day. If the whole family had been converted all would have been well, but for her alone to take the step would have been 'selfish'. She eventually decided against it. The fact that adherence to the Christian faith to a certain extent isolates the individual from his family by making it impossible for him to participate in the rituals which have the deepest meaning for the family group, is probably the biggest obstacle to conversion.

The direct impact of Christian teachings on the ordinary Tokyo dweller is slight. Less than one half of 1% of Japanese are Christians, and the number of churches and priests is relatively small. Evangelical open-air campaigners occasionally reach wider audiences than the converted, but these are mostly Americans whose impassioned hell-fire oratory loses much in the process of interpretation into less convincingly impassioned Japanese spoken with a second-generation Japanese-American accent.

23

Beliefs of 'the Uncommitted'

MOST of the residents of Shitayama-cho are uncommitted to any particular religious doctrine. The majority of them, it is true, are regular performers of rites which have an important social function in the context of the family, and which, indeed, many of them explicitly conceive in that light. The majority would, it is true, bow respectfully at a temple or shrine if they had occasion to pass directly in front of it. Some of them performed rites by which they express a sense of their own personal dependence on supernatural beings of whom they regularly request favour and protection. But few subscribe to any coherent religious doctrine and few are members of any religious association.

But this does not necessarily mean that they hold no beliefs at all concerning the problems which religious faiths try to answer. This may be so; in some cases, this probably is so; but others do hold beliefs of varying degrees of firmness and definiteness, some of which it will be the business of this chapter to examine.

Some elements of Buddhist thought have become so thoroughly absorbed into Japanese culture that they no longer depend on Buddhist institutions for their perpetuation and could be expected to persist even if those institutions were to be abolished. It is the existence of such ideas and beliefs which provides the justification for calling Japan a 'Buddhist country' despite the general lack of concern with the Buddhist faith as such. An example noted earlier (p. 357) was the high value placed on the 'state of non-self'. Many other typically Japanese attitudes and ideas—for instance, the whole complex of beliefs in the superiority of spirit over matter, or the aesthetic values embodied in such arts as the tea ceremony, the Noo drama or some schools of painting—derive in large part from the philosophical ideas of Buddhism, particularly those of the highly developed Zen sect. But in this broad sense Japan can less justly be called a Buddhist country than Britain can be called a Christian country, for in the important realm of ethics it is Confucian, not Buddhist, ideals which dominate; and it is Confucian, not Buddhist, concepts which are the currency of Japanese ethical discourse.

One element of the Buddhist world-view which is strongly in evidence in Tokugawa popular literature and which might be expected to have a strong hold on Japanese popular thought is a fatalistic determinism emphasizing the necessity of resigned acceptance of one's lot. This is, however, a belief more appropriate to a static status society than to the more individualistic type of society which is developing in urban Tokyo, a society which has a growing faith in its own material progress and places an increasing emphasis on the possibility and desirability of 'getting on'. At any rate, this sort of fatalism would appear not to be very marked among the people of Shitayama-cho today. A question to the effect, 'When people come into this world do you think their future is already fixed, or do you think that depending on a man's will and ability and effort, there's no limit to what he can become?' produced only thirteen replies which spoke of the power of fate, and of these only one used the Buddhist word *innen*; the others, apart from a few sophisticated determinists, used a word (*ummei*) which has become common as a translation of 'Fate' in Western romantic literature.

One of the crucial areas of belief in any religious system is its teachings concerning the destiny of the soul after death. Some questions on this topic which were asked of the small sample have been referred to before, but they are worth considering in more detail here.

People were asked whether they thought death was the end of everything or whether a spirit, or something like a spirit, lived on.

Table 24: Survival after Death

Answer	No.	Whether a spirit goes to Heaven or Hell, or becomes happy or unhappy depends on*				
		Actions while alive	Descendants' worship	'Faith' while alive	Others	Don't know
'Don't know at all'	12					
'Death is the end of everything'	34					
'Something survives, but no idea in what form'	5					
'Something survives but in undifferentiated form'	9					
'Spirits go to a Heaven or to a Hell'	14	11 (12)	0 (1)	0 (0)	0 (0)	3 (1)
'No Heaven or Hell, but spirits may be happy or unhappy'	26	7 (16)	1 (5)	0 (1)	4 (3)	14 (1)

* Figures in brackets represent the number choosing this alternative when these three suggestions were made by the interviewer. The preceding figures represent the replies to the previous open-ended question.

If the latter, whether there was a Heaven and a Hell for the spirits to go to, alternatively, even if there was no heaven and hell, whether there was such a thing as spirits being happy or unhappy after death. If so, what was the decisive factor in determining whether a spirit went to Heaven or Hell (or became happy or unhappy). If no answer was forthcoming to the last open-ended question, people were asked to choose between (1) Actions during life, (2) The punctiliousness or otherwise of the ritual acts of survivors, and (3) The depth of a man's 'faith' during his life. The results were as shown in Table 24.

Not many professed to believe in the existence of Heaven and Hell and of those who did a significantly high proportion were women. Where it occurs, however, belief in Heaven and Hell seems to form part of a coherent and fairly definite belief system. Nearly all of those who confessed to such a belief, immediately pointed to actions during life when asked what determined the ultimate destination of the soul. By contrast, the majority of those who agreed with the possibility of vaguely happy or unhappy states in an after-life 'didn't know' what decided the soul's fate until suggestions were made to them.

The notion of Heaven and Hell, or rather of a number of heavens and a number of hells, has a long history in Indian and Chinese Buddhist thought. In the early forms of the doctrine they are clearly rewards and punishments apportioned according to the individual's conduct while on earth. There is a special god of judgement—Emma—and there are sutras which list the types of crime for which hell is the inevitable punishment.[301] In Japan, these eschatalogical doctrines seem to have suddenly come to the forefront towards the end of the Heian period. Hell figured largely in the evangelistic teachings of the tenth century. Screens bearing pictures of the torments of Hell are mentioned in literature and they seem to have exercised a strange fascination for the Heian Court. The most famous work on this theme is the *Oojoo Yooshuu* (Essentials of Salvation),[302] a tenth-century work describing the torments of Hell as well as the delights of Heaven and accompanied by the author, Genshin's, own most skilful and horrific drawings. As these doctrines became crystallized in the so-called Pure Land sects—Joodo, Shin, Yuuzuu-nembutsu—in the twelfth and thirteenth centuries, the emphasis seems to have shifted from Hell to Heaven. The torments of Hell ceased to be a theme for artistic and literary creation, though the 'Essentials of Salvation' was still being printed and circulated in the Tokugawa period.

The new sects not only shifted the emphasis from Hell to Heaven, they also taught that entry to Heaven depended not on 'works' but entirely on faith in the saving grace of Amida who had sworn to save mankind.

The fourteen people who express their belief in Heaven and Hell do not appear to be directly influenced by any of the orthodox doctrines. Only six of them in fact belonged to one of the Pure Land sects (i.e. have a Pure Land sect temple as their family temple), and these six all say that they have never in their lives heard a sermon. The others belong to sects such as the Tendai or Zen which hold, in theory, that there is no Heaven and Hell except as picturesque descriptions of subjective states. Moreover, their doctrine of Heaven as the reward for virtue is very different from the orthodox Pure Land doctrines of Heaven as the automatic reward of faith, and the subsequent 'prodding' question suggesting this answer attracted none of them.

It would seem, then, that this idea of Heaven and Hell has been perpetuated in Japanese society outside the traditions of orthodox Buddhism. (Though priests may certainly have helped to perpetuate it, for priests do not necessarily know the doctrines of their sect in which they often receive no formal training.) The most frequent occasion for the expression of these beliefs is in the training of children. Some people spoke of being threatened with the prospect of Hell in their childhood as the inevitable punishment for naughtiness. How far parents believe it, however, and how far they succeed in making their children believe it, is a different matter. 'Heaven and Hell are the inventions of the moralizers', said one person during the interview. On the other hand, fourteen people claimed to hold this belief and it is difficult to discover a motive which could have prompted pretence.

There are various theories concerning the relation of religious belief to the social structure, and to individual personality structure which attribute to belief in a heaven and hell other functions than as a device for moral instruction. Such beliefs operate, the theory runs, first to alleviate the shock of death, particularly premature death. This by suggesting not only how the person who dies will be compensated, but also by holding out hope to the bereaved of ultimate reunion. Secondly, in a more general way, such beliefs alleviate the strains and stresses which arise when the members of a society—which holds, as all societies must hold, that some types of behaviour are good and others are bad—are brought by personal experience to the realization that the rewards which that society values—material satisfaction, power, prestige, personal happiness—do not all accrue to the 'good' nor do the punishments—poverty, lack of power and prestige, mental and physical suffering—visit only the 'wicked'. The prospects of a settling of accounts in the remote future makes apparent injustices easier to bear.

Buddhism, as we have seen, did develop such a doctrine of Heaven and Hell, but few sects gave it any central importance. The more common Buddhist method of dealing with these problems is to ascribe apparent injustices to 'fate', a 'fate' which is however, invested with a certain justice by ascribing the individual's sufferings in this life to his evil deeds in a previous existence. This was the explanation of these bewildering experiences most readily available to the thinking Japanese of a century ago. It was the one which suggested itself to the author of a little illustrated book published in 1856, describing a fire and earthquake in Tokyo some years before. In his preface he shows himself to be aware of the problem: 'How can one assess the number thus crushed to death, burnt to death, or, with arms and legs broken, made permanent cripples by this terrible disaster? These were not all evil men who were thus caught in the calamity and brought to an unnatural end. Let us not seek distinctions of good or evil. At such times not even the good escape.' [303] Later, he is commenting on the story of a filial girl who was killed while trying to save her parents. 'It is said that Heaven (*Tendoo*, see n. 287) rewards the good and punishes the wicked. Yet this girl met with disaster and was burnt alive. At such a critical juncture, she yet did not forget her parents . . . But despite such constancy of purpose she could not escape an untimely death. Is this what the Buddhists mean when they talk of "the fate of a previous existence" (*shukugoo*)?' [304]

To this agnostic Confucian the Buddhist explanation was not a satisfactory one, though the resignation which it counselled was not incompatible with the Confucian attitude to life. It is even more doubtful if the cognitive beliefs which are involved would be accepted by many Japanese today.

A possible opportunity for the expression of such beliefs in answer to the interview question about fate and effort was, as we have seen, taken by only a few people, only one of whom used the appropriate terminology. There is, however, a third type of explanation of suffering; one rarely made explicit but which can be seen underlying certain beliefs and practices which are commonly, even in Japan, called 'superstitious'.

The eschatological method of dealing with the question: 'Why? Why should this happen to me?' may be epitomized in the answer: 'Life is like that in this vale of tears. But what is this beside the happiness of eternal life which shall ultimately be yours. Then shall the wicked be laid low and the righteous shall see the Kingdom of God.' The Buddhist answer may be summarized as: 'None can escape the consequences of the sins of previous existences. Only by bearing these ills with fortitude and with faith can we hope, through the continuous cycle of birth and re-birth eventually to attain Nirvana.' The third approach is more direct, limited in its scope to this earthly existence. The 'Why?' of the suffering individual is answered quite simply: 'Because you walked under a ladder, because you did not take sufficient care to site your house in accordance with the omens, because you entered the precincts of that shrine in a state of ritual impurity. Take care in future to observe the correct rituals, to avoid that which should be avoided, and to worship those gods who would otherwise be offended by your neglect and to call on the help of those others who can help to counteract evil influences. Do this and you will escape injury.'

This latter, too, is a cohesive system which works very well until the development of the natural sciences begins to demand modification in the world-view which it entails. The performance of the rites, the avoidance of taboos, the offering up of prayers, gives the individual confidence to face life with all its dangers. Yet the ritual rules are always extremely complex and often contradictory so that some minor ones must inevitably be overlooked. Thus, whenever calamity occurs it can always be 'explained' as the result of some transgression.

In one house in Shitayama-cho a child of two died of whooping cough. This was the fourth death in the family in six years. A former wife had died in her late forties, then her child, then the husband had died soon after marrying again; now his widow had lost a child. It was a particularly lively and likeable child and the whole family were very upset. The young shop assistant who lived with the family complained with tears in his eyes that the mother had not looked after the child properly. But there were other explanations forthcoming. An old aunt, in particular, was striken with remorse. A few days before the child's death she had come up from the country, leaving home during the *Higan* festival which, according to an old superstition, means misfortune. She hadn't wanted to come but her children had laughed at her for being superstitious, so she had been emboldened to set out. (Another neighbour said in comment: 'It's like that. You think there's nothing in it; you don't believe there are going to be any ill effects. But then if anything happens afterwards—well, you can never be sure, can you? You always wish you had never done anything so dangerous.')

But this did not explain the continued series of deaths. A possible explanation of this lay in the fact that the family had some years back had a store-house built on to the North-East corner of the house. The North-East corner of Japanese houses—the *kimon* or 'devil door' as it is called—has to be handled very carefully. It is from this quarter that danger may come. Some houses in the country have little shrines in that corner to ward off evil influences; Mount Hiei to the North-East of Kyooto was made a sacred mountain bristling with temples in order to protect the Court, and the Tokugawas built the temples at Ueno for the same reason. Ordinary Tokyo houses do not normally have divine protection of this sort, but nevertheless certain precautions must be taken. The lavatory, for instance, must never be placed in the North-East corner. This is one superstition which everyone knows in Tokyo,[305] just as mirror-breaking and walking under ladders are the two typical British superstitions. It is as difficult to see why this particular one should have retained its strength in Tokyo as to see why the mirror and ladder superstitions should have done so in England.

The bereaved family had not installed a lavatory in the North-East corner and there was some doubt whether 'interfering with the devil door' to the extent of building a store-house was actually likely to have ill effects.[306] They called in professional advice.

The woman who gave advice has been referred to before as the organizer of the pilgrimage *koo* described on p. 334. She was in her late thirties, the daughter of a Shinto priest, a woman of a very strong and dominating personality, not insignificant intellectual and conversational powers, and with a bold manner which, towards men, was flirtatious in its truculence. She dressed in a black *kimono* with a white undergarment showing at the edges and called herself a *sendatsu*, an old word for a pilgrimage leader. On this occasion she had been invited to the neighbourhood by one of the pious families which had two extra *kami-sama* in its house. One of these *kami* had reached the first anniversary of its installation and the *sendatsu* was asked along to perform a short ceremony. The family which had invited her told their neighbours and by the time of her arrival there were several demands for her services. She was asked to pronounce on the store-house. She was not disposed to attach much importance to it; nevertheless, she said, having been in the house some minutes, 'Somehow or other I feel that there is an evil spirit (*mamono*) here,' and promised to come again to perform a proper purification ceremony. Another family wished to have her opinion about a rearrangement of some furniture in their entrance-hall—could it be carried out without ill consequences? Yet another wished to know what would be a propitious day on which to cut off the water supply in order to have a new pipe put in. Each of these families presented her with an envelope containing a gift of money, and finally, the family which had first invited her provided a feast at which liberal quantities of rice-wine were provided, and drunk with gusto by the *sendatsu*.

This woman also organized pilgrimages, had climbed Mount Fuji fifty times, and practised fortune-telling by palmistry as well as the more normal geomantic and calendrical operations such as advising on the siting of houses, on propitious days for weddings, removals, beginning journeys and so on. She was a regular visitor to Shitayama-cho; at least once a month some family or other would invite her, and her conversation seems to have been valued almost as much as her oracles.

The sample of a hundred persons was asked the following questions. For the first two questions the sample was split in order to test the effect of introducing bias into the question. One half received questions A, and the other half, the questions B.

<table>
<tr><td align="center">*A*</td><td align="center">*B*</td></tr>
<tr><td>1. Could you tell me one or two of the *majinai* you practise in your house?</td><td>1. Do you practise any *majinai* in your house?</td></tr>
</table>

Gave examples	6	Yes	5
No truck with them	44	No truck with them	45

2. Are you careful about 'direction-lore' in your house?   2. What sort of things in 'direction-lore' are you most careful about in your house?

Yes	9	Gave examples	16
Don't worry at all	41	Don't worry at all	34

3. But wouldn't you feel uncomfortable if you had a lavatory in the 'devil-door'?

No	60	Yes	15

4. Do you think something will happen if you are not careful?

Yes	23	—What sort of thing?
No	2	—Then why are you careful?

(*Majinai* includes both prohibitive superstitions, rituals before going on a journey, ritual disposal of milk-teeth, etc., and also empirical medical lore; cures for hiccoughs, bones in the throat, tape worms, splinters in the finger, heat-rash, whooping cough ('take some fresh vegetables and throw them in the river'), pins and needles, etc.)

A comparison of the A and B questions will show that although there is no marked difference where the *majinai* of Question 1 are concerned, in the case of Question 2, the form of question assuming already that the respondent believed in 'direction-lore' produced a higher proportion who admitted that they did. Although this difference is not quite statistically significant[307] it does suggest the possibility that there is a tendency to pretend to greater scepticism in these matters than is actually felt. It is also noticeable that another fifteen were persuaded to reconsider their attitude by Question 3. Typical of their replies is this one: 'Well, if you're ill and somebody tells you that it's because of something to do with the "devil-door", yes, then you do begin to feel worried.'[308]

There were some rationalizers who declared that they did not believe in these rules and prohibitions as superstitions, yet defended them as embodying rules of empirically demonstrable hygienic value. A contrary example of the ousting of superstition by the diffusion of scientific (?) knowledge was the remark of a man who mentioned the traditional prohibition against sleeping with the head towards the north ('like a corpse' as Confucius said, for corpses were always laid out that way in ancient China). He did not believe, he said, that these things have any particularly bad effects, 'But it's just that I would feel uncomfortable in contravening the rules. However, I've felt much less about them since I read in the Reader's Digest that from something to do with the earth's magnetic field and the daily revolution of the earth, it is actually *better* for the circulation and for growth to sleep with your head pointing north.'

It is not surprising to find that the people who are careful about directions and dates are roughly the same people who believe in the protective power of *fuda* and who are the most regular devotees of some sort of productive or protective cult. More interestingly, there is also a significant correlation between all these things and belief in the existence of a heaven and hell.[309] The 'two ways' of dealing with the problem of suffering are not, by any means, mutually exclusive alternatives. Those who are attracted by the one, are equally likely to have recourse to the other. And of the two, thoughts of a compensatory after-life would seem to be least in the forefront of people's minds. Reference to Heaven and Hell is infrequent in daily conversation, and in this contrasts with frequent references to superstitions and *kami*. Again, of the newly created post-war sects, few, in the summary of their doctrines, made any mention of an afterlife, but a high proportion of them did promise the protection and help of the *kami* in this life. In fact, one would suspect that it is only in rare instances, as for instance among the early German Protestant sects, when belief in an afterlife is at the core of a doctrine, when the religious community really is a community and when the delights of Paradise and the tortures of Hell are recurrent themes in the literature and doctrinal instructions of the Church, that this belief really has important psychological functions.

RELIGION AND MORALITY

Again, because belief in an after-life is never a very 'strong' belief, it is doubtful if its effect as a moral sanction is very important. Rather, the links between religion and morality in Japan are those we have already outlined.

1. The operation of certain rituals associated with Shinto Shrines to impress on the individual an awareness of his membership of, to a limited extent the local and to a greater extent the national, collectivity and so to reinforce his sense of obligation towards the collectivity which that membership entails.

2. The operation of certain rituals associated with the family *butsudan* to impress on the individual an awareness of his membership of his family and of his indebtedness to past generations of his

family, with the effect not only of increasing a sense of direct obligation to other members of the family, but also of giving added force to the sanction of family displeasure attaching to all infringements of the norms internalized during the process of socialization within the family.

3. Thirdly, not without relevance to moral behaviour and moral judgement is a generalized attitude of religious humility—a sense of the individual's dependence on and insignificance in the face of what may be described as Nature, the Universe, or the whole abstract world of the noumenal. This is an attitude which both Buddhist and Confucian teachers in Japan have been at pains to cultivate. It tends, inevitably, to be weakened in the townsman whose environment is more exclusively man-made and whose livelihood is more secure and less dependent on the caprices of nature. Nevertheless, traces of such an attitude were apparent in the replies of some people in Shitayama-cho to questions asking them about the word *on*—debt-incurring favours (as of parents, teachers, the Emperor, and the like) on which great stress was laid in the school-taught ethics as the foundation and justification for duties of loyalty and service towards social superiors. The question was: 'People say that we are the recipients of *on* from the moment we come into this world. What do you think?' Most of the hundred asked this question disagreed, and held that man did not begin to receive *on* until his parents began to bring him up, his teachers to teach him and so on. Five, however, answered the question by referring to the *on* of 'nature' (*shizen*, a modern word) of 'all living creation' (*shujoo, bambutsu*, the first a Buddhist, the second primarily a Confucian word) or of 'heaven-and-earth' (*tenchi*—a Confucian term). Perhaps the most direct expression of this attitude and one not expressed in any terms derived from specific historical moral teachings, was the reply of the man who said: 'I can't say directly, but, for instance, when the weather clears after a long spell of rain, somehow you feel as if you want to thank somebody.'

The sentiment expressed may have its roots in a general feeling of well-being and a diffuse sense of gratitude for that well-being. As such it has much in common with Christian praise for the goodness of God. But it is more than that; it is also an expression of humility and dependence on forces greater than man. As a moral force it tends to be a prop of tradition, since the workings of nature and the workings of society are identified as parts of a single established order. It is anti-Promethean in effect; a curb to the sin of hubris. But it can provide backing for almost any ethical principle. The woman who spoke of receiving the *on* of 'heaven-and-earth' said, in answering a further question, that it was one's duty to repay this *on* by 'working hard and living justly'.[310]

Fukuzawa Yukichi, the moralist of the Meiji enlightenment, saw clearly the moral and social implications of this sense of religious humility. One essay in his Fukuoo Hyakuwa is devoted to an attack on the doctrine of the *on* of 'heaven-and-earth' (he used the word '*tendoo*' which can be a synonym for *tenchi*) from the standpoint of his belief in a mechanistic universe. (Why should the screw feel grateful to the steam engine?) However, his essentially aristocratic sense of social responsibility caused him some subsequent qualms. He adds a note at the end of the essay to the effect that the argument may be too difficult for the ordinary run of his fellow-countrymen, and that 'there may be a danger that people will only half understand and jump to the conclusion that there is no *kami* and no *hotoke* in the world of men and that worship and the repayment of *on* are all meaningless ideas. Such people, lacking in any proper moral or intellectual cultivation, may become irresponsible and constitute a danger to the social order. The sense of indebtedness for *on* springs from a religious faith and whether or not that faith rests on illusion or on emotion, it is the task of the intellectual *vis-à-vis* the lay world not to disturb this faith and to seek to maintain the "virtuous feelings" (*tokushin*) of the untutored masses.' [311]

4. Somewhat similar are religious experiences of a more mystical kind, which are less easy to relate directly to moral sanctions and yet which cannot be entirely dismissed as having no relevance at all to moral behaviour. These are the experiences which mystics seek to communicate, experiences which in Japan are associated with the words *muga* (not-self) or *sammai* (*samadhi*, trance), states which, as we have seen, some people say it is their object to attain in prayer at shrines, temples and family altars. These experiences may be described in various ways; as 'communion' with God or with Nature, as becoming aware of the insignificance of human life in the cosmological process, as appreciating the sanctity of everyday life, or as realizing the meaning of human existence. In Japanese popular culture the pursuit of such experiences is generally seen as a means to the end of developing strength of character—the ability to transcend all passions and all the sufferings of the flesh, to concentrate the whole of one's vital forces on the perfection of a single act, to quell an enemy with the steady gaze of an unwavering eye. Pursued, such experiences are often elusive. But the capacity for such experiences may exist apart from their deliberate pursuit. One young man in Shitayama-cho, who said nothing of *muga* or of *sammai*, answered the question about the existence of spirits in these terms: 'I often wonder about death. I often think about it as I gaze at the stars. Not so much personal death as about what will happen when everything dies and the earth has run down. I get a strange feeling, almost of mystery.'

At a less sophisticated level, there was another man who frequently takes his children on pilgrimages to a mountain shrine and who revealed in describing the 'spiritual training' which these expeditions afforded, how even apparently simple productive rites can be given some philosophical significance. He tells his children that this pilgrimage is symbolic of life's journey. When they are in the train they are to imagine themselves in their mother's womb, when they leave it and climb to the first stage they are at the Nursery School, at the next stage, the Primary School, and so on until, from the ninth or tenth stage which represents 'the most trying age in a man's life, between forty and fifty', it is but a short climb to the top. This form of mountain climbing, he said, is good 'spiritual training' because it leads to 'concentration of the spirit'; it is not mere recreation or mere sight-seeing. And it would, indeed, be rash to deny that the contemplation of the responsibilities which await one in the future and of the inevitability of one's own death, even divorced from any belief concerning what is likely to follow that death, will have some effect on a man's moral behaviour.

But the major moral sanctions are not religious in character; even those which have their source in the family are only *reinforced* by religious rites. A discussion of some of the other important sanctions —the disapproval of social groups other than the family and the guilt arising from a stricken conscience—will be our partial concern in the next and final chapter.

24

Society and the Individual

THE last chapter touched briefly on the moral implications of a sense of religious humility springing from a consciousness of the individual's dependence on forces greater than man, and offered as proof that at least vestiges of this sentiment existed a number of replies to a question about *on*. The same question ('People say that we are the recipients of *on* from the moment we come into this world. What do you think?') was answered by fifteen people out of the hundred by referring to the *on* of 'society' or of 'neighbours'. In answer to other leading questions a large number of people (though by no means the overwhelming majority one would expect in view of the fact that these ideas formed an essential part of the ethics teaching in pre-war schools)[312] acknowledged that they had received *on* from their parents, from their school-teachers, from the Emperor, from 'the State', from employers, or from individuals who had helped them earlier in their lives. And most of these acknowledged further that the receipt of these favours entailed certain corresponding obligations; in part obligations of loyalty and devoted service to those who had vouchsafed these favours—filial piety towards parents, for instance, or, in the case of the Emperor and the State, obeying laws and paying taxes—in part the obligation of living up to certain generalized standards of moral conduct which these honoured superiors had enjoined.

Every Japanese, wrote Ruth Benedict, conceives himself as a 'debtor to the ages and the world.' [313] 'Every man', says another source, 'is a debtor to the world: to his parents; his schoolmaster; his friends and employers. He owes them his existence; his knowledge; his happiness and his daily bread.' [314] All his social acts must be guided and directed by an awareness of that indebtedness and of the duties towards others which it entails.

This ethic would have been explicitly acknowledged by the samurai of the Tokugawa period if he had read any of the books of moral exhortation which were written for him and if he in any way resembled the characters of contemporary fiction and drama. On his feudal lord he was quite clearly dependent for the rice income which he received as a hereditary retainer. To his ancestors and his immediate parents he was quite clearly indebted for maintaining the status of the family which allowed him to enjoy that position. That he should therefore strive to give loyal service to his lord and to maintain the honour of the family, thereby not letting down his forebears, were quite clearly duties of the highest priority. The peasant of the Tokugawa period probably did not have so easily available any such clear verbal forms for explaining to himself and to others why he should behave as he did. Nevertheless his state of dependence on others was just as real.

His was a closed society of limited opportunity and limited range of choice. In that society the forms of personal relationships which arose were limited in number:—parent and child, elder-brother and younger-brother, mother-in-law and daughter-in-law, head of tenant household and head of landlord household, young man of 20 and any unrelated househead of 50 or more—even at this level of detail a full list of the types of relationship in which a single individual might be involved would not occupy any very great space. Such relations being small in number and of such a kind as to recur with great frequency, the appropriate behaviour they required was fairly minutely regulated. Most people had a clear idea, and within the same village an identical idea, of how a tenant should behave towards a landlord. These standards of proper conduct gained the greater compulsive force, not only from the degree of their detailed elaboration and from the fact that they were universally accepted, but also from the fact that throughout the life of each individual continuing to do what his forebears had done was the dominant feature of his activity. The son, working with his father, learned from him all he needed to know in order eventually to succeed to the headship of his family—when to plant the rice and how much fertilizer to apply, what neighbours should be taken what gifts at New Year, which gods were to be propitiated with what offerings, what was the correct approach to the landlord when asking him to take a reduced rent in years of bad harvest. Tradition was the more powerful in that it provided a clear answer for almost every situation which might arise.

Not only did the standards which regulated behaviour towards other people within the village have the greater legitimacy and compulsive force in that they were part of an established and stable order, they also had the backing of strong sanctions. Every family was, in plain fact, dependent on its neighbours. The right to irrigate its ricefields at the time which should be determined by lot or by regular roster, the right to cut undergrowth as fertilizer and fodder from land held in common by the village or owned by a rich landlord, the co-operation of other villagers in protecting crops from nocturnal theft, their help at housebuilding or re-roofing, at funerals or after a fire; all these were essential to the livelihood of the family.

In some villages where property was fairly equally distributed the reciprocity of rights and duties involved in relations between families was symmetrical. In others relations of dependence were closely associated with differences of status; branch families rendered to main families, and tenant families to landlord families, service and respect in return for protection and economic opportunity.

In either case the community, or powerful individuals within the community, could make life economically impossible for those who failed to observe the established proprieties governing relations between fellow-villagers. They could make life emotionally impossible too. It is impossible to ignore the fellow-villager one meets on the two-foot-wide paths between rice fields. And suddenly to meet with blank stares and hostility could be a source of extreme emotional discomfort for the individual accustomed to feeling the security of belonging to his village—to feeling assured that he is accepted by his fellow-villagers, that he will receive their gestures of respect or friendliness and can count on their sympathy and help in trouble.

If an individual was a part of his village, he was even more a part of his family. In a large household, living in a house with few rooms divided by flimsy partitions, no part of life was private. The individual shared according to his ability in the family's productive life, and he shared according to his status in the family's consumptive life. He shared in the family's recreations and in its joys and sorrows. His interest were his family's interests; his property was family property. If he offended against the rules of propriety governing his relations with other villagers his shame was his family's shame, for his honour was his family's honour, and the maintenance of that honour was a duty not simply to the other members of his immediate household, but also towards 'the family' which lived on though the individuals composing it changed, and to 'the ancestors' who had given the family the honoured status it enjoyed and whom the family united in honouring in rites at the family altar. If his actions consistently brought the family's good name into ill-repute, the family might reject him, for without its good name, without its good standing in the economic organization of the village, the family could not survive.

The Tokugawa peasant, then, was not fully an individual. He had few private emotions, and few private ambitions. The pattern of his life was more or less determined at birth. He had only to follow the course that was expected of him. In a closely regulated system of social relations situations which presented themselves to him as offering or requiring a conscious choice between alternative courses of action were rare. When such situations did arise, it was as a representative of the family that he acted, and the responsibility for the choice was as much his family's as his own. The possibility of incurring the displeasure of, and becoming emotionally isolated from, his family and his neighbours was a sufficient sanction to prevent him departing from the established modes of conduct. For on these people he was both economically and emotionally dependent.

But his great-grandson, Mr. Risookei, in modern Tokyo is a very different person and his life is lived under different conditions. His neighbours are simply people who live next-door and in whose economic or emotional life he shares as little as they in his. His employer is simply the man to whom for the moment he sells his labour. His livelihood depends on no-one's goodwill; only on the fact that it continues to be in the interest of his employer to employ him, of his shopkeepers to serve him, and of his bank to maintain its reputation by safeguarding his savings. What employer he shall serve, which shop he shall patronize, how he shall spend his leisure time, whom he shall make his friends—these become questions which offer a conscious choice of alternatives. And, provided that his choices are not proscribed by the laws of the country, few people outside his immediate household will be concerned to show either approval or disapproval of his actions; perhaps only a small circle of workmates or neighbours, a circle which, small and constantly shifting with changes of job and of residence, is less important to his emotional well-being and has lesser power to influence his conduct by its expressions of approval and disapproval than was the case with the Tokugawa peasant and his fellow-villagers. 'The Risookei family' means little to such circles of acquaintances, and the fear that by exciting their disapproval he will bring dishonour on the good name of his family weighs little with Risookei himself.

Tradition, then, does not provide Mr. Risookei with clear directions for leading his life or regulating his relations with his fellow-men; nor does his social environment provide pressures which serve to keep him moving in traditional grooves. His sources of direction are internal. It is a duty to *himself* to live up to the aims which he has set himself, and it is he who blames himself if he fails to achieve his ambitions to acquire wealth, or prestige, or saintliness, or power, or academic qualifications. It is his own conscience whose disapproval is excited if, in dealing with the manifold situations of choice which face him, he fails to live up to certain generalized standards of conduct which he has internalized.

But the 'inner-directed' individualist, Mr. Risookei—or, to translate him into English, Mr. Ideal Type—apart from being a very incomplete characterization, is not, it will have been abundantly clear from the rest of this book, typical of the citizens of Shitayama-cho. Life certainly is less closely regulated for the average Shitayama-cho citizen than it was for the Tokugawa peasant. Tradition supplies fewer guides to conduct. Many are imbued with a desire to do better than their fathers, rather than simply to 'preserve the family', its livelihood and its good name. Their need to retain the good opinion of others is less pressing, their moral controls are more internalized, their goals, their ambitions, their emotions and their responsibilities more individual. But at the same time, as discussions in previous chapters, of the family, of employment relations, and of neighbour relations have shown, this is only a question of degree; many are involved in stable relations of personal dependence on others whose good opinion and material support they value to the extent of allowing them to become the objects of their loyalty and the arbiters of their moral conduct. Many features of the system of social relations prevailing in the Tokugawa village are still preserved in the city. Mr. Risookei is only an extrapolation; a carrying to extremes of certain trends in respect of which people in Shitayama-cho do differ from the Tokugawa villager. It will be the business of this final chapter to discuss some of these differences—differences in the nature of the principles by which conduct is guided and judged, and in the sanctions by which these are enforced.

EXPLICIT MORAL PRINCIPLES

Moral beliefs, attitudes and symbols have a dynamism of their own, and the more they are explicitly expressed in words the greater their entrenchment, the greater their power of independent survival. The ethical thinking of the modern city Japanese is strongly influenced by the fact that the system of social relations out of which the society of the Tokugawa period was built up—a system which was little questioned and which fitted the economic structure of that society—developed its own explicit ethic—just how explicit the size of a catalogue of popular moral treatises of the period would show.[315] This ethic persisted into the modern period and its strength was enhanced by wider diffusion through such means of mass communication as were available, in particular the school system. It was on this ethic that the citizens of Shitayama-cho were for the most part nurtured. It was an ethic which stressed dependence. In particular, as taught in the schools, the greatest stress was put on those vertical relations of dependence—of child on parents, servant on master, pupil on teacher, citizen on the Emperor and 'the authorities' in general—relations of dependence an adequate appreciation of which, and of the duties of obedience which they involved, was crucial to the authoritarian structure of government. But the ethic did not omit to stress horizontal interdependence also—as between neighbours, fellow-workers, fellow-pupils—and to teach the duty of maintaining harmonious relations of mutual support, in other words a full observance of the behaviour required in what were defined in Chapter 16 as *giri*-relations. The ethic had a place, too, for what might be called historic dependence, the dependence of the present on all past generations, an awareness of which should induce in the individual a humble respect for the established institutions of his society.

The circumstances of industrialization did not *enforce* any radical changes in the traditional ethic. Although the situation of the modern townsman *permitted* deviations from patterns of conduct which were obligatory in the village, it did not necessarily *demand* them. The son whose future no longer depended on eventual succession to his father in the family business or farm could defy his father, but there was no compelling reason why filial piety should not continue to be held a cardinal duty. The goodwill of neighbours may be of sufficiently minor importance for them to be safely ignored, but this does not prevent good neighbourliness from remaining a part of the definition of the upright man. Even where, in practice, all-out competition ruled rather than traditional co-operation—as between, say, school children taking entrance examinations, or rival tradesmen and manufacturers freed from the restraints of guild-regulated agreements—it was possible to justify the abandonment of one part of the traditional ethic (the duty of maintaining harmonious relations with one's fellows) in terms of another part (the duty of adding to the status, wealth or honour of one's family).

One modification was enforced in the traditional ethic by the emergence of Japan as a nation-state in competition with other nation-states. A new dimension of loyalty had to be added. The individual had to lose some of his individuality not only in his family, and in the slightly wider in-group of the people with whom he had *giri*-relations, but also in the nation. He had to develop a feeling of belonging to the nation, to take unto himself and make a part of himself the ambitions of 'Japan', to feel Japan's honour as his honour and Japan's shame as his shame. This national loyalty had on occasion to take precedence over other loyalties—over loyalty to the local community (see the discussion of Shinto in Chapter 20) and even—if the taxation system and the conscription system were to work other than by mere coercion—over family loyalty. The verbal expression of duty to the nation took the same form as for other spheres of duty. It was taught chiefly as a duty of loyalty to the personal symbol of the nation—the Emperor—and the duty was justified by the doctrine that every Japanese was a recipient of the *on* of the Emperor and was dependent on the Emperor, for without the Emperor there would be no Japan and without Japan there could be no Japanese.

The modern city Japanese was, thus, provided with standards of behaviour which were more generalized than those of the Tokugawa villager and hence more useful to him in the more varied circumstances and problems of his everyday life. (More generalized in that—to give an example which doubtless exaggerates the extent to which generalization was absent in the village—he learnt that 'One should always show respect to one's social superiors' rather than that he should always bow to Mr. A and Mr. B and members of family C, and so on.) But the principles which were thus generalized and available to form a part of his conscience were those of the traditional ethic, abstractions of the duties implied in the sort of social relations which existed in the village, specifying broad loyalties to particular categories of persons. Principles of a more universalistic kind, specifying proper behaviour applicable to all situations, were not entirely lacking; hard work, courage, honesty and frugality were traditionally virtues (see the discussion on p. 198). But, compared with the overwhelming importance attached to particularistic obligations towards persons, they were relatively little stressed.

However, partly as a result of institutional changes, partly as a result of the direct influence of foreign ideas, these and other newer principles of a universalistic kind have come to demand greater consideration in the moral scheme of things. Kindness and consideration to 'others', loyalty to principles and 'isms', the pursuit of truth, the frank expression of opinion, justice and equality before the law, the equality of the sexes, the duty of self-development, the right to seek happiness and self-fulfilment;—these phrases enshrine principles of conduct which have acquired increasing importance. And frequently they clash with the older particularistic obligations. Some examples of such conflict have already been noted in earlier chapters (see p. 262). One or two more type situations may be given in illustration.

A nephew employed in his uncle's firm as under-manager is convinced of the justice of the workers' case in a strike conflict. Should be suppress his 'sympathies' and loyally support his uncle as the ethics of *giri* prescribe? Or should he work for what he believes to be just even though it does bring on him the accusation that he does not know *giri*?

A girl is due to marry the son of her father's business partner, but she decides she does not love him but someone else. Her father explains that it would be very awkward for him if the marriage did not take place. Would the modern Japanese applaud her if she sacrificed private feelings so that the family could behave as the *giri* norms prescribe? Or would they applaud her if she sought to assert her own individuality—what the new Constitution somewhat plagiaristically calls her 'right to life, liberty and the pursuit of happiness'—and sacrificed *giri* and filial piety in the process?

Was Mr. Okazaki at the Shitayama-cho Ward Association meeting right to 'speak his mind' about the management of the Association? Or should he have kept silent in order to preserve the amicable atmosphere of harmony between neighbours which was everyone's ideal?

Which is the more upright man; the research student who, disagreeing

profoundly with the theories of the professor who secured him his place in
the university, yet refrains from ever making public his disagreement, or
the man who considers the pursuit of truth to be of more importance than
personal loyalties?

'Someone to whom you are indebted for past favours has a son who
takes the entrance examination for a certain firm. A representative of the
firm calls to ask you for a personal opinion of the son's qualities. You
happen to know that he is an unreliable person. How would you answer the
firm's enquiries? Do your best to see that he gets the job by finding some
way of praising him? Avoid giving a direct answer? Or tell the truth that
he is an unsuitable person?'

The traditional type of Japanese moral dilemma has been the
conflict of personal loyalties. Japanese moralists have always had to
be ready with answers to such problems as: 'Which is the more important—loyalty or filial piety? What should one do when the interests
of one's lord and the interests of one's parents are at variance?'
But the sort of situations outlined above present dilemmas of a
different kind, conflicts between, on the one hand, particularistic
loyalties, and on the other either individual aspirations which it is
held to be the right of everyone to hold, or generalized principles of
conduct which are held to be applicable to all situations.

Most Japanese would recognize these situations as dilemmas;
few, perhaps, would very sharply condemn the taking of either the
one course or the other. Many would admit to confusion. But there
is little doubt that the universalistic principles have gained ground
as compared with the Japan of eighty years ago. The last question
was, in fact, asked of a nation-wide sample of some 3,000 Japanese
in 1953—23% said that they would do their best to get the son accepted by the firm, 48% said that they would tell the truth about
him. The investigators also asked a group of twenty-six 'experts' to
forecast the results of the interviews. Twenty said that the former
would be the most usual reply for a Japanese to make, and thirteen
said that it would be 'most unusual' for a Japanese to say that one
should tell the truth in such a situation.[316] The experts were intellectuals who, in Japan, tend to have a low estimation of their fellow
countrymen (low, that is, by their own standards since they tend to
be strongly opposed to the old particularistic morality). Nevertheless, this illustrates well the difficulty which any Japanese in these
situations would have in knowing which course would secure the
approval of the majority of his fellow countrymen.

TYPES OF MORAL SANCTION

These conflicts of moral standards are clearly related to changes
in, and differences between, various types of sanctions on conduct

and it is to a brief consideration of these that we must now turn. The distinction is sometimes made by American cultural anthropologists between shame-cultures and guilt-cultures, those, that is, in which the major moral sanction is the fear of being ridiculed and rejected by others, and those 'which inculcate absolute standards of morality and rely on man's developing a conscience.' Ruth Benedict, whose formulation this is, considers Japan to be a shame-culture. Shame is the root of virtue, and a virtuous man is one who 'knows shame'.[317] The general assumption of the cultural anthropologists (and one which springs in part from their wholly admirable purpose to counter narrow ethnocentrism by pointing to the relativity of culture and ethics) is that these mechanisms are selected more or less arbitrarily by different cultures from a vast range of human potentialities the bounds of which are only loosely determined by the limits of adaptability of the human organism.

A more suggestive formulation of the distinction between shame-control and guilt-control, and one which relates these to other features of social organization, is that of David Riesman. In *The Lonely Crowd* he suggests that shame-control is characteristic of all 'tradition-directed' cultures, and that guilt-control is only one aspect of the 'inner-direction' of the more individuated man typical of expanding and materially progressive societies in an area of free competition.[318] If this association between guilt-control and the early development of capitalism is valid for all societies and not merely for the West, one would expect the Japanese to have become gradually less sensitive to shame and more subject to feelings of guilt.

Not far from Shitayama-cho was a poster originating from the local Fire Services' propaganda department. It said simply 'Fires (*kaji*) bring shame (*haji*)'. Another notice nearby said, 'If you have a conscience (*ryooshin*) do not deposit rubbish here.' Perfect evidence, perhaps, of the transitional phase? But further reflection must lead to the conclusion that moral sanctions in Japan cannot be easily and satisfactorily dealt with in terms of any simple shame-guilt dichotomy. It will help first to make a list of some of the possible sanctions on behaviour which are important in Japan. An individual's choice of alternative courses of action may be influenced, consciously or unconsciously, by the desire to avoid,

1. Personal shame. The ridicule and disapproval of 'the world' which would follow deviations from an expected code of conduct. The extent of 'the world' will vary for the individual, from a narrow range of neighbours, friends, relatives and workmates, to, in the case of a politician or a film star, the whole nation.
2. Family or we-group shame. That is, to avoid bringing dishonour on his family, his school, his department, with, perhaps, in the back-

ground the fear of being rejected by the group whose good name he has besmirched.

3. Punishment for breaking the law.
4. The displeasure of particular individuals resulting from failure to perform obligations towards those individuals.
5. The displeasure of particular individuals for failing in other respects to live up to certain standards of conduct which those individuals had enjoined on him.
6. The feeling of guilt which comes from failing to live up to standards which he has made his own.

In the Tokugawa village with its settled and commonly shared ways of life and standards of behaviour, the effect of all these sanctions generally coincided. The villager who was discovered secretly interfering with the weir at night in order to take into his own fields water which should properly go to his neighbour was personally ashamed to look his fellow villagers in the face the next day. The attitude of members of other branches of the family left him in no doubt that the honour of 'the family of the ancestors' was besmirched. He was punished according to the explicit rules of the village by having his own water ration reduced. He had to face the particular resentment of the neighbour from whose fields he diverted water, and the displeasure of his marriage go-between who had always taken an interest in him and was 'disappointed in him'. And probably, even before he was discovered, he had, as well as the fear of being found out, a feeling that he was 'doing wrong'.

For the modern city-dweller, these various sanctions still coincide in their effect over a wide area of conduct. Except among criminal groups (where fear of the scorn of one's fellows works in a contrary direction to the others) robbery, fraud, murder and child neglect can bring all these sanctions into operation. But their relative force has changed. The law has become clear and calculable and sharply defined in its scope; it is not represented by the paternalistic official with omnicompetent discretionary powers. Letting the family down is of lesser importance as 'the family' ceases to loom so large in the individual's consciousness. The importance of avoiding personal shame is in part maintained by the persistence of child-rearing habits of an earlier age when this sanction was a crucial one. Mothers do sometimes tell their children that 'people will laugh at' them, or they 'will be disliked' if they do such and such (although they equally often say that 'it is wrong' or 'naughty' (*ikenai*) to do such and such). For those who—as is possible in the towns—'keep themselves to themselves' the fear of shame is of lesser importance. But, as was shown in Chapter 16, the majority do not keep themselves so aloof from neighbours, at least, and those who do are often motivated by an exaggerated fear of the neighbours' criticism to which greater intimacy might expose them. To start a fire to the danger of one's neighbours still, in the words of the poster, 'brings shame' and the culprit can only try to mitigate the wrath of his neighbours by making a full and abject apology (see p. 260). Fear of 'what the neighbours will think' weighs heavily on housewives, and the close quarters at which life is lived in a densely populated Japanese city exposes a very wide range of one's life to the neighbours' thoughts. Nevertheless, the force of this sanction is weakened in that the more mobile city dweller can always move to a new district and a new job— and, as the Japanese proverb has it, 'the traveller leaves his shame behind him'.

But most city dwellers are not continually moving on. Most are involved in a network of stable personal relations of the type which were described in an earlier chapter as *giri*-relations, and it is these, the relations of 'support and be supported', to which the fourth of our list of sanctions specifically applies. What was said in that chapter (p. 258) concerning the decline in the importance of these relations—as compared with, say, the Tokugawa village—implies *ipso facto* a decline in the importance of this type of sanction. But the decline is only relative, and, as was pointed out in discussing the means of 'getting on' in Japanese society, industrial Japan has provided a new importance for *giri*-relations. In an industrializing society in which the dependent employee's advance in a bureaucratic organization has been not only the most easily available, but also the most highly valued form of social advancement, the strict fulfilment of obligations towards superiors who have taken one under their wing, and the careful avoidance of their displeasure, have been of the greatest importance for the individual's well-being.

Guilt may indeed combine with the sanctions implied by *giri* relations. In so far as, with explicit teaching of generalized principles of duties towards superiors, such obligations become internalized, conscience may support the *giri*-sanction. The man who fails to repay his department chief's kindness by covering up for him when the accountants are on the point of discovering suspicious gaps in the accounts, feels guilty about having failed to fulfil an obligation as well as uncomfortable at the department chief's displeasure. (Though in so far, on the other hand, as these relations can simply be manipulated as means to individual ends, conscience may play no part. An ex-department chief's displeasure may be easily borne and no feelings of guilt aroused as the ingrate steps into the shoes of his dismissed superior.)

Conscience gains in strength with the increasing explicitness of moral principles. A generation of parents nurtured on the school ethics text-books in some measure add their influence to that of the schools in making the principles of proper conduct impressed on their children more explicit and more generalized. We have already discussed the different types of principle which can be internalized—both those of the traditional kind stressing obligations to superiors and those of a different kind stressing duties to all fellow-men and duties to oneself. One further point deserves notice concerning the nature of the Japanese conscience, or rather, the nature of what the Japanese say about conscience and the forms in which they express feelings of guilt.

Conscience seems often to be less, in George Mead's terms, a 'generalized other' as a specific other. That is to say that it is intimately connected with what we have listed as sanction 5. 'I don't know what my mother will say when she finds out' is not very different from the typical expression of guilt: 'I don't know how to excuse myself to my dead mother' (*Shinda haha ni taishite mooshiwake ga nai*). Other expressions of guilt more familiar to the West are also frequently heard: 'I have done something wrong' (*Warui koto shimashita*), 'my conscience accuses me' (*ryooshin ga togameru* or *ki ga togameru*), 'I feel the pangs of conscience' (*ryooshin no kashaku wo kanjiru*). The idea of conscience as an innate guide which 'knows' what is right and what is wrong is not foreign to Japan. The modern word for conscience derives from Mencius, and Wang Yang Ming, who made conscience a central part of his philosophy, was not without Japanese followers. But the Neo-Confucianism orthodox in Tokugawa Japan had a different ethic. With its stress on obedience to superiors it saw knowledge of good and evil not as innate but as something taught by those superiors—taught in the history of Man by the sages of antiquity, and taught in the history of individual men by parents and teachers. The Christian who believes that his conscience is the voice of God within him feels that it is a duty to God to obey its dictates and that he has sinned in the sight of the Lord if he fails to do so. The Japanese who conceives of the voice of his conscience as the voice of his parents and teachers feels it to be a duty towards them to obey it, and if he fails to do so it is they whom he has let down. Even after their death his feelings of guilt may take the form of imagining how displeased these honoured parents and teachers would be, and his verbal expressions of that feeling may take the form 'I don't know how to excuse myself to . . .' (In those who believe in ancestral spirits, these feelings may be related to the belief in the vindictiveness and malignancy of such spirits discussed on p. 318—much as Christian consciousness of sin is related to the hell-fires of a wrathful God.)

Whether, however, this difference between the Japanese and the Western Christian in the type of imaginings and verbal expressions which accompany feelings of guilt means that the feelings of guilt themselves are different (as defined, say, in terms of their psychological genesis and functioning) is a further and debatable point. One relevant observation is that the judgement sometimes made that the Japanese 'have no sense of sin',[319] may simply be a way of saying, firstly, that feelings of guilt are not often expressed in a religious form, and secondly that matters of sexual conduct—matters which are capable of arousing the deepest emotional disturbance—are not made the centre of Japanese morality as they frequently are of the Christian.

So far we have got no nearer an answer to the main question with which we began this discussion of moral sanctions (namely; has guilt replaced shame as the major sanction?) except to show that the sort of sanction specific to the *giri*-relation (including both the possible displeasure of honoured and respected—or simply feared and utilized —superiors and that of those social equals with whom one is in constant interaction) has application to a wide area of conduct and can claim equal importance with both guilt and shame. The complaint that 'we Japanese have no civic sense'—a complaint which has recurred frequently in post-war exercises in national self-denigration in the newspapers—amounts in fact to saying that this (and the fear of the law) are the only sanctions which really work. The man who is punctilious in performing all his obligations towards people with whom he has a *giri*-relationship will, it is said, nevertheless fight tooth and nail to be the first on the train, scatter litter in public parks, sell adulterated food and fail to put himself out to help strangers in distress. 'Other people' outside of his *giri* world, people whose displeasure is of no importance to him do not count. The only way, says one newspaper writer, to prevent Japanese from using train lavatories while trains are standing in a station is to provide automatic locking devices on the doors.[320]

But the place to seek a test of the relative strengths of the various sanctions is in those situations in which their effects do not coincide but pull in opposite directions. The individual in the modern city, whose contacts may ramify into diverse groups with differing standards and values, is frequently faced with such situations. The Christian teetotaller (Japanese Christians are often non-smokers and non-drinkers) has to meet the scorn of his fellow-workers when he refuses to take a night out on pay-day. The young man who believes in marital fidelity is laughed at by his friends when he refuses to move on to a brothel after a party. But shame and guilt are not the only sanctions which conflict in their operation. Many of the situations which were given above as examples of conflicts between differing types of moral principles involve conflicting sanctions. The nephew in the strike, for instance, may reject intellectually the whole scale of values which gives priority to duties towards uncles, but opposed to the urgings of his conscience which prompt him to support the workers' claims (urgings which may be backed by fear of the scorn of his left-wing friends of university days, or of the disappointment of his hero-worshipped professor of economics) is the prospect of the outraged displeasure of his uncle and of his parents who expect that *giri* should take precedence over everything. In such situations conscience often wins, but it is a bold cultural anthropologist who will undertake to assess in any precise terms, even for a single individual, let alone for a whole society, the relative strength of conscience compared with the fear of shame or the fear of the displeasure of individual others.

In comparative terms, conscience has certainly widened its scope in Japan since the Meiji period. But, to return to Riesman's thesis, whereas the development of a competitive capitalist society in the West was accompanied by a great expansion in the sphere of conscience, the development of less competitive and more regulated forms of capitalism in the more authoritarian Japanese atmosphere has given conscience less scope. The necessity of obeying superiors has restricted freedom to obey one's own conscience, and emphasis on the moral propriety of obeying superiors has made the following of one's own inner light appear reprehensible and presumptuous. The point at issue will become clearer if we put conscience back in a wider context as a characteristic of the 'individuated' man, and conclude with a brief discussion of the ways in which one can legitimately speak of increasing individuation in recent Japanese society.

THE INDIVIDUAL AND THE GROUP

The word 'individuation' will be used rather than 'individualism' to make clear that what is meant is a descriptive category for certain characteristics of behaviour and motivation, and not a consciously held politico-economic philosophy. It may be defined first of all by contrasting reference to what might be çalled 'collectivism', or, more ponderously if less ambiguously, 'collectivity-orientation'. For the individuated person, the things he wants most are things he wants for himself or for specific individual others, not for some group—some 'we'—to which he belongs. To realize his desires he relies on his own efforts, knowledge and skills rather than on the joint effort of his group. The things which make him glad or sad are primarily things which happen to himself (or to some individual others) rather than things which happen to a wider we-group of which he feels himself a member. He selects his opinions, beliefs and moral standards not simply to conform with his immediate social environment, but in the light of strongly held principles of right and wrong which he has internalized. The responsibility for his own actions he accepts as his own, and in his conduct he is guided by the dictates of his own conscience which would make him feel guilty if he deviated from the standards which he expects of himself, rather than by the fear that by departing from the standards of his group he will be accused of having let the group down. These various traits tend to be related; they may be summarized as reflecting the extent to which the individual 'identifies with' or 'merges self in' some wider group of which he is a member.

In this country the evaluative associations of the word 'individualism' are ambiguous: we are accustomed to speak approvingly of 'independence' when concentrating on the aspect of holding one's own opinions fearlessly regardless of the opinions of others, and disapprovingly of 'selfishness' when concentrating on the aspect of giving one's own aims and desires absolute priority. In pre-war Japan 'individualism' (*kojin-shugi*—a post-Meiji translation of the European word with similar referential denotation) had much the same pejorative ring as 'selfishness' (*riko-shugi*). Since the war phrases such as 'human rights' and the 'liberty of the individual' have been written into the constitution and gained such universal currency through the press and radio that a housewife in Shitayama-cho will condemn a husband who keeps a mistress on the grounds that it is an 'infringement of the wife's human rights'. The word *kojin-shugi* (individualism) was too thoroughly a 'bad' word to be easily purified, but other formerly emotionally neutral words which had been the exclusive preserve of metaphysicans—words like 'actor-ness' (*shutaisei*, i.e. being that in which resides the power of independent action) and 'self-direction' (*jishusei*)—have been seized on as the slogans of the left-wing writers and educators, and even the counter-attack of the more conservative has generally taken the somewhat half-hearted form of stressing the responsibilities of freedom and the danger of confusing liberty with licence. These are changes in the values now upheld by the mass communication media. They may be dismissed as changes merely in the ideological superstructure, but they have undoubtedly given an extra stimulus to a long-term trend towards individuation in actual behaviour, a trend which, even before the war, despite the enshrinement of the traditional anti-individualist ethic in a position of unassailable supremacy, was nevertheless going forward concomitantly with changes in the structure of society.

Evidences of this trend have been given in earlier chapters; it may be summarized as follows. Large numbers of individuals have become more independent of their families, and the definition of 'the family' with which the individual identifies has narrowed from the wider kinship group conceived as an entity persisting through the generations to the more ephemeral household based on the conjugal family. Fewer people tend to merge their identity in wider groups outside the family, such as neighbourhood groups or occupational groups. As a countervailing tendency, more people have come to feel more strongly a sense of membership of the nation, a group of a different order from the face-to-face groups which formerly claimed the individual's loyalty. Greater individuation there is, then, than in, say, the Tokugawa village, but still less than in Western societies. Some people still explain their conduct to themselves and to others as a 'duty to the family'. The solidarity of the ex-Tokyo Imperial University clique in the civil service is still spoken of as a menace to efficient government, employees of Mitsui may still avoid mixing socially with employees of Mitsubishi, and maintaining the ward's good name is still a motive which prompts people in Shitayama-cho to give donations for the Red Cross.

And this is not the whole story. Hitherto we have considered individuation only in contrast to 'collectivity-orientation'. In dealing with Japanese society a different polar opposite to individuation deserves equal attention—that, namely, in which the individual surrenders a part of himself not to a group of which he is a member, but to particular individuals whose leadership he accepts, with whose fortunes he identifies himself, on whose help he depends for securing his own advancement or happiness, on whose goodwill he depends for his emotional security, and on whose approval he depends for his self-respect. Sometimes, when groups are characterized by authoritarian leadership, it is not always possible to distinguish between the two types of non-individuation; to distinguish, that is, between behaviour which springs from self-identification with the family, and that which springs from personal submission to the househead; between identification with the fortunes of the family-atmosphere firm, and submission to the authority and protection of the employer. Generally speaking, however, in traditional Japanese society (as, indeed, is reflected in the form in which obligations are expressed in the traditional ethical code) personal submission has been as important a structural principle as group-identification. The processes of industrialization and urbanization have had the effect of altering the forms it takes without much reducing its importance. The peasant who comes to seek his fortune in the towns finds no group which will immediately accept him into membership (even though the patterns of neighbour relations are such that he can develop a sense of belonging to his new ward or neighbour group more rapidly than in most societies). But he has a traditionally sanctioned alternative to the 'individualism by default' which Marion J. Levy finds in his urban Chinese. He can attach himself to some patron—generally his employer—who will provide him with some of the security and guidance and approval which—being unaccustomed to habits of self-sufficiency, self-guidance, and self-evaluation—he feels the need for. In

Japanese urban society, where this sort of employment relation was fully established in the Tokugawa period, patrons have not been lacking.

We have noted how, despite the depersonalization of employment relations with the increasing scale of modern industry, these types of relationship have not altogether lost their importance. It is the trade union boss, the foreman or the department chief who becomes the new patron. Dependence remains the keynote. 'A powerful backer will come to your aid and thus assure a favourable outcome' is the form in which shrine fortune-telling cards assure 'those engaged in disputes and conflicts' that they are bound to win.

Individuation can proceed, we have seen, working through the traditional patterns, in so far as personal relations become instrumentalized; a mere means to further individual ends, maintained only as long as they continue to serve those ends and thus ceasing to imply the same surrender of self as formerly—inner individuation being only cloaked by the external forms of submission. But such individuation is an incomplete and stunted growth; by destroying trust it can only lead to moral anarchy. Not backed by 'individualism' as a faith, and lacking any explicit ethic with which to justify itself, it cannot develop those mechanisms of inner control which are necessary to societies of individuated men in order that the self-seeking of one individual should still give scope to the self-seeking of others. Its logical dead end is the ruthless manipulations of such as T in Shitayama-cho, corruption in the civil service, or the career of the fraudulent money-lender-university student who became the type case of '*après-guerre* youth' when he was found dead in his office, a bottle of poison in one hand, and on the wall a placard bearing his motto: 'What belongs to me is mine, and what belongs to others is legitimate game.' [321] It is understandable that 'individualism', of which these are often represented in Japan as the typical exemplars, should seem to many a destructive philosophy involving the negation of all responsibility, and that many voices have been raised in recent years to warn against the dangers of confusing liberty with license, and to stress the responsibilities of freedom.

Democratic political institutions—with their stress on the free expression of individual opinion, the acceptance of majority decisions tempered by the forebearance to consider the wishes of the minority, and the restriction of coercive state power to spheres in which the limitation of the freedom of action of some individuals can be justified by a greater expansion of the freedom of action of other individuals—may be seen as a product of competitive individualistic capitalism, an adaptation of the individualistic ethic of the individuated man to the needs of coexistence in society. It can plausibly be asserted that it was economic individualism which laid the basis for the political emphasis on the importance of the individual which is of the essence of democracy.

But today the era of economic individualism is all but over. The later stages of capitalist development have brought a new kind of collectivism of a vaster and more impersonal kind than that of the medieval village—the collectivism of the giant industrial corporation, of State welfare services and nationalized industries, of shared fashions in clothes, enjoyments and values diffused by mass radio and television. In America where this trend has gone further than elsewhere, social scientists are beginning to mourn the disappearance of the 'inner-directed' man. His 'other-directed' supplanter, who depends increasingly on the goodwill and approval of his fellows for his emotional security and for his material well-being, values popularity above everything and develops a radar-like sensitivity to the values and standards of others which enable him to adapt chameleon-like in whatever environment he finds himself. If this is not a false prophecy of despair, and not a phenomenon specific to the American melting-pot situation, but a danger inherent in modern forms of economic organization, our only hope of avoiding the brave 1984 world of the novelists lies in the inertia of institutions, in the persistence of democratic forms of government after the type of character structure which created them has ceased to be the dominant type in our society.

The attempt has been made to transplant these institutions in Japan, in a society in which the older forms of collectivism have not disappeared, and in which the mechanisms which regulated industrial development have been imposed from above (having been borrowed from abroad) rather than worked out in the stress and conflict of clashing individual wills; a society which jumped from feudalism to the corporate stage of industrial capitalism and in which, as a consequence, the individual entrepreneur has never had much scope to gain power, nor, with the continuance of the Tokugawa preference for advancement by learning and dependent service rather than by self-seeking money-making, has he had much chance to gain prestige as the admired type, the representative of the ethos of the society. (Even in districts like Shitayama-cho where the self-employed worker sets the pace and provides a model for the aspirations of employees, the typical self-employed worker is dependent on a big wholesaler or industrial firm, and it is to the university and a good job in the civil service or a large firm that most parents want to send their sons.) Now, forms of the new collectivism have arrived before the old ethic of dependence on the group and dependence on superiors has disappeared—large industrial corporations, government economic controls and welfare services, mass communication —new forms of dependence and new pressures to conformity.

The new collectivism is not inimical to some of the trends towards greater individuation apparent hitherto—in the fields of family relations and neighbour relations, for instance. But the economic dependence of the individual grows with the decreasing scope for economic activity outside large-scale industrial and commercial organizations, and these organizations still allow for the retention within them, in a modified form, of 'personal' dependence—patron-client relations of the traditional type. At the same time, improving techniques of mass communication offer increasingly efficient means of fostering the trend exhibited in pre-war nationalism, towards a new kind of 'impersonal' dependence—emotional dependence on and identification with a vaster secondary group, be it nation, class or party, and its leaders. State social services increase this impersonal dependence at the material level. And the individual who ceases to be an articulated member of his family or small local community, as he becomes more individuated in this sense, may, for that reason—because he is deprived of the security of binding primary ties—become even more vulnerable to pressures to conform with the anonymous mass. More leisure, increasingly mass-organized, provides new spheres as well as new pressures to conformity, new sources of shame (not having the right clothes, not having seen the right film) and new impersonal dependences in the form of entertainment-addiction.

Have democratic political forms much chance to grow in a society in which independence of thought and action are not established habits and established virtues—in which the open expression of differences of opinion and the acknowledgement of conflicts o interest are not expected or easily tolerated, nor the mechanisms developed for achieving compromise agreement by appeal to accepted generalized principles of justice and fair procedure? Can independence of thought and action become and remain established habits and virtues only in societies in which independence of economic activity is, or has been, the norm? Or can they become established simply by the influence of ideas and transplanted institutions—by the establishment of the forms of representative government and by the hypothetical devoted idealism of thousands of school-teachers—and in the teeth of the plain fact that the economic basis for some of the old forms of personal dependence still remain and new forms of impersonal dependence are growing in importance?

'It is a striking phenomenon,' writes a Japanese sociologist in 1951, 'that today, when voices on all sides ring out with demands for "democratization" we should hear the words "liberalism" and "individualism" so infrequently. It may be argued that this is a reflection of a tendency to pin hopes for the future on a socialistic, rather than a capitalistic order. But if so we need to examine even more closely the spirit of dependence which seeks refuge and security in a socialistic order while avoiding the baptism of liberalism and individualism —while, that is to say, skipping over the process of individual reformation in the field of consciousness. In a typically Japanese way, the necessary revolution in individual attitudes—a revolution which is only possible through the self-awareness and effort of each individual —is being omitted.' [322]

The Westerner must guard against the fallacy of assuming (like the author quoted, together with most other Japanese intellectuals) that the stages of social development which Western countries have experienced are right and natural stages deviation from which is somehow unhealthy (for in the Westerner the historicist fallacy may become tinged with arrogance.) But it was difficult for someone who left Japan in 1951 to think other than in these terms of a nation whose leaders of opinion had decided that theirs was a 'backward country', a 'following-behind country', committed to imitating the development of the West now in its social and political as well as in its industrial forms. Japan had, owing to its peculiar circumstances, skipped a stage in the proper order of social development. The damage had to be repaired. It may be that 'the process of individual reformation in the field of consciousness' will be accomplished although all the omens are against it. It may be that the effort will be abandoned. One could hardly expect the period to last indefinitely in which the nation is prepared to take its values from, and measure its achievements by the yardstick of, other countries. (It did not, it will be remembered, last for very long in the Meiji period.) Eventually, a sensitive *amour-propre* may combine with entrenched interests to develop new goals of a different—a 'truly Japanese'—kind, and to create a new sort of society and a new sort of political regime in which the old forms of dependence are subtly combined with the new.

Enquiry Methods

THE enquiry was carried out during the months March to September 1951. A meeting was first held with officials of the ward association who agreed to give their support. I was then introduced by one of these officials to the current heads of each of the neighbourhood groups. The latter distributed on my behalf to each household in their groups a leaflet explaining the scope and purpose of the enquiry and the gift of a small towel such as might normally be given by new residents to their neighbours as a basis for initiating acquaintance. Subsequently I accompanied each interviewer on his first visit to each house.

Apart from a small number of formal unscheduled interviews with ward officials, priests, estate agent and prominent citizens, the organized parts of the enquiry consisted of the following parts.

1. Basic data concerning household composition, age, marital status and relation to household was obtained from the local food office for each household in the ward. This was checked by interviewers and expanded with details of birthplace, education, occupation, parental occupation and details of residence and household possessions. The following scheduled interviews were then conducted.

2. On household income and expenditure and domestic management. (The factual sections were addressed to housewives or to male households in the absence of a housewife, the attitude sections to housewives alone.)

3. On ancestry and kinship ties, household celebrations, religious affiliations of the household, neighbourhood ties, visiting and the form of marriage. (To housewives or male household in absence of a housewife.)

4. On leisure activities. (To one hundred individuals aged fifteen or over.)

5. On education and the bringing up of children. (To one hundred parents.)

6. On religious practice and attitudes and general *weltanschauung*. (To one hundred individuals aged 15 or over.)

7. On political attitudes. (To one hundred individuals aged 15 or over.)

8. On employment. (To a scratch collection of seventy-eight employees.) Schedules 4 to 8 contained a mixture of factual and attitude questions.

SAMPLING

The samples of one hundred for Schedules 4 to 7 were drawn by the following method. All persons over 15 were stratified into six age, two sex and three educational categories and the sample was drawn by random enumeration in such a way that it accurately reflected the age and sex composition of the total population and fairly accurately reflected its composition by educational experience.

REFUSALS AND SUBSTITUTIONS

1. *Basic Data*

Households registered at Food Office, Feb. 1951	325
Refusals	3
Removals, prolonged absences	25
Total for which information obtained	297

(Two of the refusals were from households which had no dealings with their neighbours and paid no subscriptions to the ward association. The third was a woman living with a mentally deficient brother whose domestic situation was too painful for her to wish to discuss it with interviewers and who asked through an intermediary to be left alone. In a fourth household, the husband who had resentful memories of his experiences as a post-war prisoner of the British army in Malaya, refused to co-operate, but his wife caught the interviewer and apologetically invited him in during her husband's absence.)

2. *Domestic Economy*

Some parts of this questionnaire were completed for all the above 297 households.

3. *Kinship, Neighbour Ties, etc.*

This questionnaire was completed for 255 households. Most of those excluded were single-person households in apartment blocks—floating individuals rather than households. A small number of the original households had by this time removed and others were abandoned after several failures to secure appointments for interviews. Unfortunately no record was kept of the number in each category.

4–7. *Sample Interviews*

Substitution was permitted in the case of refusals or if repeated attempts to contact the sampled individuals failed. The number of substitutes and re-substitutes was as follows.

Leisure	23
Education	16
Religion	19
Politics	31

The number of outright refusals was small. Substitutes were always drawn from the same age, sex and education cell as the individual sampled. The effect of substitution was certainly to bias the sample towards the more leisured and, perhaps, the better-off. Since, however, the population of Shitayama-cho, in the accurate image of which the sample was drawn, was not in itself accurately representative of any wider universe, this was not felt to be a serious drawback. Not much importance has been or was intended to be placed on the numerical analysis of these replies. Their chief value lay in the large number of open-ended questions which they contained combined with the possibility of a rough check on the representativeness of the views expressed.

PREPARATION OF QUESTIONNAIRES

Each schedule was composed by myself, and the first draft used for from six to ten exploratory pre-tests, as often as possible in company with a Japanese sociologist. The purpose of the pre-test was to find out how far the questions elicited the information desired and to discover what additional questions were necessary to avoid ambiguities. They were not intended as a guide to the preparation of check lists or precoding which were rarely used.

INTERVIEWS

Interviews lasting between thirty minutes and one hour for each of the schedules were carried out (apart from a small number conducted by myself) by students of Tokyo and other universities, a few of whom had previous interviewing experience. A preliminary meeting was held to discuss each schedule and a list of instructions and conventions displayed in the survey centre. Co-ordination was not, however, as efficient as it should have been and for stages 1 to 3 the quality of the interviewing varied greatly. For Schedules 4 to 8 however, it was of a generally high standard.

For Schedules 4 to 8 interviewers were instructed to get the interviewee alone as far as possible, but it frequently was not possible. The conditions under which each interview was made were recorded, but in practice no use has been made of this information in analysis.

TABULATION AND ANALYSIS

Most cross-tabulations and some simple tabulations are based on 243 households (containing 238 housewives and 200 married couples) for which a selection of data from Schedules 1 to 3 was coded and card-punched. (This represents the total, less single-person households, less fifteen households excluded owing to deficiencies or unreliability of the data.) No independent check on the coding was possible. For other simple tabulations based on schedules 1 to 3, the total varies since some interviews were not completed, some questions were not asked where the interviewer deemed them inappropriate or embarrassing, and a small number of questionnaires have been excluded where it was apparent from internal evidence that the interview was not properly conducted. The economic status scale used for cross-tabulations was a rough *ad hoc* nineteen point scale for which points were awarded on the following basis.

A. Housing

(i) Size of Dwelling

Less than 2 mats per person	0 pt.
2–3·49 ,, ,, ,,	2 pts.
3·5–6·49 ,, ,, ,,	4 pts.
More than 6·5 ,, ,, ,,	6 pts.

(ii) Occupancy Status

Sole occupier of dwelling (owner or tenant)	2 pts.
Occupier subletting part of dwelling	1 pt.
Subtenant or apartment dweller	0 pt.

B. Household Possessions

For possession of

Wireless	1 pt.
More than one gas tap	1 pt.
Sewing machine	1 pt.
Electric iron	1 pt.
Bath	2 pts.
Ice-box	2 pts.
Electric fan	3 pts.

The combinations of categories used for contingency tests were not always constant, but the most commonly used gave the following distribution.

0–2	pts.	47 households
3–5	pts.	71 households
6–10	pts.	70 households
11–19	pts.	55 households

Family Budgets

* These budgets were kept by housewives in Shitayama-cho for one month. They were not exactly concurrent but all fell within the period mid-June to late August, and where the househead is in receipt of a monthly wage they run from one pay-day to the next.

Each household keeping a budget was given a book of slips; one slip to be made out for each purchase. Each slip contained space for (*a*) the article bought, (*b*) the quantity, (*c*) price, (*d*) remarks (e.g. for whom bought, etc.), (*e*) the name of the member of the family making the purchase.

Twenty households were selected on the following principles:

(*a*) All households in Shitayama-cho were roughly stratified into three economic groups on the basis of monthly household expenditure per person according to the housewife's estimate of such expenditure as given in a previous interview. Seven households from each of the lower two strata and six from the upper were then chosen, ensuring that,

(*b*) They were housewives who had been marked by interviewers as 'extremely co-operative' during the two previous interviews.

(*c*) They were housewives who had said in the course of a previous interview that they regularly kept a family budget.

Three housewives, two from the upper and one from the middle stratum failed to complete the course. This slightly biased the sample towards the less-well-off.

On the other hand the principles of selection certainly biased the sample in favour of the methodical housekeeper, leaving the more haphazard under-represented. In any case, however, these can only be treated as a number of case studies, not as a sample which permits generalizations about the parent universe.

One factor impairing the comparability of the data is that the husband's personal expenditure is not apparently always included, despite the request that it should be. Households for which some expenditure by the husband is recorded are marked + in the column 'Husband's Expenditure', households for which no such expenditure is recorded are marked − and may well be considered under-estimated. In the case of Family 17, however, there is every possibility that this is not the case and that the husband handles no money himself.

A further defect concerns the choice of month. In some industries it is the practice to give a mid-summer bonus in June or July. This is by no means as common as the year-end bonus, and in fact makes very little difference to the average monthly earnings of workers (Statistics Bureau, Prime Minister's Office, *Consumer Price Survey*, Aug. 1950, p. 35). Nevertheless, there may be some families whose income is temporarily inflated by such a bonus for the month during which the budget was kept. Such extra income is, however, most likely to be spent on clothing and furniture which is excluded from totals in this table.

Expenditure on railway season tickets, rent, taxes, insurance, etc., which covers several months' contributions is divided by the number of months in the period covered. It is possible, however, that some other block payments covering several months were not specified and this may lead to some minor error.

Family Number		1	2	3	4
Occupation of Househead		Clerk	Police sergeant	Factory worker	Taxi-driver
Number in Family		9	5	4	4
Composition of Family†		m (64), w (57), s (31)ᶻ, s's w (29), gd (4), gd (2), s (19), s (15), d (22)ᵚ	m (37), w (30), s (7), d (4), s (3)	m (39), w (45), s (8), father (83)	m (36), w (28), d (7), d (4)
Occupation of Other Wage-earners		Clerk (y) Civil Servant (x)	—	—	—
Husband's Expenditure‡		—	+	+	+
Total Monthly Expenditure per person (excluding furniture and clothing)		2,353	2,605	2,680	2,913
Food Expenditure per person on	Rice and Bread	1,132(54·8%)	509(45·7%)	445(29·7%)	109 (8·2%)
	Fish	277(13·4%)	96 (8·6%)	162(10·8%)	301(22·5%)
	Meat and Eggs	105 (5·1%)	47 (4·2%)	193(12·9%)	225(16·9%)
	Milk, Butter and Cheese	0	6 (0·5%)	0	101 (7·6%)
	Cakes	78 (3·8%)	0	121 (8·1%)	55 (4·1%)
	Veg., Bean Curds and Pickles	259(12·5%)	237(21·3%)	276(18·4%)	312(23·4%)
	Other Foods	213(10·3%)	71 (6·4%)	225(15·0%)	57 (4·3%)
	Restaurants	0	149(13·4%)	74 (4·9%)	175(13·1%)
	All Food	2,064(100%)	1,115(100%)	1,496(100%)	1,335(100%)
Total Family Expenditure on	Food	18,578(87·7%)	5,687(43·3%)	5,986(55·8%)	5,339(45·8%)
	Rent, Water, Heat and Light	899 (4·2%)	997 (7·6%)	1,187(11·1%)	1,258(10·8%)
	Medical Exp.	160 (0·8%)	2,413(18·4%)	796 (7·6%)	20 (0·2%)
	Alcoholic Drinks	248 (1·2%)	0	0	0
	Cigarettes	0	510 (3·9%)	420 (3·9%)	0
	Entertainments, Children's Pocket money, etc.	150 (0·7%)	1,328(10·1%)	170 (1·6%)	0
	Religious Expenditure	30 (0·1%)	50 (0·4%)	0	50 (0·4%)
	Insurance and Savings	482 (2·3%)	300 (2·3%)	0	0
	Gifts	170 (0·8%)	560 (4·3%)	200 (1·9%)	280 (2·4%)
	Education, Stationery, newspapers	36 (0·2%)	632 (5·0%)	483 (4·5%)	670 (5·8%)
	Other Exp.	420 (2·0%)	651 (5·0%)	1,479(13·8%)	4,035(34·6%)¶
	Total (excluding clothing and furniture)	21,173(100%)	13,128(100%)	10,721(100%)	11,652(100%)
	Clothing and Furniture	25,552	1,935	75	5,050

Expenditures*

5	6	7	8	9	10
Warehouse porter	Writing brush carver	Radio script editor	Bank clerk	Clerk	Works manager
3	5	5	5	4	6
m (32), w (28), sister (17)	m (71), w (65), s (42), s's w (32), gd (3)	m (52), w (46), d (24), s (21), s (18)	m (52), w (52), s (18), s (15), s (12)	m (35), w (30), d (8), d (4)	m (53), w (43), d (19),² d (16), mother (73), lodger (22)
—	Engineer	—	—	—	Clerk (x)
—	+	—	—	+	+
3,138	3,758	3,780	4,535	4,538	4,615
613(38·3%)	331(24·1%)	611(27·1%)	509(27·7%)	582(22·6%)	368(15·0%)
144 (9·0%)	167(12·2%)	376(16·7%)	185(10·1%)	334(13·0%)	
142 (8·9%)	81 (5·9%)	559(24·8%)	152 (8·3%)	382(14·8%)	
0	31 (2·3%)	95 (4·2%)	0	280(10·9%)	
63 (3·9%)	184(13·4%)	91 (4·0%)	231(12·6%)	195 (7·6%)	1,598(65·1%)
314(19·6%)	140(10·2%)	283(12·6%)	209(11·4%)	459(17·8%)	
325(20·3%)	254(18·5%)	237(10·5%)	451(24·6%)	228 (8·9%)	
0	183(13·3%)	0	98 (5·3%)	115 (4·5%)	488(19·9%)
1,601(100%)	1,371(100%)	2,252(100%)	1,835(100%)	2,575(100%)	2,454(100%)
4,803(51·0%)	6,857(36·4%)	11,261(59·6%)	9,177(40·5%)	10,307(56·8%)	14,725(53·2%)
975(10·4%)	261 (1·4%)	1,057 (5·6%)	1,212 (5·3%)	687 (3·8%)	1,175 (4·2%)
0	220 (1·2%)	1,040 (5·5%)	730 (3·2%)	0	235 (0·8%)
0	480 (2·6%)	0	0	0	1,320 (4·8%)
130 (1·4%)	2,000(10·6%)	60 (0·3%)	240 (1·1%)	1,000 (5·5%)	430 (1·6%)
0	1,454 (7·7%)	900 (4·8%)	7,700(34·0)%	1,010 (5·6%)	784 (2·8%)
210 (2·2%)	250 (1·3%)	850 (4·5%)	80 (0·4%)	0	882 (3·2%)
0	4,031(21·5%)	0	303 (1·3%)	980 (5·4%)	1,465 (5·3%)
1,830(19·4%)	325 (1·7%)	1,800 (9·5%)	0	1,800 (9·9%)	2,540 (9·2%)
345 (3·7%)	315 (1·7%)	410 (2·2%)	585 (2·6%)	995 (5·5%)	1,540 (5·6%)
1,123(11·9%)	2,595(13·8%)	1,522 (8·1%)	2,650(11·7%)	1,375 (7·6%)	2,593 (9·4%)
9,416(100%)	18,788(100%)	18,900(100%)	22,677(100%)	18,154(100%)	27,689(100%)
400	16,210	260	2,430	7,245	3,820

Family Number		11	12	13	14
Occupation of Househead		Head clerk	Envelope-maker (self-emp.)	Clerk	Office Worker
Number in Family		3	4	2	4
Composition of Family†		m (38), w (35), d (18)	m (54), w (50), s (20),ᶻ s (17)	m (29), w (22)	m (51), w (43), s (16), s (14)
Occupation of Other Wage-earners		—	Gas collector (x)	—	—
Husband's Expenditure‡		+	+	+	+
Total Monthly Expenditure per person (excluding furniture and clothing)		5,344	6,821	6,864	8,747
Food Expenditure per person on	Rice and Bread	672(19·2%)	1,481(43·3%)	732(24·6%)	757(36·2%)
	Fish		349(10·2%)	208 (7·0%)	367(17·5%)
	Meat and Eggs		345(10·1%)	384(12·9%)	158 (7·5%)
	Milk, Butter and Cheese	1,018(29·0%)	157 (4·6%)	50 (1·7%)	0
	Cakes		365(10·7%)	150 (5·0%)	50 (2·4%)
	Veg., Bean Curds and Pickles		406(11·9%)	565(19·0%)	413(19·7%)
	Other Foods		275 (8·0%)	734(24·6%)	231(11·0%)
	Restaurants	1,815(51·8%)	42 (1·2%)	155 (5·2%)	117 (5·6%)
	All Food	3,505(100%)	3,420(100%)	2,978(100%)	2,093(100%)
Total Family Expenditure on	Food	10,517(65·5%)	13,682(50·1%)	5,957(43·4%)	8,371(23·9%)
	Rent, Water, Heat and Light	1,090 (6·8%)	1,277 (4·7%)	1,350 (9·8%)	2,050 (5·9%)
	Medical Exp.	0	701 (2·6%)	455 (3·3%)	244 (0·7%)
	Alcoholic Drinks	330 (2·1%)	3,051(11·2%)	0	1,988 (5·7%)
	Cigarettes	1,150 (7·2%)	30 (0·1%)	1,740(12·7%)	1,200 (3·4%)
	Entertainments, Children's Pocket Money, etc.	1,120 (7·0%)	550 (2·0%)	1,030 (7·5%)	850 (2·4%)
	Religious Expenditure	0	0	0	30 (0·1%)
	Insurance and savings	100 (0·6%)	3,500(12·8%)	0	7,842(22·4%)
	Gifts	1,000 (6·2%)	0	150 (1·1%)	3,060 (8·7%)
	Education, Stationery, newspapers	395 (2·5%)	1,135 (4·3%)	332 (2·4%)	1,790 (5·1%)
	Other exp.	332 (2·1%)	3,358(12·3%)	2,715(19·7%)	7,562(21·6%)
	Total (excluding clothing and furniture)	16,034(100%)	27,284(100%)	13,729(100%)	34,987(100%)
	Clothing and furniture	1,100	3,992	1,240	3,860

Expenditures—continued

15	16	17	National Averages		
Small factory owner	Sales clerk	Retired managerial worker	Recipients of public relief	Manual workers	Non-manual workers
4	3	2	3·5	4·56	4·70
m (51), w (42), s (20), s (17)	m (54), w (47), d (23)	m (61), w (46)	—	—	—
—	—	—	0·8 persons employed	1·40 persons employed	1·29 persons employed
+	—	—	+	+	+
11,953	13,124	13,701	1,408	2,911	3,501
792(17·4%)	2,353(43·3%)	1,360(26·7%)	522(54·9%)	601(42·2%)	582(36·6%)
544(12·0%)	309 (5·7%)	463 (9·1%)	56 (5·9%)	160(11·2%)	190(12·0%)
869(19·1%)	365 (6·7%)	1,178(23·1%)	} 19 (2·0%)	} 99 (6·9%)	} 206(13·0%)
330 (7·3%)	65 (1·2%)	300 (5·9%)			
62 (1·4%)	423 (7·8%)	50 (1·0%)	22 (2·3%)		
619(13·6%)	1,041(19·2%)	729(14·3%)	176(18·5%)	} 565(39·6%)	} 611(38·5%)
831(18·3%)	876(16·1%)	1,015(19·9%)	131(13·8%)		
500(11·0%)	0	0	24 (2·5%)		
4,547(100%)	5,432(100%)	5,095(100%)	950(100%)	1,425(100%)	1,589(100%)
18,188(38·0%)	16,297(41·4%)	10,191(37·2%)	3,325(67·5%)	6,493(48·9%)	7,469(45·4%)
1,708 (3·6%)	1,110 (2·8%)	2,954(10·8%)	494(10·0%)	1,217 (9·2%)	1,497 (9·1%)
920 (1·9%)	8,615(21·9%)	8,000(29·2%)	192 (3·9%)	710 (5·3%)	807 (4·9%)
6,400(13·4%)	935 (2·4%)	0	10 (0·2%)	(215)‖(1·6%)	(215)‖(1·3%)
600 (1·3%)	0	300 (1·1%)	67 (1·4%)	333 (2·5%)	275 (1·7%)
6,650(13·9%)	740 (1·9%)	0	38§(0·8%)	568§(4·3%)	796§(4·8%)
100 (0·2%)	1,150 (2·9%)	350 (1·3%)	see 'other expenditure'		
2,100 (4·4%)	4,610(11·7%)	357 (1·3%)	58 (1·2%)	744 (5·6%)	933 (5·7%)
2,300 (4·8%)	400 (1·0%)	300 (1·1%)	see 'other expenditure'		
680 (1·4%)	960 (2·4%)	450 (1·6%)	159§(3·2%)	190§(1·4%)	334§(2·0%)
8,165(17·1%)	4,555(11·6%)	4,500(16·4%)	586(11·9%)	2,806(21·1%)	4,127(25·1%)
47,811(100%)	39,372(100%)	27,402(100%)	4,929(100%)	13,276(100%)	16,453(100%)
5,150	11,785	750	360	1,291	1,759

National Averages

(a) *Recipients of Public Relief:* Ministry of Welfare, Health and Welfare Statistics Division: *Cost of Living Survey, No. 1 (Seikeihi Choosa Hookoku)* July 1951. These figures are based on a national survey of 3,345 households receiving public relief over the three months Sept.–Nov., 1950. Although the surveying authority and the relief-giving authority were quite distinct, there are obvious reasons for suspecting some under-reporting. It might be thought that the Ministry of Welfare officials conducting the survey would be led by the general Panglossian bias inherent in their position to correct this to some extent. On the contrary, however, if they exerted any bias at all, the evidence is that it would have been in the opposite direction, for the report of this survey seems primarily intended as a tract, highlighting the need for improved social services, in which there is every reason to think these officials sincerely believed.

(b) *Urban Manual and Non-Manual Workers.* Statistics Bureau, Prime Minister's Office, *Consumer Price Survey (Shoohisha Kakaku Choosa)*, March 1951. These figures are based on a government budget survey using a panel sample of 1,307 non-manual and 825 manual workers from 28 Japanese cities. These figures are for March 1951.

The comparability of these three sets of data is somewhat impaired by the differences in times of collection, in particular by the price rise which took place between the Ministry of Welfare Survey and the other two. The Cost-of-Living Index for the relevant periods is as follows (100 = average Jan.–Dec. 1948):

Sept.–Nov. 1950 (Recipients of Public Relief)	128·2
March 1951 (Manual and Non-manual Workers)	147·0
July 1951 (Shitayama-cho)	148·9

† Composition of Family. Family members are identified with respect to relationship to househead, thus: m=man, w=(his) wife, s=son, d=daughter, s's w=son's wife, gd=grand-daughter.

Figures in brackets represent age.

‡ Husband's Expenditure. See note *, para. 6.

§ These categories do not accurately correspond with those used for analysis of the other budgets. Exact comparison is therefore impossible.

‖ This sum for alcoholic drinks is an estimate based on the average for the whole sample of both manual and non-manual workers. In the broad classification from which this table is derived this item is included under 'other foods'. Here this sum has been subtracted from the total food expenditure to make these comparable with the other budgets.

¶ Includes remittance of 3,000 *yen* to husband's mother.

Social Insurance Schemes in Force in 1951

1. *Health Insurance.* Implemented 1927. Compulsory for workers in all concerns employing more than five workers, with the proviso, however, that 'temporary workers' need not be insured, an easy loophole for the unscrupulous employer which was particularly abused during the war. In February 1952, 7,029,000 workers were insured of a total of thirteen and a half million wage and salary workers. Contributions, graded according to wage-level, are drawn from the employer and from the employee in equal proportions (2·75% of the wage from each in 1950). The State provides only the expenses of administration. Medical treatment is provided by special panel doctors, free except for the cost of the first consultation for the insured, and at 50% of cost for their families. Money benefits, proportionate to the wage level, include sickness allowances (60% of full wages, limit six months, for tuberculosis eighteen months), maternity allowance (60% of wages for 12 weeks for a worker, 1,000 *yen* for a worker's wife) and funeral allowance (month's wages for a worker, 1,000 *yen* for a member of the worker's family).

2. *Welfare Pensions Insurance.* Implemented 1942. Compulsory to the same classes of worker as above. (In fact 6,603,000 were insured in February 1952.) Contributions totalling 3·5% of wages for miners, and 3% for other workers are shared between employer and employee in equal proportions. The State supplements this by 20% of receipts for miners and 10% for other workers, and also bears administrative costs. (It has also had to make special Exchequer grants to repair the ravages of inflation.) Pensions, graded according to wage and contribution level, are granted for old age (minimum one third of average wage during working life, from a minimum age of 50 for miners, 55 for other workers), for disablement, for widows and for orphans.

3. *Unemployment Insurance Scheme.* Implemented 1947. Compulsory for approximately the same categories as above. (In fact 6,340,000 were insured in April 1952.) Contributions equal to 1% of the wage or salary are contributed each by the employer, the employee and the State. The State also bears the cost of administration.

60% of the last wage (but with a maximum in 1951 of 9,000 *yen*) is paid for six months on unemployment.

4. *Workmen's Accident Compensation Insurance*. Implemented in 1947. Compulsory for the same classes of worker as (1) with some additions. (7,814,000 were insured in March 1952.) Contributions, paid by the employer, are graded according to the accident rate of the industry and of the individual firm. Medical treatment, sickness allowances, disablement pensions, funeral grants (two months' pay) and lump sum compensation for dependants (1,000 days' pay for death) are provided.

5. *National Health Insurance Scheme*. Permissive legislation passed in 1938 allowed local authorities or friendly societies to organize Health Insurance Schemes. (In practice the former predominate. In July 1950 approximately half of local authorities had started such a scheme, but this included only 28% of the city administrations. 5,162,000 households paid contributions covering 24 m. out of the total 83 m. population.) Contributions are levied directly or as part of local taxes. The State contributes administrative expenses. Medical treatment at reduced fees, and funeral, maternity and death benefits on approximately the same scale as (1) are provided. No such scheme was operated by the borough to which Shitayama-cho belonged.

In addition there is a special security scheme for seamen and a special pensions scheme for government employees.

Sources

For details of legislation:

Ministry of Welfare, *Collection of Laws under the Jurisdiction of the Ministry of Welfare*, 1951, pp. 274–331.
Ministry of Labour, *Japan Labour Code*, 1952, pp. 297–345, 400–45.

For details of contributions and benefits:

Shakai Hoshoo Shingikai, *Shakai Hoshoo Seido ni kansuru Kankoku oyobi Shiryoo*, 1950, pp. 49–50, 432–4.

For details of current operation:

Jiji Tsuushinsha: *Jiji Nenkan, 1953*, pp. 272–4.

Some Documents concerning the teaching of Social Studies

A. THE MINISTRY OF EDUCATION'S OUTLINE COURSE OF STUDY

THE 1951 edition of the Social-Studies Outline for primary schools begins with a general introduction setting out main principles. The aim is to 'give the children a deep and fair appreciation of society, and by making them understand their own position in it enable them to make a proper adjustment to their own society and contribute to its progress'. The method of teaching is not 'to give them a variety of disconnected information concerning society, regardless of their needs and interests', but to 'take up real problems which concern the children in their own lives and encourage them to investigate them on their own initiative'. Small problems can be expanded in their implications to involve all the disciplines of ethics, political science, economics, sociology, geography, history. Whereas in the old teaching of history and geography excessive emphasis was laid on the memorization of facts, the present aim is to cultivate 'the ability to look at problems from a historical or from a geographical point of view. . . . To see the geographical or the historical factors involved in actual problems.'

It then proceeds to a more detailed general statement of the objectives of the social-studies course.[1]

1. To give an understanding of the importance of one's own and other people's personality and individuality, and to foster an independent attitude to life.

2. Concerning such social groups as the family, the school, the local community, and the nation, to give an understanding of the nature of relations between individuals within the group, between the group and the individual, and between group and group, and to foster the attitudes and abilities which will promote individual adaptation to and the improvement of group life.

3. To give an understanding concerning the mutual inter-relations between such social functions as production, consumption, transport and communications, insurance of life and property, welfare facilities, education, culture and politics, concerning the operation of

407

these functions and their meaning for human life. And to foster the attitudes and abilities which promote active participation in co-operative social activity.

4. To give an understanding of the close relationship between human life and the natural environment, and to foster the attitudes and abilities which promote adaptation to the natural environment and its effective use.

5. To give an understanding of the nature and the development of social institutions, facilities and customs, and to foster the attitudes and abilities which promote adaptation to them and their improvement.

This is followed by an outline of the objectives of each year's course. Some examples may be given.

For the first year (age six), the ideas to be got across are listed as follows:

Adults all have some work to do.

Members of the family all have some function.

Parents are always concerned with the happiness of their children.

Our basic needs for clothes and food and shelter are provided in the home.

If we are kind to each other, then we can all be happy.

If rules are carefully obeyed, games are more enjoyable.

If we are careful to keep things tidy, and to decorate the home and the school, they become pleasant places.

The home and the school have special facilities for preserving health and safety.

A healthy body means a happy life.

People use all sorts of means of transport for travel and for carrying goods.

In order to live with other people it is necessary to be punctual.

In order to live with other people it is necessary not to make a nuisance of oneself to others.

For the fifth year (age 10) the ideas to be got across are as follows:

The development of industry is largely determined by the natural conditions of climate, topography and resources.

Industrial methods have vastly improved with the progress of science. The use of material resources has improved with the development of industry.

With the development of industry, forms of food, housing and clothing have changed.

As the use of natural resources improves, there is a danger that these resources might be wasted or exhausted.

The greater the division of labour, the more efficient life becomes. The greater the division of labour, the greater the mutual dependence of individuals in society and hence the greater one's responsibility to one's fellows.

The development of machine industry owes a great deal to new sources of power.

By the development of machine industry, men have come to have sufficient margin to concern themselves with welfare, recreation and cultural activities.

Mass production should contribute to the general welfare.

Machines help to preserve life and property, but at the same time can sometimes damage them.

It is desirable to use science to promote human happiness.

The development of industry tends to lead to the concentration of population.

Methods of trade change with social development.

The greater the scarcity of goods, the greater the necessity to make some adjustments between production and consumption.

The routes by which products reach the consumer are an important factor in determining their price.

It is necessary to plan one's personal expenditure.

When purchasing it is important to examine carefully before choosing.

The development of commerce and industry has kept in step with the development of transport.

The development of commerce and industry is often stimulated by special local conditions.

Unless people take care not to do things which they cannot thoroughly approve of, a good society is impossible.

Examples of 'grouping themes' for dealing with the above are suggested as follows:

The production of goods necessary for daily life.
From hand-craft production to machine production.
The development of commerce and consumption.

The following is an extract from the Japanese History section of the Outline Study Course for high schools (ages 15–17).[2] Japanese history was beginning to be taught as a separate division of the Social Studies course from 1950 onwards. This extract gives a good indication of the general interpretative and value bias of the authors.

Theme No. 3

'In what sort of society did the status system and master-servant relations develop?'

Summary

In the development of social life accompanying human progress there are many points of similarity throughout the world. Many countries, between an ancient society and a modern society have passed through a period of feudal society. In Japan, too, before the development of modern society there existed the feudal system in which the samurai ruled and in which the status system and master-servant relationships were established. Moreover, the period lasted so long that even today when we have reached the age of democracy feudal customs and outlook are still deeply rooted and offer a fundamental obstacle to complete modernization.

Content, and Examples of Study Methods

I. Are there not still today remnants of a 'status system' and 'master-servant relationships'?

1. Discuss what 'status system' means.

2. Find examples in our own surroundings of remnants of the 'status system' and 'master-servant relationships' and study how and when they arose.

II. What do 'feudal' and 'feudalism' mean?

1. Find out from dictionaries and by etymological study of the word *hooken* and of the English word 'feudalism'.

2. Consider two or three examples of things that today are popularly called 'feudal' and discuss their nature.

3. Read a scene from a Kabuki play such as Sendai-hagi or Terakoya and discuss the feudal elements in it.

III. By what forces was feudal society established, and what kind of lives did people lead in feudal society?

1. How did the samurai class develop and improve its social position?

(*a*) Make a list of the factors which made the rise of the samurai historically inevitable and discuss each one.

(*b*) Looking through Chinese history, pick out similar facts, and write an essay on the common features.

(*c*) Study the relations between the system of land tenure and the increasing power of the samurai.

2. How did the samurai succeed in wresting power from the aristocrats?

(*a*) Discuss the character of Minamoto Yoritomo.

(*b*) Draw maps and diagrams showing the political and geographical situation of Kamakura.

(*c*) Discuss whether the organization of the Kamakura government was suited to the internal condition of the country at the time.

The outline proceeds to discuss particular phases of the history of the feudal period on the lines of the last section.

B. COMMENT ON TRENDS IN SOCIAL STUDIES TEACHING

The following are extracts from an article in the *Asahi* of 29 July 1952 under the heading 'Is History Teaching to Swing to the Right?'

'This spring a manuscript for a text-book of Japanese History for use in the High School Social Studies Course, when sent to the Ministry of Education for approval (a legal necessity before it can be used in schools), received criticisms from a member of the Examining Committee of which the following are examples.

'In discussing relations between China and Japan in the fifth century, the word "tribute" is used. The examiner's remark is that this is undesirable since it will give the pupils an impression of inferior servility.

'Again, in discussing the marriage system of ancient Japanese society the manuscript says, "The status of women was considerably higher than in later times. There was the custom of polygamy, but the other wives besides the chief wife were still treated as wives, and were not the despised 'concubines' of later times." The comment is "undesirable to teach children about concubines".

'In discussing the family system of Tokugawa times the manuscript reads, "The ideal of male superiority was all-pervasive. It was not thought in the least wrong for a man to have concubines, but the wife was expected to give loyal service to a single husband. Although it was impossible for the wife to demand divorce, the husband could arbitrarily 'send away' his wife at any time. And not only the husband; the wife could be sent away by the arbitrary decision of the mother-in-law, too." The comment is that this description is overloaded with malicious hostility towards the Japanese family system.

'Discussing the impoverishment of the farmers at the end of the Tokugawa period, the text runs. "The burden on the farmers became gradually heavier, and in extreme cases 80% of the crop had to be paid in feudal dues. . . . The farmers, oppressed by the inhuman exactions of the feudal lords and the greed of moneylenders, were at last forced to the illegal methods of flight and finally revolt. At least 1,300 instances of peasant revolts are known to have occurred in the Tokugawa period." The comment is that the treatment appears to approve of illegal action.

'The fairly large section on the Pacific War and the post-war period has the comment that this may well be omitted since this lies well within the range of the pupils' own experience.

'Just imagine the sort of Japanese history this member of the Examining Committee would like to teach. All facts such as the sending of tribute to China which might injure the prestige of "The Great Japanese Empire" are to be omitted. Thus the pupils will be spared any sense of "inferior servility" and their hearts will warm with "pride in their Fatherland". The Japanese family system will be praised as a "noble moral custom" and it will be tabooed to refer to the contradictions of the feudalism which, to our misfortune, still persists in our family institutions today. The farmers of the feudal period led happy and contented lives. . . .

'Is this the first sign that all our efforts since 1946 to bring about a fundamental change in the teaching of history in schools is going to be all in vain, and that history teaching is to go back to its pre-war form? I trust that my fears will prove unfounded.'

At the end of 1953 a review of the first six years of Social Studies teaching was published by a group of left-wing educationalists.[3] Their intention, at a time when the conservative government, alarmed at what it considered dangerously radical tendencies in the educational world, was taking steps to restrict by Act of Parliament the activities of the extreme left-wing Teachers' Union and also discussing the possibilities of a regrouping of the Social Studies course, is obvious from the first paragraph of the preface.

'The Government's suggestion that the Social-Studies course should be reconstructed appears to us to conceal extremely dangerous intentions. The arguments that history and geography should be taught more systematically, and that moral education should be carried out in a more positive manner have a certain justice as far as they go, but the crux of the matter lies in the motives inspiring these arguments. The aim of the proponents of reconstruction does not lie in the direction of the firm establishment of individual rights and freedoms in order to promote individual happiness. The aim, on the contrary, is once more to cover up all real problems in the enveloping concept of the "State". It is not a Social-Studies course that they want, but a State-Studies course, something on the lines of the war-time Citizens' Course. These are nothing more nor less than the educational ideals of Fascism' (p. 1).

The general tone of the book is one of confidence that they can maintain their point. But they themselves are not satisfied with the teaching of social studies hitherto. One author claims for the course that,

'For the first time in the history of Japanese education, children have been brought, not merely to the knowledge, but also to the realization and consciousness, of themselves as active participants in society . . . the consciousness that within whatever social group they belong to they, as individuals, have the right to receive respect as individual personalities, and at the same time a responsibility for the existence and maintenance of the group proportionate to that respect.'

He admits, as a defect, that the design of the course 'demands too much of the ability and the effort of the teacher'. He is inclined to discount the charge that it fails to impart systematic knowledge, but he finds its greatest defect in the lack of a 'problem-consciousness', the absence of an awareness of the historical and political problems which face modern Japan, and hence a lack of any clear focus (pp. 24–5).

Others claim that, largely as a result of Social-Studies teaching, children now express themselves freely, have developed independent initiative and a spirit of enquiry, and are better able to co-operate with each other (pp. 45–71). One author is more inclined to take seriously the charge that the course fails to impart necessary factual knowledge of history and geography—children know all about slavery and the manor system, but have no idea whether the Heian period comes after the Muromachi or before; they know all about the development of railways, but are unable to find prefectures on the map (pp. 36–8). The same author gives many instances of the lack of any focus or meaning in the investigations children are en-encouraged to make—he cites trips to a tram depot by children who set themselves the task of examining the transport system, but return with exact statistics of the number of pillars supporting the tram-depot roof, and one child found standing outside the school lava-tories on a cold day counting the number of visitors per hour. (The aim was to draw a graph showing the relation between the use of the lavatories and daily temperature, but the exact educational object of the exercise was not clear) (pp. 30–2). Others point out the embarrassed bewilderment of the teacher when children's investigations reveal tax evasions and black-market dealings in the village (pp. 31, 49).

But the basic problem of the inevitability of political bias overshadows the book, though neatly sidestepped in the one essay devoted to politics. Are children to be taught to accept the social system about which they learn, or is the aim to stimulate their 'problem consciousness', to encourage them to see injustices and deficiencies? There is no doubt that the authors of this book stand by the latter aim. (One of them would reject the whole 'via-the-solution-of-problems-in-the-pupils'-own-lives' approach implicit in the Ministry of Education's Course of Study Outline, on the ground that it is too constricting for adequate arousal of 'problem consciousness' (p. 302).) But despite the fact that the authors represent the dominant stream of thought in the non-official educational world (three of them are professors at the ex-Imperial Tokyo University) and despite the recent flood of publications by young left-wing primary school teachers of essays by their pupils which leave no doubt about the attitudes communicated in the classroom, and despite the extreme left-wing leadership of the Teachers' Union, one may still doubt whether, taking Japan as a whole, the present conservative Government has a great deal to worry about.

Ward Association Annual General Meeting

THE following account of the Ward Association's General Meeting will be more intelligible if some description is given of the personalities principally involved. There were fourteen men who took an active part in the affairs of the Association, twelve who were 'in', and two who were 'out' of the leadership circle.

Sakura, the President of the Ward Association, was also President of the local primary school P.T.A. and owner of a small factory. (For his success story, see p. 197.) He had during the war been the leader of the 'new group' whose factional strife with the 'old group' had led to the election of a neutral President. With the death of the leader of the 'old group' Sakura became the obvious choice. He was the second wealthiest man in the ward and owner of a small car.

Sakura was not greatly respected in the ward; one of the chief things held against him was that on the occasion when his chimney started a fire, he was 'not man enough' to come out and apologize. On the other hand, he was thought to be open in his dealings; he was not overbearing and dictatorial in manner as some of the other aspirants to leadership might have been in his position; his slight diffidence made him approachable and few people actively disliked him.

The Vice-President, Minagawa, was a farmer's son from West Japan, aged 54, a High School graduate employed in an advertising agency. He was universally liked, and his infectious enjoyment at the ward festival communicated itself to others and added to the gaiety of the occasion. He took a great and self-confessed pleasure in organizing things, and was the real administrator of the Association.

Next in importance came two of the 'managers' (*kanji*), Kataoka, aged 44, an ambitious owner of a small factory, a middle-school graduate who was disliked for his pomposity, but was nevertheless forceful enough to have a great deal of influence at meetings where he was easily the most fluent speaker and the most adept at manipulating the ceremonial phraseology required for public occasions. He was an official of the C.P.C.T.A., of the middle-school P.T.A., and of the Worshippers' Association. Nakazawa, aged 56, was an ex-special-branch (thought control) police officer and now official of a trading firm, somewhat better liked in the ward than Kataoka, but wordy and less efficient at meetings. He was a co-opted 'advisor' of the primary school P.T.A. although he had no children at the school.

At meetings of the ward leaders at the President's house, Kataoka and Nakazawa each deferred to the other, though, after ritual exchanges ('Please! Please!'—'No! Please! Please!'—'No, you come here. It all amounts to the same thing') it was generally the former who eventually took the upper seat, sometimes above Minagawa, the Vice-President.

Next came a third 'manager', Okazaki, aged 37, a middle-school graduate and salesman. He was a vigorous organizer who made a speciality of what he called *rikurieeshon* (recreation), and was chairman of the Out-door Activities Section of the P.T.A. At meetings of the ward leaders he was fertile in suggestions and did not hesitate to express his opinions in deference to his elders. At the general meetings he appeared more impetuously inclined to over-ride opposition than the other more careful leaders and had to be restrained by the President. He made no attempt to conceal his status as 'Sakura's man'. When asked whom he was supporting for the Borough Council elections, he mentioned a candidate and explained that he was a 'good friend of Sakura's'.

These five constituted an inner circle of the 'in' group who appeared to consult each other in all matters. It was their names which appeared as 'supporters' on the election notices of the candidate for the Borough Council elections whom the ward leaders decided to support conjointly with a neighbouring ward. The remaining seven 'ins', who generally appeared at meetings of the ward leaders and of whom no-one appeared to know for certain who were 'managers' and who were not, were quiet non-entities who played little effective part in the discussions. Kobata, the 59-year-old greengrocer, and Kanazawa, a 65-year-old pottery decorator, were well-liked old residents both of whom had a good knowledge of traditional customs and came into their own during the preparations for the festival celebrations. Mikimoto and Tomita, the Treasurer and Assistant Treasurer, were younger men (aged 37 and 32 respectively), the one a watch repairer and the other an office worker, who faithfully carried out their clerical duties, but did nothing on their own initiative. Fukakusu and Makimura were also old residents (aged 59 and 45 respectively) who had lived most of their lives in the ward and had their businesses there, the first as a stationer, the second as the keeper of a spaghetti restaurant. Finally, Izumi, a talkative and pompous officer worker, aged 47, was co-opted as 'manager' after this general meeting at which he showed himself to be a 'constructive' critic, lacking the fundamental hostility of the real opposition and acting as a buffer between the latter and the leaders.

The opposition consisted of two younger men, Okazaki, aged 31, an office worker and younger brother (in a separate household) of the Okazaki of the 'in' group mentioned above and of a similar impetuous disposition, and Sunagawa, aged 42, also an office worker and the son of a former ward President. Both of these had been active organizers of the Youth Culture Society who had enjoyed a great sense of self-importance in 1946–7 and resented their eclipse by the older leaders of the re-emergent Ward Association. Neither had much following in the ward, not even among the young unmarried men, most of whom they had alienated by their overbearing leadership of the Youth Culture Society. Both were thought generally in the ward to be over-ambitious, and Sunagawa was also suspected of sharp practice in connection with a friendly society he had organized soon after the war. These two were permanently excluded from the counsels of the *yuuryokusha* because of their argumentative 'enthusiasm' (in its old pejorative sense) and their overt hostility which, in turn, their exclusion did much to augment. Their chief sin was that they were disrupters of the 'harmony' and unanimity which was everyone's ideal. They caused unpleasantness in that they used the obstructive tactics of demanding conformity with those rules (of fair play, democratic procedure, open discussion, and so on) to which lip-service was paid but which were, by mutual agreement, ignored.

FIRST MEETING

The annual general meeting was called for May 25th to consider the financial report for the year ended March 31st and the budget for the current year, and to elect officers. Twenty-nine people were present, the leaders sitting in the front, while of the remainder (mostly *tonari-gumi* chiefs) the women sat at the back. Only two women said anything during the whole course of the discussions and that was to express approval of one of the leader's suggestions in a low voice.

The meeting began an hour late. At the advertised time the only person present was the Youth Culture Association leader, Okazaki, who had copied the financial statement from the circulating notice board and came with the intention of raising objections.

(In what follows the younger Okazaki will be distinguished from his elder brother, a member of the inner circle of leaders, as Okazaki (anti) and Okazaki (pro) respectively.)

The discussion which resulted from Okazaki (anti)'s objections to the expenditure on gifts to the police, borough office, fire brigade etc., was summarized on p. 277. The discussion was finally closed when one of the leaders suggested that these objections properly belonged to a discussion of the current year's budget and suggested that the report be accepted. The President then asked 'Is everyone agreed that we accept this report?' There were shouts of 'Agreed' (*Igi-nashi*) followed by general clapping. What follows is summarized from notes taken at the meeting.

SAKURA (*President*): Well, we will go on to this year's budget. Properly this should be done by the newly elected officials, but for the sake of convenience we will get it over with now. Would the Treasurer please read the budget out. (*This was done.*) We will now go through the items individually. Perhaps Mr. Minagawa (Vice-President) would explain.

MINAGAWA: First of all, income 150,000 *yen*. This is slightly more than last year. Hitherto dues have been 'from 20 *yen* upwards' a month, and as a result there have been considerable 'ups and downs' and there have been complaints from some people to the effect that they have been asked to give too much compared with others. We decided this year to ask for from 30 *yen* upwards, though of course there is no objection—indeed it would be desirable—for the *tonari-gumi* Chief, at his or her discretion, to reduce that amount in some cases if he saw fit.

OKAZAKI (*anti*): Is this not really rather unreal. Suppose that the newly elected officers decided that a lot of the expenses were unnecessary, then there would be no need to collect 30 *yen* a head. We ought really to re-elect officials first.

There followed some sharp exchanges between Okazaki (anti) Okazaki (pro), Nakazawa, Kataoka and Minagawa. If the new officers did decide to cut down expenses, who would object? You couldn't cut down expenses anyway—the whole idea of the Association was that it should act instead of individuals in the matter of police contributions, etc. If you were going to reduce its expenses you might as well not have an Association. The discussion was getting heated when:

SAKURA: Well, as I said before, properly speaking officers should be elected first and if there is a wish that that should be done then we will. We will alter the agenda.

OKAZAKI (*anti*): That would be the democratic way.

NAKAZAWA: So it might be, but you can't go simply on theory (*riron*). You've got to consider the usual practice. You will find that in 80–90% of cases it is the practice for the budget to be decided first.

MINAGAWA: Suppose we put it to the vote.

SAKURA: No, we will do it the proper way. First of all we have to elect a Presiding Officer to supervise the elections.

OKAZAKI (*pro*): I propose Mr. Minagawa.

MINAGAWA: No, Mr. Kataoka.

KATAOKA: No, you.

TWO OTHERS: Mr. Minagawa.

SAKURA: Well, shall we ask Mr. Minagawa? (*Applause.*)

MINAGAWA (*taking the seat at the table*): We will now come to the business of electing officers. Now, what would be the best way of going about this?

OKAZAKI (*anti*): I have a proposal. There are very few people here tonight. The circulating notice boards did not go round very well and many people do not know about the meeting. I think it would be better if we asked the *tonari-gumi* chiefs to make simple little boxes and get everybody in their *tonari-gumi* to make anonymous votes for the President and Vice-President. This would be the democratic way.

KATAOKA: It seems to be proposed that we get the *tonari-gumi* chiefs to collect anonymous votes. I shouldn't think this extra trouble and labour is necessary. The chiefs of each *tonari-gumi* are here tonight and I think we can safely say that they represent the opinion of their *tonari-gumi*. It would be simplest if the *tonari-gumi* chiefs were appointed as an Electoral Committee and got together to decide on the new President and Vice-President.

MINAGAWA: Well, we have two proposals. Which shall we take?

NAKAZAWA: The first would cause a great deal of trouble and we have never done it before. As Mr. Kataoka says . . .

MINAGAWA: What do other people think?

OKAZAKI (*pro*): I support Mr. Kataoka.

ONE VOICE AT THE BACK: Hear! Hear!

MINAGAWA (looking at Okazaki (anti)): Well the majority seem to favour Mr. Kataoka's opinion, so if it is all right, I think we will do it that way.

It was while the *tonari-gumi* chiefs were gathering at the other end of the room that sharp words were exchanged between the two Okazakis, the elder accusing the dissident younger of being 'unco-operative'. One of the women present observing this said to her neighbour in criticism of the censure on Okazaki (anti), 'But it's best to speak your mind, isn't it? Opinions are opinions after all.' Nakazawa who was sitting nearby turned and said, 'Perhaps so, but not when it's carried to the point of being "unco-operative".'

Okazaki (pro) joined the *tonari-gumi* chiefs. Although not a chief himself, his pretext was that the chief of his own *tonari-gumi* was not present. He appeared to be doing all the talking. Sakura went over to them and said that he intended to refuse re-election. Nevertheless, in a very short time they had returned and Okazaki announced that they recommended Sakura as President and Minagawa as Vice-President.

Sakura refused fairly firmly. Okazaki (pro) said that it was the voice of the ward and there was no one else. Sakura said he thought new blood was necessary and the Association tended to get into a groove; in any case he was very busy these days. Minagawa also supported the idea that officers should be renewed every year.

Okazaki (pro) refused to take no for an answer. Kataoka and Nakazawa joined in.

Minagawa suggested that the Electoral Committee should go back and reconsider. Sakura suggested a paper ballot. Okazaki (pro) reluctantly agreed.

They then got together and Okazaki (pro) wrote down orally expressed votes on a piece of paper. When he had finished with the *tonari-gumi* chiefs Minagawa suggested, 'Can we ask everybody except the officials (*kambu*)—the "ordinary ladies and gentlemen" (*ippan no kata*) too.' The people excluded by this designation *kambu* (literally 'staff') were the *yuuryokusha* above, whether they were officially 'managers' or not.

The result was the same. Sakura and Minagawa. Sakura again refused firmly. He didn't mind being Vice-President. The best person for President would be O (the gentle wartime compromise President). He was in better health these days and he was an excellent man. They should send a deputation to him.

Okazaki (pro) was finally persuaded by Sakura's firmness that this was no mere polite diffidence. 'Well, if Mr. Sakura won't do it, it is either Mr. Kataoka or Mr. Minagawa.'

KATAOKA (*switching from his tailor-squat to a formal position on his knees*): May I be permitted to excuse myself. The President has to be a man who is popular and inspires confidence. On these counts I am 'zero'. I would like to decline.

MINAGAWA: But this is nonsense. I have always from the beginning been in favour of changing officers every year.

Nakazawa then suggested that perhaps the best thing to do would be to adjourn the meeting, meet again in a week's time, try to get more people to come, get the *tonari-gumi* chiefs to sound out opinion in their group, and perhaps sound out O in the meantime. This was eventually agreed on.

After the end of the meeting, Okazaki (pro) said, 'What a mess, It was all supposed to go so smoothly, too.'

SECOND MEETING

By the time of the second meeting, eighteen days later, Sakura had been prevailed on to accept the Presidency. (Probably because the *yuuryokusha* could not agree among themselves to support either Kataoka or Minagawa). This time there were thirty-six people present. Okazaki (anti) was this time absent, but was replaced by the opposition's second string, Sunagawa. The discussion was this time tape-recorded, and the parts in direct speech are verbatim translations. The full flavour of the ceremonial and respect language unfortunately cannot be conveyed in translation.

Sakura opened the meeting by asking for everyone's consent for the tape-recording and asking for 'plenty of clapping'. He then handed over to Minagawa who had been appointed Presiding Officer for the elections when the previous meeting had been adjourned.

MINAGAWA: We now come to the business of election of officers. I think that first we should appoint a Presiding Officer. Now, what, I wonder, would be the most desirable method to adopt? May I have suggestions?

NAKAZAWA: I propose that he should be nominated by the Chairman.

MINAGAWA: The Chairman's nomination is suggested. How would that be?

THREE VOICES: Agreed!

MINAGAWA: In that case I will ask Mr. Kataoka to be Presiding Officer. (*Applause.*)

KATAOKA (*moving to the table*): Ladies and Gentlemen (literally 'Everybody!') Under your nomination I have been appointed to the weighty office of Presiding Officer. As you know, as is prescribed in the rules, it is an appointment which ceases as soon as the officers are elected. Meanwhile, as Presiding Officer, I would like to ask for your co-operation and attention.

Our business is to elect officers, and the first question is the method to be adopted. For instance, we could appoint an Electoral or a Selection Committee, or there are various methods we could adopt. We will decide in accordance with the general wish. Can I have suggestions, please.

SUNAGAWA: Mr. Presiding Officer!

KATAOKA: Yes.

SUNAGAWA: May I ask, please, under what article of the constitution this meeting was called tonight?

Here Kataoka asked that the recording should be stopped while he explained that when the Association was restarted it was agreed that in the unsettled political conditions of the day it would be preferable not to commit the Association to any formal rules, but to settle everything 'in an amicable way' (*nagoyaka ni*) at the general meetings. After the Peace Treaty they hoped to arrive at some settled constitution. Sunagawa, after repeating that every association he had ever been in had rules, contented himself with expressing the hope that a constitution would soon be drafted. The recording was then resumed with Kataoka's repeated request for suggestions as to the procedure for electing officers.

NAKAZAWA: I suggest that we appoint an Electoral Committee.

SUNAGAWA: Another point I'm afraid.

KATAOKA: Yes? Please.

SUNAGAWA: Well, it seems to me, looking round, that there aren't many people here tonight, and I would think, instead of having an Electoral Committee or anything like that, it would be better, as Mr. Kataoka said just now, for everybody to join in and decide 'amicably' together.

KATAOKA: Everybody?

SUNAGAWA: Everybody present tonight.

KATAOKA: It seems a small number, but if everybody, everybody, er . . . That is to say if the whole meeting were to become an Electoral Committee, I'm not sure how that would work.

Well, I put it to the meeting. First we have the suggestion that we should appoint an Electoral Committee to elect officers, and secondly that everybody, that is to say . . .

SUNAGAWA: By everybody, I mean by ballot.

KATAOKA: By ballot. Secondly there is the suggestion that it is better to hold a ballot. Now, which shall we make it?

OKAZAKI: I'm for the Electoral Committee. (*Short silence.*)

OKAZAKI: Well, mmmm, how would it be if we took a resolution on it?

KATAOKA: All right. We have then, on the agenda, two proposals, for election by ballot or for election by an Electoral Committee. Is it agreed that we take a vote on the matter? I suggest that we take the majority decision.

A WOMAN TONARI-GUMI CHIEF: Excellent.

The voting, by a show of hands, was nineteen for an Electoral Committee and seven for a popular vote. Ten abstained.

KATAOKA: Well, it is decided that we appoint an Electoral Committee. The next question is the appointment of the Committee, the numbers, composition. . . . Mmmm. What would be the best way of going about it—the appointment of the Electoral Committee?

FUKAKUSU: I think the Presiding Officer's nomination would be good enough.

KATAOKA: The suggestion is the Presiding Officer's nomination. How would that be?

FOUR VOICES FROM THE FRONT: Agreed! Agreed!

KATAOKA: Right! Presiding Officer's nomination it is. The next question is the size of the Committee, about how many, exactly how should we proceed?

OKAZAKI: About ten people I would think.

KATAOKA: About ten. Would that meet with approval?

VOICES: Excellent; Agreed!

KATAOKA: No other suggestions? An Electoral Committee of about ten.

VOICES: Agreed! Agreed!

KATAOKA: It appears that there are no objections, so we will make it about ten members. Now, are these ten to be chosen by nomination? Ummmm, how should we proceed, I mean the selection of the committee?

NAKAZAWA: Yes, by nomination.

KATAOKA: Would the Presiding Officer's nomination meet with approval?

FUKAKUSU: That's what we said just now.

KATAOKA: The Presiding Officer's nomination it is. However, the numbers and the . . .

SAKURA: Just a moment. The question of the ten members. Ummm, I think if we go by the Presiding Officer's nomination there's a danger that the Committee might be somewhat biased. The ten people, er, that is, if we had one person from each *tonari-gumi* it would be somewhat larger of course: eighteen would it be, or nineteen?

NAKAZAWA: That is a bit too many isn't it?

SAKURA: I think that would be better.

NAKAZAWA: Judging by the way it generally goes, if we had one person from each *tonari-gumi*, that is to say, nineteen people, these nineteen people—I mean it always seem a bit too large. I would think personally that about ten would be the right number. . . .

SAKURA: Yes, ideally, about ten is just right I suppose, but . . .

NAKAZAWA: Of course, as far as nomination goes . . .

KATAOKA: In that case then, if you will permit me, I will call the roll of the *tonari-gumi* chiefs.

It was found that twelve of the nineteen *tonari-gumi* chiefs were present. They gathered at the other end of the room and were joined by Okazaki who this time had no right to be there since the chief of his own *tonari-gumi* was present. He suggested that they should give the same decision as last time just to see what happened. The oldest male was automatically appointed spokesman and soon returned to announce that Sakura was elected President and Minagawa Vice-President. Kataoka, announcing that the Treasurers, Managers and Auditors were to be appointed by the President, withdrew to make way for Sakura who took over the table amidst general applause.

SAKURA: Well, as I have several times said, I would rather have declined the honour. . . . I'm afraid that I can be of little service. . . . However, for one more term with everybody's kind co-operation . . . I put myself at your disposal. (*Bow.*)

The meeting was about to move into consideration of the budget when Kataoka said: 'One moment, I have an objection.' (This caused laughter, the very idea of one of the *yuuryokusha* having an 'objection' struck everyone as incongruous.) The suggestion was that the other officers should be nominated by the President before proceeding with the next business. Sakura replied that it would be difficult to decide so soon. He asked the Treasurer and Assistant Treasurer to continue in office. As for the 'auditors' and 'managers' (it was never clear whether *kanji* (manager) was being used as an abbreviation of *kaikei-kanji* (auditor) or as a separate office. The question was raised again at the end of the meeting but remained as obscure after the explanation as before it) he would like to increase their numbers this year and would be glad to have more time to discuss the matter with the Vice-President and the Treasurers. This was agreed to. The next year's budget was then read.

SAKURA: Now, if there are any questions, we'd be glad to have them.

IZUMI: One hears a lot about health measures these days. Is the amount put down for it here enough? What sort of things will it cover?

The Treasurer then detailed the previous year's expenditure—rubbish disposal and the provision of tea and cakes for the temporary vaccination centre. Izumi went on to describe an article he had just been reading in a weekly paper about fly-less villages, rat-less villages, mosquitoe-less villages and so on. If villagers could do this sort of thing, surely Shitayama-cho could show a little more initiative in these matters. Could not disinfectant and insecticides be purchased? When he was told by Sakura that it was an excellent idea, but the limited nature of the budget forbade this, he replied that, as it had said in the article, lack of funds was constantly used as an excuse for inadequate hygiene measures and he was sure that no-one would begrudge giving a little extra in membership fees. After all, it would be cheaper in the long run. No doctor would provide a cure for 20 or 30 *yen* if you actually became ill. The discussion revolved around these general arguments until:

SUNAGAWA: Really, when you say that there is not enough money . . . Here, in the next part of the budget we have membership fees for the Crime Prevention and Traffic Co-operation Association, and the Mothers' Society and things of that sort. Wouldn't it be possible to cut down these amounts and use the money for the sort of thing Mr. Izumi has been talking about, things that people in the ward will directly receive the benefit of? Is there no possibility of cutting down these amounts?

SAKURA: Well, just looking at the budget it might appear that way; of course we had quite a lot of discussion about that at the last meeting.

After some further sparring during which Sunagawa's main line of argument was that the time had come for the Association to pass from its simple contribution-collecting phase to a more positive administrative phase, and Nakazawa, as a palliative red-herring, suggested that they might get the C.P.T.C.A. to increase its 'kick-back' to the ward for street-lighting, Sakura eventually said:

SAKURA: Of course, if it is the general opinion . . . This Fire Prevention Co-operation Association charge, for instance. . . . If it is the general opinion that this should not be included we can take it out—omit it altogether. . . . We can take out the Borough District Office expenses, too, and the same applies to the Crime Prevention

Association. On the other hand, it would mean that we would go round to everyone and ask for contributions.

SUNAGAWA: But that wouldn't, of course, be compulsory. It would be left to each individual to give or not.

SAKURA: Of course.

The interchange between Sunagawa and Sakura continued on these lines, Sakura saying that there would be no objection to omitting these items from the budget altogether and collecting individually if that was the general wish, and Sunagawa repeating his point that it would be better to leave these contributions to individual collection and the time had come for more money to be spent on things that were of greater importance to the people of the ward. Sunagawa then asked if it was necessary even individually to pay this money to the police, etc. Sakura said there was no compulsion about it: 'If you were to say you didn't intend to pay, well, I suppose that would be that.'

NAKAZAWA: No, I disagree. The gentleman over there—Mr. Sunagawa is it? You know, you say that there's no reason to give if it can be avoided, or for emotional reasons you personally don't want to give, but we are all—if you consider that nobody is living all by himself. And when other people are doing this (i.e. presumably, making gifts to the police, etc.) you yourself, overtly or otherwise, are in some way receiving the benefits. If you realize this I think you will feel that you ought to take some of the burden yourself. And if you give in that spirit . . . I'm not talking about going beyond the law; that, I think, is wrong, but in accordance with means each should take his share. I think that is right and proper. And to talk of cutting this right out of the budget . . .

SUNAGAWA: That's not what I'm saying.

NAKAZAWA: If you cut it out completely.

SUNAGAWA: I'm not saying that it should be cut out completely. I'm suggesting that some of the money from these items should be transferred to more necessary things. That was what I . . .

NAKAZAWA: Oh? Not to cut them out completely. But I thought just now the Chairman said, or perhaps he was putting the extreme case, that we could cut it out completely.

SAKURA: No, I said that if that was the general opinion we could . . . (*Several people began talking at once.*)

IZUMI: May I ask about this 60,000 *yen*. (The total sent out of the ward in gifts.) How much does that come to per household per month?

SAKURA: Well, it's about a third of the budget, so I suppose about 10 *yen*.

IZUMI: In which case, if contributions were collected individually, I don't suppose we could get away with 10 *yen* for all three.

SAKURA: I should think that's about what it comes to.

NAKAZAWA: It's about the minimum limit.

IZUMI: In which case it comes much cheaper to do it in one lump than to have individual contributions, doesn't it—the actual burden, I mean.

SAKURA: Well, I would think so.

SUNAGAWA: But, to come back to what Mr. Izumi was talking about earlier on. If we leave this as it is and do try to, say, increase expenditure on hygiene or install more street lights, it will mean that it's impossible to do it without putting up the membership fees. But at the present time—I mean, the Peace Treaty is due soon, and Japan lost the war—as a defeated nation I think we ought to be as economical as possible and cut down. . . .

SAKURA: But at the present time, take, for instance, hygiene. I agree that it's very important, but as far as the ward's concerned, even if we spent, say, 10,000 *yen* or something, we couldn't do all that amount of work with it, and if you really made it up to a considerable sum . . .

SUNAGAWA: If the rest of the budget is left as it is, then the membership fees would have to be pretty big or you would never catch up with it.

OKAZAKI: As far as I can see, what Mr. Sunagawa and Mr. Izumi are saying is that we should try and reduce as far as possible the amount that goes out of the ward and use as much money as possible within the ward so as to improve, to enrich, you might say, the lives of the people of the ward. Isn't that it?

?: Yes, that's right.

OKAZAKI: Well, if in the future, the Chairman and the Vice-President, I mean the President and the Vice-President, depending on how they run things . . . I mean, couldn't we accept this as it is?

SAKURA: As it is?

OKAZAKI: Yes, as it is.

SAKURA: And try to take account of the opinions which have been expressed tonight . . . Mmmm . . .

OKAZAKI: And then . . .

SAKURA: Well, it was suggested that the C.P.T.C.A. contribution could be reduced. Well, I think we could cut that down a bit.

IZUMI: Well, don't try to do the impossible. (*Laughter.*) If you can get them for their part to do a bit more positive work for us. I mean if we can ask our officers to do what they can so that, for instance, we can save money by getting the borough to do more in the way of hygiene work and so on . . .

The end of his speech was lost in clapping started by the *yuuryokusha* which indicated that the budget was accepted and approved.

SUNAGAWA: Before we go on, there's one thing I'd like to say about what Mr. Nakazawa said just how. I would just like to make my position clear, I wasn't speaking simply from a personal viewpoint. Mr. Nakazawa said that one mustn't take a 'blow you, Joe, I'm all right' sort of attitude and since there is all this *tsukiai* (gifts to the police, etc.) we must think of other people. But that wasn't in the least my intention. I was only saying that the ward as a whole, that the ward should be the basis and come first, and we should do what we can to cut down what is sent outside. That was all I was saying. I don't want to be misunderstood.

SAKURA: Yes, yes. I understand.

KATAOKA: I have—it's not really a question—a suggestion, rather.

SAKURA: What is it? I think we've had enough about the C.P.T.C.A. (*Laughter*.)

KATAOKA: No, no. This is going off into quite a different subject. It may seem somewhat peculiar, since I had the honour of being consulted when the budget was being prepared, that I should now start asking questions. It is rather a case of the host and the guest getting mixed up, but I've been thinking recently about the membership fees. Our budget for this year is 150,000 *yen*, which is some 28,000 *yen* more than last year. Well, in my opinion—at present the minimum is supposed to be 20 *yen*. In my opinion, rather than saying that we will make the minimum 30 *yen*, if some people can afford only 20 *yen*, well, let it be 20 *yen*; even if we cannot iron out the ups-and-downs, well that doesn't matter. We should leave it on a voluntary basis. It may be, if you will pardon my alluding to it, that for some people even 20 *yen* is a considerable burden, and some people could easily afford 100 *yen*. I would suggest that we shouldn't make it a strict rule that the minimum should be 30 *yen*, but let those who are willing to co-operate give just what they can; 20 *yen*, 10 *yen*, or 5 *yen* or whatever it is. I don't think we should assume that we must increase the income to 150,000 *yen*.

Kataoka then went on to speculate on the possible deficit that might arise, and to make the point that there was sufficient flexibility in the budget and sufficient probability of economies being possible for the situation to be safely left to the officials to deal with.

Sakura agreed and added that it would help for this sort of thing if some of the officials were renewed annually, and that he hoped this would happen in the future.

After a request from Sunagawa that the officials should make greater efforts to make economies by buying in the cheapest market, and a confused discussion started by a question from Izumi asking what were the exact titles of the officers of the Association, the meeting closed with general applause.

Forms and Occasions of *Butsudan* Worship

THE forms of worship at the family *butsudan* fall into three main categories.

1. Those rites which involve some kind of offering, most commonly of rice and water or tea. In some families such offerings are made before every meal, in others it seems to suffice if the offering is made once a day. In most cases, however, when particular delicacies are bought or received, some will be put in the *butsudan* before any of the family begins to eat it. It is enough if one member of the household performs these rites; they would not be repeated by several individuals successively.

2. Rites which might be performed by any number of people in quick succession, which do not necessarily imply needs on the parts of the spirits. The most common ritual form is simply bowing with palms together at chest height in front of the *butsudan*. (Distinguished from the obeisance before the *kamidana* by the quiet placing together of the hands as opposed to the hand-clap preceding the bow before the *kamidana*.) Some rites, such as burning incense or reciting passages from Buddhist sutras are intermediate, some might think it natural for several people to perform them in quick succession, others might not.

3. So-called *hooji* ceremonies at which priests or other qualified persons intone prayers and passages from the sutras in the presence of the assembled family.

The first two types of worship are individual; only the third requires concerted action by the whole family. The occasions for worship are as follows:

1. The first two types of individual worship may be performed daily. In some cases it may be the regular duty of one member of the family—either the househead or his wife—to perform the offertory acts every morning. Even these acts of worship may, however, be confined to the special occasions which will be enumerated below.

2. *The Spring and Autumn Equinoxes*

The seven days centring in each equinox—*Higan* as the festival is called—were traditionally occasions for visits to family graves, for *hooji* ceremonies before the *butsudan* or at the family temple, for the baking of special cakes, and in some sects for special services at temples. The Meiji government finding everything grist for its mill, declared the days of the equinox public holidays entitled Spring (Autumn) Festival of the Imperial Ancestors (*Shunki* (*Shuuki*) *Koorei-sai*). On these days the Emperor worshipped his own ancestors with great ceremony, and school-children began their holiday with a reading at school of the Imperial Rescript on Education and with concerted bowing to the Emperor's portrait. In this way the traditional associations of the occasion with ancestor worship were associated with the nation and the Imperial Family in a way characteristic of the shrewd religious policy of the Meiji government. Since the end of the war and the enforced dissociation of national occasions and public holidays, these days have been rechristened with the neutral terms 'Spring Equinoctial Day' and 'Autumn Equinoctial Day' (*Shumbun* (*Shuubun*)*no hi*.) Such names, however, are unlikely to have any greater success than the Meiji government's ponderous creations in displacing the original Buddhist name for the day—*o-higan no chuunichi*—(the central day of *Higan*).

3. *The Bon Festival*

The central festival of the religious calendar and one primarily centring around the family *butsudan* is the Bon festival extending over a week in mid-summer. This festival, which is, in many ways complementary to the New Year celebrations[4] is essentially a family festival, though in rural districts there are generally village celebrations as well. It is the occasion when sons and daughters will make every effort to return home. Patients in hospital hope that they will be better 'to be home in time for Bon'. In most parts of Japan it is the time of the year at which women customarily return to their parental family, an indication of the fact that, particularly where the religious aspects of the family are concerned, the transference of a woman's loyalty by marriage is not entirely complete.

At the Bon festival the *butsudan* may be decorated with flowers, streamers and lanterns, and before it are laid offerings of fruit, vegetables, cakes and rice. The spirits of the dead are supposed to return to join the family in its festivities and on the last day of the festival a ceremony takes place which symbolizes the departure of the spirits for whatever is conceived to be their natural habitat. Priests may be invited (at a fee) to the house to perform a *hooji* ceremony for the assembled family, or the family may go to the family temple and (at less expense) get the priest to perform a *hooji* there.

4. *Anniversaries of Deaths*

These anniversaries (*meinichi*) are the typical occasions for a *hooji* ceremony which, though optional at Bon and Higan, are practically obligatory on certain of the anniversaries. These ceremonies are essentially periodic repetitions of the funeral ceremonies, first on every seventh day after death until the forty-ninth (though some families abbreviate this, celebrating only the seventh and the forty-ninth, or every seventh until the thirty-fifth), then at yearly intervals until the fiftieth, with special emphasis on the first, third, seventh and thirteenth anniversaries. Again, the ceremony may be held either at home or at the family temple. It is most cheaply performed by a layman friend of the family and this is the most common form in villages remote from temples. The recitation of prayers and sutras can become the leisure-time activity of any man with a good voice and a good memory and an awe for the mysteries of things. That such men can perform it indicates that the efficacy of the ceremony— either the magical effect of the prayers or the spiritual efficacy for the participants—lies in the ceremony itself and does not depend on any consecrated status of the person who performs it.

In describing the contents of the *butsudan*, the 'register of the past' was mentioned. In this, with a page to each month, are entered the anniversary days of the deaths of all past members of the family, a necessary procedure for an old established family which is conscientious in celebrating in some way or other (perhaps only by an extra flower or two) the death-days of all the ancestors.

GRAVES

At Bon and Higan, visits may be made to the family graves, on death-anniversaries to the grave of the individual concerned. The principles governing the location and types of grave may be mentioned here.

After cremation (earth burial persists only in remote country districts or among the adherents of certain modern sects) the ashes may be

- (a) immediately placed in a grave
- (b) divided between the grave and the depository of the family temple, or sometimes the depository of the chief temple of the sect often on one of the sacred mountains in central Japan.
- (c) brought home and placed on a small temporary altar.

In some families the last is customary until the forty-ninth day, after which the ashes are taken for burial. Alternatively, this may happen when, for example, an eldest son of a rural family whose ashes would normally be buried in the family grave has made his home in Tokyo and dies there. The ashes would be kept until a suitable occasion arises for transporting them to his native place. When a younger son migrates to Tokyo and founds a branch family, his ashes would normally be buried in a new grave in Tokyo, but in families with a long tradition the ashes may be divided between the Tokyo grave and the grave of the main family at his native place.

Graveyards may be attached to temples, but not necessarily so. In villages there may be many small graveyards, each used by a number of, generally related, families. In Tokyo there are many small graveyards attached to Buddhist temples and other larger graveyards, often near crematoria. Since the ashes take up little space a small grave can suffice each family. In the big secular graveyards in Tokyo, wealthy families often erect a large tomb covered with monumental decorations of stone lanterns or pillars modelled on the Buddhist *stupa*. Lettered gravestones are sometimes erected to individuals; in temple graveyards they bear the posthumous name of the deceased (in villages the stones are sometimes replaced by simple wooden boards bearing, as well as the posthumous name, an invocation in Sanskrit), in secular graveyards they most commonly bear the name borne during the individual's life. In these secular graveyards it is common to see magnificent stones inscribed with the name of some eminent citizen with, beside it, the name of his surviving widow, already cut in the stone, but with the characters picked out in red, a pledge that remarriage is not contemplated. Some graves bear only one stone, not to individuals, but to all the ancestors collectively. It is marked 'Grave of the ancestors of all generations of the —— family' (. . . *ke senzo daidai no haka*).

There are some sectarian variations in these practices, but the degree of uniformity is very wide indeed.

The Objects of Cults; Buddhism and Shinto, *Kami* and Hotoke

THE attempt will be made in this appendix to clarify more exactly the connotations of the words which were used in Chapters 18 to 23 as the names of types of supernatural beings.

It was accepted as a working definition that *kami* are the objects of worship at Shinto shrines, and the *Hotoke* are the objects of worship at Buddhist temples. Most Japanese would consider such a definition impeccable. A glance at the following table, however, will show that it requires some modification. It classifies by type (a) the *fuda* which Shitayama-cho families reported as having in their *kamidana* (excluding those of the parish and national shrines) and (b) the *fuda* or other separate objects of worship not in the *kamidana* which they referred to when asked if they had any other '*kami-sama*' besides the kitchen, lavatory and water *kami*.

It will be seen that some of these so-called *kami* are of Buddhist origin. (The betwixt-and-between deities like the originally Taoist Kooshin, and the gods of luck Daikoku and Ebisu are difficult to assign either to Shinto or to Buddhism. Of the last two all that one can say is that the former is more often to be found in Buddhist temples and the latter more often in Shinto shrines.) There can be no doubt about this: none but *kami* would be found in the *kamidana*, and as far as the separate shrines are concerned the question specifically asked 'have you any more *kami-sama*?' Moreover, of the six houses which shared these nine temple-*fuda* shrines five had *butsudan* —the proper place for *Hotoke*. Nevertheless they chose to give these deities separate shelves as *kami-sama* rather than put them in the *butsudan* as *Hotoke*.

How can this be reconciled with the previously implied definition of the *kami* as the beings worshipped with hand-claps at Shinto shrines, and *Hotoke* as the beings worshipped without hand-claps at Buddhist temples? A partial answer lies in the fact that there is a subsidiary connotation of the words *kami* and *Hotoke* already mentioned on page 331; namely that the *kami* are the forces who can

Type or Origin of Fuda	Number	
	In Kamidana	In Separate Shrines
Shinto Shrines:	26	8
Inari	5	6
Others	21	2
Mountain Cults:	44	15
Buddhist Temples (Narita, Minobu, etc.)	36	11
Shinto Shrines (Ontake, Haguro, etc.)	8	4
Shinto Sects: (Oomoto, Konkoo)	4	—
Betwixt-and-between deities	4 (Daikoku, Ebisu)	5 (Daikoku, Ebisu, Kooshin)
Buddhist deities	6 (Kannon, Fudoo, Taishaku, Kooboo-daishi)	9 (Kannon, Dainichi, Jizoo, Daruma, Taishaku, Kishimojin, Nichiren, 'The Zoozenji Temple')
Amulets	—	6
Total of *Fuda*	84	43
Total of Households	68	36

be employed to further the worshipper's material, this-worldly, interests, the *Hotoke* are more anthropomorphically conceived beings who are chiefly concerned with providing salvation in an after-life. Thus, productive this-worldly cults suggest the appropriateness of kami-worshipping attitudes, even though, as a result of long years of coalescence between Buddhist and Shinto institutions, some of the objects of these cults are in origin Buddhist. Hence, in the description previously quoted it was Shinto *gohei* which the worshipper waved and the *kami* by which he was possessed at the (Buddhist) temple to Fudoo at Narita. Hence, in a temple enclosure devoted to productive cults of one sort or another, Buddhist Jizoo jostle with Shinto Inari. Hence the *fuda* of the temple in Asakusa to the Buddhist Goddess of Mercy, Kannon, the centre of a flourishing productive cult, are brought home and enshrined as *kami*.

During the long years of coalescence between Shinto and Buddhism, not only were the Shinto *kami* found a place in the Buddhist pantheon (generally by identification with some of the minor deities which Buddhism had picked up in its journeyings across India, Tibet and China), in addition some of the *Hotoke* who had started as symbols of developed ethical and metaphysical concepts gradually became the *kami*-like objects of productive cults. Some Hotoke were more resistent to this process than others—Shaka, Miroku, Amida, do not appear in the list of *kami* in houses in Shitayama-cho, and Kannon is only represented by the *fuda* of the Asakusa temple which, like everything else in Asakusa, is a special case. The effects of these long years of fusion could not be fully undone by the Meiji government in its attempts to resuscitate a 'pure' Shinto. In any case the religious reformers were little concerned with these popular—and to their aristocratic minds undignified—mass cults.

Within the category of *kami* as thus defined, however, there does seem to be a vague distinction between those which are in origin purely Shinto and those which are in origin Buddhist. There is, first of all, a difference in their concrete forms; the latter are represented by images of human appearance, the former by no image—the 'body of the *kami*' (*shintai*) is always concealed and often consists of no more than a mirror. This difference is perhaps responsible for the fact that originally-Buddhist deities predominate among those to which one has recourse in times of illness or distress, and the Shinto deities predominate among those to which ones goes in order to get the balances of fortune weighted in one's favour. A child's illness takes one to a Kishimojin or a Jizoo—where the compassionate expression of the image may of itself be comforting. But it is to a Shinto Inarisama—where there are no images except a mass of jolly-looking toy foxes—that a man goes who has put a lot of money on a horse, a geisha who hopes that the man hiring her that evening might be a possible permanent patron, a *kabuki* actor anxious about his first appearance in a new part, or a shopkeeper who is ambitious for the expansion of his business.

We may now, perhaps, attempt to summarize the meanings generally attached to and the propositions implied in the use of the words which have been used above—*kami, hotoke, Hotoke,* etc.

Students of Shinto, from Motoori to Holtom and Haring, have expended considerable effort in an attempt to define the 'essential meaning of *kami*'. Most discussions of this sort have been vitiated by the failure to realize that while one may find a certain consistency of usage of an important term of this sort in a homogeneous culture at a given time—a consistency which does permit one to speak metaphorically of 'essential meaning'—to expect to find the same consistency throughout the thousand years of the recorded development of Japanese culture, during which time it has attained to a high degree of complexity and differentiation, is somewhat unrealistic. Etymological analysis further confuses the issue; the attempt to derive the present-day meaning of *kami* or *kami-sama* from its etymological relation to *o-kami-san* (a wife) and *o-kami* (the authorities) is about as legitimate as it would be to draw conclusions concerning the Englishman's concept of Godhead from the fact that the balcony of a theatre is called 'the Gods'.

Even Shitayama-cho was too culturally heterogeneous, its residents too diverse in origin, beliefs and ways of life, to find absolute consistency between individuals in their use of these terms. What follows is an attempt at a set of highest-common factor definitions as they might be elucidated from people who were on the whole 'believers' rather than 'sceptics'. Some uses of the terms would not at all fit into this scheme; for example, one man remarked about the *hotoke* that 'they are much more intimate than the *Hotoke*, but the *Hotoke* are of a higher standing—they are almost *kami-sama*'.

1. When people die they either become *hotoke*—as in most ordinary families—or *kami*—in the case of people who are buried according to Shinto rites, i.e. Emperors, famous men such as Ieyasu or General Nogi, the dead of ordinary families which follow Shinto rites, and all who have died in battle and are enshrined in the Yasukuni shrine.[5]

2. The *Hotoke* are associated in peoples minds with the temple images of Shaka, Kannon, Amida, Miroku and so on, images often of great beauty and compassionate expression.

3. At the *butsudan* one is concerned with the *hotoke*, and also to a lesser extent with the *Hotoke* since the *hotoke* are in the latter's care. One may also pray to both the *hotoke* and the *Hotoke* for protection, but, as we have seen, this is a minor element in *butsudan* worship. Although there is nothing really incongruous in praying to the *Hotoke* for protection and favour in this world, they are thought of chiefly as guides and guardians of the soul after death. (For evidence concerning the differentiation of the *Hotoke* and the *hotoke*, see note 257).

4. There are also other *kami* besides these which are explicitly conceived as the souls of dead persons. These are the *kami* of the mountains and fields, rivers, rice, the sun and the forces of nature. Some, according to legend, were once real people, but they are no longer thought of as such since the legends have been forgotten. Their distinguishing characteristic is that (non-family) shrines are dedicated to them. The actual fabric of the shrines and the *fuda* which are issued from them may also be called *kami*.

5. The *kami* which are explicitly conceived as the souls of dead human beings are worshipped, if at all, in the same way as *hotoke* are worshipped at the *butsudan*. At *kamidana* and at other household shines (apart from the *butsudan*) one is concerned with the other type of *kami*. There are many sub-types of these. Some are prayed to for daily protection and for special favours, and there is often considered to be a formal bond between the worshipper and the *kami* whereby the worshipper if he plays his part with due regard to the formalities,

can expect the *kami* to respond. Some *kami* are considered as forces which can be manipulated and used as a weapon. These last, however, are considered to be of inferior status. A *kami's* importance may be roughly measured by the size of the shrine devoted to it.

6. There are many other words which could be translated 'spirit': *tamashii, mitama, rei, reikon, shinrei*, etc. These may be differentiated as:

(*a*) *Tamashii, reikon, rei* are used sometimes as an alternative to *hotoke*, or to mean the 'soul' of a dead person in the intermediate period before it becomes a fully-fledged *hotoke*.

(*b*) *Mitama, rei, shinrei* are used as equivalents for *kami*, though there is sometimes a suggestion, as in words like *mitamawake* ('dividing the *mitama*', a process of setting up a new shrine by, as it were, taking a 'cutting' from an established one), that *mitama* means something like the 'essence' or the 'soul' of the *kami*. *Shinrei* are generally the inferior type of *kami* such as the *kami* in the earth which are ritually quelled or pacified before building operations, or the *kami* which operate in talismanic *fuda*.

NOTES

(The reference numbers to notes which contain only source references or figures for independence values are italicized in the text)

1. G. Gorer, *The Americans*, 1949, p. 4.
2. See e.g. Isomura Eiichi, *Toshi Shakaigaku*, 1953, pp. 62–90.
3. The Meiji Restoration, which marked the end of the Tokugawa feudal administration and the beginning of a new era of strong central government committed to modernization, took place in 1868. The reign of the Emperor Meiji lasted until 1912.
4. 'Borough' is used as a translation of *ku*, the major administrative division of the central urban area of Tokyo metropolis. (The rural periphery is divided into *shi* (cities), *gun* (rural districts) and the islands.) There are 23 *ku* with, in 1950, populations ranging from 110,000 to 400,000. (The total population of these central urban areas in this year was 5,385,000, which compares with 6,779,000 for 1940.) (Bureau of Statistics, Office of the Prime Minister, *Population Census of 1950*, vol. VII, pt. 13, p. 28.) The official post-office translation of *ku* is 'ward', which word, however, I prefer (in order to convey a better immediate impression of size to an English reader) to reserve for *choo* as in *Shitayama-cho*. (It may be noted here that the latter name—and Tokyo Osaka and Shinto—are the only intentional exceptions to the general rule that throughout the book long vowels will be indicated by doubling—as *oo, uu*.)
5. Tanaka Keiji, *Tookyoo Shinshi* (*Kyoodo Shinsho* ser. 13), 1951, p. 77.
6. Isomura Eiichi, *op. cit.*, p. 85.
7. The borough to which Shitayama-cho belongs, and indeed most of the zone between two and five kilometres from the centre of the city is calculated to have been growing at an accelerating rate until the turn of the century. Thereafter the rate of population growth rapidly declined, and after 1920 was less than 1% p.a. (Isomura, *op. cit.*, pp. 67–73.)
8. Sources: 1872–1930; Shinobu-ga-oka Shoogakkoo, *Tookyoo. Hattatsushi*, 1950 (cyclostyled), a local history compiled by a nearby elementary school. Sources are not quoted. 1950; the National Census of that date (figures kindly supplied by the Taitoo Borough Office). 1951; the writer's estimate based on the number of households surveyed (298 households, 1,181 persons), the number of refusals (3 households), and the number known to be living in the ward when the face-sheets were being prepared, but had left before interviews actually began. Some of those who left were replaced by new arrivals who were not included in the survey. Out-flow was, however, greater than in-flow. The peak was probably reached about 1947, after which the population gradually began to decline as more housing became available in other parts of Tokyo. For the purposes of the above table, 'households' includes single-person households.
9. In 1950, the density of the residential population was higher in the borough of which Shitayama-cho is part than in any other Tokyo borough, at 116 per acre. (Bureau of Statistics, Office of the Prime Minister, *Population Census of 1950*, vol. VII, pt. 13, p. 28.) This figure compares with a density of 92 per acre for Paddington, London's most densely populated borough in 1951. (*Municipal Year Book*, 1953, p. 660), and it must be remembered that Japanese houses of

more than two storeys are rare. Both these, however, are overall densities and exact comparison is difficult—one of the few parks and lakes in Tokyo was included in the area of the borough to which Shitayama-cho belonged. The area of Shitayama-cho itself had a population density of 230 persons per acre at the time of the 1950 census. (Calculated from figures kindly supplied by the Taitoo Borough Office.) This is approximately equal to the density for Soho in 1891, but still somewhat better than the highest population density for residential areas recorded in London for that period—365 per acre for the parish of Bethnal Green North. (B. S. Rowntree, *Poverty, A Study of Town Life*, 1902, p. 169.)

10. Households are defined in terms of sharing a common budget. Single-person households are excluded in the calculation of these figures. (Bureau of Statistics, Office of the Prime Minister, *Population Census of 1950*, vol. vii, pt. 13, p. 164, and vol. iii, pt. 1, p. 116.)

11. Bureau of Statistics, Office of the Prime Minister, *Population Census of 1950*, vol. iii, pt. 2, p. 129.

12. For convenience all monetary values in this chapter have been converted into approximate sterling equivalents at the current exchange rates, taking 1,000 *yen* = £1.

13. See e.g. Nooshoomushoo, *Shokkoo Jijoo*, 1903, edn. of 1947, vol. ii, pp. 153–4, and Yokoyama Gennosuke, *Nihon no Kaso Shakai*, 1899, Iwanami ed. 1949, p. 26.

14. This is not to say that the financial and industrial leaders were *not* predominantly recruited from the samurai class. They could not, however, be expected to maintain intact the samurai ideology to the same extent as those still engaged in the traditional samurai occupations of fighting and governing. No comprehensive study of the family origins of Japan's business leaders appears to exist. Such a study would be of some importance for the interpretation of Japan's recent political and social development.

15. Something of the attitude of the bureaucracy may be seen in the pages of the *Shokkoo Jijoo* which is a full and objective report on conditions in Japan's major industries prepared in 1903 by a research section of the Ministry of Agriculture and Commerce. As Professor Tsuchiya remarks in his introduction to the 1947 edition, it is 'almost entirely free from the attempts to distort the facts which characterize most official investigations' and where, in the cold recital of facts an expression of evaluation can be found it is almost invariably one of indignant sympathy for the workers.

16. Kazahaya Yasoji shows clearly the origin of the National Health Act of 1938 in pressure from the army. *Nihon Shakai-Seisakushi* (A History of Social Policy in Japan), Aoki Bunko edn. 1952, vol. II, pp. 462–6.

17. Juutaku-mondai Kenkyuukai, *Juutaku Mondai*, 1951, p. 20.

18. *Ibid.*, p. 20.

19. *Ibid.*, p. 20.

20. *Ibid.*, p. 22.

21. Nihon Tookei Kyookai, *Nihon Tookei Nenkan 1950*, p. 351.

22. Jiji Tsuushinsha, *Jiji Nenkan 1953*, p. 272.

23. The Japanese census definition of an 'ordinary household' (a group of two or more persons living together and sharing a common budget) is adopted here, except that three groups of single unrelated individuals sharing rooms but maintaining separate budgets—'quasi-households' by the census definition—are included. Thus every resident of Shitayama-cho is either counted as a member of a household or constitutes a 'single-person household'.

24. Juutaku-mondai Kenkyuukai, *op. cit.*, p. 48.

25. *Ibid.*, p. 48.

26. The extension of legal rules of exogamy to prohibit marriage between

uncles and nieces, aunts and nephews, half-brothers and half-sisters by the same father is a Meiji innovation, not found in early legal codes.

27. It would be of interest to know whether the sort of child neurosis described by Melanie Klein, which she traces so frequently to the child's observation of its parents' sexual relations, tends to be more common among Japanese children who must be more frequently exposed to such experiences. If not, the question arises: what are the other necessary conditions which obtain in the Viennese and not in the Japanese family which makes the importance of these early experiences so different?

28. Prime Minister's Office, Statistics Bureau, *Report on the Housing Census of 1948*, pp. 10 and 127.

29. Keizai Shingichoo, Choosa-bu, *Sengo no Kokumin Shotoku*, 1953, pp. 15 and 21.

30. *Ibid.*, pp. 15, 21. By 1955 this figure had fallen to 21%. (Keizai Kikakuchoo, *Shoowa-30-nen Kokumin Shotoku*, 1956, p. 11.)

31. A combination of the National Income figures (Keizai Shingichoo, *op. cit.*) and Ministry of Labour employment statistics (Jiji Tsuushinsha, *Jiji Nenkan*, 1953, p. 65) gives 155,000 *yen* per head for the wage and salary earner compared with 173,000 for the self-employed and their unpaid family workers. The peasant lags well behind with 57,000.

32. Tsuru Shigetoo, 'Sarari-man to Zeikin', in *Bungei Shunjuu*, June 1952.

33. Morita Yuuzoo, *et. al.*, *Zukai Nihon no Keizai*, 1953, p. 21.

34. Office workers also have more frequent resort to the municipal pawn shops according to the municipal pawnbroker's report for 1952. (*Ashai*, Tokyo morning ed., 11 June, 1953.) The statistics given, for what they are worth, show 54% of users to be office workers and only 16% to be manual workers.

35. Keizai Antei Hombu, *Keizai Hakusho, 1952*, p. 164. To some extent this is the result of a redistribution in favour of the peasants whose consumption level the same source estimates at 104% of pre-war (p. 170).

36. Keizai Antei Hombu, *Keizai Hakusho, 1952*, pp. 164–5.

37. Tokyo-to Minseikyoku, *Minseikyoku Nempoo*, 1950, p. 36.

38. Bureau of Statistics, Office of the Prime Minister, *Consumer Price Survey, March 1951*, p. 23.

39. Ministry of Welfare, *Kokumin Eiyoo no Genjoo*, Aug. 1952, p. 29. Other energy sources provide respectively, potatoes 3%, sugar 3%, fats 2%, pulses 5%, vegetables and fruit 4%, meat, fish, eggs and milk products 9% in the towns, and potatoes 7%, sugar 2%, fats 1%, pulses 5%, meat, fish, eggs and milk products 5% and fruit and vegetables 3% in rural areas. (Totals do not add due to rounding.)

40. Keizai Antei Hombu, Shigen Choosakai, *Shokuhin kyooka ni kansuru kankoku*, 27 May 1952.

41. The proportion of total flour consumption used in bread rose from 12% to 23% during 1932–8. (B. F. Johnston, *Japanese Food Management in World War II*, 1953, p. 81.)

42. Iwanami Henshuubu, *Tokyo, Daitokai no Kao*, 1952, p. 46.

43. *Yomiuri*, morning, 5 August 1951.

44. However, less shame attaches in Japan than in England to other illnesses such as venereal disease. This is, of course, largely a function of the general difference in attitudes towards sex. The matter-of-fact attitude towards venereal disease is best illustrated in the name of a small private hospital specializing in these diseases which advertised itself widely in the locality. It was called the *Kaishundoo*, or Hall of Spring Regained—'Spring' having in Japanese all the 'young man's fancy' associations in a rather more earthy form.

45. An American psychoanalyst, writing rather obviously under the pressure of wartime stereotypes, enumerates this as one of the eighteen symptoms of anal

compulsive neurosis in the Japanese national character. It is a reaction formation against the masochism (inverted sadism) which develops from the frustrations experienced while undergoing strict sphincter training during childhood. The masochistic nature of many traditional remedies (acupuncture, the moxa) is adduced as additional evidence of this. (Weston La Barre, 'Some Observations on Character Structure in the Orient', *Psychiatry*, vol. VIII, No. 3, 1945, p. 319.)

46. *The Chrysanthemum and the Sword*, 1946, p. 24.

47. Soorifu, Yoron Choosa Kyoku, *Shakai Hoshoo Seido Yoron Choosa, No. 1*, 1950, p. 7.

48. In the thirteenth century the word seems to have had the technical meaning of 'enter into a relation of retainership with a feudal lord', somewhat like 'commendation' although land was not necessarily involved. The *Jooei Shikimoku*, a feudal code of 1332, has the sentence, 'If you cherish those who *tanomu* you they become as your own children.' (Art. 19, *Gunsho Ruijuu* edn., vol. 22, p. 5.)

49. Crucial in this respect is the attitude of the authorities to attendance at High School by children of families receiving relief. Until April 1951, this was forbidden. Thereafter it was permitted on condition that the child attending High School was no longer counted as a member of the family for the purpose of calculating the amount of the relief grant. (*Nippon Fujin Shimbun*, 26 March 1951.) It is doubtful, however, whether this formal concession of equal rights makes any material difference to such children's chances of receiving higher education.

50. Shakai Hoshoo Seido Shingikai Jimukyoku, *Shakai Hoshoo Seido ni kansuru Hookoku*, 1948, pp. 45–7.

51. Although no attempt has been made to use Professor Talcott Parson's formulation of the social system in its entirety, certain key terms which have general value in the description of social relations have been borrowed at various points in this book. The following brief definitions might not be recognized by Professor Parsons himself (whose own elaborated definitions are to be found on pp. 46–51 and 58–67 of *The Social System*, 1951). They do, however, fairly represent the degree of precision with which the terms are used in this book.

A relation of A to B is said to be 'affective' when A's actions are coloured by the spontaneous expression of feelings towards B, and 'affectively-neutral' when this is not so.

A relation of A to B is said to be 'diffuse' when the two interact over a wide range of activity, 'specific' when their interaction is confined to a particular context.

A relation of A to B is said to be 'particularistic' when there could in the nature of the case be only one B, 'universalistic' when B can be defined by certain objective criteria which a large number of specific individuals might fulfil. Societies or institutions are said to be 'particularistic' or 'universalistic' according as relations of the former or the latter type predominate.

Sometimes the lump term 'personal' is used for relations which are affective, diffuse and particularistic, with 'impersonal' as its opposite. Thus the personal relation between husband and wife is affective, diffuse and particularistic. The impersonal relation between a booking clerk and the purchaser of a railway ticket is none of these things.

Statuses and roles are said to be 'ascribed' when they appertain to the individual by the accident of birth, 'achieved' when they are allocated on the basis of the individual's performance. Societies are said to be 'ascriptive' or 'achievementistic' according to which means of allocating statuses and roles predominates.

An individual's action is said to be 'self-oriented' when the motives inspiring it involve the achievement of goals private to himself, 'collectivity-oriented' when the goals concerned are those of a group to which he belongs. An individual can also be so described according to which type of action predominates in his behaviour.

All of these dichotomies represent, of course, not absolute categories but the extreme points on scales of infinite gradation.

52. Soorifu, Kokuritsu Yoron Choosa-sho, *Shakai Hoshoo Seido Yoron Choosa*, pt. 1, 1950, p. 2.

53. A Japanese content analyst has studied the cultural differences revealed in a comparison between Blondie and a similar Japanese domestic cartoon series, Sazae-san of the Asahi. Blondie, though in enforced thrift, the constant fear of the sack, the rent-collector and the gas-man, she suffers from all the evils inherent in monopoly capitalism, is liberated, rational, managing and socially conscious. Sazae-san, though 'positive', is positive in a feudal sort of way and is bound by the conventions of middle-class respectability. (Imamura Taihei, 'Nihon Manga to Amerika Manga', in *Me* I, 1 January 1952.)

54. $p < ·01$.

55. Between age and keeping a budget, and between educational level and keeping a budget, $p < ·001$. Between age and receptiveness to suggestions, and between education and receptiveness to suggestions $p < ·01$. Since the younger are in general better educated, the two factors of age and education obviously overlap. Partial contingency analysis suggests, however, that both factors have independent importance.

56. $p < ·05$.

57. $p < ·05$.

58. $p < ·02$.

59. $·1 < p < ·2$.

60. $p < ·001$.

61. Sir G. Sansom, *The Western World and Japan*, 1949, p. 445.

62. The Interpretation of Hozumi Nobushige, the chief advocate of the revision of the 1890 code. *The New Japanese Civil Code as Material for the Study of Comparative Jurisprudence*, Tokyo, 1904, pp. 6–12, quoted in Munroe Smith, *A General View of European Legal History*, New York, 1927, p. 371.

63. Wagatsuma Sakae, *Ie no Seido*, 1951, p. 170.

64. *Greater Learning*, 5. Legge's translation.

65. In the Chinese legal codes, and also in the Japanese eighth-century codes which were modelled on them, lack of filial piety ranked second only to treason in the hierarchy of crimes. Thus informing against one's father was always a crime meriting punishment unless the father's offence was treason.

66. The other sense in which the word is commonly used is, of course, 'the actual set of family institutions prevailing at any given time or place'. In pre-war controversies the latter sense was the one usually employed by sociologists, the former by legal scholars, often to cross-purposes. A third sense, that given by Prof. Koyama in the *Dictionary of Japanese Society and Ethnography* (Nihon Minzoku Kyookai, *Nihon Shakai Minzoku Jiten*, 1952) is 'the set of legal institutions governing family relations sanctioned by any particular political or religious authority'.

67. A considerable literature exists on such patron-client relations. The classic documentation of forms found in rural areas is to be found in Yanagita Kunio, 'Oyakata Kokata', in *Kazoku-seido Zenshuu*, Part I (Shi-ron-hen), vol. iii, 89–124. Recent studies of particular groups which have appeared in the *Japanese Sociological Review* (*Shakaigaku Hyooron*) include, on politics, Tanaka Soogoroo, 'Hambatsu, Sono Keisei o Chuushin ni' (*S.H.* 9, 1952); on street traders, Iwai Kooyuu, 'Teikya no Kenkyuu' (*S.H.* 1, 1950); on trade unions Nakano Takashi, 'Roodoo Kumiai ni okeru Ningen-kankei' (*S.H.* 7, 1952); and on labour organization, Matsushima Shizuo, 'Koozan ni okeru oyabun kobun shuudan' (*S.H.* 1, 1950) and Fujimoto Takeru, 'Kumigashira oyakata seido no Honshitsu' (*S.H.* 8, 1952). Two useful articles in English are Ishino, Iwao, 'The Oyabun-kobun: A Japanese Ritual Kinship Institution', *Amer. Anthrop.*, vol. 55, pt. 1, December

1953, and J. W. Bennett and M. Nagai, 'A Summary and Analysis of "The Familial Structure of Japanese Society" by Takeyoshi Kawashima', *South-Western Journal of Anthropology*, vol. 9, No. 2, Summer 1953, p. 239.

68. In an excellent article on the development, or rather the resuscitation, of this ideology in Japan, particularly as shown in the contrast between the 1st (1904) and the 2nd (1910) editions of the school ethics text-books, Ishida Takeshi also attributes some importance to the contemporary dominance of Hegelian doctrines of the organic state. Ishida Takeshi, 'Waga kuni ni okeru kokumin-kyooka no ichitokushitsu—Kazoku-kokka-kan no kisei katei ni tsuite', in *Tooyoo Bunka*, No. 11, 1953.

69. Ueda T. 'Kinsei Nihon no Keizai Hatten to Kazokuseido', in Kokusai Gakuyuukai, *Kaki Nihon Bunka Kooza Kooenshuu*, 1938, p. 124.

70. Hozumi Nobushige, 'Ie no Hooriteki Kannen', *Hoogaku Shimpoo*, 85 (1898), quoted by Wagatsuma Sakae, *Ie no Seido*, 1951, p. 208.

71. The *Onna Daigaku*, now known to every Japanese, is so much the epitome of the old family ideals that from the Meiji period to the present day reformist writers have frequently set out explicitly to attack it, as is indicated by the title of their books; for instance, Doi Kooka, *Shin Onna Daigaku* (A New O.D.), 1876, Fukuzawa Yukichi, *Onna Daigaku Hyooron* (A Review of the O.D.), 1898, and, as recently as 1952, Nakagawa Zennosuke, *Onna Daigaku Hihan* (The O.D. Criticized). A Translation of the *Onna Daigaku* is contained in B. H. Chamberlain, *Things Japanese*, 1890, p. 367.

72. See e.g. R. Linton, *The Cultural Background of Personality*, London 1947, p. 34, and Kingsley Davis, *Human Society* 1949, pp. 55-6. The latter expresses the distinction as that between norms which require maximum and those which require only moderate performance.

73. Use has been made of the following works. Toda Teizoo, *Kazoku no Kenkyuu* (1916), *Kazoku Koosei* (1937) and *Ie to Kazoku-seido* (1944); Fukuo Takeichiroo, *Nihon Kazoku-seido-shi* (1950); Sunagawa Kanei, *Nihon Kazoku-seido-shi Kenkyuu* (1925); Inoue Kiyoshi, *Nihon Joseishi* (1950); Nakagawa Zennosuke, *Onna Daigaku Hihan* (1952); Kawashima Takeyoshi, *Nihon Shakai no Kazokuteki Koosei* (1949); Wagatsuma Sakae, *Ie no Seido* (1951); and the *Kazoku-seido Zenshuu Part I* (*Shiron-hen*), vols. 1-5 (1937-8). This represents only a fraction of a vast literature on the family of either a historical, contemporary sociographic or polemical kind, much of it (like the works of Fukuo, Inoue and Nakagawa quoted above) aimed at a popular rather than an academic audience.

74. 'As between step-mother and step-child, and as between wife and "recognized natural son" (i.e. of the husband by another woman), the same relationships shall be deemed to exist as between parent and child.' (1898 Civil Code, Art. 728.) Adultery (defined as intercourse of a married *woman* with a man not her husband) was a crime under the old Criminal Code. (Art. 183.) Such a definition of adultery followed naturally from the nature of the marital relationship. The important aspect of adultery was not the 'unfaithfulness' involved, but the possibility of false paternity. In the terms of a later paragraph, a family which had 'borrowed a womb' had exclusive rights of usufruct. Cf. also Lord Justice Denning '(Adultery) is no bar to advancement in any of the offices of State, high or low, whereas any other *form of stealing* would mean the end of a career.' (*The Times*, 3 May, 1954. My italics.)

75. Hozumi Shigetoo, 'Rienjoo to En-kiri-dera', in *Kazoku-seido Zenshuu*, 1937 Part 1 (Shiron-hen), vol. 2, p. 271.

76. Shimonaka Y. ed. *Shintoo Daijiten*, 1937, article *Kibuku*.

77. Article 957.

78. *Kagami-gusa* (published 1669), quoted in Himeoka, T., 'Hooken Dootoku ni arawareta fuufu no jooge-kankei', *Shakaigaku Hyooron*, 15 (vol. iv, no. 3), p. 13.

79. It is interesting in this connection to note that according to the surmise of the folk-lorist Nakayama Taroo, the use at the wedding ceremony of a tray with the model pine and the dolls representing the old man and the old woman of Takasago is a later substitute for a former custom of presenting a tray mounted with vegetables cut to represent the male and female sexual organs, a practice still common in some rural districts at the turn of the century. (Nakayama Taroo, *Nihon Kon-in-shi*, 1928, pp. 339–42.)

80. A seventeenth-century example is the following *kaken* of the founder of the house of Mitsui, the great commercial concern. It is one of the earliest merchant family *kaken* recorded. In samurai families the practice is very much older.

1. A single tree will snap in the wind, but a thicket cannot be broken. In amity and co-operation strengthen the fortunes of our family.
2. The senior members of each house shall together form the Roobun (Council of Elders) and these shall be the supreme authority. Let every househead heed their commands.
3. Let there be no disputes within the family.
4. Firmly eschew all extravagance and practice rigorous economy.
5. Under a good general there are no weak troops. Exercise the greatest care to advance the wise and the able.
6. The children of each house shall spend a certain period working under the direction of shop managers and sub-managers, receiving the same treatment and living the same lives as the other assistants. Under no circumstances shall they receive favoured treatment. (Quoted from *Kokumin Seishin Soodooin*, 15 April 1938 in Toda Teizoo, *Ie to Kazoku-seido*, 1944, p. 178.)

81. Civil Code (1898), Article 744. 'The legal presumptive heir to the headship of a family may not enter another family or establish a new family, except when it is necessary for him to assume the headship of the main family' (of which his own is a branch). Evasion was just possible, if complicated. The girl's family could adopt a male heir, and after the marriage the adoption *de convenance* could be dissolved if the adoptee's parents wished to have him back.

82. Article 748 and Part 5.

83. Article 749.

84. Article 750.

85. Article 772.

86. See note 80 for an example of such a family council permanently constituted. Family councils were given legal status in the 1898 Code as *ad hoc* bodies for the regulation of succession disputes, the appointment of guardians, etc. By 1925, however, it seems to have been generally admitted that they were working badly and leading to numerous unintended abuses. (Wagatsuma Sakae, *Ie no Seido*, 1951, p. 274.)

87. The 1890 Civil Code contained a provision permitting the deposition of househeads who proved unsuitable. The 1898 Code took it out as an undesirable limitation of the househead's authority. The 1925 reform proposals favoured its restoration on the grounds that protection of the family as a whole against the inadequacies of individuals was more important than the bolstering of the authority of the househead. (Wagatsuma Sakae, *op. cit.*, pp. 186, 258.)

88. The practice of *noren-wake* (splitting the shop-blind) in the merchant classes and *hookoonin-bunke* (servant branch-family) in rural areas. The latter is a sociologist's word for which there are many dialect equivalents—*kerai-kamado, kado-wakare, niwa-wakase*, etc. Yanagita Kunio records nine such names (*Zokusei Goi*, 1943, pp. 55–70) all from N.E. Japan to which this practice seems chiefly to have been confined, at least as far as rural areas were concerned.

89. This account is largely based on Fukutake Tadashi, *Nihon Nooson no Shakaiteki Seikaku*, 1949, pp. 34–48, 69–115. There is a considerable literature

on these *doozoku* (as the sociologist calls them; there are at least twenty-six dialect names, of which *maki* is perhaps the most widespread. See Yanagita Kunio, *Zokusei Goi*, 1943, pp. 1-31). A bibliography will be found in M. Nagai, *Doozoku: A preliminary study of the Japanese Extended Family Group and its Social and Economic Functions*, Ohio State University, Research Foundation, Interim Technical Report, No. 7, September, 1953, which also contains the only detailed account of such a lineage in English.

90. Furushima Toshio *et al*, *Sanson no Koozoo*, 1949, p. 172.

91. That is from about the end of the seventeenth century onwards. It was not until that time that primogeniture inheritance—a fundamental condition for most of the other features of the Japanese family—became established in the merchant classes. (Fukuo Takeichiroo, *Nihon Kazoku-Seido-shi*, 1950, p. 207.)

92. This account owes much to the distinctions drawn between the samurai family and the 'common people's' (*shomin*) family by Kawashima Takeyoshi in his *Nihon Shakai no Kazokuteki Koosei*. See also J. W. Bennett and M. Nagai, 'A Summary and Analysis of The Familial Structure of Japanese Society by Takeyoshi Kawashima', *South-Western Journal of Anthropology*, vol. 9, no. 2, Summer 1953, p. 239.

93. Some idea of the extent of these regional variations can be seen in the pages of the *Zenkoku Minji Kanrei Ruijuu*, a collection describing customary law in various parts of Japan, compiled in 1877 and expanded in 1880 as material for the drafting of the first Civil Code. (Reprinted in *Meiji Bunka Zenshuu*, vol. 8.)

94. See e.g. Hattori Shisoo, *Bishi no Shigaku*, 1953, pp. 1-15.

95. Aizawa Seishisai, a scholar of the late Tokugawa period, was scornful of Western nations who were little better than beasts since they would rather die without heirs than take a concubine to ensure the succession. (Inoue Kiyoshi, *Nihon J* *seishi*, 1950, p. 142.)

96. Ii oue, *loc. cit.*

97. A late Tokugawa period edict recorded for a district now a Tokyo suburb directs the attention of local officials to the 'enforcement' of divorces. Some couples, divorced by the husband's parents, had been meeting secretly—to the detriment of public morality. (*Zenkoku Minji Kanrei Ruijuu* (1880), in *Meiji Bunka Zenshuu*, vol. 8, p. 212.)

98. Particularly when discussing societies undergoing change it seems of doubtful legitimacy to talk of the 'norms of a society' in a 'normative'—as opposed to a statistical—sense. I prefer, therefore, to talk of the 'norms of an individual' meaning 'patterns of behaviour the rightness of which the individual would be prepared verbally to affirm and deviations from which, in so far as he perceives them to be deviations, would be likely to arouse his disapproval'. Although this begs several questions ('perceives' and 'disapproval' for instance) it seems the nearest one can get to a meaningful definition in behavioural terms. Common norms, then, are those which statistically predominate in a group of individuals.

99. In 1920, 47%, in 1930, 49% and in 1950, 38% of the total population of Tokyo prefecture (which includes about 10% inhabitants of rural suburbs) were not natives of the prefecture. (Bureau of Statistics, Office of the Prime Minister, *Population Census of 1950*, vol. vii, pt. 13, p. 21.)

100. During the depression of the early twenties, one form of unemployment relief provided by the government was the offer of reduced fares to workers wishing to return to their native village. (Yanaibara Tadao ed. *Gendai Nihon Shooshi*, 1952, vol ii., p. 184.)

101. Thus, for instance, there is a great difference at the present day between the relation of teacher and pupil in the teaching of the traditional Japanese arts —singing, dancing, tea ceremony and so on—and in the teaching of the 'modern' arts of ballet or the piano. The former still has its psuedo-kinship nomenclature

and an explicit ideology of personal allegiance entirely lacking in the latter. (Kawashima Takeyoshi, 'Iemoto Seido', in *Me*, No. 4, March 1953, p. 21.)

102. Bureau of Statistics, Office of the Prime Minister, *Population Census of 1950*, vol. iii, pt. 2, p. 221.

103. *Ibid.*

104. Wagatsuma Sakae, *Ie no Seido*, 1951, p. 231.

105. The foremost proponent of the liberalizing recommendations in the Legal Commission of Enquiry was Minobe Tatsukichi, dismissed from his university post in 1935 for his 'organic' theory of the function of the Emperor in the Japanese Constitution.

106. For a summary of these legal changes, see Kurt Steiner, The Revision of the Civil Code of Japan: Provisions Affecting the Family, *Far Eastern Quarterly*, vol. ix, No. 2, February 1950.

107. p < ·001 for all men who have completed schooling. This result may be in part accounted for by the fact that the average family size is smaller in Tokyo and Yokohama than for the rest of the country. According to the 1950 Fertility Census, women in Tokyo aged 50–54 who had ever married had had an average of 3·86 children, whereas the corresponding figure for the same age-group was 5·19 for all rural districts and 5·96 for the most fertile agricultural prefecture, Miyagi. (Bureau of Statistics, *Population Census of 1950*, vol. iii, pt. 1 (10% sample), pp. 169–74.)

108. Conflict is not, however, universal. One family in Shitayama-cho was renowned among neighbours for the mutual affection and good humour which characterized the relations of mother-in-law and daughter-in-law. The fact that it was commented on, however, is sufficient indication that it was thought exceptional. There were also three instances of widows or divorcees living with parents-in-law. In one case a widow had married again, but on being divorced had returned to live with the parents of her first husband. In another, a couple were separated, but it was the son of the family, not his wife, who had gone to live elsewhere.

109. In August 1953, the Government Public Opinion Research Institute asked in the course of a survey 'If you had to choose, which would you think was preferable, a household in which although the parents and children did not get on too well, the husband and wife were happy together, or one in which although the husband and wife did not get on too well, the relations between parents and children was a good one?' The results were:

Replies placing greatest emphasis on parent-child relation	21%
Replies placing greatest emphasis on husband-wife relation	54%
Depends on the circumstances	15%
Don't know	10%

(Kawashima Takeyoshi, *Kekkon*, 1954, p. 182.)

110. ·05 < p < ·2 (s.d. of diff.).

111. *Nippon Fujin Shimbun*, 6 April 1951.

112. Oohama Hideko, *Oya o yashinawanai ko*, Tokyo, 1953.

113. *Nippon Fujin Shimbun*, 21 April 1951. See also an article on 'Old People's Day' in the *Yomiuri* (morning, 30 June 1951) which stresses the need for more old people's homes.

114. In the last six months of 1950 there were 182 such cases out of a total of 613 appeals for maintenance presented to the Tokyo tribunals. (Oohama Hideko, *op. cit.*, pp. 143–4.)

115. ·2 < p < ·3.

116. In this chapter 'househead' is used exclusively in the sense of head of a household, not in the pre-war legal sense of head of an *ie*, which could include several households.

117. In his recent book on marriage, Kawashima Takeyoshi attributes

considerable importance to these factors in effecting changes in the structure of authority in the family since the war. (*Kekkon*, 1954, pp. 63, 135.)

118. Kawashima Takeyoshi, *Kekkon*, 1954, p. 18.

119. Wagatsuma Sakae, *Ie no Seido*, 1951, pp. 264, 275.

120. It would appear that childlessness was frequent formerly in Japan. The 1940 Fertility Census gave a total proportion of 14·6% of completed families as childless. (A. Okazaki, *Nihon Jinkoo no Jisshooteki Kenkyuu*, 1951, p. 286.) The 1950 Census indicates a gradual improvement; the proportion of childless women among those 'still married' and aged over 55 years was 11%, among those 'still married' and aged 45–55, 9%. (Bureau of Statistics, Office of the Prime Minister, *Population Census of 1950*, vol. iii, pt. 1, p. 188.) The difference between 14·55% and 11% is so great (they refer to the same cohort) that it must indicate either some fault with the surveys or a very high rate of childlessness among those who have died between 1940 and 1950. One reason suggested by Okazaki for the improvement (or rather specifically as an explanation of the differentials between regions and occupational groups in 1940) is improved treatment of venereal disease.

121. The Tokugawa period saw a gradual extension of the permitted scope of adoption in samurai laws, including a removal of original restrictions to kinsmen. Tokugawa society was so completely organized as a network of relations between families, that the disappearance of any one family unit in the upper strata of the network, by rendering unemployed its retainer families, created a social problem. It was particularly after the revolt in 1651 of Yui Shoosetsu, the leader of a body of such masterless men, that the Bakufu widened the adoption laws.

122. A phrase of Saikaku suggests that the wife's dominance in such households extended even to the couple's sexual relations—'Every night to bed at dusk, the adopted husband grows thinner and thinner.' 'Nanshoku Ookagami' in *Saikaku Zenshuu* (Koten Zenshuu ed. 1946), vol. iv, p. 10—an incidental indication that restraint and frigidity were not expected of seventeenth-century merchant class wives in Oosaka.

123. There appears to be some local variation in this, however. It is reported that in Shikoku adopted sons-in-law seem to suffer no loss of prestige and occupy positions of high status in the village community. (R. J. Smith, Co-operative Forms in a Japanese Agricultural Community, *Occasional Papers*, Centre for Japanese Studies, Univ. of Michigan, no. 3, 1952, p. 59.)

124. Nakagawa Zennosuke, 'Daikazoku to Bunke', in *Kazoku-seido Zenshuu*, Part I (Shiron-hen), vol. iv, p. 254. He shows that the proportion of son-in-law adoptions to total marriages was 5·6% for the whole country in 1920 and 5·2% in 1932.

125. Wagatsuma Sakae, *Ie no Seido*, 1951, p. 267. In the nineties, on the other hand, it appears that the protagonists for equal inheritance laid the greatest stress on economic arguments; increased circulation, the expansion of credit and the encouragement of individual enterprise. (*Ibid.*, pp. 196–7.)

126. Toda Teizoo, *Kazoku no Koosei*, 1942 (3rd ed.), pp. 295–8.

127. At the present moment (July 1954) some demands are being made, admittedly by the near-lunatic fringe of Japanese politicians, for 'the restoration of the family system'.

128. In the conjugal family from which the father is for most of the time absent, the mother tends to be the model for children of both sexes. For the boy, however, a switch to a masculine and a rejection of the feminine model is required in the process of attaining adulthood, quite apart from the Oedipus implications of his relation with his mother. This is not so for the girl. This idea is elaborated by Talcott Parsons, 'The Social Structure of the Family', in R. Anshen, ed., *The Family: Its Function and Destiny*, 1949.

129. This point is made by Talcott Parsons, in 'The Social Structure of

the Family', in R. Anshen, ed., *The Family: Its Function and Destiny*, 1949, p. 183.

130. Talcott Parsons seems to suggest that emphasis on 'love' is a 'functional imperative' of the conjugal family, but in this I fail to follow him. The argument seems to rest in part on a confusion between 'relations' and 'roles' in the sense used above. (*Op. cit.*, p. 184.)

131. According to Kawashima Takeyoshi, at the beginning of the nineteen-thirties there was a deliberate relaxation of police controls on obscene publications and other forms of commercialized sex, and also (by Ministry of Education order) in the school authorities' strict control over adolescent friendships. This was a temporary measure aimed at reducing labour unrest and taking the students' minds off politics. (*Kekkon*, 1954, p. 221.)

132. A story vouched for by Kawashima (*op. cit.*, p. 15). Much of the material for this and the following few pages is derived from Professor Kawashima's most percipient, if somewhat hasty, work.

133. Kawashima Takeyoshi, *Kekkon*, 1954, pp. 171–2.

134. Tamaki Hajime, 'Shoo', in *Kazoku Seido Zenshuu*, Part I, vol. 1, p. 191.

135. Wagatsuma Sakae, *Ie no Seido*, 1951, pp. 260–2.

136. Tsurumi Shunsuke, 'Sasaki Kuni no Shoosetsu ni arawareta Tetsugaku-Shisoo', in *Shishoo no Kagaku*, vol. iii, no. 2.

137. *Kindai no Renai-kan*, published in Aoki-Bunko series, 1950.

138. Fujin Kurabu, *Endan to Konrei Isshiki*, 1930, p. 49.

139. See Kuro Hyoosuke, 'Nikutai Bungaku no Seiri', *Shisoo no Kagaku*, vol. iv, no. 3.

140. Kawashima Takeyoshi, *Kekkon*, 1954, p. 55.

141. *Tokyo Nichi-Nichi*, 22 July 1949, reprinted in *Daini-Burari Hyootan*, 1952, p. 26.

142. *Asahi Shimbun*, morning, 18 July 1953.

143. Tamaki Hajime, *Kazoku* (*Shakaika Zensho* series), 1952, pp. 32–7.

144. *Yomiuri Shimbun*, morning, 13 April 1951.

145. Kawashima Takeyoshi, *Kekkon*, 1954, p. 40.

146. *The Family Revolution in Modern China*, 1949, *passim*.

147. Legal registration is not of itself an important condition of respectability. Even in the most impeccable cases, registration is often delayed some months after the ceremony which gives the marriage social recognition.

148. F. Le Play; *Les Ouvriers Européens*, 1855, p. 290.

149. In a small country town near Hiroshima, after the wedding of a shopkeeper's son the bride's trousseau was displayed in the shop window. Crowning the display were her Girls' High School leaving certificate and her tea and flower diplomas. Status-asserting display is an important element of weddings particularly in small communities. The very name for the wedding feast—*hiroo-shiki*—means 'display ceremony'.

150. A pre-war guide to marriage advises go-betweens, always to offer such reasons for refusals. (Kawashima Takeyoshi, *Kekkon*, 1954, p. 41.) The decline in the extent to which these superstitions really affect the arrangement of marriage is illustrated by the fate of women born in 1906. This was the year of the Horse in Fire Major, and women born in that year (recurring once every six decades) make notoriously bad wives. Enough parents, solicitous of their daughter's future welfare, delayed or back-dated the birth-registration to make a considerable alteration in the sex ratio of births for that and the two surrounding years. In 1904 it was 105·1 (a normal figure), in 1905, 102·7, in 1906, 108·7, in 1907, 102·7 and in 1908 back to normal with 104·6. Their horoscope has, however, had little effect on the marriage chances of those unfortunate enough to be born too near the middle of the year for falsification to be possible. Of women alive in

Tokyo at the time of the 1950 census, the following percentages remained un-married. (Something under one-quarter of the 43-year-olds and something over three-quarters of the 44-year-olds were born in 1906.) Age 42—3·24; age 43—3·28; age 44—3·01; age 45—2·55, age 46—2·43. (Bureau of Statistics, Office of the Prime Minister, *Population Census of 1950*, vol. vii, pt. 13, p. 40.) This could be due to a higher suicide rate among the ill-fated spinsters, and indeed there are some grounds for thinking that the present sex ratios of the relevant age-groups (age 43—98·4; 44—104·2; 45—100·2 for the whole country) represent a slight increase in the sex imbalance of the 1906 group as compared with the actual birth registrations. This, however, is more likely to be due to a proportion of married women born in 1906 sticking to a false story about their age which had, perhaps, helped them to get married. Spinsters would be unlikely to falsify since the circumstances of their birth provide a face-saving explanation of their spinsterhood (unless they were still hopeful at 44). Demographers constructing a generation life table would be advised to leave the 1906 group severely alone.

151. Fujin Kurabu, *Endan to Konrei Isshiki*, 1930, p. 48.

152. Word counts of some sixty-one hit songs showed 'weep' as the most frequent verb with 'part' as runner up; 'smile' is used infrequently and mostly in the negative. Of natural phenomena the most favoured are 'wind' ('biting', 'evening', 'cold') and 'rain'. Minami Hiroshi, 'Nihon no Ryuukooka' in Shisoo no Kagaku Kenkyuukai, *Yume to Omokage*, 1950.

153. *Eitaigura, Saikaku Meisakushuu* (Edo Bungei edn., 1929), vol. 2, p. 98.

154. Quoted from the *Yomiuri Shimbun*, 9 April 1952, in Kawashima Take-yoshi, *Kekkon*, 1954, p. 190. The scope of the sample is not given.

155. *Yomiuri Shimbun*, 11 April 1951. A nation-wide stratified random sample of 3,000. The force of the comparison is rather weakened by the insertion of the indecorous element of walking arm in arm.

156. R. Merton, 'Social Structure and Anomie: Revisions and Explanations', in R. Anshen, ed., *The Family: Its Function and Destiny*, 1949, p. 230.

157. For men in their thirties, the distribution is

	Education		
	Elementary	Middle	Higher
Love Marriage	3	13	5
Arranged Marrage	15	21	3

A chi square test, though of dubious accuracy with the small expected frequencies in the Higher group, yields ·05 < p < ·1.

158. Shishi Bunroku, *Jiyuu Gakkoo*, 1951, p. 344.

159. Independence values for this and subsequent associations are given in Table 21, p. 177.

160. A note might not be out of place here concerning the validity of these indices *qua* indices of the dimensions described. Although the interpretation was based largely on *a priori* grounds, there is some justification to be found in the inter-correlations of the indices. As far as the second dimension is concerned, sending New Year cards and claiming property are very significantly associated (p < ·01), though neither of these indices when correlated with the wife's having visitors yields an independence value higher than ·3 < p < ·5. For the third dimension, the husband's helping in the home and deciding jointly on 'condo-lence money' amounts are associated at the p < ·06 level, but the husband's having visitors, which correlates very significantly with the former (p < ·01) shows no association at all with the latter. There would thus appear to be other important specific factors involved besides the common factor defined as the 'dimension'.

161. The results of Japanese studies on Kinseyan lines have been recently published (Shinozaki Nobuo, *Nihonjin no Sei-seikatsu*, 1953) but they do not give the impression of great reliability and yield few significant breakdowns by

age, region, education or occupation. As might be expected, features which are often considered as evidence of a 'co-operative' attitude to sex relations, such as experimentation in coital positions and indulgence in fore-play, are reported to be rarer in Japan (within marriage) than in America. (40% of couples never indulge in any sort of foreplay though it is progressively more common with the younger age groups (*op. cit.*, p. 66) a fact which, however, is capable of more than one interpretation.) On the other hand, there seem to be no complaints in the birth-control literature that husbands are unco-operative, and Shinozaki notes (p. 152) that among contraceptive methods used, according to various surveys, those requiring the husband's initiative predominate.

162. *Nippon Fujin Shimbun*, 24 August 1951.

163. Kawashima Takeyoshi, *Kekkon*, 1954, p. 229.

164. Kawashima provides some evidence for this. (Kekkon, pp. 193–5). The change is, of course, towards an increase in non-commercial premarital sexual relations. Shinozaki reports (*Nihonjin no Sei-Seikatsu*, 1953, p. 241) that of a sample of married men in the Shitamachi districts Tokyo 71·2% had had premarital sexual experience and of a sample from Yamanote districts, 71·8%, but of these only 10·3% and 8·7% respectively had had intercourse with women other than prostitutes. The number of married women who reported premarital sexual experience was small. It is interesting to note that in a newspaper opinion survey slightly more men than women thought that a woman should be a virgin on marriage (87·3% as compared with 86·1%), and slightly more women than men thought virginity important for the man (75·9% compared with 73·2%). (*Yomiuri*, 11 April 1951. The exact form of the questions is not given; the size of the sample (stratified random for all Japan) was 3,000, which makes the second, but not the first, of these differences significant at the 5% level.) This is in contrast with England where, according to Geoffrey Gorer, women tend to be more insistent on chastity for both sexes than men ('English Ideas about Sex', *Encounter*, December 1953.)

165. *Yomiuri Shimbun*, 27 August 1951.

166. These figures represent, of course, the dissolution of registered marriages. Since marriage was only registered, particularly in rural districts, when it seemed after a trial period that the bride would make the grade, the actual number of divorces was much higher. There is reason to think, however, that the delay between marriage and registration was decreasing throughout the period, so that the real decline in divorce was greater than the figures indicate.

167. Yasu Iwasaki, 'Divorce in Japan', *American Journal of Sociology*, vol. 36, 1930, p. 441.

168. In 1949, 96·9% of divorces were by consent—i.e. ended by the simple act of registration, 2·6% by Family Tribunal mediation, and 0·4% as the result of court decisions in cases where one party refused consent to the divorce. (Oohama Hideko, 'Kaji Jiken kara mita Kazoku no Tenshon', in Nihon Jimbun Kagakkai, *Shakaiteki Kinchoo no Kenkyuu*, 1953, p. 65.)

169. Kawashima Takeyoshi, *Kekkon*, 1954, p. 186.

170. *Nippon Fujin Shimbun*, 8 June 1951.

171. Lump-sum alimony can be awarded if the case is taken for mediation to the Family Tribunal, but there are no means of enforcing its awards unless the case is taken to the ordinary courts. Of the respondents to a questionnaire sent to all concerned in decisions reached by the Family Tribunals in 1949 (about one-seventh of the total replied), 36% reported that the Tribunal's decisions were being ignored. (*Yomiuri*, 30 April 1951.)

172. A good analysis of the hero of popular fiction is to be found in Tsurumi Shunsuke, 'Nihon no Taishuu-Shoosetsu', in Shisoo no Kagaku Kenkyuukai, *Yume to Omokage*, 1950.

173. *The Chrysanthemum and the Sword*, 1946, pp. 43, 57, 95.

174. Watsuji Tetsuroo, 'Ruth Benedict "*Kiku to Katana*" no ataeru mono: Kagakuteki Kachi in taisuru Gimon', in *Minzokugaku Kenkyuu*, vol. xiv, no. 4, 1949, p. 27.

175. Quoted in Inoue Kiyoshi, *Nihon Josei-shi*, 1949, p. 162.

176. This was not, however, true of one of the largest sects, the Shinshuu. Shinshuu priests were allowed to marry and as a result hereditary succession prevailed, though sometimes modified in favour of ability by the practice of adoption.

177. Carmen Blacker, 'Kyuuhanjoo by Fukuzawa Yukichi', *Monumenta Nipponica*, vol. ix, nos. 1–2, p. 305.

178. The Okayama school, for instance, contained a separate boarding establishment for the children of commoners, though the principles by which entrants were selected are not clear. (Mombushoo, *Kyooikushi Shiryoo*, 1890, vol. 2, p. 581.)

179. For attacks on *meiri no tame no gakumon*, see e.g. Kumazawa Banzan, *Shuugi Washo* (first printed *c.* 1710), Yuuhoodoo edn., 1928, pp. 401–2, and Matsudaira Sadanobu, *Taikan Zatsuwa* (1793–1800), in *Nihon Zuihitsu Zenshuu*, 1928, vol. 14, p. 177.

180. This is apparent in some of the central government edicts of 1869 and 1870 concerning the establishment of elementary schools for the masses. (Kokumin Seishin Bunka Kenkyuujo, *Nihon Kyooikushi Shiryoo-sho*, 1937, vol. 5, pp. 56, 150.) At the same time some of the provincial administrations were pushing ahead with educational re-organization on strictly egalitarian lines. (*Ibid.*, pp. 47–50.)

181. Kaigo Tokiomi *et al.*, *Nihon Kyooikushi*, 1943, p. 268.

182. Jean Floud in D. V. Glass, ed., *Social Mobility in Great Britain*, 1954, p. 103.

183. Matsuzaki Minoru, *Bummei Inaka Mondoo*, 1879, reprinted in *Meiji, Bunka Zenshuu*, vol. 20, 1920, p. 277.

184. Kumagaya Kaisaku, *Nihon Kindaihoo no Seiritsu*, 1955, p. 95.

185. Wagatsuma Sakae, *Ie no Seido*, 1950, p. 178.

186. It has been suggested that the number of non-samurai children who reached the Middle Schools in the Meiji period was extremely small. (Kaigo Tokiomi, *Kyooiku no Shakai Kitei*, 1949, pp. 168–9.) But precise evidence is not available and Professor Kaigo's value orientation is such as, if anything, to lead him to overestimate the rigidity of the Meiji system.

187. The *shosei-bushi* or 'Song of the Shosei' was one of the popular songs of the Meiji period. The first line 'Don't look down your nose at the poor *shosei*' was a constant, the second line was subject to variation. 'Eventually I'll be a government official' is recorded for 1874–5. 'Ministers and Counsellors were all *shosei*' and 'Even French Napoleon was once a *shosei*' for 1881, and for 1897 the less self-assertive 'Back in my home town nobody knows'. (Koodansha, *Ryuukoo Kayoo Daizen*, 1937.)

188. Mombushoo, *Kootoo Shoogakkoo Shuushinsho*, 4 vols., 1905–6, and Mombushoo, *Jinjoo Shoogakkoo Shuushinsho*, 6 vols., progressively revised from 1918 to 1930.

189. A work of 1928 gives a list of starting salaries in various prominent firms according to qualifications. Thus one learns that, for instance, in Mitsubishi a graduate of an Imperial University could expect to start at 90 *yen* a month, a graduate of one of the lesser private universities at only 65 *yen* a month. (Maeda Hitoshi, *Sarari-man Monogatari*, 1928, p. 70.)

190. Maeda Hitoshi, *op. cit.*, p. 9.

191. The second question, separated from the first by some twenty minutes of questions on other topics, was intended as a check on the first. As such it is, perhaps, very revealing of the general value of abstract questions in interviews of

this sort. There was a great deal of changing sides between the two questions; in fact only three of the ten who gave the 'status' answer to the first question were amongst the twelve who answered 'blacksmith' to the second. A partial explanation may be that although the second part of the first question clearly juxtaposed and contrasted the two symbols *mibun* (status—but a much commoner word than 'status' is in English) and *shusse* ('getting on'), the first part was taken by some to refer to 'living within one's means' in the economic sense, and the whole question therefore gave a somewhat confusing impression.

192. *Yomiuri Shimbun* (morning), 30 July 1951.

193. A Girls' High School teacher said that in many of his girls' homes the mother was anxious for her daughter to get to a university, but the father lukewarm or hostile. One woman in Shitayama-cho whose girlhood ambition to become a doctor had been thwarted by parents was determined that her daughter should get to a medical school.

194. Statistics Bureau, Prime Minister's Office, *Population Census of 1950*, vol. vii, pt. 13, p. 21. The proportions for girls are 10·7% and 2·5% respectively.

195. *Yomiuri Shimbun* (morning), 17 June 1951.

196. In 1951, a fairly reliable sample survey showed nearly one-quarter of the city populations to be regularly practising contraception, and another 20% said that they would like to limit their families if the means were available. (Population Problems Research Council, The Mainichi Shimbun, *A Survey of Public Opinion on the Readjustment of Overpopulation* (Population Problems, Series 3), 1951, pp. 19–25.)

197. $r = ·41$ ($p < ·01$).

198. According to a newspaper report, of total expenses of 900 million *yen* for Tokyo High Schools, 750 million derived from public funds in 1951, the rest from fees. (*Yomiuri Shimbun* (morning), 23 August 1952.)

199. A scholarship grant, in itself not sufficient to cover school expenses let alone maintenance, was provided for 3% of High School pupils in 1951. It was hoped to increase this proportion to 5% during the following year. (*Yomiuri Shimbun* (morning) 12 August 1951.)

200. Intelligence tests are used only for preliminary weeding out of candidates for the entrance examinations to some of the public universities. A leading feature article on these tests in a popular weekly suggests that they are extremely unpopular. (*Shuukan Asahi*, 6 December 1953.)

201. Sumiya Mikio, 'Shihon to Roodoo', in Nihon Jimbun Kagakkai, *Hooken Isei*, 1951, p. 130.

202. Kawashima Takeyoshi, 'Risshin Shusse', in *Temboo*, September 1951.

203. The use of respect language has declined in Japan as it tends to decline in other Asian societies which are being industrialized. The decline of status-consciousness in general is doubtless one cause, another is that in an industrialized society the hierarchical ranking of individuals is by no means as distinct, and the marks of status by no means as clear in dress and bearing as in a static society of fixed hereditary statuses. Should a newspaper reporter defer to a civil servant, or vice versa? There are obvious conveniences in dropping the whole thing. (In Indonesia it is said that the spread of Bahasa Indonesia has been facilitated by the fact that it permits of neutrality with regard to respect levels, something which is almost impossible in Javanese.) As Kawashima notes, however, within stable relationships in which super- and subordination are clearly marked, respect language remains. The respect-language system also operates on two other quite different levels: (*a*) As a reflection of horizontal, not vertical, social distance—of the degree of familiarity or unfamiliarity of the speakers. Thus two individuals who would both consider themselves on a footing of equality, would *both* use 'respectful' forms at the beginning of an acquaintance and both use less polite forms as they became more familiar. (*b*) And this largely in the

case of women, the use of respect language can be a means of affirming one's sex or social status. The use of respect forms is 'lady-like', a demonstration that the woman is not lacking in essential femininity. Further, the use of the more elaborate respect forms demonstrates that one possesses the breeding which enables one to use them. Competitive displays of such refinement by upper-class women are a frequent source of amusement to the Japanese themselves.

204. See Nakano Takashi, 'Roodoo Kumiai ni okeru Ningen Kankei', *Shakai-gaku Hyooron*, no. 7, 1952.

205. A survey by the Central Wages Commission shows the very wide gap between wages in the large (generally unionized) firms and the small ununionized firm. In May 1950 average wages in enterprises employing 5–29 workers were in few industries more than two-thirds and in some (metal industries and pottery industries) less than a half of the average in firms employing 30 or more workers. (*Yomiuri Shimbun* (morning), 1 August 1951.)

206. The Registration Law of 1898 still required this information. The revised 1914 Law required it only 'if the househead was of samurai or of aristocratic stock' (i.e. the former designation 'commoner' was replaced by a blank). In 1938, however, although the law remained unchanged, a new regulation required the registers to be printed henceforth without a space for 'status', although aristocrats and samurai could still have it written in.' (Nemoto Matsuo, *Koseki-hoo*, 1940, pp. 14–16 and Futaguchi Hideaki, *Koseki-hoo Hikkei*, 1930, p. 141.)

207. In 1951, even if one takes the manufacturing industries alone, only 57% of the total number employed were in establishments with more than 30 workers. (Soorifu Tookeikyoku, *Nihon Tookei Nenkan 1952*, p. 39. Figures derived from the 1951 Establishment Census.)

208. $\cdot 05 < p < \cdot 1$ for a four-fold table taking mentions of 1 and 3 v. mentions of 2 and 4.

209. To the question (in the religious attitudes questionnaire), 'Towards whom do you feel an *on*', only three people mentioned the Emperor (out of a hundred; this compares with fifty-three who offered the reply 'parents'). A further prod, 'What about the Emperor' produced forty-four positive replies. In another similar survey carried out by a Japanese sociologist in a village not far from Tokyo, only 30% (of a sample of sixty-four) were prepared to acknowledge the Emperor's *on*. (Kawashima Takeyoshi, 'On no ishiki no Jittai', *Chuuoo Kooron*, March 1951.)

210. *Kokumin* is etymologically 'the people of the country', in some contexts it is best translated 'nation', but it is distinct from 'the people' in Communist contexts (as in the Chinese People's Republic), which is *jimmin*.

211. Tsurumi Shunsuke, 'Kotoba no O-mamori-teki Shiyoohoo ni tsuite', *Shisoo no Kagaku*, vol. i, no. 1.

212. 'Anyone who has ever peeped into a primary school staff meeting will certainly have an entirely new slant on the Japanese language. You will find even the venerable headmaster contorting his vocal organs to discuss what is to be done about the *koka-koramu*, the importance of *skoppu* or of *shiiken*. You may be tempted to ask what language it is he is talking.

'*Koa-karikyuramu* (core curriculum), *Sukoopu* (scope) and *Shiikuensu* (sequence) and the rest are now such thoroughly acclimatized Japanese words and have so lost touch with their originals, that perhaps the venerable headmaster is to be forgiven for getting mixed up with Coca-Cola.' (Takata Tamotsu, *Daini Burari-Hyootan*, 1952, p. 96.) Another writer, deploring the tendency to use foreign words without much appreciation of their meaning, claims to have overheard the remark, 'That's a very good school. They say they have a *karikyuramu* (curriculum) there.' (Gotoo Iwao *et al.*, *Zooho Atarashii Kyooikuhoo*, 1949, p. 129.)

213. Shuppan Nyuusu, *Shuppan Nenkan* 1951, pp. 840–1. This does not include text-books which account for another 15% of the total book production.

214. One of my most vivid impressions of the mixture of new techniques and traditional attitudes resulted from a visit to the headmaster of a village school in the mountains of central Japan. Soon after our arrival he walked to the microphone in the corner of his room and relayed a message throughout the school asking Teacher Suzuki to come to the headmaster's room. Teacher Suzuki, the only woman member of the staff, arrived from her class, not to be introduced to the visitors, but to pour water from the always simmering kettle into the teapot and to serve us tea.

215. A newspaper opinion survey reported that 63% believe that children are worse behaved than before the war. The most common reason given by the 14% minority who thought that they were better behaved was that they have 'learnt to speak up for themselves frankly and clearly' and that they are 'more open and active'. (*Yomiuri Shimbun*, 4 May 1951. A large sample of Tokyo dwellers.)

216. *Yomiuri*, 31 March 1951.

217. At one of the cheap hostel-type hotels in the mountains not far from Tokyo, the clientele was said to consist mostly of *abekku* who stayed in the private rooms and the *bangaroo* and *hyutte* (bungalows and hütte) dotted on the hillside, and parties of students who stayed in the single large dormitory room. According to a rough check of the four-hundred-odd people who signed the register (one person for each party) in one spring month in 1951, 69% were office workers, 31% students, 7% manual workers and 3% miscellaneous. 90% were between the ages of 17 and 30. Users of this sort of youth-hostel type of hotel some way from the nearest railway are, of course, different from the visitors to the more popular resorts. Of eleven married men in Shitayama-cho who had recently been to a hot-spring resort, all had been with male friends, mostly with fellow employees and often on a trip organized by the firm. Of seven married women, three had gone with husband and children or with husband and other neighbours, the rest with women friends, with children, or with their own relatives.

218. According to one audience survey, 80% of an opera audience and 77% of a 'modern theatre' audience was below 30—compared with only 34% under 30 in a *Shinkokugeki* audience (the jazzed-up form of *kabuki* with female actresses and at least one sword-fight every quarter of an hour). (Minami Hiroshi, 'Engeki no Kankyakusoo', in Shisoo no Kagaku Kenkyuukai, *Yume to Omokage*, 1950, pp. 256–7.)

219. A group of Japanese content analysts has studied this type of popular fiction which they consider to embody and uphold 'essentially Japanese' values, in particular those most resistant to democratic processes. (See Shisoo no Kagaku Kenkyuukai, *Yume to Okakage*, 1950, and for a summary of their work, R. P. Dore, 'The Tokyo Institute for the Science of Thought', *Far Eastern Quarterly*, vol. XIII, no. 1, November 1953.)

220. Including factory, school, university and neighbourhood leisure-time associations, and also trade or professional associations (but excluding employees' unions and Parent-Teacher Associations, Ward Associations and the like in which membership is conferred *ipso facto* by residence), twenty-five people out of a sample of 104 aged 15 or more reported membership in thirty-one associations. This ·3 : 1 ratio of membership to total population compares with the ratio of 1·4 : 1 reported for an English country town of some 15,000 inhabitants and similar ratios for American towns of similar size. The ratio would doubtless be less for an English city population, but probably not sufficiently so to reduce significantly the gap in this respect between Japan and England. (Thomas Bottomore, 'Social Stratification in Voluntary Organizations', in D. V. Glass, ed., *Social Mobility in Great Britain*, 1954, p. 355 n.)

221. ·02 < p < ·05.

222. ɒ < ·01.

223. *The Chrysanthemum and the Sword*, 1946, p. 133.

224. It is at least a possible hypothesis that the high degree of formalization of social intercourse in Japan is related to the predominance of forms of economic co-operation in the Japanese village and that the latter is related to the nature of the Japanese family. Traditional forms of inheritance and adoption making for the continuance of the stem family ensured that the composition of a village in terms of the number and identity of the family units composing it remained stable over a long period of time. The fact that the continuing family, rather than short-lived individuals, could act as the locus of rights and duties made possible long-term forms of co-operation—such, for instance as thatching groups providing for the re-thatching of each member's house every twenty or thirty years—which would have been unworkable under a different system of family organization. It is still the household, rather than the individual, which acts as the unit in neighbour relations.

225. Isomura Eiichi, *Ku no Kenkyuu*, 1936, p. 254.

226. See Appendix V, p. 424.

227. Almost all feminine emotional outbursts are designated *histeri* (hysteria), and largely, perhaps, as a result of the post-war popularity of sexological literature, are generally assumed to have a sexual origin.

228. This description of the Edo city administration is based on Kooda Naritomo, 'Edo no Shisei', in Kokushi Kenkyuukai, *Iwanami Kooza: Nihon Rekishi*, vol. 3, 1933, and Takikawa Masajiroo, *Nihon Hooseishi*, 1941, pp. 441–61.

229. These were, respectively, *tsuki-gyooji, nanushi, machi-doshiyori* and *machi-bugyoo*.

230. Called variously, *kumiai, gonin-gumi, sewanin-kai*, etc.

231. A source of 1791, a time when the non-samurai population of Edo was somewhere around the half-million mark, gives the number of landlords as 18,876 and the number of agents as 16,727, though other sources for the same year speak of more than 20,000 agents. (Kooda, *op. cit.*, p. 21.)

232. Mitsuda Shinzoo, 'Tokugawa-jidai ni okeru chooson-jichi no han-i', *Shigaku-Zasshi*, vol. x, no. 9, 1899, p. 927 (date of edict not stated).

233. Of the ward associations existing in 1935, 36% had been founded between 1923 and 1927. (Isomura Eiichi, *Ku no Kenkyuu*, 1936, p. 242.)

234. Doomei Tsuushinsha, *Jiji Nenkan 1939*, p. 612.

235. Jiji Tsuushinsha, *Jiji Nenkan 1948*, p. 217.

236. Robert Guillain, *Le Peuple Japonais et La Guerre*, Paris, 1947, p. 141.

237. The final regulation ordering the disbanding of these associations was not issued by the Japanese Government until January 1947. (Jiji Tsuushinsha: *Jiji Nenkan 1948*, p. 217.)

238. Such institutionalized forms of mutual exhortation are a common feature of Japanese social life. Injunctive, didactic, or edifying public notices abound. One small branch-line signal box, for example, had its walls covered with a variety of such notices ranging from 'Loose screws: Loose attention' to 'Germs thrive in a dirty workplace'. Like the phrase in the description of the *tonari-gumi* translated as 'be ever watchful for themselves and for others', these may be considered as expressions of the collectivist assumptions of Japanese society. Every man is, and is expected to be, his brother's keeper. The same attitude accounts for the 'Let us' form in which these exhortations are often couched. Instead of 'Fishing Prohibited', the notice in the Imperial Palace moat reads 'Let us love the fishes'; instead of 'Take care on the Roads', 'Let us avoid accidents and make a bright and happy Tokyo'.

239. Early in 1956 the Department of Justice ordered the immediate dissolution of all bodies such as the C.P.T.C.A.

240. Before the Borough Council elections in 1951, Sakura called a meeting of the leaders at his house to discuss policy. He started off by saying that it would be a good thing if someone from this ward were elected; the only way

anything could be done in the borough was by pressure exerted by a councillor. Unless someone with an interest in the ward was elected, the roads in the ward would never be made up and the school would never get its other wing repaired. It was also necessary to have a 'man of character', not someone who was interested in the salary which nowadays, under the deplorable new system, was paid to borough councillors. There was general agreement on this and the discussion proceeded on generalized and abstract lines for some time until Minagawa, the Vice-President, came rather hesitantly to the point and suggested that Sakura himself should stand. There was little apparent enthusiasm for the idea, and Sakura, somewhat discouraged, said something about the expense of electioneering being more than he could manage out of his own pocket. The opportunity was quickly seized to jump back to generalities with a discussion of various examples of lavish and parsimonious campaigns, of the minimum anyone could hope to get elected on, and how many times this exceeded the official expense allowance. In a lull, someone then suggested that Kataoka, another of the inner group, was thinking of standing. This he denied. There was an air of some embarrassment until Minagawa suggested that perhaps after all it would be better to put the weight of the ward behind a certain candidate from a neighbouring ward who would be grateful for the extra votes, was equally concerned with the local primary school where he had been the P.T.A. President before Sakura, and could be relied on as a quid pro quo to get the main road through the ward metalled. This was taken up with alacrity; it would, moreover, said one, involve less danger of arousing petty jealousies and resentments in the ward. The Shitayama-cho leaders appeared at the adoption meeting of the neighbouring candidate, the names of the inner circle were duly appended as 'supporters', on his election posters and the word was passed round that the interests of Shitayama-cho demanded his support. By and large he got the support; the number of his votes showed that many must have come from Shitayama-cho. Eighteen months after his election the main road through Shitayama-cho was metalled.

241. The question arises here, of course, how far my own presence affected the situation. At the second meeting the Chairman, certainly, when faced with the awkward question why there was no constitution, asked that the tape-recording should be stopped while he gave his explanation in terms of the unsettled political situation, but he stuck to his point without concessions, nevertheless. For the general question of observer distortion, see pp. 8–9.

242. See e.g. Paul S. Dull, 'The Senkyoya System in Rural Japanese Communities', Centre for Japanese Studies, University of Michigan, *Occasional Papers*, no. 4, 1953.

243. See Isomura Eiichi, *Ku no Kenkyuu*, 1936, pp. 252–4. The author's opposition seems to be based not simply on the pragmatic grounds that such ward associations were likely to be ineffective, but also on the value grounds that they were undesirable. This in part because they provide scope for the exercise of petty tyranny by local 'powerful men', and in part because 'progress' demanded that in Japan as in the West city life should become more and more *gesellschaftlich* and less and less *gemeinschaftlich* and it was a bad thing to set one's face against progress. The influence of such evolutionary sociological theories on Japanese official thinking was apparent also in discussion of social services (see pp. 71–3).

244. According to the report of a public opinion survey conducted by the Tokyo Metropolis (early in 1953?) 32% of a sample of residents in the borough areas of Tokyo said that *tonari-gumi* had been re-formed in their ward. Ward associations without formal *tonari-gumi* sub-groups were apparently somewhat more frequently reported. (Isomura Eiichi, *Toshi Shakaigaku*, 1953, pp. 223–6.) As far as official policy is concerned the Local Government Office of the Central Government issued a statement on September 23, 1952 pointing out that the order banning the associations was due to lose its effect a month later, and that

the government had no intention at that date of either encouraging or forbidding the revival of such associations.

245. See e.g. *Asahi* (Tokyo, morning) 6 October and 24 October 1952.

246. In the opinion survey quoted above, of the 32% who reported that *tonari-gumi* existed in their district, 3% thought it a bad thing. (20% thought it a good thing and 8% didn't know.) Of the 53% who reported no *tonari-gumi* (13% didn't know whether *tonari-gumi* had been revived or not and 2% were not reported). 17% were opposed to the idea of their revival. (16% were in favour, 20% didn't know.) (Isomura, *op. cit.*, p. 225.)

247. Throughout the following discussion 'shrine' will be used for Shinto and 'temple' for Buddhist places of worship.

248. A typical prayer for such a ceremony runs: 'Before our Holy Shrine, I, ——, priest, humbly speak. To ——, child of thy family, of number ——, —— street, in this town of —— wherein Thou makest Thine abode, on the —— day of the —— month, was born, thanks to the revered and gracious favour of Thee and Thy Fellow-*kami*, a son. Daily waxing in strength he has grown like the young bamboo and today, being his ——th day, he has come into Thy presence in joyful thanks for Thy Holy Favour. On this happy and propitious day he has come, offering up the ribbon of thank-offering, to make his first visit to Thy Shrine in respectful thanksgiving. Quietly and calmly take note of him, we pray, and guard him hence, night and day, that he may be unharmed by the tricks of the evil *kami* and that he may grow up in loyalty and sincerity to be a fine and beautiful child of Thy Family. In firm and humble intercession, thus I pray.' (Jinja Shimpoosha, ed. *Norito Bunrei-shuu*, vol. II, 1951, p. 25.)

249. Shisoo no Kagaku Kenkyuukai, ed., *Watashi no Tetsugaku*, vol. 1, 1950, p. 220.

250. An interesting indication of the undiminished importance of the religious bond in some rural communities is provided by the simultaneous conversion to Catholicism of a whole village in Kyooto prefecture in 1949. Conversion of a section of the village might be expected seriously to disrupt the village system of social relations. Not until a majority was prepared for conversion did it become possible and then everyone had to follow suit. (Ministry of Education, *Shuukyoo Nempoo (Year-Book of Religion)*, 1950, p. 22.)

251. *Analects*, Bk. VI, ch. 20, Legge's translation. Whether or not Waley's alternative interpretation (by showing respect to *keep them* at a distance) is correct the relevant fact is perhaps that the traditional interpretation of the passage in Japan has been that of Legge, and the word concerned—*keien suru* —is in common use in the sense 'to keep a respectful distance from'.

252. Hara Zen, *Sentetsu Soodan*, Yuuhoodoo ed., p. 188.

253. *Chuushin koomon ni izuru.*

254. $p < \cdot 05$ (sd of d). The questions on marriage concerned are those detailed on p. 126. It would be an interesting question for further study whether, if the common factor in the association could be isolated, it could best be called traditionalism versus anti-traditionalism, or authority-acceptance versus rebellion, that is, whether the dichotomy appears at the ideological level and the relevant factor is the cognitive acceptance or rejection of traditional ethical beliefs, or only at the attitudinal and behavioural level in conformity or non-conformity to patterns of submissive or deferential behaviour. The present material will not bear such an analysis.

255. The sharpness of this statement of the contrast in attitudes may somewhat exaggerate the actual situation. The '1940 conception' of the *kami* was, of course, that held by the conscious Shinto revivalists of the Tokugawa period and the popular pilgrimages to the Ise shrine during the period may be cited as evidence that such ideas had more general currency. (Such pilgrimage years occurred at about fifty-year intervals and for one of these years—1705—the improbable

figure of three and a quarter million is recorded as the number of pilgrims reaching the shrine.) Such pilgrimages, however, appear to have been part of a sun-worshipping productive cult, similar in nature to many of the modern mountain cults, rather than a cult of the ancestors of the Emperor about whom the mass of the people of the Tokugawa period knew little or nothing. (Kishimoto Hideo, ed., *Meiji Bunka-shi*, vol. 6 (*Shuukyoo-hen*), 1954, pp. 42, 500, Shimonaka Y., ed., *Shintoo Daijiten*, 1937, article *o-kagemairi*.)

256. Asahi Shimbunsha, *Asahi Nenkan, 1952*, p. 235.

257. Evidence for this statement may be found in the answers given to the question: 'Would you say that there was a difference between the *hotoke* which your ancestors have become, and *hotoke* like, say, Shaka or Amida and so on? Or would you say that they were the same?' Fifty-one people out of a hundred said that there was a difference, forty that there was not. (Six didn't know, and three were scornful of the whole affair.) One would guess, however, that this underestimates the extent to which there is a difference of conceptualization and in attitudes. To say that there was no difference was the easiest way of answering the question; it obviated the necessity of explaining how they differed, and it is significant that there is an extremely high correlation between the answer 'same' to this question and the answer 'don't know' to an immediately preceding question: 'How do you picture the *hotoke-sama*?' Moreover, to analyse the difference required a certain degree of introspective analysis of which not everyone would be capable; 'I suppose since they have the same name they are the same' may be taken to represent a typical thought process. At the same time, the answer 'same' sometimes conceals a much greater degree of sophistication, as in the case of a woman who elaborated her answer by saying that 'they are the same in that they both live in the heart of the worshipper'.

The differences pointed out by the other fifty-one fall into two main categories. Firstly, the *hotoke* are much more 'intimate' and more important to the worshipper than the *Hotoke*. Secondly, the *Hotoke* are of higher rank than the *hotoke* in some supposed hierarchical scale.

258. Thus, whereas Buddhists hold ceremonies every seventh day until the forty-ninth after death, Shintoists hold ceremonies every tenth day until the fiftieth. The present Shinto burial rites, though it is claimed that they represent original Shinto traditions which had been kept alive during the millennia of Buddhist ascendancy among such groups as the priests of the Ise shrine, are a creation of the nineteenth century. Some attempts to revive Shinto burial rites had been made earlier in the Tokugawa period by the forerunners of the Shinto revivalist movement, but it was only in the first years of Meiji, when the Government gave official encouragement to the attempt to make Shinto into a comprehensive religion which could replace Buddhism that Shinto burial rites became fully formalized, more widely practised and compulsory for Shinto priests (who hitherto had been buried according to Buddhist rites). The Government ordinance of 1882 which deprived Shinto priests of their teaching functions and marked the end of this policy, in favour of the creation of a 'civic' Shinto which could be backed by State compulsion and yet not offend against the principle of religious freedom which was to be embodied in the Meiji Constitution, also deprived Shinto priests, in principle, of their right to officiate at funeral services. However, a qualification to this ordinance, which was never subsequently amended, permitted priests of lesser shrines to officiate at funerals 'for the time being'. The prohibition did not, of course, apply to the priests of the Shinto Sects (see pp. 350–52) which became independent of State Shinto at about this time. Priestly officiation is not, however, necessary for a Shinto burial service—the chief mourner among the relatives is strictly the chief officiator—and there has always been a body of opinion within Shinto doctrine that death was a defilement from which Shinto priests should dissociate themselves as far as possible. (Cabot

Colville, 'Shinto, Engine of Government', *Trans. Asiatic Society of Japan*, 3rd ser., vol. I, p. 17), Hiraoka Yoshifumi, *Zassai Shikiten-han*, 1944, pp. 381–7. Kishimoto Hideo, ed., *Meiji Bunka-shi*, vol. 6 (*Shuukyoo-hen*), 1954, pp. 99–102.)

The small proportion of families who today practice Shinto burial rites are generally either (*a*) descendants of Shinto priests, (*b*) descendants of families which during the Tokugawa period lived in one of the few fiefs such as Aizu or Mito where the feudal lord favoured the Shinto revivalists and was strong enough to ignore Tokugawa regulations which insisted on regular declarations of adherence to the Buddhist faith, (*c*) descendants of families which lived in fiefs such as those of Southern Kyuushuu where, in the first flush of Shinto revivalism in the early years of Meiji, the feudal-lord-turned-prefectural-governor ordered his whole fief to adopt Shinto rites, (*d*) individuals or the descendants of individuals who have been persuaded by the same ideology, or (*e*) adherents of the Shinto Sects (see pp. 350–2).

259. *Arigatai O-Tera-Sama* quoted in Shisoo no Kagaku Kenkyuukai, *Yume to Omokage*, 1950, p. 336.

260. Ministry of Education, *Shuukyoo Nempoo, 1950*, p. 472.

261. According to one informant, however, it used to be by no means uncommon in samurai families for *ihai* of the wife's parents to be preserved in the family *butsudan*.

262. As has been pointed out by Radcliffe Brown, who considers, indeed, that his own sociological theory of the function of religion in society is already explicit in Hsün Tzu. (*Structure and Function in Primitive Society*, 1952, pp. 157–60.)

263. *Hsün Tzu*, ch. 19, as translated by Derk Bodde in Fung Yu-Lan, *A History of Chinese Philosophy*, 1937, p. 351.

264. *Hsün-Tzu*, ch. 19, translation of Arthur Waley, *Three Ways of Thought in Ancient China*, 1934, p. 25.

265. *Li Chi*, ch. 21, Fung Yu-Lan, *op. cit.*, p. 350.

266. *Hsün Tzu*, ch. 19, Waley, *op. cit.*, p. 25.

267. *Mo Tzu*, ch. 48, Fung Yu-Lan, *op. cit.*, p. 91.

268. *Mo Tzu*, ch. 30, Fung Yu-Lan, *op. cit.*, p. 98–9.

269. Respectively, *O-taku no shuukyoo wa nan desu ka?* and *Anata wa kojin to shite nanika wo shinjin shite imasu ka?*

270. Shisoo no Kagaku Kenkyuukai, *Sengoha no Kenkyuu*, 1951, p. 101.

271. The *kami* also, apparently, help those who help themselves. A pair of grey moss-covered stones had been placed by a merchant devotee as a decoration for the entrance to an Inari shrine not far from Shitayama-cho. It bore in elegant lettering of a type which suggested that it might be contemporaneous with the translation and subsequent vogue of Samuel Smile's *Self Help*, 'So-and-so's Emporium, No. so-and-so, So-and-so Ward. For all stockinets, flannels and silks'.

272. $p < \cdot 01$.

273. $p < \cdot 05$.

274. One advantage of respect language is that one can ask this sort of question in Japanese without bringing the interview to an immediate and unpleasant conclusion.

275. $\cdot 05 < p < \cdot 1$.

276. A recent large-sample survey of the prestige ratings of various occupations in Japanese industrial cities found that the Buddhist priest was rated twelfth out of twenty-eight occupations, immediately below a newspaper reporter and an elementary school-teacher and immediately above an owner of a small retail store and a local government clerk. (Japan Sociological Association, *Social Stratification and Mobility in Japan*, in *International Sociological Association*, *Liege Congress Papers*, 1953, Section I.)

277. These figures and, unless otherwise stated, all other information of a factual nature concerning post-war religious sects, is derived from Ministry of Education, *Shuukyoo Nempoo* (*Yearbook of Religion*), 1950.

278. *Ibid.*, p. 184.

279. Such, for example, as W. G. Aston, *Shinto the Way of the Gods*, 1905; G. Kato, *A Study of Shinto, The Religion of the Japanese Nation*, Tokyo, 1926; D. C. Holtom, *The National Faith of Japan*, 1938, and *Modern Japan and Shinto Nationalism*, revised edition, 1947.

280. See translation, R. K. Hall, ed., *Kokutai no Hongi*, 1949.

281. E.g. 'It is in the subduing of those who refuse to conform to the august influence of the Emperor's virtues that the mission of our Imperial Military force lies' (*Ibid.*, p. 170).

282. Ministry of Education, *op. cit.*, p. 352.

283. By December 1951 the number of shrines affiliated to the Jinja Honchoo had grown to just over 88,000. (Ministry of Education, *Shuukyoo Benran*, 1954, p. 532.)

284. According to an analysis of post-war religious publications (Ministry of Education, *Shuukyoo Benran*, 1954, pp. 428–36) the Central Bureau of Shrines issued only two works of a doctrinal character between January 1946 and August 1952. The Shinto sects (see below, p. 350 ff.) were, however, considerably more active in the publishing field.

285. D. C. Holtom, *The National Faith of Japan*, 1938.

286. *Ibid.*, p. 245. There is also a full and sympathetic description of one of these sects in C. W. Halpern, *The Kurozumi sect of Shinto*, Tokyo, 1945.

287. The lack of popular comprehension of the doctrine of the Buddha as a principle of which the individual Buddhas were only incarnations may be cited as a further example of this tendency. It would be wrong, however, to suggest that there has never been any idea of a universal deity in Japan. The Chinese *T'ien* or *Shang-ti* (a description of which, may be found in Feng Yu-Lan, *A History of Chinese Philosophy* (translated by D. Bodde), London, 1937, p. 31, J. Spae, *Ito Jinsai*, Pekin, 1948, p. 111, and, Tsuda Sookichi, 'Joodai Shina ni okeru Ten oyobi Jootei no kannen', in *Tooyoo Gakuhoo*, vol. 12, no. 3) has, under the guise of *Ten*, *Tendoo*, or *Tenchi*, found some acceptance among Japanese thinkers (cf. also note 310) and *Ten* as a semi-anthropomorphic supreme deity is in fact incorporated into the doctrines of several of these thirteen sects. More relevant here is the fact that this concept of *Ten* also finds a place in popular thought. The writer recalls a woman who described an incident in which she had been wronged and misunderstood. She concluded with a shrug of the shoulder and the words '*De mo Ten ga mite iru*'—'However Heaven sees all' (and understands that it was not I who was in the wrong).

288. Ministry of Education, *Shuukyoo Benran*, 1954, pp. 532–43.

289. Ministry of Education, *op. cit.*, p. 208.

290. Ministry of Education, *Shuukyoo Nempoo 1950*, p. 295.

291. *Ibid.*, p. 295.

292. *Ibid.*, p. 71. In the *1952 Yearbook*, however (by which time the membership claimed had risen to 143,000) reference to the bombing incident is deleted, the leader is said simply to have been imprisoned 'for a certain reason'. (Ministry of Education, *Shuukyoo Benran*, 1954, p. 116.)

293. By the time of the *1952 Yearbook*, four sects had restored loyalty and filial piety to the catalogue of virtues.

294. Ministry of Education, *Shuukyoo Nempoo 1950*, p. 284.

295. *Ibid.*, p. 312.

296. B. Watanabe, *Gendai Nihon no Shuukyoo*, 1950, p. 42. The last technique has a long and honoured history as the *hooben* of Buddhism.

297. Ministry of Education, *op. cit.*, p. 73.

298. Jiji Shimpoosha, *Jiji Nenkan*, 1952, p. 301.
299. J. Naruse on Female Education in S. Okuma, ed. *Fifty Years of New Japan*, 1910, vol. 1, p. 219.
300. M. Kawaguchi, in Shisoo no Kagaku Kenkyuukai, ed. *Yume to Omokage*, 1950, p. 136.
301. See *Bukkyoo Daijiten*, article *Jigoku*.
302. See the translation by A. K. Reischauer, 'Genshin's Ojo Yoshu', in *Trans. Asiatic Society of Japan*, Second Ser. 7 (1930), pp: 16–97.
303. Hattori Choozen, *Ansei Kemmon-roku*, 1856, vol. I, f. 6.
304. *Ibid.*, f. 13.
305. A recent survey shows that it is not universally diffused. In some parts of Japan superstitions unknown in Tokyo are strongly believed in; another example of the wide regional variations in culture which still exist. Ministry of Education, Meishin Choosa Kyoogikai (Council for Research on Superstitions), *Meishin no Jittai* (The Degree of Superstitious Belief), 1950, pp. 34–44.
306. Almost anything can constitute 'interference' with the devil-door. An interviewer's note concerning another family runs as follows: 'Their staircase is in the "devil-door" and since they recently "interfered" with it they have had nothing but misfortune. The eldest son's bride has turned out to be a "bad 'un" and had to be sent home; then the husband died (aged 65). So now they are not using the stairs at all until they have them seen to, and the mother and her two sons are living entirely in the two small rooms downstairs.'
307. $\cdot 1 < p < \cdot 2$.
308. It is interesting to note that a Ministry of Education questionnaire completed by the parents of children at three schools in Tokyo (one near Shitayama-cho, one in an agricultural and one in a fishing village) produced 73% who said that they were careful about the 'devil-door'; a noticeable contrast with Shitayama-cho. (Ministry of Education, Council for Research on Superstition, *op. cit.*, p. 35.)
309. $\cdot 01 < p < \cdot 05$ (sd of d).
310. Although it is unlikely that she had ever heard of him, she was in fact, repeating something like the teachings of the seventeenth-century Confucian philosopher Kaibara Ekken. *Tenchi* for him was an anthropomorphic, or at least an anthropopathic, deity responsible for all creation. (See note 287.) We acknowledge the *on* of our parents who feed and educate us, and of our feudal lord who provides us with a living; how much more, then, should we acknowledge the *on* of *Tenchi* who created our parents and our feudal lord, created the rice and the clothes which we receive from them; is, in fact, our 'Great Father and Mother' (a phrase taken from the Chinese Book of History). Just as we repay our parents and our feudal lord by loyal service, so we must requite this even greater debt by loyal service to *Tenchi*. This could be done by fostering all the works of creation (which includes being kind to animals) but more especially by keeping in a state of pristine purity the essentially good nature with which *Tenchi* has endowed us (for he followed Mencius in believing in Original Virtue), i.e. by leading a moral life. (His clearest statement of this doctrine is contained in the *Yamato Zokukun*, 1710. See *Ekken Jikkun*, Yuuhoodoo, edn.,1928, vol. 1, p. 67.) Thus, in the same way as in the Christian religion, the goodness of God is directly linked to exhortations to just and moral behaviour. Kaibara had no followers and founded no sect. Nor was this particular doctrine of his incorporated in the official code taught in Japanese schools (which had its religious basis in the Shinto pantheon rather than his monotheistic or pantheistic *Tenchi*). This is another example of the persistence of relatively simple beliefs (cf. also the doctrines of heaven and hell p. 365) outside of the established doctrines of the religious sects.
311. *Fukuoo Hyakuwa*, first published 1896, 43rd ed. 1907, p. 34.
312. That the proportion giving unprompted 'text-book' answers to questions

about *on* was surprisingly small was also the conclusion of a similar survey conducted by a group of Japanese sociologists in a village not far from Tokyo in 1950. It was found, however, that the word *on* was used spontaneously and appeared to have much greater significance for its users, of certain other relations of dependence, not much stressed in the school-taught ethic, but having considerable economic importance in village society. (Kawashima Takeyoshi, 'On no ishiki no jittai', *Chuuoo Kooron*, March 1951.)

313. *The Chrysanthemum and the Sword*, 1946, ch. 5.

314. This succinct statement of the *on* doctrine derives from a recent advertisement of the Esso Petroleum Company. (*Listener*, 23 September 1954, p. 494.)

315. The *Kokusho Kaidai* (ed. Samura Hachiroo, 1926) lists 400 popular moral treatises published in printed editions before 1868.

316. Hayashi Chikio, 'Kokuminsei no Kenkyuu', in *Kyooiku Toookei*, August 1954, pp. 28–36.

317. *The Chrysanthemum and the Sword*, 1946, pp. 222–7.

318. *The Lonely Crowd*, 1950, chs. 1–2. My debt to this stimulating book will be apparent in other parts of this chapter.

319. See e.g. Sir George Sansom, *Japan, A Short Cultural History*, rev. ed., 1946, pp. 483, 496.

320. *Yomiuri* (morning), 14 May 1951.

321. Minami Hiroshi, *Nihonjin no Shinri*, 1953, pp. 34–6.

322. Iizuka Kooji, *Nihon no Seishinteki Fuudo*, 1952, p. 69.

NOTES TO APPENDICES

1. Mombushoo, *Shoogakkoo Gakushuu Shidoo Yooryoo, Shakaika-hen* (MEJ2105), 1951. This is the third attempt at a Course of Study and one which meets with the general approval of such people as the authors of the book quoted at the end of this appendix. The first two attempts (particularly the first of 1947) were strongly criticized as bad translations of an extremely vague and unhelpful description of the American Virginia Plan.

2. Mombushoo, *Chuugakkoo, Kootoogakkoo, Gakushuu Shidoo Yooryoo, Shakaika-hen*, III, (MEJ2125), 1951, pp. 29–31.

3. Katsuta Shuichi, Miyahara Seiichi, Munakata Seiya, *et al.*, *Nippon no Shakaika*, October 1953.

4. The old New Year Festival centred on the 15th of the first (lunar) month, and with Bon ending on the 15th of the seventh the two occasions divided the year into two halves and are traditionally days of debt settlement and gift-giving. Some districts now celebrate Bon on the 15th of Gregorian July. In many rural districts, however, the lunar calendar is still followed since the time coincides with a slack period in the agricultural cycle. A compromise is to hold it 'a month late' on the 15th of Gregorian August.

5. The publisher's blurb of a recent translation of the minority report of the Indian judge at the Tokyo War Crimes Trials, published in Japan under the title *Japan, Not Guilty* quotes the following sentence from a review: 'This is a book I would like to offer up to all the *kami* in the Yasukuni shrine.'

Index

abacus, 62
abekku (a 'couple'), 159
abortion, 68, 205
achievement, n.51
acupuncture, 66
adolescent friendships, 236-7
adopted son-in-law, 147
adoption, 74, 100, 103, 132, 144, 145, 147, n.81, n.121, n.124
adultery, 97, 119, 161, n.74
advertisement, forms of, 17, 245, n.271
affectivity, n.51
age, and status, 232; differences, 86, 171, 174-7, 181, 244, 336
agnosticism, 314, 326-8, 335-8, 366, 369
agriculture, 85, 117, 132, 293
Aizawa Seishisai, n.95
Alcock, R., 356
alcohol, 176, 208, 368, 400-3
Altar of the Buddhas, 149, 151, 312-28, 427-31
Amaterasu, 309
ambition, *see* social mobility
America, 9, 67, 70, 80, 83-4, 170, 182, 239, 259, 358
American Educational Mission, 227
Amida, 312, 321, 329, 364, 433
amulets, 335, 432, 435; *see also fuda*
ancestor worship, 94, 99, 101, 103, 112, 119, 142-6, 149, 159, 211, 292, 312-28, 352, 356, 361, 370, 376, 427-30
Anglo-Japanese alliance, 9
anomie, 167, 170
anonymity, of the city, 267, 287, 392
Anti-Crime Association, 17
apaato (apartment blocks), 15, 23, 29, 37, 45, 78, 82
apologies, 260
apprenticeship, 34, 104, 333; *see also shosei*
aristocracy, 34, 217; feudal 11, 14
army, 41, 217, 348, n.16, n.281; criteria of promotion, 192; *see also* conscription
arranged marriage, 167-71; *see also miai*
Asahi newspaper, 161, 163, 204
Asakusa, 331
ascription, definition, n.51
assassination, 354
associations, 246-8; membership in, n.220
Aston, W. G., n.279
astronomy, 167

authority, 114-15, 240, 285, 321, 387 n.254; of parents, 307; in the family, 136-141; *see also* househead

bachelors, 122
ballet, 244, n.101
barbers, 270
bath-houses, 15, 17, 41, 151, 159, 248, 268
bedding, 16, 47
beliefs, 338, 362-73; consistency of, 325-8
Benedict, R., 7, 67, 176, 186, 191, 192, 200, 206, 208-9, 253, 261-2, 324, 374, 382
Bennet, J. W., n.67, n.92
beri-beri, 59
Beveridge Report, 71
Bible, 359, 360
birth, 300, 333; control, 82, 205, 246, n.196
birthdays, 249
birthplace, 18
birth-rates, 205
Blacker, Carmen, n.177
Blondie (cartoon strip), 84, n.53
Bodde, Derk, n.263
Bohemianism, 161
bombing, 13, 15, 29, 37, 42, 78, 143, 151, 228, 296, 301, 314
Bon festival, 316, 318, 342, 428, 461n.
book publishing, 227
borough (definition of), n.4
borough government, 271-2, 277, 286
borrowing, between neighbours, 263-4
bossu (a boss in local politics), 70, 221, 222
Bottomore, T., n.230
branch families, 96, 101-6, 111-12, 123, 148-56
bread, 58-60, 82, n.41
bribery, 57, 208, 260, 262
brothels, *see* prostitution
Browning, R., 161
Buber, M., 349
Buddhas, 313
Buddhism, 60, 87, 143, 149, 192-3, 211, 246 307, 312-28, 330-2, 334, 340-7, 353, 371, 427-35, n.258, n.287; and Japanese culture, 362; development of, 291-4; *see also* temples
builders, speculative, 15
building controls, 42